OZ CLARKE'S
WINE
GUIDE
1995

ELEVENTH EDITION

Contributors to *Oz Clarke's Wine Guide 1995*

William Bolter lives and works in Bordeaux, where he is a wine broker, winemaker and wine writer; **Nicholas Faith** is a financial journalist and the author of books on Champagne and Cognac as well as the classic study of the Bordeaux wine trade, *The Wine Masters*. **Rosemary George MW** is the author of many wine books and is currently working on a book on New Zealand wines. **Stuart Walton** is a freelance wine and food writer; **Tom Stevenson** writes for many leading wine publications and is the author of the leading work on the wines of Alsace. **Redmond O'Hanlon** writes about wine as well as teaching French at University College, Dublin, and **Stephen Brook** is the wine correspondent for *Vogue* and the author of *Sauvignon Blanc & Sémillon* as well as a recent travel book, *The Claws of the Crab: Georgia and Armenia*. He is currently completing a book on Sauternes. **David Gleave MW** runs the Italian specialist merchant Winecellars and is the author of *The Wines of Italy*. He is currently writing a book on Tuscan wines. **John Radford** is a wine writer with a particular interest in Spain. **Suzy Atkins** is a regular contributor to many magazines, including *WINE* and *Which Wine Monthly*. **Richard Mayson** has written a book on *The Wines of Portugal,* and California-based wine writer **Larry Walker** is a contributor to many British publications. **Bob Campbell** is a leading New Zealand wine writer and **Charles Metcalfe**, as well as writing about wine, has a weekly wine slot on Granada Television's *Good Morning*.

Reviews of previous editions

'Packed with insider information and opinion, and worth every penny.' Derek Cooper

'...the guide gets better with every vintage. Clarke writes with enthusiasm virtually steaming off the page. Here is someone who loves wine.' *The Guardian*

'If you haven't bought a copy, there is little hope for you.' *The Sunday Telegraph*

'An enthusiastic, opinionated and entertaining survey of the world's wines and a price guide to wines on the shelves of Britain.' *The Sunday Times*

'... typically up-to-date, irreverent but informative.' *The Independent*

'Scholarly, funny and thought-provoking.' Robert Parker

'*Webster's Wine Guide* is both passionate and quite unpretentious, in true Oz Clarke fashion.' *The Newcastle Journal*

OZ CLARKE'S
WINE GUIDE 1995

ELEVENTH EDITION

'WEBSTER'S'
THE COMPLETE WINE
BUYER'S HANDBOOK

WEBSTERS
MITCHELL BEAZLEY
LONDON

Editorial Director Sandy Carr
General Editor Margaret Rand
Art Director Jason Vrakas
Price Guides Editor Lorna Bateson
Editorial Assistants Jennifer Mussett, Matthew Barrell
Designer Adelle Morris
DTP Jonathan Harley
Editorial Consultant Rosemary George
Database Consultant Alexandra Boyle
Indexer Naomi Good
Cover photograph James Merrell

Advertising Sales
Logie Bradshaw Media Limited,
Swan House, 52/53 Poland Street,
London W1V 3DF,
tel 071-287 2876, fax 071-734 3840

Created and designed by
Websters International Publishers Limited,
Axe and Bottle Court, 70 Newcomen Street,
London SE1 1YT
in association with Mitchell Beazley
International Limited, Michelin House,
81 Fulham Road, London SW3 6RB

Oz Clarke's Wine Guide 1995 Edition
© Websters International Publishers
and Mitchell Beazley Publishers 1994

ISBN 1 85732 375 0

Printed and bound in the UK by
Cox & Wyman, Reading

CONTENTS

INTRODUCTION

Am I reading this right? Do I need glasses or what? There are all these doctors suddenly telling me to drink more wine. It depends. If it's an English or an American doctor, they will go public on a 'little' more wine and go private on 'drink what you want to, within reason. Just don't overdo it. If it's a Danish doctor, they'll reckon you could double your recommended consumption – in other words they'll step into line with what doctors around the Mediterranean have been saying for as long as I can remember. But wherever they hail from, this year has at last seen the medical profession do an about turn and begin to promote the idea that a reasonable amount of wine, preferably red, drunk on a regular basis, will not only make you a happier, less stressed, nicer person to know, but it will probably make you live longer by a matter of several years or more.

When attempts were made at the beginning of the nineties to publish 'good news' stories about alcohol, editors of newspapers simply didn't want to touch them, yet they were more than pleased to carry stories about the abuse of alcohol. Until the *60 Minutes* television programme in America relayed the news to almost 22 million households that a little bit of what you fancy does you good.

Thank goodness for Serge Renaud of the French National Institute of Health Research. It was his assertion on *60 Minutes* that red wine drinking was the crucial factor in keeping French heart disease levels low despite their eating large amounts of animal fat, that overnight made wine drinking respectable in America. Another survey I have notes that the 32 million Americans who do drink wine save America $1billion a year in health costs; if the 141 million Americans who don't drink wine were to down three glasses a week, the report concludes, there'd be a further health saving of $2.2 billion a year. Now in 1994 he writes that in a further study of heart patients he has found that red wine drunk within the context of a low animal fat 'Mediterranean' diet was found to have a 70–80 per cent success rate in both preventing and curing heart disease.

Stress reducer

I might add that it's not just the Mediterranean diet plus a couple of glasses of wine that is regarded as an aid to healthy living. Other studies showed that the south-west of France, where animal fat based foods like *confit d'oie* and *foie gras* are part of the normal diet, has one of the highest life expectations in the world. Two factors are crucial. Most of the fat is poultry- and game-based. And secondly, tannic red wine is part of the normal diet. Is there a connection? Tell me there isn't. And another thing the anti-alcohol lobby may care to think about: a bottle of wine shared is a great way to reduce stress. And stress may well be the greatest killer of them all. Now that doctors across the world are coming out with the results of their studies into wine drinking and alcohol use, and now that the media is prepared to carry such stories, we'll all be that much closer to finding out whether the old German saying that there are more old wine drinkers than old doctors has any truth to it.

But it's quality as well as quantity that counts, so what will we be drinking this year? Well, after the sordid demise of two leading companies involved in *en primeur* claret sales and the criminal disappearance of thousands of cases of young claret from another company's cellar, don't expect me to be buying *en primeur*. There's nothing that needs buying before it's bottled at the moment anyway. Companies – indeed very respectable companies – have been touting '93 clarets *en primeur*. Away with you! I'm increasingly unhappy about advising non-professionals to buy *en primeur* (apart from a few small super-trendy properties). If we look back at the last 14 years, you will have benefitted in financial terms from buying *en primeur* only once, in the case of the 1982 vintage. The 1989s have risen a little in value since they were offered, but the price was ludicrous in the first place. The '88s and the '90s will both offer equally good drinking in time and you won't have had to pay extra to finance American hype.

Elastic labels

Hype comes in all shapes and sizes, but what counts ultimately is the wine in the glass, not the label on the bottle. Give me a decent flavour and I'll pay a fair price for the wine. I happily accept Chardonnays from Moldova, Pinot Noir from Romania and Cabernet from the Crimea. I love the idea of Malbec from Argentina and Tannat from Uruguay. And when it comes to France, Australia, New Zealand, South Africa or Spain, I'm not going to say – hey, I've got reason to believe you've been elastic in your interpretation of grape and place on this label. I'll just say – is this good grog, is it worth me fishing out the folding ones?

I accept there are some particular *terroirs* that are worth perfecting. The gravel banks of St Julien and Pauillac are special, as is the heart of Pomerol. Many of the vineyard sites in Burgundy's Côte d'Or, in Italy's Barolo or Barbaresco, in Germany's Mosel Valley, or indeed in New Zealand's Hawkes Bay or Australia's Coonawarra are special. But the law is often an ass when it comes to appellations. Political pressure allows all kinds of hangers-on to famous appellations, or allows enormous generic appellations to bask in reflected glory. No-one believes that all the wines in Bordeaux, Burgundy, Muscadet or Champagne, in Piesport, Chianti, Napa Valley or Coonawarra are worth an appellation. Many of the vineyards were growing wheat or sugar beet before they switched to grapes to make more money.

It's especially disturbing to see master blenders like Australia and New Zealand being tempted to a French-style geographically-based appellation of origin system. Origin doesn't give you the flavour in the bottle; it's the man or woman who is dedicated enough to express that origin who does that. Just because one grape variety always grew there doesn't mean that another grape variety wouldn't be better. I hope these countries, and others sniffing at the appellation bait, remember that it was their exuberant freedom from bureaucratic interference that allowed them to create the flavours that the general public now loves.

In a mood of devilry, I've just done an experiment in my kitchen. I took a heady, unbalanced figgy £10 Chardonnay proudly displaying the Tasmanian appellation. Yuk. So I blended it 50-50 with a neutral white from a co-op in southern Portugal costing all of £2.39. The result? A very enjoyable, balanced, attractively fruity Chardonnay. Well, sort of Chardonnay. Sort of Australian. Half the price, too. I did the same with a tough, aggressive £16 Napa Valley Cabernet Sauvignon. I mixed this with some French Gamay de Touraine (£4.98) and a healthy splash of southern French Grenache/Syrah (£2.69). The result: fruit, brightness, a reasonable level of tannin and oak. Althogether a thoroughly enjoyable California Cabernet – well, sort of Cabernet. Sort of California.

100 BEST BUYS

These are the best of the best: our pick of this year's *Guide*. If you see certain regions missed out, this might be because the wines are good value across the board (like Bulgarian reds) or because (as in the case of Beaujolais) we think there's better value elsewhere. Nor have we always picked the cheapest wines, though we've picked the cheapest stockists of those wines. Happy drinking!

Sweet White Bordeaux
1990 Clos St-Georges (SAI) £6.95
1984 Les Cyprès de Climens (VIC) £10.29

Red Burgundy
1991 Gevrey-Chambertin, Rossignol-Trapet (OD) £9.99
1989 Savigny-lès-Beaune, Pavelot (GE) £8.75

White and Sparkling Burgundy
Crémant de Bourgogne, Cave de Lugny (WAI) £6.25
1992 St-Aubin le Charmois, Leflaive (LAY) £10.95

Rhône Red
1992 Côtes du Rhône Parallèle 45, Jaboulet (HOG) £4.61
1990 Crozes-Hermitage, Cave des Clairmonts (WAI) £5.65
1990 Côtes du Rhône Guigal (OD) £4.95
1985 St-Joseph le Grand Pompée, Jaboulet (HOG) £8.61

Rhône White
1990 Lirac la Fermade, Dom Maby (YAP) 6.25
1987 Condrieu, Vernay (SEC) £8.99

Loire
1993 Pouilly-Fumé les Loges, Saget (MAJ) £5.99
1993 Sauvignon du Haut Poitou, Cave Co-op du Haut-Poitou (WAI) £3.99
1992 Sauvignon de Touraine, Confrérie d'Oisly et Thésée (OD) £3.99
1992 Coteaux du Giennois, Balland-Chapuis (OD) £4.99
1990 Vouvray, Domaine de l'Epinay (ASD) £5.75
1990 Vouvray, Ch de Vaudenuits (GRE) £6.25

Alsace
1993 Pinot Blanc Cave Co-op, Turckheim (BOT, THR) £4.49
1992 Gewürztraminer Réserve Prestige, Cave Co-op. Turckheim (NI) £6.70
1991 Sylvaner Vieilles Vignes, Ostertag (MV) £5.90

Languedoc-Roussillon
VeP de l'Herault Muscat Sec, du Bosc (WS) £4.60
1992 VdP d'Oc Chardonnay, Philippe de Baudin/Chais Baumière (SAI) £3.99
1992 VdP d'Oc Cépage Chardonnay, Ryman £4.95
1992 VdP d'Oc Chardonnay, Fortant de France (WAI) £3.99
1992 VdP d'Oc Cépage Chardonnay, Ryman (SAI) £4.95
1992 VdP d'Oc Cépage Merlot, Domaine des Fontaines (WAI) £2.99
1992 Coteaux du Languedoc Cépage Syrah, les Vignerons de la Carignano (OD) £3.99
1992 Côtes de la Malepère, Ch de Festes (BEK) £3.71
1991 VdP des Côtes Catalanes, Château de Jau (OD) £2.99
1991 VdP d'Oc La Cuvée Mythique, DuBernet/Vign. de Val d'Orbeiu (NI) £6.59
1991 VdP d'Oc Syrah, la Fadèze (LAY) £5.69
1990 Lirac la Fermade, Dom Maby (YAP) £5.95
1990 Corbières, Ch de Caraguilhes (SAF) £4.39
1990 Collioure, les Clos de Paulilles (OD) £6.49
1990 Corbières, Ch de Lastours (WCL, BU) £5.85-£5.95
1990 Faugères Cuvée Spèciale, Gilbert Alquier (SUM) £7.54
1989 Minervois, Ch de Fabas (GE) £3.95

South-West France
1993 Bergerac, Ch la Jaubertie Rosé (NI) £5.65
1992 Côtes de St-Mont, Producteurs Plaimont (SOM) £2.95

The codes given in brackets after the wine names indicate the merchants stocking the wines at these prices in the summer of 1994 The same codes are used in the price guides which begin on page 262. The key to the codes will be found on page 263.

1992 Côtes de Frontonnais, Ch Bellevue-la-Forêt (SAI) £3.95

1991 Gaillac, Ch Clement Termes (HOG) £3.93

1990 Bergerac, Ch la Jaubertie rouge (NI) £4.99

Germany

Rheingau Riesling, Schloss Reinhartshausen (SO) £3.25

1991 Kreuznacher Riesling Spät., Paul Anheuser (TES) £4.49

1990 Trittenheimer Apotheke Riesling Aus., F-W-Gymnasium (EY) £9.90

1989 Eltviller Sonnenberg Riesling Kab., von Simmern (WAT) £5.39

1989 Wachenheimer Rechbachel Riesling Kab., Bürklin-Wolf (ASD) £5.99

1986 Falkensteiner Hofberg Riesling Kab., F-W-Gymnasium (VIC) £5.39

1985 Eltviller Sonnenberg Riesling Kab., von Simmern (RAE) £5.95

1983 Oestricher Doosberg Riesling Kab., Schönborn (SO) £5.79

Italy

1993 Soave Classico Superiore, Masi (PIP) £4.85

1993 Orvieto Classico Abboccato, Antinori (GRE) £4.70

1993 Bardolino Classico Ca' Bordenis, Santi (HOG) £4.02

1993 Valpolicella Classico, Allegrini (WCL) £4.99

1993 Spanna, Travaglini (EL) £3.62

1992 Soave Classico Monte Tenda, Tedeschi (AD) £5.10

1992 Teroldego Rotaliano, Gaierhof (WAI) £4.25

1992 Dolcetto d'Acqui, Viticoltori dell'Acquese (AD) £4.50

1992 Recioto della Valpolicella Classico, Allegrini (LEA) £7.95

1992 Rosso Conero San Lorenzo, Umani Ronchi (NI) £4.39

1992 Carmignano Barco Reale, Capezzana (WCL) £5.99

1991 Chianti Rufina, Villa di Vetrice (GRE, AME, PIP, VA) £3.99–£4.29

1991 Chianti Classico, Rocca delle Macie (MAJ, SAF, DAV) £4.89–£4.99

1991 Nebbiolo d'Alba San Rocco, Mascarello (GRE) £7.65

1990 Valpolicella Classico Superiore Valverde, Tedeschi (AD) £5.10

1990 Pinot Nero, Puiatti (WCL) £8.79

1990 Chianti Rufina, Villa di Vetrice (SOM) £3.65

1990 Parrina Rosso, La Parrina (POR) £4.49

1989 Sassella, Nino Negri (HOG) £5.15

1988 Barolo, Aliberti (BY) £6.53

1988 Barbera d'Asti, Viticoltori dell'Acquese (BUT) £3.96

1988 Carmignano, Villa Capezzana (SOM) £6.95

1986 Recioto Amarone, Zenato (VA) £9.99

Sherry

Valdespino Fino (WAT) £4.23

Manzanilla de Sanlúcar, Barbadillo (AME, OD) £4.99

Dos Cortados Old Dry Oloroso, Williams & Humbert (HOG) £9.00

Tio Diego Amontillado, Valdespino (WAT) £7.50

Palo Cortado de Carrascal, Valdespino (WAT) £8.16

Port

Graham 10-year-old Tawny (NI) £10.95

1988 Quinta de la Rosa Port (HAM) £10.70

1983 Smith Woodhouse (PIP) £10.75

United States

1991 Ridge Paso Robles Zinfandel (AMI) £8.95

1991 Renaissance Riesling (AD) £7.20

1990 Calera Jensen Pinot Noir (PIP) £11.11

1989 Carneros Creek Pinot Noir (WCL) £7.49

Australia

1993 Brown Bros Dry Muscat (PIP) £4.99

1992 Hill-Smith Old Triangle Riesling (ASD) £3.99

1992 Charles Melton Nine Popes (SOM) £7.75

1992 Baileys Bundarra Shiraz (OD) £4.99

1991 Mount Langi Ghiran Shiraz (SOM) £6.80

1990 Penfolds Coonawarra Shiraz Bin 128 (SOM, HOG) £5.70–£5.84

1990 Lindemans Pyrus (POR, SAI, OD) £9.75–£9.99

1990 Rockford Basket Press Shiraz (WCL, AUS) £9.95–£9.99

1988 Coldstream Hills Cabernet Sauvignon (CV) £5.88

New Zealand

1990 Matua Valley Late Harvest Gewurztraminer half (LEA) £4.95

South Africa

1991 Backsberg Pinotage (HOG) £4.06

Other Regions

1991 Nemea, Boutari, Greece (OD) £3.85

1987 Château Carras, Côtes de Meliton, Greece (CV) £6.35

1987 Negru de Purkar, Moldova (NO) £4.89

1986 Tamaioasa, Romania (GRE) £3.70

1960 Tamaioasa, Romania (BU) £7.75

PENINSULA WARFARE

I'd better say this right away. We award 30 wines a star rating in our annual *Webster's* tasting. We expect to find at least that many wines that rise triumphantly to our challenge and fill us with exhilaration at the end of a hard day's tasting. We expect to raise our standards every year, not drop them.

Last year we awarded six wines a three star rating – this year we awarded two. Last year we awarded nine wines two stars – this year we awarded six. And last year we awarded 15 wines one star – this year we awarded 22. So the standard of wines was lower this year. But that's only half the story.

If we had kept to last year's marking criteria, only one of the three star wines would have made the grade. Five of this year's two star wines would have been marked down to one star, and of the 22 one star wines, ten would have got no rating of any sort. We had to lower our own judging standards to get a top 30. And we're not happy.

We had decided to have a look at Spain and Portugal this year because we've kept getting reports, both from people paid to disseminate such ideas, and from impartial tasters, that both countries were finally starting to make exciting wine

Lurching to Port

Both countries already do, of course. Portugal has Port and Madeira – at their best, two sublime fortified wines. Her table wines have lurched from the frankly atrocious to the fascinating but eccentric. But I always knew the potential was there. Every time I tasted young, fresh wine straight from the vat, the strange but delicious flavours of Portugal's indigenous grape varieties were apparent. But most winemaking in Portugal seemed based on aging the wine too long in the wrong sort of barrel: the sort of treatment guaranteed to flog the fruit and perfume out of any wine. Every time I begged the winemakers to bottle the wines while they were young and juicy, they looked at me as if I was deranged.

Spain was different. Sherry (from the right producer) is a superb fortified wine. Rioja used to be able to produce world class wines in the era when only the suitable land was planted with vines, when yields were lower and when the locals had a little more confidence in what they were doing. Penedès would occasionally come up with something special, as would Ribera del Duero, but the all pervasive feeling in the vast Spanish vineyard was one of boredom.

The legion of fascinating grape varieties that Portugal possesses and yet seems unable to benefit from, is not present in Spain. Spain has only a handful of native vines of any personality. Talented and determined winemakers can turn this handful to good effect, even in unpromising areas; conversely, in supposedly top regions like Penedès, Rioja and Ribera del Duero, poor winemaking can leave one sorrowing at so much wasted quality, seeping away in a sea of volatility, sulphides and bacterial contamination.

Indeed, we decided to exclude Rioja from our tasting. Partly this was out of common sense – we already had the better part of 200 wines to look at, Rioja would have added a whole pile more. But it was equally a question of – well, what? Correct: boredom again. To be honest, the most encouraging Riojas I've seen recently are the fruit-first no-oak youngsters that show what a splendid grape Tempranillo is for making bright, vibrant reds even if most producers have lost sight of how to make it age. Funnily enough, Rioja got a lot of its ideas about barrel-aging from Bordeaux, but Bordeaux still does it better.

Penedès would like to claim the role of pretender to Rioja's throne, but relentlessly fails to do so. The quality-oriented wine companies always seem to promise more than they deliver, and the incidence of faulty wine still is much too high.

But I had hoped Navarra would draw clear of the long shadow cast by Rioja, its immediate neighbour. Pound for pound, Navarra wines are the better bet.Their fruit is more focussed, their oak seems better handled, and the authorities have been far more relaxed about experimentation with grape varieties. But here too there are too many examples of a good initial release of a vintage or a brand being followed up by inferior shipments.

There are two areas where you really can find fruit in the bottle, and they operate at different levels. As soon as you have a Ribera del Duero wine in a tasting, you get thwacked by the fruit. Bravo. This wild, high river valley produces ripe, dark red grapes from the Tempranillo vine (here called Tinto Fino). But in that case, why do so few figure in our star wines? Winemaking, pure and simple. I kept wondering how wines can be so young, so ripe and yet so flat. Ribera del Duero until recently was famous only for Vega Sicilia, Spain's legendary top red. Then came other attention-grabbers like Pesquera (whose over-hyped wine did not manage to earn a star with us) and a bandwagon began to roll. Spain really does have a problem producing wines of the highest class. Ribera del Duero may well have the red grapes to do just that, but there's a lot of basic winemaking to get right yet.

But the area where they are getting the winemaking right, where the grapes are proving to be of remarkably good quality and where the price never exceeds that quality is the vast swathe of land south of Madrid – the treeless, sunscorched ranges of La Mancha and Valdepeñas.

There's a lot of bad wine in La Mancha – indeed only 2 million hls of the annual production of about 17 million hls are declared as DO, and by no means all of the 100 or so co-ops actually know what they're doing. But there is a bigger concentration of export-minded, eager-to-please wine growers here and in Valdepeñas than anywhere else in Spain.

Airén filings

Until recently, I would have said that the region's curse is the white Airén grape which grows like a weed everywhere – almost 80 per cent of the half a million acres of vine here are Airén. I've actually described it as the world's most boring grape variety. Well, I take it back.

Modern winemaking methods are proving that the Airén is ideally suited to producing soft, light, appley whites for quick consumption. The other major grape here is the red Cencibel, or Tempranillo. Under one name or another this pops up just about everywhere in Spain. Cencibel used to be blended with Airén and sold in the cafés of Madrid. Now that they're suddenly trying to make decent stuff they've realised that in Cencibel they've got some of the best grapes in Spain.

So why haven't I given any stars to wines from La Mancha and Valdepeñas? Because they are concentrating, both in red and whites, on producing decent, attractive wines at decent prices – not adding the extra that wins awards, and I totally support that approach. But pricewise they were between £1.99 and £3.99,

- and every one was a decent drink. That probably deserves at least a star for consistency.

Most of the 'extra' in Spain so far is being provided by the inclusion of international grape varieties, or, in the case of the high quality aromatic white grapes of northern Spain, by adopting an international approach. Spain has resisted the attraction of 'flying winemakers', be they French, English or Australian, more successfully than most, but they are now beginning to appear.

International grape varieties like Chardonnay and Cabernet Sauvignon cause many Spaniards to work up a most dreadful lather. Yet most of their own grapes are incapable of achieving any great heights. Why not spice them up a bit with other internationally tried and tested varieties? It won't be the first time that winemakers have shown that the right blend is more than the sum of its parts. Swallow your pride, Señores. Sure, make the best of what you do have, but if you relentlessly stick to Spanish grape varieties vinified in a traditional Spanish way, you're going to be as bored as we are.

As for Portugal, thank goodness for Sogrape. And it's not just me who should be thanking Sogrape, it's the whole Portuguese winemaking fraternity. Now, I'm one of the least likely people to start crowing in praise of a massive megabucks operation like Sogrape, and my hackles rise and my bullshit detector leaps to red alert whenever I come anywhere near most of the big wine companies of the world – but Sogrape seems to be different. For one thing, it delivers the goods.

Sogrape makes Mateus Rosé. So long as you get it fresh it's perfectly good. But that's not the point. What matters is that Sogrape sells well over 30 million bottles of the stuff every year. That equals serious money, and serious profit. It cost Sogrape £6m to build a spanking new winery in Dão, the area that used to delude itself that it was making Portugal's best red wine. In fact it was a dustbin of lazy self-interest dominated by a co-operative movement of a particularly antediluvian character. Quiet persuasion wasn't going to work in that time warp. Any company that wanted anything done in Dão was going to have to do it itself.

And it's working. Not only are Sogrape's Duque de Viseu Dãos already the best commercial examples on the market, but there are single estate wines in the pipeline and the crusty monopoly of the co-ops has been broken.

That's Dão. Sogrape also has a major winery in Bairrada. Its Terra Franca was the only Bairrada red to get any stars. Its Bairrada whites both got stars. No other white Bairrada did.

Its white Vinho Verde, Chello Dry, got a star too – something no other Vinho Verde managed. In fact the only Portuguese white stars apart from Sogrape were a Chardonnay and a Muscat made by an Australian.

Pink with embarassment

You could say – fair enough, but rosés and reds are Portugal's strengths. Yes you could. I'm not so sure you'd be right, but you could. Let's look at the rosés. The showing was pathetic. Sogrape's Nobilis wasn't up to star standard but is a reasonably attractive fresh, dryish style. As for the rest of the dirty laundry bag full of failed Mateus look-alikes – well, all I can say is that they were as bad as the Spanish – and that was bad.

Back to reds. The north of Portugal is supposed to produce all the great Portuguese reds. If Dão and Bairrada were pretty feeble, what about the Douro? Well, guess what? Our best wine came from the Douro. Our third best did as well.

Both are made by Sogrape-owned Ferreira. Otherwise? Nothing.

So what about the South? The Oeste, the Ribatejo, the wide vistas of the Alentejo are supposed to be one of the great grape baskets of Europe, a land packed with vineyards full of interesting indigenous varieties that bristle with flavour and personality. And yes, I found a three star Alentejo wine from Sogrape. And a good Cabernet/Periquita from Quinta de Panças in Alenquer. The latter, astonishingly, was the only non-Sogrape Portuguese red to gain a star. Take away Sogrape and Portugal gets one single star.

What on earth is going on? Not just with the winemaking, but also with the British importers and retailers. Don't these people taste the wines they import?

What a difference a year makes

At the moment I except the Almeirim co-op from these criticisms. Its Leziria and Ramada brands are both well-made and enjoyable. Yet I can remember these wines a year ago, when they were far better. I remember the burst of gorgeous damsony fruit, the magnificent muddle of conflicting flavours and sensations all bound together by a ripe, rich black-fruited power.

A year ago Leziria and Ramada would both have walked into the ratings. Now they get acceptable marks because the wines are still clean and enjoyable and have some character. This year Leziria shows interesting fern and pepper, celery and sloes in its flavour. Ramada shows aggressive cranberry and redcurrant. What's missing? The ripeness. The damsons, the raspberries and plums. The wines are now stretched and dilute. Still okay, but obviously struggling to keep up with demand.

But what about Borba? My notes say 'light, tannic, lean, dilute raisin and redcurrant'. Yet a few years ago Borba was a star.

What about Terras del Rei? My notes say – well, perhaps I should leave out the unsavoury details of precisely what my notes say. A few years ago Terras del Rei, too, was a star. And I've got other notes from the Alentejo and Ribatejo and Terras Vedras regions that make me want to bang my head with frustration. All of them are at best pale imitations of what they were a few years ago. I've probably stuck my neck out in support of the southern Portuguese reds more than any other British critic in recent years. Now I feel like an idiot.

This short-termism – stretching the wines to meet current demand with no thought for the future – is a worrying trend. Because these co-ops aren't actually poor. They've had millions of ECUs pumped into them since accession to the European Union. The prices of things like Borba and Terras del Rei aren't so cheap when you compare them to the offerings of some other European co-ops. Someone's making some money out of these wines. Who is it? And what are they doing with their profits?

What they should be doing is re-investing, employing good oenologists at decent rates of pay, and perhaps buying hearing aids to help them hear their critics clearly as we attempt, albeit harshly, to tell them what the export market wants. They might also buy a few cases of southern French, South African, Australian and New Zealand wines from our high streets to show what is possible with the grape varieties the world already knows.

And then they could get get their acts together and show us what they can do with their own varieties, probably the greatest untapped treasure store of original flavours in the wine world today.

OZ CLARKE'S TOP THIRTY

WINE	RATING	SAMPLE PRICES
1991 Alentejo Sogrape Vinha do Monte, red, P	★★★	£5.25
1985 Barca Velha, red, P	★★★	£24.00
1993 Sauvignon Blanc, Hermanos Lurton, Rueda, S	★★	£3.99
1993 Quinta des Pedravites, Bairrada white, P	★★	£4.99
1985 Viña Magana Meriot Reserva, red, S	★★	£19.99
1985 Viña Magana Reserva, Navarra, red, S	★★	£11.49
1982 Castillo de Ayud Reserva, Bodegas Langa, red, S	★★	c£.5.00
1984 Ferreira Reserva Especial, red, P	★★	£9.99
1990 Cova da Ursa Chardonnay, JP Vinhos, white, P	★	£6.99
1992 João Pires, VR Terras do Sado, white, P	★	£3.99- £4.69
1992 Chardonnay vino de mesa, Bodegas de Crianza de Castilla la Vieja, white, S	★	£5.65
Sainsbury's Viño de la Tierra Blanco, Extremadura, S	★	£2.59
1993 Palacio de Bornos, Rueda white, S	★	£3.95
1993 Solana, Bodega Alanis, Torrontes & Treixadura, Ribeiro, white, S	★	£3.99
1993 San Trocado, Bodega Alanis, Ribeiro, white, S	★	£4.99
1991 Vinas del Vero Chardonnay, Somontano, Compania Vitivinicola Aragonesa, white, S	★	£5.45 - £6.10
1992 Augustus Chardonnay, Cellers Puig & Roca, Penedés, white, S	★	£8.49
1993 Principe de Viana Chardonnay, Navarra, S	★	£4.49
Chello Dry Vinho Verde, white, P	★	£3.79
1991 Bairrada Reserva, Sogrape, white, P	★	£5.39
1990 Quinta de Pancas, red, P	★	£4.99
1990 Raïmat Abadia, Costers del Segre, red, S	★	£4.49
1990 Vinas del Vero Pinot Noir, Somontano, Compania Vitivinicola Aragonesa, red, S	★	£6.59- £7.00
1989 Tinto F Callejo, Bodegas Felix Callejo, red, S	★	£7.09
1989 Las Campanas Cabernet Sauvignon, Navarra, S	★	£3.99 - £4.49
1988 Monte Ducay, Bodegas San Valero, Cariñena, red, S	★	£3.99
1987 Senorio de Nava Crianza, Ribera del Duero, red, S	★	£5.99
1990 Bairrada Terra Franca, red, P	★	£3.49-£4.40
1990 Dão Duque de Viseu, red, P	★	£4.99
1992 Valle de Raposa, red, P	★	£4.49

Prices are as supplied to us by merchants in June 1994. Vintages may change.

IBERIAN WINES

TASTING NOTES	STOCKISTS
Gorgeous sweet stewy dates and plums, fresh blackcurrant and tobacco.	WS,SAF
Treacle, liquorice, prunes and plums, blackberries, cherries and herbs.	OD
Snappy stuff: aggressive elderflower, grapefruit, passion fruit, peardrops.	VIC, SAI
Apricot, lime pith, a hint of kid glove leather and a sprinkling of classy talc.	OD
Lovely fat, ripe fruit: rich, thick-textured blackcurrant and raspberry.	BOD
Full, with raspberry freshness and a dark tarry blackberry, blueberry core.	BOD
Mature, old-fashioned: marrons glacés and sultanas, beefed up with dates.	Contact Rioja Wine Co: 0824 703 407
Port without the sugar and strength; liquorice, bilberry black chocolate; dry.	OD
Thick, peach syrup and grilled nuts; horny-handed traditional Aussie style.	TES, WR
Breezy, grapy, with nice citrus lash and a good whiff of floral loo freshener.	SAI, TES, SAF, OD
Simple, attractive creamy Chardonnay showing a little oak.	Contact C&D Wines: 081 650 9095
Bright, fresh nectarine and ripe apple flavours with a hint of spice.	SAI
Aggressive grapefruit, lemon pith and Granny Smith apple peel – but it works.	Contact C&D Wines: 081 650 9095
Spritzy, lively white with lemon pith and grapefruit and a splash of honey.	OD
Sandalwood-dry and pearskin-scented, like Imperial Leather aftershave.	OD, PLA
Strange, rich old-style Chardonnay mixing syrup with chickpeas and humus.	CB, SAF, ROB, RES, RE
Old-style Chardonnay again, rich, figgy, nutty, with tropical fruit syrup.	FUL
Sharp, tangy nectarine- and peach-scented, and a little clove spice.	BOD
Spritzy bubbles, lemon zest and a dusty dryness. Good, typical Vinho Verde.	SAI
Lanolin and leather: will go lemony and butter-caramelly in a year or two.	SAF, GA
Deep, gutsy, blackcurrant skins, coffee beans and earth.	GA
Fairly mature blackcurrant and raspberry fruit with fairly smoky oak.	SAI, TES, VIC, THR
Interesting leafy, twiggy Pinot Noir with volatile but attractive cherry fruit.	SAF, PLA, BIB
Smoky, creamy oak on slightly acid but refreshing blackcurrant fruit.	WS
Overripe, almost too sultana-ish, but strong new-wave damson saves it.	OD
Good, quite rich blackberry and raisin fruit, though it also has a lean streak.	MOR
Deep, dark, ripe plumskins texture and a pleasant spiciness too.	ASD, SAF, FUL
Aggressive meaty stuff, blackcurrant and cranberry with lovage and bay.	SAI, BEK, SAF
Deep, young; loganberry, fruitcake spice emerge after several hours' opening.	SAF, BEK
Lovely juicy fruit and gorgeous, unexpected floral perfume.	SAF

For a key to stockists and codes, see page 263. (Shipments may vary.) S= Spain; P=Portugal

IDEAL CELLARS

This is where I start handing out cheques. Every year I give some lucky wine merchants and the odd writer budgets of £100, £500 and £1000 and I say – okay, what would you buy? And just look at the sort of wines they come up with: wines with fruit, wines with flavour, wines that you don't have to mortgage your house for. And where are they from? From Australia, from New Zealand, from the Rhône and from Italy, that's where: all those places where the winemakers know how to get the best out of their grapes. My sort of winemakers, my sort of wines.

PETER AMEY

AMEY'S WINES

I've had to restrict myself – but even so, I've managed to sample most of my favourite regions.

£100

Four stylish wines for enjoyable everyday drinking, with elegance from France and rich concentration from Australia.

Syrah Vin de Pays des Collines Rhodaniennes, Cave de Tain l'Hermitage *Delicious, soft, smoky, peppery Syrah from the northern Rhône.* **6 for £22.74**

1992 David Wynn Dry Red, Australia *A super flavour-packed blend of Cabernet, Pinot and Shiraz, from the talented Adam Wynn of Mountadam Vineyard near Adelaide* **6 for £27.08**

1992 Vin de Pays des Côtes de Gascogne, Domaine de Maubey *I am always impressed with the quality of this wine. It is a blend of Colombard, Ugni Blanc and Gros Manseng, with a lovely fragrant nose, fresh, rich palate and zippy acidity.* **6 for £22.74**

1993 Salisbury Estate Chardonnay/ Sémillon *A great value-for-money white from Victoria, fresh and full of ripe peachy, melony flavours, with just a touch of new oak; wonderfully gluggable.* **6 for £25.60**

Total cost: £98.16

£500

This cellar allows me a wonderful choice of wines, with real quality and individuality from all round the world. These are not for laying down, though.

1992 Muscadet de Sèvre et Maine Sur Lie, Château de Chasseloir *An example of how good Muscadet can be. The old vines of this property make big intense wine with superb balance and length.* **12 for £68.28**

1993 Mount Langi Ghiran Riesling, Australia *Although famous for his long-living Shiraz, winemaker Trevor Mast produces several other stunning varietals, including one of Australia's finest Rieslings. It it quite dry, with intense tangy, honeyed, citrus fruit, and goes wonderfully with oriental food.* **12 for £70.56**

1993 Te Mata Castle Hill Sauvignon Blanc *New Zealand has become justly famous for the quality of its delicious, intensely-flavoured Sauvignon Blancs. This one is a superb example, with a lovely, pure, elegant style.* **12 for £88.35**

1991 Chianti Classico, Felsina Berardenga *One of my favourite Chianti houses, which regularly produces a rich, deeply-flavoured wine with great structure, even in difficult years like 1991.* **12 for £83.79**

1989 Huntington Estate Cabernet/Merlot *A new find for me, and one with which I am delighted. The vineyard is in Mudgee in New South Wales, and makes beautifully stylish, complex reds.* **12 for £87.66**

1987 Château de la Rivière, Fronsac *A wonderful wine from what is generally rated a lesser year in Bordeaux. It has powerful, rich, minty, plummy fruit, complex and long.* **12 for £102.48**

Total cost: £501.12

£1000

With £1000 to spend I can indulge myself a little. Some of these I shall be happy to lay down for a while – providing I can have my other two cellars in the meantime.

1991 Taltarni Clover Hill Tasmania Sparkling Chardonnay *Let's start with a classy new sparkling wine from Taltarni's Tasmanian vineyard. A delight now, with its elegant pineapply fruit and yeasty complexity, this will continue to improve over the next few years.* **12 for £113.43**

1991 Alsace Gewürztraminer, Leon Beyer *Delicious spicy Gewürztraminer with excellent balance.* **12 for £95.19**

1992 Te Mata Elston Chardonnay *This has got to be my favourite among the many New Zealand Chardonnays. They're more subtle, anyway, than the Aussies.* **12 for £136.68**

1991 David Wynn Patriarch Shiraz, Australia *Adam Wynn buys up parcels of Eden Valley Shiraz from old vines to produce this stunning wine of great concentration, with wonderfully intense spicy fruit and rich oak, and an excellent finish.* **12 for 107.73**

1989 Beaune 1er Cru Les Epenottes, Vallet Frères *Excellent deep, long-flavoured Burgundy with new oak complexity. When Pinot Noir is this good, it's worth spoiling oneself.* **12 for £202.35**

1988 Brunello di Montalcino, Argiano *A wonderfully intense, rich combination of ripe blackcurrant, pepper and dark chocolate – tannic, long and superbly complex.* **12 for £167.46**

1982 Warre's Quinta da Cavadinha Port *I love port, and Warre's terrific single-quinta vintage has got to be one of the best buys around, with its gorgeous rich, spicy fruit.* **12 for 182.28**

Total cost £1005.12

MIKE CONOLLY

SAINSBURY'S

How do my cellars this year differ from those I put together last year? Well, France seems to be making something of a comeback, with eight of the 19 wines selected, and I've gone for Spain, too – even though Oz doesn't agree! I've come up with a fairly mixed bag, but I've tried to cover as many styles as reasonably possible – though I'm afraid my own two Champagnes sneaked in again. I'm certain there's something here for every wine lover. Enjoy!

£100

1993 Rueda Sauvignon Blanc, Hermanos Lurton *A New-World-style Sauvignon, made by a Frenchman in a little known area of Spain. This may be taking the Flying Winemaker idea to extremes, but it works. Excellent flavour.* **6 for £23.94**

1993 Chapel Hill Hungarian Chardonnay *A flying winemaker again – Kim Mylne this time – and remarkable value.* **6 for £17.94**

Who but Sainsbury's would let an Australian loose in an Italian vineyard?

The Australian is one Geoff Merrill, wine maker of great renown and apparently second owner of Merv Hughes' moustache.

The vineyards, selected from hundreds throughout Italy, and those of Gruppo Italiano Vino (GIV).

The marriage broker was Sainsbury's, with more than a little self interest.

Sainsbury's wanted Geoff to improve the blend of their own label Italian wines by extracting as much flavour as possible from the grapes whilst remaining true to the wine style.

Then to use his antipodean expertise and GIV's extensive facilities to produce new and interesting wines.

Both tasks turned into a labour of love.

Unimpressed by the potential of the trebbiano grape, he travelled to the north in search of the chardonnay and cabernet sauvignon.

Just before harvest time 'Buffalo Bill' as the Italians called him, drove 1,600 kilometres in a day checking the ripeness of the grape.

He de-stemmed everything 'because I didn't want those coarse, stalky tannins'.

And from the press he used only the free-run juice, which was immediately cooled to preserve the fresh fruit flavours.

He imported the yeasts he uses in Australia.

He insisted on oak barrels. And eliminated oxygen at all stages.

The result?

Four new blends of Sainsbury's Italian classics including the Orvieto Classico, a delicate dry white with a hint of citrus.

And six wines new to Sainsbury's. (Try the fresh plummy flavours of our Teroldego Rotaliano or the unique , blackcurrant flavours of Cabernet Sauvignon Delle Tre Venezie.)

All have great character. Like their maker.

1991 Sainsbury's Tempranillo/Cabernet Sauvignon, Navarra *A superb blend from a go-ahead winery. The Cabernet Sauvignon gives just enough grip to balance the lustiness of the Tempranillo.*   **6 for £23.70**

1990 Saumur Champigny, Domaine Les Hauts de Sanziers *Cabernet Franc at its best – cool and brambly. Very good slightly chilled.*   **6 for £41.70**

Total cost: £107.28

£500

You'll need several trolleys for this lot.

Fino Quinta, Osborne *Drink it as they do in Jerez – chilled to the bone (the* fino *that is) and at one sitting.*   **12 halves for £39.48**

Sainsbury's NV Champagne *Sorry to repeat myself, but our blend from Duval is good, year in, year out. The style is now perhaps slightly lighter and fruitier than, say, five years ago.*   **12 for £143.40**

1992 Ménétou-Salon, Henri Pellé *Good Loire Sauvignons are never cheap, but this has a lovely combination of delicate fruit and firm backbone.*   **12 for £77.40**

Sainsbury's Chardonnay delle Tre Venezie *The first fruits of a growing collaboration between Sainsbury's and the Italian company G.I.V. An Italian white with fruit and flavour.*   **12 for £43.08**

1990 Château Beaumont Haut-Médoc *First rate Cru Bourgeois Haut-Médoc at an excellent price. Very drinkable now, but will keep for several years.*   **12 for £89.40**

1990 Pyrus Lindemans *The archetypal Aussie blockbuster. Bring a sharp knife and cut a slice or two of this wine's fabulous fruit.*   **12 for £119.40**

Total cost: £512.16

£1000

Sainsbury's Oloroso *Dry, full, intense: a great winter warmer.*   **12 halves for £40.68**

1989 Sainsbury's Champagne *I couldn't leave this out. Powerful, distinguished wine, not for casual consumption.*   **12 for £167.40**

1993 Geoff Merrill Grenache Rosé *A wonderfully fruity but dry Aussie rosé from larger-than-life Geoff Merrill.*   **12 for £58.88**

1993 Kesselstatt Estate Riesling *All the race and flint of a top Mosel, from a superb winery. Remarkable value.*   **12 for £55.80**

1991 Sainsbury's Copertino Riserva *Warm, robust red from the deep south of Italy, the Mezzogiorno.*   **12 for £47.80**

1989 Château Lamothe-Bergeron *A magnum is always good fun when there are six or more round the table and this mid-weight, fruity Haut-Médoc is a favourite of mine.*   **6 magnums for £191.40**

1992 Church Road Chardonnay *Deliciously balanced NZ wine,with plenty of weight but a lightness of finish which leaves you wanting more.*   **12 for 95.40**

1990 Château de Rully Rouge,Rully, Rodet *This Côte Chalonnaise shows that even now you don't have to pay the earth for a quality Burgundy.*   **12 for 107.40**

1989 Château Maucaillou, Moulis *A staple in Sainsbury's fine wine range for many years: supple, velvety, middle-weight and seductive.*   **12 for £143.40**

Sainsbury's 10-Year-Old Tawny Port *A versatile port, capable of finishing a really good meal without excessive hangover potential, or very attractive lightly chilled as an apéritif.*   **12 for £121.80**

Total cost: £1029.96

LANCE FOYSTER MW

HAMPDEN WINE COMPANY

We are independent merchants buying wherever we like: direct from producers, or indirectly through agents. We do seem to have a European bias, mainly, I think, because my partner Ian and I know these countries so well.

£100

Even when one's choosing wines for every day, one doesn't have to stick entirely to familiar appellations.

1986 Marius Reserva, Almansa *Medium-bodied, typical Spanish flavours, and plenty of oak to match the soft, fruity Tempranillo.* **6 for £28.20**

1992 Moyston Shiraz/Cabernet, Australia *Ripe fruit and rich chunky flavours from this classic Australian blend of grapes. This is a style that the Australians have really made their own.* **6 for £25.65**

1993 Château Calabre, Montravel Sec *A delicious, crisp aperitif: an unoaked Sémillon / Sauvignon blend from a little-known* appellation *near Bergerac. (It's not so long ago that one would have said something pretty similar about Bergerac itself.)* **6 for £27.07**

1992 Picpoul de Pinet, Coteaux de Languedoc *Soft, but with nice balancing acidity from the Picpoul grape. This wine is organic.* **6 for £28.20**

Total cost £109.12

£500

For £500 I can have wonderful concentrated but subtle flavours from all over Europe and far, far beyond. Cheap at the price, I say.

1993 Château Puy Servain, Montravel Sec *Another Montravel, and this time a superior pure Sauvignon from Château Calabre, near Bergerac. Unoaked, concentrated Loire-like flavours from old vines.* **12 for £63.27**

1991 Alsace Pinot Blanc, Marcel Deiss *You could drink this as an aperitif or have it with food. It comes from a top Alsace grower, it has fruity, aromatic, off-dry flavours, and it's deliciously full and fat in the mouth.* **£72.96**

1992 Dr Loosen Riesling Kabinett *This is low in alcohol, but rich in classic, delicate Mosel flavours, and it comes from a top grower. In fact some would say that Ernst Loosen is the best producer in the whole of the Mosel.* **12 for £83.40**

1992 Quinta La Rosa, Douro *A blend of traditional Douro flavours and modern, fruit-enhancing wine-making. Brilliant wine, hugely successful.* **12 for £56.43**

1990 Buena Cepa, Ribera del Duero *A rich, deep-coloured Spanish red from an increasingly successful area, with soft, warm grape flavours dominating the oak tannins.* **12 for £63.84**

1989 Château St Jacques, Bordeaux Supérieur *Typical Médoc flavours from a wine made at Château Siran. This is dry and cedary, with lots of rich, ripe fruit. A good year, too.* **12 for £79.23**

1990 Kanonkop Pinotage *I think this is the very best example in South Africa of this cross-bred vine. Its sweet plummy fruit has a nice spicy edge, enhanced by brief oak aging.* **12 for £87.21**

Total cost: £506.34

£1000

This doesn't pretend to be a cellar for all occasions; just one filled with wines I love.

1991 Alsace Gewürztraminer, Marcel Deiss *Dry, but with the mouth-filling richness typical of the grape.*   **12 for £102.03**

1990 Rully La Chaume Jacques Dury *Classic Burgundian flavours at a non-classic price: soft, rounded Chardonnay, with that unmistakable dry Burgundian nuttiness.*   **12 for £101.46**

1993 Moss Wood Chardonnay Margaret River, Australia *Always a favourite. Even fatter, richer and more buttery than the rest.*   **12 for £132.00**

1987 Alentejo, Quinto do Carmo *This is a long-established vineyard in central Portugal, where old vines produce super-ripe and concentrated fruit, helped along with plenty of new oak.*   **12 for £111.15**

1987 Rioja Reserva Contino *A single-estate Rioja with strong fruit flavour still dominant over the oak. Will continue to age impressively.*   **12 for £111.15**

1990 Carignano Tenuta Cappezzana *From a superb estate in Tuscany. A drop of Cabernet Sauvignon in the blend seems to add extra fruit to what is an already rich style.*   **12 for £96.90**

I'll have two half-cases of dessert and fortified wines to drink or keep:

1989 Vouvray demi-sec Le Haut Lieu, Huet *Lots of concentrated sweetness and noble rot, despite the* demi-sec *title. An example of the exceptional richness this region attained in 1989.*   **6 for £76.00**

1992 Château Puy Servain Moelleux, Haut Montravel *All the time-consuming love and care necessary for top Sauternes are lavished on this. Only nobly-rotten grapes, vinified in new oak, end up as a smooth, creamy dessert wine lacking only a little of the power of the great names.*   **6 for £66**

10 year Malmsey Madeira, H.M. Borges *Only with Madeira this old (and older) do the genuine and unique flavours show themselves: warm, tangy baked fruit, with overtones of prunes and figs. Lusciously sweet, with delicious crisp, clean acidity to balance.*   **6 for £88.00**

1987 Vintage Port, Quinta da Eira Velha *The wine from this privately-owned estate in the Douro used to be absorbed into Cockburns' blends, but now it's making vintage wine under its own label. Its very deep colour and rich sweet, nicely baked fruit flavours make it ready for drinking, though traditionalists will want to hold on to it.*   **6 for £85**

Total cost: £969.69

ROSEMARY GEORGE MW

My cellar this year is based on Riesling, which in my book is the world's finest white grape. Its range of flavours is unparalleled, and how else could I get classic wines from top growers at these prices? They come from Germany unless stated otherwise; I would have liked to have included some Austrians but the best, which are very fine, are unavailable here.

£100

I'll drink the Jackson Estate as an aperitif, and have the Dr Loosen or the Saar with salmon.

1992 Dr Loosen Riesling *The simplest wine from one of the Mosel's top producers. Everyday classic style.*   **6 for £36**

1993 Jackson Estate Marlborough Dry, New Zealand *The label doesn't say so, but this is pure Riesling and it is delicious, flowery and fragrant.* **6 for £36**

1990 Ayler Kupp Riesling Spätlese, Saar Winzerverein *Lovely steely flavours with underlying honey.* **6 for £30**

Total cost: £102

£500

Don't think that Spätlesen are always sweet. Most are medium, with wonderfully taut balancing acidity. I'd be happy to lay all these bottles down for another few years.

1989 Freinsheimer Goldberg Riesling Spätlese, Lingenfelder *Delicious delicate honey with balancing acidity, from one of the great names of the Pfalz.* **12 for £84.00**

1992 Wehlener Sonnenuhr Riesling Kabinett, Dr Loosen *Slaty nose and honeyed fruit; very elegant.* **12 for £100.80**

1993 Serriger Schloss Saarsteiner Riesling Kabinett *Lightly peachy, with good Saar acidity.* **12 for £93.60**

1992 Haardter Herzog Riesling Trocken Spätlese, Müller Catoir *I don't usually like German trockens, but this is an exception, with real fruit and balance.* **12 for £120.00**

1990 Piesporter Domherr Riesling Spätlese, von Kesselstatt *All that fine Mosel should be, with honey and elegance.* **12 for £121.80**

Total cost: £520.20

£1000

With lots of loot to hand I can afford some sweet wines as well, and some top Alsace. 1989, 1990 and 1992 were all excellent years in Germany – most of these will see a decade out.

1992 Niederhauser Steinberg Riesling Kabinett, Staatliche Weinbaudomäne *The producer is the local state domaine, and it's very reliable. This has appealingly delicate fruit which will develop well in bottle for several years.* **12 for £79.80**

1992 Scharzhofberger Riesling Kabinett, von Kesselstatt *Delicate fruit, balanced with steely acidity.* **12 for £82.20**

1990 Graacher Himmelreich Riesling Auslese, Friedrich-Wilhelm-Gymnasium *Wonderful honeyed concentration and elegance. This is getting sweet enough for many puddings.* **12 for £138.60**

1993 Brauneberger Juffer Riesling Auslese, Max. Ferd. Richter *Still very closed but with plenty of potential. Put it away for a decade, then have it after dinner – or with baked apples.* **12 for £130.80**

1990 Schloss Reichartshausener Riesling Spätlese, Balthasar Ress *Spicy hints on the nose with a complex honeyed palate. Good gutsy Rheingau structure.* **12 for £147.60**

1989 Alsace Riesling Schlossberg, Paul Blanck *Lovely slaty Riesling fruit from one of the region's best names.* **12 for £110.40**

1990 Alsace Riesling Grand Cru Saering, Schlumberger, Alsace *Superb fruit, with Alsace steeliness and weight. Alsace Riesling can be more approachable than German.* **12 for £139.29**

1992 Redwood Valley Late Harvest Rhine Riesling, New Zealand *Luscious fruit from one of the star Riesling producers of the Antipodes.* **12 halves for £72.00**

1985 Alsace Riesling, Clos Ste-Hune, Trimbach *From the finest vineyard in Alsace. I'd prefer a whole case, but I've run out of cash.* **3 for £90.00**

Total cost: £990.69

JAMES HOGG

J.E. HOGG

These aren't meant to constitute balanced cellars – merely suggestions on how to spend your money. My tastes are very traditional, and my own cellar would have lots of claret, Burgundy, Alsace and Germany, but I've mainly recommended wines that come from elsewhere but have a similar subtlety and balance. The brasher sort of wine is not here.

Claret features, though, because the recent run of lighter vintages necessitates some stockpiling of 1990. Southern France provides a vast range of styles – our selections from there and from other countries are at the lighter end of the spectrum.

£100

This cellar is entirely red, but I feel that as an example of value for money it would be hard to beat. You may just have to give up fish for the duration.

1991 Château de Laurens, Faugères *Fills every corner of the mouth without being heavy or aggressive.*   **6 for £22.14**

1991 Syrah Vin de Pays de l'Aude, Domaine de Thelin *Very smooth and mellow without any of the pungency so often found in cheaper Syrah from the south of France.*   **6 for £22.92**

1990 Château Guionne, Côtes de Bourg *This has good presence and is drinkable now, but there's no hurry, because it will develop well.*   **6 for £29.16**

1991 Chianti Rufina Remole, Frescobaldi *There's excellent concentration of fruit here with a full, traditional, nutty flavour. This is serious Chianti.*   **6 for £26.70**

Total cost: £100.92

£500

Apart from the first wine this is an entirely New World selection, but of a kind to appeal to a decidedly Old World wine merchant. I haven't got any sparkling wine yet, but that can wait until I've got more money.

1989 Domaine de Rimauresq Rouge, Côtes de Provence *Another find from southern France. This has real elegance, style and subtlety of flavour.*   **12 for £67.68**

1990 Houghton's Gold Reserve Cabernet Sauvignon *Western Australian wines are usually too strongly flavoured for me, but this is very moreish.*   **12 for £65.64**

1990 Firestone Cabernet Sauvignon *Unlike many California wines this always seems to say, as claret does, that it comes from a particular piece of ground.*   **12 for £103.80**

1991 Bouchard Finlayson Blanc de Mer, South Africa *Just a beautifully balanced light white that disappears alarmingly rapidly from the glass.*   **12 for £67.68**

1992 Redwood Sauvignon Blanc, Nelson, South Island   **12 for £82.56**
1991 Babich Irongate Chardonnay, Hawkes Bay   **12 for £110.16**
A couple of New Zealand whites that are much less intense than many, but with a breadth of flavour that makes them an excellent accompaniment to food.

Total cost: £497.52

£1000

These are distinctly serious wines. You may think this cellar a little heavy on the Pinot Noir, but it's a wonderful grape and I haven't had any at all until now.

1988 Brunello di Montalcino Castelgiocondo, Frescobaldi *Drinking exceptionally well despite its youth. Gutsy but still elegant, this will appeal to even the most dedicated claret drinker (like me, possibly).* **12 for £111.72**

1988 Chianti Classico Riserva Ducale Oro, Ruffino *Probably needs another year or two, but the balance and concentration of fruit are quite superb.* **12 for £133.20**

1990 Nuits-St-Georges, Champy *It has often been difficult to justify the price of red Burgundy, but this one speaks for itself – it's a village wine, rather than anything grander, but it's a very complete wine of great charm and flavour. It's drinking beautifully already, but will keep well for several years.* **12 for £187.08**

1990 Tyrrell's Vat 6 Pinot Noir, Hunter Valley **12 for £128.40**
1991 Pipers Brook Vineyard Pinot Noir, Tasmania **12 for £136.08**

There's been a steady improvement in Australian Pinot Noir in recent years, and these two are outstanding. Tyrrell's has great charm, and Pipers Brook is very complete.

1982 Conde de Valdemar Gran Reserva Rioja *A remarkable, velvety wine from the company of Martinez Bujanda with a marvellous structure and long, lingering flavour.* **12 for £140.28**

1989 Moulin de Duhart, Pauillac *A very pleasant, uncomplicated, archetypal claret. It's the second wine of Château Duhart-Milon, and it slips down the throat very nicely.* **12 for £121.44**

Crémant d'Alsace Cuvée Julien, Dopff au Moulin *Some sparkling wine to use up the cash; this is a much underrated* appellation *that offers great value for money. This wine is dry, with lots of flavour and real character.* **5 for £40.30**

Total cost: £998.50

NEIL MACFARLANE

BUTE WINES

André Simon was close to the mark when he wrote, 'Wine is a friend, wine is a joy, and like sunshine, wine is the birthright of all.' You don't have to spend a fortune to indulge in it either.

1989 Alsace Gewürztraminer St-Hippolyte, Charles Koehly *Koehly's wines are yet to be discovered. Clean and dry, this is above all fruity and richly scented.* **6 for £46.68**

Total cost: £95.58

£100

Even with a limited budget, you can still enjoy fine wines from the best regions. An Alsace provided my first foray into the delights of wine, while Burgundy, I believe, still produces the world's greatest.

1990 Bourgogne Passetoutgrains, Volpato *At its best this appellation can offer perhaps the finest value in Burgundy, with rich colour, spicy bouquet and concentrated flavours.* **6 for £48.90**

£500

Okay, I'm a francophile: you might have guessed by now. I might drink the pink sparkler in the garden; but imagine sitting down to a grand dinner and being presented with the rest of this array of French wines.

Baron de Charmeuil Rosé Sec NV *Loads of strawberry fizz –great fun, and a good-value price.* **12 for £69.60**

1990 Chablis Villages, Laurent Tribut
*Jean Dauvissat's son-in-law produces
elegant, graceful wines.*   **12 for £114.36**

1987 Château Greysac, Haut-Médoc *Ready
for drinking now, and quite hard to resist.
Rich, fruity flavours.*   **12 for £87.84**

1989 Bourgogne Rouge, Edmond Cornu
*Superb generic Burgundy from this
underrated producer. The quality would
surprise you.*   **12 for £82.92**

1989 Vouvray Moelleux, Domaine la
Saboterie *You need not spend a fortune on
Sauternes when this luscious, peachy
Vouvray is available. This was an excellent
year for sweet wines in the Loire, too, with
lots of botrytis.*   **12 for £72.84**

Lillet White Apéritif *A spicy French blend
of fruit liqueurs and white wine. Okay, it's
not strictly speaking a wine,but to my
mind it's still a treat.*   **12 for £84.36**

Total cost: £511.92

£1000

*Wines of this quality should be shared with
close friends, and then only those who will*

*appreciate them. However, I think I would
be tempted to restrict them to the most
exclusive of company – myself.*

Bicentenaire Patrimoine Brut NV, Canard-
Duchène *A medium-bodied Champagne
offering outstanding value.*   **12 for £182.28**

1989 Alsace Riesling Reserve Particulière,
Domaine Weinbach *One of the great estates
of Alsace. Wonderfully balanced wine from
the meticulous Mme Faller.*   **12 for 121.80**

1990 Chardonnay, Cape Mentelle *The best
of Australian Chardonnays, full of rich
apricot flavours.*   **12 for £145.20**

1989 Chambolle-Musigny, Domaine Dujac
*Even with his so-called lesser Burgundies,
Jacques Seysses produces the finest on offer
anywhere in the world.*   **12 for £193.92**

1988 Château de Fonsalette, J Reynaud
*Unquestionably one of the greats from the
Côtes-du-Rhône.*   **12 for £136.68**

1988 Château Coutet, Sauternes *Typically
luscious Sauternes from the traditionally-
minded Marcel Baly.*   **12 for £243.12**

Total cost: £1023.00

DAVID PINCHARD

AVERYS OF BRISTOL

The real skill of the merchant is to find
wines that taste more than they cost. To
pursue flavour rather than pomposity, in
other words. Here goes...

£100

*This cellar won't last long in our house
where guests seldom leave a glass unfinished.*

1992 Averys Fine White Burgundy *Crisp
fruit, and an elegant, slightly honeyed
finish.*   **6 for £33**

1992 Nobilo Marlborough Sauvignon
Blanc, New Zealand *Classic grassy, tangy
flavour that lasts and lasts – except, as I
say, in our house.*   **6 for £33**

Tyrrells Long Flat Red, Australia *Tasty,
consistent Syrah-Cabernet blend from this
long-established Hunter Valley family firm.
The Long Flat of the name doesn't refer to
the flavour, by the way – it's the name of the
vineyard.*   **6 for £33**

Total cost: £99

£500

I'll keep these away from my guests for a while, because they can all improve further.

Deinhard Heritage Hochheim *This wine first appeared in Britain on the day my youngest son was born, nearly six years ago. It is a superior dry German from the tiny growing area around Hochheim. Smoky, minerally Riesling.* **12 for £112**

1990 Swanson Merlot, Napa Valley *Balanced, rounded, juicy fruit. This is Merlot with proper backbone. Pomerol watch out.* **12 for £128**

1990 Alsace Tokay-Pinot Gris, Kuentz-Bas *Not cheap but deliciously full of incredible spice and individuality.* **12 for £132**

1987 Château Musar, Lebanon *The first time I met winemaker Serge Hochar he had been holed up in his flat in Beirut for ten days being shelled. The Bekaa is the world's most dangerous vineyard, and the wine is a miracle. Buy some to help keep civilization alive. This vintage, incidentally, is the best for years.* **12 for £112**

Total cost: £484

£1000

What I have looked for are wines that are the best of their kind for the price. Despite my New World bias, when I'm rich enough France still wins the game a lot of the time.

Averys Special Cuvée Champagne *I know it sounds partisan but I love our Special Cuvée from Epernay. It has a lovely full-bodied savoury character, and it always benefits from six months' rest after arrival in this country.* **12 for £149.16**

Lustau Almacenista, Manzanilla Pasada de Sanlúcar *Quite simply the best sherry of all: dry. refined, full of character and well-*

aged. But once it's open, drink it all at once before it goes stale. You'll find it hard not to, anyway.   **12 for £149.46**

1990 Givry Blanc Le Preferé du Roi Henri IV, Remoissenet *White Givry is a rare find. This is lovely Burgundian Chardonnay from a real master – and very good value, too, since it's from the cheaper Côte Chalonnaise.*   **12 for £129.58**

1993 Chablis Château de Viviers, Lupe Chollet *Superb steely Chardonnay from a first-class year. It'll keep for a few years, too.*   **12 for £104.34**

1989 Chambolle-Musigny, Avery *Not for nothing are Avery's Burgundian bottlings world famous, even in these days of grower-worship. This village wine has a lovely vegetal Pinot nose, silky-smooth palate and great length.*   **12 for £205.86**

1989 Rustenberg Gold, South Africa *This estate is 300 years old, which makes it one of the oldest in the country. Its classic Bordeaux blend of Cabernet Sauvignon, Cabernet Franc and Merlot, on the other hand, is still young, but it is going to be great.*   **12 for £114.63**

1990 Les Meysonnières, Chapoutier *What are the two Chapoutier brothers doing? Whatever it is they seem to have found the secret of making Rhône Syrah taste magnificent younger. 1990 is also a great year.*   **12 for £125.93**

Blandy's 10-Year-Old Malmsey Madeira *Sadly, I have very little money left for this; but at about £14 a bottle I think I can stretch to one. I shall just have to make it last.*   **1 for £14**

Total cost: £992.96

VICTORIA ROSS

GAUNTLEYS OF NOTTINGHAM

I didn't set out to put together predominantly Rhône and southern French cellars, but there is just so much quality and value there, and so many stunning flavours. I've also taken advantage of our discount of five per cent off everything if you (or I, come to that) buy more than 12 bottles.

£100

The wines I have selected for my £100 cellar are all superbly made. The Lumian was too expensive for a whole half case, so I've limited myself to five – and still overspent.

1990 Domaine Fontaine du Clos Merlot, Vin de Pays de Vancluse *One of our many great finds last year, and now a firm favourite. Superbly made* vin de pays *with great character and class which belie the price.*   **6 for £32.40**

1990 Côtes du Rhône, Lumian *A real old-fashioned style of Côtes du Rhône with rich aromas of black fruits and spices – highly concentrated with soft, velvety fruit and ripe, round tannins.*   **5 for £29.00**

1990 Domaine de Joy, Côtes de Gascogne *A lovely clean, fresh, dry white wine with stone-fruit flavours and zippy acidity. Superb value.*   **6 for £25.20**

1990 Cépage Syrah, Domaine de Montmiran, Vins de Pays des Côtes de Thongue *This domaine in the Côtes de Thongue specializes in single grape varieties – but not Cabernet and not Chardonnay. This Syrah has delicious, perfumed, soft berry fruits, is beautifully balanced and silky smooth.*

6 for £26.40

Total cost less discount: £107.30

£500

With a bit more cash in my pocket I can afford to dabble in Bordeaux and Alsace, but I'm still not going to desert the Rhône and the South. In fact, I'll have even more.

1991 Côtes de Roussillon Vendange, Cépage Mourvèdre, Les Vignerons de Rivesaltes *Black / purple in colour, and with a bouquet of toasty new oak and black fruit, this is akin to a Côte-Rôtie or Hermitage. It has outstanding depth and richness and full-bodied, highly extracted fruit flavours. It's a real pleasure to drink now, although it should last for ten years or more.* **12 for £83.40**

1991 Domaine Gramenon Syrah, Côtes du Rhône *Must rank alongside Fonsalette as a fine examples of southern Rhône Syrah. It's all black fruits, liquorice, smoke and coffee, held together with soft, ripe tannins. It's drinking now, too.* **12 for £94.80**

1990 Domaine Gramenon Ceps Centenaire, Côtes du Rhône *This is a blockbuster. It's almost like port, it's so rich and thick, and it's full of concentrated cherries, hickory and toffee.* **12 for £118.80**

1991 Château Castelnau Vieilles Vignes, Entre-Deux-Mers *Made from 100-year-old Sémillon vines and vinified in new oak, this is a wine to rival the finest white Graves, except in price.* **12 for £94.80**

1991 Rockford Dry County Grenache, Barossa Valley *Full bodied, with rich, peppery, jammy fruit flavours, and from Australia.* **12 for £91.20**

1991 Clos St-Imer Gewürztraminer, Ernst Burn *Packed with roses, smoke and exotic spices. I can only afford three bottles, so I'll have to make it last.* **3 for £38.70**

Total cost less discount: £495.60

£1000

With £1000 I shall have some really good Champagne – though you'll notice how restrained I've been on quantity. In fact, so keen am I to get as many magnificent Rhônes as possible that I've had to break the rules on full cases.

1991 Cornas Special Cuvée, Chapoutier *Chapoutier made this old vine cuvée for Gauntleys. It's intense and concentrated, typically Chapoutier in style with pure, creamy fruit flavours.* **12 for £166.80**

1990 Châteauneuf-du-Pape, Pegau *Wow – what a wine. It's full of complex tar, spice and liquorice, with great structure and length.* **12 for £154.80**

1991 St-Joseph, Domaine Jean Marsanne *I'd have this for the nose alone: all violets and cassis and followed, on the palate, by mouthwatering fruit.* **12 for £126.00**

1992 Côtes du Rhône Viognier, Gramenon *Even with £1000 I can't afford much Condrieu, so I'll have this instead. It must be the most exciting Viognier produced outside Condrieu, and it has a bouquet of pungent, perfumed apricots that leaps from the glass.* **12 for £153.00**

Now for a rather unlikely split case – half Hermitage, half Alsace Gewürztraminer. I had the latter in my last cellar, but this version is even better.

1990 Hermitage La Sizeranne, Chapoutier
6 for £155.40
1991 Alsace Gewürztraminer Clos
Windsbuhl, Zind-Humbrecht **6 for £118.20**
*No cellar should be without at least one
1990 Hermitage, and this Gewürztraminer
is opulent and scented. Too good for smoked
salmon.*

1983 Champagne Louis Roederer *I could
live quite happily with a cellar full of*

*nothing but Roederer. Compromises,
compromises...* **3 for £98.55**

1990 Le Haut Lieu Moelleux 1er Trie,
Gaston Huet *I've spent so much on Rhônes
that I haven't got much left for that
essential of life, pudding wine. But 1990
was a superb year for it in the Loire, so I'll
sneak in just three bottles.*
3 for £79.50
Total cost less discount: £999.64

ELEANOR SMITH

ROBERSON

Because of the eccentricities of my nature,
I have chosen to avoid all the good clarets
for which Robersons is known, and have
decided instead to go for something
completely different.

£100

*It was very tempting to go all out for
quantity at this stage, buy the cheapest
wine and throw the biggest party, but in the
end quality won the day.*

1992 Côtes du Lubéron, Vieille Ferme
Blanc *A spicy, savoury white, great for an
evening in with a bowl of popcorn and a
good video.* **6 for £28.22**

1992 Montepulciano d'Abruzzo, Citra *Big,
rich and concentrated – an excellent
accompaniment to my favourite style of
food, which is* piccante. **6 for £21.95**

1990 San Pedro Merlot, Lontue Valley,
Chile *All too easily gulpable red. It reminds
me of soft plum crumble with an extra
helping of cream.* **6 for £25.65**

Inocente Fino, Valdespino *This reminds me
of lazy days in Jerez. Bring on the
castanets...* **6 halves for 25.65**

Total cost: £101.47

£500

*With this amount of money I can afford to
indulge myself and friends in elegant
sufficiency.*

1989 Chablis, Etienne Defaix *Eighteen
months on the lees and not a hint of oak –
distinctive and profound, with extra flavour
and finesse.* **12 for £138 75**

1992 Riesling QbA, Dr Loosen, Mosel *Crisp
and refreshing with delicate, elegantly-
wrought lime cordial fruit.* **12 for £72.15**

Seppelt Sparkling Shiraz Brut nv *Big, bold
and brassy.* **12 for £110.45**

1991 Nebbiolo d'Alba San Rocco, Giuseppe
Mascarello *Violets, truffles, cherries – I
could eulogize for hours.* **12 for £92.69**

Manzanilla Papirusa, Emilio Lustau *Who
said sherry is for grannies? Tangy fresh sea
salt – get those tapas out. Drink it cold and
don't leave any.* **6 for £44.12**

Campbells Liqueur Muscat, Australia *The
ideal remedy for coughs and colds – far
more palatable, twice as effective and you
won't need a prescription.* **3 for £30.39**

Total cost: £488.55

£1000

I've never had so much money.

1991 Rias Baixas, Lagar de Cervera Albariño *The fewer people who know about the merits of this wine, the better I shall like it. All the more for me.*   **12 for 96.66**

1991 Alsace Grand Cru, Riesling Saering, Schlumberger *Peach melba with grated cinnamon on the nose.*   **12 for 127.98**

1991 Arneis Blangé, Ceretto, Piedmont *Nut crush and vanilla, overlaid with poached pears.*   **12 for £118.26**

1991 Ridge Paso Robles Zinfandel, San Luis Obispo *Pure blueberry pie in liquid form.*   **12 for £118.26**

1988 Brunello di Montalcino Poggio Antico, Tuscany *A towering, intense, individual red Could only be Italian. A huge wine in every sense.*   **12 for £215.46**

1985 Cornas, Guy de Barjac, Rhône *Reminds me of my gumboot days on the farm – a glorious ripe nose that lingers on and on, and keeps me coming back for more.*   **12 for 193.86**

1992 Coteaux du Layon Cuvée de Paon, Domaine des Baumard *Like a honeymoon – pure sticky bliss.*   **6 for £69.93**

Champagne Roederer Rich nv *A glass of this with my mum's fruit cake and I'm in seventh heaven.*   **3 for £59.27**

Total cost: £999.68

OZ CLARKE

I can hear this voice chanting away in my brain. It sounds so familiar. It's the clarion call of the nineties once again: fruit, fruit and more fruit. How did we ever manage to drink cheaply before they unlocked the simple secret of keeping the flavour of fruit in our wines? And for value for money and fruit – I'm heading east.

1992 Bulgarian Sliven Vat 2462 Cabernet Sauvignon
Even better than the Young Vatted, succulant blackberry and loganberry fruit. And it's cheaper – just £2.49 a bottle. Weird.   **6 of each for £49**

Total cost: £101

£100

1993 Hungarian Leanyka/Müller-Thurgau
Lovely perfumed gentle white.
1993 Hungarian Szeksard Chardonnay
Full, ripe open-flavoured fruit.
1993 Moravian Grüner Veltliner *Snappy witch hazel and white pepper, fresh, cheap and from Safeway.*   **6 of each for £52**

1993 Bulgarian Young Vatted Merlot
1993 Bulgarian Young Vatted Cabernet Sauvignon
These two appeared in Safeway last year and revolutionized the way we look at Bulgarian reds. These new vintages are just as good.

£500

I really did intend to spend lots more money on far more expensive wines for my £500 cellar. Really I did. And then I went through the year's tasting notes and there was so much brilliant stuff at way under a fiver that I simply had to include it. So hang on: you'll get your fix of high prices later.

1993 Côtes de Roussillon, Château de Belesta
1993 Côtes du Roussillon, Mas Segala
1993 Corbières, Château de Cabriac
1993 St Chinian, Château Maurel Fonsalade

Brilliant red flavours are bursting out all over the south of France at the moment. Lots are from international grape varieties like Cabernet and Merlot. But these estates have spurned the interloper grapes and made stunning, juicy, herb-steeped reds– and look at the price. **6 of each for £93**

1992 Carignanissime, Daniel Domergue, Minervois *An astonishing pepper and celery and sweet raspberry gum red. It's 100 per cent Carignan.*
1992 Pinot de Pech, Pech-Celeyran, Vin de Pays d'Oc *Tastes as though it's made from pine rather than Pinot Noir, but it's smashing stuff.* **6 of each for £66**

1993 Domaine Ste François Sauvignon Blanc, Vin de Pays d'Oc
1993 Domaine Ste Pierre Chardonnay, Vin de Pays d'Oc
Just find me anything from anywhere that's as good as these two whites at this kind of price. **6 of each for £45**

Right – Change of language. To English. Or rather to Italian. Kiwi/Australian winemaker Kim Mylne has been at the Centele winery in Puglia in the south of Italy doing wonders with both native and international varieties.
1993 Negroamaro Rosato, Centele *Wonderful gutsy rosé.*
1993 Primitivo, Centele *Action-packed palate buster from Puglia's best red grape variety.*
1993 Chardonnay de Barrique, Centele *Stunning top quality oaky Chardonnay from an area that's even laughed at by other Italians.* **6 of each for £81**

1993 Mount Hurtle Grenache, Maclaren Vale
1993 Rosé of Virginia, Charles Melton, Barossa
Rosés, eh? Rosés in a £500 cellar? Well, the Negromaro is man's stuff, but the next two are made for monsters. (And by monsters, as it happens.) **6 of each for £69**

How am I doing? Loads of dosh left. I'd better get a move on. Those pinkos have given me a taste for the New World, so let's stay there.
1993 Fairview Estate Sauvignon Blanc/Sémillon, South Africa
1992 Fairview Estate Shiraz/Merlot, South Africa
Fairview is leading the way in quality at a fair price on the Cape. **6 of each for £50**

I was going to give Chile a miss because I've had so many disappointments recently. But the 1993 vintage from two new winemakers put the pale offerings of most of their colleagues to shame.
1993 Cono Sur Pinot Noir, Chile
1993 Carmen Reserve Merlot, Chile
1993 Carmen Reserve Cabernet Sauvignon, Chile
These are absolutely brilliant red wines, just bursting with fruit and structure, tannin and oak, all bound together. It's about time Chile produced something like this. **6 of each for £87**

Yalumba Sparkling Cabernet, Australia
*Oh my God. I've just noticed. No authentic
Aussie sparkling 'Burgundy'. My cellar
would not be my cellar without the
glistening, foaming ruby juice that makes
even the sternest Ocker's face crumple into a
smile. But I've only got £8 left. None of the
celestials, then, but a bottle of this should
do nicely.*   **1 for £8**

Total cost: £499

£1000

Well, I suppose I could just stock my entire
cellar with sparkling Shiraz from
Australia. Once you get hooked on this
gorgeous dark purple foaming brew, all
other wines seem a bit serious and sober-
sided. But, just in case there isn't £1000's
worth of bottles of this nectar in Britain,
I'll choose some other bottles of a saner
sort.

1993 Freycinet Cabernet Sauvignon,
Tasmania
1993 Spring Vale Pinot Noir, Tasmania
*Well, not that much saner. Tasmanian
Cabernet and Pinot Noir? These red grapes
don't usually ripen in Tassy, but on the east
coast there is a tiny warm microclimate
that produces some of the most sensational
fruit in Australia.*   **6 of each for £150**

1993 Matua Valley Ararimu Cabernet
Sauvignon
1993 Te Motu Cabernet Sauvignon *While
I'm musing about classics from unlikely
areas, what about some of the world's
greatest red wine from New Zealand? The
North Island round Auckland had a
stunning vintage in 1993 and I've chosen
the two best Cabernets.*   **6 of each for £180**

1989 Newton Napa Valley Cabernet
Sauvignon, California
1990 John Riddoch Coonawarra Cabernet
Sauvignon, Australia
1991 Mas de Daumas Gassac, Vin de Pays
de l'Herault
*Actually, I could do with a bit more
Cabernet. Bordeaux hasn't been that lucky
in the last couple of years but there's lots of
brilliant Cabernet from elsewhere
equalling the best that Bordeaux has to
offer. Cabernet on its own can be a bit
gaunt and lean, but these three match
power with perfume.*   **4 of each for £150**

1992 Dalwhinnie Shiraz, Victoria
1992 Bailey's Shiraz, Victoria
1992 Coriole Shiraz, MacLaren Vale
1992 Bowen Estate Shiraz, Coonawarra
*Okay, I'm ready to begin walking on the
wild side again. The Australians have re-
discovered their pride in Shiraz in a big
way, largely thanks to the enthusiasm with
which we Brits have clamoured for the
stuff.*   **6 of each for £220**

1992 Tim Adams Sémillon, Clare
1991 Amberley Sauvignon Blanc/Sémillon,
Western Australia *Room for a bit more
Southern Seas magic? I think so. These are
tip top quality and the price is low for that
quality. I'll keep these for a few years
because they'll age superbly, though they're
smashing already.*   **6 of each for £100**

1992 Meursault l'Ormeau, Alaine Coche
1992 Chassagne-Montrachet les
Chevenottes, Jean-Marie Gagnard *Right,
back to the mainstream, but only because
the quality of the 1992 vintage for white
Burgundy is so good it softens even the
heart of an anti-traditionalist like me.
These are very traditional and stunningly
good. I shan't be opening them until the
end of the decade.*   **6 of each for £175**

Peter Rumball Sparkling 'Burgundy',
Australia *You're not going to stop me
throwing caution to the wind and getting
two bottles – well, if I can chisel the price a
bit – of the king of the cherry red sparkling
brigade.*   **2 for £25**

Total cost : £1000

FRANCE

How we see French wine, and what we actually buy, are two very different things. Ask the drinker on the street (an unfortunate phrase, perhaps, but you know what I mean) about his or her view of French wines and you will probably get words like 'high quality' and 'expensive' being bandied about.

Yet we know it's not true. The third most popular wine in Britain is *vin de pays*, behind Liebfraumilch and Lambrusco, neither of which are known for their quality. Australian white, way down in eighth place, is far more exclusive.

Clever old France. For years it succeeded in convincing the world that all its wines were the finest that were to be had, simply because just a few were extremely good. And all the time much of the rest was some of the most dreary, fruitless stuff ever to see the inside of a bottle.

But note that I use the past tense. Because France has woken up. It's starting to compete with places like Australia; and some of the hardest competition is coming from *vins de pays*. *Vins de pays* have improved beyond recognition, particularly if they're from the South. It's here that visiting winemakers have brought an insistence on wines with fruit, wines with flavour, and wines at affordable prices. No, they haven't been to every *chai* that makes *vin de pays*. Yes, there is still *vin de pays* that tastes of stale old wood and dirty dishcloths. But an awful lot is some of the most attractive wine to be found anywhere.

Ironic, isn't it? One of the most popular wines in Britain is also one of the best. Has that ever happened before? I doubt it. It means that the wine-making revolution is affecting us all, not just those who can afford good claret, and that's some of the best news I've had all year. Clever old France.

QUALITY CONTROL

The French have the most far-reaching system of wine control of any nation. The key factors are the 'origin' of the wine, its historic method of production and the use of the correct grape types. There are three defined levels of control – AC, VDQS, and *Vin de Pays*.

Appellation d'Origine Contrôlée (AC, AOC) To qualify for AC a wine must meet seven requirements:
Land Suitable vineyard land is minutely defined. **Grape** Only those grapes traditionally regarded as suitable can be used. **Degree of alcohol** Wines must reach a minimum (or maximum) degree of natural alcohol. **Yield** A basic permitted yield is set for each AC, but the figure may be increased or decreased year by year after consultation between the growers of each AC region and the Institut National des Appellations d'Origine (INAO).
Vineyard practice AC wines must follow rules about pruning methods and density of planting. **Wine-making practice** Each AC wine has its own regulations as to what is allowed. Typically, chaptalization – adding sugar during fermentation to increase alcoholic strength – is accepted in the north, but not in the south. **Tasting and analysis** Since 1979 wines must pass a tasting panel.

Vin Délimité de Qualité Supérieure (VDQS) This second group is, in general, slightly less reliable in quality. It is in the process of being phased out. No more *vins de pays* are being upgraded to VDQS but there is still no news on when existing ones will be upgraded to AC (or downgraded to *vin de pays*).

Vin de Pays The third category gives a regional definition to France's basic blending wines. The rules are similar to AC, but allow a good deal more flexibility and some wonderful cheap wines can be found which may well surprise. Quality can be stunning, and expect fruit, value and competent wine-making.

Vin de Table 'Table wine' is the title for the rest. No quality control except as far as basic public health regulations demand. *Vins de pays* are always available for approximately the same price, and offer a far more interesting drink. Many Vins de Table here are dull and poorly made.

LOIRE   Main wine regions
CAHORS   Other regions

RED BORDEAUX

In 1993 it was finally acknowledged in Bordeaux that there was an international economic crisis, and that France was part of it.

Consumers felt the financial pinch and stopped buying wine. The fall in the rate of inflation had removed one of the great arguments for buying wines *en primeur,* and the 1993 vintage, after promising well, fell victim to rain during the harvest, making it the third difficult vintage in a row, after the frosts of 1991 and the dilute, underripe wines of 1992. To add to Bordeaux's woes, the 1993 devaluation of the pound added ten per cent to sterling prices.

The general weakening of the market was seen in such spectacular sales as those of Châteaux Latour, Gruaud-Larose and Rausan-Ségla. Latour, which had been a prestige possession of Allied Lyons, was presumably found to be an expensive luxury and was sold off to a French multi-millionaire, François Pinault, who at another period might have bought a racehorse or a Rembrandt. Gruaud-Larose, one of the loveliest of the Médoc châteaux in the middle of some of the best located vines in St-Julien, was sold off rather quietly to the Alcatel group, a powerful conglomerate more active in trains (the TGV) and telecommunications than in wine. Rausan-Ségla was sold after no more than a few years as a George Walker toy to the American branch of the Chanel perfume company.

The buyers in each of these sales bought both the property and the wine stocks, but it is not known for how much; two-thirds of the going price in, say, 1989, at the top of the market, seems a reasonable estimate. Given that prices in 1989 were quite outrageously high and unrelated to any likely return on investment, if the vendors got two-thirds they must be pretty pleased. Certainly, it is difficult to see a return even now at any likely bottle price of the wines in question. But perhaps it's worth it for the pleasure of drinking your own Latour.

Decline and fall

The most significant event of the year, however, was not the sale of a clutch of famous châteaux: it was the failure of a major merchant, SDVF, of which *Webster's* readers have probably never heard. But if the aftermath of that failure had gone worse than it did, SDVF might have become very famous indeed, because for a while Bordeaux feared that a major crash might be precipitated.

Behind the initials was a company, Societé Distribution des Vins Fins, and a man called Antoine Hernandez, who had successfully reacted to a previous Bordeaux crisis, that of the 1970s. He started off in that decade selling large quantities of expensive Bordeaux at low margins. His success was enormous, and his company had in Bordeaux the charisma which these days attaches to the likes of Amstrad and Lonrho. He became one of the two or three major players in the field of Classed Growth Bordeaux; and then he fell.

SDVF had had an early start and developed a persuasive track record that enabled it to outpace its rivals for 15 years or so. It had attracted the enthusiastic co-operation of more than ten banks, but nevertheless lacked a solid capital base. It had investments in the Loire and in Beaujolais, and began to handle the wines of lots of small châteaux – in which overheads are a higher percentage of the sale price than is the case with big châteaux. That might not have helped; but in the end it was that lack of a firm capital base compounded by some errors of management that caused the SDVF edifice to topple.

Now the company has been acquired from the liquidator by the Cointreau group, but when rumours began to circulate in the summer of 1993 that all was not well at SDVF it was feared that no buyer might be found for the company, and that the liquidator would release the firm's huge stocks at knock-down prices. That might have been the last straw for the battered Bordeaux market.

At the time of writing, though, Bordeaux is starting to breathe again. The '93s are selling well, except in Britain and the USA, and people are more optimistic

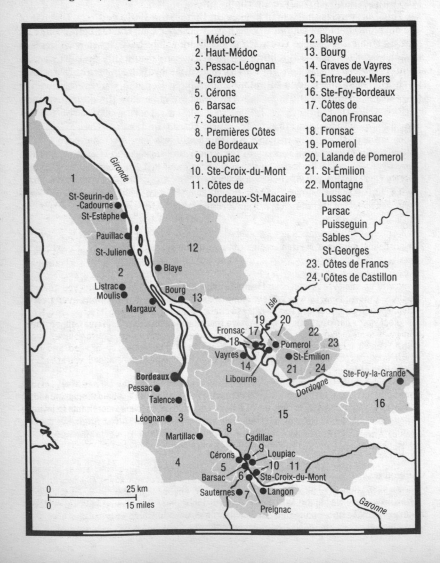

1. Médoc
2. Haut-Médoc
3. Pessac-Léognan
4. Graves
5. Cérons
6. Barsac
7. Sauternes
8. Premières Côtes de Bordeaux
9. Loupiac
10. Ste-Croix-du-Mont
11. Côtes de Bordeaux-St-Macaire
12. Blaye
13. Bourg
14. Graves de Vayres
15. Entre-deux-Mers
16. Ste-Foy-Bordeaux
17. Côtes de Canon Fronsac
18. Fronsac
19. Pomerol
20. Lalande de Pomerol
21. St-Émilion
22. Montagne
    Lussac
    Parsac
    Puisseguin
    Sables
    St-Georges
23. Côtes de Francs
24. Côtes de Castillon

than they were in the early spring. But the situation, nevertheless, is very different to that which obtained only a few years ago.

It used to be that merchants bought the off-vintages like 1984 because loyalty to the châteaux in these years would earn them enough brownie points to allow them a crack at the top vintages. Not now. Nowadays merchants will pay a high price for good years like 1989 in order to get less exciting years like 1991 at a low price. The logic is that while the best, hyped vintages will go to collectors no matter what the price, there is solid demand in between for second or third-rate years from restaurateurs who want to put famous names on their wine lists, but who want to be able to charge affordable prices.

That, anyway, is the case in France. In Britain the 1991s and '92s, because of the devaluation of the pound, will be hardly cheaper than the far better '89s and '90s. So go for the Classed Growths, where there will be bargains in both the '91s and the '92s: good wines at a fair price for fairly early drinking. The 1993 vintage should be worth buying *en primeur* provided it's bought for drinking and not with any misguided idea of making money. It is not a vintage to buy for investment, even though its price when bottled will be appreciably higher than when first offered.   **WILLIAM BOLTER**

BUYING CLARET *EN PRIMEUR*

Some well-publicized company failures in the last year have highlighted the problems of buying wine this way. Basically, buying *en primeur* means that you order your wine each spring when the château proprietors announce an opening price for their new wines. You buy the wines through your wine merchant, pay in advance and sit back and wait until the wine is delivered, after bottling, 18 months or so later. It is common then to leave the wine in the merchant's care, either in the merchant's own warehouse (if duty has been paid) or in bond (if it has not).

Most of the time the system works admirably well. Things can go wrong, though, if the merchant goes bankrupt. One of the guarantees that buyers have always been advised to ask for, and that merchants have always freely given, is that that your name is written on every single case of wine that you have bought, while it is in the warehouse. This (along with written title to the wine) is supposed to prove to the Official Receiver that you have a right to those cases. (If one merchant goes bankrupt before the wine has even been shipped to Britain, you have roughly a cat's chance in hell of ever seeing it.)

Last year's bankruptcies, however, have revealed that this doesn't always happen; the only way to make sure that your name is on your wine is to visit the warehouse yourself and look. Even so, it is not common practice for wine stored in bond to be so labelled; and if a merchant goes bankrupt before your wine has even been bottled and shipped, you are also unlikely to see your purchase.

It is up to the vast majority of honest wine merchants to improve the service they give to their customers, in order to shore up the credibility of the trade as a whole. Some, indeed, have been spurred to do just this, and it is becoming more common for merchants to invite customers to inspect their duty-paid wines. A handful of merchants (John Armit, Corney & Barrow, Adnams, Laytons, Lay & Wheeler, Tanners and Yapp) have got together to form what they call The Bunch (the object seems to be to exchange ideas and information over a good lunch) and they offer precisely this service.

One of the major warehouses, Octavian Ltd, of Hertfordshire, have launched a scheme called 'Protection Plus' which is intended to ensure that in the event of a merchant bankruptcy you will get your wine no matter what. Anybody thinking of buying wine *en primeur* and not taking delivery at the earliest opportunity simply must investigate the safeguards. And if your merchant doesn't offer them, go somewhere else.

GRAPES & FLAVOURS

Fine claret has the most tantalizing and unlikely combination of flavours of any red wine. There's the blast of pure, fragrant blackcurrant essence of the basic fruit, and then the exotic, dry perfumes of lead pencil shavings, fresh-wrapped cigars and the intense smell of cedar resin to weave an endlessly fascinating balance of sweet and dry tastes. Increasingly nowadays this is also blended with the buttersweet overlay of new oak barrels.

Bordeaux's vineyards are so poised on the knife-edge of being able to ripen their grapes or failing to do so that every vintage is fascinatingly, absorbingly different. The relatively temperate air in this coastal region is a crucial factor in the quality of the wine. In all but the very hottest years, the sunshine is tempered by cool breezes off the Atlantic. If the year nevertheless gets too hot, as in 1959 and 1976, and in some cases 1982, 1989 and 1990, the flavour can be rich, strong and burnt, more like the Californian or Italian attempts at claret. If the summer rains and autumn gales roll in off the Bay of Biscay and the grapes can't ripen, then the taste may be thin and green, resembling the Cabernets of the Loire valley. But in the years of balance, like 1966, '70, '78, '83, '85, '86, '88, '89 and '90 those astonishing sweet and dry, fruity and tannic flavours mix to produce the glory that is claret.

CABERNET SAUVIGNON It comes as a surprise that this world-famous Bordeaux grape covers only a fifth of the vineyard area. In the Médoc and Pessac-Léognan, however, more than half the vines are Cabernet Sauvignon, and the grape has a greater influence on flavour here than elsewhere in Bordeaux. Crucially, a wine built to age needs tannin and acidity, and the fruit and extract to keep up with them. Cabernet Sauvignon has all these in abundance. It gives dark, tannic wine with a strong initial acid attack, and a stark, pure blackcurrant fruit. When aged in new oak, it can be stunning. It's the main grape of the Haut-Médoc, but other varieties are always blended in to soften it and add a further dimension.

CABERNET FRANC A lesser Cabernet, giving lighter-coloured, softer wines than Cabernet Sauvignon, sometimes slightly earthy but with good, blackcurranty fruit. It's always blended in Bordeaux. In St-Émilion and Pomerol it can give very fine flavours and is widely planted. Château Cheval Blanc in St-Émilion is two-thirds Cabernet Franc.

MERLOT Bordeaux has more Merlot than Cabernet Sauvignon. It covers almost a third of the vineyard, and is the main grape in St-Émilion and Pomerol, whereas in the Médoc and Graves it's used to soften and enrich the Cabernet. It ripens early and gives a gorgeous, succulent, minty, blackcurrant- or plum-flavoured wine, which explains why Pomerols and St-Émilions take less effort to enjoy than Médocs. It also makes less long-lived wine than Cabernet, and is likely to peak and fade sooner.

MALBEC A rather bloated, juicy grape, little seen nowadays in Bordeaux, though it appears in some blends, especially in Bourg and Blaye. In Bordeaux it tastes rather like a weedy version of Merlot, soft and low in acidity. Upriver in Cahors it has real style, which probably explains why there's lots of it in Cahors and little in Bordeaux.

PETIT VERDOT A dark, tough grape with a liquorice-and-plums taste, and a violet perfume, used for colour. Little planted in the past but on the increase now because it adds quality in a late, ripe year.

WINES & WINE REGIONS

BORDEAUX ROUGE, AC Unless qualified by one of the other ACs below, this is the everyday wine of Bordeaux, either from co-ops, from properties in undistinguished localities, or wine disqualified from one of the better ACs. It can come from anywhere in Bordeaux. Still reasonably priced, for drinking young, it is a delicious, appetizing meal-time red when good, and a palate-puckering disappointment when bad.

BORDEAUX SUPÉRIEUR, AC Similar to Bordeaux Rouge but, in theory, a bit more interesting. It must have more alcohol and be produced from a slightly lower yield. The same comments on quality apply, but from a good estate the wines can be delicious – and age for a number of years. Best results increasingly are from properties producing white Entre-Deux-Mers and from the Premières Côtes on the right bank of the Garonne river. Best châteaux: *Brethous, Cayla, Domaine de Terrefort, Fayau, la Gabory, le Gay, Grand-Moüeys, Gromel Bel-Air, Jalousie-Beaulieu, Jonqueyres, du Juge, Lacombe, Méaume, Peyrat, Pierredon, Reynon, la Roche, Tanesse, Thieuley, de Toutigeac, de la Vieille Tour.*

CÔTES DE BOURG, AC A reasonable-sized area across the river to the east of the Médoc, with its best vineyards looking directly across the Gironde to Margaux. Their rather full, savoury style is backed up by sweet Merlot fruit and occasionally a touch of new oak. As Médoc and St-Émilion prices spiral, Bourg wines are slowly coming into their own. Best châteaux: *de Barbe, du Bousquet, Brûle-Sécaille, la Croix, Dupeyrat, Grolet, Guionne, Haut-Guiraud, Haut-Rousset, de Millorit* and wines from the co-op at *Tauriac*.

CÔTES DE CASTILLON, AC and **CÔTES DE FRANCS, AC** Two small regions east of St-Émilion on the road towards Bergerac, which are turning out an increasing number of exciting wines. They can be a little too earthy, but at their best they combine a grassy Cabernet Franc freshness with a gorgeous, juicy, minty Merlot sweetness, even honeyed in the best châteaux. Best châteaux: *Beau-Séjour, Belcier, Brisson, Canon-Monségur, Ferrasses, Fonds Rondes, Grand Taillac, les Hauts-de-Grange, Lessacques, Moulin-Rouge, Parenchère, Pitray, Rocher-Bellevue.* On the extreme eastern edge of the Gironde is the department's latest rising star. The scions of a number of well-known wine-making families are producing fruity, light, delicious wines to drink early, using a lot of Cabernet Franc. Best châteaux: *la Claverie, de Francs, Lauriol, du Moulin-la-Pitié, la Prade, Puygueraud.*

CÔTES DE FRONSAC, AC (now usually called simply Fronsac) with the (in theory) superior **CANON-FRONSAC, AC**, is a small area just west of Pomerol. The wines can be a bit grassy and tannic, but they can also be excellent, often having the sweet fruit of St-Émilion, the mineral depth of Pomerol, and a slightly cedary perfume. Nevertheless the general standard has been increasing recently, greatly helped by the interest shown by the firm and family of *Jean-Pierre Moueix*, the best merchants in Libourne. Best châteaux: *Canon-de-Brem, Canon-Moueix, Cassagne Haut-Canon, Dalem, de la Dauphine, Fonteuil, Mayne-Vieil, Mazeris, Moulin Haut-Laroque, Plain Point, la Rivière, la Truffière* (super since 1985), *Toumalin, la Valade.*

GRAVES, AC Since 1987 the Graves, the vast region south of Bordeaux town, has been deprived of its most prestigious properties, the ones nearest the city, and

The price guides for this section begin on page 265..

now grouped in a separate AC, Pessac-Léognan. The southern two-thirds had a bad reputation as a semi-sweet white area, which it has taken a decade to overcome. These efforts have been intensified by the lopping off of Pessac-Léognan.

Red Graves run the gamut of claret flavours, and are less easy to sum up than others. There are various soils, and though the Cabernet Sauvignon is the dominant grape in the North, as in the Médoc, there's less stress on Cabernet, more on Merlot, so slightly softer wines. They tend to have some of the blackcurrant and cedar of the Médoc, but without the sheer size of, say, Pauillac: they have some of the full, plummy richness of St-Émilion yet it never dominates; and there is a slightly gravelly quality in many of them, too. The less well-known châteaux are cheapish, and pretty good. Local merchant Pierre Coste has developed a style of young-drinking Graves which is deliciously drinkable (available in Britain at Adnams, Haynes, Hanson & Clark, Tanners and others).

HAUT-MÉDOC, AC Geographically, the prestigious southern part of the Médoc, nearest Bordeaux – from Blanquefort in the South to St-Seurin de Cadourne in the North. The AC covers the less exciting vineyards in between because there are six separate ACs within the region where the really juicy business gets done. These are Margaux, St-Julien, Pauillac, St-Estèphe, Listrac and Moulis. Even so, the AC Haut-Médoc has five Classed Growths including two superb ones – *Cantemerle* and *la Lagune* – and an increasing number of fine *bourgeois* properties like *Beaumont, de Castillon, Cissac, Hanteillan, Lamarque, Lanessan, Liversan, Pichon, Sociando-Mallet* and *la Tour-du-Haut-Moulin* – plus lots of lesser properties, such as châteaux *Bernadotte, Cambon-la-Pelouse, Coufran, le Fournas, Grandis, du Junca, Larose-Trintaudon, Malescasse, Maucamps, Moulin de Labarde, Quimper, Sénéjac* and *Verdignan*.

LALANDE-DE-POMEROL, AC Pomerol's northern neighbour, a region as tiny as Pomerol itself, is often accused of being overpriced, but since it can produce rich, plummy wines with a distinct resemblance to those of Pomerol at a distinctly less painful price, this criticism is not entirely justified. The best châteaux are *Annereaux, Bel-Air, Belles-Graves, Bertineau-St-Vincent, Clos des Moines, Clos des Templiers, la Croix Bellevue, la Fleur St-Georges, Grand Ormeau, Haut-Ballet, les Hauts-Tuileries, Lavaud-la-Maréchaude, Siaurac, les Templiers, Tournefeuille*.

LISTRAC, AC One of the less prestigious communes of the Haut-Médoc, just to the west of Margaux. Grown on clay-dominated soils, the wines contain a higher proportion of Merlot. They are generally tough, rather charmless, only slightly perfumed wines, lacking the complexity of the best villages, but the meteoric rise in quality amongst the *bourgeois* wines since the '82 and '83 vintages has made its mark, though without quite the same show of fireworks. But some properties rise above this such as *Clarke, la Bécade, Cap-Léon-Veyrin, Fonréaud* (since 1988), *Fourcas-Dupré, Fourcas-Hosten, Fourcaud, Lestage* and the *Grand Listrac* co-op.

MARGAUX, AC Of the famous Haut-Médoc communes, this is the nearest to Bordeaux, covering various villages making rather sludgy, solid wines at one extreme, and at the other extreme the most fragrant, perfumed red wines France has yet dreamed up. The great wines come from round the village of Margaux itself. People pay high prices for them and still get a bargain. The best châteaux include: *d'Angludet, la Gurgue, d'Issan, Labégorce-Zédé, Margaux, Monbrison, Palmer, Prieuré-Lichine, Rausan-Ségla, du Tertre*. Among the next best are châteaux *Durfort-Vivens, Giscours, Marquis d'Alesme-Becker, Marquis de Terme, Siran* and *la Tour-de-Mons*.

MÉDOC, AC This name covers the whole of the long (80km) tongue of land north of Bordeaux town, between the Gironde river and the sea, including the Haut-Médoc and all its famous communes. As an AC, it refers to the less regarded but important lower-lying northern part of the area, traditionally known as the Bas-Médoc. AC Médoc reds, with a high proportion of Merlot grapes, are drinkable more quickly than Haut-Médocs and the best have a refreshing, grassy, juicy fruit, backed up by just enough tannin and acidity. Easily the best property is *Potensac*, where Michel Delon of Léoville-Las-Cases makes wine of Classed Growth standard. Other good wines are *le Bernadot, Cardonne, Cassan d'Estevil, David, d'Escot, la Gorce, Greysac, Grivière, Haut-Canteloup, Lacombe-Noaillac, Noaillac, Ormes-Sorbet, Patache d'Aux, la Tour-de-By, la Tour-St-Bonnet, Loudenne, Vieux-Château-Landon*. Most of the co-ops – especially *Bégadan, Ordornac* and *St-Yzans* – make good fruity stuff.

MOULIS, AC Another lesser commune of the Haut-Médoc next door to, and similar to, Listrac, but with more potentially outstanding properties and a softer, more perfumed style in the best which can equal Classed Growths. Best are *Bel Air Lagrave, Brillette, Chasse-Spleen, Duplessis-Fabre, Dutruch-Grand-Poujeaux, Grand-Poujeaux, Gressier-Grand-Poujeaux, Maucaillou, Moulin-à-Vent, Poujeaux*.

PAUILLAC, AC The most famous of the Haut-Médoc communes, Pauillac has three of the world's greatest red wines sitting inside its boundaries, *Latour, Lafite* and *Mouton-Rothschild*. This is where the blackcurrant really comes into its own. The best wines are almost painfully intense, a mixture of blackcurrant and celestial lead pencil sharpenings that sends well-heeled cognoscenti leaping for their cheque books. Best: *D'Armailhacq* (formerly known as *Mouton-Baronne-Philippe*), *Grand-Puy-Lacoste, Haut-Bages-Avérous, Haut-Bages-*

Libéral, Lafite-Rothschild, Latour, Lynch-Bages, Mouton-Rothschild, Pichon-Baron, Pichon-Lalande. Next best: *Batailley, Clerc-Milon-Rothschild, Duhart-Milon, Grand-Puy-Ducasse, Haut-Bages-Monpelou*.

PESSAC-LÉOGNAN, AC An AC in its own right since September 1987 for the area traditionally the Graves' best and containing all the *crus classés*. The AC covers ten communes but only 55 châteaux. In recent years the growers have fought back with increasing success against the tide of suburbia, replanting and improving their wines, above all the whites which, at their best, offer a depth surpassed only by the best Burgundies. The reds have a biscuity, bricky warmth. Best: *Carmes-Haut-Brion, Cabannieux, Cruzeau, Domaine de Chevalier, Domaine de Gaillat, Domaine la Grave, Ferrande, de Fieuzal, Haut-Bailly, Haut-Brion, Haut-Portets, la Louvière, Malartic-Lagravière, la Mission-Haut-Brion, Pape-Clément* (since 1985), *Rahoul Rochemorin, de St-Pierre, Smith-Haut-Lafitte* (since 1988), *Roquetaillade-la-Grange, la Tour Martillac, Tourteau-Chollet*.

POMEROL, AC Tiny top-class area inland from Bordeaux, clustered round the town of Libourne. The Merlot grape is even more dominant in Pomerol than in St-Émilion, and most Pomerols have a deeper, rounder flavour, the plummy fruit going as dark as prunes in great years, but with the mineral backbone of toughness preserving it for a very long time. Pomerol has no classification, but it harbours the world's greatest red wine, *Château Pétrus*. Any vineyard that has been picked out by Jean-Pierre Moueix or influenced by enologist Michel Rolland can be regarded as being of good Classed Growth standard. Best châteaux: *le Bon Pasteur, Bourgneuf-Vayron, Certan-de-May, Certan-Giraud, Clinet, Clos René, Clos du Clocher, Clos l'Église, la Conseillante, la Croix de Gay, l'Église Clinet, l'Évangile, le Gay, la Grave-Trigant-de-Boisset, Lafleur, Lafleur-Gazin,*

La Fleur Pétrus, Lagrange à Pomerol, Latour-à-Pomerol Petit-Village, Pétrus, le Pin, Trotanoy, Vieux-Château-Certan.

PREMIÈRES CÔTES DE BLAYE, AC
There is a shift to red in this historically white area across the river from the Médoc. The wines are too often a little 'cooked' in taste and slightly jammy-sweet. They're cheap, but have a lot more improving to do. Good names: *Bas Vallon, Bourdieu, Charron, Crusquet-Sabourin, l'Escadre, Fontblanche, Grand Barail, Haut-Sociando, Jonqueyres, Peybonhomme.*

PREMIÈRES CÔTES DE BORDEAUX,
AC This long, south-facing slope stands opposite Bordeaux town and slides down the river Garonne to about opposite Barsac. In spite of its rather grand name, its only claim to fame until recently has been the production of rather half-baked Sauternes lookalikes. But it is now producing some very attractive reds. The 1985, '88 and '89 vintages produced numerous wines with a surprising amount of soft fruit and durability. Best châteaux: *de Berbec, Brethous, Cayla, Fayau, Grands-Moüeys, du Juge, Lamothe, de Lucat, Peyrat, la Roche, Reynon, Tanesse.*

ST-ÉMILION, AC
Soft, round, and rather generous wines, because the main grape is the Merlot, aided by Cabernet Franc and Malbec, and only slightly by Cabernet Sauvignon. St-Émilions don't always have Pomerol's minerally backbone, and the sweetness is usually less plummy and more buttery, toffeed or raisiny. Top wines add to this a blackcurranty, minty depth. It's a well-known name, yet with few famous châteaux. It has its own classification, but is very sprawling, and has two top châteaux, *Cheval-Blanc* and *Ausone*, plus a dozen excellent ones. Some areas also annex the name, like St-Georges-St-Émilion or Puisseguin-St-Émilion. They're often OK, but would be better value if they didn't trade greedily on the St-Émilion handle.

Best in satellites: *St-Georges, Montaiguillon, Tour du Pas St-Georges* (St-Georges-St-Émilion)*; Haut-Gillet, de Maison Neuve* (Montagne-St-Émilion)*; Bel Air, la Croix-de-Berny* (Puisseguin-St-Émilion)*; Lyonnat* (since 1983) (Lussac-St-Émilion). Best châteaux: *l'Angélus, l'Arrosée, Ausone, Balestard-la-Tonnelle, Beauséjour-Duffau-Lagarosse, Canon, Canon-la-Gaffelière, Cheval-Blanc, Clos des Jacobins, la Dominique, Figeac, Fonroque, Larmande, Magdelaine, Pavie, Pavie Decesse, Soutard, Tertre-Rôteboeuf, Troplong-Mondot.* Next best: *Belair, Cadet-Piola, Berliquet, Cap de Mourlin, Cardinal Villemaurine, Carteau, Côtes Daugay, Clos Fourtet, Corbin-Michotte, Couvent des Jacobins, Destieux, de Ferrand, Trappaud, Fombrauge, Franc-Mayne, la Gaffelière, Grand-Mayne, Gravet, Villemaurine, Magnan-la-Gaffelière, Mauvezin, la-Tour-du-Pin Figeac, Monbousquet, Pavie-Macquin, Rolland-Maillet, Tour-des-Combes, Trottevieille.*

ST-ESTÈPHE, AC
This northernmost of the great Haut-Médoc communes is a more everyday performer. There aren't many famous names, and most are relatively cheap. Best: *Calon-Ségur, Chambert-Marbuzet, Cos d'Estournel, Haut-Marbuzet, Lafon-Rochet, Marbuzet, Meyney, Montrose, les Ormes-de-Pez, de Pez.* Next best: *Andron-Blanquet, Beausite, du Boscq, Cos Labory, le Crock, Lavillotte, Phélan-Ségur.*

ST-JULIEN, AC
There are two main styles. One is almost honeyed, a rather gentle, round, wonderfully easy-to-love claret. The other has glorious cedar-cigar-box fragrance mixed with just enough fruit to make it satisfying as well as exciting. Best châteaux to look for: *Beychevelle, Ducru-Beaucaillou, Gruaud-Larose, Lagrange* (in recent vintages especially), *Lalande-Borie, Langoa-Barton, Léoville-Barton, Léoville-Las-Cases, St-Pierre, Talbot.* Next best: *Branaire-Ducru, Gloria, Hortevie, Léoville-Poyferré* and *Terrey-Gros-Caillou.*

THE 1855 CLASSIFICATION

This is the most famous and enduring wine classification in the world – but it was never intended as such, merely as a one-off guide to the different Bordeaux wines entered for the Great Paris Exhibition of 1855, made up by various local brokers and based on the prices the wines had obtained over the previous century or so. Those brokers would be dumbfounded if they returned today to find we still revered their rather impromptu classification.

An interesting point to note is that the wine name was classified, not the vineyard it came from. Some of the vineyards that make up a wine are now completely different from those of 1855, yet, because the name got into the lists, the level of classification remains. There are endless arguments about the quality ratings, but the only change so far occurred in 1973, when Mouton-Rothschild got promoted from Second to First Growth level after 50 years of lobbying by its late owner. In general, those properties which are classified do deserve their status, but that's never yet stopped anyone from arguing about it.

First Growths (1ers Crus)
Latour, *Pauillac*; Lafite-Rothschild, *Pauillac*; Margaux, *Margaux*; Haut-Brion, *Pessac-Léognan* (formerly *Graves*); Mouton-Rothschild, *Pauillac* (promoted in 1973).

Second Growths (2èmes Crus)
Rausan-Ségla, *Margaux*; Rauzan-Gassies, *Margaux*; Léoville-Las-Cases, *St-Julien*; Léoville-Poyferré, *St-Julien*; Léoville-Barton, *St-Julien*; Durfort-Vivens, *Margaux*; Lascombes, *Margaux*; Gruaud-Larose, *St-Julien*; Brane-Cantenac, *Cantenac-Margaux*; Pichon-Longueville, *Pauillac*; Pichon-Longueville-Lalande (formerly Pichon-Lalande), *Pauillac*; Ducru-Beaucaillou, *St-Julien*; Cos d'Estournel, *St-Estèphe*; Montrose, *St-Estèphe*.

Third Growths (3èmes Crus)
Giscours, *Labarde-Margaux*; Kirwan, *Cantenac-Margaux*; d'Issan, *Cantenac-Margaux*; Lagrange, *St-Julien*; Langoa-Barton, *St-Julien*; Malescot-St-Exupéry, *Margaux*; Cantenac-Brown, *Cantenac-Margaux*; Palmer, *Cantenac-Margaux*; la Lagune, *Ludon-Haut-Médoc*; Desmirail, *Margaux*; Calon-Ségur, *St-Estèphe*; Ferrière, *Margaux*; Marquis d'Alesme-Becker, *Margaux*; Boyd-Cantenac, *Cantenac-Margaux*.

Fourth Growths (4èmes Crus)
St-Pierre, *St-Julien*; Branaire-Ducru, *St-Julien*; Talbot, *St-Julien*; Duhart-Milon-Rothschild, *Pauillac*; Pouget, *Cantenac-Margaux*; la Tour-Carnet, *St-Laurent-Haut-Médoc*; Lafon-Rochet, *St-Estèphe*; Beychevelle, *St-Julien*; Prieuré-Lichine, *Cantenac-Margaux*; Marquis-de-Terme, *Margaux*.

Fifth Growths (5èmes Crus)
Pontet-Canet, *Pauillac*; Batailley, *Pauillac*; Grand-Puy-Lacoste, *Pauillac*; Grand-Puy-Ducasse, *Pauillac*; Haut-Batailley, *Pauillac*; Lynch-Bages, *Pauillac*; Lynch-Moussas, *Pauillac*; Dauzac, *Labarde-Margaux*; d'Armailhacq (formerly Mouton-Baronne-Philippe), *Pauillac*; du Tertre, *Arsac-Margaux*; Haut-Bages-Libéral, *Pauillac*; Pédesclaux, *Pauillac*; Belgrave, *St-Laurent-Haut Médoc*; de Camensac, *St-Laurent-Haut-Médoc*; Cos Labory, *St-Estèphe*; Clerc-Milon-Rothschild, *Pauillac*; Croizet-Bages, *Pauillac*; Cantemerle, *Macau-Haut-Médoc*.

Webster's *is an annual publication. We welcome your suggestions for next year's edition.*

CHÂTEAUX PROFILES

These properties are valued according to how they are currently performing; a five-star rating means you are getting a top-line taste – not just a well-known label. Some big names have been downgraded, some lesser-known properties are promoted – solely on the quality of the wine inside the bottle. A star in brackets shows that the wine can achieve the higher rating but does not always do so.

The £ sign shows which are offering particularly good value – that does not mean any of these wines will be cheap but look for recessionary price reductions.

L'ANGÉLUS *grand cru classé St-Émilion* ★★★★ One of the biggest and best known *grands crus classés*. A lot of Cabernet in the vineyard makes for a reasonably gutsy wine, although rich and soft. Since 1979 new barrels have helped the flavour. The 1985 and '86 are, by a street, the finest yet, with excellent '87, '88 and '89.

D'ANGLUDET *cru bourgeois Margaux* ★★★ £ *Bourgeois* easily attaining Classed Growth standards. Owned by Englishman Peter Allan Sichel, the wine has much of the perfume of good Margaux without ever going through the traditional lean period. Fairly priced. Tremendous value. The 1980s have seen Angludet on a hot streak. The '83 and '90 are the finest *ever*, and the '85, '86, '88 and '89 are big and classy.

D'ARMAILHACQ *5ème cru classé Pauillac* ★★★ (Formerly known as Mouton-Baronne-Philippe) A wine of very good balance for a Fifth Growth, with the perfume particularly marked, this obviously benefits from having the same ownership as Mouton-Rothschild. 1986 and '83 are very good, with '82 not bad either.

AUSONE *1er grand cru classé St-Émilion* ★★★★(★) The phoenix rises from the ashes. For many years people referred to Ausone as they would to a slightly mad aunt, who then marries the most popular boy in town. The boy in question is Pascal Delbeck, who has been at the château since 1976 and has worked at returning Ausone to its proper position as one of St-Émilion's two First

Growths. Potentially great wine at its best. The 1985, '86, '89 and above all the '90, should be especially good.

BATAILLEY *5ème cru classé Pauillac* ★★★ £ Batailley's reputation has been of the squat, solid sort rather than elegant and refined, but recently the wines have performed that extremely difficult Pauillac magician's trick – they've been getting a lot better, and the price has remained reasonable. Drinkable young, they age well too. The 1983, '85, '86, '88, '89 and '90 are excellent, available – and affordable.

BELAIR *1er cru classé St-Émilion* ★★★ The arrival of Pascal Delbeck at Ausone had a dramatic effect on Belair too, since it's under the same ownership. It looked as though it was rapidly returning to a top position as a finely balanced, stylish St-Émilion, but some recent bottles have been strangely unconvincing.

BEYCHEVELLE *4ème cru classé St-Julien* ★★★★ Certainly the most expensive Fourth Growth, but deservedly so, since traditional quality puts it alongside the top Seconds. It takes time to mature to a scented, blackcurrant, beautifully balanced – and expensive – wine. At the end of the 1970s and beginning of the 1980s the wines were rather unconvincing, but the sale of the château (to a civil servants' pension fund) in 1985 dramatically improved matters through greater selectivity. 1989 and 1990 are sublime.

BRANAIRE-DUCRU *4ème cru classé St-Julien* ★★★ Used to be soft, smooth wine with a flavour of plums and chocolate, gradually achieving a classic, cedary St-Julien dry perfume in maturity. The 1981, '82, '85 and '86 are good. But the 1980s have been very erratic, with rather dilute flavours and unclean fruit. '82, '85 and '86 were clean and fruity, but '83, '87 and '88 were strangely insubstantial. 1989 and '90 saw a welcome return to form, thanks to a change of ownership, with wine of sturdy fruit and backbone.

BRANE-CANTENAC *2ème cru classé Margaux* ★★ A big and famous property which has been underachieving when most of the other Second Growths have been shooting ahead. It has had chances in the last eight years to prove itself, but remains behind the rest of the field. Even its supposedly inferior stable-mate Durfort-Vivens has produced better wine in recent years.

CALON-SÉGUR *3ème cru classé St-Estèphe* ★★★(★) The château with the heart on its label. This is because the former owner, Marquis de Ségur, though he owned such estates as Lafite and Latour, declared 'my heart belongs to Calon'. An intensely traditional claret, it's certainly good on present showing, but doesn't set many hearts a-flutter. 1986 and '88 were promising though.

CANON *1er grand cru classé St-Émilion* ★★★★(★) Mature Canon reeks of the soft, buttery Merlot grape as only a top St-Émilion can. Recently, it has been getting deeper and tougher, and although we'll probably miss that juicy, sweet mouthful of young Merlot, the end result will be even deeper and more exciting. The wines seem to get better and better; marvellous 1982s and '83s were followed by a stunning '85 and a thoroughly impressive '86. 1988 was excellent. '89 and '90 are keeping up this high standard.

CANTEMERLE *5ème cru classé Haut-Médoc* ★★★(★) For some years after 1983 the Cordier company controlled this Fifth Growth and the wine is now often up to Second Growth standards, although sometimes a little light. The 1988 and '89 are the best recent vintages by a long way, and the '83 was really good, but though the '85, '86 and '90 are beautifully perfumed, they are a little loose-knit. Interestingly, the perfumed style quite suits the '87.

CHASSE-SPLEEN *cru bourgeois Moulis* ★★★(★) A tremendously consistent wine, at the top of the *bourgeois* tree, and a prime candidate for elevation. It already sells above the price of many Classed Growths. The wines were impressive, chunky and beautifully made right through the 1980s, except for a rather 'over-elegant' 1985. Choose 1982 and '86, followed by lovely '87 and tip-top '88. The 1989 is a bit fierce, but the '90 is first class, with lots of blackberry fruit backed by a firm structure. Even the '91 and '92 are impressive.

CHEVAL-BLANC *1er grand cru classé St-Émilion* ★★★★★ The property stands on an outcrop right next to Pomerol, and seems to share some of its sturdy richness, but adds extra spice and fruit that is unique, perhaps due to the very high proportion of Cabernet Franc. Good years are succulent. Lesser years like 1980 can be successes too, and only 1984 and 1987 haven't worked. The 1982 is unbelievably good, and the '81, '83, '85 and '86 are not far behind. '88 is one of the top wines of the vintage, but '89 and '90 are not quite of the intensity I would want.

CISSAC *cru grand bourgeois Haut-Médoc* ★★★ £ Traditionalists' delight! This is one of the best known *bourgeois* growths, dark, dry and slow to mature with lots of oak influence, too – the oak perhaps a little more apparent than the fruit. It is best in richly ripe years like 1982 and '85, and can be a little lean in years like '86. '88, '89 and '90 were very good indeed.

COS D'ESTOURNEL *2ème cru classé St-Estèphe* ★★★★★ £ The undoubted leader of St-Estèphe, this has much of the fame of the top Pauillacs. The wines are dark, tannic and oaky: classically made for long aging despite a high percentage of Merlot. A 'super-second' but less expensive than its rivals – the 1992 is a real bargain. The quality was so good in '85, '88 and '89 that they are probably undervalued. Even the '91 is decent. Second label Château Marbuzet is good.

DOMAINE DE CHEVALIER *cru classé Pessac-Léognan* ★★★★(★) The red and white are equally brilliant. The red has a superb balance of fruit and oak, and the white is simply one of France's greatest. You have to book ahead even to see a bottle of the white but you might find some red. Buy it. It's expensive and worth every penny. The hottest years are not always the best here, and despite an impressive richness in 1982, the '81, '83, '85, '86 and '88 may yet turn out better. 1987 is a resounding success in a light vintage, as is 1984. 1989 and '90 were classy in an area of Bordeaux where results seem uneven.

DUCRU-BEAUCAILLOU *2ème cru classé St-Julien* ★★★(★) One of the glories of the Médoc. It has now distanced itself from most other Second Growths in price and quality, yet the flavour is so deep and warm, and the balance so good, it's still worth the money. With its relatively high yields, it has a less startling quality when young than its near rivals Léoville-Las-Cases and Pichon-Longueville-Lalande. The mid-'80s saw problems with the barrels, so while '82 and '85 are top drawer, and '81, '79 and '78 fit for the long haul, most recent vintages must be approached with caution.

L'EVANGILE *Pomerol* ★★★(★) Top-line Pomerol, lacking the sheer intensity of its neighbour Pétrus, but perfumed and rich in a most irresistible way. Output isn't excessive, demand is. 1982, '85, and '88 are delicious, with first-rate '87 too. '89 is packed with multi-layered, firm, luscious fruit, and '90 is another blockbuster.

DE FIEUZAL *cru classé Pessac-Léognan* ★★★★ One of the stars of Pessac-Léognan, the white only just behind Domaine de Chevalier, the red well ahead. The red starts plum-rich and buttery, but develops earthiness and cedar scent allied to lovely fruit. It made one of the finest 1984s, outstanding '85s and '86s as well as lovely '87s and thrilling '88s. '89 was top-notch, the '90 very good. The white, though unclassified, is scented, complex, deep and exciting. Even the '92 is worth buying.

FIGEAC *1er grand cru classé St-Émilion* ★★★★ Figeac shares many of the qualities of Cheval-Blanc (rare gravelly soil, for a start) but it's always ranked as the – ever-reliable – star of the second team. A pity, because the wine has a beauty and a blackcurranty, minty scent uncommon in St-Émilion. High quality. High(ish) price. Figeac is always easy to drink young, but deserves proper aging. The excellent 1978 is just opening out, and the lovely '82, '85 and '86 wines will all take at least as long. '89 and '90 are already seductive.

LA FLEUR-PÉTRUS *Pomerol* ★★★★ This wine is in the top flight, having some of the mineral roughness of much Pomerol, but also tremendous perfume and length. Real class. We don't see much of this in the UK since the Americans got their teeth into it, but the 1982 and '89 are without doubt the best recent wines; the '85 and '86 seem to lack that little 'extra' class.

GAZIN *Pomerol* ★★★(★) This can produce the extra sweetness and perfume Nenin usually lacks. Although fairly common on the British market, it wasn't that great up to about 1985. Now controlled by Moueix, '87 and '88 are an improvement, and '89 and '90 are really very fine, so we can all start buying it again.

GISCOURS *3ème cru classé Margaux*
★★★ This property excelled right through
the 1970s and into the '80s, and made some
of Bordeaux's best in years like '75, '78 and
'80. But something's gone wrong since 1982.
Although 1986 is good, and '87 reasonable
for the year, '83, '85 and '88 are not up to par.
1989 and '90 showed a return to form.

GLORIA *cru bourgeois St-Julien* ★★(★)
Owing to the high-profile lobbying of its
late owner, Henri Martin, Gloria became
expensive and renowned. The quality of
this quick-maturing wine has not always
been faithful to the quality of the rhetoric.
1986, '88 and '89 show some signs that the
wine is becoming worthy of the price.

GRAND-PUY-DUCASSE *5ème cru classé
Pauillac* ★★★ £ Every recent vintage has
been a success, and, with a price that is not
excessive, its slightly gentle but tasty
Pauillac style is one to buy. The 1979 is
lovely now, and the '82 and '83 are very
nice without causing the hand to tremble
in anticipation. Since 1984 there has been
a discernible rise in tempo and '85 and '86
look to be the best wines yet, but little
exciting wine was made in the late 1980s.

GRAND-PUY-LACOSTE *5ème cru classé
Pauillac* ★★★★ £ This combines perfume,
power and consistency in a way that shows
Pauillac at its brilliant best. Blackcurrant
and cigar-box perfumes are rarely in better
harmony than here. Not cheap but worth it
for a classic. The 1978 is sheer class, the
'82, '83, '86 and '88 top wines, and the '84,
though very light, is gentle and delicious.
1989 is deliciously perfumed with robust
fruit – a real star, as is the super 1990.

GRUAUD-LAROSE *2ème cru classé St-
Julien* ★★★★(★) Another St-Julien that
often starts rich, chunky and sweetish but
will achieve its full cedary glory if given
time, while still retaining a lovely sweet
centre, typical of the wines (like Talbot)
formerly owned by the Cordier family.

The remarkable run of 1982, '83, '84 and
'85 continued with a great '86, an attractive
'87, exceptionally impressive '88 and '89
and, keeping up the standards, almost
unnervingly juicy, ripe '90.

HAUT-BAILLY *cru classé Pessac-Léognan*
★★★★ Haut-Bailly tastes sweet, rich and
perfumed from its earliest youth, and the
high percentage of new oak adds to this
impression even further. But the wines do
age well and, though expensive, are of a
high class. 1981, '82, '85, '86, '88 and '89 are
the best recently.

HAUT-BATAILLEY *5ème cru classé
Pauillac* ★★★ Once dark, plummy and slow
to sweeten, this is now a somewhat lighter,
more charming wine. In some years this
has meant it was somehow less satisfying,
but 1989 is the best yet, marvellously
concentrated. 1986 and '88 are the best of
earlier wines, with '82, '83 and '85 all good,
but just a touch too diffuse and soft.

HAUT-BRION *1er cru classé Pessac-
Léognan* ★★★★★ The only non-Médoc red
to be classified in 1855. The wines are not
big, but are almost creamy in their gorgeous
ripe taste, deliciously so. If anything, they
slightly resemble the great Médocs.
Although 1982 is strangely insubstantial,
the next four vintages are all very fine and
'88 and '89 are outstanding, while the 1990,
although worthy of the château, could not
quite compete with its predecessors. There
is also a delicious, if overpriced white
Haut-Brion – the 1985 is spectacular.

D'ISSAN *3ème cru classé Margaux* ★★★★
One of the truest Margaux wines, hard
when young (though more use of new oak
recently has sweetened things up a bit),
but perfumed and deep-flavoured after ten
to 12 years. Fabulous in 1983, '88 and '90,
first rate in '85 and '86, with a good '87 too.
1989 has excellent fruit, while 1990 is a
star, rich and concentrated, with lots of
liquorice fruit on the palate.

LAFITE-ROTHSCHILD *1er cru classé Pauillac* ★★★★★ The most difficult of all the great Médocs to get to know. It doesn't stand for power like Latour, or perfume like Mouton. No, it stands for balance, for the elegant, restrained balance that is the perfection of great claret. And yet, till its day comes, Lafite can seem curiously unsatisfying. I keep looking for that day; at last I am finding satisfaction. 1990, '89, '88 and '86 are undoubtedly the best recent vintages, followed by 1982, and this fabled estate seems to be dishing up fewer fairy tales and more of the real stuff that dreams are made of.

LAFLEUR *Pomerol* ★★★★★ This tiny property is regarded as the only Pomerol with the potential to be as great as Pétrus. So far, they couldn't be further apart in style, and Lafleur is marked out by an astonishing austere concentration of dark fruit and an intense tobacco spice perfume. The 1982 almost knocks you sideways with its naked power, and the '83 and '85 are also remarkable. 1989 is superbly fruity and displays tremendous finesse already.

LAFON-ROCHET *4ème cru classé St-Estèphe* ★★★(★) Since the 1970s, an improving St-Estèphe, having as much body, but a little more perfume than most of them. 1982, '83 and '85 are all good, though none of them stunning, while '86, '87, '88, '89 and '90 show real class and a welcome consistency of style.

LAGRANGE *3ème cru classé St-Julien* ★★★(★) Until its purchase by the Japanese Suntory whiskey group in 1984, Lagrange had always lacked real class, though '82 and '83 were reasonable. But the vineyard always had great potential, even when the wine was below par, and investment is making its presence felt; '85, '86, '88, '89 and '90 are impressive and '87 was good too. Another bandwagon is rolling. Make sure you concentrate on more recent vintages.

LA LAGUNE *3ème cru classé Haut-Médoc* ★★★★ Certainly making Second Growth standard wine, with a rich, soft intensity. It is now becoming more expensive, but the wine gets better and better. The 1982 is a wonderful rich, juicy wine, with '85 and '88 not far behind, and '83 not far behind that. 1986 is burly but brilliant stuff, as is '89. 1987 is more delicate but good.

LANESSAN *cru bourgeois Haut-Médoc* ★★★ 'Grand Cru Hors Classe' is how Lanessan describes itself. This could be a reminder of the fact that a previous owner felt it unnecessary to submit samples for the 1855 Classification, so its traditional ranking as a Fourth Growth was never ratified. Nowadays, the wine is always correct, if not distinguished. But this may be because the owner resolutely refuses to use new oak and therefore his wines are more discreet when young. The '82 and '83 are both exhibiting classic claret flavours now, '88 looks set for the same path and '90 is a wine of balance and depth.

LANGOA-BARTON *3ème cru classé St-Julien* ★★★★ £ This wine is very good, in the dry, cedary style, and although sometimes regarded as a lesser version of Léoville-Barton, this is patently unfair. The wine has exceptional character and style of its own, and is reasonably priced. 1982 and '85 are exciting, '86 and '87 very typical, but the '88 may be the best for 30 years. The '89 almost matched Léoville for elegance and the '90 was fully its equal.

LASCOMBES *2ème cru classé Margaux* ★★★ Lascombes made its reputation in America, and that's where it still likes to be drunk. Very attractive early on, but the wine can gain flesh and character as it ages. It's been a little inconsistent recently, but the 1985 and '83 are good, and the '86 is the most serious effort for a long time. '87 is also good, but '88 is so light you'd think they'd included every grape on the property. The '89 and '90 are more hopeful.

LATOUR *1er cru classé Pauillac* ★★★★★
This is the easiest of all the First Growths
to comprehend. You may not always like it,
but you understand it because it is a huge,
dark, hard brute when young, calming
down when it ages and eventually
spreading out to a superb, blackcurrant
and cedar flavour. It used to take ages to
come round, but some recent vintages have
seemed a little softer and lighter, yet
usually retaining their tremendous core of
fruit. Let's hope they age as well as the
previous ones, because the 1984 was more
true to type than the '85! And though the
'82 is a classic, both '83 and '81 are very
definitely not. '86 and '88 seem to be back
on course, and '89 looks splendidly
powerful. With the '89 and '90 the new
management showed that power and
richness were part of their inheritance. The
'91 and '92 are the best wines of their
years. The second wine, Les Forts de
Latour, is getting better and better, while
the third wine, Pauillac de Latour, is now
made in most years to preserve the quality
of the two greater wines.

LÉOVILLE-BARTON *2ème cru classé
St-Julien* ★★★★★ £ The traditionalist's
dream. Whoever described claret as a dry,
demanding wine must have been thinking
of Léoville-Barton. Despite all the new
fashions and trends in Bordeaux, Anthony
Barton simply goes on making superlative,
old-fashioned wine for long aging, and
resolutely charging a non-inflated price for
it. All the vintages of the 1980s have been
attractive, but the 1982, '83, '85 and '86 are
outstanding, the '87 delicious, and the '88
and '90 are two of the best wines of the
Médoc. 1989 keeps up the standard. All are
wonderfully fairly priced.

LÉOVILLE-LAS-CASES *2ème cru classé
St-Julien* ★★★★★ Because of the owner's
super-selectivity, this is the most brilliant
of the St-Juliens, combining all the sweet,
honeyed St-Julien ripeness with strong, dry,
cedary perfume. The wine is justly famous,

and despite a large production, the whole
crop is snapped up at some of the Médoc's
highest prices. The 1982 is more exciting
every time a bottle is broached, and all the
vintages of the 1980s are top examples of
their year. The second wine, Clos du
Marquis, is better than the majority of
Classed Growths, if only because Michel
Delon puts into it wines which any other
owner would put into his *grand vin*.

LÉOVILLE-POYFERRÉ *2ème cru classé
St-Julien* ★★★★ The Léoville that got left
behind, not only in its unfashionable
reputation, but also in the quality of the
wine, which until recently had a dull,
indistinct flavour and an unbalancing
dryness compared with other top St-
Juliens. Things are now looking up with
new investment and new commitment and
I feel more confident about this property
with every vintage. The 1982, '85, '86 and
even the '87 are considerable
improvements, and '88, '89 and '90
continue the progress, but it still has some
way to catch up in terms of power and
concentration with its peer group.

LOUDENNE *cru bourgeois Médoc* ★(★)
The château is owned by Gilbey's and the
wine is seen a lot in such chains as Peter
Dominic. The red has a lot of Merlot and is
always fruity and agreeable, but a little too
soft to lay down for long.

LYNCH-BAGES *5ème cru classé Pauillac*
★★★★★ This château is so well known that
familiarity can breed contempt, and its
considerable quality be underestimated. It
is astonishingly soft and drinkable when
very young, and yet it ages brilliantly, and
has one of the most beautiful scents of
minty blackcurrant in all Bordeaux. The
most likely to show that character are the
1986 and '83, and, remarkably, the '87, but
for sheer exuberant starry-eyed brilliance,
the '88, '85 and particularly the '82 are the
ones. '89 is unusually big and powerful,
while the '90 is more restrained and classic.

MAGDELAINE *1er grand cru classé St-Émilion* ★★★★ A great St-Émilion, combining the soft richness of Merlot with the sturdiness needed to age. They pick very late to maximize ripeness, and the wine is made with the usual care by Jean-Pierre Moueix of Libourne. Expensive, but one of the best. 1982 and 1985 are both classics, '88 and '89 tremendously good.

MALARTIC-LAGRAVIÈRE *cru classé Pessac-Léognan* ★★★ £ While its near neighbour, Domaine de Chevalier, hardly ever produces its allowed crop, this property frequently has to declassify its excess. Even so, the quality is good, sometimes excellent, and while the white is very attractive young, the red is capable of long aging. 1987, '86, '85, '83 and '82 are all successful, with '88 and '89 the finest yet, but the '90s are disappointing.The red, in particular, is rather wishy-washy.

MALESCOT-ST-EXUPÉRY *3ème cru classé Margaux* ★★(★) A property which seems to have lost its way. Traditionally it started out lean and hard and difficult to taste, but after ten years or so it began to display the perfume and delicate fruit only bettered by such wines as Palmer and Margaux. Yet after tasting and re-tasting the wines of the 1980s, the conclusion is that they are made too light and lacking in depth for this thrilling scent ever to develop. The '88 and 1990 may prove me wrong.

MARGAUX *1er cru classé Margaux* ★★★★★A succession of great wines have set Margaux back on the pedestal of refinement and sheer, ravishing perfume from which it had slipped some years ago. The new Margaux is weightier and more consistent than before, yet with all its beauty intact. 1978 and 1979 were the harbingers of this new 'Mentzelopoulos era', the '80 was startlingly good in a tricky vintage, and '82, '83 and '86 are just about as brilliant as claret can be, while the '88 may well be the wine of the vintage. The deep, concentrated

'89 doesn't seem to match up to the '88, but the 1990 is as fragrant and powerful as the 1986 – which is saying a lot. In '91 and '92 the wines, though not up to Latour's level, were better than most of the First Growths.

MEYNEY *cru bourgeois St-Estèphe* ★★★(★) £ This epitomizes St-Estèphe reliability, yet is better than that. It is big, meaty and strong, but never harsh. Vintages in the 1970s lacked personality, but recent wines are increasingly impressive and although the wine is difficult to taste young, the '82, '83, '85, '86, '88 and '89 are remarkable and the '84, '87 and '90 good.

LA MISSION-HAUT-BRION *cru classé Pessac-Léognan* ★★★(★) La Mission likes to put itself in a class apart, between Haut-Brion and the rest. Yet one often feels this relies more on weight and massive, dark fruit and oak flavours than on any great subtleties. For those, you go to Haut-Brion or Domaine de Chevalier. '82, '85 or '86 are recommendable of recent vintages.

MONTROSE *2ème cru classé St-Estèphe* ★★★★ Traditionally famous for its dark, tannic character, and its slow, ponderous march to maturity. For a wine with such a sturdy reputation, some recent vintages have seemed faintly hollow. 1986 made amends with a really chewy, long-distance number, and '87 was densely structured, if hardly classic, but it's taken until '89 and '90 for the wine really to return to form. The château, which tends to pick rather early, came into its own in '89 and '90, and even made a decent '91 and a better '92. The second wine, Dame de Montrose, has been a bargain these past four years.

MOUTON-ROTHSCHILD *1er cru classé Pauillac* ★★★★★After years of lobbying, Baron Philippe de Rothschild managed to raise Mouton to First Growth status in 1973. Of course it should be a First Growth. But then several Fifths should probably be Seconds. The wine has an astonishing flavour, piling intense cigar-box and lead-pencil perfume on to the rich blackcurrant fruit. The 1982 is already a legend, the '86 and '89 are likely to join '82, and the '85, '84 and '83 are well worth the asking price.

NENIN *Pomerol* ★★ A thoroughly old-fashioned wine. It quite rightly pleases the royal family, who order rather a lot of it. But in fact it is rather chunky and solid and has quite a tough core for a Pomerol, which doesn't always disperse into mellow fruitfulness. The 1985 and '86 aren't bad, but, really, the '82, the '83 and the '88, all good vintages, were pretty feeble.

PALMER *3ème cru classé Margaux* ★★★★ 'Most expensive of the Third Growths?' asks one of Palmer's owners. 'No. Cheapest of the Firsts.' There's (some) truth in that. Until 1978 Palmer used to out-Margaux Margaux for sheer beauty and perfume. And it still can occasionally out-perform some of the First Growths in tastings. It was consistently brilliant in the 1960s and 1970s (excepting '64), but the 1980s have seen it lose some of its sure touch, and the '83 lacks some of its neighbours' class. '87 and '88 are very good too, but are closer in style to out-Beychevelling Beychevelle. '89 is cedary and elegant, rich but tannic, in a year when not all Margaux wines had great depth of fruit. In 1990 Palmer was better than most, but not all, of its neighbours.

PAPE-CLÉMENT *cru classé Pessac-Léognan* ★★★★(★) One of the top properties in Pessac-Léognan, capable of mixing a considerable sweetness from ripe fruit and new oak with a good deal of tough structure. 1975 was great, but then we had a very poor decade until 1985. The last five vintages are outstanding, with the 1990 an example of Pessac-Léognan at its best.

PAVIE *1er grand cru St-Émilion* ★★★★ The biggest major property in St-Émilion, with high yields, too. Until recently good without being wonderful, stylish without

being grand. Still, Pavie does have the true gentle flavours of good St-Émilion and recent releases are showing a deeper, more passionate style which puts it into the top flight. 1990, '89, '88, '87, '86 and '85 are good examples of the new, '82 of the old.

PETIT-VILLAGE *Pomerol* ★★★★ A fairly pricy wine, it is not one of the soft, plummy Pomerols, and until recently there was a fair amount of Cabernet giving backbone. The wine is worth laying down, but the price is always high. 1985, '83 and the absurdly juicy '82 are all very good, but the '88, '89 and '90 look likely to be the best yet.

PÉTRUS *Pomerol* ★★★★★ One of the world's most expensive reds, and often one of the greatest. Astonishingly, its fame, though surfacing briefly in 1878, has only been acquired since 1945, and in particular since 1962, when the firm of Jean-Pierre Moueix took a half-share in the property. This firm has given the kiss of life to many Pomerol properties, turning potential into achievement, and with Pétrus it has a supreme creation. Christian Moueix says his intention is to ensure no bottle of Pétrus ever disappoints. 1982 and 1989 were stupendously great. 1985 isn't far off it, nor is '81, and the only example from the last 20 years which seemed atypical is the rather Médoc-like 1978.

DE PEZ *cru bourgeois St-Estèphe* ★★★ One of the most famous *bourgeois* châteaux, the wine is almost always of Classed Growth standard, big, reliable, rather plummy and not too harsh. 1982 and '83 were very attractive, though some prefer the more unashamedly St-Estèphe wines of the 1970s, which saw a bit of a comeback with the excellent '86.

PICHON-LONGUEVILLE *2ème cru classé Pauillac* ★★★★★ (since 1987) Often described as more masculine than its 'sister', Pichon-Longueville-Lalande, this tremendously correct but diffident Pauillac (formerly Pichon-Longueville-Baron) was until 1987 only hinting at its potential. Drier and lighter than Lalande, it was also less immediately impressive, despite aging well. 1987 saw the property being bought by the AXA insurance company and Jean-Michel Cazes of Lynch-Bages being brought in to run it. The '87 was very good, the '88 superb, the '89 *tremendous*, broodingly intense, while the '90 is one of the Médoc's greatest wines.

PICHON-LONGUEVILLE-LALANDE

2ème cru classé Pauillac ★★★★(★) Pichon-Longueville-Lalande (formerly Pichon-Lalande) produced a stunning 1970, and since then has been making a rich, oaky, concentrated wine of tremendous quality. Its price has climbed inexorably and it wishes to be seen as the equal partner of St-Julien's leading pair, Léoville-Las-Cases and Ducru-Beaucaillou. 1982, '83 and '85 all brim with exciting flavours, and '86 may be even better. Nothing since then reaches the same standards, though '87 and '88 are good. Both '89 and '90 are below par, and easily outclassed by the wines of rival estate Pichon-Longueville over the road. Lalande only got back on form in '92 and '93.

PONTET-CANET *5ème cru classé Pauillac* ★★★ The biggest Classed Growth of them all. Famous but unpredictable, and still trying to find its traditionally reliable form. 1985 and '86 are hopeful, '87 and '88 less so, '90 hopeful again as the owners become more selective.

POTENSAC *cru bourgeois Médoc* ★★★(★) £ The most exciting in the Bas-Médoc. It is owned by Michel Delon of Léoville-Las-Cases, and a broadly similar style of wine-making is pursued. This gives wines with a delicious, blackcurrant fruit, greatly improved by a strong taste of oak from once-used Las-Cases barrels. Not expensive for the quality. Beats many *crus classés* every year for sheer flavour.

PRIEURÉ-LICHINE *4ème cru classé Margaux* ★★★ One of the more reliable Margaux wines, and in years like 1970, 1971 and 1975 it excelled. Recently it has been fairly priced and although not that perfumed, a good, sound Margaux. 1983, '86, '88 and '89 are all good, but '90 is the first really exciting wine for some time, and 1991 and '92 continue the improvement.

RAUSAN-SÉGLA *2ème cru classé Margaux* ★★★★(★) Up to and including the 1982 vintage this lovely property, rated second only to Mouton-Rothschild in the 1855 Second Growths, had been woefully underachieving for a couple of generations. But a change of ownership in 1983 saw a triumphant return to quality – in the very first year. 1983, '85 and '86 were triumphs. 1987 was declassified as Château Lamouroux but is still delicious. The '88 is a supreme achievement which the '89 matches and the '90 surpasses.

RAUZAN-GASSIES *2ème cru classé Margaux* ★★ Right behind Rausan-Ségla, but the wine is leagues below most Second and Third Growths in quality, and so far hasn't taken the hint from Ségla that quality pays in the end.

ST-PIERRE *4ème cru classé Médoc* ★★★★ Small St-Julien property producing superb, underrated, old-fashioned wine. Once under-priced, but the image-conscious Henri Martin of Gloria stopped that when he took over in 1982. Still, the quality has been worth it. While the 1970 and '75 were underrated stars, the wines of the 1980s are possibly even better. Martin died in 1991, and the family are carrying on the tradition.

DE SALES *Pomerol* ★★★ £ An enormous estate, the biggest in Pomerol by a street. This vastness shows in a wine which, though it is good round claret, doesn't often excite. The 1985 is very nice, the '83 and '82 are very nice.

SIRAN *cru bourgeois Margaux* ★★★
Sometimes mistaken for a Classed Growth
in blind tastings, this property is indeed
mostly made up from the land of
Châteaux Dauzac and Giscours. The '85
and '83 are the most successful wines of
recent years, but all vintages have been
good lately. The '88 was a bit clumsy, but
the 1989 and 1990 vintages are showing
well.

TALBOT *4ème cru classé St-Julien*
★★★★ One of the most carefully made and
reliable of the fleshier St-Juliens,
suffering only in comparison with its sister
château in the former Cordier stable,
Gruaud-Larose, and always offering value
for money and tremendous consistency.
Maybe the name Talbot just lacks the right
ring? Whatever the reason, you must
seek out the exciting 1986, the super-
classy '85, '83 and '82 and the ultra-stylish
'84, as well as the impressive '88 and the
big, rich '89. The '90, however, seems to
lack something in the way of
concentration.

DU TERTRE *5ème cru classé Margaux*
★★★(★) This wine is unusually good, with
a lot of body for a Margaux, but that weight
is all ripe, strong fruit and the flavour is
direct and pure. Funnily enough, it's not
cheap for a relative unknown but neither is
it expensive for the quality. The '85 is rich
and dense and yet keeps its perfume intact,
while the '86, '83 and '82 are rich and
blackcurranty – already good and sure to
improve for ten years more. '88 was not
quite so good, for some reason, but '89 was
back to normal.

TROTANOY *Pomerol* ★★★★ If you didn't
know Pétrus existed, you'd say this had to
be the perfect Pomerol – rich, plummy,
chocolaty fruit, some mineral hardness,
and tremendous fat perfume. It's very, very
good, and makes Pétrus' achievement in
eclipsing it all the more amazing. The '82 is
brilliant, and although the '85 is also
wonderfully good, the vintages of the mid
and late 1980s haven't been quite as
thrilling as have previous examples of this
château.

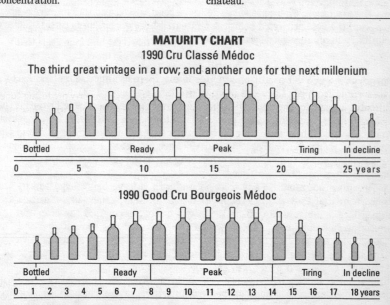

MATURITY CHART
1990 Cru Classé Médoc
The third great vintage in a row; and another one for the next millenium

| Bottled | Ready | Peak | Tiring | In decline |

0   5   10   15   20   25 years

1990 Good Cru Bourgeois Médoc

| Bottled | Ready | Peak | Tiring | In decline |

0   1   2   3   4   5   6   7   8   9   10   11   12   13   14   15   16   17   18 years

SECOND WINES

Second wines were a phenomenon of the 1980s. They have existed for as long as anyone alive can remember, and will live on until everyone can afford Lafite for Sunday lunch, but the period of their most spectacular growth was that wonderful ten years from 1981 to 1990 when it was thought that only fools or villains could not make great wine.

This is where second wines came in. Initially they came only from the major châteaux who practise quality control by selecting only the best vats for their *grand vin*. Anything else – the produce of young vines, or any lots of wine that because of quirks of weather don't quite make the grade – goes into the second wine, called something like Les Forts-de-Latour or Pavillon-Rouge-de-Château-Margaux. These two examples sell above the £15 mark, but most second wines are cheaper, at under a tenner, and they give more than an inkling of the style of the *grand vin*.

Second wines are not generally offered *en primeur*, and one considerable advantage in buying them is that it is possible to taste at less expense and, the wine being generally faster maturing, with greater pleasure, before buying.

The fact that the wine is sold under a second label is less alarming than it sounds to the consumer: almost all proprietors get rid of anything really inferior by selling it off under a generic label. Château Latour has not only Les Forts-de-Latour, but also a third wine, a Pauillac. Many proprietors take the easy way out by selling off the lesser wine (anything not good enough for a second, or even a third wine) to merchants who use it for blending.

The quality of second wines varies even more from château to château than does the *grand vin*. There are very shoddy second wines, and there are very good ones, and the best are listed below. A château whose *grand vin* is unsatisfactory is unlikely to produce good second wine.

Second-rate years

However, since 1990 conditions in Bordeaux have changed. The best second wines come from big harvests of good quality, but both 1991 and 1992 were difficult vintages for the main wines and nothing really good was left over for the junior siblings. In addition, the prices of the top wines of those châteaux which produce second labels were themselves much lower in these vintages. From the consumer's point of view, too, 1991 and 1992 are not years in which to buy second wines. Who wants the rejects of off-vintages? Although, that being said, the Dame de Montrose '92 is very good.

This does not mean to say that second wines have been forgotten by the growers, or that they will not reappear if good quality, generous quantities and high prices again coincide. After 1991 (when frost decimated the crop and the recession began to bite), 1992 (when the vintage was unexciting and the recession bit harder) and 1993 (when a wonderful vintage was snatched away by rain at the harvest and the recession dominated everything), it is difficult to feel confident that second wines will ever be as common as they were in 1989, but things change quickly in Bordeaux and on its markets. Who knows? In two years' time it may again be chic to serve second wines rather than those vulgarly expensive major châteaux.   **WILLIAM BOLTER**

RECOMMENDED WINES

Most of these (and we have starred the ones we feel are the best bets) are from the Haut-Médoc, since properties there are larger and the opportunities for selection much greater. But when you buy a second wine, don't feel you're buying a second rate modern invention. Château Margaux produced its first Pavillon Rouge du Château Margaux in 1908, and Léoville-Las-Cases created its second label, Clos du Marquis, in 1904. But the habit faded in the 1930s as the owners rushed to sell everything as *grand vin* simply to survive. Only recently has it been revived.

Haut-Médoc

1st Growth: ★les Forts-de-Latour (Latour), Moulin-des-Carruades (Lafite), ★Pavillon-Rouge-du-Château-Margaux (Margaux).

2nd Growth: ★le Baronnet-de-Pichon (Pichon-Longueville), ★Clos du Marquis (Léoville-Las-Cases), ★la Croix (Ducru-Beaucaillou), la Dame de Montrose (Montrose), Domaine de Curebourse (Durfort-Vivens), ★Lamouroux (Rausan-Ségla), ★Marbuzet (Cos d'Estournel), Moulin-Riche (Léoville-Poyferré), Notton (Brane-Cantenac), ★Réserve de la Comtesse (Pichon-Longueville-Lalande), ★St-Julien (Léoville-Barton), ★Sarget de Gruaud-Larose (Gruaud-Larose), ★les Tourelles-de-Longueville (Pichon-Longueville).

3rd Growths: ★Fiefs de Lagrange (Lagrange), ★St-Julien (Langoa), de Loyac (Malescot St-Exupéry), Ludon-Pomies-Agassac (la Lagune), Marquis-de-Ségur (Calon-Ségur), ★Réserve du Général (Palmer).

4th Growths: de Clairefont (Prieuré-Lichine), Connétable-Talbot (Talbot), des Goudat (Marquis de Terme), Moulin-de-Duhart (Duhart-Milon-Rothschild), ★Réserve de l'Amiral (Beychevelle), St-Louis-le-Bosq (St-Pierre).

5th Growths: Artigue-Arnaud (Grand-Puy-Ducasse), Enclos de Moncabon (Croizet-Bages), ★Haut-Bages-Avérous (Lynch-Bages), les Hauts-de-Pontet (PontetCanet), ★Lacoste-Borie (Grand-Puy-Lacoste), ★Villeneuve-de-Cantemerle (Cantemerle).

Good Bourgeois Châteaux: Abiet (Cissac), ★Admiral (Labégorce-Zédé), Bellegarde (Siran), Bory (Angludet), ★Clos Cordat (Monbrison), Domaine de Martiny (Cissac), Domaine Zédé (Labégorce-Zédé), Ermitage de Chasse-Spleen (Chasse-Spleen), Labat (Caronne-Ste-Gemme), Granges-de-Clarke (Clarke), ★Lartigue-de-Brochon (Sociando-Mallet), ★Lassalle (Potensac), Moulin d'Arrigny (Beaumont), Prieur de Meyney (Meyney), Réserve du Marquis d'Evry (Lamarque), ★Tour de Marbuzet (Haut-Marbuzet)' ★Salle-de-Poujeaux (Poujeaux).

Graves, Pessac-Léognan

★Abeille de Fieuzal (Fieuzal), Bahans-Haut-Brion (Haut-Brion), ★Batard-Chevalier (Domaine de Chevalier), ★Coucheroy (la Louvière), ★Hauts de Smith-Haut-Lafitte (Smith-Haut-Lafitte), ★la Parde-de-Haut-Bailly (Haut-Bailly).

St Emilion

Beau-Mayne (Couvent des Jacobins), ★Domaine de Martialis (Clos Fourtet), ★Franc-Grace-Dieu (Canon), Jean du Nayne (Angelus), Grangeneuve-de-Figeac (Figeac), ★des Templiers (Larmande).

Pomerol

Chantalouette (de Sales), Clos Toulifaut (Taillefer), ★Fleur de Clinet (Clinet), la Gravette-de-Certan (Vieux-Château-Certan), Monregard-Lacroix (Clos du Clocher), ★la Petite Église (l'Église Clinet).

Bordeaux Supérieur Côtes de Francs,

les Douves de Francs (de Francs), ★Lauriol (Puygueraud).

CLARETS OUT OF THEIR CLASS

Trying to rearrange the Classification of 1855 is a regional pastime. These days there is many a Fifth Growth that should perhaps be a Second or Third, and some Seconds or Thirds that should be Fourths or Fifths.

One of the most exciting things for a claret devotee is to catch a château at the beginning of a revival in its fortunes. While a reputation is being built or re-built, the quality will keep ahead of the price. However, the price will rise – and nowadays you can go from mediocrity to magnificence in two or three years.

The problem for the drinker is complicated by the competitive nature of the growers who, naturally, see price as a yardstick of quality. In the late 1970s, there was a handful of Second Growths – most obviously Ducru-Beaucaillou, Pichon-Lalande and Léoville-Las-Cases – which rose above their peers, in price and quality, while others – notably Cos d'Estournel and Léoville-Barton – kept quality up and prices (relatively) down. The same process was repeated in the late 1980s with the emergence of some excellent but over-priced 'super' *crus bourgeois*. Monbrison, Poujeaux-Thiel, Chasse-Spleen, Sociando-Malet, all got above themselves. Fortunately 1991 sobered them up.

Médoc

Minor châteaux performing like top bourgeois *wines:* Andron-Blanquet, Cartillon, le Fournas Bernadotte, de Junca, Lamothe, Malescasse, Maucamps, Moulin-de-Laborde, Patache-d'Aux, Peyrabon, Ramage-la-Bâtisse, la Tour-de-By, la Tour-du-Haut-Moulin, la Tour-Pibran, la Tour-St-Joseph, Victoria.

Top bourgeois *performing like Classed Growths:* d'Angludet, Brillette, Chasse-Spleen, Chambert-Marbuzet, Cissac, la Gurgue, Hanteillan, Haut-Marbuzet, Gressier-Grand-Poujeaux, Hortevie, Labégorce-Zédé, Lanessan, Maucaillou, Meyney, Monbrison, les Ormes-de-Pez, de Pez, Potensac, Poujeaux, Siran, Sociando-Mallet, la Tour-de-Mons.

Classed Growths outperforming their classification: Camensac, Cantemerle, Clerc-Milon-Rothschild, Grand-Puy-Lacoste, Haut-Bages-Libéral, d'Issan, Lagrange, la Lagune, Langoa-Barton, Léoville-Barton, Lynch-Bages, Marquis d'Alesme-Becker, Rausan-Ségla, St-Pierre, du Tertre, la Tour-Carnet. Since 1987 Pichon-Longueville has been top flight.

Graves

Outperformers: Cabannieux (white), Domaine la Grave (white), Montalivet (red and white), Rahoul (red), Roquetaillade-la-Grange (red and white), Cardaillan.

Pessac-Léognan

Outperformers: Carbonnieux (white), Couhins-Lurton (white), Cruzeau, de Fieuzal (red and white), la Louvière (red and white), Malartic-Lagravière (red and white), Rochemorin, Smith-Haut-Lafitte (white, and red since 1988), la Tour-Martillac.

Pomerol

Outperformers: Bertineau St-Vincent (Lalande-de-Pomerol), Belles Graves (Lalande-de-Pomerol), le Bon-Pasteur, Bourgneuf-Vayron, Certan de May, Clinet, Clos du Clocher, Clos René, L'Eglise Clinet, Feytit-Clinet, la Fleur-St-Georges (Lalande-de-Pomerol), Franc-Maillet, Grand Ormeau (Lalande-de-Pomerol), la Grave-Trigant-de-Boisset, les Hautes-Tuileries (Lalande-de-Pomerol), Latour-à-Pomerol, Lavaud la Maréchaude (Lalande-de-Pomerol), Siaurac (Lalande-de-Pomerol), les Templiers (Lalande-de-Pomerol).

St-Émilion

Outperformers: l'Arrosée, Balestard-la-Tonnelle, Bellefont-Belcier, Berliquet, Cadet-Piola, Cardinal-Villemaurine, la Dominique, de Ferrand, Fombrauge, Larmande, Monbousquet, Montlabert, Pavie-Decesse, St-Georges, la Serre, Tertre-Rôteboeuf, Troplong-Mondot, Vieux-Château-Mazerat.

Sauternes

Outperformers non-classed: Bastor-Lamontagne, Chartreuse, de Fargues, Gilette, Guiteronde, les Justices, Liot, Menota, Raymond-Lafon, St-Amand.

Outperforming Classed Growths: d'Arche, Doisy-Daëne, Doisy-Védrines, de Malle, Nairac.

CLARET VINTAGES

Claret vintages are accorded more importance than those of any other wine; so much so that good wine from a less popular vintage can get swamped under all the brouhaha. We have had a parade of 'vintages of the century', although the fuss more usually starts in Bordeaux itself or on the volatile American market than in more cynical Britain.

Wines age at different rates according to their vintage. They may get more delicious or less so as they mature; some may be at their best before they are fully mature, because, although their balance may not be terribly impressive, at least they've got a good splash of young fruit. Wines also mature differently according to the quality of the property.

The generic *appellations* – like Bordeaux Supérieur – rarely need any aging. So a 1985, for instance, from a *premier cru*, might take twenty years to be at its best, a good *bourgeois* might take ten, and a *petit château* might take five years.

The grape variety is also important. Wines based on the Cabernet Sauvignon and/or Cabernet Franc (many of the Médocs and the Graves) will mature more slowly than wines based on the Merlot (most Pomerols and St-Émilions).

In the following tables, A = quality; B = value for money; C = drink now; D = lay down.

1993 This year will go down in the memory of wine drinkers as the vintage which might have been. Until ten days before the harvest in the third week of September, the condition of the grapes was excellent, and they gave promise of what the owner of Château Léoville-Las-Cases described as a vintage better than 1961.

But then the rain started. It rained regularly and relentlessly; this was not a year in which a grower could gamble on a dry period and be rewarded with outstanding wine, or when a brave proprietor could engage 500 pickers and pick the harvest in a day, before the rains came: everyone got wet and everyone suffered the same conditions.

Fortunately the grapes were in very good condition after a dry summer, and ripe enough to permit fairly good wine to be made in spite of the weather.

In general, the Merlot-based wines have come out better than those based on Cabernet Sauvignon or Cabernet Franc, both of which lack power. But unlike in most wet years, there was very little rot.

Leaving aside the major *appellations,* the best reds were made by winemakers who took account of the dilution of the juice and aimed for well-balanced wines with fruit and charm rather than wines for the long haul. Those in the lesser *appellations* of Bordeaux, Bordeaux Supèrieur and the Côtes who worked hard to extract tannins have quite often produced austere wine lacking in charm. This is a year in which the best buys among the cheaper wines are fresh and for early drinking. Merchants' basic claret will probably give more pleasure than many a petit château from, say, the Côtes de Bourg.

The Médocs are quite varied in style.

The best, including most of the top châteaux, are good, though without the power or longevity of a great vintage. Below the top level the picture becomes more uneven, with wines that range from attractive but short to unattractive and even shorter.

The reds of the Graves and particularly of Pessac-Léognan are, at their best, elegant, delicate and subtle. The less successful ones are thin, but the general level of quality is pretty high.

The most successful wines of the vintage are from St-Émilion and Pomerol. The best here have excellent colour and above all a power and concentration not seen elsewhere. If any 1993 clarets keep, it will be these. The less good Pomerols are very deep coloured but rustic, and the less good St-Émilions lack personality.

1992 This was the wettest summer for at least 50 years and Bordeaux had less sunshine than in any year since 1980.

Conscientious growers went through the vineyard again and again, in order, said Peter Sichel, 'to remove those grapes that now had no hope of reaching a decent degree of ripeness.' But there was so much rain that the growers could not keep up with the grapes' production of yet more watery juice.

By then it was clear that there was no hope of decent quality, and although the first part of September was rather cheerier, many of the grapes did not ripen, reaching only a miserable seven or eight degrees of potential alcohol, a mere two-thirds of the level they had reached in 1990.

Only a few managed to bring in their whole crop before the rain set in more seriously and continuously in early October – the only blessing was that the weather was too cold to allow rot, so that the grapes were mostly healthy, if watery. Even in the best estates the wines risk dilution – most obviously with the Merlot, where some of the grapes were as bloated as small plums.

But despite the size of the total crop,

the market won't be flooded. The selectivity continued into the vats. Every estate worth the name has a second wine, many a third, and most are prepared to declass some of their wine even more completely. The result will be that they will be offering less than half their total as their *grand vin*. It has become a matter of pride to insist on how small a percentage of the wine goes into the *grand vin*.

1991 After the Great Frost a miserable May and June did not help matters, though hopes rose after an August which was the hottest on record.

Trouble started again in late September, just as the harvest was beginning in the Médoc. Rain fell heavily, and those growers who waited a few days for the grapes to ripen but managed to pick before 14 October stood the best chance of making decent wines. At that point the rain started in earnest and all hope for improvement had to be abandoned. The result was a small and wildly variable vintage, but not as small as has been suggested by merchants anxious to dispose of their stocks of earlier years.

This is one of those difficult years (like 1987) when you stick to the very best estates, stars like Margaux, Latour, Pichon-Longueville and Léoville-Las-Cases. Montrose also stood out: Jean-Louis Charmolüe is famous for picking early, so he got his grapes in before the onset of the rains. Even his second wine (Dame de Montrose) is good value. Among the *crus bourgeois* reliable estates like Chasse-Spleen and Sociando-Malet came up to scratch. In the Graves a few estates like Smith-Haut-Lafitte and La Tour Martillac made decent wines.

But all the growers faced problems. I agree with merchants Lay & Wheeler that 'the best are fragrant and attractive, but they are not wines to lay down'. In the Libournais the situation was still worse, with nine-tenths of most crops simply wiped out in the frost. Few reputable growers are marketing 1991 wines under their château labels, preferring instead usually to ship the little wine they did make under a generic label, although there were a few more-than-acceptable wines, notably Gazin.

And the prices? Happily, unlike in 1984, they reflected the lower quality of the wine. The first-growths dropped FF40 to FF160 (Haut Brion sold at FF150) and there has been a corresponding 20 per cent drop elsewhere, bringing an excellent wine like Haut-Bages-Libéral down to a mere FF32. But, frankly, stick to the bargains. These will never be great wines.

1990 (AD) For the third consecutive year and for the eighth time in a decade, the harvest was excellent if not superlative.

It was generally the old vines with deep roots which coped best with the extreme heat, and a water-collecting, clay-based sub-soil proved an advantage: those vines grown on well-drained pebbles (chiefly Cabernet Sauvignon) had a hard time. With some notable exceptions, the Merlot-based wines did better than those made from Cabernet Sauvignon. Some Médoc properties (Latour is unusual in this) have a subsoil of clay.

On the whole the very hot summer and lack of rain during the ripening season meant that the acidity was low and the alcohol high. Some wines may be very good and exceptionally ripe; but they were not made to be stashed in the farthest corner of your cellar or to be laid down for your first-born's 21st.

The quality was uneven. In the north of the Médoc (the area that used to be called the Bas-Médoc), the wines fared well. Also good were St-Estèphes from the most northerly of the Médoc Classed Growths; as you go further south, however, through Pauillac, St-Julien and Margaux, quality is far more variable: some very nice wines, yes, but to be chosen with care. Across the Gironde where the Merlot dominates, the alcohol in the wines tends to be too high to produce wines of the elegance which is

meant to typify Bordeaux in a good year.

It is now clear that 1990 was the last of the 'trois glorieuses' along with 1988 and 1989. Of the three it now seems clear that anyone looking for a classic Bordeaux vintage (albeit a tough and tannic one) should opt for the 1988; the last two vintages having been too unusual to produce wines in the old claret mould, though many were splendid, if richer and fruitier than old-style claret buffs would like. Modern drinkers, immersed in rich Australian reds, will lap them up.

1989 (AD) For those who like to designate a Bordeaux vintage as either a Merlot year or a Cabernet year, this was one in which the Cabernet Sauvignon couldn't fail to ripen well. Merlot was more of a problem, and in most cases was fully ripe at the beginning of September. It became a balancing act, attempting to catch the grapes *before* acidity got too low but *after* the tannins were ripe.

Prices, needless to say, went up, even though this was a gigantic crop. But the growers claimed that the 1988 First Growths increased in value by 50 per cent within a year of picking; they felt little pressure on them to keep prices down.

So to specifics. In the Haut-Médoc, Cantemerle stood out, followed by La Tour de By, Coufran, Citran and Lanessan. In Margaux, Rausan-Ségla was back on form. Giscours, d'Issan, du Tertre, Lascombes and Cantenac-Brown were very successful, but overall it may not be a Margaux year.

Elsewhere in the Haut-Médoc the wines seem better constructed for the long haul. In St-Julien, Langoa-Barton, Léoville-Barton, Beychevelle, Gruaud-Larose, Talbot, Branaire-Ducru were excellent with Ducru-Beaucaillou a notch above. In Pauillac, Haut-Batailley looks back on form, sturdy, rich Pichon-Longueville a lovely counterpoint to the elegance of Pichon-Longueville-Lalande, Latour impressively magnificent, combining power with finesse.

In St-Estèphe Montrose attracted

attention with a triumphant return to the top, and also successful were Cos Labory, Meyney and Lafon-Rochet.

Over on the right bank, St Émilion and Pomerol defied a Cabernet year with Merlots of charm and richness. Best are Canon-la-Gaffelière, Balestard la Tonnelle, Larmande, Cap-de-Moulin, Troplong-Mondot for good value. Elsewhere there is Canon, La Conseillante, Gazin, Clinet, L'Evangile, Clos Fourtet, Pavie, an especially powerful L'Angélus, and a Cheval-Blanc of tremendous concentration and fragrance.

The Graves and Pessac-Léognan were more uneven, and although Domaine de Chevalier and Pape Clément are as classy as you would hope, only de Fieuzal, La Louvière and Haut-Bailly stood out.

1988 (AD) A difficult year, saved by a long warm summer – a vintage which could be the most classically balanced of the '80s.

Graves/Pessac-Léognan yielded a remarkable range of wines, which showed how they are getting their act together. Special efforts from La Louvière, Larrivet-Haut-Brion, de France, Smith-Haut-Lafitte (a joyous return to the top rank), Fieuzal, Olivier (another wine coming out of the shadows), La Tour-Martillac, Malartic-Lagravière, Pape-Clément, Haut-Bailly and Domaine de Chevalier. In the Médoc, La Lagune was good and Cantemerle as good as the inspiring '83. Margaux was less exciting, but there were good wines from Angludet, d'Issan, Tertre, Prieuré-Lichine, Palmer, Durfort-Vivens (at last) and superb efforts from Monbrison, Rausan-Ségla and Margaux. Chasse-Spleen and Poujeaux were the best of the Moulis while St-Julien had beautiful wines from Beychevelle, Gloria, St-Pierre, Talbot, Gruaud, Ducru-Beaucaillou, Langoa-Barton and Léoville-Barton. Pauillac did very well, with Lafite, Grand-Puy-Lacoste, Haut-Bages-Libéral and Pichon-Longueville-Lalande all excellent, tip-top Lynch-Bages and the triumphantly reborn Pichon-Longueville. St-Estèphe made its best vintage for years, with high quality from Cos d'Estournel, Calon-Ségur, Les Ormes-de-Pez, Meyney, Cos Labory and Lafon Rochet. The northern Médoc was a success too, in particular at Cissac, Hanteillan, Sociando-Mallet, La Tour-de-By, Potensac.

Pomerol made some excellent wines, and should have made more, but overproduction diluted the quality in many cases. Best are Clinet, Beauregard, Évangile, Moulinet, l'Enclos, Vieux-Château-Certan, with improved efforts from La Croix-de-Gay and La Pointe. St-Émilion was superb, as good as 1985 and '82. Cheval-Blanc and Figeac lead the way, followed by Canon, Pavie, L'Angélus, Larmande, Fonplégade, Canon-la-Gaffelière, Balestard-la-Tonnelle, Couvent-des-Jacobins and Clos des Jacobins.

1987 (BCD) There *are* lean, unbalanced edgy wines from 1987 – often made by the same uninspired proprietors who made mediocre '88s. But the overall style of the

MATURITY CHART

1989 Cru Classé Médoc
Rich fruit combines with ripe tannins, mainly for the long term

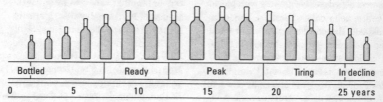

| Bottled | Ready | Peak | Tiring | In decline |

| 0 | 5 | 10 | 15 | 20 | 25 years |

1989 Good Cru Bourgeois Médoc

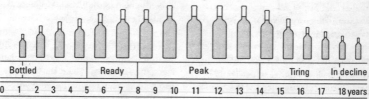

| Bottled | Ready | Peak | Tiring | In decline |

| 0 | 1 | 2 | 3 | 4 | 5 | 6 | 7 | 8 | 9 | 10 | 11 | 12 | 13 | 14 | 15 | 16 | 17 | 18 years |

1988 Cru Classé Médoc
Classic Bordeaux vintage destined for a long life

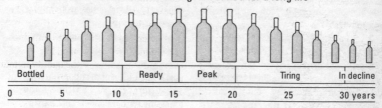

| Bottled | Ready | Peak | Tiring | In decline |

| 0 | 5 | 10 | 15 | 20 | 25 | 30 years |

1988 Good Cru Bourgeois Médoc

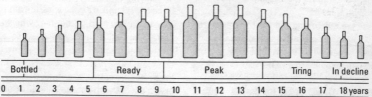

| Bottled | Ready | Peak | Tiring | In decline |

| 0 | 1 | 2 | 3 | 4 | 5 | 6 | 7 | 8 | 9 | 10 | 11 | 12 | 13 | 14 | 15 | 16 | 17 | 18 years |

wonderfully soft and drinkable, the soft Merlot fruit combining with good new oak to produce light but positively lush reds. You should start drinking these now: the green unripeness is beginning to appear.

1986 (AD) These wines incline to the lean and austere in style, but the fruit is rather thick and jammy, with a slight rasp. That said, the wines are good, sometimes very good, and mostly for the 10 to 20 year haul, though some will be attractive earlier. I think you should have some in your cellar, but if I had only one fistful of £5 notes and '86 and '88 to choose between, I'd choose '88.

1985 (ACD) These are so delicious you can drink them now. The top wines will age as long as any sensible person wants to age them – but like, I'm told, 1953, they'll *always* be good to drink. The *petits châteaux* are still gorgeous, the *bourgeois* probably the best ever at many properties and most of the Classed Growths and Graves/Pessac-Léognans are ravishing.

1984 The cheaper wines have deservedly sunk unloved into their fruitless grave. But the best Médoc Classed Growths are showing some surprising lean but fragrant Cabernet class.

1983 (ABD) A true Bordeaux classic, still relatively well-priced. Though tannic now, the wines will flower into a lovely dry cedar and blackcurrant maturity – but it'll take another year or two. AC Margaux made its best wines for a generation.

1982 (ACD) Fabulous year, unbelievably ripe, fat, juicy and rich. They're going to make great drinking right to their peak in 5 or so years' time, although some of the lesser wines, while marvellous now, are not likely to last over five years.

1981 (BCD) Good but not spectacular. Quite light, but classic flavours from top properties which should still age a bit.

1980 (BC) Nice light, grassy claret, which should have been drunk by now.

1979 (ABCD) Many of these wines demand another couple of years at least. You can keep your top wines, but hurry up and drink the lesser ones.

1978 (ACD) Virtually all the Classed Growths are lovely now, though lesser wines are beginning to dry out. Graves and St Emilion are delicious and won't improve.

1976 (C) Rather soft and sweet on the whole. Not inspiring, apart from a few exceptions in St-Émilion and Pomerol. Drink it up.

1975 (A) A difficult vintage. The very harsh tannins frequently didn't have fruit ripe enough to mesh with, and the flavour went stale and brown before the wine had time to soften. The best may yet bloom. Some time.

1970 (ACD) Now re-emerging with the fruit intact to make lovely current drinking – but the top wines will age a decade yet.

1966 (AC) All the wines are ready, with many at their peak. Yet some lesser wines which seemed to be dying out have taken on a new lease of life.

1961 (AC) Still wonderful. I marvel at how great claret can match richness and perfume with a bone-dry structure of tannin and acidity.

Most other vintages of the 1960s will now be risks; '69 and '67 are basically past it, '64 can still be good, rather big, solid wines, and '62, one of the most gorgeous, fragrant vintages since the war, is just beginning to show the ladders in its stockings. If your godfather's treating you, and offers '59, '55 or '53, accept with enthusiasm. If he offers you '49, '47 or '45, get it in writing before he changes his mind.

WHITE BORDEAUX

As far as their respective markets go, the makers of white Bordeaux might as well be on a different planet to those of the red. For one thing, all categories of red Bordeaux will sell. They may not always make a handsome profit, but a hard-working grower can expect to make a living.

The brutal truth is that this is not the case for white wine, especially dry white wine. The production costs of basic Bordeaux Blanc work out at FF4500 to FF5000 per tonneau (equal to 1200 bottles). The going rate for the wine is FF2500 to FF4000. If you're a family concern you probably don't add labour costs or depreciation of equipment into the equation; if you did you would not be able to make the books balance.

For famous châteaux the situation is different, of course: at the time of writing Domaine de Chevalier white is selling for twice the price (on the Bordeaux market) as the same estate's 1993 red. The good dry whites of the Graves sell, and individual wines like Doisy-Daëne Sec fetch good prices. But it is the mass of *petits châteaux* I am talking about; and comparing the way that the growers have striven to improve the quality of their wines over the last ten years with the way the market has deteriorated over the last five, one begins to wonder what they will do next.

For many, many years, dry white Bordeaux was over-sulphured and under-fruited. It tasted, on the whole, pretty nasty, and it was cheap. It was particularly beloved of banqueting managers and, so rumour had it, of French manual workers who found that the best preparation for their morning shift was a glass of Bordeaux Blanc at the local bar.

Great leap forward

The great stride forward in the making of dry white wines in Bordeaux came in the 1980s. The standard bearer of the new approach was and is Denis Dubourdieu of the Institut d'Oenologie de Bordeaux, the teaching and research establishment, in which the Ribereau Gayon family and Professor Emile Peynaud have played such a huge role in improving standards throughout Bordeaux. Denis Dubourdieu is the son of a well-known winemaker with an enterprising and innovative approach to vinification of both white and red wines. The basic changes in approach with Dubourdieu brought about included the importance he attached to picking at the best moment, the clearing of the grape juice before the vinification process is allowed to start, and temperature control during fermentation. The single most important change was, however, one of attitude. Younger white-winemakers no longer work according to ideas handed down by their fathers, and they taste their own and other people's wines critically.

This revolution in vinification required better and different cellar equipment from that which was in use, and the investment in stainless steel vats and cooling systems, the minimum required for wine-making the new way, was and remains a serious matter for those growers making wines that will always be modest and never great – and therefore never expensive. It took courage to make such an investment – and they presumably only made it because they believed it would pay off. And yet now, with the equipment installed and working, practising the new methods of wine-making, the wines have no known market. New drinkers turn to Jurançon or to such relatively unsophisticated wines as Vin de Pays de Cotes de Gascogne, but not to Bordeaux Blanc. However clean and fruity it is, it can't get past the barrier of consumer prejudice.

So what will these growers do? Some will replant with red vines, or graft their vineyards over; others will be forced into selling up. Others again will try and hang on in the hope that the market will change, but even for them there must be a limit to how long they are prepared to wait.

Dry insurance

The problems of semi-sweet wines are largely the same as those of dry wines, but the problems of the makers of Sauternes and Barsac are different. It is now clear that there is a market for them: enough people are willing to pay the high prices which their production requires; but only in years when the quality is exceptional.

In Sauternes and Barsac they are of course used to the situation, and those who make good wines there do so out of passion – and perhaps make a dry white to tide them over the bad years. This is an essential insurance policy; and if they only get FF30 a bottle for it, the difference in cost means that it is no less profitable than Sauternes at FF70.　　　　　　　　　　　　**WILLIAM BOLTER**

GRAPES & FLAVOURS

SAUVIGNON BLANC There has been a rush to plant more of this fashionable grape in Bordeaux in recent years, but with a couple of exceptions – such as Malartic-Lagravière, Couhins-Lurton and Smith-Haut-Lafitte – Sauvignon by itself here often gives rather muddy, tough wine. Even so, many dry white Bordeaux are entirely Sauvignon, particularly at the cheaper end, and can be fresh and flowery if made by careful winemakers like Mau, Dourthe, Ginestet and Coste. But the best are almost always blended with Sémillon. A little Sauvignon adds acidity and freshness to Sauternes and the other sweet whites of the region, too.

SÉMILLON The most important grape of Sauternes, and very susceptible to noble rot. Sémillon is vital to the best dry wines, too, though it has become sadly unfashionable. With modern techniques one can hardly tell a good dry Sémillon from a Sauvignon, except that it's a little fuller. But ideally they should be blended, with Sémillon the main variety. It gives a big, round dry wine, slightly creamy but with an exciting aroma of fresh apples and leaving a lanolin smoothness in the mouth. From the top estates, fermented cool and aged in oak barrels, the result is a wonderful, soft, nutty dry white, often going honeyed and smoky as it ages to a maturity of between 7 and 15 years. Like this it produces one of France's great white wines, and is an antidote to anyone getting just a little tired of varietals.

MUSCADELLE A very little (up to five per cent) of this headily perfumed grape often goes into the Sauternes blend and has proved particularly good in wines from Loupiac and Ste-Croix-du-Mont. In dry white blends a few per cent can add a very welcome honeyed softness. It is now being produced in small quantities as a single varietal; dry, lean, but perfumed.

The price guides for this section begin on page 294.

WINES & WINE REGIONS

BARSAC, AC (sweet) The only one of the Sauternes villages with the right to use its own name as an official *appellation* (it may also call itself Sauternes – or Sauternes-Barsac for that matter). Barsac has chalkier soils than the other Sauternes villages, and tends to make lighter wines. Even so, wines from good properties are marvellously rich despite a certain delicacy of texture.

BORDEAUX BLANC, AC (dry) This AC covers a multitude of sins. It is the catch-all name for all white Bordeaux, and as such is the label on some of France's dullest medium-to-dry whites, as well as on many fresh, simple, well-made wines. With the sudden surge of interest in Bordeaux's dry whites spurred on by the idiotic pricing shenanigans of its rivals in the Loire and Burgundy, there is simply no excuse for the – happily decreasing – amounts of over-sulphured sludge still coming on to the market. Thank goodness every year sees another surge of good guys beating back the bad. Château wines are usually the best and should generally be drunk as young as possible. Recommended names include: *Birot, Grand-Mouëys, du Juge, Lamothe, Reynon*. Good blends are possible from *Coste, Dourthe, Dubroca, Ginestet, Joanne, Lurton, Mau, Sichel* and *Univitis*. Some classy properties in red areas make good, dry white which is only allowed the AC Bordeaux. Château Margaux's white, for instance, is a simple AC Bordeaux. Many great Sauternes châteaux have started to make a dry wine from the grapes unsuitable for Sauternes. These use the 'Bordeaux Blanc' AC and often their initial letter – as in 'G' of Guiraud, 'R' of Rieussec and 'Y' of Yquem. 'Y' can really be spectacular.

BORDEAUX BLANC SUPÉRIEUR, AC (dry) Rarely used, but requires higher basic strength and lower vineyard yield than Bordeaux Blanc AC.

CADILLAC, AC (sweet) In the south of the Premières Côtes de Bordeaux, just across the river from Barsac; can produce attractive sweet whites, but since the price is low, many properties now produce dry white and red – which do *not* qualify for the AC Cadillac. The AC is in any case so involved that few growers bother with it.

CÉRONS, AC (sweet) Enclave in the Graves butting on to Barsac, making good, fairly sweet whites, but many growers now prefer to produce dry whites, which can sell as Graves. *Château Archambeau* is typical, producing tiny amounts of very good Cérons and larger amounts of good, fresh dry Graves. *Château Cérons* makes splendidly complex sweet whites worthy of the AC of Barsac. Other good names: *Grand Enclos du Château Cérons, Haura*.

ENTRE-DEUX-MERS, AC (dry) Large Bordeaux area between the Garonne and Dordogne rivers. The AC is for dry whites, which are of varying quality, but every vintage produces more examples of good, fresh, grassy whites. Many properties make red, and these can only be Bordeaux or Bordeaux Supérieur. Best: *Bonnet, Ducla, de Florin, Fondarzac, Moulin-de-Launay, Tertre du Moulin, Thieuley, Union des Producteurs de Rauzan*.

GRAVES, AC (dry) Famous, or perhaps infamous area south of Bordeaux, on the left bank of the Garonne. The infamy is the result of the endless turgid stream of sulphurous, flabby, off-dry white that *used* to flow out of the region. However, modern Graves is a dramatic improvement. Even at the level of commercial blends it can be sharply fruity and full in style, while at the best properties, with some oak aging employed, the wines are some of the most delicious dry whites in France. As from the 1987 vintage the wines from the northern Graves bear the *appellation* 'Pessac-

Léognan'. Best châteaux: *Archambeau, Bouscaut, Cabannieux, Carbonnieux, Domaine de Chevalier, Couhins-Lurton, de Cruzeau, Domaine la Grave, de Fieuzal, la Garance, la Garde, Haut-Brion, Landiras, Laville Haut-Brion, la Louvière, Malartic-Lagravière, Montalivet, Rahoul, Respide, Rochemorin, Roquetaillade-la-Grange, Smith-Haut-Lafitte* and *la Tour-Martillac.*

GRAVES SUPÉRIEURES, AC (sweet or dry) White Graves with a minimum natural alcohol of 12 degrees. Often made sweet. Best property: *Clos St-Georges.*

LOUPIAC, AC (sweet) These white wines from the lovely area looking across the Garonne to Barsac are not as sweet as Sauternes, and many properties until recently made dry white and red without the Loupiac AC because of difficulties in selling sweet whites. With rising prices has come a welcome flood of lemony-honeyed Barsac styles. Best châteaux: *Domaine du Noble, Loupiac-Gaudiet, Ricaud.*

PESSAC-LÉOGNAN, AC (dry) The AC for reds and whites declared in 1987 and created out of the best and northernmost part of Graves. Fifty-five estates are involved, including all the *crus classés*, so quality ought to be high. Yields are lower than for Graves and the percentage of Sauvignon is higher (at least a quarter of the grapes used). This might change the style of some estates, but the crucial point is that the new AC will be further motivation for improvement in what is rapidly becoming one of France's most exciting white areas. The best wines start out with a blast of apricot, peach and cream ripeness and slowly mature to a superb nutty richness with a dry savoury finish. Best châteaux: *Bouscaut, Carbonnieux* (from 1988), *Couhins-Lurton, Domaine de Chevalier, de Fieuzal, Haut-Brion, la Louvière, Malartic-Lagravière, Rochemorin, Smith-Haut-Lafitte* and *la Tour Martillac.*

PREMIÈRES CÔTES DE BORDEAUX, AC Some very attractive reds and excellent dry whites from the right bank of the Garonne in the bang-up-to-date, fruit-all-the-way style, as well as some reasonable sweetish wines. The sweet wines can be AC Cadillac, but you still get some under the Premières Côtes mantle, sometimes with their village name added, as in *Château de Berbec*, Premières-Côtes-Gabarnac.

STE-CROIX-DU-MONT, AC (sweet) The leading sweet white AC of the Premières Côtes de Bordeaux. Can be very attractive when properly made. *Château Loubens* is the best-known wine, but *Lousteau-Vieil* is producing better wine every year, and *Domaine du Tich, La Grave, la Rame, des Tours*, and the sadly minuscule *de Tastes* are also good.

SAUTERNES, AC (sweet) The overall *appellation* for a group of five villages in the south of the Graves: Sauternes, Bommes, Fargues, Preignac and Barsac. (Barsac wines may use their own village name if they wish.) Concentrated by noble rot, the

---

**1855 CLASSIFICATION OF SAUTERNES
Grand premier cru** Yquem (Sauternes).

Premiers crus Climens (Barsac); Coutet (Barsac); Guiraud (Sauternes); Haut-Peyraguey (Bommes); Lafaurie-Peyraguey (Bommes); Rabaud-Promis (Bommes); Rayne-Vigneau (Bommes); Rieussec (Fargues); Sigalas-Rabaud (Bommes); Suduiraut (Preignac); la Tour-Blanche (Bommes).

Deuxièmes crus d'Arche (Sauternes); Broustet (Barsac); Caillou (Barsac); Doisy-Daëne (Barsac); Doisy-Dubroca (Barsac); Doisy-Védrines (Barsac); Filhot (Sauternes); Lamothe (Sauternes); Lamothe-Guignard (Sauternes); de Myrat (Barsac) (now extinct); Nairac (Barsac); Romer-du-Hayot (Fargues); Suau (Barsac); de Malle (Preignac).

THE COST OF A BOTTLE

1989 Sauternes Cru Classé	£18.95	
VAT	2.82	
Mark-up	4.84	
Duty	1.01	
Distribution	0.17	
Shipping	0.16	
Wine	9.95	

Sémillon, along with a little Sauvignon and Muscadelle, produces at its glorious best a wine that is brilliantly rich and glyceriny, combining honey and cream, pineapple and nuts when young, with something oily and penetrating as it ages and the sweetness begins to have an intensity of volatile flavours, rather like a peach, bruised and browned in the sun, then steeped in the sweetest of syrups. These are the fine wines. Sadly, owing to economic pressures, much Sauternes outside the top Growths used to be made sweet simply by sugaring the juice and stopping the fermentation with a massive slug of sulphur. In recent years the average quality has soared, and the wines are infinitely less turgid and sulphury, as indeed they ought to be given their rising prices. And in bad years those châteaux that can afford it can now practise cryoextraction – which isn't some form of torture but a method of freezing the grapes before fermentation which can increase the richness of the juice pressed out. Best châteaux: *Bastor-Lamontagne, Climens, Doisy-Daëne, Doisy-Védrines, de Fargues, Gilette, Guiraud, Lafaurie-Peyraguey, Lamothe-Guignard, Rabaud-Promis, Raymond-Lafon, Rayne-Vigneau, Rieussec, St-Amand, Suduiraut, La Tour Blanche, d'Yquem.*

CHÂTEAUX PROFILES

I have valued these properties according to how they are currently performing; a five-star rating means you are getting a top-line taste – not just a well-known label. Some big names have been downgraded, some lesser-known properties are promoted – solely on the quality of the wine inside the bottle. A star in brackets shows that the wine can achieve the higher rating but does not always do so.

The £ sign shows which wines are offering particularly good value for money – although that does not mean any of these wines will exactly be cheap.

D'ARCHE *2ème cru Sauternes* ★★★(★) A little-known Sauternes property now beginning to make exciting wine after a long period of mediocrity. 1983, '86, '88, '89 and '90 are particularly good and show great promise for the future

BASTOR-LAMONTAGNE *cru bourgeois Sauternes* ★★★ £ Unclassified property making marvellous, widely available and easily affordable wines, as rich as many Classed Growths. 1983, '86, '88, '89 and '90 epitomize high quality Sauternes at a remarkably fair price.

BROUSTET *2ème cru classé Barsac* ★★★ A reliable, fairly rich wine, not often seen, but worth trying. The 1988 and '90 are especially good, the dry white disappointing.

CABANNIEUX *Graves* ★★★ £ One of the new wave of non-classified Graves which is radically improving its white wine by the use of new oak barrels. The red is good, too. 1986, '88, '89 and '90 show the way.

CARBONNIEUX cru classé Pessac-Léognan ★★★(★) This large property used to make decent enough old-style white that aged surprisingly well, but since 1988 they have been using 50 per cent new oak – and can you taste the difference! The 1990 is the best yet, and '92 is good..

CLIMENS *1er cru Barsac* ★★★★★
Undoubtedly the best property in Barsac, making some of the most consistently fine sweet wines in France. 1983, '86, '88, '89 and '90 are all excellent. It also makes a delicious second wine called Les Cypres that is well worth seeking out.

COUHINS-LURTON *cru classé Pessac-Léognan* ★★★★ 100 per cent Sauvignon dry white fermented in new oak barrels, producing a blend of grassy fruit and oaky spice. Recent vintages have been excellent.

COUTET *1er cru Barsac* ★★(★) A great property which in recent years has not been living up to its previous exacting standards.

DOISY-DAËNE *2ème cru Barsac* ★★★(★)
A very good, consistent property providing relatively light, but extremely attractive sweet wine. Doisy-Daëne Sec is a particularly good dry white.

DOISY-VÉDRINES *2ème cru Barsac* ★★★★ £ A rich, concentrated wine, which is usually good value. 1980, '83, '86 and '89 are very good.

DOMAINE DE CHEVALIER ★★★★★ (for white). See Red Bordeaux.

DE FARGUES *cru bourgeois Sauternes* ★★★★(★) Small property owned by Yquem, capable of producing stunning, rich wines in the best years.

DE FIEUZAL ★★★★(★) The white is unclassified, but, with its burst of apricot fruit and spice, is one of Bordeaux's leading dry whites. See Red Bordeaux.

FILHOT *2ème cru Sauternes* ★★(★) Well-known Sauternes property producing pleasant but hardly memorable wines, though the 1988 looks a bit more hopeful.

GILETTE *cru bourgeois Sauternes* ★★★★ Remarkable property which ages its wines in concrete tanks for 20 to 30 years before releasing them. Usually delicious, with a dry richness unique in Sauternes thanks to long maturation and absence of wood. The 1967 is heavenly, and only just released. Seriously!

GUIRAUD *1er cru Sauternes* ★★★★(★)
Fine property owned since 1981 by a Canadian who has revolutionized the estate and brought the wines back to peak, and pricy, form. The wines are difficult to taste when young but are very special, and the 1983, '86, '88, '89 and '90 are going to be outstanding.

HAUT-BRION *cru classé Pessac-Léognan* ★★★★(★) Small quantities of very fine, long-lived wine, also appealing when young. See Red Bordeaux.

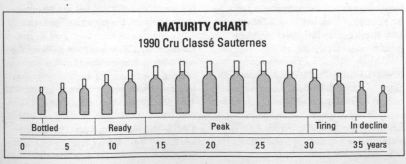

MATURITY CHART
1990 Cru Classé Sauternes

| Bottled | Ready | Peak | Tiring | In decline |

| 0 | 5 | 10 | 15 | 20 | 25 | 30 | 35 years |

LAFAURIE-PEYRAGUEY *1er cru Sauternes* ★★★★(★) Fine property, returning to top form after a dull period in the 1960s and '70s. Remarkably good in the difficult years of '82, '84 and '85, it was stunning in '83, '86, '88, '89 and '90.

LAMOTHE-GUIGNARD *2ème cru Sauternes* ★★★ Since 1981 this previously undistinguished wine has dramatically improved. 1983, '86 and '88 show the improvement as will '89 and '90.

LAVILLE-HAUT-BRION *cru classé Pessac-Léognan* ★★★★ This should be one of the greatest of all white Pessac-Léognan, since it is owned by Haut-Brion, but despite some great successes, the general effect is patchy – especially given the crazy prices.

LA LOUVIÈRE *cru bourgeois Pessac-Léognan* ★★★★ This property has been making lovely, modern, oak-aged whites since the mid-70s but is only now achieving the acclaim it deserves. Since 1987, the quality has climbed even higher.

MALARTIC-LAGRAVIÈRE *cru classé Pessac-Léognan* ★★★ £ Tiny quantities of perfumed Sauvignon; recently more variable, if not disappointing.

DE MALLE *2ème cru Sauternes* ★★★ Good, relatively light wine from a very beautiful property set partly in the Graves and partly in Sauternes. It went through a bad patch in the early and mid-'80s when the owner died after a long illness, but since '88 his widow has been making wines fully worthy of the name.

RABAUD-PROMIS *1er cru Sauternes* ★★★(★) At last! The 1986, '88, '89 and '90 are excellent and show a long-awaited return to First Growth quality.

RAHOUL *cru bourgeois Graves* ★★★ A leader of the new wave of cool-fermented, oak-aged whites among the Graves

properties, having an effect on all the growers in the region. Also increasingly good red. Ownership changes are worrying, though, and the '88, '89 and '90 were not as special as previous vintages, though still good. Domaine Benoit and Château Constantin also good in the same stable.

RAYMOND LAFON *cru bourgeois Sauternes* ★★★★ Owned by the former manager of neighbouring Yquem, this is fine wine but not quite as fine as the increasingly daunting price would imply.

RIEUSSEC *1er cru Sauternes* ★★★★(★) One of the richest, most exotic Sauternes, and particularly good wines during the 1980s. The 1982 is good, the '83, '86 and '88 really special, the '89 and '90 wonderful.

ST-AMAND *cru bourgeois Sauternes* ★★★(★) £ Splendid property making truly rich wines that age well, at an affordable price. Also seen as Château de la Chartreuse. Since the 1970s each decent vintage has produced a delicious example.

SMITH-HAUT-LAFITTE *cru classé Pessac-Léognan* ★★★★ A late convert to cool fermentation and oak-aging, but since 1985 making superb wines. Also increasingly good, and better-known, reds.

SUDUIRAUT *1er cru Sauternes* ★★★(★) Rich, exciting wines, frequently deeper and more intensely perfumed than any other Sauternes – except for its neighbour, d'Yquem, but unfortunately not as reliable as it should be. A remarkable 1982 was followed by a fine '83, a very good '85 but disappointing '86 and ditto in 1988. 1989 was a leap up again, though.

D'YQUEM *1er grand cru classé Sauternes* ★★★★★ The pinnacle of achievement in great sweet wines. Almost every vintage is a masterpiece and its outlandish price is almost justified, since d'Yquem at its best is the greatest sweet wine in the world.

SWEET WHITE BORDEAUX VINTAGES

The 1980s brought Sauternes a share in the good fortune that was drenching the red wines of Bordeaux with great vintages. About time too, because 1983 created a much needed surge of interest in these remarkable, super-sweet wines and 1986, '88, '89 and '90 can continue it. The astonishing run of Indian summer vintages that saved red Bordeaux year after year from 1977 was not always so kind to Sauternes. In 1978 and 1981, the botrytis just didn't quite develop, and in 1982 the rains came at exactly the wrong time, diluting potentially perfect grapes. But the vintages of the late 1980s are more than making amends. It's worth remembering that Sauternes can be drunk very young or very old, depending entirely on whether you like the startlingly sweet shock of young wine or the deep, nutty, golden honey of older wines. The best can last a very long time. The *en primeur* prices have the wine merchants listing the best Barsac at around £250 a case and the finest Sauternes at over £300.

1993 This is not a year for fine Sauternes. The best wines are the semi-sweet ones made by sensible but unimaginative growers. These are perfectly sound wines but lack any very distinctive character and, above all, they lack botrytis. The producers who tried to make something more exciting made wines that are at best flowery with agreeable sweetness and charm, at worst smelling of ignoble rot.

1992 A handful of châteaux managed to harvest some botrytized grapes in September, but most of the little wine that was made then will not be 'true' Sauternes but *passerrillés,* wine made from ripe grapes which have not been attacked by botrytis. The October rains washed the grapes too thoroughly and ensured that they would never attain the desired degree of over-ripeness and were too clean to rot. Oh well...

1991 A very difficult year in Sauternes, as in the rest of Bordeaux. In Sauternes the impact of the frost was greatest on the Sémillon, leaving yet another source of imbalance in an overly high proportion of Sauvignon. Such wines as are being let onto the market are correct or better, but only Climens seems to have produced a stunner.

1990 The most extraordinary year in Sauternes since 1893. The weather was tropical, and the grapes were so ripe that when it rained heavily in late August the botrytis really took off, and there was no stopping it.The wines are so big and so varied, even within the same estate, as to be almost impossible to judge young — because no-one, even in Sauternes, has any point of comparison. Whether they will remain too big, rich and heavy to be truly enjoyable is possible, but I doubt it: they should all, the lesser wines as well as the classed growths, be treated as if they were old-style claret, to be left for a decade before being sampled. Then, I believe, they will prove to be the treat (though not, alas, the bargain) of a lifetime.

1989 A vintage that has not developed as in theory it should. The wines are turning out to be wildly inconsistent. In theory the growers who picked early – before the rains which set in on October 19 – did best. So stick to the stars – apart from Lafaurie-Peyraguey, which had an off-year.

1988 In 1988 every Sauternes and Barsac château and many in Cadillac, Loupiac and Ste-Croix-du-Mont, had the chance to make the greatest wine in a generation. It was a dry year and patience was needed while botrytis developed. Sadly, one or two leading properties were seen harvesting long before noble rot had run its full course. Many other producers went through the vines again and again, picking only the well rotted grapes: the wines are already destined to be classics.

1987 The rains came far too early this year, long before noble rot could get going on the grapes. Even so some pleasant, light wines were made, especially by those properties

➤

who used the cryoextraction method of freezing the grapes to concentrate what sugar there was. But some estates bottled no wine from this vintage.

1986 Another marvellous year, when noble rot swept through the vineyards, and any proprietor who cared to could make great sweet wines. At the moment the best wines seem to be even better than 1983 and 1988 but it is notoriously difficult to judge young Sauternes, so I could well reverse my opinion in a year or two. By which time the '89s and '90s can join the debate.

1985 Quite pleasant lightish wines, but only a handful of outstanding wines from estates with the courage to wait for botrytis in a very dry year.

1983 Superbly rich, exciting wines to be ranked alongside 1986 and 1988, 1989 and 1990. Which vintage will finally turn out best is going to entail a large amount of comparative tasting over the next decade. What a jolly thought.

1981/80/79 Three attractive mid-weight vintages. The 1981s are a touch graceless, but the best 1980s have been underrated and will still improve.

1976 Fat, hefty, rich. Some haven't quite developed as hoped, but lots of 'lanolin' oiliness and lusciousness in those that have.

1975 Another lovely year. Not quite so utterly indulgent as 1976 but perhaps a little better balanced.

DRY WHITE BORDEAUX VINTAGES
Using cool fermentation, and a greater percentage of Sauvignon Blanc, many white Bordeaux are not now being made to age, but all Graves/Pessac-Léognan should be kept for at least two to three years, and the best 10 to 20 years.

1993 The rain stopped the dry whites from being outstanding, but the general level is more uniform than among the red. The only real problems were in the few vineyards with a high proportion of Muscadelle, a variety which does not take kindly to rain. Overall the wines are well-balanced and without aggressive acidity; a pronounced Sauvignon nose is common. The wines from the top châteaux of Pessac-Leognan are perfectly sound, but appear to outstrip their humbler neighbours rather less convincingly than usual.

1992 The Graves alone was able to bring in a decent crop of perfectly pleasant, albeit unremarkable wines. Unfortunately the French are snapping them up so you can't look for any real bargains. Nevertheless there are some serious well-structured wines, like Fieuzal, La Louvière, Smith-Haut-Lafitte and Domaine de Chevalier.

1991 The April frost that damaged just about the whole of Bordeaux hit the Graves particularly badly, so there simply won't be much dry white from there that year. What there is, though, could be rather good: concentrated by the frost damage, and well-balanced. Try and get somebody else to buy it for you: it won't be cheap.

1990 Even hotter and drier than 1989, and considerably less successful. The Graves seems especially disappointing. Be very selective.

1989 Unlike 1988, the problem was with overripe rather than underripe grapes. In years to come the dry wines will inevitably be overshadowed by the sweet ones.

1988 Some of the 1988 dry whites lack a little oomph. Even so, most 1988s from good producers are delicious, and some are outstandingly good.

1987 Even the top wines are already drinking well, although those from Pessac-Léognan can happily take further aging.

BURGUNDY

It was a flamboyant action, and Bouchard Aîné made the most of it. This old-established merchant house has been billing Bernard Repolt, its new winemaker, as 'the man who threw away 90,000 bottles of wine'. It is no exaggeration, for Repolt's first action on being appointed was to get rid of stock which didn't measure up to his standards (though he found another half million bottles which did).

Repolt's expensive gesture was perhaps the most dramatic example of the revolutionary changes which have swept Burgundy in the wake of a recession which has reduced wine prices by over half in the space of five years. The most fundamental, symbolized by the fact that Repolt is also the firm's general manager, is the recognition that the names of famous communes on the labels is no longer enough: to make wine that is saleable to the punters, good wine-making and strict selection are required.

We knew it all the time, of course: it's part of the standard advice handed out to novices of Burgundy wines. But understanding Burgundy has been difficult enough without adding a galaxy of interrelated growers with the same names but different standards to the equation. Thus too many winemakers have been getting by for far too long on the region's ancient reputation.

Repolt fulfills the same role, in another old-established firm – Jaffelin – as he does at Bouchard Aîné. Both are owned by Frank Boisset, who is known for a more hustling style than Burgundy has been accustomed to these past thousand years. Boisset bought Bouchard from the receivers, and Jaffelin from Robert Drouhin, the man who is regarded as the epitome of the best in the 'old' Burgundy, in terms both of his personal style and that of his wines, which range from the reliable to the superb. But he, even he, has been hurt by the recession.

A question of upbringing

The revolution, which is still in full swing, is a reaction against forces whose existence the Burgundians themselves still do not admit. First among these forces is the market itself and, within it, competition from wines from the New World. But even if the Burgundians don't officially accept that they have a problem, nevertheless they are trying to solve it. For example, the committee responsible for making and selling the wine from Burgundy's Holy of Holies, the vineyards owned by the Hospices de Beaune, is contemplating some major changes, like actually improving the wine-making and not allowing the buyers at the Hospices' sale in November to cart it off in cask straight away and mature it any old how.

The Hospices committee's belated recognition of the need for quality and authenticity in its wines has a lot to do with a four-year slide in the prices they fetch. Not only has this slide averaged 20 per cent a year; but it could accelerate if the sale's stoutest supporter and bidder, the legendary octogenarian André Boisseaux, were soon to depart for the Burgundian heaven situated somewhere between Le Montrachet and Romanée-Conti.

The Hospitaliers, like the rest of Burgundy, have discovered the crucial importance of 'rapport qualité prix' or value for money, not a phrase much employed previously in Burgundy. But let the figures tell the story. In 1992–3

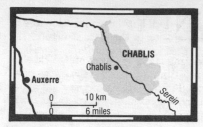

CHABLIS

Chablis

Auxerre

Serein

0   10 km
0   6 miles

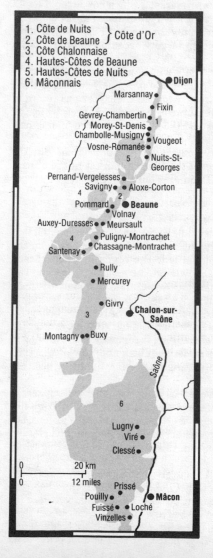

1. Côte de Nuits } Côte d'Or
2. Côte de Beaune
3. Côte Chalonnaise
4. Hautes-Côtes de Beaune
5. Hautes-Côtes de Nuits
6. Mâconnais

Dijon

Marsannay
Fixin
Gevrey-Chambertin
Morey-St-Denis
Chambolle-Musigny
Vougeot
Vosne-Romanée
Nuits-St-Georges
Pernand-Vergelesses
Savigny
Aloxe-Corton
Pommard
Beaune
Volnay
Auxey-Duresses
Meursault
Puligny-Montrachet
Chassagne-Montrachet
Santenay
Rully
Mercurey
Givry
Chalon-sur-Saône
Montagny
Buxy

Saône

0   20 km
0   12 miles

Lugny
Viré
Clessé

Prissé
Pouilly
Mâcon
Fuissé
Loché
Vinzelles

CLASSIFICATIONS

Burgundy has five different levels of classification:

Non-specific regional appellations with no geographical definition, e.g. Bourgogne, which may come from inferior land or young vines.

Specific regional appellations, e.g. Côte de Beaune-Villages, generally a blend from one or more villages. Côte de Nuits-Villages is usually better.

Village commune wines Each village has its vineyards legally defined. The village names are traditionally used for vineyards with no special reputation, which are thus usually blended together under the village name. But there is a growing move towards even relatively unknown vineyards appearing on the label. These unclassified vineyards are called *lieux-dits* or 'stated places'. They can only appear on the label in letters half the size of the village name.

Premier cru It's typical of Burgundy that *premier cru* or 'First Growth' actually means 'Second Growth', because these are the second best vineyard sites. Even so, they contain some of Burgundy's finest wines. They are classified by both village and vineyard names, e.g. Gevrey-Chambertin, Combe-aux-Moines. The vineyard name must follow the village name on the label, and it may be in the same size print. Confusingly, some growers use smaller print, but the appellation should make it clear whether it is a *premier cru* or a *lieu-dit*.

Grand cru These are the real top growths. Not every village has one. The reds are mostly in the Côte de Nuits, the whites in the Côte de Beaune. A *grand cru* vineyard name can stand alone on the label without the village – for example, Chambertin from the village of Gevrey-Chambertin. (By long tradition, a Burgundy village is allowed to tack on the name of its *grand cru* vineyard, and use the compound name for wines that have nothing to do with *grand cru*, for instance Puligny-Montrachet.)

sales of wine in volume terms were up by over a third but the actual value rose by a mere four per cent, representing a further erosion in the price structure. The result is that in real terms the prices being asked for many *appellations* are back to where they were 20 years ago after the first oil shock.

As a result of their new-found lack of greed the growers sold slightly more red wine than even in the boom years (and 38 per cent more than they managed in 1991–2), and far more white than ever before. The most dramatic increase has been in domestic consumption in both senses of the term: the wines were bought by the French (shopping increasingly in supermarkets, which now account for 43 per cent of home-drinking sales), who bought them for drinking at home. Those parting with their money were paying an average of a mere FF25 a bottle, down from FF33 the previous year, a drop which largely accounts for Burgundy's comeback on the domestic market.

The sales increases were greatest in white wines, where the total sales of 272,000 hectolitres were a third greater than in the previous year, which itself had been a near-record. Sales of red narrowly topped their previous record of 1987–8. In other words the reds were recapturing an older market, while the whites, above all the wines from Chablis and the Mâconnais, were finding new buyers.

Abroad sales recovered, as the military would put it, on a broad front. But, the Brits should notice, there is no mention of the British market in the official literature. There is talk of Japan and Denmark, but not of us. We no longer matter that much to the Burgundians.

Style wars

This is of less importance to the consumer than the changes in wine-making that have been creeping into Burgundy. The most obvious of these has been the arrival of consultant winemakers from outside the region. The increased importance of the (to the Burgundians) newfangled oenologists has had two major effects. For almost the first time since wine-making began all those millennia ago there are arguments about styles based on the winemaker rather than on the hitherto all-important *terroir*. So it is that Guy Accad, the Lebanese-born *wunderkind* now making wine for a fair number of top growers, is attacked for the over-tannic nature of his wines. Yet many of his competitors are moving in the same direction, towards making the modern equivalent of the long-lasting, well-structured wines of yesteryear, forgetting the easier, lighter wines that developed in the 1980s.

The second, and most important consequence is that the better winemakers in Burgundy are finding it possible to make fine, elegant wines even in years like 1991 and 1992, which the French would describe as *'jaloux'* – literally jealous, but more accurately translated as requiring constant skilled attention (though even their greatest skills have not proved enough to save the largely-unripe white 1993s).

One by-product of the revolution has been to give the merchants an increased role in an age that worships the grower-winemaker. There has been an increasing, and largely unspoken, recognition that most domaines were ill-equipped to make wine properly, a lesson rubbed in by their inability to sell their wines except to the French hypermarkets, organizations which are traditionally indifferent to quality and simply buy village names at rock-bottom prices. The many owners so treated are either handing the management over to proper winemakers employed by merchants (or other, better-equipped estates) or, secure in the knowledge that they're good at actually growing the grapes, handing them over to be turned into wine – a practice which forms the basis for Olivier Leflaive's success. Perhaps the best example, however, has been the Domaine Jacques Prieur, one of the best in Burgundy, but one where the wine-making was so haphazard that, as one wine merchant puts it, 'there are simply no older vintages worth tasting.' The wines are are now made by the redoubtable Nadine Gublin, an oenologist employed by merchants Antonin Rodin – and very good they are too.

The cost of the revolution, though, has been an enormous strain on the merchants themselves, who often held excess stocks of wines. This was compounded by the fact that much of those stocks consisted of wines sold by growers who kept their best for themselves. Hence the sorting-out; and hence, as we shall see, the increasing importance of the name of the producer on the bottle, rather than the provenance, however impressive that may be.

RED WINES

The competition from foreigners (in Burgundian terms, that means anyone north or west of Dijon) is less pronounced in the field of red wines. The Pinot Noir is proving to be just as unreliable a grape variety outside Burgundy as it is within it. And because the wines from regions like Oregon and Carneros (Burgundy's only real competitors) are now expensive the Burgundians have been granted a breathing space.

The opportunity has been seized by individual growers throughout the province. There are even a handful of wines being made in the Hautes-Côtes de Nuits (notably the luxury *cuvées* made by the the co-operative) that are worth looking at. And Joseph Roty even makes a decent Grand Ordinaire – most misleading of names – as well as an elegant Marsannay.

This is typical: the best merchants, and the domaines which employ proper winemakers, are really showing their form in the lesser communes. Boillot is a name to look for in several, and other good-value growers' wines include the Chorey-lès-Beaune from Tollot-Beaut, the Marsannay made by Domaine Bruno Clair, and the Savigny-lès-Beaune made by Luc Camus on his Domaine Pavelot. In the Côte Chalonnaise, the Burgundian equivalent of the Cru Bourgeois which performed so well in Bordeaux in the 1980s, Mercurey can be especially good value because of the amount of land under vine. Faiveley is well-placed because of its large holdings, though its supremacy is being challenged by a feisty grower, Emile Juillot.

Faiveley remains reliable everywhere as does Jadot (good Fixin, in particular), Jaffelin (including a reliable Monthélie) while Labouré-Roi is a name which, like the others, is a far more reliable indicator of quality than the grandest *appellations*. There you really do have to stick to the best names, because, bluntly, the revolution has barely touched the majority of the smaller domaines, who can sell the relatively small quantities of wine they make to (almost invariably ignorant) French tourists, or, at a pinch, to supermarket buyers anxious to have a Gevrey or a Vosne on their shelves. NICHOLAS FAITH

GRAPES & FLAVOURS

PINOT NOIR The sulkiest, trickiest fine wine grape in the world is the exclusive grape in almost all red Burgundies. It needs a more delicate balance of spring, summer and autumn climate than any other variety to achieve greatness.

It used to be true to say that no other part of the world could produce a Pinot Noir to match those of Burgundy. But isolated growers in Oregon, California, New Zealand, Australia and South Africa are now making very fine examples. Even so, Burgundy is still the only place on earth where fine Pinot Noirs are made in any great quantity. The problem is, awful Pinot Noirs abound too, heavy, chewy and sweet-fruited or thin and pallid. Good

Burgundian Pinot Noir should generally be *light*, fragrant, marvellously perfumed with cherry-and-strawberry fruit, sometimes meatier, sometimes intensely spicy, but, as a rule, *light*. It needs time to mature, but it can be so delicious young that it doesn't always get the chance.

GAMAY Most Burgundy has by law to be 100 per cent Pinot Noir, but the Gamay (the Beaujolais grape) can be used in wines labelled 'Burgundy' or 'Bourgogne' which come from the Mâconnais and the Beaujolais regions, or from elsewhere in Burgundy in wines labelled 'Bourgogne Passe-Tout-Grain', 'Bourgogne Grand Ordinaire' or 'Mâcon'.

WINES & WINE REGIONS

ALOXE-CORTON, AC (Côte de Beaune) Ten years ago, this village at the northern end of the Côte de Beaune was the best of all buys for full-flavoured, balanced Burgundy. More recently, most Aloxe-Corton has been pale stuff indeed. Its production is overwhelmingly red, and it has the only red Grand Cru in the Côte de Beaune, Le Corton, which is also sold under various subdivisions like Corton-Bressandes, Corton Clos du Roi and so forth, and is seen on the market rather more frequently than one might expect a Grand Cru to be. Go for *Jadot, Drouhin, Jaffelin* and *Tollot-Beaut.* Also good are the following: *Chandon de Briailles, Dubreuil Fontaine, Faiveley, Juillot, Daniel Senard, Michel Voarick, Bouzerot-Gruère.*

AUXEY-DURESSES, AC (Côte de Beaune) One of the villages behind the Côte d'Or itself, with a deservedly high reputation for full, but fairly gentle, nicely fruity reds. After a slump in the early '80s there have been excellent wines made recently by a handful of good growers, especially in the years from 1987 to 1990. Look for *Ampeau,*

Diconne, Alain Gras, Duc de Magenta, Leroy, Roy, Prunier and *Thévenin.*

BEAUNE, AC (Côte de Beaune) One of the few reliable commune wines, usually quite light, with a soft, 'red fruits' sweetness and a flicker of something minerally to smarten it up nicely. The wines are nearly all red. Beaune has the largest acreage of vines of any Côte d'Or commune, and they are mostly owned by merchants. It has no Grands Crus but many excellent Premiers Crus, for example Grèves, Marconnets, Teurons, Boucherottes, Vignes Franches and Cent Vignes. In general, the 1983s were better than elsewhere, the 1986s a bit light but the 1987s much better, the '88s, '89s and '90s outstanding and selected '91s and '92s worth hunting out. The best growers are *Lafarge* and *Morot,* and good wines are made by *Besancenot-Mathouillet, Borley, Drouhin, Germain, Jadot, Jaffelin, Morey, Tollot-Beaut.*

BLAGNY, AC (Côte de Beaune) Tiny hamlet on the boundary between Meursault and Puligny-Montrachet. The red wine is usually a bit fierce, but then this is white wine heartland, so I'm a bit surprised they grow any red at all. Best producers: *Leflaive, Matrot*.

BONNES-MARES, AC (Côte de Nuits) Grand Cru of 15.54 hectares mostly in Chambolle-Musigny, with a little in Morey-St-Denis. Usually one of the most – or should I say one of the very few – reliable Grands Crus, which ages extremely well over 10 to 20 years to a lovely smoky, chocolate-and-prunes richness. Best names: *Domaine des Varoilles, Drouhin, Dujac, Groffier, Jadot, Roumier, de Vogüé*.

BOURGOGNE GRAND ORDINAIRE, AC Très Ordinaire. Pas Très Grand. Rarely seen outside Burgundy, this is the bottom of the Burgundy barrel. It may be made from Pinot Noir and Gamay, and even a couple of obscure grapes, the Tressot and César, as well.

BOURGOGNE PASSE-TOUT-GRAINS, AC Often excellent value, lightish wine made usually in the Côte d'Or or the Côte Chalonnaise from Gamay blended with a minimum of one-third Pinot Noir. In some years it may well be mostly Pinot. *Rodet* and *Chanson* make it well, but as usual, the growers make it best, particularly in the less famous Côte d'Or and Hautes-Côtes villages; *Rion* in Nuits-St-Georges, *Léni-Volpato* in Chambolle-Musigny, *Henri Jayer* in Vosne-Romanée, *Thomas* in St-Aubin, *Chaley* or *Cornu* in the Hautes-Côtes, and many others like them. But even at its best, true Burgundy it ain't.

BOURGOGNE ROUGE, AC The basic red AC from Chablis in the North to the Beaujolais *crus* in the South. Unknown Bourgogne Rouge is best avoided – much of it is very basic indeed. Most Bourgogne Rouge is made exclusively from Pinot Noir, but Gamay can be used in the Beaujolais (if declassified from one of the ten *crus*) and Mâconnais, and the César and Tressot are

permitted in the Yonne around Chablis. Wine from the ten Beaujolais *crus* can be declassified and sold as Bourgogne – and *that* should generally be from the Gamay grape alone. Domaine-bottled Bourgogne Rouge from good growers – and a handful of merchants – can be excellent value. Look for those of *Bourgeon, Coche Dury, Germain, d'Heuilly-Huberdeau, Henri Jayer, Juillot, Lafarge, Mortet, Parent, Pousse d'Or, Rion* and *Rossignol*. Good merchants include *Drouhin, Faiveley, Jadot, Jaffelin, Labouré-Roi, Latour, Olivier Leflaive, Leroy, Rodet, Vallet*. The co-ops at *Buxy* and *Igé* are also good as is the *Caves des Hautes-Côtes*. Their 1987s are still good now; their 1988s and 1989s are better, and their '90s will be best of all. As elsewhere, a few '91s will be decent if unremarkable.

CHAMBERTIN, AC (Côte de Nuits) Most famous of the eight Grands Crus of Gevrey-Chambertin, this 13-hectare vineyard should make wines that are big, strong and intense in their youth, mellowing to a complex, perfumed, plummy richness as they mature. Good ones need 10 to 15 years' aging. Best producers: *Drouhin, Faiveley, Leroy, Mortet, Ponsot, Rebourseau, Rousseau, Tortochot*.

CHAMBERTIN CLOS-DE-BÈZE, AC (Côte de Nuits) Grand Cru in the village of Gevrey-Chambertin next to Chambertin both geographically and in quality. Can keep ten years in a good vintage. The wines may also be sold as Chambertin. 1988, 1989 and 1990 are tops. Best names: *Drouhin, Bruno Clair, Faiveley, Gelin, Mugneret-Gibourg, Rousseau*.

CHAMBOLLE-MUSIGNY, AC (Côte de Nuits) This village towards the southern end of the Côte de Nuits can make light, cherry-sweet, intensely perfumed, 'beautiful' Burgundy, but sadly most commercial Chambolle will be too sweet and gooey to retain much perfume. The best producer is *Georges Roumier*, with wonderful wines in every vintage between 1985 and 1990. For other producers the years to go for are 1988 and '90: *Barthod-Noëllat, Château de Chambolle-Musigny, Drouhin, Dujac, Groffier, Hudelot-Noëllat, Rion, Serveau, Volpato-Costaille, de Vogüé.*

CHAPELLE-CHAMBERTIN, AC (Côte de Nuits) Small Grand Cru vineyard (5.4 hectares) just south of the Clos-de-Bèze in Gevrey-Chambertin. Typically lighter and more delicate than the other Grands Crus. But over-lightness – from over-production – is their curse. The best producer is *Louis Jadot.*

CHARMES-CHAMBERTIN, AC (Côte de Nuits) At 31.6 hectares, this is the biggest of the Grands Crus of Gevrey-Chambertin. It can be fine, strong, sensuous wine, but as with all the Gevrey-Chambertin Grands Crus, it can also be disgracefully light. Best producers: *Bachelet, Drouhin, Rebourseau, Roty, Rousseau, Tortochot.*

CHASSAGNE-MONTRACHET, AC (Côte de Beaune) Down in the south of the Côte de Beaune, about half the wine Chassagne-Montrachet produces is red, even though its fame lies in its large share of the white Grand Cru vineyard of Le Montrachet. The reds from here, though, are a puzzle. At their best they're good value, if a bit heavy, plummy and earthy. Best names: *Bachelet-Ramonet, Carillon, Colin, Jean-Noël Gagnard, Duc de Magenta, Gagnard-Delagrange, René Lamy, Albert Morey, Moreau, Jean Pillot, Ramonet-Prudhon.*

CHOREY-LÈS-BEAUNE, AC (Côte de Beaune) This is a good lesser commune near Beaune, producing good value soft, fruity reds. Because the village isn't popular or hyped, these are some of the few affordable wines Burgundy can offer in top vintages such as 1988, 1989 and 1990. *Germain* and *Tollot-Beaut* are the best producers.

CLOS DE LA ROCHE, AC (Côte de Nuits) Largest and finest Grand Cru of Morey-St-Denis, on the border with Gevrey-Chambertin. When not made too lightweight, this can be splendid wine, full of redcurrant-and-strawberry richness when young, but coming to resemble pretty good Chambertin after ten years or so. Best names: *Amiot, Dujac, Leroy,* both *Hubert* and *Georges Lignier, Ponsot, Rousseau.*

CLOS DES LAMBRAYS, AC (Côte de Nuits) A Grand Cru only since 1981, this nine-hectare vineyard in Morey-St-Denis belongs to a single family (*Saier*), which is unusual in Burgundy. In the 1970s the estate became very run down and the wines were not only very rare but also not very tasty. Wholesale replanting in 1979 means that no real style has yet emerged, but old-timers say that the Clos des Lambrays could potentially make one of Burgundy's finest, most fragrant reds.

CLOS DE TART, AC (Côte de Nuits) Grand Cru of Morey-St-Denis owned by Beaujolais merchants *Mommessin*. At its best Clos de Tart is a light but intense wine which lasts a surprisingly long time.

CLOS DE VOUGEOT, AC (Côte de Nuits) This 50-hectare vineyard dominates the village of Vougeot. Over 80 growers share the enclosure and, while the land at the top is very fine, the land by the road is not. That rare thing, a good bottle of Clos de Vougeot, is fat, rich, strong and thick with the sweetness of perfumed plums and honey, unsubtle but exciting. It is only found in top vintages, like 1988 and 1990, and then only from the best producers. Best names: *Arnoux, Château de la Tour, Jacky Confuron, Drouhin-Laroze, Engel, Grivot, Gros, Hudelot-Noëllat, Jadot, Lamarche, Leroy, Mugneret, Raphet, Rebourseau.*

CLOS ST-DENIS, AC (Côte de Nuits) The village of Morey-St-Denis gets its name from this Grand Cru but the villagers probably should have chosen another one – like the much better known Clos de la Roche – because this small 6.5 hectare vineyard has rarely achieved great heights and is probably the least famous of all the Grands Crus. I'd give my vote to *Georges* or *Hubert Lignier,* or *Ponsot,* though *Dujac* is the best known.

LE CORTON, AC (Côte de Beaune) This is the only red Grand Cru vineyard in the Côte de Beaune, situated on the upper slopes of the famous dome-shaped hill of Corton. Ideally, Corton should have something of the savoury strength of Vosne-Romanée to the north, and something of the mouth-watering, caressing sweetness of Beaune to the south, but the wines labelled Corton have been strangely insubstantial in recent vintages, and wines from subdivisions of Le Corton itself, such as Corton-Pougets, Corton-Bressandes and Corton Clos du Roi, more regularly reach this ideal. Best producers include: *Chandon de Briailles, Dubreuil-Fontaine, Faiveley, Gaunoux, Laleur-Piot, Maldant, Prince de Mérode, Quenot, Rapet, Ravaux, Reine Pédauque, Daniel Senard, Tollot-Beaut, Michel Voarick.*

CÔTE CHALONNAISE, AC This is the name given to the area immediately south of the Côte d'Or, the full name of which is Bourgogne Rouge (or Blanc) Côte Chalonnaise. The vineyards come in pockets rather than in one long swathe like those of the Côte d'Or, but the top three villages of Rully, Mercurey and Givry all produce good wines, with a lovely, simple strawberry-and-cherry fruit.

CÔTE DE BEAUNE The southern part of the Côte d'Or, fairly evenly divided between red and white wines. There is a tiny AC Côte de Beaune which can produce light but tasty reds in warm years. Best producers: *Bouchard Père et Fils, René Manuel, J Alexant.*

CÔTE DE BEAUNE-VILLAGES, AC

Catch-all red wine *appellation* for 16 villages on the Côte de Beaune. Only Aloxe-Corton, Beaune, Volnay and Pommard cannot use the *appellation*. Rarely seen nowadays and rarely exciting, it used to be the source of much excellent soft red, as many lesser-known but good villages would blend their wines together. Still, it *is* worth checking out the wines of *Jaffelin, Lequin-Roussot* and *Bachelet*.

CÔTE DE NUITS

The northern part of the Côte d'Or, theoretically producing the biggest wines. Frequently it doesn't and many of Burgundy's most disappointing bottles come from the top Côte de Nuits communes. It is almost entirely devoted to Pinot Noir.

CÔTE DE NUITS-VILLAGES, AC

Covers the three southernmost villages of Prissey, Comblanchien and Corgoloin, plus Fixin and Brochon in the North. Usually fairly light and dry, they can have good cherry fruit and the slightly rotting veg delicious decay of good Côte de Nuits red. Look out for *Durand, Rion, Rossignol* and *Tollot-Voarick*, and especially *Chopin-Groffier* and *Domaine de l'Arlot*.

CÔTE D'OR

The source of Burgundy's fame – a thin sliver of land worth its weight in gold. It's only 30 miles long, and often less than a mile wide, and it runs from Dijon to Chagny. It has two halves, the Côte de Nuits in the North and the Côte de Beaune in the South.

ÉCHÉZEAUX, AC

(Côte de Nuits) Large Grand Cru of Vosne-Romanée. Best producers: *Domaine de la Romanée-Conti, Engel, Faiveley, Louis Gouroux, Grivot, Henri Jayer, Lamarche, Mongeard-Mugneret, René Mugneret*.

EPINEUIL, AC

Tiny region near Tonnerre, producing light but fragrant styles of Pinot Noir.

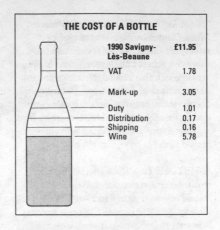

THE COST OF A BOTTLE

1990 Savigny-Lès-Beaune	£11.95
VAT	1.78
Mark-up	3.05
Duty	1.01
Distribution	0.17
Shipping	0.16
Wine	5.78

FIXIN, AC

(Côte de Nuits) A suburb of Dijon, Fixin can make some of Burgundy's sturdiest reds, deep, strong, tough but plummy when young, but capable of mellowing with age. Such wines are slowly reappearing. If you want to feel you're drinking Gevrey-Chambertin without shouldering the cost, Fixin from the following producers could fit the bill: *Bordet, Charlopin-Parizot, Bruno Clair, Fougeray, Roger Fournier, Gelin, Guyard, Joliet, Moillard, Philippe Rossignol*.

FLAGEY-ÉCHÉZEAUX, AC

(Côte de Nuits) Commune that sells its basic wines as Vosne-Romanée but, in Échézeaux and Grands-Échézeaux, has two Grands Crus.

GEVREY-CHAMBERTIN, AC

(Côte de Nuits) The start of the big time for reds. Gevrey-Chambertin has eight Grands Crus, and two of them, Chambertin and Chambertin Clos-de-Bèze can be some of the world's greatest wines. They should have rough, plumskins and damson strength, fierce when young, but assuming a brilliant, wafting perfume and intense, plummy richness when mature. Many of the best wines are made by young growers who do not own as much land in the top vineyards as the larger, old-established estates, but whose commitment to quality shines through. *Bachelet, Boillot, Burguet,*

Michel Esmonin, Philippe Leclerc, Mortet, Naddef and *Rossignol-Trapet* are the names to look out for. Of the old estates, *Rousseau* is best but *Domaine des Varoilles* is also good. Also look out for *Frédéric Esmonin, René Leclerc, Maume* and *Roty*, and for the merchants' bottlings, *Drouhin, Jadot, Faiveley* and *Jaffelin*. But there are still some over-priced horrids bearing the sacred name.

GIVRY, AC (Côte Chalonnaise) Small but important red wine village. At its best, deliciously warm and cherry-chewy with a slightly smoky fragrance but there are too many mediocre bottles around, especially from *négociants*. *Baron Thénard* is the best estate, but *Chofflet, Clos Salomon, Joblot, Lespinasse, Mouton* and *Ragot* are also worth investigating.

LA GRANDE RUE, AC (Côte de Nuits) Wholly owned by the Lamarche family. Elevated to Grand Cru status in 1990, more because of its potential – it is situated between La Tâche and La Romanée-Conti, the two greatest vineyards in Burgundy – than because of the wines it has recently produced.

GRANDS ÉCHÉZEAUX, AC (Côte de Nuits) A slightly second-line Grand Cru, but capable of delicately scented, plum-and-wood-smoke flavoured wine which will go rich and chocolaty with age. Best names: *Domaine de la Romanée-Conti, Drouhin, Engel, Lamarche, Mongeard-Mugneret*.

GRIOTTE-CHAMBERTIN, AC (Côte de Nuits) One of the smallest Grands Crus of Gevrey-Chambertin – 5.58 hectares. Best producers: *Drouhin, Ponsot, Roty*.

HAUTES-CÔTES DE BEAUNE and **HAUTES-CÔTES DE NUITS** A happy hunting ground, this hilly backwater behind the line of famous villages and vineyards on the Côte d'Or. The 28 Hautes-Côtes villages make fairly good, light, strawberry-like Pinot at a decent price. The grapes do not always ripen fully every year, but they had no problems in 1988, '89 or '90. Look out for the Hautes-Côtes de Nuits wines of *Cornu, Domaine des Mouchottes, Jayer-Gilles, Thévenet* and *Verdet* and the Hautes-Côtes de Beaunes of *Bouley, Capron Manieux, Chalet, Guillemard, Joliot, Mazilly* and *Plait*. The *Caves des Hautes-Côtes* is beginning to produce some of the best value reds in the whole of Burgundy.

IRANCY, AC Mostly Pinot Noir from vineyards just to the south-west of Chablis, sometimes with a little of the darker, tougher local grape, the César. Rarely deep in colour, but always perfumed, slightly plummy and attractive, good at two years old and usually capable of aging several years more. It must legally be labelled 'Bourgogne Irancy'. Good producers: *Léon & Serge Bienvenu, Bernard Cantin, André & Roger Delaloge, Gabriel Delaloge, Jean Renaud, Simmonet-Febvre, Luc Sorin*.

LADOIX-SERRIGNY, AC (Côte de Beaune) An obscure village, overshadowed by Aloxe-Corton next door. Worth looking out for though, as *Capitain, Cornu, Prince de Mérode, Chevalier* and *Ravaut* all make decent, crisp wines at very fair prices.

LATRICIÈRES-CHAMBERTIN, AC (Côte de Nuits) Small Grand Cru vineyard in Gevrey-Chambertin and very similar in style to Chambertin though without the power. So long as the producer hasn't pushed the yields too high, it is at its best at 10 to 15 years. Best producers: *Camus, Ponsot, Leroy, Rossignol-Trapet*.

MÂCON ROUGE, AC There's a lot of red wine made in the Mâconnais but it's usually fairly lean, earthy Gamay without the spark of Beaujolais' fruit. If you like that sort of thing, try the wines of *Igé* and *Mancey*, or *Lafarge*'s wine from *Bray*. *Lassarat* is improving things by using new oak, and I'm sure more will follow.

MARSANNAY, AC (Côte de Nuits) Used to produce mostly rosé under the name Bourgogne Rosé de Marsannay, but the introduction of an *appellation* for reds in 1987 has encouraged growers to switch. The first results of this new seriousness are most encouraging and some lovely wines are already emerging, usually quite dry and cherry-perfumed, sometimes more full-blown and exciting. One to watch. Best producers: *Bouvier, Charlopin-Parizot, Bruno Clair, Collotte, Fougeray, Fournier, Geantet-Pansiot, Huguenot, Jadot, Naddef.*

MAZIS-CHAMBERTIN, AC (Côte de Nuits) 12.5 hectare Grand Cru in Gevrey-Chambertin, far more reliable than most of the neighbouring Grands Crus. Mazis can have a superb deep blackberry-pip, damson-skin and blackcurrant fruit which gets more exciting after six to 12 years. Best: *Faiveley, Hospices de Beaune, Maume, Rebourseau, Roty, Rousseau, Tortochot.*

MAZOYÈRES-CHAMBERTIN, AC (Côte de Nuits) Grand Cru of Gevrey-Chambertin, rarely seen since producers generally take up the option of using the Grand Cru Charmes-Chambertin instead.

MERCUREY, AC (Côte Chalonnaise) The biggest Chalonnais village, producing half the region's wines. Indeed many call the Côte Chalonnaise the 'Région de Mercurey'. It's mostly red wines, and they are often fairly full, with attractive strawberry fruit and a little smoky fragrance. As with the other Chalonnais reds, Mercurey's problems are infuriating inconsistency of quality, allied to callous exploitation of the name by some *négociants. Château de Chamirey, Chandesais, Chanzy, Domaine La Marche, Dufouleur, Faiveley, Jacqueson, Juillot, de Launay, Meix-Foulot, Monette, Antonin Rodet, Saier* and *de Suremain* are all good.

MONTHÉLIE, AC (Côte de Beaune) Monthélie shares borders with Volnay and Meursault, but fame with neither. It's a red wine village, and the wines deserve recognition, because they're full, dry, rather herby or piney, but with a satisfying rough fruit. Often a good buy but beware the insidious growth of *négociants'* labels from firms who never traditionally noticed the AC. Best producers: *Boussey, Caves des Hautes-Côtes, Deschamps, Doreau, Garaudet, Château de Monthélie, Monthélie-Douhairet, Potinet-Ampeau, de Suremain, Thévenin-Monthélie.*

MOREY-ST-DENIS, AC (Côte de Nuits) Once obscure and good value, the wines of Morey-St-Denis are now expensive and in general suffer from overproduction and over-sugaring. They should have less body and more perfume than Gevrey-Chambertin, and slight savouriness blending with rich, chocolaty fruit as they age. Most are too light, but there are some outstanding growers. *Pierre Amiot, Bryczek, Dujac, Georges* and *Hubert Lignier, Marchand, Ponsot, Serveau, Charloppin, Perrot-Minot* and *Vadey-Castagnier.* Their 1987s, '88s, '89s and '90s are all excellent.

MUSIGNY, AC (Côte de Nuits) Extremely fine Grand Cru which gave its name to Chambolle-Musigny. All but a third of a hectare of the 10.65 hectare vineyard is red, capable of producing Burgundy's most heavenly-scented wine, but few recent offerings have had me lunging for my cheque book. Best names include: *Château de Chambolle-Musigny, Jadot, Leroy, Jacques Prieur, Georges Roumier, de Vogüé.*

NUITS-ST-GEORGES, AC (Côte de Nuits) When it's good, this has an enthralling decayed – rotting even – brown richness of chocolate and prunes rising out of a fairly light, plum-sweet fruit – quite gorgeous, whatever it sounds like. It used

The price guides for this section begin on page 300.

to be one of the most abused of all Burgundy's names and virtually disappeared from the export markets, but is now fairly common, expensive but immeasurably better, and increasingly reliable. From companies such as *Jadot, Jaffelin, Labouré-Roi* and *Moillard*, it's even becoming possible to buy good merchants' Nuits once more. *Labouré-Roi* is the most consistent merchant, although *Moillard* and *Jadot* are increasingly good particularly at Premier Cru level. The most famous growers are *Robert Chaillon, Gouges, Michelot* and *Daniel Rion*, but excellent wines are also made by *Domaine de l'Arlot, Ambroise, Chicotot, Jean-Jacques Confuron* and the amazingly deep (and amazingly expensive) *Leroy*. There were problems with rot in 1986 and with hail in 1987 so it is best to stick to top vintages such as 1985, '88, '89 and '90.

PERNAND-VERGELESSES, AC (Côte de Beaune) Little-known village round the back of the hill of Corton. Some quite attractive, softly earthy reds, mostly on the lean side. *Besancenot-Mathouillet, Caves des Hautes-Côtes, Chandon des Briailles, Delarche, Dubreuil-Fontaine, Laleure-Piot, Pavelot, Rapet* and *Rollin* are the best producers.

POMMARD, AC (Côte de Beaune) From good producers, Pommard can have a strong, meaty sturdiness, backed by slightly jammy but attractively plummy fruit. Not subtle, but many people's idea of what red Burgundy should be. The most consistently fine wines are made by *de Courcel* and *de Montille*, but also look out for the wines of *Billard-Gonnet, Boillot, Château de Pommard, Girardin, Lahaye, Lejeune, Jean Monnier, Mussy, Parent, Pothier* and *Pousse d'Or*.

RICHEBOURG, AC (Côte de Nuits) Exceptional Grand Cru at the northern end of the commune of Vosne-Romanée. It's a wonderful name for a wine – Richebourg – and, at its best, it manages to be fleshy to

the point of fatness, yet filled with spice and perfume and the clinging richness of chocolate and figs. Best producers: *Domaine de la Romanée-Conti, Gros, Henri Jayer, Leroy, Méo-Camuzet*.

LA ROMANÉE, AC (Côte de Nuits) This Grand Cru is the smallest AC in France, solely owned by the Liger-Belair family and sold by *Bouchard Père et Fils*. It is usually adequate, but nowhere near the quality of the next-door vineyards owned by the *Domaine de la Romanée-Conti*.

LA ROMANÉE-CONTI, AC (Côte de Nuits) This tiny Grand Cru of almost two hectares is capable of a more startling brilliance than any other Burgundy. The 7000 or so bottles it produces per year are seized on by the super-rich before we mere mortals can even get our tasting sheets out. It is wholly owned by the *Domaine de la Romanée-Conti*.

LA ROMANÉE-ST-VIVANT, AC (Côte de Nuits) 9.54 hectare Grand Cru in the village of Vosne-Romanée. Far less easy to taste young than its neighbouring Grands Crus and needs a good 12 years to show what can be a delicious, savoury yet sweet personality. Best names: *Arnoux, Domaine de la Romanée-Conti, Latour, Leroy*.

RUCHOTTES-CHAMBERTIN, AC (Côte de Nuits) The smallest Gevrey-Chambertin Grand Cru at 3.1 hectares, with wines of deeper colour and longer-lasting perfumed richness than most of the village's other Grands Crus. Best producers: *Georges Mugneret, Roumier, Rousseau*.

RULLY, AC (Côte Chalonnaise) Village just a couple of miles below Santenay, initially known for its sparkling wine, but gradually gaining a reputation for light but tasty reds and whites. Best producers: *Chanzy, Château de Rully, Delorme, Domaine de la Folie, Duvernay, Faiveley, Jacqueson, Jaffelin*.

ST-AUBIN, AC (Côte de Beaune) Some of Burgundy's best value wines, especially from *Bachelet, Clerget, Lamy, Prudhon, Thomas* and *Roux*. The 1988s, '89s and '90s are delicious and reasonably priced.

ST-ROMAIN, AC (Côte de Beaune) Even more out of the way than St-Aubin. Full, rather broad-flavoured, cherry-stone dry reds. On the whole sold cheaper than they deserve. Look for *Bazenet, Buisson, Gras, Thévenin* and *Thévenin-Monthélie*. Go for top vintages such as 1985, '88 and '90.

SANTENAY, AC (Côte de Beaune) Rough and ready red. At its best, with a strong, savoury flavour and good strawberry fruit, though frequently nowadays rather lean and mean. Best: *Belland, Girardin, Lequin-Roussot, Morey, Pousse d'Or, Prieur-Bonnet, Roux*. Even here, there can be variation.

SAVIGNY-LÈS-BEAUNE, AC (Côte de Beaune) Not famous, but pretty reliable. Light, with an attractive earthiness and strawberry fruit. Often good quality at a fair price. Try *Bize, Camus-Bruchon, Capron-Manieux, Chandon de Briailles, Ecard-Guyot, de Fougeray, Girard-Vollot, Guillemot, Pavelot-Glantenay, Tollot-Beaut*. The 1985s, '87s and many '89s are drinking well now; the '88s and '90s need longer.

LA TÂCHE, AC (Côte de Nuits) Another Grand Cru monopoly of the *Domaine de la Romanée-Conti*. As famous as Romanée-Conti, but not so totally unobtainable, since the 6.06 hectare vineyard can produce all of 24,000 bottles a year. The wine is heavenly, so rich and heady the perfumes are sometimes closer to age-old brandy than table wine and the flavour loaded with spice and dark autumn-mellow fruits and the acrid richness of dark chocolate.

VOLNAY, AC (Côte de Beaune) Volnay is one of the most perfumed red Burgundies, with a memorable cherry-and-strawberry spice, but also, in its Premiers Crus, able to turn on a big, meaty style without losing the perfume. The best at the moment are *Lafarge* and *de Montille*. Their 1985s, '88s, '89s and '90s are superb. Other good names: *Ampeau, Blain-Gagnard, Boillot, Bouley, Clerget, Comtes Lafon, Delagrange, Glantenay, Marquis d'Angerville, Pousse d'Or, Vaudoisey-Mutin, Voillot*.

VOSNE-ROMANÉE, AC (Côte de Nuits) The greatest Côte de Nuits village, right in the south of the Côte. Its Grands Crus sell for more money than any red wine on earth, and, remarkably for Burgundy, they are dominated by a single estate, *Domaine de la Romanée Conti*. These vineyards make wines capable of more startling brilliance than any other red wine in France, with flavours as disparate yet as intense as the overpowering, creamy savouriness of fresh *foie gras* and the deep, sweet scent of ripe plums and prunes in brandy. You may need to re-mortgage your

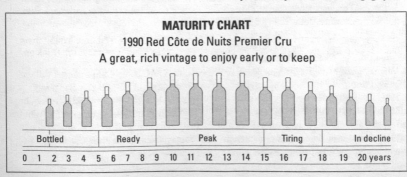

MATURITY CHART
1990 Red Côte de Nuits Premier Cru
A great, rich vintage to enjoy early or to keep

| Bottled | Ready | Peak | Tiring | In decline |

0 1 2 3 4 5 6 7 8 9 10 11 12 13 14 15 16 17 18 19 20 years

house in order to experience this, though. There are also fine Premiers Crus, and the village wines, though not so reliable as they once were, can sometimes reflect their leaders. The 1987s and '89s are good; the '85s, '88s and '90s are unutterably great. Apart from the Domaine, look for *Arnoux, Sylvain Cathiard, Confuron-Coteditot, Engel, Grivot, Jean Gros, Hudelot-Noëllat, Georges Jayer, Henri Jayer, Henri Lamarche, Leroy, Méo-Camuzet, Mongeard-Mugneret, Georges Mugneret, Pernin-Rossin, Rouget, Daniel Rion* and *Jean Tardy*.

VOUGEOT, AC (Côte de Nuits) A village famous only because of its Grand Cru, Clos de Vougeot, which at its best is plummy and broad. However, there are some decent wines made outside the Clos – most notably from *Bertagna* and *Clerget*.

RED CÔTE D'OR VINTAGES

1993 What could have been a marvellous vintage was badly affected by the late September rain. At their best the reds are long and aromatic and, the locals claim, with enough structure to last. The acid level is low but the levels of tannins are higher than at any time in the past five years, and the colour is terrific.

1992 A large vintage of wines with attractive ripe fruit, if not a great deal of concentration and structure. Many will be pleasing early on, in a style similar to 1989. A few first-rate wines from producers who kept their yields low.

1991 A small crop, partly because of hail damage, and spoilt by rain at vintage time. Even so, there were some very good reds made – and with some yields as low as 10 hectolitres per hectare, they can have extraordinary concentration. It's a very patchy vintage, but the good wines will be ones to keep, because of that concentration.

1990 The long, warm summer produced yet another large crop. The 1990s are brilliantly fruity, naturally high in sugars. Most producers now consider this the best of the great trio of '88, '89 and '90. Lesser wines will be ready early; the best are sumptuously rich.

1989 A lot of good wines were made in this warm year, but only a few exceptional ones. They are softer than the 1988s, though some are superbly concentrated, particularly in the Côte de Beaune. Some may prove better than the '88s.

1988 There was potential to make great wine in 1988, though it was hardly a textbook year. Some grapes were rather short on sugar, but those who waited to pick were walloped by the rain. Throughout the Côte d'Or a surprising number of growers did not overproduce, did pick fully ripe grapes before the rains came, and have made delicious wines – more joyously fruity than 1987, and quite a bit deeper and riper than 1986.

1987 The good producers made quite small amounts of well-coloured, concentrated wine which in some cases is better than their 1985s. The best '87s are very good indeed, Côte de Beaune having the edge over Côte de Nuits. Further down the scale the wines aren't as good as '85, but are better than '86.

1986 Over the last year the wines have been shedding toughness, and now exhibit their best feature, perfume. Stick to decent producers, because there was some rot. Drink up.

1985 When the 1985s were young, they were terrific. Some have gone from strength to strength. Some seem stuck in a 'dumb' phase. Some shot their bolt early.

1983 The best wines display impressive flavour. If you can wait another decade you may have the most impressive old-style Burgundies made in the last 20 years, but I'd avoid Vosne-Romanée, Chambolle-Musigny and Morey-Saint-Denis.

1982 Ridiculously over-praised to start with. The best wines are from the Côte de Beaune and are delicate, perfumed, nicely balanced and need drinking.

WHITE WINES

Burgundy's whites are now the benchmark, and the target, for thousands of wines from dozens of countries. Australia and the rest are hard on its heels – and, lo and behold, Burgundy is fighting back. Of the top wines there is little to say – they are only ever available in tiny quantities and at prices far above even those of the Premiers Grands Crus from Bordeaux. It is the wines below this level that concern most of us; and it is precisely here that the developments have been most dramatic.

It wasn't so long ago that the average Burgundian grower would barely admit that anybody else made Chardonnay, far less that it might be as good as the stuff made by himself, or his father, or his great-great-grandfather. Now, along with the realization that the world is both bigger and smaller than he thought, has come the revelation that he, as an individual, has to do better, or an Aussie will do it for him. Suddenly Burgundy has become self-critical.

New improved whiteness

This concern for quality means that the best value white Burgundies – and, for the first time in years one can talk in these terms – come from a handful of larger domaines. Some have historically respected names, like the many branches of the Delagrange family in Puligny, or the Pillots. But others have been transformed, like the Domaine Jacques Prieur, or L'Arlot, which has been unrecognizable since 1986, when it was bought by the insurance giant, AXA.

Easier to find are wines from trustworthy merchants like Drouhin, Faiveley, Jadot, Labouré-Roi – which produces a delicious and widely available Côte de Beaune Blanc at a mere £6.99 – and the inescapable (but undeniably reliable) Olivier Leflaive. But the improvement is now spreading throughout the merchant community – noisily, as with Bouchard Aîné, quietly through takeover as with Champy, or through the recognition of new reality, as with Ropiteau, a merchant which was in the past a no-go area for consumers, and with Boisset, now a maker of reliable cheapos.

As a result the areas to be avoided are shrinking. Take Chablis, for instance. An awful lot of the stuff being churned out, even from the Premiers Crus, is pretty characterless and simply lacks the depth of concentration required. But buyers with clout and taste can extract good wines even from the co-operative, La Chablisienne (Marks & Sparks has done just that). Otherwise you have to rely on a handful of reliable names, like the Domaine Laroche and the Domaine des Malandes, which makes one of the best of the under-£10 Chablis.

The same theme, of surprising success even from co-operatives, and a lot of disappointment in theoretically better wines, applies right through the vineyard, from Mâcon north to Corton. The Mâconnais has been, historically, a region dominated by value-for-money quaffing Chardonnay, lighter, more delicate, and, yes, classier than the Antipodean variety, but equally reliable. The co-operative at Viré is still the best-known, but in the South names like Clessé and Prissé are cropping up in the quality stakes, especially for their better *cuvées*, with names like St-Véran Vieilles Vignes from Prissé. As always, the best wines from these 'lesser' *appellations* come from individual estates, like that owned by the Thévenet family in Mâcon. But on the other hand you have communes like St-

Véran, which may be popular, but are still producing an lot of mediocre wine.

There are parts of Burgundy where the standard has risen so dramatically that the wines can, in general, be recommended. Wines from the Côtes Chalonnaise, from Rully and Montagny in particular, are not of course as potentially fine as those from Corton, Puligny and Chassagne, but, crucially, they are made in reasonable quantities on relatively large estates by increasingly sophisticated winemakers. Many of the latter are employed by highly competitive merchants such as Faiveley and Antonin Rodet. They (above all the omnipresent Olivier Leflaive) are opening new markets for the wines. Even in that difficult year 1992 Leflaive and his winemaker Frank Grux produced excellent, well-structured wines from Montagny, Mercurey and Rully, while Rodet's Château de Rully is one of my favourites.

A handful of individuals are even making worthwhile wines from that (usually correctly) despised grape the Aligoté. The original standard-bearer was Aubert de Villaine, part-owner of the Domaine de la Romanée-Conti, with his Aligoté from the tiny commune of Bouzeron. But he has now been joined by Guy Roulot (who also makes an excellent generic Meursault) and Lamy-Pillot.

Chardonnay like any other

Looking at all these changes it is possible to discern a pattern which is adding up to a revolution. Consumers of white Burgundy the world over are now so much more discerning than they were in the past, and the prices of the greatest wines are still at such stratospheric levels even after the recent falls, that white Burgundy, even more than red (because the quantities are smaller, the prices often higher, the competition from outside the region so much more severe) is going to be judged by the same criteria as lesser beverages.

This sounds like a bit of an anti-climax. But it isn't. It means that, in future, the Pulignys and the Chassagnes will be assessed on their quality, as they have been to an increasing extent over the past few years. For the first time in Burgundian history the village or vineyard name alone will no longer be enough.

Of course, we as consumers always knew that the name of the producer mattered, just as much as the name of the village. Too many producers, though, coasted along on the reputation of their villages. It is the realization among the growers that they count that has produced the turnaround.

There is a second corollary: that in the many 'lesser' communes, notably on the Côte Chalonnaise, white Burgundy has created what it previously lacked: a solid, reputable middle class, a group of 'crus bourgeois' which buyers will judge, not on the commune, but on the reputation of the winemaker or merchant. And if that means that the Château du Rully, or the Mercurey from M Juillot, fetches double the price of old-fashioned, sloppily-made wines from the same commune, as happens all the time in Bordeaux, so be it. This drinker, for one, will be happy.

Unfortunately these revolutionary changes may be too late. In the 1993 International Wine Challenge, Burgundy's white wines performed much better in the 'unoaked' than in the 'oaked' section, and this may not conform to modern tastes. At a recent tasting at the Reform Club in London, a classic 'traditional' outlet, the members clearly preferred two sturdier, oakier, fuller wines from Australia and California respectively to a Montagny from Leflaive, which they clearly found too delicate for palates brutalized by oak, vanilla, sawdust and butter over the years.   NICHOLAS FAITH

GRAPES & FLAVOURS

CHARDONNAY In a world panting for Chardonnay, Burgundy makes the most famous Chardonnay of all. Even in the decidedly dicky Burgundian climate, it produces a fair to considerable amount of good to excellent wine almost every year. Its flavour depends on where it is grown, and how the wine is made. Chardonnays made without the use of oak barrels for aging will taste very different from barrel-aged wines. A Mâcon produced in stainless steel will have rather appley fruit as well as something slightly fat and yeasty or, in a hot year, a slightly exotic peachiness. Côte Chalonnaise Chardonnay is generally rather taut and chalky-dry, but given some oak, it can become delicately nutty. Chablis, too, generally produces lean wine, but in riper years and with some oak treatment it can get much rounder and mouth-filling. The Côte d'Or is the peak of achievement for Chardonnay, and a top wine from the Côte de Beaune manages to be luscious, creamy, honeyed yet totally dry, the rich, ripe fruit intertwined with the scents of new oak into a memorable and surprisingly powerful wine – from the right producer, the world's greatest dry white. It is this that has so enticed the New World wineries – and quite a few in the Old World, too, outside France – into trying to mimic the success of Burgundian Chardonnay.

ALIGOTÉ Not planted in the best sites – though there are a few vines in Corton-Charlemagne. Aligoté used to be merely sharp, spritzy café wine, but from old vines it can produce a lovely, refreshing wine, scented like buttermilk soap yet as sharp and palate-cleansing as a squeeze of lemon juice.

PINOT BEUROT Known elsewhere as Pinot Gris. Very rare in Burgundy, but it produces rich, buttery wine usually blended in to soften the Chardonnay. There is a little unblended Pinot Beurot in the Hautes-Côtes.

PINOT BLANC There is a little of this about in the Côte d'Or – in Aloxe-Corton, for instance, where it makes a soft, rather unctuous, quick-maturing wine. Rully in the Côte Chalonnaise has a good deal and it ripens well in the Hautes-Côtes. There is also an odd white mutation of Pinot Noir – as at Nuits-St-Georges where the Premier Cru La Perrière produces a very savoury white, and in the Monts Luisants vineyard in Morey-St-Denis.

WINES & WINE REGIONS

ALOXE-CORTON, AC (Côte de Beaune) This most northerly village of the Côte de Beaune has one of the Côte's most famous Grands Crus, Corton-Charlemagne. It can be a magnificent, blasting wall of flavour, not big on nuance, but strong, buttery and ripe, which traditionally is supposed to require long aging to show its full potential. Do not expect this sort of quality from the simple village wine, however; recent vintages of Corton-Charlemagne have mostly been disappointing and one is left wondering if they're not trying to produce too much wine.

AUXEY-DURESSES, AC (Côte de Beaune) Tucked away in the folds of the hill rather than on the main Côte de Beaune slope, Auxey-Duresses has never been well known, but has always had some reputation for soft, nutty whites. Recently, though, too many have been disappointingly soft and flabby, but the new confidence of the lesser villages is evident here too and 1992, '90, '89 and '88 have all produced good wine. Producers like *Ampeau, Diconne, Duc de Magenta, Jadot, Leroy* and *Prunier* are still producing pretty decent stuff.

BÂTARD-MONTRACHET, AC (Côte de Beaune) Grand Cru of Chassagne and Puligny lying just below Le Montrachet and, from a good producer, displaying a good deal of its dramatic flavour, almost thick in the mouth, all roast nuts, butter, toast and honey. Can be exciting, if inevitably expensive. Good names: *Blain-Gagnard, Clerc, Jean-Noël Gagnard, Leflaive, Bernard Morey, Pierre Morey, Michel Niellon, Pernot, Poirier, Claude Ramonet, Ramonet-Prudhon, Sauzet.*

BIENVENUES-BÂTARD-MONTRACHET, AC (Côte de Beaune) Tiny Grand Cru in Puligny below Le Montrachet, and inside the larger Bâtard-Montrachet – whose wines are similar though the Bienvenues wines are often lighter, more elegant and may lack a tiny bit of Bâtard's drive. Best producers: *Carillon, Clerc, Leflaive, Pernot, Ramonet-Prudhon.*

BOURGOGNE ALIGOTÉ, AC Usually rather sharp and green except for sites near Pernand-Vergelesses where old vines can make exciting wine, but the locals add Crème de Cassis to it to make Kir – which tells you quite a lot about it. Look out for *Coche-Dury, Confuron, Diconne, Jobard, Monthélie-Douhairet, Rion, Rollin.*

BOURGOGNE ALIGOTÉ DE BOUZERON, AC (Côte Chalonnaise) The white wine pride of the Côte Chalonnaise is made not from Chardonnay but from the Aligoté grape in the village of Bouzeron. The vines are frequently old – this seems to be more crucial for Aligoté than for most other wines – and the buttermilk soap nose is followed by a very dry, slightly lemony, pepper-sharp wine, too good to mix with Cassis. It got its own AC in 1979. It owes its sudden fame to the interest of the *de Villaine* family, who own a substantial estate there making the best of all Aligotés, rich and oaky. *Chanzy* and *Bouchard Père et Fils* are also good.

BOURGOGNE BLANC This can mean almost anything – from a basic Burgundy grown in the less good spots anywhere between Chablis and the Mâconnais to a carefully matured wine from a serious producer, either from young vines or from parts of his vineyard that just miss a superior AC, especially on the borders of Meursault. Best producers: *Boisson-Vadot, Boyer-Martenot, Boisson-Morey, Henri Clerc, Coche-Dury, Dussort, Jadot, Javillier, Jobard, Labouré-Roi, René Manuel, Millot-Battault* and *Buxy* co-op (*Clos de Chenoves*).

CHABLIS, AC Simple Chablis, mostly soft, sometimes acidic, covers the widest area of the *appellation*. Well it would, wouldn't it? They've included most of what used to be Petit Chablis for a start. But at the rate they're now extending the Premier Cru status to virtually anything that grows, maybe Premiers Crus will soon overtake Chablis in acreage. Chablis covers a multitude of sins, with a lot of wine going under *négociants'* labels, and a lot being sold by the co-op – they make most of the *négociants'* stuff too. Some of the co-op's best *cuvées* are outstandingly good, but many of the cheaper *cuvées* are too bland and soft. A good grower is more likely to give you something steely and traditional. Good producers: *Christian Adine, Jean-Marc Brocard, La Chablisienne, Jean Collet, René Dauvissat, Defaix, Jean-Paul Droin, Joseph Drouhin, Jean Durup, William Fèvre, Vincent Gallois, Alain Geoffroy, Jean-Pierre Grossot, Michel Laroche, Bernard Légland, Louis Michel, Guy Mothe, François & Jean-Marie Raveneau, Regnard, Simmonet-Fèbvre, Philippe Testut, Robert Vocoret.*

CHABLIS GRAND CRU The seven Grands Crus (Blanchots, Preuses, Bougros, Grenouilles, Valmur, Vaudésir and Les Clos) come from a small patch of land just outside the town of Chablis, on a single slope rising from the banks of the river Serein. The wines *can* be outstanding, though still unlikely to rival the Grands Crus of the Côte de Beaune. To get the best out of them, you need to age them, preferably after oaking, although *Louis Michel*'s oak-free wines age superbly. The last six vintages have seen a considerable increase in the use of oak by the better producers, and the results are deeper, more exciting wines which may well benefit from six to ten years' aging in bottle.

CHABLIS PREMIER CRU Some 30 names, rationalized into 12 main vineyards. Once upon a time, this used to be a very reliable classification for good, characterful dry white, if less intense than Grand Cru, but again, there has been this expansion mania, meaning that many hardly suitable pieces of vineyard are now accorded Premier Cru status. Given that there is a price difference of £3 to £4 a bottle between Chablis and Premier Cru Chablis, the quality difference should be plain as a pikestaff. Sadly it rarely is. However, in the nineties there has been a definite move towards quality by the better growers and *La Chablisienne* co-op.

CHASSAGNE-MONTRACHET, AC (Côte de Beaune) Only half the production of this famous vineyard at the south of the Côte de Beaune is white, but that includes a large chunk of the great Montrachet vineyard. The Grands Crus are excellent, but the Premiers Crus rarely dazzle quite like those of nearby Puligny-Montrachet. The Chassagne '86s are mostly at their best now, and should be drunk; the '89s are wonderfully ripe and concentrated and can be drunk now or kept for years. The '90s will be magic, the '92s pure magic. Best producers include: *Blain-Gagnard, Carillon, Chartron et Trebuchet, Colin, Duc de Magenta, Fontaine-Gagnard, Jean-Noël Gagnard, Gagnard-Delagrange, Génot-Boulanger, Lamy-Pillot, Laguiche, Château de la Maltroye, Moreau, Albert Morey, Bernard Morey, Niellon, Fernand Pillot, Ramonet. Jaffelin* is the best merchant.

CHABLIS VINEYARDS
Grands Crus

Blanchots, Bougros, Les Clos, Grenouilles, Preuses, Valmur, Vaudésir. La Moutonne, considered a Grand Cru, is from a parcel in Preuses and Vaudésir.

Premiers Crus

Fourchaume (including Fourchaume, Vaupulent, Côte de Fontenay, Vaulorent, l'Homme Mort); Montée de Tonnerre (including Montée de Tonnerre, Chapelot, Pied d'Aloup); Monts de Milieu; Vaucoupin; Les Fourneaux (including Les Fourneaux, Morein, Côte des Prés-Girots); Beauroy (including Beauroy, Troesmes); Côte de Léchet; Vaillons (including Vaillons, Châtains, Séché, Beugnons, Les Lys); Mélinots (including Mélinots, Roncières, Les Epinottes); Montmains (including Montmains, Forêts, Butteaux); Vosgros (including Vosgros and Vaugiraut); Vaudevey.

CHEVALIER-MONTRACHET, AC (Côte de Beaune) Grand Cru vineyard of Puligny, directly above Le Montrachet. The higher elevation gives a leaner wine, but one with a deep flavour as rich and satisfying as a dry white wine can get. Good examples will last 20 years. Best: *Bouchard Père et Fils, Clerc, Jadot, Latour, Leflaive, Niellon*.

CORTON, AC (Côte de Beaune) Corton-Charlemagne is the white Grand Cru here in Aloxe-Corton, but tiny patches of the Corton Grand Cru grow Chardonnay and Pinot Blanc. The finest wine, the *Hospices de Beaune*'s Corton-Vergennes, is all Pinot, and *Chandon de Briailles* makes Corton-Bressandes that is half Pinot Blanc.

CORTON-CHARLEMAGNE, AC (Côte de Beaune) This famous Grand Cru of Aloxe-Corton and Pernand-Vergelesses occupies the upper half of the dome-shaped hill of Corton. It is planted almost entirely with Chardonnay, but a little Pinot Blanc or Pinot Beurot can add intriguing fatness to the wine. Good names: *Bitouzet, Bonneau du Martray, Chandon de Briailles, Chapuis, Dubreuil-Fontaine, M. Juillot, Hospices de Beaune, Laleure Piot, Latour, Rapet.*

CÔTE CHALONNAISE, AC As the ordered vines of the Côte de Beaune swing away and dwindle to the west, the higgledy-piggledy vineyards of the Côte Chalonnaise hiccup and splutter into life as a patchwork of south- and east-facing outcrops. Light, usually clean-tasting Chardonnay predominates among the whites – although at long last the idea of oak-aging is catching on. But the Côte Chalonnaise has one star that cannot be overshadowed by the famous Côte d'Or: the village of Bouzeron makes the finest and the most famous Aligoté in all France.

CÔTE D'OR This famous strip of vineyard, running south-west from Dijon for 30 miles, sprouts famous names right along its length, with a fine crop of illustrious whites in the southern portion. But in fact it produces only about 16 per cent of Burgundy's white. (Mâconnais is the chief white producer, with the Côte Chalonnaise a distant second.) Fortunately, prices are down, and quality up from the late '80s.

CRÉMANT DE BOURGOGNE, AC What used to be simple, pleasantly tart fizz based on slightly green Chardonnay and Aligoté grapes, excellent for mixing with cassis, is sharpening up its act. Competition from other regions and countries, added to the increase in Champagne prices, has led to co-operatives, such as the *caves* of Viré or St-Gengoux-Clessé in the Mâconnais, and the *Cave de Bailly* in the Yonne and *Delorme* in Rully, producing excellent, eminently affordable fizz, increasingly from 100 per cent Chardonnay. Crémant de Bourgogne is becoming a wine that can face competition from most non-Champagne sparklers.

CRIOTS-BÂTARD-MONTRACHET, AC (Côte de Beaune) Tiny 1.6 hectare Grand Cru in Chassagne-Montrachet nuzzled up against the edge of Bâtard itself. Hardly ever seen but the wines are similar to Bâtard, full, strong, packed with flavour, perhaps a little leaner. Best producers: *Blain-Gagnard, Fontaine-Gagnard.*

HAUTES-CÔTES DE BEAUNE, AC and **HAUTES-CÔTES DE NUITS, AC** A lot of reasonably good, light, dry Chardonnay from the hill country behind the Côte de Beaune and Côte de Nuits. Best producers: *Caves des Hautes-Côtes, Chalet, Cornu, Goubard, Jayer-Gilles, Alain Verdet* (organic).

MÂCON BLANC, AC It seemed, a few years ago, that the spiralling price of Pouilly-Fuissé – the region's only white wine star – was acting as a spur for the producers to improve quality. As Pouilly-Fuissé came spinning back to earth – a wiser but better, and cheaper, wine – upping the price of Mâcon to patently unrealistic levels seemed to have been the only effect. Now prices are back down again, and quality has yet to show any great improvement. Most Mâcon simply cannot compete with the best-value New World wines.

MÂCON BLANC-VILLAGES, AC One step up from basic Mâcon Blanc, this must come from the 43 Mâcon communes with the best land. The rare good ones show the signs of honey and fresh apples and some of the nutty, yeasty depth associated with fine Chardonnay. You can expect the better wines from those villages, notably **Viré, Clessé, Prissé** and **Lugny**, that add their own village names (Mâcon-Viré, etc). Full, buttery yet fresh, sometimes spicy: look for that and, if you find it, consider paying the price. You will find it occasionally in the 1989s and '90s – but only rarely in other vintages. Prices went silly in the mid-1980s but, as elsewhere in Burgundy, have now collapsed to reasonable levels. Best producers: *Bicheron, Bonhomme, Danauchet, Goyard, Guillemot-Michel, Josserand, Lassarat, Manciat-Poncet, Merlin, Signoret, Talmard* and *Thévenet-Wicart*.

MERCUREY, AC (Côte Chalonnaise) This village, all by itself, makes over half the wine of the Côte Chalonnaise. Most of the production is red – the whites used to be rather flaccid afterthoughts from the less good land, but as the price of white rose in the Côte de Beaune, several producers started making a bigger effort with interesting results. Good examples come from *Chartron et Trebuchet, Château de Chamirey, Faiveley, Genot, Boulanger, M Juillot*.

MEURSAULT, AC (Côte de Beaune) Situated halfway down the Côte de Beaune, this village is the first, working southwards, of the great white wine villages. It has by far the largest white production of any commune in the Côte d'Or, and this is one of several reasons why its traditionally high overall standard is gradually being eroded. The wines should be big and nutty and have a delicious, gentle lusciousness, and sometimes even peachy, honeyed flavours. Meursault has more producers bottling their own wine than any other village. These are some of the best: *Ampeau, Pierre Boillot, Boisson-Vadot, Boyer-Martenot, Buisson-Battault,*

Coche-Debord, Coche-Dury, Comtes Lafon, Gauffroy, Henri-Germain, Jean Germain, Grivault, Patrick Javidier, François Jobard, René Manuel, Matrot, Michelot-Buisson, Millot-Battault, Pierre Morey, Prieur, Roulot.

MONTAGNY, AC (Côte Chalonnaise) White-only AC in the south of the Côte Chalonnaise. In general the wines are a bit lean and chalky-dry, but now that the use of oak is creeping in, some much more interesting wines are appearing. Best producers: *Arnoux*, co-op at *Buxy, Latour, B Michel, de Montorge, Alain Roy, Vachet*. Best merchants: *O Leflaive* and *Rodet's Les Chagnots*.

LE MONTRACHET, AC (Côte de Beaune) This is white Burgundy at its greatest, the finest of fine white Grands Crus in the villages of Puligny and Chassagne. Does it mean most enjoyable, most happy-making? Not really. In fact the flavours can be so intense it's difficult sometimes to know if you're having fun drinking it or merely giving your wine vocabulary an end of term examination. So be brave if someone opens a bottle of Montrachet for you and let the incredible blend of spice and smoke, honey and ripeness flow over your senses. Good producers include: *Amiot-Bonfils, Bouchard Père et Fils, Domaine de la Romanée-Conti, Jadot, Comtes Lafon, Laguiche, Pierre Morey, Prieur, Thénard* and, since 1991, *Leflaive*.

MATURITY CHART
1992 White Côte de Beaune Premier Cru
Well balanced vintage which may benefit from some ageing

Bottled	Ready	Peak	Tiring	In decline

| 0 | 1 | 2 | 3 | 4 | 5 | 6 | 7 | 8 | 9 | 10 | 11 | 12 years |

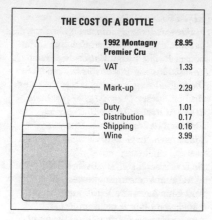

THE COST OF A BOTTLE

1992 Montagny Premier Cru	£8.95
VAT	1.33
Mark-up	2.29
Duty	1.01
Distribution	0.17
Shipping	0.16
Wine	3.99

MUSIGNY, AC (Côte de Nuits) Just 0.3 hectares of this predominantly red Grand Cru of Chambolle-Musigny are planted with Chardonnay, owned by the *Domaine de Vogüé*, and most of it seems to be consumed on the premises.

PERNAND-VERGELESSES, AC (Côte de Beaune) The village wines can be good, – with the some of the best Aligoté in Burgundy. The Chardonnays are generally fairly lean and need time to soften, but can be gently nutty and very enjoyable from a good producer. Can also be very good value. Best names: *Dubreuil-Fontaine, Germain, Laleure-Piot, Pavelot, Rapet, Rollin.*

PETIT CHABLIS There used to be lots of this grown on the least good slopes. But the growers objected that it made it sound as though their wine was a lesser form of Chablis. Nowadays, of course, pretty well the whole lot is called 'Chablis' – so *we* can't tell what's what, *they're* all richer, they're happy, we're not... I give up.

POUILLY-FUISSÉ, AC (Mâconnais) This once ridiculously overpriced white has dropped its price considerably in the last few years. This tumble came about partly because the Americans stopped buying – although they were the ones who made it famous in the first place – and partly

because the general quality from this co-op-monopolized, *négociant*-abused AC was a disgrace. Best producers: *Barraud, Béranger, Corsin, Duboeuf*'s top selections, *Ferret, M Forest, Guffens-Heynen, Leger-Plumet, Loron's les Vieux Murs, Manciat-Poncet, Noblet, R Saumaize, Vincent* at *Château Fuissé.* Adjoining villages **Pouilly-Loché, AC** and **Pouilly-Vinzelles, AC** have borrowed the name and make similar wines at half the price.

PULIGNY-MONTRACHET, AC (Côte de Beaune) The peak of great white pleasure is to be found in the various Montrachet Grands Crus. Le Montrachet is peerless, showing how humble words like honey, nuts, cream, smoke, perfume and all the rest do no honest service to a white wine that seems to combine every memory of ripe fruit and subtly worn scent with a dry, penetrating savouriness. There are several other Grands Crus less intense, but which offer the same unrivalled mix. There are Premiers Crus as well. While 'village' Meursault may be good, it's always worth buying a single vineyard wine in Puligny-Montrachet. Much of the wine that's produced is sold in bulk to *négociants* whose offerings vary between the delicious and the disgraceful, but look for the wines of *Amiot-Bonfils, Boyer-Devèze, Carillon, Chartron et Trebuchet, Clerc, Drouhin, Jadot, Labouré-Roi, Laguiche,* both *Domaine Leflaive* and *Olivier Leflaive, Pernot, Ramonet-Prudhon, Antonin Rodet, Sauzet, Thénard.*

RULLY, AC (Côte Chalonnaise) This village gets my vote for the most improved AC in Burgundy. It was originally known for fizz, and then for pale, nutty, dull Chardonnay, but the use of oak to ferment and age the wine has turned a lot into wonderfully soft, spicy Burgundies of good quality – and low price. Best names: *Bêtes, Chanzy, Cogny, Delorme, Dury, Duvernay, Domaine de la Folie, Jacqueson, Jaffelin, Olivier Leflaive, Rodet.*

ST-AUBIN, AC (Côte de Beaune) Some of Burgundy's best value white wines, full and racy, come from this tiny, forgotten Côte de Beaune village behind the far more famous Puligny-Montrachet and Meursault. Two-thirds of the vineyards are Premiers Crus and it really shows. Starting with '82 it became clear that St-Aubin's Premiers Crus could rival the more famous wines of Meursault and Puligny-Montrachet. The 1989s are rich, the '92s (need I say it?) magic. Other good producers in the commune are *Bachelet, Bouton, Clerget, Colin, Delaunay, Duvernay, Jadot, Jaffelin, Lamy, Albert Morey, Prudhon, Roux* and *Thomas.*

ST-ROMAIN, AC (Côte de Beaune) The flinty, dry whites that emerge from this out of the way Côte de Beaune village right up near the Hautes-Côtes are often decent quality and pretty good value. Best are: *Bazenet, Buisson, Germain, Gras, Thévenin, Thévenin-Monthélie.*

ST-VÉRAN, AC (Mâconnais) Pouilly-Fuissé's understudy, capable of simple, soft, quick-maturing but very attractive, rather honeyed white Burgundy. There are some great 1989s and '90s but '92 has produced the highest recent quality across the board. Best producers: *Corsin, Dépardon, Dom. des Deux Roches, Duboeuf, Grégoire, Lassarat, de Montferrand, Saumaize, Thibert, Vincent* – and, above all, *Drouhin.*

SAUVIGNON DE ST-BRIS, VDQS Wine of AC quality grown south-west of Chablis that languishes as a VDQS just because Sauvignon Blanc is not a permitted AC grape in the area. Often one of the most nettly, most greeny-gooseberryish of all France's Sauvignons, but recent ones have been more expensive and less exciting. It has not really faced up to the competition from New Zealand – and Bordeaux. Good names: *Louis Bersan, Jean-Marc Brocard, Robert & Philippe Defrance, Michel Esclavy, André Sorin, Luc Sorin.*

WHITE BURGUNDY VINTAGES

White Burgundy is far less prone to vintage fluctuation than red, and in most years can produce a fair amount of pretty good wine.

1993 Virtually all the wines are too lean to be attractive. The grapes simply did not ripen in the cold, rainy weather which marked September, though the locals are confident about their fruitiness. Not a purchase, given the availability (and reasonable price) of the 1992s.

1992 A far better vintage for the whites than for the reds. The 1992s have masses of exuberant fruit and seemingly better acidity than their 1991 counterparts. The best white vintage since 1989, but in a less alcoholic, more elegantly balanced style than most 1989s.

1991 Patchy in quality, though without the reds' occasional brilliance. That vintage-time rain did more damage to the Chardonnay than to the Pinot Noir, in terms of rot, and some of the picking had to be pretty hasty. The whites don't match up to the previous three vintages in quality, but the Mâconnais wines are drinking well now.

1990 Though the growing season was in many ways similar to 1989 the 1990s have some of the structure of the '88s and some of the richness of the '89s. They are less austere than the '88s and probably won't last as long. The Chardonnay crop was very large, so the whites are proving to be inferior to the reds. A good rather than a great vintage for white Burgundy.

1989 An outstanding year for white Burgundy, in the hands of competent winemakers. Hailed as the best white vintage of the 1980s, almost all the best growers' wines are beautifully balanced, despite their richness. As one Burgundy importer put it: 'a richer version of the structured and seriously undervalued 1985s'. However, a number of wines have worryingly low acidity levels, and some are already showing signs of premature aging.

1988 The fruit was, if anything, a little cleaner and fresher than in 1987. Numbers of Mâconnais wines had a bright, fresh fruit not seen down that way for a few years. Chablis prices went up by 10 to 15 per cent, but you couldn't honestly say that its quality went up in parallel.

1987 Good producers made attractive, quite light wines, sometimes with a slightly lean streak of acidity. Try the exciting new growers in the Côte Chalonnaise and Mâconnais. The Côte d'Or produced wines that were often frankly dull, but Chablis has turned out well.

1986 There's an interesting debate over the relative qualities of '86 and '85. Initially 1986 was given a better reception even than '85 because, whereas the latter seemed to rely on sheer power, 1986 seemed to have finer acidity, a more focused fruit and even a hint of richness. The balance has been redressed a bit now. The good 1985s have proved to be much better balanced than previously thought, and whilst a few '86s have closed up somewhat, others have suddenly started to tire. Chablis had that classic blend of leanness and restrained ripeness which can make it the logical, if not the emotional choice for so many fish dishes. Grands Crus still need several years. The Mâconnais promised much, but few bottles really delivered.

1985 This is on the way back. Along with the strength are increasing signs of a proper acid balance and an outstanding concentration of fruit. Pity nobody waited to find out because most '85s were consumed long ago. If you do see one from a good producer, go for it – well, perhaps not, I've just remembered the price it'll be. Chablis started out with a lesser reputation, but wines from good producers can still improve.

1983 Frequently heavy, rather unrefreshing, soggy-flavoured wines (from overripe, rot-affected grapes) which rapidly lost their fruit. Some rare examples may turn out to be wonderful, but they aren't ready yet.

BEAUJOLAIS

Beaujolais is rather like the little girl in the nursery rhyme, a wine that swings between the extremes of very good and horrid. When it is good, there is nothing better. It is redolent of ripe plummy fruit and full of beguiling drinkability, a wine with instant appeal. But when it is bad, it epitomizes the worst in wine-making: thin, acidic and dilute, confected and overchaptalized. Too little of the former and too much of the latter has caused a certain disenchantment with Beaujolais, particularly in its Nouveau form, and sales have fallen.

Generally Beaujolais-Villages offers more satisfying flavours, with more fruit and richness, while the *crus* provide wines with longer staying power, especially from Moulin-à-Vent, Chénas and Morgon. The producers of Morgon have introduced what they call Morgon Age, by which the wine must remain in the cellar for 18 months before sale, and the wine is labelled accordingly. Wines like this begin to acquire some of the vegetal flavours of Pinot Noir from the Côte d'Or. The inhabitants of Beaujolais would say that *'il pinotte'*.

Some of the *crus* are better known than others. Côte de Brouilly deserves to be thought of as more than just an adjunct to plain Brouilly, for the vineyards are quite different and the flavours more concentrated. Chénas, the tiniest of the ten *crus*, is rather overshadowed by its more prestigious neighbour, Moulin-à-Vent. St-Amour owes its popularity to its name, as does Fleurie, while Juliénas is underrated. Regnié, in retrospect, has suffered from its elevation to *cru* status, for instead of being at the top of the hierarchy of Beaujolais-Villages, it is now at the bottom of the pecking order *crus*, and prices have dropped accordingly.

Pièces at any price?

The Beaujolais market has gone through a period of volatility. After crazy price rises at the end of the 1980s, prices plummeted sharply with the 1991 and 1992 vintages. The *négociants*, who account for 85 per cent of all Beaujolais sales, were reluctant to buy the 1992s. Consequently the growers, who had wine in their cellars and the prospect of nowhere to stock the next vintage, panicked and dropped their prices. Some 1991s were sold for as little as FF1100 per *pièce* of 216 litres, when the cost price per *pièce* is generally considered to be about FF1800. The sharp drop in prices certainly had the effect of encouraging sales, so that stock moved, with the result that the prices of the 1993s have gently risen.

A price bracket of between FF2050 and FF2450 per *pièce*, which was instigated by the Union Interprofessionelle des Vins de Beaujolais to prevent prices from falling too low, is now preventing prices from rising too high. Most growers consider FF10 a litre to be a suitable return for their labours and reasonable people are hoping for an element of stability in the market, but this is always difficult to achieve with a fluctuating agricultural crop. The yield for 1993 was 100,000 hectolitres less than 1992, but that was probably no bad thing. Nonetheless, Beaujolais is not a cheap wine to produce. The stubby goblet-trained vines make mechanization in the vineyards very difficult and the grapes must be hand-picked in order to conform to *appellation* regulations.

If a wine is expensive to produce there is no point in making it badly. The *Chartre de Qualité,* instigated in 1991, is dismissed by all reputable producers as merely stating what they already do. It was seen as a way of reminding their more careless colleagues how to make wine properly and to encourage them to tighten up on some of the basics that were in danger of being overlooked. So it was not exactly revolutionary and in any case was never binding. But whether as a result of the charter or not, there has been some investment in new equipment, with tighter control of fermentation temperatures; greater care is also being taken with the maceration of the grapes, and this is being done in shallower vats which allow for a higher ratio of grapes to juice. More attention is being paid to work in the vineyard, with less use of fertilizers and tighter control of yields. You still see large old barrels (used simply for storage, rather than for imparting any oak flavour to the wine), but there is nothing wrong with these if they are well-maintained. In contrast the occasional new barrique does nothing more than deform the intrinsic flavour of Beaujolais.

The region still has to look to its laurels. For years, by concentrating on one grape variety, one basic style and a good marketing policy, it led the field in the easy-drinking-reds stakes. Now competition is likely to do more for quality in Beaujolais than any number of charters – and that competition is coming not just from the New World but also from its own doorstep, the Midi, which is increasingly making the sort of flavoursome, juicy wines that Beaujolais used to do so well.   ROSEMARY GEORGE MW

GRAPES & FLAVOURS

CHARDONNAY Chardonnay does make some white Beaujolais, and it's usually quite good. Grown in the North, it has a stony dryness closer in style to Chablis. In the South it is much nearer to the fatter, softer, wines of southern Burgundy.

GAMAY The Gamay grape produces pretty dull or tart stuff in most places. But somehow, on these granite slopes, it has the ability to give one of the juiciest, most gulpable, gurgling wines the world has to offer. The Gamay has no pretensions. Ideally Beaujolais is simple, cherry-sharp, with candy-like fruit, sometimes with hints of raspberry or strawberry. The wines from the *crus* go further, but in the main the similarity they share through the Gamay grape is more important than the differences in the places they come from. All but the wines of the top villages should be drunk as young as you can find them, although years like 1988, 1989 and 1991 produced wines at *cru* levels that are now aging well. The *cru* wines from 1993 will also repay some keeping.

BEAUJOLAIS, AC This covers *all* the basic wines, the produce of the flatter, southern part of Beaujolais, stretching down towards Lyon. Most of the best is now sold as Nouveau. Run-of-the-mill Beaujolais, apart from Nouveau, is likely to be pretty thin stuff, or beefed up illegally with something altogether different. In fact, since you're allowed to re-label Nouveau as 'Beaujolais', some of the best wine in the new year (much appreciated by those who scoff at Nouveau) will be none other than re-labelled Nouveau. Good producers include *Blaise, Carron, Charmet, Château de la Plume,* co-op at *Bully, Duboeuf Bouteille Cristal, Garlon, Labruyère, Loron, Pierre-Marie Chermette* of the *Domaine des Vissoux.*

BEAUJOLAIS BLANC, AC To be honest, Beaujolais Blanc is usually quite expensive and in its rather firm, stony-dry way is rarely as enjoyable as a good Mâcon-Villages. Most of the examples we see come from the North, often bordering on St-Véran in the Mâconnais, so despite being rather closed in, you expect it to blossom sometimes – but it doesn't. I'd plant Gamay instead if I were them. *Charmet* is the most interesting producer, but his vineyards are in the South. *Tête* is good.

BEAUJOLAIS ROSÉ, AC I never thought I'd waste space on this apology for a wine until I tasted an absolute stunner from *M Bernard* of Leynes: it was one of the best pinks I'd had all year. The co-op at *Bois d'Oingt* has also shown that it can make exciting Beaujolais rosé. But it's usually too expensive.

BEAUJOLAIS NOUVEAU (or **PRIMEUR**), **AC** The new vintage wine of Beaujolais, released in the same year as the grapes are gathered, at midnight on the third Wednesday in November. It is usually the best of the simple wine, and will normally improve for several months in bottle, but in good Nouveau vintages like 1989 and 1991 it can improve for years. I always keep a bottle or two to fool my wine-buff friends – and it always does: they're usually in the Côte de Beaune at about £12 a bottle. I'm sniggering in the kitchen.

BEAUJOLAIS SUPÉRIEUR, AC *Supérieur* means that the basic alcoholic degree is higher. It doesn't ensure a better wine, and is in any case rarely even seen on the label.

BEAUJOLAIS-VILLAGES, AC Thirty-five villages can use this title. They're mostly in the north of the region and reckoned to make better than average wines, with some justification because there are quite major soil differences that account for the demarcation of Beaujolais and Beaujolais-Villages. The wines are certainly better than basic Beaujolais, a little fuller and deeper, and the cherry-sharp fruit of the Gamay is usually more marked. However, look for a wine bottled in the region, and preferably from a single vineyard, because an anonymous blend of

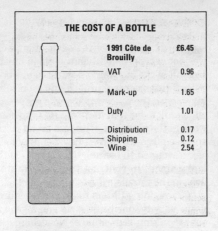

THE COST OF A BOTTLE

	1991 Côte de Brouilly	£6.45
	VAT	0.96
	Mark-up	1.65
	Duty	1.01
	Distribution	0.17
	Shipping	0.12
	Wine	2.54

Beaujolais-Villages may simply mean a heftier version of an ordinary Beaujolais. *Noël Aucoeur, Domaine de la Brasse, Domaine de la Chapelle de Vatre (Sarrau), Jacques Dépagneux, de Flammerécourt, Château Gaillard, Gutty Père et Fils, André Large, Château des Loges, Jean-Charles Pivot, Jean-Luc Tissier, Trichard* and *Château des Vergers* are good and local, but most domaines are bottled by one of the merchants in the region. Labelling by the domaine is on the increase.

BROUILLY, AC Southernmost and largest of the Beaujolais *crus*, Brouilly has the flattest of the *cru* vineyards, and usually makes one of the lightest *cru* wines. There is some variation in style between the more northerly villages and those in the South where granite produces a deeper, fuller wine, but in general Brouilly rarely improves much with keeping. In fact, it makes a very good Nouveau. A few properties make a bigger wine to age – but even then, nine months to a year is quite enough. Good names include *Château de la Chaize, Domaine Crêt des Garanches, Château de Fouilloux, Hospices de Belleville, Château de Pierreux, Domaine de Combillaty (Duboeuf), Domaine de Garanches, André Large, Château de Nevers. Château des Tours*, although lovely young, can age longer.

CHÉNAS, AC This second-smallest *cru* makes strong, dark wines, sometimes a bit tough, that can be drunk a year after the harvest, or aged to take on a Pinot Noir-like flavour. Exceedingly fashionable in France. Look out for the wines of *Louis Champagnon, Charvet, Château de Chénas, Domaines des Brureaux, Domaine Chassignon, Domaine de la Combe Remont (Duboeuf), Pierre Perrachon, Emile Robin*.

CHIROUBLES, AC Another *cru* for early drinking, grown on hillsides towards the southern end of the Beaujolais *crus*. The wines are naturally light, similar to Beaujolais-Villages in weight, but with a perfumed, cherry scent that makes this France's favourite Beaujolais *cru*. Good names include *Georges Boulon, René Brouillard, Cheysson, Château Javernand, Château de Raousset, Jean-Pierre Desvignes, Duboeuf, Méziat* and *Georges Passot*.

CÔTE DE BROUILLY, AC The Mont de Brouilly, a pyramid-shaped hill in the middle of the *cru* of Brouilly, makes quite different wine to Brouilly itself. The soil is of volcanic origin, and the slopes lap up the sun. Best: *Château Thivin, Conroy, Domaine de la Pierre Bleue, Jean Sanvers, Lucien Verger, Chanrion*.

CRU The ten *crus* or growths (Fleurie, Moulin-à-Vent, Brouilly, Chénas, Côte de Brouilly, Chiroubles, Juliénas, St-Amour, Morgon, Regnié) are the top villages in the steeply hilly, northern part of Beaujolais. All *should* have definable characteristics, but the produce of different vineyards and growers is all too often blended to a mean by merchants elsewhere. Always buy either a single estate wine, or one from a good local merchant like *Chanut Frères, Duboeuf, Dépagneux, Ferraud, Loron, Sarrau, Thomas la Chevalière, Louis Tête, Trenel*.

FLEURIE, AC Often the most delicious of the *crus*, gentle and round, its sweet cherry-and-chocolate fruit just held firm by a touch of tannin and acid. Very popular in Britain and the US, and often too pricey. Try *Château de Fleurie (Loron), Chauvet, Chignard, Colonge, Domaine de la Grand, Grand Pré (Sarrau), Domaine de la Presle, Domaine des Quatre Vents, Duboeuf*'s *la Madone, Bernard Paul, Verpoix*, the *Fleurie* co-op's *cuvées, Cuvée Presidente Marguerite* and *Cuvée Cardinale*.

JULIÉNAS, AC Juliénas *can* be big wine, with tannin and acidity, but many of the best more closely resemble the mixture of fresh red fruit and soft, chocolaty warmth that makes for good Fleurie. Good ones include *Château du Bois de la Salle, Domaine des Bucherats, Château des Capitans, Château de Juliénas, Domaine de la Dîme* and *Domaine de la Vieille Eglise*. Also good: *Pelletier* and *Duboeuf*.

MORGON, AC The wines of this *cru* can be glorious. They can start thick and dark, and age to a chocolaty, plummy depth with an amazing cherries smell. Morgon Age has to be kept for at least 18 months before release. *Jacky Janodet* is intense. Look also for *Aucoeur, Château de Pizay, Château de Raousset, Descombes, Desvignes, Domaine de la Chanaise, Domaine Roche St Jean, Dom. de Ruyère, Drouhin, Gobet, Lapierre, Félix Longepierre* and *Georges Vincent*.

MOULIN-À-VENT, AC Enter the heavy brigade. These *cru* wines should be solid, and should age for three to five years and more from years like 1985 and '91. The best have a big, plummy, Burgundian style, and their toughness doesn't give you much option but to wait. It rarely resembles anyone's view of straight Beaujolais – it takes itself far too seriously – but quite a few of the 1991s are already very good. *Louis Champagnon*'s is good, as is *Brugne*,

The price guides for this section begin on page 319.

Charvet, Château des Jacques, Château du Moulin-à-Vent, Château Portier, Domaine de la Tour de Bief, Jacky Janodet, Raymond Siffert and *Héritiers Maillard* (formerly *Héritiers Tagent*). *Georges Duboeuf* is experimenting with new oak barrel-aging.

REGNIÉ, AC Since the 1988 vintage, Beaujolais' tenth *cru*. Makes wine quite similar to Brouilly in ripe vintages but a bit weedy when the sun doesn't shine. *Duboeuf Bouteille Cristal* the best so far.

ST-AMOUR, AC Among the most perfect Beaujolais, this pink-red wine from one of the least spoilt villages usually has freshness and peachy perfume and good, ripe fruit all at once. It isn't that common here (though the French love it), and yet it is frequently the most reliable and most enjoyable *cru*. Sadly, the news has leaked out and prices are leaping up. Look out for *Château de St-Amour, Domaine des Billards (Loron), Buis, Domaine des Ducs, Domaine du Paradis, André Poitevin, Francis Saillant, Paul Spay*.

BEAUJOLAIS VINTAGES

With Beaujolais the rule is, drink it as young as possible. Only the top wines from the best villages will benefit much from aging, although Nouveau may improve with a month or two's rest.

1993 Most of France suffered from rain at the vintage and Beaujolais was no exception. However, August had been hot, so most of the grapes were ripe and picked before the heavens really opened on 20 September. Nevertheless, the crop was 100,000hl smaller than 1992, the result of spasmodic hailstorms during the summer. There are some good wines among the *crus.*

1992 An above-average crop of below-average wines. Late rains and high yields combined to produce thin, light wines. Moulin-à-Vent and St-Amour suffered hail damage. There are some decent wines to be found, but only from quality-conscious producers.

1991 Unlike most of France, Beaujolais had an excellent year in 1991. Largely spared the April frosts, the grapes were ripe two weeks before the cold wet weather which set in in late September. Beaujolais from the 1991 vintage has good colour and relatively high tannin levels.

1990 Yet another corker of a vintage – very good quality and plenty of it. The harvest yielded very fruity, typical Beaujolais with rich Gamay character. Easy-drinking but full flavours reach right across the board, with the ordinary Beaujolais, the Villages and all of the *crus* emerging well.

1989 Along with other vineyard areas of France, and indeed Europe, the 1989 vintage in Beaujolais was one of the earliest ever. The heat meant that colour was unusually deep, but the aromas were also much more pungently fruity than expected after such a summer. But this was the year higher prices really started to bite. In terms of value for money, less well-known *cru* names like Chénas and Côte de Brouilly were worth a try.

1988 There's no doubt that 1988 was an exceptional year in Beaujolais. There is a marvellous quality of luscious, clear, ripe fruit about the best wines. Even the Nouveaus were terrific. I remember a string of delicious Beaujolais-Villages. And some really delightful St-Amour and Brouilly. Pressure on supply meant overproduction in some quarters. Even so the best are now getting their second wind.

1985 No vintage has ever given so much sheer pleasure as 1985 with its riot of fruit and spice. Some of the wines are still excellent – but they've grown up, become serious. Many will be enjoyable, but the days when they made you dance with delight are over.

CHAMPAGNE

The Champenois have now completed the revolution on which they embarked four years ago, a series of dramatic changes whose benefits will continue to echo for decades. What is more they are now prepared to talk about Before and After, and admit to previously unmentionable practices, like buying ready-made bottles of wine *sur lattes* (that, is wine that has completed the second fermentation but has not yet been disgorged and is being aged in bottle), using the *tailles* (the coarsest wine from the final, hardest pressing of the grapes) using Pinot Meunier (a grape often publicly decried for its quality, but much used just the same), and using grapes from unfashionable communes. Glasnost, perestroika, the lot, summed up in an unprecedented insistence on the fact that Champagne ought to be a fine wine which sparkles, not just fashionable fizz.

The revolution came about through the Champenois' arrogance, expressed in a combination of ever-rising prices and increasingly unreliable quality. This had allowed the competition to flourish: what made matters worse, many of the best rivals came from the New World and carried the names of some of Champagne's best firms, like Deutz, Roederer and so on.

Today virtually all the *grande marques* – itself a term which is being redefined – are making wines which have their own style. And although there are still a lot of ultra-cheapos (what the the French call *premier prix* Champagnes) on the market, the supply is slowly drying up as the results of the revolution trickle through – but it is bound to be a long process given Champagne's time cycle.

The first, and what will be seen by historians as the crucial step, the storming of the Bastille as it were, came in 1990 when the famous 'contract' was broken. This was a relic of the bad old days before the war when the Champagne firms performed a crucial social role in guaranteeing a minimum price for then largely unwanted grapes. But by the 1980s growers had the upper hand: prices had risen, and, far more importantly, buyers had to take what they were given under an allotment system heavily skewed against those houses wanting to maintain quality and in favour of those looking for expansion.

Cheaper and better

Once the market had been opened, market forces came into play, and the Great Slump of the early 1990s gave the houses their chance. Since then, not only have grape prices fallen dramatically, from a maximum of FF32 in 1990 to FF20 three years later, but the firms can now, and not before time, impose ever-increasing quality standards.

As dutiful readers of *Webster's* will recall, these new improved standards cover every aspect of winemaking: yields have been reduced so that fewer grapes may be picked from a hectare of vines (down to 8500 kilos in 1993); less juice may be pressed from a kilo of grapes, because of the suppression of the third pressing, the *deuxième taille* which furnished the juice for the acid ultra-cheapos, and less wine may be made from a given quantity of juice. There is also a small increase in the maturation period, from a year to 15 months – this latter is the only step which still needs taking further. Harvest dates are more precisely controlled than they were, and there has been a considerable tightening-up in the quality and the modernity of the presses.

The revolution has even forced the Champagne nobility to rethink the qualifications for admittance to their ranks. Pressured by the launch of Bollinger's Charter of Quality, the Syndicat des Grandes Marques was forced to change its rules, so that only firms following far stricter criteria than those legally required will be allowed to continue in the club (the biggest groups have led the way by allowing some of their secondary brands, like Mercier and Canard-Duchêne, to be thrown out). These same groups have also drawn back from their previously over-lavish use of their names on the sparklers they make outside Champagne – whose quality, not coincidentally, shows their mastery of the process.

Champagne for sale

It is worth dwelling on these changes to show just how far-reaching they are. But only because the Champagne houses now want them to be: they would merely have been hollow legal requirements had not the majority of large firms seized on them to tighten up quality, and show, sometimes for the first time in a generation, just how different one house is from another. And it was only in the course of a week spent questioning the technical directors of 14 major firms that I realized that every house follows a different path at every stage; and even when two firms are supposedly doing the same thing, they are often doing it in different ways – Billecart-Salmon's definition of 'cool fermentation', for instance, is at least 3°C below anyone else's.

At the macro-economic level, the changes are already showing in a recovery in sales throughout the world, especially in Britain, and supply is now being roughly equated with demand. But, at a micro-level, the economic problems have hit – as they so often do – just as the recovery is under way. There were strikes, riots, sit-ins, lock-ups, the whole caboodle, when the Moët & Chandon group declared redundancies, which could have been effected peacefully a few years earlier. As a result there have been great upheavals: the bosses of Moët and Veuve-Clicquot have been changed and Moët is headed, for the first time in its history, by an outsider. Smaller firms are suffering from the ill-effects of holding too much stock in times of high interest rates. Roederer, the most profitable company in Champagne, rescued the fine family firm of Deutz, Gosset was taken over by a family from Cognac, and rumours are swirling round other small family concerns. But, so far, the new buyers are cherishing the image of the enterprises they have bought. NICHOLAS FAITH

MATURITY CHART
1988 Champagne
A surperb vintage which will repay keeping

| Bottled | Disgorged | | Ready | | Peak | | | Tiring | In decline |

0 1 2 3 4 5 6 7 8 9 10 11 12 13 14 15 16 17 18 years

GRACES & FLAVOURS

GRAPES & FLAVOURS

CHARDONNAY The grape of white Burgundy fame here tends to produce a lighter, fresher juice, and the resulting Champagnes are certainly the most perfumed and honeyed. They have been criticized for lacking depth and aging potential. Not true. Good Blancs de Blancs have a superb, exciting flavour that is improved by aging, especially those from the southern end of the Côte des Blancs.

PINOT NOIR The grape that makes all the finest red Burgundies also makes white Champagne. Pinot Noir has enough difficulty in ripening in Burgundy, and further north in Champagne it almost never attains any great depth and strength of colour or alcohol, which is fair enough since the general idea here is to produce a *white* wine. Very careful pressing of the grapes in traditional vertical presses is the best way to draw off the juice with as little colour as possible, and the rest of the reddish tinge generally precipitates out naturally during fermentation. Even so, the juice does feel quite big: a Champagne relying largely on Pinot Noir is certain to be heavier and take longer to mature.

PINOT MEUNIER The other black grape, making a softer, fruitier style of wine, important for producing easy wines for drinking young, and crucial for toning down the assertive flavours of Pinot Noir.

WINES & WINE STYLES

BLANC DE BLANCS Champagne made exclusively from Chardonnay. Has become increasingly fashionable as drinkers look for a lighter style of wine. Should not only be fresh but creamy and bright as well. Some firms, notably *Billecart-Salmon, Henriot, Pol Roger* and *Roederer* make excellent NV Blanc de Blancs, and the *Union Co-operative* at Avize makes the best of its position at the heart of the Côte des Blancs. A handful of firms sell vintage Blanc de Blancs (watch out for *Pol Roger*'s '86) and a couple also make luxury *cuvées* purely from Chardonnay. Historically, *Taittinger*'s Comtes de Champagne was the benchmark but it is now being challenged by the delightful *Dom Ruinart*.

BLANC DE NOIRS This white style is made from black grapes only and is common throughout the Marne Valley. Few have the quality and longevity of *Bollinger*'s *Vieilles Vignes*, but none are even half as expensive. Most are rather solid. *Pierre Vaudon* is an exception, elegant and well-balanced; *Barancourt* is more expensive, and beefy; *H Billiot* is fine.

BRUT Very dry.

BUYER'S OWN BRAND (BOB) A wine blended to a buyer's specification, or more probably, to a price limit. The grapes are of lesser quality, the wines usually younger, and cheaper. *Maison Royale (Victoria Wine), Sainsbury, Tesco, Waitrose* are all pretty consistent, *M&S* less so but can be the best of all.

CM In the small print on the label, this means *co-opérative-manipulant* and shows that the wine comes from a co-operative, whatever the brand name implies.

COTEAUX CHAMPENOIS Still wines, red or white. Overpriced and generally rather acid. A village name, such as Cramant (white) or Bouzy (red) may appear. *Alain Vesselle*'s Bouzy is one of the few exciting reds.

The price guides for this section begin on page 322.

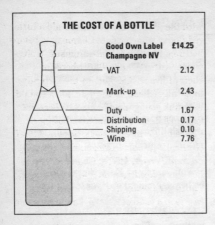

THE COST OF A BOTTLE

Good Own Label Champagne NV	£14.25
VAT	2.12
Mark-up	2.43
Duty	1.67
Distribution	0.17
Shipping	0.10
Wine	7.76

CRÉMANT Until recently used for fizz with half the pressure of normal Champagne. The best was *Mumm's* uniquely creamy *Crémant de Cramant*. The Champenois have now had to abandon the description as part of a deal which gave them the monopoly of the term 'méthode Champenoise'. And *Mumm's* delight has been flatly renamed *Mumm de Cramant*.

DE LUXE/CUVÉE DE PRESTIGE/ CUVÉE DE LUXE A special highly prized blend, mostly vintage. Some great wines and some gaudy coat-trailers. Most are in silly bottles, and overpriced, but a few do deliver. In general drunk *far* too young. Most need a good ten years to shine. Best: *Bollinger RD, Dom Pérignon, Dom Ruinart, Krug Grande Cuvée, Laurent Perrier Grand Siècle, Pol Roger Cuvée Sir Winston Churchill, Roederer Cristal, Taittinger Comtes de Champagne, Cuvée NF Billecart, Cattier Clos du Moulin, Philipponnat Clos des Goisses, Perrier-Jouët Belle Epoque*.

DEMI-SEC Medium sweet. Rarely very nice, but *Louis Roederer* is outstanding, and *Mercier* is surprisingly fresh and floral.

DOUX Sweet. *Louis Roederer* is excellent.

EXTRA DRY Confusingly, this is less dry than 'Brut', but drier than 'Sec'.

GRANDE MARQUE Ambiguous term meaning 'great brand'. It was a self-styled group of 28 houses, including the 15 or so best known (recently replaced by the new Club des Grandes Marques, which has fewer members). The term *should* be synonymous with quality – better grapes, older reserve wines and more rigid selection. It wasn't, but *should* be in future.

NM In the code on the label, this means *négociant-manipulant* (merchant-handler) and should show that the wine was bottle-fermented by the house on the label.

NON-DOSAGE Most Champagne has a little sweetness – a 'dosage' – added just before the final cork. A few are sold bone-dry and will have names like Brut Zero. Best are *Laurent Perrier, Piper-Heidsieck*. Designed to show that it's the wine, not the dosage that provides the quality.

NON-VINTAGE The basic non-vintage wine is the one by which a producer should be judged. Until the early 1990s many firms were not making a wine of any consistent quality, let alone a recognizable house style. But now they are. The wines are generally based on a single vintage and usually aged for three years. But many of them provide a greater depth and age and ensure consistent quality by using up to 40 per cent of *vins de reserve*, still wines kept back from previous vintages, and a few (notably *Laurent Perrier*) reduce their output of single-vintage wines to ensure that their non-vintage contains some of their best. Apart from *Laurent Perrier*, the best of the bunch, running from light to vinous are *Billecart-Salmon, Pol Roger, Perrier-Jouet, Charles Heidsieck* (now a benchmark for the standard brands), *Louis Roederer,* and, worth the extra couple of quid, *Bollinger*. They all, especially the lighter wines, benefit from a few extra months in bottle after purchase even though most firms allow wine destined for Britain an additional six months in bottle.

RC A new designation indicating *récoltant-co-opérateur* – for a grower selling wine produced at a co-op. It should stop growers pretending they've made it themselves.

RECENTLY DISGORGED A term used for Champagnes that have been left in the cellars, drawing flavour from their yeast deposits, for much longer than usual before disgorging. The wines can happily rest for 20 to 30 years on the lees but are usually released after seven to ten years. *Bollinger RD* is the most famous; wines also from *Deutz, Alfred Gratien* and *Laurent Perrier*.

RICH The sweetest Champagne.

RM Means that the wine comes from a single grower, a *récoltant-manipulant*, literally 'harvester-handler'. RM indicates that he has made his Champagne himself, rather than taking it to the local co-op. Best: *Bara, Beerens, Billiot, Bonnaire, Brice, Cattier, Clouet, Fliniaux, Michel Gonet, André Jacquart, Lassalle, Albert Lebrun, Leclerc-Briant, Legras, Vesselle, Vilmart*.

ROSÉ Traditionally, the pink colour is gained by a short, careful maceration of the black Pinot Noir and Pinot Meunier skins with the juice. Other producers add a little red Bouzy wine to white Champagne before bottling. Ideally rosés are aromatic, fruity wines, with a delicious strawberry or cherry flavour. Sadly, many are virtually indistinguishable from white. Most should be drunk young. Best producers: *Besserat de Bellefon, Billecart-Salmon, Bollinger, Charbaut Certificate, Dom Ruinart, Alfred Gratien, Jacquart la Renommée, Lassalle, Laurent Perrier, Moët et Chandon, Louise Pommery, Roederer* and *Roedererer Cristal, Taittinger Comtes de Champagne. Krug rosé* is in a class of its own, and so it should be at the price.

SEC Literally 'dry', but any Champagne so labelled will actually be medium dry.

SR Société de Récoltants. Label code for a family company of growers.

VINTAGE Wine of a single, good year, generally fuller than non-vintage, but almost always nowadays released too young. Best: *Billecart-Salmon, Bollinger, Gosset Grande Millésime, Alfred Gratien, Henriot, Krug, Bruno Paillard, Joseph Perrier, Perrier-Jouët, Pol Roger, Louis Roederer, Ruinart, Veuve Clicquot*.

CLASSIFICATIONS

The classification system in Champagne is based on vineyards. The approved areas for vineyards are strictly demarcated and the vineyard land graded according to suitability for black and white grapes, going from 100 per cent for the finest Grand Cru villages through 90–99 per cent for the 41 Premier Cru villages and on to 80 per cent for the least favoured.

If the guideline price is 20 francs per kilo of grapes, a 100 per cent village grower receives the full 20 francs. An 80 per cent grower will receive only 80 per cent – 16 francs – and so on, it's all quite simple. The whole system is now less rigorous than it was 50 years ago, when percentages ranged from 50 to 100.

Champagne houses boast about how high their 'average percentage' of grapes is. Some Champagne labels will say either '100 per cent Grand Cru' or 'Premier Cru' and even a village name as well, Avize, for example, if the wine comes entirely from one single top village.

Hardly surprisingly, no one ever bothers to declare on the label percentages in the 80s or lower 90s, but in actual fact many of the best value Champagnes on the UK market come from these so-called 'lowly' villages. There is no reason why careful vineyard managment and vinification should not produce good results.

CHAMPAGNE HOUSE PROFILES

BILLECART-SALMON ★★★★(★)
Terrifically elegant Champagne from a
family-owned house. Very refined, delicate
wines and a lovely rosé. Its vintage, Cuvée
NF Billecart, is also excellent.

BOLLINGER ★★★★ Like Krug, makes
'English-style' Champagnes: warm, rich
and oaky. For a time its reputation was
marred because the wines were released
too young, but it's now back on song. RD,
for Récemment Dégorgé, its luxury *cuvée*,
is kept on its lees until just before sale.
Also Vieilles Vignes. Bollinger has been at
the centre of the latest reforms.

ALFRED GRATIEN ★★★★ Serious, oak-
fermented wine at a much lower price than
Krug. Very long-lived vintage.

KRUG ★★★★★ The classic heavy, serious
Champagne. Grande Cuvée, oak-fermented
is outstandingly good, and weightier than
any competitor. Expensive rosé has an
incomparable Pinot Noir cherry-fruitiness.
Even more expensive Clos de Mesnil is a
delicate, single vineyard Blanc de Blancs.

LANSON ★★(★) Until recently had (well-
deserved) reputation for excessive acidity.
New ownership is not finding life easy and
future quality is uncertain. Classic, long-
maturing vintage.

LAURENT PERRIER ★★★★ One of the
most reliable of all the non-vintage blends.
Excellent, reasonably-priced rosé. Prestige
brand Grand Siècle is (sensibly) blend of
several vintages. Good value.

MOËT & CHANDON ★★(★) Brut
Imperial infuriatingly unreliable –
sometimes as good as any NV, at other
times tasting bland and characterless.
Vintages usually show well but are
released too young.

MUMM ★(★) Traditionally rich wine (I'm
told), but all too frequently unimpressive.
Delicate, creamy Mumm de Cramant. You
can't help wishing its class would rub off on
the NV and vintage.

PERRIER-JOUËT ★★★Back making
light, classic Champagne. Best known for
Belle Époque in a pretty bottle, all flowery
elegance, echoed in fresh, slightly unripe-
cherry feel of the wine.

POL ROGER ★★★★ Model family firm,
producer of Churchill's favourite fizz.
Delicious, delicate Blanc de Blancs. NV,
vintage and Cuvée Sir Winston Churchill
all top class. New are vintage Blanc de
Chardonnay, vintage rosé and a Demi-sec.

POMMERY ★★(★) A curious wine. At its
best it can have a light, flowery elegance.
But it can also be inexplicably bland.

LOUIS ROEDERER ★★★★(★) Most
famous for Cristal, invented for sweet
toothed Russian Tsars. Now the most
natural of all the prestige *cuvées*, reflecting
the quality of each vintage. Cristal is made
(in small quantities) even in theoretically
bad years – like 1974 and 1977 – when its
almost vegetal sweetness comes through.
NV usually one of the best despite needing
more age. Good Demi-sec and Doux.

TAITTINGER ★★★(★) Splendidly light,
modern, Chardonnayish style, carried
through in its model Blanc de Blancs,
Comtes de Champagne.

VEUVE CLICQUOT ★★★ For a century
and a half greatly loved by the British. The
NV can still have the rich, warm style first
made famous by the formidable Madame
Veuve Clicquot-Ponsardin. Prestige *cuvée*
La Grande Dame almost chocolate-rich –
its 1985 was a classic.

CHAMPAGNE VINTAGES

In theory Champagne firms only make single-vintage wines in especially fine years. But only a few firms, like Bollinger and Laurent-Perrier, follow the theory. At the other extreme comes Roederer which controls its own supply of grapes so totally that by means of ultra-careful selection it is able to release its de luxe vintage Cristal (albeit in tiny quantities) even in generally disastrous years like 1974 and 1977. Other firms are liable to fall into two traps: either opting too readily for vintage wines in marginal years or, increasingly common, releasing wines after only five years in bottle, which may be okay for French tastes but leaves the average Brit with an acid stomach. Nevertheless, even firms like Moët, whose non-vintage is variable, generally come up with a decent vintage – although the current crop of 1988s badly needs an extra couple of years in bottle before being drunk.

1993 After an excellent summer – despite some local hailstorms in May – the skies opened in September and the result was, inevitably, some dilution of the quality of the juice. And if the yield had not been restricted, the 29,000 hectares of grapes, a total increased by 5000 hectares in the previous ten years, would have produced enough wine to fill over 400 million bottles, nearly twice the current worldwide demand. And the quality? Probably not outstanding.

1992 One of the largest harvests of all time. Decent, but no more, with some problems of rot.

1991 Another large crop, and one better for stiffening the non-vintage than for single-vintage wines.

1990 The late sunshine produced a record crop. Most Champenois are likely to offer vintage Champagnes, many of them superb, although because grapes reached record prices that year the wines are likely to be expensive.

1989 Like 1988, the wines from Champagne echo the qualities, above all the richness, found in other regions. A vintage year with wines which could be ready after a mere five years, like the '82s of blessed memory.

1988 A classic year, marked by a harvest which began on 19th September, well before the usual date. The wines have bite, backbone and fruit, but will be drunk too young. Try and buck the trend and put some aside for a few more years.

1987 A lot of wine, but even the Champenois are not enthusiastic about its quality. Only Pommery declared a vintage. Why, we ask ourselves?

1986 Useful wines, despite some rot. They would have made a decent, if slightly hard vintage, but got sold far too young.

1985 An *annus mirabilis*. Very heavy frosts in January – down to –25°C in the Aube – blighted some of the vineyard area, but, as is so often the result, the final wines were fine, very typical, without any of the hardness associated with some vintages. Buy when you can get them.

1984 Oh dear: a year when the *grandes marques* had to dig deep into the *vins de reserve* to maintain the quality of their non-vintage wines. Not all succeeded.

1983 The second of the record-breaking vintages which stopped all talk of a Champagne drought and which was much drunk in its day by that now virtually extinct breed, the yuppy. Still high-grade, if a little lean, which is more than could ever have been said for yuppies.

1982 A year when Nature was generous, allowing Champagne to make luscious wines which were virtually all ready within five years but are still on song – if you can get them.

RHÔNE

The first surprise, I suppose, is that good white wines should be grown here at all. It's so uncompromisingly hot and dry, so relentlessly sunbaked and, by the end of summer, so bleached, with the only colour coming from the red tiles of the roofs, the struggling green of the vines and the blue-white of the sky, that it bears little resemblance to the more classic white wine landscapes of Europe. Think of the gentle, mellow Côte d'Or, the calm, turretted Loire or even Germany, with its precipitous slopes and cloudy skies. None of them are remotely like the Rhône Valley.

But then the most typical vineyard landscape in Australia would feature grass browned to the colour (and texture) of old shoe leather surrounding a patch of emerald vines – and those vines, as likely as not, produce whites as crisp and fresh as are to be found anywhere. In fact, they may even be Viognier, because the fame of the Rhône Valley's most distinctive white grape is spreading beyond its borders. There's a fair bit in California, as well. What was once a local curiosity is becoming an international jet-setter.

Planting mania

Viognier used to be the Rhône's great rarity. A bottle of it, from Condrieu, will cost you £20 or so, and you'd better drink it within two or three years, before its apricot and acacia fruit fades. In 1965 there were just eight hectares of Viognier planted in Condrieu out of a possible total of 100 ha; now there are 80 ha, 3.7 of which have recently been sold to top grower Marcel Guigal. (The other 100 per cent Viognier AC, Château Grillet, has just three hectares of vines – and isn't as good.) They consist of terraces that climb the hill behind the town; they overlook a broad bend of the Rhône, and most of them were planted in the late eighties. That means that most of the vines are young – indeed, not all are even in full production yet – but don't expect the price of Condrieu to tumble to affordable heights just because there's going to be more of it about. Yields are low: the law says 37 hl/ha is the maximum, though that went up from 32hk/ha in 1987. Moves have been made to make the working of umpteen tiny, terraced plots easier, by jointly-funded helicopters for spraying, but production costs are still pretty high. And presumably the growers feel they have as much right to a reasonable living as anybody else.

They're enjoying their new success. They're celebrating it with experimentation: sweet Viognier, oak-aged Viognier, you name it. Sweet (or at least semi-sweet) Viognier in fact harks back to the past: it often used to be made this way (from overripe grapes, and a few botrytised ones if there were any) but it had pretty well died out by the end of the eighties and given way to a steely dryness. Given the fact that many of the young *vignerons* making sweet Condrieu now have never tasted one of the older generation of sweet wines it's difficult to make comparisons, but the modern wines are certainly likely to be fresher, with more involvement of stainless steel.

Oak is another matter. Viognier, unoaked, is one of the most aromatic and opulent grapes around and it's hard to see what new oak does for it except mask the aroma and increase the price. Luckily most of the growers don't seem to be succumbing to the temptation.

However, in a sense it's only when a grape is planted outside its traditional home that one really begins to learn what it tastes like. Viognier is popping up all over the Vaucluse and Gard *départements*: fermented cool for maximum, international-style fruit, these wines have got the flavour, yes. They're often packed with apricots and peaches, and they have the distinct advantage of not requiring a bank loan every time you feel like a bottle. But no, they don't taste like Condrieu. They don't have the same rusticity, the same gutsy earthiness underlying their opulence – though when you're paying double for gutsy earthiness they begin to look rather attractive. They'll get better, too, as the vines get older: already some of the wines that tasted a bit stretched in their early vintages have considerably more depth.

So who's good? The Perrins of Château de Beaucastel took cuttings from Château Grillet, and they sell it as white Côtes du Rhône Coudoulet de Beaucastel. Guy Steinmaier's Côtes du Rhône from Domaine Ste-Anne is better, and Château de St-Esteve, also in Côtes du Rhône, looks promising.

All roads lead to aroma

But Viognier doesn't have to be made as a varietal; it can add aroma to the other white grapes of the southern Rhône, just as it does at Domaine Pélaquié when mixed with Grenache Blanc, Clairette and Bourboulenc. Luc Pélaquié has doubts as to whether Viognier in the South can ever attain the weight of Condrieu, but now that the trend for southern whites up to and including Châteauneuf is for fruit and freshness, the Grenache Blanc (high on alcohol, prone to oxidation and low on aroma) is becoming pushed out of the blends in favour of Bourboulenc, Roussanne and Clairette as well as Viognier.

Roussanne seems to be ahead on points at the moment, with some going into new oak at Beaucastel (which makes a wine with 80 per cent Roussanne and another with 100 per cent, from old vines), Château de la Gardine and Château La Nerthe, all in Châteauneuf. Not that it's an easy grape to handle, since it's prone to both rot and oidium and is difficult to control during fermentation. And white Châteauneuf, even with these improvements, is all too often stronger on technology than it is on concentration of flavour.

The more modern school of Châteauneuf is based on early picking and cold fermentation – 16°C is not unusual – to preserve acidity and freshness. The wines are bottled early and usually forego the malolactic fermentation: again, acidity is the reason.

The traditionalists (and there are good wines in both schools) pick later, ferment at around 20° to 25°C and age the wine for six months or so in oak, either old or new. Châteaux Rayas, Fortia and de Beaucastel, Domaine Pierre André and Clos des Papes are masters of tradition; Château Mont-Rédon and Domaines du Vieux Telegraphe and Font-de-Michelle are modernists. Not surprisingly, the modern versions are steelier and leaner; they can be drunk early or, like the traditional wines, they can be aged. A peculiarity of a white Châteauneuf, and one it shares with white Hermitage, is that it retires into itself for a couple of years after its first youth, and emerges at five or six years old with much more depth and complexity.

That's the ideal, anyway. There's no reason why more white Châteauneuf shouldn't be as good as the best – no reason, that is, apart from lack of will. It's certainly nothing to do with the landscape.   MARGARET RAND

RED WINES

Northern Rhône reds are really the different manifestations of a single grape variety – the Syrah. It is virtually the only red grape grown in the North (and certainly the only one for *appellation contrôlée* wine) and it can range from light, juicy and simple in the more basic St-Joseph and Crozes-Hermitage offerings, to something rich, extravagant and wonderfully challenging in the top wines of Hermitage, Côte-Rôtie and Cornas.

Southern Rhône reds are usually made from a range of grape varieties, none of which, except the Syrah, Mouvèdre and very occasionally the Grenache are able to produce wine of dramatic individuality on its own, and that means basic fruit flavours across the whole area are very similar. These are usually raspberry-strawberry, often attractively spicy, slightly dusty, and sometimes livened up with some blackcurrant sweetness or wild herb dryness. The introduction of carbonic maceration – the Beaujolais-type method of vinification – in the Rhône has meant that many wines, even at the cheapest level, can have a deliciously drinkable fruit; but with a certain uniformity of style.

GRAPES & FLAVOURS

CARIGNAN This grape is much maligned because in the far South it used to, and sometimes still does, produce tough, raw, fruitless wines which form the bulk of France's red contribution to the wine lake. Old vines can produce big, strong but very tasty wines that age well, and the use of carbonic maceration can work wonders.

CINSAUT Delicate, uneven and with low acidity. A pure Cinsaut wine will not age; but when yields are kept low it can add real finesse, as at *Château Rayas*.

COUNOISE Rich, spicy, floral flavours, and highly regarded at *Beaucastel* and *Durieu* in Châteauneuf du Pape. Could be promising.

GRENACHE The most important red grape in the southern Rhône, with loads of alcohol and a gentle, juicy, spicy fruit perked up by a whiff of pepper, ideal for rosés and easy-going reds. But it's not good at flowering successfully.

MOURVÈDRE An old-fashioned, highly flavoured wine, low in alcohol, which doesn't always ripen fully (its base is Bandol, right on the Med). But it has an excellent, rather berryish taste, and a strong whiff of tobacco spice that is making it increasingly popular with the better growers.

SYRAH The northern Rhône is dominated by this one red grape variety. The Syrah makes some of the blackest, most startling, pungent red wine in France, and, although it is grown elsewhere, it is here that it is at its most brilliant. From Hermitage and Cornas, it rasps with tannin and tar and woodsmoke, backed by the deep, ungainly sweetness of black treacle. But give it five or ten years, and those raw fumes will have become sweet, pungent, full of raspberries, brambles and cassis. Syrah is less common than the Grenache in the southern Rhône, but as more is planted, the standard of southern Rhône reds is sure to rise.

VIOGNIER This aromatic white grape can be used as up to 20 per cent of the blend of red Côte-Rôtie to add fragrance, and it really does: Côte-Rôtie made purely of Syrah lacks the haunting beauty of one blended with Viognier.

WINES & WINE REGIONS

CHÂTEAUNEUF-DU-PAPE, AC This can be delicious, deep, dusty red, almost sweet and fat, low in acidity, but kept appetizing by back-room tannin. *Can* be. It can also be fruit-pastilly and pointless, or dark, tough and stringy. Thirteen different red and white grapes are permitted, and the resulting flavour is usually slightly indistinct, varying from one property to another. The occasional 'super-vintage' like 1978 gives wines that can stay stunning for ten years and more. Around one-third of the growers make good wine – and as much as two-thirds of the wine sold probably exceeds the permitted yields. So it makes sense always to go for a domaine wine and certainly not one bottled away from the region. Good, full ones include: *Château de Beaucastel, Château Rayas* and *Clos du Mont-Olivet, Château Fortia, Château St-André, La Nerthe, Chante Cigale, Clos des Papes, Chante-Perdrix, Le Vieux Donjon, la Jacquinotte, Font de Michelle, Font du Loup, Brunel, Quiot, Dom du Grand Tinel, Dom de Mont-Redon, Dom du Vieux Télégraphe, Dom Durieu, Bosquet des Papes, Lucien Gabriel Barrot, Les Clefs d'Or, Fabrice Mouisset, Chapoutier's La Bernadine* and *Henri Bonnot.*

CORNAS, AC Black and tarry tooth-stainers, from the right bank of the Rhône, opposite Valence. Usually rather hefty, jammy even, and lacking some of the fresh fruit that makes Hermitage so remarkable, yet at ten years old this is impressive wine. There have been quite big price rises in recent years, but then quality seems to improve year by year, too. Excellent blockbusters are made by *Auguste Clape, Robert Michel* and *Noël Verset.* It's also worth looking out for *René Balthazar, de Barjac, Colombo* (good 1992 *Domaine des Ruchets), Delas, Juge, Leménicier, Allemand, Maurice Courbis* and *Jean Lionnet* (good 1992 *Cuvée Rochepertuis), Alain Voge.*

COSTIÈRES DE NÎMES, AC The growers here have opted for being in the Rhône, even though the wines are more Languedoc in style: decent rosés and meaty, smoky reds. They're improving: try *Ch La Tuilerie, Dom de l'Amarine, Ch de Campuget, Mas Carlot.*

COTEAUX DU TRICASTIN, AC Fast-improving, good value, spicy, fruity reds. Best producers: *Domaine de Grangeneuve, Tour d'Elyssas* (especially its 100 per cent Syrah), *Producteurs Réunis Ardéchois* (co-op), *Domaine Saint-Luc, Domaine du Vieux Micocoulier.*

CÔTE-RÔTIE, AC The admixture of the white Viognier grape makes this one of France's most scented reds when properly made. But the AC has been extended on to the plateau above the traditional 'roasted slope', and unless something is done to differentiate the two, the reputation of this highly-prized, highly-priced vineyard will be in tatters. Local producers are currently advocating a system of site names, like the *climats* of Burgundy. At best, from *Gentaz-Dervieux, Jamet, Guigal* and *René Rostaing,* Côte-Rôtie is delicious. Look also for *Gilles* and *Pierre Barge, Bernard Burgaud, Jasmin, Dervieux-Thaize, Vidal-Fleury* and *Delas Cuvée Seigneur de Maugiron.*

CÔTES DU LUBÉRON, AC Upgraded from VDQS in 1987, Lubéron makes some decent reds, usually rather light, but capable of stronger personality. The Val Joanis rosé is one of the best in the South. Try also *Château de Canorgue, Château de l'Isolette, Mas du Peyroulet, Val Joanis* (also to be seen under own label as *Domaines Chancel* or *Domaine de la Panisse), Vieille Ferme.*

The price guides for this section begin on page 328.

CÔTES DU RHÔNE, AC This huge AC covers 80 per cent of all Rhône wines. Well-made basic Côtes du Rhônes are delicious when young, wonderfully fresh and fruity, like a soft Beaujolais. Or they can be fierce, black, grape-skins-and-alcohol monsters. *Coudoulet de Beaucastel* is beefy, and many of the weightiest are made by Châteauneuf or northern Rhône producers like *Guigal*. *Château du Grand Moulas* is spicy and attractive, with plenty of body. Also good: *Caves C.N. Jaume, Château de Deurre, Château de Fonsalette, Château de Ruth, Château de Goudray, Clos du Père Clément, Dom de Bel Air, Dom de la Cantharide, Dom de St-Estève, Domaine des Aussellons, Jean Lionnet* and *Chapoutier*'s rosé.

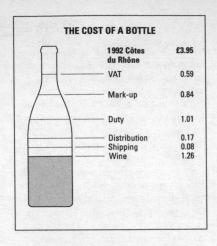

THE COST OF A BOTTLE

1992 Côtes du Rhône	£3.95
VAT	0.59
Mark-up	0.84
Duty	1.01
Distribution	0.17
Shipping	0.08
Wine	1.26

CÔTES DU RHÔNE-VILLAGES, AC One of the best areas for good, full reds that can also age, combining earthy, dusty southern heat with spicy, raspberry fruit. They come from higher quality villages, 17 of which can add their names on the label, including Vacqueyras, Cairanne, Chusclan, Valréas, Beaumes-de-Venise and Rasteau. Good growers: (Laudun) *Domaine Pelaquié;* (Rasteau) *Domaine de Grangeneuve;* (Sablet) *Jean-Pierre Cartier, Château de Trignon, Domaine de Boisson, Domaine St-Antoine, Domaine de Verquière;* (Cairanne) *Domaine de l'Ameillaud, Dom Brusset, Dom l'Oratoire St-Martin, Dom de la Présidente, Dom Rabasse-Charavin;* (St-Gervais) *Dom Ste-Anne;* (Séguret) *Dom Courançonne, Dom de Cabasse;* (Valréas) *Roger Combe, Dom des Grands Devers, Le Val des Rois;* (Vacqueyras) *Château de Montmirail, Clos des Cazaux, Dom la Fourmone, Dom des Lambertins, Le Sang des Cailloux.*

CÔTES DU VENTOUX, AC Good area producing lots of fresh, juicy wine, of which the red is the best. Can even be quite special. Best: *Domaine des Anges, Jaboulet, Pascal, Vieille Ferme, Vieux Lazaret.*

CROZES-HERMITAGE, AC A large AC providing a lot of fairly strong and slightly tough and smoky Hermitage-type wine which at its best has a lovely juicy fruit as well. *Etienne Pochon (Château de Curson), Graillot*'s *La Guérande* and *Jaboulet's Thalabert* brand are outstanding; also good are *Desmeures, Ferraton, Albert Belle, Stephane Cornu, Laurent Combier, Tardy & Ange,* the *Tain* co-op, and *Gabriel Viale.*

GIGONDAS, AC Big, chunky, plummy wines that can be short on finesse. This is Grenache country, and proud of it. *Domaine de St-Gayan* is very good, as are *Château de Montmirail, Clos des Cazeaux, Château du Trignon, Domaine les Gouberts, Domaine de Longue-Toque, Domaine l'Oustau Fauquet, Domaine les Pallières, Domaine Raspail-Ay.*

HERMITAGE, AC Grand, burly red from a small, precipitous vineyard area around the hill of Hermitage. Strong and fierily tough when young, it matures to a rich, brooding magnificence. There is always a stern, vaguely medicinal or smoky edge to it, and an unmatchable depth of raspberry and blackcurrant fruit. Although a number of people produce Hermitage of sorts, there have traditionally been only two stars, the marvellously good *Chave*, who produces small amounts of impeccable wine, and the ebullient, export-orientated *Paul Jaboulet*

Aîné, who produces larger amounts of more variable wine. To them should be added *Chapoutier*'s *Le Pavillon*. Also good: *Delas Cuvée Marquise de la Tourette, Desmeure, B. Faurie, Guigal, Sorrel, Belle, Faurie* and *Jean-Louis Grippat*.

LIRAC, AC An excellent, often underrated area south-west of Châteauneuf whose wines it can frequently equal. The reds are packed with fruit, often tinged with a not unwelcome mineral edge. The rosés are remarkably fresh for so far south. Whites can be first-class if caught young. Best: *Château d'Aquéria, Domaine de Château St-Roch, Domaine des Causses et St-Eymes, Domaine les Garrigues, Domaine la Fermade, Maby, Domaine de la Tour*.

ST-JOSEPH, AC Almost smooth and sweet compared to their tougher neighbours, these reds, especially those from the hills between Condrieu and Cornas, can be fairly big, fine wines, stacked with blackcurrant in good years. There has been some planting on less suitable land, but quality is mostly high, and though there have been price rises, the wines *were* undervalued. *Chave, Coursodon, Florentin, Gripa, Grippat, Jaboulet, Maurice Courbis* and *Trollat* are leading names. The co-op at *St-Désirat Champagne* makes lovely Beaujolais-type St-Joseph.

TAVEL, AC The AC only applies to one colour of wine – pink. The wines are quite expensive, certainly tasty, but too big and alcoholic to be very refreshing. Any of the Rhône grapes will do, but generally it's Grenache-dominated, with the addition of a little Cinsaut. Best producers: *Château d'Aqueria, Château de Trinquevedel, Domaine de la Forcadière, Domaine de la Génestière*.

VACQUEYRAS, AC The newest of the Rhône ACs makes reds and rosés of character and structure, the best being from the Garrigue plateau, 300ft above the village. Cinsaut fanatic *Château de Montmirail* is good, as are *Domaine de Verquière, Clos des Cazeau, Domaine de la Fourmone, Le Sang des Cailloux*.

VIN DE PAYS DES COLLINES RHODANIENNES A usually impressive and expanding northern Rhône area, particularly for inexpensive, tasty Syrah reds, though Gamay can also be good.

VIN DE PAYS DES COTEAUX DE L'ARDÈCHE This straggly, upland Rhône *département* puts into a nutshell what the *vins de pays* should be trying to achieve. A mixture of go-ahead co-ops and outside influences decided to plant grapes to make wine that would *sell*: delicious Nouveau-style Gamay, first class Syrah, good Cabernet, and they've planted Sauvignon Blanc, Pinot Noir – and Chardonnay, both for *Louis Latour*'s Chardonnay de l'Ardèche and the local co-ops (higher quality, far lower prices).

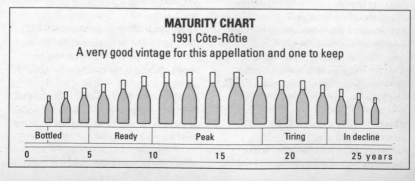

MATURITY CHART
1991 Côte-Rôtie
A very good vintage for this appellation and one to keep

Bottled	Ready	Peak	Tiring	In decline

| 0 | 5 | 10 | 15 | 20 | 25 years |

WHITE WINES

The two main styles of northern Rhône white could hardly be more different. The wines based on Marsanne and Roussanne – Hermitage, Crozes-Hermitage, St-Joseph and St-Péray – are in general weighty, strong, initially lacking in perfume and charm, but capable of a great, opulent, even pompous richness, given the decade or so they need to mature. Some modern versions, like those of Jaboulet, are less ambitious but ready within the year. The wines based on the Viognier are heavenly – totally different in style, bursting with the fruit flavours of apricots and pears and a mad, heady perfume like flower gardens in spring. Very special.

The interest in southern Rhône whites is fairly recent because it had always been assumed, with justification, that white wine from the region's non-aromatic grapes, produced on parched vineyards in the baking summer heat, could not possibly be anything but dull and flabby and fruitless. Now that many leading producers have invested in refrigerated equipment, and adopted cool fermentation techniques, it is quite remarkable what delicious flavours are beginning to appear. The vintage of 1989 was particularly good and so was 1990 – where growers were careful not to overproduce.

GRAPES & FLAVOURS

CLAIRETTE Makes sparkling Crémant de Die, but is a bit dull unless livened up with the aromatic Muscat. In the South it makes rather big, strong whites, sometimes creamy, but more often dull and nutty. Needs careful handling and early drinking.

GRENACHE BLANC A widely planted variety in the southern Rhône producing appley wines with a strong whiff of aniseed. Good, but soft, so drink young.

MARSANNE The dominant of the two grapes that go to make white Hermitage and Crozes-Hermitage, as well as white St-Joseph and St-Péray. Its wine is big and weighty but with a rather good, rich, sweet scent. Further south it makes big, burly wine, fat, lanoliny, but capable of rich exotic peach and toffee flavours, too. A good quality producer.

MUSCAT Used to great effect blended with Clairette to make the sparkling Clairette de Die, but more famous for Muscat de Beaumes de Venise.

ROUSSANNE Altogether more delicate and fragrant than the Marsanne, but it is inconveniently prone to disease and a low yielder, so it is increasingly losing ground to Marsanne. Found chiefly in Hermitage and St-Péray in the North, though it also makes light, fragrant wines further south in Châteauneuf. Look out for Château de Beaucastel's *Vieilles Vignes* version.

UGNI BLANC Boring workhorse grape planted all over the South to produce basic gulping stuff. The same as the Trebbiano of Italy, where it is hardly more exciting.

VIOGNIER The grape of Condrieu and Château Grillet. It has one of the most memorable flavours of any white grape because it blends the rich, musky scent of overripe apricots with that of spring flowers. The wine is made dry, but it is so rich you hardly believe it. Sweet versions are making a comeback. Viognier is, in its quiet way, becoming a bit of a cult, with plantings increasing in the southern Rhone, in California and even Australia.

WINES & WINE REGIONS

CHÂTEAU GRILLET, AC A single property in the far north-west of the northern Rhône, and the smallest AC in France at only three hectares, excepting a couple of Vosne-Romanée Grands Crus in Burgundy. This wine should have that magic reek of orchard fruit and harvest bloom about it. Sometimes it does.

CHÂTEAUNEUF-DU-PAPE BLANC, AC Only three per cent of the AC is white, but the wines can be outstandingly perfumed with a delicious nip of acidity, leaving you wondering how on earth such aromatic wines could come from such a hot, arid region. Magic or technology; or it might be such delights as the Roussanne and Picpoul varieties adding something to the base of Grenache Blanc, Clairette and Bourboulenc. Wonderful wines can be produced in the most unlikely places – and this just happens to be one of them. Although the wine can age, you lose that perfumed rush of springtime madness after a year. Best: *Beaucastel* (their pure Roussanne *Vieilles Vignes* – and the new Viognier white), *Clefs d'Or, Clos des Papes, Font de Michelle, Grand Tinel, Mont-Redon, Nalys, Rayas, Vieux Télégraphe*.

CLAIRETTE DE DIE, AC New rules mean that the unexciting Champagne method wine (which used to be called Clairette de Die) is now called Crémant de Die, and what used to be called Clairette de Die Tradition, made by the ancient *méthode dioise ancestrale*, is now the only wine allowed to be called Clairette de Die. Made half from Clairette, half from Muscat, it's delicious, light and off dry. The still wine is Coteaux Diois.

CONDRIEU, AC From a small area at the northern end of the northern Rhône, this is wonderful when made properly, with apricot scent that leaps out of the glass, and an exciting balance of succulent fruit and gentle, nipping acidity. But its sudden popularity has led to great replanting, sometimes by people concerned more with high prices than high quality. Yet the potential quality is so stunning that with luck the *arrivistes* will realize that the real thing is worth striving for. The potential area is 100 hectares, and about 80 are planted. There is some *cépage* Viognier, which will show what the fuss is about – at half the Condrieu price. (Yapp has one.) Top names: *Château du Rozay, Delas, Dumazet, Guigal, Multier,* (who, like some others, is using new oak), *Niero Pinchon, Jean Pinchon* and *Georges Vernay*.

COTEAUX DU TRICASTIN, AC Fresh, fruity and quite full-flavoured southerly whites, not as exciting as the reds. Best bet: *Producteurs Réunis Ardéchois*.

CÔTES DU LUBÉRON, AC Usually pleasant and light southern wine but little more, though recent innovations have started to produce much more fragrant, interesting styles at such properties as *Château de l'Isolette, Mas du Peyroulet, Val Joanis* and *Vieille Ferme*.

CÔTES DU RHÔNE BLANC, AC; CÔTES DU RHÔNE-VILLAGES BLANC, AC Increasingly fresh, fruity and gulpable especially from the villages of Laudun and Chusclan. *Domaine Pelaquié* at Laudun is the leading estate, and *Domaine Ste-Anne* at St-Gervais is good.

CROZES-HERMITAGE, AC Generally a rather dull, strong northern Rhône white, but there are good ones from *Desmeure, Fayolle, Jaboulet* and *Pradelle*.

HERMITAGE, AC Often a bit heavy and dull, but curiously it ages tremendously well to a soft, rich nuttiness. Some of the finest is made by *Chapoutier, Chave, Desmeure, Ferraton, Grippat* and *Sorrel*.

LIRAC, AC The whites can be good young, resembling a less exotic Châteauneuf: less exotic flavour; less exotic price.

ST-JOSEPH, AC Northern AC with some fair, nutty white and better red. *Grippat* is good. *Florentin* does an intense old-style headbanging white unlike any other.

ST-PÉRAY, AC Made in the southern bit of the northern Rhône, this was once France's most famous sparkling wine after Champagne. Not any more. It tends to be rather stolid and short of freshness. And the still whites are just dull. The occasional better bottle will come from *Chaboud, Clape, Grippat, Juge* or *Voge.*

FORTIFIED WINES

MUSCAT DE BEAUMES DE VENISE, AC This Côtes du Rhône village is the only place in the Rhône to grow the Muscat grape. The golden sweet wine – a *vin doux naturel* – has become a real fad drink, but for once the fad is a good one, because it's supremely delicious. Grapy, fresh, rich but not cloying. Look for *Domaine de Coyeux, Domaine Durban, Jaboulet* and the *Beaumes de Venise* co-op.

RASTEAU, AC The Côtes du Rhône village of Rasteau also makes a few big, port-like fortified wines – *vins doux naturels* – both red and off-white. Young ones can have a delightful raspberry scent from the Grenache Noir. The whites are made from Grenache Blanc and can be frankly unpleasant. Production is pretty small. Try *Domaine de la Soumade, Co-opérative de Rasteau.*

RHÔNE VINTAGES

1993 A light year for fairly early drinking: reds from top growers are fruity and elegant, not very tannic, and whites need drinking before they lose their fruit.

1992 A fairly rotten year, but the best growers were able to make something of it. In Châteauneuf and the South a few made decent wines for early drinking. Some 'correct' wines in the North. Buy only from top growers and drink up quickly.

1991 Many northern Rhône growers had their fourth very good year in succession; in Côte-Rôtie at least the wines are generally better than the 1990s. In the South yields were tiny, and the wine only moderately good.

1990 On the whole the North survived the drought best though rain affected picking in Côte-Rôtie. Choose 1990 for the North (though Côte-Rôtie is dodgy); 1989 for the South.

1989 Drought in much of the region, and some poor Hermitage and Cornas was made by growers unable to master it. Small crops meant concentrated Châteauneuf for keeping.

1988 There is certainly *some* great 1988, mostly in Côte-Rôtie, Hermitage and Châteauneuf-du-Pape. There is also a fair amount which is far too tannic for its own good.

1987 Côtes du Rhône reds and northern Rhônes can be good.

1986 A rather joyless vintage for reds. Some very good Châteauneuf and Hermitage but the ambitious Côtes du Rhône names made some of the best. Some white still improving.

1985 Brilliant Côte-Rôtie, St-Joseph and Cornas. Châteauneuf is delicious and juicy.

1983 Outstanding dark, rich, complex Hermitage and very good Côte-Rôtie for keeping. Southern reds are good, but the failure of the Grenache left some a bit tough.

1982 Good, rather simple northern reds; a difficult, hot vintage in the South.

LOIRE

Things are looking up in the Loire. After 1991's frost disaster, and the relatively dull, unfocussed quality of many of the the '92s, the 1993 vintage looks particularly promising. In Muscadet, they are all but hanging out the bunting; 1993 wines from the better producers (such as Bossard and Métaireau) should be full of savoury concentration.

Much of France suffered a rather sodden vintage in 1993 but, uncharacteristically, the greater part of the Loire was spared. August was mostly quite hot and even the early-October rainfall around Saumur didn't really upset the applecart. There, botrytis took hold of the Chenin Blanc more pervasively than in any vintage since 1990, and there should be some great sweet wines to look forward to from Coteaux du Layon and Bonnezeaux. Chenin wines from a little further east in Vouvray and Montlouis haven't quite the ripeness to be any sweeter than *demi-sec*, by and large, but these will provide some very attractive, fruity wines at a year to 18 months old.

Cabernet Franc reds from the Loire are not always appreciated even now. To some extent, this is understandable. In a poor year, the grape can produce ghastly, vegetal brews with fretsaw tannins and a stink of green pepper skin, while in a light vintage like 1992, they just seem bleached and pointless. The '93s should be the vintage to convince the sceptical: in Anjou and Saumur, they have turned out many ripe-fruited reds, with velvety tannins imparting strength without brutality.

Gooseberries on a plateau

In the upper Loire, where Sauvignon Blanc comes into its own, prices for the top *appellations* of Pouilly-Fumé and Sancerre seem to have reached a plateau for the time being, with Sancerre – for my money – being distinctly the more reliable for those unfamiliar with individual producers. The big news in these parts, though, is Ménétou-Salon, just to the west of Sancerre. At a slightly gentler price, the best of these wines (such as those from Pellé) possess all of the bracing, raw-gooseberry steeliness of their more illustrious neighbour. Sauvignon generally has much better aromatic definition than in the previous vintage, and will hold for longer if mature dry white is your thing.

Anjou is also the home of some of France's best rosé wines, which, suffering the fate of most pink wine, tend not to be taken seriously. Don't think of all rosés as either lipstick-pink sweet bubblegum stuff, or onion-coloured fruit-free brutes with too much alcohol. Vinified sensitively, they can give a refreshingly dry mouthful of happy, raspberry-scented fruit. The co-operative at the southern-Loire outpost of Haut-Poitou makes a dry, appetizing Cabernet rosé for a very fair price. Waitrose has it.

In this amorphous and very various region, a fair amount of Champagne-method sparkling wine is also produced. Quantities this year may be reduced as producers prefer to use their top-quality grapes for their still wines, but Huët's sparkling Vouvray is always outstanding. Crémant de Loire can also be a very pleasant surprise, with the non-vintage rosé of Château Langlois exhibiting plenty of strawberries-and-cream appeal.

Now, if it could only be this good every year...   STUART WALTON

WHITE GRAPES & FLAVOURS

CHARDONNAY Increasingly widespread in the Loire and producing lean, light but tangy results in Haut-Poitou, in Anjou as Vin de Pays du Jardin de la France and in Orléans as Vin de l'Orléanais (where it's called Auvernat: *Clos St-Fiacre* is terrific). It also occurs in Muscadet (*Le Chouan* and *Domaine Couillaud* are good) and adds character and softness to Anjou Blanc.

CHASSELAS Makes adequate but dull wine at Pouilly-sur-Loire; it's actually best as a table grape, in a fruit salad.

CHENIN BLANC A grape that cries out for sun and ripens (if that's the word) well after the other varieties. Experiments with allowing the skins to steep in the juice before fermentation, and the quiet addition of a bit of Chardonnay, are beginning to produce outstanding peachy whites.

It also performs superbly on the Loire in a few warm and misty microclimates (especially Quarts de Chaume and Bonnezeaux), where noble rot strikes the Chenin with enough frequency to make it worthwhile going through all the pain and passion of producing great sweet wine, with steely acidity and honeyed, ripe-apple fruit. These wines can seem curiously disappointing when young, but fine sweet Chenin manages to put on weight and become sweeter for perhaps 20 years before bursting out into a richness as exciting as all but the very best from Germany or Bordeaux. And then it lasts and lasts...

MELON DE BOURGOGNE The grape of Muscadet, light and neutral. It's good at producing fresh, surprisingly soft, slightly peppery, dry white wine with a salty tang, generally for drinking young, though a good domaine-bottled *sur lie* can mature surprisingly well.

SAUVIGNON BLANC The grape of Sancerre, and the main white grape of Pouilly and Touraine, with a whole range of fresh, green, tangy flavours that might remind you of anything from gooseberries to nettles and fresh-cut grass, and there's sometimes even a whiff of newly roasted coffee. The wines are usually quite tart – but thirst-quenching rather than gum-searing – and have loadsafruit. Sauvignon can age interestingly in bottle, but the odds are against it, except for the high-priced oak-aged *cuvées*.

WHITE WINES & WINE REGIONS

ANJOU BLANC SEC, AC France's cheapest AC dry white made from the hard-to-ripen Chenin Blanc, grown anywhere in Anjou upriver from the Muscadet region, often tart, sulphured and sour. But it *can* be good, steely and honeyed, especially from Savennières with its two tiny special ACs, Coulée-de-Serrant and La Roche aux Moines, and from names such as *Domaine Richou* who mix Chardonnay with their Chenin, for extra flavour, fruit and body. They are allowed up to 20 per cent Chardonnay or Sauvignon Blanc. Some have planted a little bit more on the side, and it's no bad thing. Other good names:

Mark Angelli (Cuvée Christine), Baranger, Château de Valliennes, Domaine de la Haute Perche, Jaudeau.

BONNEZEAUX, AC One of the most unfairly forgotten great sweet wines of France. After a long period of decline, this small AC inside the Coteaux du Layon is on the up again. The vineyard area has grown from 42 hectares in 1975 to 157 hectares in 1985 and prices for the lovely noble-rot-affected wines are rising fast. So much the better; they were far too cheap before, and if you don't make it profitable for the growers to make great sweet wine, they'll give up and plant apples. Look out for the outstanding wines of *Mark Angelli* (from old vines), *Jacques Boivin* of *Château de Fesles*, *Goizil*, *Renou* and *Denéchère*.

CHEVERNY, AC Elevated to AC status in 1993, this Touraine region is improving fast. Its claim to fame is the teeth-grittingly dry Romorantin grape, but there is also Chenin, Sauvignon and Chardonnay. *Domaine des Huards* makes fine, delicate wines, while the *confrèrie* at Oisly-et-Thésée produces a crisp Sauvignon/Chardonnay blend. Others: *Cazin, Gendrier, Gueritte, Tessier*.

COTEAUX DE L'AUBANCE, AC A rambling *appellation* south of Anjou giving pleasant semi-sweet whites, quite cheaply. Good producers: *Domaine des Rochettes, Jean-Yves Lebreton* and *Domaine Richou*.

COTEAUX DU LAYON, AC A large AC producing varying qualities of sweet white wine, at its best rich and tasty with a taut acidity that allows the wine to age for a long time. *Domaine Ambinois, Château de la Guimonière, Ogereau, Domaine du Petit Val, Domaine de la Pierre St Maurille, Domaine des Quarres, Château de la Roulerie, Clos Ste-Catherine* and *Domaine de la Soucherie* are worth trying. There are also six Coteaux du Layon-Villages ACs that usually offer higher quality.

CRÉMANT DE LOIRE, AC Sparkling wine AC intended to denote higher quality but not much used. Compared with Saumur AC fizz, the yield must be lower (50 rather than 60 hectolitres per hectare), the juice extract less (150kg of grapes as against 130kg for one hectolitre of juice), and the wine must lie on its lees for 12 months rather than 9 after its second fermentation. The product is usually softer and nicer than the frequently harsh wines of Saumur, but the merchants have built up Saumur and don't seem inclined to put much effort into Crémant de Loire. Laudable exceptions are the first-rate house of *Gratien & Meyer*,

Langlois-Château, St-Cyr-en-Bourg co-op, and the small *Cave des Liards*.

GROS PLANT, VDQS Gros Plant rejoices in being one of the rawest wines in France, and the prosperity of dentists in Nantes is thanks in no small measure to the locals' predilection for the stuff. That said, it *does* go amazingly well with seafood and seems to suit oysters. *Bossard's* is soft and honeyed. *Métaireau* and *Sauvion* have also tamed its fury. *Clos de la Sénaigerie* and *Clos de la Fine* from *Domaine d'Herbauges* are good.

HAUT-POITOU, VDQS Produced in an isolated area south of the main Loire vineyards. Chardonnay and Sauvignon from the *Cave Co-opérative du Haut-Poitou* are good but tending to the lean side.

MENETOU-SALON, AC Small, growing AC to the west of Sancerre making pretty good Sauvignons (and some fair reds and rosés). The *Vignerons Jacques Coeur* co-op produces about half the Sauvignon. *Henry Pellé* makes the best in Menetou, followed by *Jean-Max Roger* and *Domaine de Chatenoy*.

MONTLOUIS, AC Chenin area south of Vouvray. Makes similar wines, but often more robust – which, when it comes to the Chenin grape, isn't always a good idea. *Dominique Moyer, Domaine des Liards* and *Jean-Pierre Trouvé* are good, but lots are short on fruit, long on sulphur.

MUSCADET, AC Simple, light, neutral wine from the Nantes area. Straight Muscadet, without any further regional title, is usually flat and boring. But at least it's light – the Muscadet ACs are the only ones in France to impose a *maximum* alcohol level (12.3 per cent).

The price guides for this section begin on page 338.

MUSCADET DE SÈVRE-ET-MAINE, AC

The biggest Muscadet area, making the most but also the best wine. A good one may taste slightly nutty, peppery or salty, even honeyed, sometimes with creaminess from being left on the lees, sometimes a chewy apricot-skin taste and sometimes with a slight prickle. It should always have a lemony acidity, and should feel light. Buy domaine-bottled wine only, and check the address, looking out for *St-Fiacre* and *Le Pallet*, two of the best villages.

MUSCADET DES COTEAUX DE LA LOIRE, AC

A small area along the banks of the Loire east of Nantes. In quality, it's between Muscadet and Muscadet de Sèvre-et-Maine. *Pierre Luneau* is good.

MUSCADET SUR LIE

This is the most important thing to look for on a Muscadet label – even though not all producers use the term honestly. Traditionally indicates that the wine has come straight from the lees (the yeast sediment from fermentation), thus having more character than usual and a slight prickle. In the best cases this is so, but the law only says that the wine must be bottled before 30 June in the year after the vintage – not a guarantee of much, except perhaps freshness. It's best to buy only *sur lie* labelled *mise en bouteille à la propriété / château / domaine*. Some merchants, like *Sauvion*, have portable bottling lines, and bottle properly *sur lie* at the grower's cellar. Its *Château du Cléray* and *Découvertes* range are very good. *Guy Bossard* makes good organic *sur lie*. Also notable: *Domaine de Coursay-Villages, Domaine du Grand Mouton, Pierre Luneau, Domaine de la Montaine, Château de Chasseloir, Clos de la Sénaigerie, Jean-Louis Hervouet, Domaine du 'Perd-son-pain'*, any from *Louis Métaireau* including *Domaine du Grand Mouton, Cuvée LM, Cuvée One,* unfiltered *Huissier* and oddities like *25 August 1989*, the result of a single day's harvest; both *Michel* and *Donatien Bahuaud*'s single domaine wines, *Bonhomme* and *Guilbaud*.

POUILLY-FUMÉ, AC

Just over the river from Sancerre and very similar. They are said to smell of gunflint because of their smokiness. They can be fuller than Sancerre, and the best have a mineral complexity, but given the prices, there are still too many under-achievers. Best: *J C Châtelain, Didier Dagueneau* (Pouilly's most brilliant winemaker), *Serge Dagueneau, Château Favray, Masson-Blondelet, André Figeat* and the too-expensive *Baron de L.*

POUILLY-SUR-LOIRE, AC

Made from the dull Chasselas grape which makes good eating but not memorable drinking. *Serge Dagueneau* makes a good example.

QUARTS DE CHAUME, AC

A tiny 40-hectare AC in the Layon valley with a perfect microclimate for nobly-rotten sweet wines. They are rare and expensive, not quite as sweet as top Sauternes, but they can be even more intense, with high acid stalking the rich apricot and honey fruit. *Jean Baumard* is superb; also *Château de Bellerive* and *Château de l'Echarderie*.

QUINCY, AC

Fairly pungent Sauvignon Blanc wines grown west of Sancerre. *Domaine de Maison Blanche, Pierre Mardon, Jacques Rouzé* and the co-op *Jacques Coeur* make good examples.

REUILLY, AC

Light, fragrant Sauvignon Blanc wines from near Quincy, west of Sancerre. *Gérard Cordier* and *Claude Lafond* are the important growers. (There is also some tasty red and rosé.)

SANCERRE, AC

Green, smoky, tangy wine from the Sauvignon Blanc grape grown at the eastern end of the Loire. Drunk young when it's at its best, it should be super-fresh and fruity, with a flavour and fragrance like gooseberries or fresh-cut grass, and a brilliant balance between sharpness and ripe, round body. But all too often it smells sulphurous or meaty, and tastes simply flabby. Look for single-domaine wines – especially those of *Pierre Archambault, Joseph Balland-Chapuis, Henri Bourgeois, Francis & Paul Cotat, Lucien Crochet, Pierre & Alain Dézat, Domaine Laporte, Alphonse Mellot, Paul Millérioux, Henri Natter, Bernard Noël-Reverdy, Jean-Max Roger, Pierre Riffault, Domaine Vacheron* and *André Vatan*.

SAUMUR, AC Champagne-method wine made from Chenin grapes, sometimes with the welcome addition of Chardonnay, Sauvignon or even Cabernet Franc, any of which can give a bit more roundness to the acid Chenin. Well-made sparkling Saumur (including a little rosé) is lively and appley but too many are just too rough to revel with. Best producers: *Ackerman Laurance, Bouvet-Ladubay, Gratien & Meyer* and *Langlois-Château*.

SAUMUR BLANC, AC White, usually ultra-dry, though it can occasionally be sweet, similar to Anjou Blanc.

SAVENNIÈRES, AC Some of the steeliest, longest-living, diamond-dry white wines in the world come from this tiny Anjou *appellation* just west of Angers. One vineyard, Savennières Coulée-de-Serrant, has its own AC within Savennières, and *Madame Joly*'s wines from the *Clos de la Coulée-de-Serrant* are extremely fine. Look out also for wines from *Yves Soulez* from the *Château de Chamboreau, Clos du Papillon, Jean Baumard (Clos Ste-Catherine), Domaine de la Bizolière* and the *Domaine aux Moines*.

TOURAINE, AC Everybody sees Touraine Sauvignon, with some justification, as a Sancerre substitute. The *Confrérie des Vignerons de Oisly-et-Thésée* sell to half the British wine trade, and their wines are good, as are *Paul Buisse, Château de l'Aulée, Domaine de la Charmoise (Marionnet), Château de Chenonceau, Domaine des Corbillières, Domaine Joël Delaunay* and *Domaine Octavie*.

VIN DE PAYS DU JARDIN DE LA FRANCE The general *vin de pays* of the Loire valley. Usually unmemorable, though pleasant, but the results can be impressive, especially when based on Sauvignon and Chardonnay. *Biotteau's Château d'Avrille Chardonnay* and *Domaine des Hauts de Saulière's Chardonnay* have lovely fruit.

VOUVRAY, AC Sparkling wine and still whites ranging from the tangily dry to the liquorously sweet, though usually caught in the middle. In fact Vouvray is best at producing the off-dry *demi-sec* style, and from a good producer this Chenin wine, initially all searing acidity and rasping dryness, over a number of years develops a deep, nutty, honey-and-cream flavour. Most commercial Vouvray is poor. Good producers are: *Daniel Allias, Domaine des Aubuisières, Brédif, Chamalou, Château Gaudrelle, Château Moncontour, Foreau, Huet, Prince Poniatowski* and *Domaine de Vaugoudy*.

RED GRAPES & FLAVOURS

CABERNET SAUVIGNON This doesn't always ripen too well in the Loire, but even so it adds some backbone to the wines. It is really at its best in the ripest years.

CABERNET FRANC The great quality grape of Anjou and Touraine. All the best reds are based on Cabernet Franc, and the styles go from the palest, most fleeting of reds to deep, strong, proud wines of great character and considerable longevity.

GAMAY This rarely achieves the lovely, juicy glugginess of Beaujolais, but when made by a careful modern winemaker it can have a fair amount of fruit, though always with a tough edge.

PINOT NOIR In and around Sancerre this can, in warm years, produce a lovely, light, cherry-fragrant wine that will be either a rosé or a light red. But really interesting examples are rare in the Loire.

RED WINES & WINE REGIONS

ANJOU ROUGE CABERNET, AC Until a few years ago Anjou Rouge was a byword for raw, rasping red fit to drive a chap to Liebfraumilch. Now it's likely to be light and dry from the co-ops, and spicy, strong and capable of aging from the best domaines. It can rival Bourgueil. Best producers: *Mark Angelli (Cuvée Martial), Château d'Avrille, Château de Chamboureau (Soulez), Clos de Coulaine, Domaine de la Petite Croix, Domaine du Petit Val, Domaine des Rochettes (Chauvin), Logis de la Giraudière (Baumard), Richou, Roussier*.

ANJOU ROUGE GAMAY, AC Rarely more than adequate, but in the hands of someone like *Richou*, the 'rooty' character is replaced by a fresh, creamy fruit that is sharp and soft all at once, and *very* good. *Domaine des Quarres* is also worth a try.

ANJOU-VILLAGES, AC Cabernets Franc and Sauvignon from the 46 best villages in Anjou. Some are labelled 'Anjou-Villages Val-de-Loire'. *Domaine de Montgilet, J-Y & H Lebreton, Domaine Ogereau* and *Richou* are good. Go for the concentrated 1990s or fresh 1993s.

BOURGUEIL, AC Some of the best reds of the Loire come from this AC in Touraine. When they are young they can taste a bit harsh and edgy, but give them a few years and they will have a piercing blackcurrant fruitiness, sharp and thirstquenching. They can age remarkably well, developing complex leathery, meaty flavours. Best: *Audebert* (estate wines), *Pierre Breton, Caslot-Galbrun, J-F Demont, Domaine des Forges, Domaine des Ouches, Pierre-Jacques Druet, Lamé-Delille-Boucard*.

CABERNET D'ANJOU, AC (Rosé) There is a reasonable chance of a pleasant drink here, because the Cabernets – mostly Franc, but often with Cabernet Sauvignon too – do give pretty tasty wine, usually less sweet than simple Rosé d'Anjou. Best: *Dom Baranger, Dom de Hardières, Dom de Richou, Château de Valliennes.*

CHEVERNY, AC Red Cheverny tends to be light and crisp, with a healthy dollop of Gamay perhaps beefed up with Cabernet Franc. *Oisly-et-Thésée*'s is strawberryish with a fair bit of Pinot Noir in it.

CHINON, AC In a ripe year (1988, '89, '90), Chinon can be delicious, exhibiting a great gush of blackcurrant and raspberry. There's earthiness too, but it is soft and cooling, and after a few years it seems to dissolve into mouthwatering fruit. Domaine wines are *far* better than *négociant* wines, which can be thin. Best: *Bernard Baudry, Jean Baudry, Domaine du Colombier, Couly-Dutheil, Druet, Gatien Ferrand, René Gouron, Charles Joguet, Alain Lorieux, Pierre Manzagol, Jean François Olek, Jean-Maurice Raffault, Raymond Raffault, Domaine du Roncée, Domaine de la Tour.*

HAUT-POITOU, VDQS Fairly 'green' but reasonably enjoyable reds from the Loire hinterland, usually made from Gamay.

ROSÉ D'ANJOU, AC The omnipresent and frequently omnihorrid French rosé. It is based on a pretty feeble grape, the Groslot, and suffers in the main from lack of fruit and excess of sulphur. A few like the co-op at *Brissac* can make it fresh.

ROSÉ DE LOIRE, AC A little-made dry rosé from Anjou or Touraine.

SANCERRE ROUGE, AC Pinot Noir, and in general overrated, but occasionally you can find a fleeting cherry fragrance and sweetness of strawberries that can survive

a year or two in bottle. Silly prices, though. *Henri Bourgeois, Domaine Vacheron, Pierre & André Dezat* and *Domaine de Chatenoy* at the nearby Menetou-Salon AC are good.

SAUMUR ROUGE, AC Usually very light and dry Cabernet Franc from 38 villages round Saumur. Light, but the fruit is often marked and attractively blackcurranty. The co-op at *St-Cyr-en-Bourg* is good, as is Château Fouquet from Paul Filliatreau.

SAUMUR-CHAMPIGNY, AC Cabernet red from the best villages in Saumur. It is way above other Loire reds thanks to a firm structure and velvety softness, fruit that is slightly raw and rasping, yet succulent and rich at the same time. Although the term 'vieilles vignes' is open to interpretation it is always the best bet for quality. *Domaine Filliatreau* makes an outstanding one, as well as *Primeur,* for immediate drinking. Also good: *Château de Chaintres, Château du Hureau, Château de Targé, Domaine Dubois, Domaine Lavigne, Domaine Sauzay-Legrand, Denis Duveau, Dom de Nerleux, Dom des Roches Neuves, Dom du Val Brun.*

ST-NICOLAS DE BOURGUEIL, AC These Cabernet reds from an AC within Touraine AC are grown on gravelly soil, so they tend to be lighter and more forward than nearby Bourgueils. They can be good, but stick to warm years. The wines of *Claude Ammeux, Caslot-Jamet, Jean-Paul Mabileau* and *Joël Taluau* seem best.

TOURAINE, AC The reds aren't usually very exciting, being rather green and stalky on the whole. They are often Gamay-based but may be made from a variety of grapes, including Cabernet. The *Domaine de la Charmoise (Marionnet),* and the co-op of *Oisly-et-Thésée* produce fair Gamays. *Château de Chenonceau* is also good.

VIN DE PAYS DES MARCHES DE BRETAGNE These wines from the mouth of the Loire are usually fairly flimsy numbers, but a good grower can use the denomination to produce something unusual and exciting. *Guy Bossard,* for instance, a leading Muscadet producer, makes an amazingly fragrant and fruity red from Cabernet Franc.

LOIRE VINTAGES

Loire vintages are very important, and can be radically different along the river length. In poor vintages, Muscadet is most likely to be OK, while in hot vintages Sauvignon goes dull, but the Chenin finally ripens. The red grapes need the warm years.

1993 Good, flinty Sauvignon from Touraine and the upper Loire is matched by crisp Anjou Chenin. Reds too look potentially mouth-watering and capable of aging. Selected producers in Coteaux du Layon will have fine, botrytis-affected wines of powerful concentration. Young Muscadet will be as good as it gets from the smart operators.

1992 A large crop of wines that generally lack concentration. The reds are very light.

1991 Devastating weather meant that in some areas, notably Muscadet, no wine was made at all. Sancerre and Pouilly-Fumé were down by half. Quality was average.

1990 Another *annus mirabilis.* The sweet white Chenins, luscious and built to last, may even exceeed the great '89s. Great reds too. Sancerre and Pouilly can be low in acidity, but once again late-harvest Sauvignon has given an encore.

1989 An exceptional year, particularly for sweet Chenin Blancs, which are comparable with the legendary '47s. The reds were ripe, but some dry whites lack acidity. Oddity of the year: sweet, botrytis-affected Sancerre in new oak.

1988 Delicious Sancerres and Pouilly-Fumés, and first-class Muscadet.

ALSACE

A few people in Britain – just a very few – are addicted to Alsace wines. But the vast majority, those who are not addicted, never go near them.

How do I know this? Because the *per capita* consumption of Alsace wine here is just two centilitres, which is barely a mouthful. On the other hand, more than 90 per cent of Alsace wine is consumed by just two per cent of the population.

Alsace, although it is well-publicised, still manages to be undiscovered. Yet if these wines were to appear out of the blue today, not in Europe but in Australia, they would create a cult following. Wines would be flying off the shelves. They're so fruity, so well made, people would cry. And so they are, both fruity and well made. So what's the problem?

I think I know. Alsace wine is not cheap. The cheapest comes from the co-operatives but even so, there's not much around under £5; and if you want something more exciting from one of the region's best producers, you'll be in for nearer twice that. But of course in Britain most people never pay more than a fiver for a wine; and a fiver gives them lots of delicious wines to choose from, from all over the world. A committed Alsace drinker will happily pay for the finest wines from his favourite producer, but most of the rest consider even the generic *cuvées* from famous names like Trimbach, Hugel, Zind-Humbrecht, Schlumberger and Domaine Weinbach to be far too expensive. If most consumers cannot be tempted to try the first rung of wine from the region's best producers, how will they ever know what the greatest Alsace wines taste like? The answer is that they won't. In the long run, then, the famous houses will fail to gain new customers, sales will decline further, aficionados will be charged ever-higher prices, and the wines will be put even further out of reach of ordinary consumers.

Alsace escape route

Not a very cheerful prospect. I believe there is only one way out of this vicious circle, and Alsace's producers have to act both collectively and radically. They have to introduce a new budget line, one rung below their generic wines, where every varietal sells at between £3.99 and £4.99.

I am not suggesting that they should drop their standards or cut the quality of any of their established *cuvées*. These producers make some of the most classic wines in Alsace and it would be a dark day when they stopped doing that. They must realize, however, that the existence of a quality image for Alsace in Britain depends on their taking the initiative. Recent events in Alsace virtually demand it, for the growth of *vendange tardive*, *sélection de grains noble* and Grand Cru wine over the last ten years has skimmed more and more cream off the top of the Alsace pot. The only logical way to redress the situation is to siphon off a new range of wines from the bottom.

What I am arguing for is a range of wines structured in a way that is logical and comprehensible. The best wines should be expensive and worth every penny, produced from low-yielding vines in the best spots. If you think that the introduction of 50 well-advertised Grand Cru sites has achieved this structure, think again: prices have indeed risen, but the volume of Grand Cru wine produced has increased from 18,000 hectolitres in 1985 to 40,000 at the moment – and when the new vines planted by growers attracted by the higher prices come on stream, production will rocket. Alsace will soon be thoroughly top-heavy.

The best move would be to create a new *vin de pays*, Vins de Pays du Côtes d'Alsace. This would both take advantage of the *vin de pays* consumer boom and give the growers a freer hand to make good-value wines from the high-yielding vineyards on the fertile plains, leaving the slopes for the generic AC wines and the Grands Crus. And I believe that the growers should use the freedom of the *vin de pays* denomination to produce blended wines.

Blends have a long and honourable history in Alsace, even though the AC regulations provide for varietal wines only. Edelzwicker is a blend, but a pretty debased one. The two *vins de pays* that currently exist, those of the Haut-Rhin and the Bas-Rhin, are also for varietals only, and in any case only apply to the outlying areas. Blended *vins de pays* would give a distinct character to the lowest rungs of the Alsace ladder, and far from harming the image of Alsace, as some producers fear, the reverse would be the case. *Vins de pays* are seen as good quality these days, for the simple reason that most of them are. In fact the producers could charge a higher price for a good *vin de pays* than they can for a nasty Edelzwicker. And would we mind? No, I don't think we would. We wouldn't expect the richness, body or potential longevity of the region's finest, but the technology exists to produce soft and appealing wines of true regional definition, as refreshing and as fruity as all Alsace wines should be. And they would leave the producers' hands free to make their generic varietals as good as they can be.

If you're one of the two per cent of consumers drinking most of the Alsace sold in this country, then presumably you have a vested interest in maintaining the quality and affordability of the better wines. If you're one of the 98 per cent – well, wouldn't you at least like to know what you're missing?   TOM STEVENSON

GRAPES & FLAVOURS

In Alsace wines are generally labelled according to their grape variety. Blends of two or more varieties are allowed, but account for just four per cent of the total production, and are mostly sold as cheap Edelzwicker. For this reason, recommended producers are listed here under the name of the appropriate grape.

AUXERROIS This variety is officially only tolerated in Alsace. It's fatter and more buttery than Pinot Blanc, with a touch of spice and musk. Look for *André Kientzler, Marc Kreydenweiss, Jos Meyer, Landmann-Ostholt, Rolly Gassmann, Bruno Sorg.*

CHASSELAS Rarely found now in Alsace, Chasselas has never been complex, but the few true examples can be vibrantly fruity and must be drunk fresh. Best: *André Kientzler, Jos Meyer, Schoffit.*

CLASSIC BLENDS These can be superb, and their producers avoid the Edelzwicker designation like the plague. Go for specific

cuvées: *Hugel Gentil, Marc Kreydenweiss Clos du Val d'Eléon, Co-op de Ribeauvillé Clos du Zahnacker, Schlumberger Réserve, Jean Sipp Clos du Schlossberg, Louis Sipp Côtes de Ribeauvillé.* Best in riper years.

EDELZWICKER Mostly lacklustre blends. Occasionally an Edelzwicker with an extra dollop of Gewürztraminer or Tokay-Pinot Gris will be good. *Schlumberger Cristal-Maree* has been on good form lately.

> The price guides for this section begin on page 345.

GEWÜRZTRAMINER Gewürztraminer is the least dry of all Alsace. The high street ones are usually decent, and *Beyer Cuvée des Comtes d'Eguisheim* and *Trimbach Cuvée des Seigneurs de Ribeaupierre* are bone dry. Gewürztraminer is the most voluptuous, upfront and fattest of all Alsace wines, overflowering with exotic aromas. Young Gewürz often smells of banana and the more it does so, the more finesse it will have when mature. Best: *Kuentz-Bas, Ostertag, Trimbach, Weinbach, Willm Clos Gaensbroennel, Zind-Humbrecht.*

MUSCAT Light, fragrant, wonderfully grapy. Imagine crushing a fistful of green grapes and gulping the juice. That's how fresh and grapy a good Muscat should be, but sadly too much is either too old or from the wrong vintage. Hotter years do not suit Muscat; at the moment look for 1991 and 1993. Look for *Becker, Ernest Burn, Joseph Cattin, Dirler, Marc Kreydenweiss, Kuentz-Bas, Rolly Gassmann, Bruno Sorg, Weinbach, Zind-Humbrecht.*

PINOT Some of these are labelled Pinot Blanc, but the rules permit any variety of Pinot for this wine. Not very long ago, many were so light and neutral that an honest Edelzwicker was a better bet. Now reduced yields, stricter selection and better vinification are giving plumpness, rich, ripe fruit with apple or floral overtones and a lovely long, rich and creamy finish. Best: *JB Adam, Camille Braun, Théo Cattin, Co-opérative de Cléebourg, Marcel Deiss, Hugel, Charles Koehly, Albert Mann, Rolly Gassmann, Martin Spielmann, Zind-Humbrecht.* Can also be called Klevner.

TOKAY-PINOT GRIS These are rich, musky and honeyed at best, though can run to flab if badly handled. Even the lighter ones are luscious behind their dry fruit. The best can age well. Best: *Lucien Albrecht, Barmès-Buecher, Léon Beyer, Ernest Burn, Claude Dietrich, Robert Dietrich, Pierre Frick, Marc Kreydenweiss, Kuentz-Bas, Frédéric Mallo, Schlumberger, Schoffit, Bruno Sorg, Co-opérative de Turckheim, Weinbach, Zind-Humbrecht.*

PINOT NOIR The Burgundy grape makes light reds and rosés, although many are darker than they used to be and oak aging is common. Typically they are strawberryish, with a fine perfume, though they lack complexity. Best include *JB Adam, Jean Becker, Marcel Deiss, René Fleith, Albert Hertz, Hugel, Jacques Iltis, Albert Mann, Co-opérative de Pfaffenheim, Co-opérative de Turckheim, Wolfberger.*

RIESLING The grape of the great wines of Germany. Here as steely and, as it ages, as wonderfully 'petrolly': Alsace at its most serious. Best: *Jean Becker, Leon Beyer, Paul Blanck, Deiss, Dirler, Pierre Freudenreich, Pierre Frick, Mader, Frederic Mallo, Frederic Mochel, Edgar Schaller, Schlumberger, Sick-Dreyer, Jean Sipp, Louis Sipp, Bruno Sorg, Trimbach, Weinbach, Winsch & Mann, Zind-Humbrecht*

SYLVANER Light, tart, slightly earthy and usually one-dimensional. With age it tastes of tomatoes, for some reason. Best: *Christian Dolder, J Hauller, Ostertag, Rolly Gassmann, Martin Schaetzel, Schoffit, Albert Seltz, Zind-Humbrecht.*

CLASSIFICATIONS

ALSACE or VIN D'ALSACE, AC This is the simple generic *appellation* that covers the whole Alsace region, and it is normally used in conjunction with a grape name. Thus: 'Riesling – Appellation Alsace Contrôlée'.

CRÉMANT D'ALSACE, AC White, Champagne-method fizz, made mainly from Pinot Blanc. The few who use a touch of Riesling make more interesting, flowery-fragrant versions and there are one or two good 100 per cent Rieslings worth trying.

Look for wines from *Paul Blanck, Robert Dietrich, Dopff & Irion, Dopff Au Moulin, Laugel, Co-opérative de Pfaffenheim, Co-opérative de Turckheim, Wolfberger.*

GRAND CRU In 1983 50 historically-excellent vineyards were classified as Grand Cru. They must meet stricter regulations than ordinary Alsace, and can only be planted with Riesling, Tokay-Pinot Gris, Gewürztraminer or Muscat. Notably lower (but still high) yields apply. They are recognized by the words *Appellation Alsace Grand Cru Contrôlée* on the label.

The 50 Grands Crus cover 1550 hectares, which is less than 8 per cent of the 20,250 ha classified as AC Alsace. But only 13,500 ha are planted and less than 600 ha are producing some 40,000 hectolitres of Grand Cru wine: just over 4 per cent of the production area and just under 4 per cent of the total yield of Alsace. In theory, any Grand Cru should be better than ordinary

Alsace. But delimitations are generous, and varieties like Sylvaner are excluded from sites where they always did well. In difficult years like 1986 or 1988, the better siting of the Grands Crus was crucial.

SÉLECTION DE GRAINS NOBLES The higher of the two 'super-ripe' legal descriptions based on the very high sugar content in the grapes. It only applies to wines from Riesling, Tokay-Pinot Gris, Muscat (very rare) and Gewürztraminer and corresponds to a Beerenauslese. Don't expect German acidity levels, especially not from Pinot Gris or Gewürztraminer.

VENDANGE TARDIVE The first of the 'super-ripe' categories, made from late-picked grapes. Only applies to Riesling, Tokay-Pinot Gris, Muscat (rare) and Gewürztraminer. They are very full, fairly alcoholic and vary in sweetness from richly dry to dessert-sweet.

ALSACE VINTAGES

1993 A good to average year with few high notes. This suited the low-acid varietals like Muscat and Gewürztraminer, which are fresher, crisper and more aromatic than they are in bigger, richer years.

1992 An easy vintage after a hot, dry summer. The best producers thinned the crop in the summer to reduce yields. The wines are healthy, and range from dilute to excellent.

1991 Alsace was lucky in the French context this year: unscathed by frost, the main problem, after a splendid summer, was late September and October rains. Careful vinification will have produced fresh, clean wines, but it is not a late-harvest year.

1990 Some of the older growers say 1990 is the best they have ever vinified. With healthy grapes and no noble rot, 1990 was a *vendange tardive* year. The early harvest was already too hot for Muscat. Rieslings are powerful and will age well, while the Pinots look majestic.

1989 Exceptional weather produced an abundant harvest of very good but not top quality. They have lively fruit, though some are low in acidity. Look for Grand Cru sites and better producers.

1988 Rain at harvest-time made for pleasant, but hardly inspiring wine. Tokay-Pinot Gris and Riesling are the most successful.

1987 Not great, but better than first thought. Good single vineyard wines.

1986 The best are at their peak. Good *vendange tardive* and even some *SGN*.

1985 An absolute corker – wonderful wines to drink now but they will keep.

1983 A great year, but only at the top level. These are brilliant – rich, ripe and bursting with character – and will still keep.

1976 Brilliant, deep, late-picked wines bursting with flavour and richness, but still dry.

SOUTH-EAST FRANCE

The Languedoc is on the move. It has been since the early eighties, when the dynamic and cultured leader of the local Syndicat Interprofessionel, or growers' organization, persuaded his members that the party was over; that the time had come either to make quality wine or to shut up shop. By the mid-eighties the changes were becoming palpable, with new techniques like the limited use of carbonic maceration to soften the often fruitless red grapes of the Midi, and, glory be, cold fermentation giving freshness to whites that had previously tasted of tarpaulin.

Now the changes come so fast one can hardly keep up with them. Write off a commune one year, and the next you will find three new domaines turning out clean whites and tasty reds; and the latest step in this transformation is an openness to international tastes not known in French vineyards since the English owned Bordeaux. There are British winemakers, Australian winemakers and many, many French winemakers who have brought the success of their native regions to the hot South. All are busy spreading the word: the South is France's most exciting wine region. It can make New World styles or updated traditional styles.

Last year's vintage was successful, although the Mourvèdre didn't ripen fully everywhere. But most of the harvest was in by 22 September when the storms struck hard; quantity was down, but quality is splendid. REDMOND O'HANLON

RED & ROSÉ WINES

BANDOL, AC The magnificent, pine-protected, terraced vineyards of Bandol reign over the sea beneath. The reds can be world class. Here Mourvèdre is king, but is assisted by the classic southern grapes: Grenache, Cinsaut and Syrah make herby, tobaccoey, character-laden wines. The serious spicy rosés can also be excellent. Best estates: *Ch Pradeaux, Ch Ste-Anne, Dom de la Bastide Blanche, Dom du Cageloup, Dom le Galantin, Dom de Pibarnon, Dom Ray-Jane, Dom Tempier, Dom Terrebrune, La Tour du Bòn* and the splendid co-op, *Moulin de la Roque*.

BELLET, AC There are a few good, dark reds made in *Ch de Bellet* and *Ch de Crémat*, near Nice.

CABARDES, VDQS The aromatic originality and liveliness of these wines, from a region just north of Carcassonne,

derive from the influence of two different climates, one from the Atlantic and one from the Mediterranean, and from the marriage of southern and south-western grape varieties, such as Merlot, Cabernet, Fer Servadou and Cot (Malbec). Bordeaux varieties are planted in the heavier, deeper clay soil, whereas the Mediterranean varieties are grown in chalky soil. The excellent *Ch de la Bastide* does a delicious crushed raspberry Cot. Also *Ch de Rayssac, Dom Jouclary, de Brau, Ventenac*.

CASSIS, AC Some flavoursome reds and rosés can be unearthed here, notably *Dom du Bagnol* and *Dom de la Ferme Blanche*.

COLLIOURE, AC Startling, intense reds, dominated by Grenache, with increasing contributions from Mourvèdre. This ancient vineyard, tucked in between the Pyrenees and the Med, boasts several fine estates, such as *Dom de la Rectorie, Dom du Mas Blanc, Clos des Paulilles* and *Mas Casa Blanca*.

CORBIÈRES, AC This region stretches from the beaches near Narbonne to the dramatic peaks of the Hautes Corbières. Its wines can be dramatic too, ranging from juicy upfront carbonic maceration wines to the powerful, serious, traditionally made wines like the marvellous *La Voulte-Gasparets*. Best: *Ch Cabriac, Etang des Colombes, Ch Hélène, Ch Les Ollieux, Les Palais, Caraguilhes, Fontsainte, Villemajou, St-Auréol, Dom du Révérend*.

COTEAUX D'AIX-EN-PROVENCE, AC An increasing use of Cabernet and Syrah, more rigorous selection and subtle use of new oak are combining to make several interesting individual reds and rosés in a Provençal/Bordeaux style – such as *Ch Vignelaure*. Also good: *Ch de Fonscolombe, Ch de Calissanne* and *Ch du Seuil*.

COTEAUX D'AIX-EN-PROVENCE-LES BAUX, AC More intense and complex than their big brothers, these wines are often produced in vineyards blasted from the rock. There are interesting whites, splendid rosés and several startlingly good reds, like the organic *Domaine de Trévallon*, a Cabernet/Syrah blend which makes most analogous Aussie wines look vulgar. Other organic wines are made at *Mas de la Dame* and *Mas de Gourgonnier*. *Mas Ste-Berthe* also produces a good red.

COTEAUX DU LANGUEDOC, AC This consists of three *crus* and 12 *terroirs*, running from Narbonne to Nîmes. Since 1985 it has all been happening here. The classic southern grapes are used, and the growing presence of Syrah and Mourvèdre can be discerned in the complexity and breed of many recent wines. Some of the myriad outstanding producers: *Ch Moujan, Calage, Flaugergues, Pech-Redon, Lascaux, Dom de la Coste, de la Roque, d'Aupilhac,*

de Terre-Mégère and *Dom de l'Hortus*, where I tasted the finest serious rosé I've ever drunk, and drunk, and drunk. The co-ops at *Cabrières, Montpeyrous, Neffiès, St-Saturnin and Gabian (La Carignano)* are setting very high standards. But perhaps the greatest genius of all in the *appellation* is the young, gangling *Olivier Julien*, who's always trying something new, and always succeeding, whether it's red, white, rosé, or a Sauternes-style *moelleux*.

COTEAUX VAROIS, VDQS This large region can produce some very good, cheap reds and rosés, such as *Ch St-Jean de Villecroze, Ch St-Estève* and *Dom du Loou*, whose wines are impeccably clean.

CÔTES DE LA MALEPÈRE, VDQS Lying west-south-west of Carcassonne, this is another fascinating *terroir*, with a huge variety of soil composition. Using grape varieties similar to those of Cabardès, it is also entitled to draw on Cabernet Franc, which thrives in this milieu, where the Atlantic influence is even more pronounced. The Malepère co-op produces *Ch de Festes* which shone in last year's *Webster's* southern French tasting. The *Cave du Razès*, harnessing passion to high tech, produces an array of splendid wines. *Dom de Matibat* makes a really fine Bordeaux-style wine.

CÔTES DE PROVENCE, AC A sprawling area which far too often spews out millions of trivial *petits rosés d'été* for the fried beach potatoes of the Provençal coast. There are, however, many growers who do take their calling seriously and proffer top-grade wines – such as the *Commanderie de Peyrassol, Domaines de la Bernarde, St-Baillon, Rimauresque, Richeaume, Jas d'Esclans, Aumerade, Château de Selle* (too expensive), *Mas de Cadenet* and the very distinguished *Domaine de Courtade*. The co-op of the *Presquîle de St-Tropez* produces wines of surprisingly good quality.

FAUGÈRES, AC One of the three *crus* in Languedoc. The vines grow in schist soil and engender wines of real depth, class and character in which cassis, black cherries and liquorice predominate. In mature Faugères, complex game and leather aromas can often emerge. *Alquier, Louison, Lubac, Ollier-Taillefer, Vidal* and the co-op at *Laurens* must be in anyone's top ten.

FITOU, AC A good, generous, old-style red in which Carignan has traditionally been dominant (to a maximum of 75 per cent). Grenache and, increasingly, Syrah and Mourvèdre are being used to add interest. *Paul Colomer* and *Robert Daurat-Fort* are the leading lights, along with co-ops at *Villeneuve* and at *Tuchan (Mont Tauch)*.

MINERVOIS, AC This AC is producing more and more interesting reds with good peppery berry fruit – such as those made by the co-op at *La Livinière*. *J-P Ormières*, with a magic formula of Grenache, Syrah, Mourvèdre, new oak and baroque music in the cellars makes subtle, distinguished, wine at *Ch Fabas*. Other serious producers: *Ch de Gourgazaud, Villerambert-Julien, La Combe Blanche, Ch du Donjon, Dom Maris, Ste-Eulalie, La Tour Boisée* and the co-op at *Peyriac*.

PALETTE, AC A tiny AC dominated by *Château Simone*. The rosé beats the others.

ROUSSILLON, AC While many good, fruity, dusty reds are made here, there isn't quite the same sense of pioneering adventurousness as there is in the Languedoc. The ACs of Côtes de Roussillon and Côtes de Roussillon-Villages come from much the same ares, with the latter being the best *cuvées*. *Vignerons Catalans* uses carbonic maceration very skilfully: its *Mas Camo* and *Château Cap de Fouste* are excellent. Other serious winemakers here include the delightful, innovative *Cazes* brothers, plus *Ch Corneilla* and *Dom Sarda-Malet*.

ST-CHINIAN, AC Another Languedoc *cru*, where the soil can be either schist or clay-chalk, the latter giving wines with greater aging potential. Among the top must be *Dom des Jougla, Dom Madalle, Ch Cazal-Vieil, Ch Coujan, La Dournie* and *Ch Milhau-Lacugue* (especially for its brilliant rosé). The co-ops at *Roquebrun* and *St-Chinian (Berlou)* are outstanding.

VIN DE CORSE, AC Corsican growers use the southern French grapes plus the indigenous Nielluccio and Sciacarello. *Dom de Torraccia* makes a tasty red redolent of spices and rosemary. Also good: *Clos Landry, Capitoro, d'Alzeto, Dom Filippi* and *Dom Peraldi*. There are interesting whites, too.

VIN DE PAYS This is where it's all happening. With no aging AC rules to tie them in knots, the most innovative winemakers love the *vin de pays* classification for the freedom it gives them. There's plenty of Cabernet Sauvignon being used here, but some of the most exciting flavours come from Syrah and the other flavoursome grapes of the South, like Grenache or Mourvèdre. Look for the medal-devouring wines of *Fortant de France, La Grange des Quatre Sous, Dom de Condamine-L'Evêque, Dom de la Colombette* and *Dom de l'Arjolle*, not to mention the mouth-watering, inky black *Dom de Limbardié*. And then there are the great coups being brought off by the Anglo-Australian infiltrators at *Chais Baumière* and *Dom Virginie*.

In the Gard, knee-deep in salt marshes and corralled by Camargue horses, *Listel* is living proof that a thriving empire can be built on sand. In the same region, *Dom de Gournier* and *Mas Montel* are the ones to watch; and, in the Roussillon, *Chichet, Laporte* and *Vaquer*.

The ultimate accolade here must go, however, to the ebullient, combative Aimé Guibert, whose *Mas de Daumas Gassac* reds are explosively concentrated.

WHITE WINES

BELLET, AC An unusual nutty white with a good local reputation. *Ch de Crémat* and *Ch de Bellet* are worth seeking out, though like everything near Nice, they're expensive.

BANDOL, AC These can be delicious, with a lovely aniseed-and-apple bite to them. *Dom de Pibarnon* and *Dom Lafran Veyrolles* are among the most interesting: both of these vineyards have a soil constituent, blue marl, which is very rare around here and seems to give an extra dash of elegance to their wines.

CASSIS, AC A fine but expensive white from a breathtakingly beautiful vineyard area hedged in by Marseille and Toulon. The addition of Sauvignon Blanc to the classic southern varieties gives a welcome zingy lift to the wines. Look out for *Dom du Paternel* and *Clos Ste-Magdelaine*.

CLAIRETTE DU LANGUEDOC, AC The Clairette can be a difficult grape to vinify, but the quality of wines like *Dom de la Condamine Bertrand,* the co-op at *Cabrières* and *Dom St-André* show just what can be done.

COTEAUX DU LANGUEDOC, AC White wine-making is being taken more and more seriously here, and among the best are those from La Clape, based on Bourboulenc (*Chamayrac* and *Boscary* are the stars). Another rediscovery is the Picpoul de Pinet grape which has been grown around the Etang de Thau since the Middle Ages. It is dry, medium-bodied with tingling grapefruit flavours and a touch of pepper on the finish. Delicious with seafood, it would knock many a good Muscadet off its perch. Best producers: *Claude Gaujal* and the co-ops at *Pinet* and *Pomérols.* The Chenin-based *Le Lucian* from the co-op at *St-Saturnin* is another find.

CÔTES DE PROVENCE, AC The brilliant whites of *St-André de la Figuière* and *Réal Martin* are blazing the trail here – the latter with a 100 per cent Ugni Blanc. Who said the Ugni was always only a dull workhorse variety?

LIMOUX, AC Brilliant AC Chardonnays are finally seeping into the consciousness of the *cognoscenti* and causing Burgundians to reach for their worry-beads. The sophisticated *Cave du Sieur d'Arques* is at the bottom of this dastardly plot and and there is no limit to its audacity: Mauzac, Chenin, Cabernet – you name it, it can do it, and very well, too. It also makes a fine range of sparkling Blanquette de Limoux and Crémant de Limoux (the latter must contain 40 per cent Chardonnay and/or Chenin Blanc). Other excellent Crémants are made by *Antech, Robert, Philippe Collin* and *Sev Dervin*, a spy who came in from the cold of Champagne: he couldn't lick 'em, so he joined 'em.

VIN DE PAYS The same companies that are producing some of Europe's most exciting red wines in the South of France are working on the whites, as well. They're not yet as thrilling as the reds – they're still a little too correct and 'manufactured'-tasting. But they're about a million times better than the stale old tastes that were there before, and they'll go on improving. Look for *Fortant de France, Chais Baumière* (alias *Philippe de Baudin*), *Domaine Virginie, Domaine du Bosc*'s *Muscat Sec, Listel* and the sumptuous and unusual *Mas de Daumas Gassac* white.

The price guides for this section begin on page 350..

FORTIFIED WINES

BANYULS, AC (*Vin doux naturel*) This Grenache-based (50 per cent minimum) wine comes from old, low-yielding vines on terraces above the sea. It can be red or tawny, sweet or dryish, and can come, too, in a maderized *rancio* style with burnt caramel flavours. *Dom de la Rectorie, Mas Blanc* and *Mas Casa Blanca* are good.

MAURY, AC (*Vin doux naturel*) Grenache again, without the finesse of Banyuls, but more explosive in its nutty, toffee, prunes-in-brandy intensity. It, too, can be *rancio*. Try *Mas Amiel* and the co-op at *Maury*.

MUSCAT (*Vin doux naturel*) These can range from the syrupy *Tradition* made by the *Frontignan* co-op to the elegant *Ch de la Peyrade* (Frontignan), *Dom de la Capelle* (Mireval), *Grés St-Paul* (Lunel), *Dom de Barroubie* and the co-op in *St-Jean de Minervois*. The co-op at Frontignan also makes an elegant, floral Muscat – with the help of Bordeaux white-wine whizz Denis Dubourdieu. All of these are made from the Muscat à Petits Grains which gives more finesse than the Muscat d'Alexandrie, used in Muscat de Rivesaltes (*Cazes* is the master here).

SOUTH-WEST FRANCE

The *appellations* of south-west France look to Bordeaux as their inspiration. The grape varieties spill over, and often it is merely the departmental boundary that separates them. However, the further you travel from Bordeaux, the more the grapes and flavours depart from those of the Gironde.

The most individual white of the South-west is Jurançon, from the Pyrenees, where Gros Manseng and Petit Manseng provide some intriguing flavours. Nearby Madiran has benefitted from a new generation of growers, who are working hard to improve the traditional flavours of the sturdy Tannat grape that must account for a large proportion of the blend.

The same is true of Cahors, where again a new generation is successfully rejuvenating the *appellation* and making finer, more subtle wines from the unforgiving Malbec. Even those *appellations* closest to Bordeaux are establishing their own identities, with Bergerac, Côtes de Duras, Buzet and even the recently promoted *appellation* of Côtes du Marmandais producing some rewarding alternatives to claret.   **ROSEMARY GEORGE MW**

RED & ROSÉ WINES

BÉARN Red and rosé from the far South-west. The reds are predominantly from the Tannat grape, but with other local varieties and both Cabernets thrown in. In spite of this they are basically undistinguished but you could try the wines of the *Vignerons de Bellocq* co-op, or the co-op at *Crouseilles*.

BERGERAC, AC An eastward extension of the St-Émilion vineyards, Bergerac is a kind of Bordeaux understudy, but with more mixed results. The rosés are often extremely good, deep in colour, dry and full of fruit, but the reds are more exciting, with the fruit and bite of a good, simple Bordeaux without the rough edges. Like

St-Émilion, it relies on the Merlot grape, with help from both Cabernets and Malbec, but the Bergerac reds are less substantial than St-Émilions. Sadly, most British merchants cut the prices too much for the potential of the area to be seen, so that what we get here is frequently tough, meaty, medicinal and charmless. Bergerac Rouge is usually at its best at between one and four years old, depending on vintage and style. *Ch la Jaubertie* is very good and has also produced a wood-aged *'Reserve'*. *Château le Barradis* and *Château Belingard* are also good, and *Château Court-les-Mûts* makes a delicious rosé and a good red. Most of the wines in the UK originate at the large central co-op, and quality depends on whether someone paid a few extra centimes for a better vat.

BUZET, AC Used to be labelled Côtes de Buzet. The most exciting of the claret lookalikes from a region that was historically considered part of Bordeaux. Made from Bordeaux grapes with Cabernet predominant, they can combine a rich blackcurrant sweetness with an arresting grassy greenness. They are for drinking at between one and five years old, depending on vintage and style. Look out for the wines of the co-op, which dominates the area: its *Château de Gueyze, Château Padère* and *Baron d'Ardeuil* are all pretty special. It also has a real rarity – its own cooper. Almost all the wine spends at least a couple of months in wood, and this contributes massively to Buzet's serious-but-soft appeal.

CAHORS, AC Of all the south-western country wines, Cahors is the most exciting. It's grown on both banks of the River Lot in the region of Quercy, practically due east of Bordeaux (though hotter, because it's well away from the influence of the sea). It's at least 70 per cent Auxerrois (Bordeaux's Malbec), the rest being made up of varying proportions of Merlot and Tannat.

Two hundred years ago, it was one of France's most famous wines, and the 'Black Wine of Cahors' is still held up as an example of how it used to be done. The wine was made black by the simple trick of giving the grapes a quick crushing and then, literally, boiling the must. Just as boiling gets the stain out of a shirt, so it gets the tannin and colour out of a grape skin. Fruit? Er, no, but strength (it was sometimes even fortified) and stability and massive aging potential – yes. Though without fruit, it's difficult to know what age was expected to do.

Adopting modern wine-making methods has added some lovely sweet fruit to the still dark, but now less aggressively tannic wines. There's a clear whiff of fine wine about some of the big, firm products of private growers. With age, they are often almost honeyed and raisiny, with plummy fruit that gets deeper, spicier and darker, often resembling tobacco and prunes. But another sort of Cahors has sprung up, too, lighter and less inspired, for drinking young. It can sometimes be very good. The raw materials for these are quite different: the best, traditional land of Cahors is up in the hills, but most grapes are now grown in easier vineyards on the valley slopes. One third of the wine comes from the co-op, *Côtes d'Olt*, which, after a pusillanimous, fruitless start, is beginning to produce wine with real style. Its *Ch des Bouysses* is the sort of thing, and it's responsible for ten other châteaux. Its basic wine is on the light side. Good names: *Ch de Cayrou, Ch de Chambert, Ch de Haute-Serre, Clos de Gamot, Ch St-Didier, Ch de Treilles, Dom du Cèdre, Clos la Coutale, Clos Triguedina, Dom Eugénie, Dom de Gaudou, Dom de Paillas* and *Dom de Quattre*.

CÔTES DE BERGERAC, AC This is to Bergerac what Bordeaux Supérieur is to Bordeaux: from the same region, but with slightly higher minimum alcohol. It should be better, and often is. Many are still basic Bergerac, although the excellent *Château Court-les-Mûts* now uses the AC.

CÔTES DE DURAS, AC Light, grassy claret lookalikes. *Ch de Pilar* and *Le Seigneuret* from the co-op are quite good and cheap.

CÔTES DU FRONTONNAIS, AC This makes reds largely from the local Négrette grape, plus both Cabernets, Malbec and Fer Servadou. At their best they are silky and plummy, sometimes with a touch of raspberry and liquorice. The distinctive Négrette grape is wonderfully tasty and there are now some 100 per cent Négrettes from *Bellevue-la-Forêt* and *Flotis*. Great value, but drink young, as the Négrette needs the Cabernets for staying power. There is some new oak too, but it deforms the flavour of Négrette. Best are *Dom de Baudare, Ch Bellevue-la-Forêt, Ch Flotis, Ch Montauriol, Ch la Palme*.

CÔTES DU MARMANDAIS, AC Simple, soft, fruity wines for drinking young, made from the two Cabernets, Merlot, Fer and Abouriou. A few are for more serious aging, but it doesn't suit them.

GAILLAC, AC One of the best known of the south-west wines. There are two styles: Duras plus Fer Servadou and Syrah, or Duras plus Merlot and Cabernet. Mostly, this is co-op land, but the growers who care make remarkable red. *Dom Jean Cros* is an especially delicious one. Others are *Lastours, Mas Pignou, Labarthe, Larroze*.

IROULÉGUY, AC A small AC in the Basque country. The co-op dominates, and the wine is mostly roughish, Tannat-based red, though Cabernet is increasing. Try *Domaine Brana* and *Domaine Ilarria*.

MADIRAN, AC Grown near Armagnac, Madiran is often likened to claret, but only rarely approaches its finesse. Generally about half Tannat, along with the Cabernets and occasionally Fer, it spends 20 months minimum in wood. It can be astringent and too tannic, though a new generation of growers is improving its sturdy flavours. Some are even producing a pure Tannat with some success, while others soften it with Cabernets Sauvignon and Franc. New oak barriques are popping up, too. Good ones include *Ch d'Arricau-Bordes, Ch d'Aydie* (alias *Dom Laplace*), *Ch Montus* (the only Madirans I find I really like), *Ch Boucassé, Ch Peyros, Dom du Crampilh, Dom Meinjarre, Laffitte-Teston, Dom Berthoumieu* and *Dom Moureou*.

PÉCHARMANT, AC The best red wine of Bergerac from the best slope of the region, east of Bordeaux, this must be aged for a minimum of a year before sale to distinguish it from Bergerac, which can be sold after only six months. It is deliciously blackcurranty when young. *Ch de Tiregand* is very good indeed, but *Dom du Haut-Pécharmant* is even better, resembling a top-line Médoc.

WHITE WINES

BERGERAC SEC, AC A Bordeaux lookalike from east of Bordeaux, planted largely with Sémillon and Sauvignon. *Château Belingard, Château Court-les-Mûts* and *Château de Panisseau* are good but the star is *Château la Jaubertie* where tremendous flavour and panache are extracted from a Sauvignon, Sémillon and Muscadelle blend; this last grape is now being made into a 100 per cent varietal.

CÔTES DE DURAS, AC Fairly good Sauvignon-based white that can be as fresh as good Bordeaux Blanc, but just a little chubbier. *Château de Conti* is good, as is *Le Seigneuret* from the co-operative.

GAILLAC, AC North-east of Toulouse and south of Cahors, Gaillac makes more white wine than red. It can be *moelleux* (medium sweet), *perlé* (very faintly bubbly) or dry;

the dry is usually a little terse, though a few have a quite big apple-and-liquorice fruit. The sparkling wines can be superb: peppery, honeyed, apricotty and appley all at the same time. From producers like *Boissel-Rhodes*, *Canto Perlic* (a newcomer), *Cros* or *Robert Plageoles*, they are very good value. Other still wine producers to look out for are *Ch Larroze*, *Dom du Bosc Long* and *Dom de Labarthe*. The co-op at *Labastide de Lévis* is the main, and improving, force in the area. One to watch.

JURANÇON, AC Sweet, medium or dry (though rarely *very* sweet and never *totally* dry) wine from the Pyrenean foothills. Based on the Petit Manseng, Gros Manseng and Courbu, the dry wines are usually rather nutty and dull, but the sweet wines are honeyed, raisiny and peachy, yet with a lick of acidity. New oak is appearing in some cellars. Most wine is from the local co-op, but I'd plump for a grower's wine. The pace-setter is *Henri Ramonteu*, who is experimenting avidly with different blends, picking times, and the aging of both sweet and dry whites in oak. His latest innovation is a dry white wine made only from Petit Manseng, the grape more commonly reserved for the sweet wines. Other good producers are *Clos de la Vierge* (dry), *Cancaillaü* (sweet), sweet *Cru Lamouroux*, *Clos Uroulat* (sweet), *Dom de Cauhapé*, *Dom de Souch*, *Dom Bru-Baché* (dry), *Clos Thou* (dry), *Dom Larredya*, *Clos Lapeyre*, *Dom Castera*.

MONBAZILLAC, AC This is one of the most famous names in the sweet wine world. The occasional true Monbazillac is fine, rich and honeyed, yet never as good as a top Sauternes – more like a good Loupiac or Ste-Croix-du-Mont. There are few quality-conscious single properties making the real thing, and with the banning of machine harvesting matters are improving. Ones worth seeking out include *Ch du Treuil de Nailhac*, *Ch Haut-Bernasse* and *Clos Fontindoule*. The 1990s are on the

market now, and coming from one of the hottest, most botrytized vintages for years, the best are a bargain.

MONTRAVEL, AC Dry white from the Dordogne. Côtes de Montravel is *moelleux* from the same area; Haut Montravel is a separate area and sweeter. All are mostly sold as Bergerac or Côtes de Bergerac.

PACHERENC DU VIC-BILH, AC From the Madiran area near Armagnac, this is one of France's most esoteric whites, a blend of Gros and Petit Manseng and Arrufiat – a grape peculiar to the AC. At its best when dry and pear-skin-perfumed – and sometimes when rich and sweet. Best are: *Château d'Aydie*, *Château Boucassé* and *Domaine du Crampilh*.

VIN DE PAYS CHARENTAIS The Charente produces some good, grassy-fresh whites with fairly sharp acidity – which sometimes gets the better of the fruit.

VIN DE PAYS DES CÔTES DE GASCOGNE The table wine of Armagnac, and the star of this corner of France. The Ugni Blanc is the major grape, in more abundant supply since the drop in Armagnac sales, and the Colombard adds a touch of class. They're trying out the Gros and Petit Manseng, Chardonnay, and Sauvignon too, and oak aging and *vendanges tardives*. The co-op of *Plaimont* supplies many of those on sale in Britain at reasonable prices but variable quality. However, the mood of change sweeping the south-western co-ops is evident here too. There are several labels available from the *Grassa* family estates – notably *Dom de Plantérieu* and *de Tariquet*, which are very good, full, dry and acid. Also good are *Dom St-Lannes*, *Dom les Puts* and *San Guilhem*.

The price guides for this section begin on page 355.

JURA

The wines of the Jura are best summed up in the words of one of the leading producers, Christian Bourdy. 'Oenologically all the wines of the Jura are sick, but we like them like that and we do not want to cure them.' Help! you might think. But he is right: the dominant theme in many of the wines of this isolated, mountainous region of eastern France is oxidation.

It is, however, controlled oxidation, and it is the mark of most of the region's white wine, and particularly of *vin jaune*.

Happily the red and pink wines – the distinction can be somewhat blurred – tend to have the soft raspberry flavours of Pinot Noir, sometimes blended with Poulsard and Trousseau. There is also an occasional move towards more conventional white wine production. Rollet Frères produce a Chardonnay with recognizable varietal character and at Château d'Arlay the younger generation is experimenting with Savagnin that has not been near a stave of wood. The first release of the 1992 promises well. Meanwhile the growing number of sparkling wine producers are hoping for a new *appellation* of Crémant du Jura; but it won't happen this year, and it probably won't happen next. ROSEMARY GEORGE MW

WINES & WINE REGIONS

ARBOIS, AC The general *appellation* for wines of all types from the northern part of the Jura around the town of Arbois. Reds are mostly Trousseau and thuddingly full of flavour. Savagnin weaves its demonic spells on the whites, though Chardonnay is sometimes used to soften it. Interestingly there are some attractive light reds and rosés from Pinot Noir or Poulsard which seem positively out of place, they are so delicate. *Henri Maire* is the biggest producer, but the best wines come from the village of Pupillin, where the co-op produces delicious Chardonnay and a fizz.

CÔTES DE JURA, AC These are the wines, of all colours, from the centre and south of the Jura. They are virtually indistinguishable from Arbois wines, though they are sometimes a little less disturbing in their weirdness.

L'ÉTOILE, AC Small area in the south producing whites from Savagnin and Chardonnay and, occasionally, from the red Poulsard, vinified without the colour-giving skins. Also Savagnin *vins jaunes*.

VIN JAUNE The kind of wine of which more than a small glass makes you grateful it is as rare as it is. It grows the same yeasty flor as dry sherry, and its startlingly, painfully intense flavours just get more and more evident as it matures. It seems virtually indestructible, as long as the cork is healthy.

Château-Chalon AC – the 'Montrachet' of *vin jaune*! Well, that's what they think, anyway. This is the most prized – and pricy – of the *vins jaunes*, and is difficult to find even in the region. *Vins jaunes* are sold in small 62cl *clavelin* bottles, which of course the EU tried to ban. That left me in two minds. I felt that 75cl of *vin jaune* would be just too much for anyone to handle, and indeed 37.5cl might be more like it. But I was blowed if the EU was going to destroy yet another great original in the stultifying name of conformity. The EU backed down and the 62cl *clavelin* lives. Actually there *is* a reason for the 62cl size, in that 100 litres of wine, kept in barrels for six years without being topped up, reduceş to 62 litres, or 100 bottles. So they can order in nice round numbers.

SAVOIE AND THE BUGEY

The main problem with the wines of Savoie and the Bugey is that they are not sold outside the region – those not drunk by the local population are consumed by holiday-makers. The one Savoyard company with aspirations to an international profile is Varichon & Clerc, whose best wine, a Seyssel Mousseux, is made in the classical manner from Molette, a traditional Savoyard variety, as well as some Roussette; it is sold under the brand name of Royal Seyssel.

Otherwise the principal *appellation* is simply Vin de Savoie, with its 16 *crus*, a handful of which are worth seeking out. There are Abymes and Apremont, for steely whites made from the Jacquère grape, and Chignin, which has the curiosity Chignin Bergeron – a tiny enclave of the Roussanne grape of the northern Rhône. Mondeuse, grown in Arbin and also featuring in the *cru* of Chautagne, sometimes has some earthy, berry fruit and may benefit from some barrel-aging; Chasselas, otherwise known as Fendant, grows in the vineyards closer to Lake Geneva and Switzerland. A simple Vin de Savoie, with a grape variety and no *cru*, can also be worth trying, as can a Vin du Bugey Chardonnay. Otherwise the wines of the Bugey maintain their splendid isolation, rarely travelling further than the nearby city of Lyon.   ROSEMARY GEORGE MW

WINES & WINE REGIONS

BUGEY, VDQS This little VDQS half-way between Savoie and Beaujolais, is a rising star in France for its deliciously crisp Chardonnays, although it also uses the other Savoyard grapes for whites and reds. It is one of the most refreshing, zippy Chardonnays in France, and has become a fad wine with some of the local Michelin-starred restaurants – which means the growers will keep producing it.

CRÉPY, AC The least interesting Savoie region, south of Lake Geneva, where the Chasselas produces an even flimsier version of the Swiss Fendant, if that's possible. Drink young and fast, or not at all.

ROUSSETTE DE SAVOIE, AC This can be the fullest and softest of the Savoie whites. It is usually a blend of as much as 50 per cent Chardonnay with Altesse (also known as Roussette), unless it is produced in one of the four villages or *crus*, of which Frangy is the the best known, in which case it is pure Altesse. Even at its basic level, it's good, crisp, strong-tasting white.

SEYSSEL, AC and **SEYSSEL MOUSSEUX, AC** The Roussette (blended with a little Molette) makes quite full, flower-scented but sharp-edged whites in this zone of the Haute-Savoie and the Ain. Sparkling Seyssel, with its Molette base, is also good, light but pepper-pungent and available in the UK from *Varichon et Clerc*.

VIN DE SAVOIE, AC Vin de Savoie covers the whole Savoie area, but produces the most interesting results in the South. These alpine vineyards are some of the most beautiful in France and produce fresh, snappy wines. The white, from the Jacquère, Chardonnay or Chasselas, can be excellent, dry, biting, but with lots of tasty fruit. Avoid aging them for too long. The reds from Pinot Noir or Gamay are subtly delicious, while the Mondeuse produces some real beefy beauties when the vintage is hot enough. A *cru* name is often tacked on to the best wines. Ones to look out for are Abymes, Apremont, Chignin, Cruet and Montmélian, with Chautagne and Arbin quite important for reds.

VINS DE PAYS

A *vin de pays* can provide some of the best and some of the worst drinking in France. Contrast the superstar, Mas de Daumas Gassac, made from Cabernet Sauvignon and a smattering of other varieties, with a Vin de Pays de l'Hérault from a regional co-operative, made from whatever grapes its conservative-minded members have delivered, be it Carignan and Cinsaut or even Aramon and Alicante Bouchet. There are plenty of the latter sort of *vins de pays* still around, particularly in the South, but there are increasing numbers of the former sort – and yes, they're in the South as well.

The Midi is in fact full of experimentation, for the producers are untrammelled by *appellation* regulations. If they wish to plant Roussanne or Gamay, they may; if they wish to try Viognier or Pinot Noir, why not? The new heroes in particular are Sauvignon, Viognier, Roussanne and Marsanne, while Syrah and Mourvèdre are increasingly recognized for their contribution to the regional *appellations*, as well as for varietal *vins de pays*.

In some varietal *vins de pays* the grape character may be far from obvious, often because the vines are still very young. I have yet to find a Sauvignon from the Midi that truly has the taste of Sauvignon, while the more traditional varieties like Terret Blanc and Grenache Blanc are benefitting from the improved control of fermentation temperatures. Similarly the taste of Carignan has improved enormously with vinification by carbonic maceration.

Foreign investment is already arriving in the Midi, and increasingly those who can't compete on quality terms will go under. And when they do they'll take their Aramon and Alicante Bouchet with them.   **ROSEMARY GEORGE MW**

Vins de pays come in three categories:

VINS DE PAYS RÉGIONAUX There are four of these, which between them cover a major portion of France's vineyards. Vin de Pays du Jardin de la France covers the whole Loire basin across almost to Chablis and down to the Charente. Vin de Pays du Comté Tolosan is for the South-West, starting just below Bordeaux, and covering Bergerac, Cahors, the Tarn and down to the Pyrenees, but not including the Aude and Pyrénées Orientales. Vin de Pays des Comtés Rhodaniens includes the northern Rhône and Savoy; Vin de Pays d'Oc covers Provence and the Midi right down to the Spanish border.

VINS DE PAYS DÉPARTEMENTAUX These are also large groupings, and each one is defined by the boundaries of the *département*. So, for instance, any wine of *vin de pays* quality grown in the *département* of Vaucluse will qualify for the title 'Vin de Pays du Vaucluse'.

VINS DE PAYS DE ZONE These are the tightest-controlled of the categories, and can apply to actual communes or at least carefully defined localities. The allowed yield is lower and there may be more control on things like grape varieties. So, for example, we could have a Vin de Pays de la Vallée du Paradis which is in the Aude, and could also be sold as Vin de Pays de l'Aude, or under the widest, least demanding description, Vin de Pays d'Oc.

GERMANY

From year to year the state of the British market for German wines remains much the same: the worst wines sell strongly in supermarkets and high street chains, while the great estate wines sell in tiny quantities to a band of loyal connoisseurs. Indeed, fine German wines are all but absent from the shelves of large retailers, with a handful of exceptions such as Oddbins.

Those of us who love German wines – notably Riesling – continue to clutch our heads and moan. The problem is not one of price. Fine German wines are perfectly competitive in relation to good wines from Alsace and Sancerre, not to mention Burgundy.

Perhaps the British don't like the flavour of fresh, invigorating young Riesling, or lush, honeyed yet ever-so-delicate old Riesling. But that isn't my experience. Lunching with an abstemious friend, I found a glorious Mosel from J. J. Prüm listed as a bin-end on the wine list. I expected to drink the lot, but my friend took one sip of her first-ever Riesling, purred with pleasure, and then took more than her fair share of what remained in the bottle. Privileged guests at my home are offered venerable Rieslings as an apéritif and discover, contrary to expectation, that they do like German wine after all.

What can be done to spread the word? For Christopher Tyrrell, the owner of the superb Karthäuserhof estate in the Saar, the solution is simple: 'Market from the top'. Few estate proprietors would disagree. The point has been made often enough: the German wine industry, dominated by co-operatives and wholesalers, has put most of its efforts into promoting cheap bulk wines. Over the years this has led to the almost universal impression in Britain that German wine is synonymous with sugary, flavourless, liquid pap.

From cheap to cheerful

The French produce equally awful wines, but don't promote them at the expense of great Bordeaux. As Dirk Richter, owner of a fine Mosel estate, puts it: 'The wine-lover who enjoys Beaujolais may one day switch to good Burgundy. But the British family that routinely drinks cheap German wine doesn't move up to fine estate wines. It'll switch to New World Chardonnay instead.'

Richter, who sells quite successfully in Britain, is not too concerned about the modest performance of good German wine in this country. 'We only produce two per cent of the wine made in the EU. It's not that difficult to sell the best that we make, even if little of it comes to Britain. The real crisis is with the bulk wines. Prices are so low and competition between co-operatives in regions such as Rheinhessen so intense that the growers no longer find it worthwhile to grow grapes.' But even in top wine-growing regions, prices have plummeted. In the Nahe there were, until recently, three estates owned by various members of the Anheuser family. Only one remains. In the Mosel you can buy vineyards for a quarter of the price that would have been demanded ten years ago.

The Germans blame this state of affairs on the wine laws of 1971. Their legitimate complaint is that the laws ignored differences in quality between the thousands of individual vineyard sites, and imposed a system so full of loopholes that unscrupulous producers could fool customers unfamiliar with the niceties of the law into believing that rubbish was fine wine. Great names were debased and the reputation of German wine inevitably suffered. A furious Ernie Loosen, perhaps the most dynamic grower in the Mosel, once said to me: 'The 1971 laws allow too many lies. You're allowed to take a few casks of Riesling Auslese, blend in a cask of cloying blowsy Auslese from a poor grape such as Ortega, and still label the wine as Riesling.'

Last year there was excited talk of a 'proposed update' of the 1971 laws. The talk continues, but there has been little action. If the quality-conscious growers have their way, the revised law will abolish the 'Grosslage', the collective name for a whole group of vineyards. A simple example: here are two Rheingau Rieslings, one labelled Oestricher Lenchen, the other Oestricher Gottesthal. The first comes from a fine vineyard; the second, with a Grosslage name, comes from anywhere in the Oestrich district and possibly beyond. The first is likely to be a good wine, the second mediocre. Only consumers with an encyclopedic knowledge of German vineyards can detect the difference from the label.

Worse, many Grosslagen names pay homage to renowned names. 'It's a scandal,' says Ernie Loosen, 'that famous names, associated for centuries with

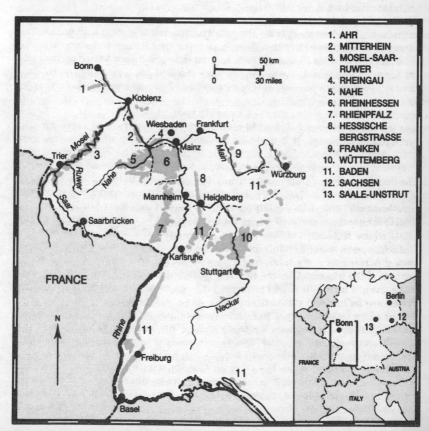

1. AHR
2. MITTERHEIN
3. MOSEL-SAAR-RUWER
4. RHEINGAU
5. NAHE
6. RHEINHESSEN
7. RHIENPFALZ
8. HESSISCHE BERGSTRASSE
9. FRANKEN
10. WÜTTEMBERG
11. BADEN
12. SACHSEN
13. SAALE-UNSTRUT

great Riesling, such as Piesporter and Niersteiner, can now be given to wines that are rubbish and contain not a drop of Riesling.'

Resistance to the abolition of Grosslagen is strong, and the change may not take place. Stefan Ress, head of the prestigious VDP (Verband Deutscher Prädikats und Qualitätsweinguter) growers' association in the Rheingau, is not too bothered. 'I don't worry too much about changes in the wine law. I prefer to find my own path. I'm now selling village wines such as my Oestricher Riesling. The wines is good but I don't want to sell it as a single vineyard wine. I keep my vineyard-designated labels for the finest wines. Hattenheimer Nussbrun is a great site, but I won't use any wine for it that is below Spätlese quality.'

This is all very admirable. But with every grower devising his own strategy in each region, the result will be chaos.

Bernhard Breuer of Rüdesheim has more radical ideas. He wants to see a vineyard classification. The best sites, perhaps a quarter of the present area, would be given Grand Cru status. Once these Grand Cru vineyards had been defined, producers should be prohibited from using traditional vineyard names for unclassified sites. Anything from lesser vineyards would be bottled as village or estate Riesling. A version of the Alsace system, in short.

Sounds fine, but it won't happen. The great estates would benefit, since they own most of the best vineyards. The small conscientious grower with good but not great vineyards wouldn't take kindly to being told he can't use any vineyard names on his labels. Some growers tell me they are happy to see certain sites designated as Grand Cru – as long as they can still put lesser sites on the label too. That way madness lies, as it will complicate German wine labels further.

Curiosity red

Meanwhile, the move towards the internationalization of German wine production continues. It is understandable that Germany, dominated by white wine production, should seek to produce more red wine for home consumption, but that is no excuse for trying to foist it on us. For about ten years Heinrich Vollmer in the Rheinpfalz has been making Cabernet Sauvignon, bravely stocked here by Augustus Barnett. A tasting of four vintages convinced me that the wine has curiosity value, like a talking horse, but beyond that it is of little worth. You can find passable Pinot Noir in Germany, but except in hot vintages such as 1990 or 1992 the wine is rarely memorable. But to grow Cabernet in Germany is as pointless as growing Syrah in Suffolk. The New World, not to mention France, will outclass you every time. As for Trollinger and Lemberger, the indigenous reds of Wurttemberg, the less said the better, at least to judge from the wines brought to London in 1994 by the region's major co-operatives. Dornfelder, a newish variety widely grown in the Pfalz, has a better future.

The Pinot varieties, however, can give excellent results, especially in Baden. Our supermarkets do stock the fairly disgusting Baden Dry, but instead they should be offering us the delicious and reasonably priced Pinot Blanc, Pinot Gris, or Pinot Noir rosés from the many outstanding co-operatives in Baden.

Still, for all the troubles besetting the German wine industry, we have an easy time of it in Britain. Almost all the top estates are available, and slow sales mean there are ample supplies of great vintages such as 1988, 1989, and 1990 from specialist merchants. At bin end sales I was still buying delicious '85s at silly prices. Thus the Germans' headaches are our bonanza.   STEPHEN BROOK

CLASSIFICATIONS

The German classification system is based on the sugar levels, and therefore the potential alcohol, of the grapes when they are picked. The main categories are as follows:

DEUTSCHER TAFELWEIN Ordinary German table wine of supposedly tolerable quality; low natural strength, sugared at fermentation to increase alcohol, no specific vineyard origin. Deutscher Tafelwein must be 100 per cent German. From a good source, like the major supermarkets, it can be better than many QbAs. The most commonly available are labelled Rhein (or Hock) or Mosel and bear some resemblance to QbAs from the Rhine or Mosel areas. Cheaper wines labelled EC Tafelwein are not worth looking at – they are usually bottled in Germany from very cheap imported wine. However, at the other end of the price spectrum are expensive 'designer table wines', red and white wines from adventurous producers who may age them in oak barriques.

LANDWEIN German *vin de pays*, slightly up-market and drier table wine from one of 20 designated areas. It can be *Trocken* (dry) or *Halbtrocken* (half-dry).

QbA (Qualitätswein bestimmter Anbaugebiete) Literally 'quality wine from designated regions' – the specific areas being Ahr, Hessische Bergstrasse, Mittelrhein, Nahe, Rheingau, Rheinhessen, Rheinpfalz, Franken, Württemberg, Baden, Mosel-Saar-Ruwer, plus two regions in what was East Germany: Saale-Unstrut and Sachsen. QbAs can be mediocre, but are not necessarily so. In modest vintages such as 1987 and 1991 they can be very good indeed, as QbAs may be chaptalized, giving wines of better body and balance than minor Kabinetts. They may also include the products of of prestigious single vineyards, where growers set standards far above those required by the law. These wines can offer outstanding value for money when produced by top estates.

QmP (Qualitätswein mit Prädikat) Quality wine with special attributes, classified in ascending order according to the ripeness of the grapes: Kabinett, Spätlese, Auslese, Beerenauslese, Eiswein, Trockenbeerenauslese. Chaptalization is not allowed, and in each category up to and including Auslese, the sugar content may range from almost non-existent to positively luscious. Drier wines may be either Trocken (dry) or Halbtrocken (half-dry). Depending on the vintage conditions, some or all of the following QmP categories will be made.

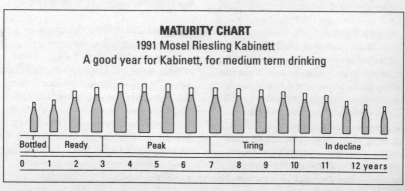

MATURITY CHART
1991 Mosel Riesling Kabinett
A good year for Kabinett, for medium term drinking

| Bottled | Ready | Peak | Tiring | In decline |

| 0 | 1 | 2 | 3 | 4 | 5 | 6 | 7 | 8 | 9 | 10 | 11 | 12 years |

KABINETT Made from ripe grapes from a normal harvest. Usually lighter in alcohol than ordinary QbA, and often delicious.

SPÄTLESE From late-picked (therefore riper) grapes. Often moderately sweet, though there are now dry versions.

AUSLESE From selected bunches of very ripe grapes. Usually sweet and sometimes touched by noble rot. In many southern regions, such as Baden, they are fermented dry, giving full wines packed with flavour.

BEERENAUSLESE (BA) From selected single grapes almost always affected by 'noble rot', a fungus that concentrates the sugar and acidity in the grapes. BA from new, non-Riesling grapes can be dull: Huxelrebe takes to noble rot so easily that you can make a BA before you've even picked Riesling. But Riesling BA, and many a Scheurebe or Silvaner, will be astonishing.

EISWEIN Just that – 'ice wine' – often picked before a winter dawn when the grapes are frozen. They are dashed to the winery by the frost-bitten pickers; once there, quick and careful pressing removes just the slimy-sweet concentrate; the water, in its icy state, stays separate. Eiswein always has a high acidity that needs to be tamed by bottle-age, though you do lose the lovely frosty, green apple flavours of youth.

TROCKENBEERENAUSLESE (TBA) 'Shrivelled berries gathered late.' That's a pedestrian translation of one of the world's great tastes. To be TBA, juice has to reach about 22 degrees potential alcohol, and can reach 30 or more. But that stifles the yeasts – so much so that fermentation may hardly get going, and a year later the liquid may have five to six degrees alcohol but 15 to 20 degrees of unfermented sugar. A top Sauternes might be picked with 22 degrees potential alcohol, but end up with 13 degrees or more, so that TBAs are usually among the sweetest wines in the world. But the tendency is to produce a slightly drier, more alcoholic style. Few growers try to make TBAs because of the risk and the cost. Remember that the vines are making a glass of wine each instead of a bottle, and the weather can easily ruin it all anyway. That's why TBAs are expensive – usually starting at £20 a half-bottle ex-cellars. But, even then, a grower won't make money; it's his pride that makes him do it. And the wines can age for as long as most of us.

GRAPES & FLAVOURS

RIESLING About 90 per cent of the most exciting wines in Germany are made from Riesling. This slow-ripening grape generally grows on the best slopes in the best villages, and when yields are controlled, it produces wonderful flavours: from steely, slaty, and dry as sun-bleached bones through apples, peaches, apricots, even lychees – more or less sweet according to the ripeness of the grapes and the intentions of the winemaker, and finally arriving at the great sweet wines, which can be blinding in their rich, honeyed concentration of peaches, pineapples, mangoes, even raisins, with an acidity like a streak of fresh lime that makes them the most appetizing of great sweet wines.

MÜLLER-THURGAU The most widely-planted German grape, this cross was propagated in 1883 to get Riesling style plus big yields and early ripening. Just like saying, 'Hey, I've just found a way to turn this plastic bowl into a gold chalice.' You can't do it. Now the workhorse, it produces soft, grapy wines when ripe – and grassy, sharp ones when not. The name Rivaner is used in general for dry wines. By reducing yields a few growers do make good wines, sometimes briefly aged in barriques.

SILVANER This was the German workhorse before Müller-Thurgau. At its worst it's a broad, earthy wine – dull, fat and vegetal. It is at its best in Franken, where it makes impressive, powerful, earthy wine which develops honeyed weight with age and suits the local porky cookery.

WEISSBURGUNDER or WEISSER BURGUNDER The Pinot Blanc is increasingly grown in Nahe, Rheinhessen, Rheinpfalz and Baden to make full dry whites, often as a Chardonnay substitute. It ripens more easily than Chardonnay though and in the right hands can produce soft, creamy wines with a touch of nuttiness. Walnuts, to be precise.

KERNER Another competitor in the 'Riesling-without-the-heartache' stakes. This was recently hailed as 'Riesling in type, but with bigger yields, and earlier ripening'. Is it? Of course not. It does ripen quickly, but the wine ages quickly, too, though with some peachy style.

RULÄNDER The French Pinot Gris. As Ruländer the style is strong, sweetish, rather broad-shouldered, with a whiff of kasbah spice and a splash of honey. When sold as Grauburgunder it is firm, dry, often aged in small oak barriques and can make exciting drinking. Some growers also call it Pinot Gris to help it sell abroad.

SCHEUREBE A tricky grape. When it's unripe, it can pucker your mouth with a combination of raw grapefruit and cat's pee. But properly ripe, it is transformed. The grapefruit is still there, but now it's a fresh-cut pink one from Florida sprinkled with caster sugar. There's honey too, lashings of it, and a crackling, peppery fire which, in the Rheinhessen, Rheinpfalz and even in the Rheingau, produces dry wines as well as sweeter, sometimes outstanding Auslese and Beerenauslese.

SPÄTBURGUNDER The Pinot Noir produces a more thrilling display further south in Burgundy. In Germany they have tended in the past to make gently fruity, slightly sweet, vaguely red wines. Now growers like *Becker* (Rheingau), *Lingenfelder* (Pfalz), *Karl-Heinz Johner* (ex Lamberhurst) and *Joachim Heger* in Baden and *Meyer-Näke* (Ahr) are doing more exciting things. Their wines have good colour and tannin, are dry and often have a spell in oak.

DORNFELDER A red variety grown mainly in the Rheinhessen and Rheinpfalz which at its best produces deep-coloured reds with great fruit concentration combined with firm structure. Made in two styles, either reminiscent of Beaujolais and for early drinking (try *Lingenfelder's*) or aged in barriques for longer keeping. *Siegrist* produces one of the best.

WINES & WINE REGIONS

AHR This small area contrives to be famous for red wines, though the flavour and the colour are pretty light, and its Rieslings are in fact more interesting. The *Staatliche Weinbaudomäne* is the best producer of old-style Spätburgunder. *Meyer-Näkel* represents the new school.

BADEN In the distant, balmy south of the country, Baden makes some red and a lovely rosé in the hills near Freiburg. Dry Ruländer and Weisser Burgunder can be really special – more reliable than the fine examples from Alsace, only ten minutes' drive away. Gewürztraminer is often dense and spicy, and even grapes like Müller-Thurgau and Silvaner can get quite interesting. There's only a little Riesling, but it's good; Spätburgunder is definitely on top. Some good value comes from small co-ops, while the area is dominated by the vast *Badische Winzerkeller*. Top producers: *Karl-Heinz Johner, Dr Heger*, the co-op at *Königsschaffhausen* and *Salwey*.

DEUTSCHER SEKT Often a sure route to intestinal distress and sulphur-led hangover, although Deinhard manages to express the lovely, lean grapiness of the Riesling; *Lila* is especially good, as is *Dr Richter*'s. *Georg Breuer*'s is outstanding, but expensive. Avoid at all costs the stuff made from imported wines, labelled Sekt (not Deutscher Sekt), or worse, Schaumwein.

FRANKEN (Franconia) This is dry wine country. The slightly earthy, slightly vegetal, big and beefy Franken wines in their flagon-shaped 'Bocksbeutel' bottles are usually based on Silvaner or Müller-Thurgau. The quality is, happily, good, but you can often get something much more interesting from elsewhere in Europe for a good deal less money. The best producers are Church and State – the *Juliusspital* and *Bürgerspital* and the *Staatlicher Hofkeller* – though *Johann Ruck* and *Hans Wirsching* at Iphofen are also good. The *Castell'sches Domänenamt* merits a detour.

HALBTROCKEN Half-dry. The general run of German wines used to go from slightly sweet to very sweet, and this 'half-dry' classification was created primarily to satisfy the Germans' own desire for dry wines to drink with food. First efforts were mean and unbalanced but three ripe vintages have shown that producers are learning how to preserve the fruit without oversweetening. At Kabinett and Spätlese level there are some quite good wines – but they're *not* cheap. Riesling Halbtrockens need at least three years to soften.

HESSISCHE BERGSTRASSE A tiny Rhine side valley running down to Heidelberg, where, presumably, most of its wine is drunk – because it never gets over here. The central town of Bensheim has one of the highest average temperatures of any wine region in Germany, so the wine is worth seeking out. In general the Rieslings are of good quality. The *Staatsweingut Bergstrasse* is the best producer.

LIEBFRAUMILCH Liebfraumilch is a brilliant invention, an innocuous, grapy liquid, usually from the Rheinhessen or Pfalz, that has dramatically fulfilled a need in the UK and US: as the perfect 'beginner's wine', it has broken through the class barriers and mystique of wine. In a way, the rest of German wine has let Liebfraumilch down, since if Liebfraumilch is the base, you should be able to move on to other things – yet many supposedly superior QbAs and even some Kabinetts, for all their high-falutin' names, are *less* satisfying than a good young Liebfraumilch.

MITTELRHEIN The Rhine at its most beautiful, providing all the label ideas for castles clinging to cliffs high above the boats and river-front cafés. It really is like that, and tourists sensibly flock there and just as sensibly drink most of its wine. One grower whose wines have got away is *Toni Jost* – his racy Rieslings are worth trying.

MOSEL-SAAR-RUWER When they are based on Riesling and come from one of the many steep, slaty, south-facing sites in the folds of the river, or strung out, mile upon mile, along the soaring, broad-shouldered valley sides, these northerly wines are unlike any others in the world. They can achieve a thrilling, orchard-fresh, spring flowers flavour, allied to an alcohol level so low that it leaves your head clear enough to revel in the flavour. Most Mosel comes from the river valley itself, but two small tributaries have been incorporated in the designation: the Saar and the Ruwer, with even lighter, perhaps sharper, perhaps more ethereal wines. Some of the best come from *Bischöfliches Konvikt, Bischöfliches Priesterseminar, Wegeler-Deinhard, Dr Loosen, Friedrich-Wilhelm-Gymnasium, Hohe Domkirche, Zilliken, Fritz Haag, von*

The price guides for this section begin on page 358.

Hövel, von Kesselstatt, Karthäuserhof, Egon Müller-Scharzhof, J.J. Prüm, Mönchhof, S.A. Prüm, M.F. Richter, Schloss Saarstein, von Schubert, Selbach-Oster, Bert Simon, Studert Prüm, Thanisch, Vereinigte Hospitien and *Weins-Prüm.*

NAHE Important side-valley off the Rhine, snaking south from Bingen. Many of the best Kabinetts and Spätlesen come from its middle slopes, wines with a grapy taste, quite high acidity and something slightly mineral too. Away from this hub of quality, the wines are less reliable. Top names: *Paul Anheuser, Crusius, Hermann Dönnhoff, Schloss Plettenberg, Prinz zu Salm Dalberg, Schlossgut Diel* and, a long mouthful to build up a thirst, *Verwaltung der Staatlichen Weinbau-domänen Niederhausen-Schlossböckelheim.*

PFALZ This used to be called the Rheinpfalz, and is still sometimes known in English as the Palatinate. The northern half clusters round some extremely good villages like Forst, Wachenheim, Deidesheim and Ruppertsberg. There's lots of fiery Riesling; Scheurebe is also excellent. The south is Germany's great success story of recent years, with fewer big names but an astonishing improvement in quality. The Pfalz is now challenging for the Rheingau for the title of top region. Look for *Basserman-Jordan, von Buhl, Bürklin-Wolf, Wegeler-Deinhard, Koehler-Ruprecht, Müller-Catoir, Pfeffingen, Rebholz, Georg Siben Erben, Siegrist* and *Lingenfelder.* There are some good, true-to-type wines from co-operatives.

RHEINGAU This fine wine area spreads north and east of Bingen. It is here, in the best sites, that the Riesling is at its most remarkable – given a long ripening period and a caring winemaker. The Rheingau contains more world-famous villages than any other German vineyard area, and even its lesser villages are well aware of their prestige. It seems a shame to grow lesser grapes here, because the Riesling picks up the minerally dryness, the tangy acidity and a delicious, grapy fruitiness, varying from apple-fresh in a good Kabinett to almost unbearably honeyed in a great TBA. Even Kabinetts have body and ripeness. Around 45 good Rheingau producers have formed the *Charta Association.* The wines, off-dry Rieslings, need four years in bottle, and are recognisable by the embossed arches on the bottle. Best: *Balthasar Ress, J.B. Becker* (also very good red), *G. Breuer, Deinhard, Johannishof, Knyphausen, Künstler, von Mumm, Nägler, Schloss Groenesteyn, Schloss Johannisberg, Schloss Reinhartshausen, Schloss Schönborn, Schloss Vollrads, Langwerth von Simmern, Staatsweingut Eltville, Dr Weil.*

RHEINHESSEN The Rheinhessen, despite having one village as famous as any in the world – Nierstein – is packed with unknown names. Wines from steep river-facing slopes at Nierstein and its unsung neighbours Nackenheim, Oppenheim and Bodenheim can be superb, softer than Rheingaus, still beautifully balanced, flowery and grapy. Otherwise, we're in Liebfraumilch and Bereich Nierstein land, and a great deal of Rheinhessen ends up in one of these two. The village, rightly, feels aggrieved, since its own reputation – traditionally sky-high – is compromised by the mouthwash that oozes out under the Bereich name. Even this is a distortion of Rheinhessen's old reputation, which was built on light, flowery Silvaner. A recent revival of this has seen the emergence of some well-made drier styles from the steep sites on the so-called Rhine Terrace. Top names: *Balbach, Carl Koch Erben, Gunderloch-Usinger, Heyl zu Herrnsheim, Rappenhof, Gustav Adolf Schmidt, Villa Sachsen, Guntrum.*

SAALE-UNSTRUT Three large producers dominate the largest of the wine regions in what we used to call East Germany. The climate is similar to Franken, the grapes are mainly Müller-Thurgau and Silvaner.

SACHSEN Germany's easternmost region in the former GDR, and previously called Elbe Tal. The vineyards are near the banks of the river Elbe, close to the cities of Dresden and Meissen, and are dominated by Müller-Thurgau. They're getting a lot of help from the West now, but there's still a lot to be done.

SEKT bA (Sekt bestimmter Anbaugebiete). Deutscher Sekt increasingly comes from private estates, and is sometimes made by the traditional Champagne method. If the wine comes from one specific quality region it can be labelled accordingly – Rheinhessen Sekt for instance – and is generally a step above Deutscher Sekt. Riesling Sekt bA is especially worth looking out for. (Try *Schloss Wachenheim* or *Winzersekt*, or *Dr Richter's*.)

TROCKEN Dry. The driest German wines. Back in the early 1970s these were painfully, searingly horrid creatures, but things improved with a series of warm vintages. Grapes high in alcohol tend to give better dry wines, so don't hesitate with Trockens from Franken of Baden, but be wary of those from Saar or Mosel.

WÜRTTEMBERG We haven't seen much Württemberg wine here because most has been drunk on the spot. Württemberg's claim to fame – if fame is the right word – is for red, which accounts for half of the production. The best grape is Lemberger, which makes dark, spicy wines suited to oak aging. Worth trying, especially from *Graf Adelmann* or *Staatliche Lehr- und Versuchsanstalt für Wein-und Obstbau. Schlossgut Hohenheilstein* is also good.

REGIONAL DEFINITIONS

German wine is classified according to ripeness of grapes and provenance. The country is divided into wine regions (alphabetically listed on these pages – Rheingau, Rheinhessen etc, and two in the former East); inside these there are three groupings. There is widespread agreement that the law needs reform, but the conflicting interests of small growers and large co-operatives is delaying the process.

Bereich This is a collection of villages and vineyard sites, supposedly of similar style, and grouped under a single name – generally that of the most famous village. So 'Bereich Nierstein' means 'a wine from the general region of Nierstein'. It could come from any one of 50 or more villages, regardless of quality.

Grosslage A group of vineyards supposedly all of similar type, based on one or more villages. The plan was to make sense of thousands of obscure vineyard names. But it doesn't work. Among the 152 designated names, there are a few good Grosslagen – like Honigberg, which groups the vineyards of Winkel in the Rheingau, or Badstube which covers the best sites in Bernkastel. In these Grosslagen, a blend of several different vineyard sites produces wine of good quality and local character. But most Grosslagen debase the whole idea of a 'vineyard' identity. Take Germany's most famous Grosslage, Niersteiner Gutes Domtal. Gutes Domtal was originally a not terribly special vineyard of 34 hectares in Nierstein. The Niersteiner Gutes Domtal Grosslage covers 1300 hectares almost all of which share no quality traits with Nierstein whatsoever.

Einzellage This is a real single vineyard wine, corresponding to a 'cru' in Burgundy or Alsace. There are about 2600 of these, ranging from a mere half hectare to 250 hectares. All the best wines in Germany are from Einzellagen, though only a distressingly small proportion actually have real individuality. Some growers are using Einzellage names less, and emphasizing their estate and grape names more, or naming QbA and QmP wines simply with the village name, such as Nierstein or Deidesheim. These wines, often from top growers, are likely to be better than many from a Grosslage.

WINERY PROFILES

FRIEDRICH-WILHELM-GYMNASIUM
★★★(★) (Mosel-Saar-Ruwer) Large Trier
estate. The best wines are textbook Mosel,
but can be inconsistent.

**FÜRSTLICH CASTELL'SCHES
DOMÄNENAMT** ★★★★ (Franconia)
Princely estate in the Steigerwald hills
which produces excellent Müller-Thurgau,
Silvaner, Riesling and as a speciality in top
years, wonderfully concentrated Rieslaner.

SCHLOSSGUT DIEL ★★★★ (Nahe)
One of the Nahe's top estates. Production is
mainly of beautifully balanced dry wines,
though sweeter styles from the warm
concentrated vintage of 1990 will be well
worth waiting for. Impeccably made,
barrique-aged dry Grauburgunder.

MÜLLER-CATOIR ★★★★★ (Pfalz)
Superbly-concentrated Riesling, Rieslaner
and Scheurebe. The jewel in its crown,
however, is probably the Grauer
Burgunder. The dry 1990 won the *Gault
Millau* Pinot Gris wine Olympics.

STAATLICHE WEINBAUDOMÄNE
★★★★ (Nahe) The State Domaine at
Niederhausen is one of the great white
wine estates of the world, producing
Rieslings which combine Mosel-like flowery
fragrance with a special mineral intensity.
Prices are very reasonable, considering the
very good quality.

VON SCHUBERT ★★★★★ (Mosel-Saar-
Ruwer) Exquisitely delicate, fragrant
Rieslings are grown on the slopes above the
Maximin-Grünhaus, a former monastic
property on the tiny Ruwer. The best
vineyard at the top of the hill is called
Abtsberg, because the wine was reserved
for the abbot: the scarcely-less-good middle
slope is called Bruderberg, and was kept
for the monks. Superlative at every level.

WEGELER-DEINHARD ★★★(★) (Mosel-
Saar-Ruwer) Koblenz-based shipper with
substantial holdings in Rheingau, Pfalz
and M-S-R. Wines from all three estates are
impeccably made. It has scaled down its
operations recently and now bottles only a
little under vineyard names. Still makes
exquisite Bernkasteler Doctor and
Wehlener Sonnenuhr.

WEINGUT BALTHASAR RESS ★★★(★)
(Rheingau) Stefan Ress's beautifully fresh,
clean Riesling wines have performed
consistently well in blind tastings. Highly
successful at both traditional-style
Spätlesen and Auslesen and off-dry wines
under the Charta group label.

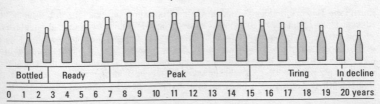

MATURITY CHART
1990 Rheingau Riesling Spätlese
Riesling Spätlese develops a more refined character after
three years in bottle

Bottled	Ready	Peak	Tiring	In decline

0 1 2 3 4 5 6 7 8 9 10 11 12 13 14 15 16 17 18 19 20 years

WEINGUT DR BÜRKLIN-WOLF★★★★
(Pfalz) The wines of this large and famous estate had plenty of aristocratic elegance until recently (particularly its top Wachenheim wines), but while the '89s and '90s are excellent, the '92s seem substandard. It might be a blip, or it might be because of recent management changes.

WEINGUT LOUIS GUNTRUM ★★★(★)
(Rheinhessen) Louis Guntrum wines are always reliable: the top Rieslings and Silvaners from the Oppenheimer Sackträger vineyard are impressively powerful, with a touch of earthiness to their fruit.

WEINGUT HEYL ZU HERRNSHEIM
★★★★ (Rheinhessen) An estate that is scandalously underrated in Britain, producing magnificent, traditional-style Riesling Spätlese, ripe yet beautifully balanced, from the red slate vineyards of Nierstein.

WEINGUT LINGENFELDER ★★★★
(Pfalz) Dynamic small estate in the northern Pfalz, producing excellent Riesling and Scheurebe, both dry and 'traditional' in style, as well as remarkably deep-coloured, full-bodied red Spätburgunder (alias Pinot Noir) and deliciously juicy red Dornfelder.

WEINGUT J.J. PRÜM ★★★★★ (Mosel-Saar-Ruwer) Legendary estate with large holdings in the great Wehlener Sonnenuhr vineyard. These are wines for the long haul: often prickly with carbon dioxide when young, and high in acidity, they develop a marvellous peachy richness with time. Wonderful stuff.

VINTAGES

1993 A warm summer promised another fine, possibly great, vintage. Rain in mid-September led to botrytis, so there was an abundance of sweet wines, with exceptional Auslesen. Yet acidity levels were mostly higher than in 1992. The Mosel and Saar had their best vintage since 1990, though with significant local variations. The Nahe and Rheingau were less successful. For Franken, it was a great year.

1992 Very good, and already being compared to 1983 and 1989. Like 1989 its problem may be acidity, making for opulent wines which may be short on bite. In the Mosel rain put paid to hopes of making much Auslese, but Spätlese quality should be excellent. Rigorous selection in Sachsen and Saale-Unstrut shows that they may be catching on.

1991 Yields were low, thanks to frost, and gave very good wines in the Saar and Ruwer, and drought led to a preponderance of QbA wines in the Mosel and Rhine. While not equalling the three preceding vintages, 1991 is not a vintage to write off. Its well-balanced Rieslings should give ample pleasure while the mega-vintages mature.

1990 The third great vintage in a row and some say the best of all. Some producers made their first sweet wines for a decade, saying the acidity was too high for dry wines. A great year for Spätlesen and Auslesen, though with little noble rot. In youth the wines have wonderful ripe fruit flavours but they will need several years for all that acidity to soften.

1989 The most forward of the trinity of great vintages, though some of the wines are a little short on acidity. From Auslese upwards the wines are luscious.

1988 Wonderful, wonderful wines. Lovely fresh acidity, a beautiful clear, thrilling fruit and remarkable array of *personalities* – you really can see the differences between sites.

1987 A pleasant, not entirely ripe vintage of sturdy QbAs. Drink it up.

1986 Not very ripe, not very clean, not very exciting. Buy only from top producers.

ITALY

Since he is based in Rome, I think I can understand why Gazza alternately bursts into tears and goes missing from Lazio's training sessions: he is trying to keep abreast of the new Italian wine laws.

A year ago, it seemed so simple. There was a new law, 164, the Goria law – so named after the Minister of Agriculture who steered it through parliament – that was going to drag Italian wine into the latter part of the twentieth century. Indeed, the cloth of Italian wine was going to be cut and tailored in a style fit to see in the new millennium. Out would go the garish check of *vino da tavola*, and in would come the smart new material of Indicazione Geografiche Tipici (IGT), similar to that used to fashion the French *vin de pays*. The classic colours of DOC and DOCG remained, but were to be used in a more intelligent manner, modern and classic at the same time.

Indeed, it was too simple. A year later, Goria is trying to steer a different course, to keep himself out of jail on corruption charges. And his law, which seemed so various, so beautiful, so new, is already looking tattered. The great powers of Italian wines – the co-operatives and the large merchants – have, in fact, torn it into pieces rather than see it fashioned into something too sleek to fit their plump, sagging bodies.

In Verona, we seem to have had the worst example of this petulance. The new law laid out quite clearly a maximum permitted yield for DOC wines, something which would have seen Soave reduced to a reasonable 85 hectolitres per hectare. On the hills of Soave Classico, where the wines are better and the yields lower anyway, this is not a problem, but on the plains, where the high-trained vines groan under the weight of the grapes the farmers force them to sustain, this would, by conservative estimates, cut yields in half. Of course this would be financially painful for the farmers, but they are in any case on a hiding-to-nothing if they carry on producing large volumes of neutral wine that fewer and fewer people want to drink. Better to change course now while they still have a market, rather than wait a few years for their wine to lose all shred of reputation, and have to start over again.

Soave on steroids

The new law gives them just such an opportunity. They could, for instance, apply for an IGT, spice up the grape mix a bit, alter the aspects of their system of training that do to the vines what steroids did to Ben Johnson and then sell their wines as Bianco Veronese or something other than Soave. Leave Soave to the hills of the Classico region, and create a new wine to replace the commonplace style *Webster's* readers would never dream of drinking. 'Why should we do this?' ask the producers. If they went and bought wines from Australia, Chile, Hungary or southern Italy, they'd have the answer.

So what did they do? They put forward the extraordinary argument that the Garganega grape, the mainstay of Soave, does not perform well if yields are reduced to such a level. What rubbish. Outdated vineyards, the sort upon which the original laws were based (and eventually foundered) are being used to undermine all the promises of law 164. So will it survive?

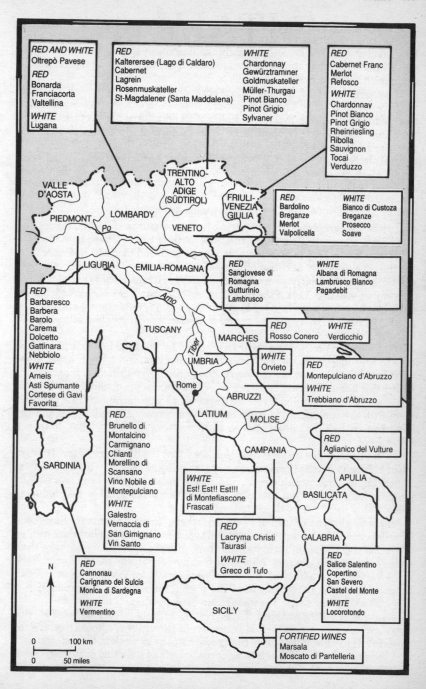

RED AND WHITE
Oltrepò Pavese

RED
Bonarda
Franciacorta
Valtellina

WHITE
Lugana

RED
Kalterersee (Lago di Caldaro)
Cabernet
Lagrein
Rosenmuskateller
St-Magdalener (Santa Maddalena)

WHITE
Chardonnay
Gewürztraminer
Goldmuskateller
Müller-Thurgau
Pinot Bianco
Pinot Grigio
Sylvaner

RED
Cabernet Franc
Merlot
Refosco

WHITE
Chardonnay
Pinot Bianco
Pinot Grigio
Rheinriesling
Ribolla
Sauvignon
Tocai
Verduzzo

RED
Bardolino
Breganze
Merlot
Valpolicella

WHITE
Bianco di Custoza
Breganze
Prosecco
Soave

RED
Sangiovese di
Romagna
Gutturinio
Lambrusco

WHITE
Albana di Romagna
Lambrusco Bianco
Pagadebit

RED
Rosso Conero

WHITE
Verdicchio

WHITE
Orvieto

RED
Montepulciano d'Abruzzo

WHITE
Trebbiano d'Abruzzo

RED
Barbaresco
Barbera
Barolo
Carema
Dolcetto
Gattinara
Nebbiolo

WHITE
Arneis
Asti Spumante
Cortese di Gavi
Favorita

RED
Brunello di
Montalcino
Carmignano
Chianti
Morellino di
Scansano
Vino Nobile di
Montepulciano

WHITE
Galestro
Vernaccia di
San Gimignano
Vin Santo

WHITE
Est! Est!! Est!!!
di Montefiascone
Frascati

RED
Aglianico del Vulture

RED
Lacryma Christi
Taurasi

WHITE
Greco di Tufo

RED
Salice Salentino
Copertino
San Severo
Castel del Monte

WHITE
Locorotondo

RED
Cannonau
Carignano del Sulcis
Monica di Sardegna

WHITE
Vermentino

N

FORTIFIED WINES
Marsala
Moscato di Pantelleria

VALLE
D'AOSTA

TRENTINO-
ALTO
ADIGE
(SÜDTIROL)

FRIULI-
VENEZIA
GIULIA

LOMBARDY

PIEDMONT

Po

VENETO

LIGURIA

EMILIA-ROMAGNA

Arno

TUSCANY

MARCHES

Tiber

UMBRIA

Rome

ABRUZZI

LATIUM

MOLISE

CAMPANIA

APULIA

BASILICATA

SARDINIA

CALABRIA

SICILY

0   100 km

0   50 miles

If we move further south, to Tuscany, the sleek locomotive of the Italian quality wine revolution, perhaps we will find that the new spirit of law 164 has been greeted with less cynicism. Surely the flow of cheap Tuscan wine into the sea of Chianti, all that stuff that used to be sold in straw-covered flasks, will be dammed by this new law?

It seems not. Instead, the consortium of Chianti growers has applied for a new law for something called Chianti Superiore. At least here there are many positive aspects to their request: maximum yields of 52 hectolitres per hectare, with no more than three kilos per plant (a far more important consideration than the yield per hectare); no blending with wines from outside Chianti, and minimum natural alcohol of 11 per cent. All this makes sense, but is destined to fail for one simple reason: they are still relying on the name bestowed on them by the laws of 1963 and 1932.

Chianti: a fiasco?

Chianti is a geographical term, referring to the communes of Radda, Gaiole and Castellina, which are situated in the hills north of Siena. These borders were defined by law in 1716 in an attempt to curtail the fraud that was widespread at the time. Yet over the next two centuries, the delimitation became increasingly elastic, and in the early years of this century, virtually every wine zone in Tuscany wanted to be part of the magic name of Chianti. They were granted their wish by their fairy godfather, Mussolini, in 1932, and many small zones, previously home to wines of quality and character, were thereafter submerged in Chianti.

This misappropriation was further legalized by the 1963 law, but now is the time to set things right, to rediscover those lost wines. But we will never know what is there as long as the *consorzio* (the region's governing body) persists in using the name Chianti to cover every red wine produced from Pisa to Pontassieve and from Siena to Sinalunga. Once again, the new law provides them with the opportunity to carve out smaller, more individual DOCs, but the opportunity, like that presented to Italian voters in March 1994, has been squandered.

With examples like these, it is little wonder that the fine fabric of law 164 is in shreds. Bright patches remain, particularly in the South, where quality is improving at a remarkable rate, and in Piedmont, where three marvellous vintages have shown that this is one of the the world's great wine-producing areas.

There is also the beacon of Bolgheri, where leading producers Sassicaia, Ornellaia and Grattamacco have grouped together to frame the law they wanted to see. Bolgheri Superiore will provide them with the opportunity to make their wines from either Cabernet, Merlot or Sangiovese, or any blend of any of the three varieties. In addition, Sassicaia seems set to be granted its own DOC, Bolgheri Sassicaia, in recognition of the work it has done, with a production of only 100,000 bottles a year, to establish the concept of fine Italian wine.

Would that others wrapped themselves so wholeheartedly in law 164. But there are too many with vested interests in the old ways, and they are too powerful. The will to initiate real change seems to be as weak in the *consorzi* as it is in the voting booths. If the Italians carry on as they have this past year, Gazza won't be the only one with tears in his eyes.   **DAVID GLEAVE MW**

RED WINES

Whereas France used always to be the model for New World exploits, Italy's great red grapes are now being taken up by the new generation of producers in California, Australia and Argentina. Having seen the heights that can be scaled with the likes of Nebbiolo, Barbera, Dolcetto and Sangiovese in Italy, they have risen to the challenge to forge the sort of flavours that their predecessors could never have created, for Italy's native red grapes are wholly individual.

GRAPES & FLAVOURS

AGLIANICO A very late-ripening grape of Greek origin, grown in the South. At its most impressive in Aglianico del Vulture (Basilicata) and Taurasi (Campania).

BARBERA The most prolific grape of Piedmont and the North-West. The wines traditionally have high acidity, a slightly resiny edge and yet a sweet-sour, raisiny taste or even a brown-sugar sweetness. But they don't have to be like this: witness some of the lighter but intensely fruity Barberas from the Asti and Monferrato hills. The grape reaches its peak in the Langhe hills around Alba where growers like *Altare, Conterno Fantino* and *Gaja* have used low yields to great effect. Experiments with barrique-aging are also encouraging, and wines like *Aldo Conterno*'s are outstandingly rich. *Alfredo Prunotto*'s *1990 Pian Romualdo Barbera d'Alba* is rather special.

BONARDA Low acid, rich, plummy reds, often with a liquoricy, chocolaty streak and sometimes a slight spritz. Most common in the Colli Piacentini of Emilia-Romagna where it is blended with Barbera as Gutturnio; also in the Oltrepò Pavese.

CABERNET SAUVIGNON The debate over the way in which Cabernet's powerful character swamped the local character of the native grapes has subsided. Fevered brows have been soothed as traditionalists have realised that the French interloper will not replace their beloved native vines, while the flag-waving revolutionaries have

reduced the prominence that Cabernet once had. Cabernet has come of age in Italy – it is now part of the intelligent new DOC for Bolgheri Superiore – but so have the producers. It is still important in the North-East and Tuscany, but it is no longer regarded as a panacea for all ills.

CABERNET FRANC Fairly widely grown in the north-east of Italy, especially in Alto Adige, Trentino, Veneto and Friuli. It can make gorgeous grassy, yet juicy-fruited reds – wines that are unnervingly easy to drink young but also capable of aging.

DOLCETTO Piedmont's answer to Gamay but, as you might expect from the region that gave us Barolo, slightly more robust. From the hills of Asti, it is light and refreshing, while from some producers in Alba, notably Mascarello, it is Dolcetto with attitude. The 1993s are delicious.

LAGREIN Local grape of the Alto Adige (Südtirol) and Trentino, making delicious, dark reds, strongly plum-sweet when they're young, aging slowly to a smoky, creamy softness. It also makes one of Italy's best rosés, called Lagrein Kretzer.

MERLOT Widely planted in the North-East. Often good in Friuli; provides lots of jug wine in the Veneto but when blended with Cabernet Sauvignon by *Loredan Gasparini* (Venegazzù) or *Fausto Maculan* (Brentino) achieves greater stature. Other Cabernet/Merlot blends are produced by

Mecvini in the Marche and Trentino's *Bossi Fedrigotti* (Foianeghe). *Avignonesi* and *Castello di Ama* in Tuscany are getting promising results, while *Ornellaia*'s *Masseto* is outstanding.

MONTEPULCIANO A much underrated grape. Yes, it is tough, but it also has lots of plummy, herby fruit. *Banfi* in Montalcino has high hopes for it. It grows mostly on the Adriatic Coast.

NEBBIOLO The big, tough grape of the North-West, making – unblended – the famous Barolos and Barbarescos as well as Gattinara, Ghemme, Carema, Spanna and plain Nebbiolo. This is a surly, fierce grape, producing wines that can be dark, chewy, unyielding and harsh behind a shield of cold-tea-tannin and acidity for the first few years; but which then blossom out into a remarkable richness full of chocolate, raisins, prunes, and an austere perfume of tobacco, pine and herbs. In the past, sloppy wine-making has been all too evident in the wines on sale here but shops are now more willing to fork out for the best.

The latter half of the 1980s saw a transformation. Whereas once the wines were unapproachable until about five years after the vintage, now the 1990s, which are bursting with fruit, seem ready to be drunk almost immediately. True, there is still a fairly hefty whack of tannin in most, but clever winemaking seems to have sheathed this in sleek and velvety fruit. A few growers (Elio Altare, Clerico, Conterno Fantino and Voerzio) are producing some

superb vini da tavola by aging their wines in barrique, or blending it with Barbera, or both, as in *Sebaste*'s *Briccoviole*.

SANGIOVESE This grape, the mainstay of Chianti and all the other major Tuscan DOCGs, is the Scarlet Pimpernel of Italian viticulture. Numerous experiments are being carried out into its nature, but they seem to produce as many questions as answers. The problem is that it is very sensitive to its environment, and changes it character completely when planted in the cool hills of Chianti, the warm clay soil of the coastal strip or the arid slopes of Montalcino. This sensitivity, which once led people to assume that the problem lay in clones, also accounts for the fact that many of the vineyards in Chianti Classico, for instance, don't produce the quality they should. Hardly surprising: the soil is too rich, the slopes too gentle and the density of planting too high. The sensitive Sangiovese might respond better if it were moved up the hill a bit, where the soil is stonier. This is the lesson people are now learning, and early results show wines of great colour, depth and vibrancy. The austere edge remains, but is balanced by the flesh, which augurs well for the future.

SCHIAVA Light reds with a unique taste that veers between smoked ham and strawberry yoghurt. An Alto Adige (Südtirol) grape, Schiava is at its best in Kalterersee (Lago di Caldaro Scelto) and Santa Maddalena. The locals, who mostly speak German, call it Vernatsch.

WINES & WINE REGIONS

AGLIANICO DEL VULTURE, DOC
(Basilicata) High up gaunt Monte Vulture, in the wilds of Italy's 'instep', the Aglianico grape makes a superb, thick-flavoured red wine. The colour isn't particularly deep, but the tremendous almond paste and chocolate fruit is matched by a tough, dusty feel and quite high acidity. What's more,

it's *not* very expensive. Two good producers are *Paternoster*, *Fratelli d'Angelo*. D'Angelo's barriqued *Canneto d'Angelo* is good.

ALTO ADIGE Also called Südtirol as the majority of the population is German-speaking. Although the UK drinks mostly the whites, the attractive light reds made of the Vernatsch/Schiava grape – especially Kalterersee and St Magdalener – have until recently been the most famous offerings. However, Cabernet, Pinot Nero, Lagrein and the tea-rose-scented Rosenmuskateller all make Alto Adige reds – and rosés – with a lot more stuffing and personality to them.

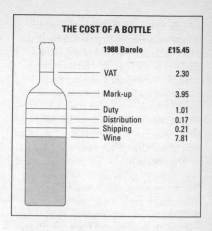

THE COST OF A BOTTLE

1988 Barolo	£15.45
VAT	2.30
Mark-up	3.95
Duty	1.01
Distribution	0.17
Shipping	0.21
Wine	7.81

BARBARESCO, DOCG (Piedmont) Toughness and tannin are the hallmarks of the Nebbiolo, Barbaresco's only grape, and they can often overshadow its finer points: a delicious soft, strawberryish maturity, edged with smoke, herbs and pine. The Riserva category (four years' aging) still exists, but most producers these days stick to the minimum two years' aging (one in wood) the law requires. When it works, the Nebbiolo can show more nuances and glints of brilliance than any other Italian grape. Best: *Luigi Bianco, Castello di Neive, Cigliuti, Glicine, Giuseppe Cortese, Gaja, Bruno Giacosa, Marchesi di Gresy, Moresco, Pasquero, Pelissero, Pertinace, Pio Cesare, Produttori del Barbaresco, Roagna, Vietti* and *Scarpa*.

BARBERA, DOC (Piedmont and others) Barbera is Italy's most widely planted red vine, and makes a good, gutsy wine, usually with a resiny, herby bite, insistent acidity and fairly forthright, dry raisin sort of fruit. It is best in Piedmont, where it has four DOCs, Barbera d'Alba, d'Asti, del Monferrato and Rubino di Cantavenna, and in Lombardy under the Oltrepò Pavese DOC; also found in Puglia, Campania, Emilia-Romagna, Liguria, Sicily, Sardinia.

BARDOLINO, DOC (Veneto) A growing number of pale pinky reds with a frail wispy cherry fruit and a slight bitter snap to the finish are appearing from the banks of Lake Garda, along with some lovely Chiaretto rosés and some excellent, *very* fresh-fruited Novello wines. There are also a few fuller, rounder wines like *Boscaini*'s *Le Canne* which can take some aging. As

quality has risen, so have the prices. Also *Arvedi d'Emilei, Guerrieri-Rizzardi, Lenotti, Masi* (*Fresco* and *La Vegrona*), *Portalupi* and *Le Vigne di San Pietro*.

BAROLO, DOCG (Piedmont) Praise be – I'm a Barolo fan! Who'd have thought it: some years ago I couldn't find *any* I liked. The raw material is still the Nebbiolo grape, a monstrously difficult character that has had to be dragged squealing and roaring into the latter half of the twentieth century. But many growers are trying to stress fruit rather than raw, rough tannins and not only will these wines be enjoyable younger – in five years rather than 20 – they will (according to the basic tenet of the modern school) actually *age better* because you can't age a wine without balance, and balance, too, makes a wine enjoyable young.

It would be easy to say only expensive Barolo is any good, just as it is easy to say that only expensive Burgundy is any good. The efforts of some of our High Street buyers show that bargains can be found, though the very nature of the zone, with only 1,200 hectares of low yielding Nebbiolo planted, makes it impossible to get anything respectable for under a fiver. But to glimpse the real majesty of Barolo, you need, as in the Côte d'Or, to step up to the great names, where the remarkable flavours of the Nebbiolo – plums and cherries, tobacco and chocolate, liquorice and violets – whirl like a maelstrom in the glass. The modernisation that has taken place in the past decade – better control during fermentation, a closer eye on aging and earlier bottling – has accentuated these flavours. This is nowhere more evident than in the glorious 1989s and 1990s, though the lighter 1991s, due out in 1995, should be more accessible.

The area of production is small, around 1200 hectares in total, and is divided into five main communes, all with individual styles. La Morra is the largest and makes the most forward and perfumed wines, ripe and velvety from around five years. Barolo itself tends to make wines of more richness and weight, but without the concentration and structure of the wines from Castiglione Falletto, and which need aging. Monforte, the southernmost commune, is known for rich and powerful wines often needing ten years in bottle. To the east, Serralunga is famous for the tough, jaw-locking style which ages more slowly than the others.

Over the last 20 years, producers have been fighting for official classification of the top sites: the new law should do this. Many are already citing vineyards on the label; for now, the ones to look for are: Arborina, Monfalletto, Marcenasco Conca, Rocche, Rocchette, Brunate, La Serra and Cerequio (La Morra); Cannubi, Sarmassa, and Brunate and Cerequio which straddle the two communes (Barolo); Bricco Boschis, Rocche, Villero, Bric del Fiasc (Castiglione Falletto); Bussia Soprana, Santo Stefano and Ginestra (Monforte); Marenca-Rivette, Lazzarito, La Delizia, Vigna Rionda, Prapo, Baudana and Francia (Serralunga). Best producers: *Altare, Azelia, Borgogno, Bovio, Brovia, Cavallotto, Ceretto, Clerico, Aldo* and *Giacomo Conterno, Conterno Fantino, Cordero di Montezemolo, Fontanafredda* (only its *cru* wines), *Bruno Giacosa, Marcarini, Bartolo Mascarello, Giuseppe Mascarello, Migliorini, Pio Cesare, Pira, Prunotto, Ratti, Sandrone, Scarpa, Scavino, Sebaste, Vajra, Vietti* and *Voerzio*.

BONARDA (Lombardy) Delicious, young, plummy red with a dark bitter chocolate twist from Lombardy and Emilia. *Castello di Luzzano* is particularly good, with great tannic length, the right fruit impact and gently peppery push.

BREGANZE, DOC (Veneto) Little-known but excellent claret-like red from near Vicenza. There's Pinot Nero, Merlot and Cabernet (Sauvignon and Franc) and these Bordeaux grapes produce a most attractive grassy, blackcurranty red, with a touch of cedar. Very good stuff... *Maculan* ages it in new wood, which makes it more exciting.

BRUNELLO DI MONTALCINO, DOCG (Tuscany) A big, strong neighbour of Chianti traditionally better known for its ridiculous prices than for exciting flavours, but slowly coming to terms with a world in which people will pay high prices, but demand excellence to go with them. The reason why the wine can be disappointing is that it can lose its fruit during the three and a half years' wood aging required by law. But in the right hands, in a good, clean cellar, the fruit can hold out, and then the wine can achieve an amazing combination of flavours: blackberries, raisins, pepper, acidity, tannin and a haunting sandalwood perfume, all bound together by an austere richness resembling liquorice and fierce black chocolate. Such wines are a growing minority, especially with the excellent 1988 vintage, though scary prices are still the norm. The best wines come from *Altesino, Argiano, Campogiovanni, Caparzo, Casanova, Case Basse, Il Casello, Castelgiocondo, Col d'Orcia, Costanti, Pertimali, Il Poggione, Talenti* and *Val di Suga*. *Biondi Santi* is the most famous and the most expensive producer but I've never had a bottle that justified the cost.

The price guides for this section begin on page 364.

CAREMA, DOC (Piedmont) The most refined of the Nebbiolo wines, this comes from a tiny mountainous zone close to Val d'Aosta. *Luigi Ferrando* is the best producer, especially his 'black label', but almost all are good – and need five to six years to be at their best.

CARMIGNANO, DOCG (Tuscany) Although the advent of Cabernet Sauvignon in Tuscany is often talked of as being an entirely recent development, Carmignano – a small enclave inside the Chianti zone just to the west of the city of Florence – has been adding in 10 to 15 per cent of Cabernet Sauvignon to its wine ever since the nineteenth century. The soft, clear blackcurrant fruit of the Cabernet makes a delicious blend with the somewhat stark flavours of the Sangiovese, which is the majority grape. There is also some good toasty, creamy rosé and some *vin santo*. The zone rose to DOCG status in 1990. *Capezzana* is the original estate and the only one which is regularly seen over here. Its 1985 and 1988 Riservas are special.

NORTH-WEST ITALY VINTAGES

North-West vintages are difficult to generalize about because it isn't always easy to catch them at their best, and a good year for Nebbiolo may not have been a good one for Dolcetto. And vice versa. Also, styles of wine-making may vary from one producer to the next. In general, Dolcetto needs drinking in its youth, Barbera can last but is often at its best young, when the fruit is most vibrant, and although there are Barolo and Barbaresco wines which you can drink after five years or so, the best last for 20 years or more. Whites should be drunk as young as possible.

1993 High hopes in September were dashed by October rains, though the long, hot and dry summer had given thick-skinned grapes that were better able to withstand the downpours than they had been in 1992. As a result, the colour is deeper and the fruit richer, and some excellent wines have been made. Particularly good for Dolcetto.

1992 Quality was diluted by September rains, which meant grey hairs for the producers and light, early drinking wines.

1991 A very fragmented year. Those wines picked before the rains in Piedmont, Gattinara and Gavi were good. It was difficult in Lombardy but there was good Valtellina and some exceptional whites. Fair to good overall.

1990 A fabulous vintage: wines of tremendous colour, richness and perfume, Barolo and Barbaresco for long aging and delicious Barbera. Wonderful Dolcetto again.

1989 Unlike the rest of Italy, Piedmont basked in glorious sunshine in 1989. Dolcetto looks even better than in the last five (excellent) vintages, and the Barbera is very good.

1988 Dolcetto and Barbera look really good, a little tough to start with perhaps, but the concentration and fruit are there. Nebbiolo got caught by the rain, but the good growers left the vineyards to dry out and picked healthy ripe grapes.

1987 Very good for Dolcetto and the whites, but patchy Barolo and Barbaresco.

1986 Barbaresco and Barolo are overshadowed by the great '85s but quality is good.

1985 An exciting vintage when more growers decided to emphasize fruit and perfume.

1983 All but the best are fading.

1982 Excellent, big ripe reds which have the fruit to age.

1978 Loads of concentrated fruit: a traditionalist's delight.

CHIANTI, DOCG (Tuscany) The first few times I had real Chianti, fizzy-fresh, purple-proud, with an invigorating, rasping fruit, I thought it was the most perfect jug wine I'd ever had. It still can be. But following the introduction of DOC in 1963, vineyards expanded all over the place to meet a buoyant demand. Chianti and especially Chianti Classico suffered more than their fair share of investors who cared only about profit and knew nothing about wine.

But Chianti might have stood more chance if the chief grape, the Sangiovese, had not been debased, first by planting the sensitive Sangiovese in poor, easily workable sites, and second by the traditional admixture of too much white juice from Trebbiano and Malvasia grapes with the red. Growers could at one time legally mix in almost one-third white grapes – yes, white grapes in red wine – and the inevitable result was wines that faded before they even made it into bottle.

Thankfully DOCG regulations now limit the proportion of white grapes to two to five per cent. This seems to have stemmed the flow of thin Chianti, and own-label examples from companies like Asda can be very good indeed.

Another development in the Chianti region has been the emergence of Cabernet Sauvignon as a component of the red wines. Although not really permissible for more than ten per cent of the total, a number of growers use it to delicious effect, though as clonal selection of better Sangiovese develops, there may come a day when this is no longer necessary. The Chianti Classico Consorzio has set in train an operation called 'Chianti Classico 2000' which is intended to ensure that as replanting takes place only top clones of Sangiovese and Canaiolo are used. By 2000 we may well be classing Chianti Classico, at least, as one of the world's great red wines once again.

The Chianti region is divided into seven

regions as follows: Classico, Colli Aretini, Colli Fiorentini, Colli Senesi, Colline Pisane, Montalbano and Rufina. Classico and Rufina are almost always marked on the label, where appropriate, but most wines from the other zones are simply labelled 'Chianti'.

CHIANTI STYLES There are two basic styles. The first is the sharp young red that used to come in wicker flasks and just occasionally still does. This starts out quite purple-red, but quickly takes on a slightly orange tinge and is sometimes slightly prickly, with a rather attractive taste, almost a tiny bit sour, but backed up by good, raisiny-sweet fruit, a rather stark, peppery bite and tobacco-like spice. This style is traditionally made by the *governo* method, which involves adding – immediately after fermentation – either a small quantity of grapes dried on racks, or concentrated must, together with a dried yeast culture, so that the wine re-ferments. Apart from the prickle, this leaves the wine softer, rounder and more instantly appealing, but it also makes it age more quickly.

The second type has usually been matured for several years and, in the bad old days before the advent of DOCG, had all the acidity and tannin it needed. Unfortunately the only fruit on show was a fistful of old raisins and a curious, unwelcome whiff of tomatoes. Nowadays there are enough exceptions around to reckon that the good wines are becoming the rule. The Chiantis of top estates, especially in fine vintages such as 1985, 1986, 1988 and 1990 are gaining a range of slightly raw strawberry, raspberry and blackcurrant flavours backed up by a herby, tobaccoey spice and a grapeskinsy roughness that makes the wine demanding but exciting. Top estates making wines to look for include *Badia a Coltibuono, Castellare, Castello di Ama, Castello dei Rampolla, Castello di San Polo in Rosso, Castello di Volpaia, Felsina Berardenga,* *Fontodi, Montesodi* and *Nipozzano (Frescobaldi), Isole e Olena, Pagliarese, Peppoli (Antinori), Riecine, San Felice, Selvapiana, Vecchie Terre di Montefili* and *Villa di Vetrice.*

DOLCETTO, some **DOC** (Piedmont) At its best, delicious, a full but soft, fresh, and dramatically fruity red, usually for gulping down fast and young, though some will age a few years. Wonderful ones come from *Altare, Castello di Neive, Clerico, Aldo Conterno, Giacomo Conterno, Marcarini, Mascarello, Oddero, Pasquero, Prunotto, Ratti, Sandrone, Scavino, Vajra, Vietti* and *Voerzio.*

FRANCIACORTA ROSSO, DOC (Lombardy) Raw but tasty blackcurranty wine from east of Milan. *Contessa Maggi, Bellavista, Ca' del Bosco* and *Longhi De' Carli* are all good.

FRIULI Six different zones (of which Grave del Friuli DOC is by far the most important quantitatively) stretching from the flat lands just north of Venice to the Slovenian border. The wines are marked by vibrant fruit. In particular, 'international' grapes like Cabernet Franc and Merlot have an absolutely delicious, juicy stab of flavour; and Refosco has a memorable flavour in the tar-and-plums mould – sharpened up with a grassy acidity. There is some good Cabernet from *Ca' Ronesca* and *Russiz Superiore. La Fattoria* and *Collavini* make excellent Cabernet and Merlot too and *Pintar* in the Collio area makes good Cabernet Franc. *Borgo Conventi*'s reds are very good and worth looking out for.

GATTINARA, DOCG (Piedmont) This is good Nebbiolo-based red from the Vercelli hills in Piedmont, generally softer and quicker to mature than Barbaresco or Barolo, but also less potentially thrilling. *Brugo, Dessilani* and *Travaglini* are important producers.

KALTERERSEE/LAGO DI CALDARO, DOC (Alto Adige) Good, light, soft red with an unbelievable flavour of home-made strawberry jam and woodsmoke, made from the Schiava (alias Vernatsch) grape in the Alto Adige (alias Südtirol). It is best as a young gulper. Best producers: *Gries* co-op, *Lageder, Muri-Gries, Hans Rottensteiner, St Michael-Eppan* co-op, *Tiefenbrunner* and *Walch*.

LAGREIN DUNKEL, some **DOC** (Alto Adige) Dark, chewy red from the Alto Adige (Südtirol) with a remarkable depth of flavour for the product of a high mountain valley. These intense wines have a tarry roughness jostling with chocolate-smooth ripe fruit, the flavour being a very successful mix between the strong, chunky style of many Italian reds and the fresher, brighter tastes of France. The *Gries* co-op, *Lageder, Muri-Gries, Niedermayr* and *Tiefenbrunner* are all good names to seek out. *Tiefenbrunner* also makes very good pink Lagrein Kretzer.

LAMBRUSCO, some **DOC** (Emilia-Romagna) Good Lambrusco – lightly fizzy, low in alcohol, red or white, dry to vaguely sweet – should *always* have a sharp, almost rasping acid bite to it. Real Lambrusco with a DOC, from Sorbara, Santa Croce or Castelvetro (and it will say so on the label), is anything but feeble and is an exciting accompaniment to rough-and-ready Italian food. But most Lambrusco is not DOC and is softened for the British market for fear of offending us. *Cavicchioli* is one of the few 'proper' ones to brave British shelves.

MONTEPULCIANO D'ABRUZZO, DOC (Abruzzi) Made on the east coast of Italy from the gutsy Montepulciano grape, a good one manages to be citrus-fresh and plummily rich, juicy yet tannic, ripe yet with a tantalizing sour bite. Fine wines are made by producers such as *Mezzanotte* and *Pepe*, while the standard of co-ops such as *Casal Thaulero* and *Tollo* is high. Other good names to look for include *Colle Secco* (from Tollo), *Illuminati* and *Valentini*.

CLASSIFICATIONS

Only 10 to 12 per cent of the massive Italian wine harvest is regulated in any way at present, and the regulations that do exist are treated in a fairly cavalier manner by many growers. At the same time producers, rebelling against the constraints imposed on their originality and initiative, have often chosen to operate outside the regulations and classify their – frequently exceptional – wine simply as *vino da tavola*, the lowest grade. This situation looks set to change, with up to 20 per cent of Italy's wines becoming subject to the law, and wines like Sassicaia probably getting their own appellation, but for the time being the following are the main categories:

Vino da Tavola This is currently applied to absolutely basic stuff but also to maverick wines of the highest class such as Sassicaia or Gaja's Piedmontese Chardonnay.

Indicazione Geografiche Tipici (or IGT for short) This will apply to table wines with some reference to place, and maybe grape type, but which do not qualify for DOC.

Denominazione di Origine Controllata (DOC) This applies to wines from specified grape varieties, grown in delimited zones and aged by prescribed methods. Nearly all of Italy's traditionally well-known wines are DOC, but more get added every year. In future, the wines will also undergo a tasting test (as DOCG wines do now).

Denominazione di Origine Controllata e Garantita (DOCG) The top tier – a tighter form of DOC with more stringent restrictions on grape types, yields and a tasting panel. First efforts were feeble, but a run of good vintages in 1983, '85, '86, '88 and '90 gave the producers lots of fine material to work with. The revised DOCG should give due recognition to particularly good vineyard sites in future.

MORELLINO DI SCANSANO, DOC A Tuscan backwater DOC that occasionally comes up with something interesting, like *Le Sentinelle Riserva* from *Mantellassi*. With a similar grape-mix to that of Chianti, its wines have a fine, dry austerity with earthy tannins, deep, ripe fruit, and remarkable, tarry spice.

OLTREPÒ PAVESE, some **DOC** (Lombardy) This covers reds, rosés, dry whites, sweet whites, fizz – just about anything. Almost the only wine we see is non-DOC fizz, usually Champagne-method, and based on Pinot Grigio/Nero/Bianco. Most Oltrepò Pavese is drunk in nearby Milan, where regularity of supply is more prized than DOC on the label. We see some red – ideally based on Barbera and Bonarda, which is good, substantial stuff, soft and fruity – though if you happen to drink it in Milan, don't be surprised to find it's fizzy.

POMINO, DOC (Tuscany) A DOC for red, white and the dessert wine *vin santo* in the Rufina area of Chianti. The red, based on Sangiovese with Canaiolo, Cabernet and Merlot, becomes rich, soft, velvety and spicy with age. The only producer is *Frescobaldi*.

ROSSO CONERO, DOC (Marches) A very good, sturdy red from the east coast of Italy opposite Florence and Siena. Combining the tasty Montepulciano grape and up to 15 per cent Sangiovese, Rosso Conero blends herb and fruit flavours; sometimes with some oak for richness. Look for *Bianchi, Garofoli, Marchetti* and *Mecvini*.

ROSSO DI MONTALCINO, DOC (Tuscany) DOC introduced in 1984 as an alternative for producers of Brunello who didn't want to age wine for Brunello's statutory four years, or who, like the top châteaux of Bordeaux, wanted to make a 'second wine'. Softer, more approachable and cheaper than Brunello di Montalcino.

ROSSO DI MONTEPULCIANO, DOC (Tuscany) This is to Vino Nobile de Montepulciano what Rosso di Montalcino is to Brunello di Montalcino: for 'lesser' Montepulciano, aged for less time in the cellar. Pretty much the same style as its big brother, but lighter and more approachable.

SPANNA (Piedmont) A Nebbiolo-based wine with a lovely raisin and chocolate flavour in the old style. Even cheap Spannas are usually a pretty good bet.

TAURASI, DOC (Campania) Remarkable, plummy yet bitingly austere red grown inland from Naples. To be honest, I'm *not* totally convinced, and am still waiting for a really exciting follow-up to the remarkable 1968. Recent releases haven't had the fruit or, as with the 1983, are impossibly tannic. *Mastroberardino* is the most important producer here.

TORGIANO, DOC and **DOCG** (Umbria) A region south-east of Perugia whose fame has been entirely created by *Lungarotti*. The reds are strong, plummy, sometimes overbearing, usually carrying the trade name *Rubesco*. Single vineyard *Monticchio* and *San Giorgio* Cabernet Sauvignon are exciting. In 1990 Torgiano Rosso Riserva became DOCG. White wines here are also clean and good. Lungarotti also makes a good flor-affected sherry-type wine called *Solleone*.

TRENTINO, DOC Just south of the Alto Adige (Südtirol), making reds either from local varieties such as Lagrein, Teroldego and Marzemino or from international grapes like Cabernet, Merlot and Pinot Noir. Too often their attractive fruit is hopelessly diluted by overcropping; a pity, because lovely Cabernet and Teroldego in particular has come from good producers, such as *Conti Martini Foradori, Istituto di San Michele, Gonzaga, Guerrieri, Pojer e Sandri, de Tarczal* and *Zeni*.

VALPOLICELLA, DOC (Veneto) Uses a variety of local grapes, especially Corvina, Rondinella and Molinara. Valpolicella *should* have delicious, light, cherry-fruit and a bitter almond twist to the finish – a bit fuller and deeper than nearby Bardolino with a hint more sourness. But it's a pretty forlorn quest unless you can find *Tedeschi*'s *Capitel Lucchine*. It's worth going for a Classico or a single-vineyard wine. The Superiore has higher alcohol, but these are wines you must drink young. Producers with good flavours are *Allegrini, Boscaini, Guerrieri-Rizzardi, Quintarelli, Le Ragose, Santi, Tedeschi, Masi* and *Zenato*.

There are a few single-vineyard wines, like *Masi*'s *Serègo Alighieri*, which are way ahead of the 'generic' stuff. They cost more, but *Allegrini*'s *La Grola* or *Tedeschi*'s *Ca' Nicalo* show what Valpolicella should be about. You might also look for wine made by the traditional *ripasso* method. In this system, new wine is pumped over the skins and lees of Recioto or Amarone, starting a small re-fermentation and adding an exciting sweet-sour dimension. *Masi, Quintarelli* and *Tedeschi* all do this well.

But the wine which can be really great is the weird and wonderful Recioto Amarone della Valpolicella. This is a wine that is imitated nowhere else. *Amaro* means bitter, and this huge wine, made from half-shrivelled Valpolicella grapes, *is* bitter, but it also has a brilliant array of flavours – sweet grape skins, chocolate, plums and wood smoke – which all sound sweet and exotic and, up to a point, they are. Yet the genius comes with that shocking, penetrating bruised sourness which pervades the wine. The good stuff is usually about three times the price of simple Valpolicella, but it's still good value for a remarkable wine. If the label simply says 'Recioto della Valpolicella', the wine will be sweeter and may still be excellent but, to my mind, a little less strangely special. Fine examples come from *Allegrini, Bertani, Masi, Quintarelli, Le Ragose, Tedeschi* and *Tramanal*.

VALTELLINA, DOC (Lombardy) Nebbiolo wine from along the Swiss border, north-east of Milan. I find it a little stringy, but someone must be drinking it because it has the largest output of Nebbiolo of any DOC, including all those in Piedmont.

VINO NOBILE DI MONTEPULCIANO, DOCG (Tuscany) A neighbour of Chianti, with the same characteristics, but more so. Usually, this means more pepper, acid and tannin at a higher price; but increasingly fine Vino Nobile is surfacing, deep wines with a marvellously dry fragrance reminiscent almost of sandalwood, backed up by good Sangiovese spice, and a strong plumskins-and-cherries fruit. Time was when you wouldn't go out of your way to find it, but that's not the case any more. There's also more of it about.
producers: *Avignonesi, Bindella, Boscarelli, di Casale, La Casalte, Fassati, Fattoria del Cerro, Fognano, Poliziano* and *Trerose*.

WHITE WINES

Italy's vinous strength is undoubtedly in its reds. They make the selection of native white varieties look very impoverished indeed: where for instance is the Nebbiolo, Sangiovese or Corvina of white varieties?

This lack of raw material has been exacerbated by a highly technocratic approach in the cellar, where the army of Italian winemakers emerging annually from the great schools of Conegliano and Alba are taught that cleanliness is paramount. There must be no flavours other than the fresh fruity ones of the the grape. Never mind that a bit of weight might be added to the wine by leaving it in contact with the lees, for example, or even (heaven forbid) a touch of complexity.

People are bored with this sort of neutrality (compounded as it is by high yields) and as a result a new generation of Italian white wine is emerging. Greater attention is being paid not only to international styles (see Sainsbury's Chardonnay del Veneto and its Italian-made Geoff Merrill wines) but also to weight and texture (as in the best Pinot Grigios of the North-East) and complexity, best exemplified by the barrel-aged Chardonnays from Tuscany. All are from imported varieties, simply because the native ones, notably Trebbiano, have few redeeming features.

The one bright spot for native whites is, oddly enough, in the South. Greco and Falanghina have wonderfully delicate perfumes that with the judicious use of technology can now be preserved.

GRAPES & FLAVOURS

CHARDONNAY The new law should alter Chardonnay's DOC status. The typical Italian style is unoaked: lean, rather floral and sharply-balanced from the Alto Adige and usually more neutral, Mâconnais-style from elsewhere. There is exciting, creamy, spicy, barrique-aged wine being made by the likes of *Gaja, Marchesi di Gresy* and *Pio Cesare* in Piedmont, *Zanella* in Lombardy, *Maculan* in the Veneto and both *Caparzo (Le Grance)* and *Avignonesi (Il Marzocco)* in Tuscany. However the best of the 'oak-free' lobby are producing some ravishing stuff by focusing on low yields and picking at the optimum moment. *Zeni* (Trentino) and *Gradnik* (Friuli) make prime examples.

GARGANEGA The principal grape of Soave. Well, it's *supposed* to make up the majority of the blend, and when well made it is refreshing, soft, yet green-apple fresh. However, it has to compete with Trebbiano Toscano in cheaper blends, and often loses.

Good producers use Trebbiano di Soave, which is much better, or Chardonnay.

GEWÜRZTRAMINER Although this is supposed to have originated in the Alto Adige (Südtirol) village of Tramin, most of the plantings there now are of the red Traminer, rather than the spicier, more memorable Gewürztraminer of Alsace. Gewürztraminer can be lovely, needing some time in bottle to develop perfume.

GRECO/GRECHETTO An ancient vine introduced to southern Italy by the Greeks, it makes crisp, pale and refreshing wines with lightly spicy overtones in Calabria and Campania and, as Grecanico, in Sicily. Grechetto is part of the same family and its delicious, nutty, aniseed character adds dramatically to Trebbiano-dominated blends in central Italy as well as sometimes surfacing under its own colours in Umbria where *Adanti* makes a splendid version.

MALVASIA This name and the related Malvoisie seems to apply to a range of grape varieties, some not related. Malvasia is found mostly in Tuscany, Umbria and Latium, where it gives a full, creamy nuttiness to dry whites like Frascati. It also produces brilliant, rich dessert wines with the density of thick brown-sugar syrup and the sweetness of raisins, in Sardinia and the island of Lipari north of Sicily.

MOSCATO The Alto Adige (Südtirol) has various sorts of Muscat, including the delicious Rosenmuskateller and Goldmuskateller, making dry wines to equal the Muscats of Alsace and sweet wines of unrivalled fragrance. But it is at its best in Piedmont, where Asti is a delicious, grapy, sweetish fizz and Moscato Naturale is a heartily-perfumed sweet wine, full of the fragrance of grapes, honey, apples and unsmoked cigars. It is best young, but *Ivaldi*'s Passito from Strevi can age beautifully. It also makes fine dessert wines on the island of Pantelleria, south of Sicily.

MÜLLER-THURGAU This is a soft, perfumy workhorse grape in Germany, but on the high, steep Alpine vineyards of the Alto Adige it produces glacier-fresh flavours; not bad in Trentino and Friuli either.

PINOT BIANCO Produces some of its purest, honeyed flavours in the Alto Adige (Südtirol), and can do very well in Friuli where the best are buttery and full.

RHEINRIESLING/RIESLING RENANO The true German Riesling is grown in the Alto Adige (Südtirol), making sharp, green, refreshing, steely dry wines – as good as most Mosel or Rhine Kabinett in Germany. It can be OK, and slightly fatter, in Friuli and Lombardy. Riesling Italico, nothing to do with real Riesling, is the dreaded Olasz/Laski/Welsch Rizling, which so despoils Riesling's name across Eastern Europe.

SAUVIGNON BLANC Quite common in the North, and gives some acid bite to far-southern blends like Sicily's Regaleali. It can be spicy, grassy and refreshing from the Alto Adige and Friuli, though the style is usually more subtle than New World Sauvignon. *Volpaia* and *Castellare* have started making it in Chianti land as have *Banfi* in Montalcino; others will follow.

SYLVANER Grown very high in the northern valleys of the Alto Adige, at its best this can be chillingly dry, lemon-crisp and quite delicious. But there are still quite a few fat, muddy examples around.

TREBBIANO The widely-planted Trebbiano Toscano is a wretched thing, easy to grow, producing vast quantities of grapes with frightening efficiency. It is responsible for an awful lot of fruitless, oxidized, sulphured blaagh-ness. However, attempts to pick it early and vinify it sharp and fresh are having some effect, and at least its use in red, yes *red* Chianti is now severely restricted. Trebbiano di Soave, the Veneto clone, is much better. Lugana is a Trebbiano DOC of character (*Zenato's* is widely available and good). Abruzzi has a strain which *can* be tasty from producers like *Tenuta del Priore, Pepe* and *Valentini*.

VERNACCIA There are several types of Vernaccia – including some red – but we mostly just see two. Vernaccia di Oristano in Sardinia is a sort of Italian version of sherry, best dry – when it has a marvellous mix of floral scents, nutty weight and taunting sourness – but also medium and sweet. Vernaccia di San Gimignano *can* be Tuscany's best traditional white – full, golden, peppery but with a softness of hazelnuts and angelica. *Fagiuoli, Teruzzi & Puthod*, and *Sainsbury's* own-label show what can be done. Some producers have tried putting it in barrique, but so far *Teruzzi e Puthod is* the only one to understand that you need an abundance of fruit in order to balance the oak.

WINES & WINE REGIONS

ALBANA DI ROMAGNA, DOCG
(Emilia-Romagna) I resent putting DOCG against this uninspiring white, which some not particularly cynical people say was made DOCG *(a)* because it was the first to apply, *(b)* because they *had* to have a white DOCG and all the others were too frightful to contemplate and *(c)* because the politicos in Bologna have a lot of clout. What's the wine like? Well, it's dry or sweet, still or slightly fizzy, or very fizzy; you see what I mean. At least these days it's less likely to be oxidized and, at its best, the dry version can be delicately scented with an almondy finish. The only really decent producers are *Fattoria Paradiso* and *Zerbina*.

ALTO ADIGE, various **DOCs** The locals up here by the Austrian border answer more warmly to *grüss Gott* than to *buon giorno* so this area is often referred to as Südtirol. Wines from these dizzily steep slopes are much more Germanic than Italian. Most are red, but this is one of Italy's most successful white regions. The wines are light, dry and intensely fresh, with spice and plenty of fruit. The best are from *Tiefenbrunner,* in his uplifting, aromatic style and *Lageder* who makes fuller, rounder wines. Both are experimenting with barrel maturation to good effect. Also *Haas*, a young producer of promise, *Hofstätter, Schloss Schwanburg, Walch* and *Terlan, Schreckbichl*, and *St Michael-Eppan* co-ops.

ARNEIS (Piedmont) Potentially stunning, apples-pears-and-liquorice-flavoured wines from an ancient white grape of the same name, with high prices to match – but since there's a feel of ripe white Burgundy about the best of them, that's not such a turn-off. Unfortunately it is trendy so some may bear the name and not much more. *Arneis di Montebertotto* by *Castello di Neive* is intense yet subtle. *Bruno Giacosa's* softer, sweeter one has a taste of hops. *Deltetto, Malvirà, Negro, Vietti, Voerzio* are good.

CENTRAL ITALY VINTAGES

1993 Another year that did wonders for sales of the ulcer drug Zantac. Things were going well until late September, when the rains came. Those grapes that ripened early, like the whites, or those zones, like Montalcino, where they harvest earlier, were lucky. The late ripeners were less fortunate, though quality seems substantially better than in 1992.

1992 Those who reduced yields have produced decent, light to medium bodied reds that are not up to '91 but will make for good drinking over the next couple of years. Early picking in Carmignano produced wines nearly as good as 1990. The Marches was also fortunate.

1991 In Tuscany, outstanding wines seem likely, including excellent Brunello. Red and white Torgiano from Lungarotti should be very good. The Marches overall look good.

1990 Excellent in Tuscany: deeply-coloured wines of tremendous perfume, built to last.

1989 The spring was good, the summer and early autumn wet. Buy good producers only.

1988 Anyone who couldn't make good wines this year ought to give up. Exciting reds.

1987 Reasonable reds such as Carmignano and nice young Chiantis.

1986 Some people are now rating 1986 Chianti Riserva more highly than the 1985s.

1985 Hardly a drop of rain from the Lords Test to the end of the season in September, so some of the wines are positively rich, but this vintage shows what DOCG is made of.

1983 In Chianti, the best '83s have aged well and are better balanced than the '82s.

ASTI, DOCG (Piedmont) Elevation to DOCG status means that the tacky 'Spumante' has been dropped from the name of the wine. Other more serious attempts are being made to improve quality, and the fact that prices have risen rapidly since DOCG came into effect on 1 February 1994 cannot be a million miles removed from the fact that there were rumoured to be about 12 million bottles of fraudulent Asti on the market. If promotion to DOCG status does nothing more than eliminate these fraudsters and take us back to the wonderfully frothy, fruit-bursting young wine that is Asti at its best, then I'll gladly open a bottle or two to toast its success.

BIANCO DI CUSTOZA, DOC (Veneto) Thought of as a Soave lookalike, though I wonder if Soave isn't a Bianco di Custoza lookalike. It contains Tocai, Cortese and Garganega, as well as Trebbiano, which helps. But the lack of pressure to make any old liquid as cheaply as possible must be as important. *Gorgo, Portalupi, Santa Sofia, Tedeschi, Le Tende, Le Vigne di San Pietro* and *Zenato* are good.

CORTESE DI GAVI, DOC (Piedmont) Cortese is the grape here, Gavi the area. The wine is dry and sharp, like Sauvignon minus the tang, and fairly full, like Chardonnay without the class. So it should be a refreshing, straight-up gulper at a pocket-easy price. But restaurant chic in Italy coos over it. The only ones I've enjoyed at anything like a reasonable price have been the fresh *Deltetto* and *Arione*, and the atypical oaked *Gavi Fior di Rovere* from *Chiarlo*.

ERBALUCE DI CALUSO, DOC (Piedmont) Half the price of Gavi, with a soft, creamy flavour, this is clean-living, plumped-out, affordable white. *Boratto, Ferrando* and *Marbelli* are good; *Boratto* also makes a rich but refreshing *Caluso Passito*.

FIANO DI AVELLINO, DOC (Campania) After numerous attempts to stomach this inexplicably famous wine from near Naples I got hold of a bottle of *Mastroberardino*'s single-vineyard *Fiano di Avellino Vignadora* and found a brilliant spring flowers scent and honey, peaches and pear skins taste. But it may have been a flash in the pan.

FRASCATI, DOC (Latium) True Frascati remains a mirage: most relies on bland Trebbiano or is spoilt by mass production. But with enough Malvasia to swamp the Trebbiano and careful wine-making, it has a lovely, fresh, nutty feel with an unusual, attractive tang of slightly sour cream. Antonio Pulcini is way ahead with *Colli di Catone, Villa Catone* and *Villa Romana;* his *cru Colle Gaio* is very special. *Fontana Candida*'s limited releases are also worth a try.

FRIULI, some **DOC** Some very good fruity and fresh whites from up by the Yugoslav border in the North-East. There's above-average Pinot Bianco, good Pinot Grigio, Chardonnay, better Gewürz, Müller-Thurgau, Riesling Renano, Ribolla and Sauvignon, and the brilliantly nutty and aromatic white Tocai, all capturing the fresh fruit of the varietal for quick, happy-faced drinking. Prices are generally in the mid- to upper range, but they are good value, especially from names like *Abbazia di Rosazzo, Attems, Borgo Conventi, Villa Russiz, Collavini, Dri, Eno Friulia, Volpe, Gravner, Jermann, Livio Felluga, Puiatti, Ronchi di Cialla, Schiopetto, Pasini.* Of the big names *Collavini* is best, but getting pricy. The almost mythical Picolit sweet wine is beautifully made by *Al Rusignul* – who is the *only* producer I've found who took this difficult grape variety seriously.

GALESTRO, DOC (Tuscany) Created to mop up the Trebbiano and Malvasia no longer used in red Chianti. Low alcohol, simple, lemony, greengage taste, high-tech style.

GAVI DI GAVI, DOC (Piedmont) (See *Cortese di Gavi*.) Grossly overpriced, clean, appley white from Piedmont. If it's labelled Gavi dei Gavi, double the number you thought of and add the price of your train fare home: Waterloo-to-Woking for the more sensible wine shops, King's Cross-to-Edinburgh for the more poncy restaurants.

LACRYMA CHRISTI DEL VESUVIO, DOC (Campania) The most famous wine of Campania and Naples. It can be red, white, dry or sweet: *Mastroberardino*'s is good.

MOSCATO D'ASTI, DOCG (Piedmont) Celestial mouthwash! Sweet, slightly fizzy wine that captures all the crunchy green freshness of a fistful of ripe table-grapes. Heavenly ones from *Ascheri, Dogliotti, Gatti, Bruno Giacosa, I Vignaioli di Santo Stefano, Michele Chiarlo, Rivetti* and *Vietti. Gallo d'Oro* is the most widely available.

ORVIETO, DOC (Umbria) Umbria's most famous wine has shaken off its old, semi-sweet, yellow-gold image and emerged less dowdy and rather slick and anonymous. It used to be slightly sweet, rich, smoky and honeyed from the Grechetto and Malvasia grapes. Its modern, pale, dry style owes more to the feckless Trebbiano. I must say I'm looking forward to Orvieto getting back to its golden days and there are signs that good producers are starting to make this happen. *Scambia* is lovely, peach-perfumed wine; *Barberani* and *Palazzone* are even better. *Decugnano dei Barbi* is good, while exciting wines, fragrant, soft and honeyed, come from *Bigi*, whose *Cru Torricella Secco* and *Cru Orzalume Amabile* (medium-sweet) are exceptional and not expensive. *Antinori*'s is a typical over-modern, under-flavoured dry, though its medium is delicious, and a new Chardonnay, Grechetto, Malvasia and Trebbiano *vino da tavola* called *Cervaro della Sala* is outstanding. Sweet, unctuous, noble-rot affected wines (*Antinori*'s *Muffato della Sala* and *Barberani*'s *Calcaia*) are rarely seen but delicious.

PROSECCO, some **DOC** (Veneto) Either still or sparkling, a lovely fresh, bouncy, light white, often off-dry, at its best from the neighbourhoods of Conegliano and Valdobbiadene. *Sainsbury's* does a typical easy-going crowd-pleaser; also look for *Canevel, Le Case Bianche, Carpené Malvolti, Collavini.*

SOAVE, DOC (Veneto) At last turning from the tasteless, fruitless, profitless mass-market bargain basement to show as an attractive, soft, fairly-priced white. The turn-around in the last few years has been quite amazing. More often than not now an own-label Soave from a good shop will be pleasant, soft, slightly nutty, even creamy. Drink it as young as possible. *Pasqua, Bertani* and *Zenato* are supplying a lot of the decent basic stuff. On a higher level *Anselmi* is outstanding, if expensive (try *Capitel Foscarino*) and *Pieropan*, especially single-vineyard wines *La Rocca* and *Calvarino*, is very good. Other good ones are *Boscaini, Zenato, Costalunga, Bolla's Castellaro, Santi's Monte Carbonare, Tedeschi's Monte Tenda* and the local co-op's *Costalta. Anselmi* also makes a *Recioto di Soave dei Capitelli* which is shockingly good in its sweet-sour way, and *Pieropan's* unoaked *Recioto* is gorgeously redolent of apricots.

TOCAI, DOC (Friuli) Full, aromatic, sometimes copper-tinged, sometimes clear as water, this grape makes lovely, mildly-floral and softly nutty, honeyed wines in Friuli, as well as increasingly good wines in the Veneto. Best producers: *Abbazia di Rosazzo, Borgo Conventi, Cà Bolani, Livio Felluga, Caccese, Collavini, Lazzarini, Maculan, Schiopetto, Villa Russiz, Volpe Pasini.*

Webster's is an annual publication. We welcome your suggestions for next year's edition.

TRENTINO, DOC This northern region, below Alto Adige, can make some of Italy's best Pinot Bianco and Chardonnay, as well as some interesting whites from Riesling, Müller-Thurgau and excellent dry Muscat. But until they stop grossly over-producing we're never going to see the full potential. The tastiest come from the mountainous bit north of the town of Trento. Look especially for *Conti Martini, Gaierhof, Istituto di San Michele, Mandelli, Pojer e Sandri, Spagnolli* and *Zeni*. Trentino also makes sparkling wine from Chardonnay and Pinot Bianco (*Ferrari* and *Equipe 5*), and fair Vino Santo (equivalent to Tuscan dessert wines) comes from *Pisoni* and *Simoncelli*.

VERDICCHIO, DOC (Marches) Of Italy's numerous whites, only Soave makes more than Verdicchio. It comes from the grape of the same name (with a little Trebbiano and Malvasia added) on the east coast opposite Florence and Siena. The wines are reliable rather than exciting – usually extremely dry, lean, clean, nutty with a streak of dry honey, sharpened by slightly green acidity. Occasionally you find fatter styles, and *Fazi-Battaglia's* single vineyard *vino da tavola Le Moie* shows the the area's potential. There is also a Verdicchio fizz. The two leading areas are Verdicchio dei Castelli di Jesi and Verdicchio di Matelica. The rarer Matelica wines often have more flavour. Good producers include: *Brunori, Bucci, Fabrini, Fazi-Battaglia, Garofoli, Mecvini, Monte Schiavo, Umani Ronchi, Zaccagnini*.

VERDUZZO, DOC (Friuli and Veneto) This is usually a soft, nutty, low acid yet refreshing light white. The DOC also includes a lovely, gentle fizz, and in Friuli Colli Orientali there are some of Italy's best sweet wines, in particular *Dri's Verduzzo di Ramandolo* and *Abbazia di Rosazzo's Amabile*.

VERNACCIA DI SAN GIMIGNANO, DOCG (Tuscany) The DOCG applies from the 1993 vintage, and officially sanctions a long-standing practice of adding up to ten per cent of Chardonnay to the blend. Can be attractively nutty, but is too often a model of bland neutrality. Exceptions are produced by the following: *Frigeni, Fagiuoli, Falchini, San Quirico, Teruzzi & Puthod* and *La Torre*.

NORTH-EAST ITALY VINTAGES

1993 The North-East seems to have escaped most of the autumn rain, or at least picked its grapes earlier. The whites from Verona, the South Tyrol and Friuli have more richness, perfume, length – well, more of everything than the 1992s, while the reds are excellent, a whisker away from the fabled 1990s.

1992 The wines picked before the rains are good, with the whites ripe and perfumed if lacking the body of 1991, and the reds medium bodied and forward. Only where yields were low is the quality good.

1991 Veneto blessed its good fortune. It was more difficult in Trentino-Alto-Adige, and some excellent reds and elegant whites were made in Friuli.

1990 Being compared with the legendary 1964. Friuli too fared extremely well. The best wines show impressive balance and concentration.

1989 Good, aromatic whites; the reds, though, were less concentrated.

1988 The quantity was reduced, but the quality was tremendous, in particular for reds.

1986 A good, balanced vintage, but there was too much overproduction for it to be exciting. It was superb for Amarone and not bad for Ripasso Valpolicella.

FORTIFIED WINES

The best known Italian fortified wine is Marsala from Sicily. The good examples may be sweet or dryish and have a nutty, smoky character which can be delicious. The off-shore island of Pantelleria produces Moscato which can be even better. Sardinia is strong on fortified wines, particularly from the Cannonau (or Grenache) grape. In general, however, the rich, dessert wines of Italy are made from overripe or even raisined grapes, without fortification.

MARSALA This Sicilian wine has, at its best, a delicious, deep brown-sugar sweetness allied to a cutting, lip-tingling acidity that makes it surprisingly refreshing for a fortified dessert wine. The rare Marsala Vergine is also good – very dry, lacking the tremendous concentration of deep brown texture that makes an old *oloroso seco* sherry or a Sercial Madeira so exciting, but definitely going along the same track. But a once great name is now also seen on bottles of 'egg marsala' and the like. A few good producers keep the flag flying; *De Bartoli* outclasses all the rest, and even makes an intense, beautifully aged, but *unfortified* non-DOC range called *Vecchio Samperi*. His *Josephine Dore* is in the style of *fino* sherry.

MOSCATO PASSITO DI PANTELLERIA From an island closer to Tunisia than Sicily, a big, heavy wine with a great wodge of rich Muscat fruit and a good slap of alcoholic strength.

VIN SANTO Holy Wine? Well, I wouldn't be too pleased with these if I were the Almighty because too much *vin santo* is vaguely raisiny and very dull. It *should* have all kinds of splendid, rich fruit flavours – apricots, apples, the richness of ripe grape skins, the chewiness of toffee, smoke and liquorice. But it's sadly rare and only *Isole e Olena* has provided me with this thrill so far. If you can't get a bottle of that try *La Calonica* or *Avignonesi* in Tuscany or *Adanti* in Umbria.

VINI DA TAVOLA

The angry young men of the 1960s have mellowed to become today's establishment. Mick Jagger is now a wealthy businessman, part-time pop star and full-time socialite, while Tom Hayden, a leading student activist, campaigner against the Vietnam war and former husband of Jane Fonda, is running for governor of California.

Italy's young turks of the wine world, the *vini da tavola*, have followed a similar career curve. When these wines first burst on to the scene, they outraged the DOC establishment, who refused to believe that mere table wines would be accepted by the market. But Cabernet, Chardonnay and French oak barrels were soon all the rage; as was a certain 'me-too' philosophy. High priced, fancily named *vini da tavola* from all sorts of regions proliferated until it was impossible to keep track of them all

Today, the likes of Sassicaia and Tignanello, once the most outrageous of these rebels, are conservative choices on a wine list. They have become established as great wines, and serve as soberly suited ambassadors for Italian wine. And such is their power in Rome that Sassicaia will become, from the 1994 vintage, the first estate in Italy to be granted its own private DOC.

This was made possible by the Goria law, passed through parliament in January 1993. This same law also made it virtually impossible for the *vini da tavola* to continue outside the DOC system, but by then they had proved their point. The proof of their victory lies in the great changes wrought by the Goria law, changes which augur well for the future of Italian wine – if, that is, they are used to good advantage.

The Goria law provides Italian wine with a more logical structure, introducing Indicazione Geografiche Tipici at the same same level as Vin de Pays in France, and allowing a DOC region to be as small as a single estate: the idea is that all high quality Italian wines will be brought under its wing, and none will be able – or will find it necessary – to work outside the system.

In any case, the great innovators of today are those working to return the likes of Chianti, Barolo or Valpolicella to their former glories; 20 years ago, people working both inside and outside the DOC laws were trying to destroy these names. And today, the non-classic areas, especially those in the South, are giving us a whole new generation of innovative DOCs to enjoy. Within a few years, the vini da tavola, like the yuppie and the Filofax, will be relics of the past, although (unlike the yuppie) they will leave a legacy of quality and innovation behind them.   DAVID GLEAVE

SANGIOVESE AND CABERNET SAUVIGNON

ALTE D'ALTESI A 30 per cent Cabernet, 70 per cent Sangiovese blend from Altesino, aged for about a year in new barriques. The '86 has good colour, fruit and elegance.

BALIFICO Volpaia's 'special', two-thirds Sangiovese, one-third Cabernet Sauvignon aged for 16 months in French oak. Exciting, exotic, oaky-rich wine, rather French in its youth, more Tuscan as it ages.

CABREO IL BORGO From Ruffino in Tuscany, vervy wines with variegated flavours: blackcurrants one moment, raspberries and brambles the next.

CA' DEL PAZZO Brunello and Cabernet from Caparzo in Montalcino. Powerful wine behind juicy blackcurrant and vanilla oak.

CAMARTINA From Querciabella, an estate high in the hills of Chianti Classico. A blend of about 80% Sangiovese and 20% Cabernet, this is one of the best of the breed.

GRIFI Avignonesi's Sangiovese/Cabernet Franc blend. It's cedary and spicily rich but lacks the class of Grifi's Vino Nobile di Montepulciano. The '85 is the best yet.

SAMMARCO Castello dei Rampolla's blend of 75 per cent Cabernet Sauvignon, 25 per cent Sangiovese. Magnificently blackcurranty, Sammarco is built to last.

TIGNANELLO First made in 1971 by Antinori, when it was Canaiolo, Sangiovese and Malvasia, it is now about 80 per cent Sangiovese and 20 per cent Cabernet. In the late 1970s it set standards that the others could only aspire to. 1988 and 1990, are excellent, rich, plummy and fleshy, and put this groundbreaker back at the top of the Super Tuscan table.

CABERNET SAUVIGNON

CARANTAN Merlot with both Cabernets, this, from Marco Felluga in Friuli, is big, savoury and tannic. The 1988 still has to come together, but shows terrific promise.

GHIAIE DELLA FURBA Made at Villa di Capezzana from roughly equal parts of both Cabernets and Merlot, and better each vintage. The 1990 is outstanding, 1989 less than impressive.

MAURIZIO ZANELLA Both Cabernets and Merlot, from Ca' del Bosco in Lombardy. Expensive but impressive, with roasted, smoky fruit. The '88 is potentially the best, with '89 and '87 not far behind.

ORNELLAIA The creation of Ludovico Antinori, brother of Piero, so presumably first cousin to Sassicaia. It's mostly Cabernet Sauvignon plus some Merlot and Cabernet Franc, made in a winery built for the purpose, and prices are sky-high. Quality is pretty terrific, too, particularly in 1990.

SASSICAIA Cabernet (Sauvignon and Franc) from Bolgheri, south-east of Livorno, it has an intense Cabernet character but a higher acidity and slightly leaner profile than most New World Cabernets. It needs about eight to ten years to begin to show at its best; '68 was the first vintage, and remains, with '72 and '82, one of the best, but '85, '88 and '90 are also excellent.

SOLAIA Piero Antinori's attempt to match Sassicaia. A blend of 80 per cent Cabernet Sauvignon and 20 per cent Sangiovese. Sassicaia beats it for beauty of flavour but Solaia does have tremendous rich fruit and a truly Tuscan bitterness to balance.

TAVERNELLE Villa Banfi's 100 per cent Cabernet from young vines at Montalcino. It has good style and varietal character.

SANGIOVESE
CEPPARELLO Very fruity rich wine from Isole e Olena, the oak beautifully blended: one of the leaders of the super-Sangioveses.

COLTASSALA Castello di Volpaia's Sangiovese/Mammolo blend, leaner and less rich than most; lovely, austere wine, needing time to soften and blossom.

FLACCIANELLO DELLA PIEVE
Fontodi's Sangiovese, aged in barrique and with a little *governo* used. Cedary, tightly grained fruit, oak and elegance.

FONTALLORO 100 per cent Sangiovese from Felsina Berardenga, fatter and richer than the Flaccianello, with a spicy rather than a cedary oak character, which takes a long time to come out of its tannic shell.

PALAZZO ALTESI 100 per cent Brunello, aged for about 14 months in new barrique at Altesino in Montalcino, packed with a delicious fruit and oakiness, and though it needs five years to develop and display its full splendour, its brilliant blackberry fruit makes it drinkable much younger.

LE PERGOLE TORTE From Monte Vertine, the first of the 100 per cent Sangiovese, barrique-aged wines. It is intensely tannic and oaky when young, and needs at least five years to open up.

SANGIOVETO Made from carefully selected old vines (about 40 years old) at Badia a Coltibuono in Chianti Classico. Yields are minute (15 to 20 hectolitres per hectare) giving tremendous concentration.

IL SODACCIO 85 per cent Sangiovese, 15 per cent Canaiolo from Monte Vertine. It could have been a Chianti, but was too oaky when young. Elegant; drink young.

I SODI DI SAN NICCOLÒ One of the most distinctive of the new-wave wines. A little rare Malvasia Nera adds wonderfully sweet and floral perfume. to the Sangiovese.

VINATTIERI ROSSO Barrique-aged blend of Sangiovese from Chianti Classico and Brunello, getting better each vintage, with the 1985 showing superb rich Sangiovese fruit and sweet oak.

WHITES
CHARDONNAY In Umbria, Antinori's *Cervaro della Sala* combines Chardonnay with Grechetto for extra-rich fruit and oak. Felsina Berardenga's *I Sistri* is fresh, zingy and grapy with an ice-cream core; Ruffino's *Cabreo La Pietra* is succulent and oaky.

TUSCAN WINERY PROFILES

MONTALCINO

ALTESINO One of the first of the new style producers in Montalcino, now making an excellent Brunello – the 1988 shows a return to form after an indifferent patch in the middle of the decade – and some good *vini da tavola*, notably under the name of Palazzo Altesi.

BANFI Oenologist Ezio Rivella's space-age winery in the hills of Montalcino, created with the money of the Mariani brothers, who brought Lambrusco to the USA. Wines include Brunello di Montalcino, Pinot Grigio, Fontanelle Chardonnay, Sauvignon, Tavernelle Cabernet Castello Banfi, a blend of Pinot Noir, Cabernet Sauvignon and Sangiovese, and Moscadello Liquoroso. New versions of Pinot Noir and Syrah will be released soon. The Banfi Spumante is one of Italy's best.

BIONDI SANTI A legendary family making a fabulously priced, but not necessarily legendary wine; however there are indications that quality is improving again, with some modernization in the cellars of its Il Greppo estate. 1988 saw its celebration of the centenary of Brunello di Montalcino.

CAPARZO is one of the new wave of Montalcino estates; investment from Milan has turned it into a serious wine producer of not only Brunello and Rosso di Montalcino, but also oak-fermented Chardonnay called Le Grance, and Ca' del Pazzo, a barrel-aged blend of Cabernet Sauvignon and Sangiovese.

FATTORIA DEI BARBI is owned by one of the old Montalcinese families, the Colombinis. Traditional methods produce serious Brunello and Rosso di Montalcino, as well as Brusco dei Barbi, and a single-vineyard wine, Vigna Fiore.

MONTEPULCIANO

AVIGNONESI An old Montepulciano family, but a relative newcomer to the ranks of serious producers of Vino Nobile, also two excellent Chardonnays: Terre di Cortona, without oak, and Il Marzocco, oak-fermented and aged wine of considerable depth. I Grifi is a barrel-aged blend of Prugnolo and Cabernet Franc.

FATTORIA DEL CERRO Traditional producers of Vino Nobile now experimenting with barriques. Its best wine remains the DOCG Vino Nobile: both 1985 and '86 were excellent and '88 will be even better.

VERNACCIA DI SAN GIMIGNANO

TERUZZI & PUTHOD Commonly acknowledged to be the best producers of Vernaccia di San Gimignano. Most expensive is the oak-aged Terre di Tufo. Also Chianti Colli Senesi and Galestro.

CHIANTI

ANTINORI Indisputably one of the great names of Chianti, boasting 600 years of wine-making. Excellent Chianti Classico from its estates Peppoli and Badia a Passignano; it also initiated the moves towards modern wine-making in Tuscany, with the development of wines like Tignanello, the archetypal barrique-aged Sangiovese, Cabernet blend. Its Orvieto estate, Castello della Sala, is the source of exciting experiments with white grapes.

FONTODI Sleek Sangiovese, in the form of single estate Chianto Classico or *vino da tavola* Flaccianello, mark this out as one of Tuscany's top names. From 1991 it has also been the source of one of Tuscany's best Pinot Noirs.

CASTELLO DI AMA Excellent single-vineyard Chianti Classico: San Lorenzo, La

Casuccia, Bellavista; also a Merlot that had critics raving in 1990. Promising Chardonnay and Pinot Grigio.

FELSINA BERARDENGA Winery very much on the up. Vigneto Rancia is a single-vineyard Chianti, I Sistri a barrique-aged Chardonnay. Fontalloro is a Sangiovese, aged in barrique for 12 months.

FRESCOBALDI The best Frescobaldi estate is Castello di Nipozzano, with a special selection Montesodi, from Chianti Rufina. It is also the producer of some excellent Pomino, including an oak-aged white, Il Benefizio. It now owns the Castelgiocondo estate further south near Montalcino, and has produced an excellent 1988 Brunello. It also makes a good white wine under the new Predicato label. Mormoreto is a fine, Cabernet-style red.

ISOLE E OLENA is rapidly increasing a reputation for fine Chianti Classico. Also Cepparello, a rich pure Sangiovese wine, made from the oldest vines of the estate; outstanding *vin santo* and a superb varietal Syrah.

RICASOLI As well as sound Chianti, Brolio makes a host of other Tuscan wines.

RUFFINO One of the largest producers of Chianti. Riserva Ducale is its best wine.

PIEDMONT WINERY PROFILES

ABBAZIA DELL'ANNUNZIATA (Barolo, La Morra) One of the greats. All the wines are full of excitement, strongly perfumed and develop wonderfully.

ELIO ALTARE (Barolo, La Morra) New wave producer – wines of firm structure and tannin behind perfumed fruit. Highly successful 1984 Barolo. Very good Barbera and Dolcetto and barrique-aged Barbera Vigna Larigi and Nebbiolo Vigna Arborina.

BRAIDA DI GIACOMO BOLOGNA (Rochetta Tanaro) Saw early the potential of Barbera in barrique: *cru* Bricco dell' Uccellone continues to impress with depth, balance and richness. An equally good Bricco della Bigotta. Unoaked, youthful Barbera, La Monella. Good Moscato d'Asti and sweetish Brachetto d'Acqui.

CASTELLO DI NEIVE (Barbaresco, Neive) Impeccable, finely crafted, austerely elegant Barbaresco from Santo Stefano. Barriqued Barbera from single *cru* Mattarello and firm, classic Dolcetto from three sites topped by Basarin. Revelatory Arneis.

CERETTO Known for both Barolo and Barbaresco. Barolo Bricco Rocche Bricco Rocche (yes) and Barbaresco Bricco Asili are legendary with prices to match. Also Barolos Brunate, Prapo, Zonchera, and Faset in Barbaresco. Light Barbera and Dolcetto. Arneis is disappointing.

CLERICO (Barolo, Monforte) Top-notch producer using barrique to fine effect in Nebbiolo/Barbera blend Arte. Barolo from two *crus* (Bricotto Bussia, Ciabot Mentin Ginestra) are among the best moderns.

ALDO CONTERNO (Barolo, Monforte) Great Barolo, traditionally made, slow to mature but worth the wait. Bussia Soprana is very special, Cicala and Colonello quite remarkable. Gran Bussia is made from selected grapes in the best years only. Il Favot (barrique-aged Nebbiolo), powerful Barbera, Dolcetto and Freisa also good.

CONTERNO FANTINO (Barolo Monforte) Guido Fantino and Diego Conterno have earned a reputation for fine Barolo from the Ginestra hillside. Rich but forward, perfumed wines, should age well.

CARLO DELTETTO (Roero, Canale) Good understated, intriguing whites from Arneis and Favorita. Reliable Roero and Gavi.

ANGELO GAJA (Barbaresco, Barbaresco) Uses barriques for most wines, including all Barbarescos: Costa Russi, Sori San Lorenzo, Sori Tildin. In vanguard of Piedmontese Cabernet (Darmagi) and Chardonnay (Gaia and Rey) production. Two Barberas (straight and *cru* Vignarey), two Dolcettos (straight and *cru* Vignabajla), Freisa and now top Barolo from the Marenca Rivette vineyard.

BRUNO GIACOSA (Barbaresco, Neive) Traditional wines of, at their best, mind-blowing quality, especially Barbaresco *cru* Santo Stefano and, best of all, Barolo from Serralunga's Vigna Rionda. Outstanding wines: rich, concentrated not overbearing, elegant. Also white Arneis and good fizz.

MARCHESI DI GRESY (Barbaresco, Barbaresco) The leading site, Martinenga, produces Barbaresco, two *crus* – Camp Gros and Gaiun, and a non-wood aged Nebbiolo called Martinenga. Elegant wines; fine '85s.

GIUSEPPE MASCARELLO (Barolo, Castiglione Falletto) Superb *cru* Monprivato at Castiglione Falletto. Also Villero and other *crus* from bought-in grapes. Barbera d'Alba Ginestra is notable. Excellent inky Dolcetto comes from a different vineyard each year; in 1993 it was Pian Romualdo.

PAOLO CORDERO DI MONTEZEMOLO (Barolo, La Morra) Wines with the accent on fruit. Standard-bearer is *cru* Monfalletto from La Morra; for some the holy of holies. *Cru* Enrico VI is from Castiglione Falletto, refined, elegant scented. Barbera, Dolcetto etc also made.

FRATELLI ODDERO (Barolo, La Morra) Barolo, Barbera, Dolcetto etc from own vineyards in prime sites in the area and Barbaresco from bought-in grapes. Wines of good roundness, balance, style, value.

PIO CESARE (Barolo, Alba) Full spread of Barolo, Barbaresco, Nebbiolo d'Alba, Dolcetto, Barbera, Grignolino and Gavi. Wines are gaining elegance, losing a bit of punch but gaining harmony and balance. Experiments with barriques; also Nebbio (young-drinking Nebbiolo), Piodilei (barriqued Chardonnay).

GIUSEPPE RIVETTI (Asti, Castagnole Lanze) Smallish quantities of magical Moscato d'Asti which sell out in a flash.

LUCIANO SANDRONE (Barolo, Barolo) A small producer making tiny quantities of perfumed Barolo with lovely raspberry and black cherry flavours from the Cannubi-Boschis vineyard. Also excellent Dolcetto.

PAOLO SCAVINO (Barolo, Castiglione Falletto) Hailed locally as one of the emerging masters of Barolo, Scavino makes superb wines which combine purity of fruit with depth and structure. Barolo Bric' del Fiasc' is his top wine; Cannubi and straight Barolo are not far behind. Delicious Dolcetto and Barbera.

VIETTI (Barolo, Castiglione Falletto) Goes from strength to strength. Classically perfect wines of their type, with a punch of acidity and tannin, plus elegance and class. Barolo (straight plus *crus* Rocche, Villero and Brunate) and Barbaresco (*normale* plus *crus* Masseria, Rabajà) are intensely complex wines. Dolcetto and Barbera also very good. Also one of the top Moscato d'Astis. Highly enjoyable Arneis.

ROBERTO VOERZIO (Barolo, La Morra) Ultra-modern approach. Attractive and fine wines, full of fruit and perfume, made with great skill, giving Roberto (not to be confused with brother Gianni) the reputation as an up and coming great. Produces Barolo, Dolcetto d'Alba, Barbera d'Alba, Freisa, and delicious barrique-aged Barbera/Nebbiolo blend Vignaserra, as well as fine Arneis.

SPAIN

Spain has gone through some testing times lately. There have been new ideas, new developments and new attitudes and, from time to time, it's been a case of two steps forward, one step back as projects were curtailed by lack of cashflow and dreams died on the rack of recession. That was the atmosphere that prevailed 18 months ago, when quite a few Spanish wine producers had begun to doubt whether all the work they'd put in and all the investment they'd made was ever going to pay off.

However, it seems they needn't have worried: 1993-94 saw an unprecedented upturn in interest by wine drinkers in Britain and throughout the world, followed by a commensurate increase in exports. At least one British retail chain (Thresher's) has a Spanish list today that 25 years ago would have done credit to a specialist independent. Statistically, Spain lies fourth in the top five countries imported into Britain, after France, Germany and Italy and (just) in front of Australia. Interestingly enough, France, Germany and Italy all registered a three-year decline to 1993, while Spanish imports increased by more than a quarter. Overall, the British market for light wines grew by 2.2 per cent in the years from 1990 to 1993, while Spanish wine imports grew by 26.5 per cent in the same period.

So, what's going on around the regions? Best performer of 1993-94 is undoubtedly Cava, with nearly a 19 per cent increase over the previous year.

This is probably due to a new realization amongst Cava producers that the export market demands something a little lighter and fresher than the traditional earthy, rooty style of fruit that knocks 'em dead in the bars of Barcelona. After initial trials with Chardonnay, which were only patchily successful, more attention to the health of the grapes on the vine, the speed with which they're transported to the winery and the delicacy with which they're pressed and fermented has resulted in a new style of Cava, best exemplified by Aria from Segura Viudas.

If there were a moving-up-on-the-rails trophy it would probably go to Ribera del Duero, which has virtually re-invented itself in the last five years. The success of Pesquera from Alejandro Fernández has encouraged a large number of growers and winemakers to re-think their approach and, given the unique attributes of the region, wake up their ideas. Even a year ago, the market for these wines was dominated by the big names of the region: Vega Sicilia, obviously, followed by Pesquera, Torremilanos, Protos and a few minor players. But the *Webster's* tasting of Spanish and Portuguese wines this year (see page 10) contained no fewer than 18 wines from Ribera del Duero, although they didn't exactly steal the show.

Pesquera with cabbages

The success of Pesquera in the late 1980s had two immediate effects. It reminded existing growers and winemakers that they lived and worked in what was potentially one of the best grape-growing regions of Europe, with a climate, soils and altitude ideally suited to the making of top-quality wines. And it galvanized the younger generation of winemakers – those whose parents had grown grapes and sold them to the local co-op or independent winery for years – into action on their own account. Quite a bit of land registered for vineyards – rich in chalk, quartz and trace elements – had been replanted during the mid-1980s with cereals and cabbages, as Ribera del Duero wine – apart from the few big-name front-runners – stubbornly refused to get off the ground in the export market-place. Quite a few of this younger generation of vineyard-owners had also been to agricultural colleges and oenological universities to study the latest techniques and technology in grape-growing and winemaking. They had seen the future and returned with a mission to create it.

Ironically, Ribera del Duero's natural advantages had been its problem: it's so easy to produce good quality wine there that even the laziest, most dinosaur-like co-op could turn out something saleable without really trying. However, once Pesquera had proved (as, indeed, Vega Sicilia had been demonstrating for 120 years) that with a little extra effort and attention to detail it was possible to aspire to more, the work began in earnest. Smallholdings started to sprout tiny wineries with stainless steel fermenting vessels, as husband-and-wife, father-and-son and brother-and-sister teams started to make their own wine in their own way on land their parents had farmed for years without ever tapping its true potential.

Outside investors began to show a serious interest, and several new wineries – perhaps most spectacularly the pink monument that is Bodega Hacienda Monasterio, in Pesquera – have replanted their vineyards, installed the very latest winemaking equipment and, in the particular case of Hacienda, bought in one-year-old Limousin barriques from châteaux in the Médoc for their first-year wines. The only things that seem to be in short supply in Ribera del Duero are qualified oenologists, with the result that the top winemakers are making a fortune moonlighting for small family wineries on their way home from the big bodega.

New technology is also the rage in Rioja: in Haro, Bodegas CVNE built a brand-new £12 million winery in 1990 which came into full service for the 1992 vintage, employing brand new technology, in which neither grapes nor wine are ever pumped, to avoid bruising them. CVNE's new installation is like a steel Mezquita – endless archways of pillars support 80 tanks, while a carousel affair rotates beneath the de-stalker to take the grapes on board. When each tank is full, it's hoisted over one of the fixed tanks and emptied. When fermentation is complete, the loose tank is pushed underneath the fixed tank on a trolley to take the grape pulp.

Justifying the DOC

If CVNE has the most high-profile installation in Rioja, other bodegas are working no less hard to make the DOC (Denominaciòn de Origen Calificada) grading, which the region won in 1991, into a reality. What they desperately need is a thumping good vintage to allow them to show off what they really can do, but nature has yet to provide it: 1992 and 1993 were both classified (in the uninformative Spanish way) as *Buena* (good), and the last *Excelente* was in 1982. But wines from the 1989 vintage (*Muy Buena* – very good) are starting to drink very well indeed. Other developments towards quality in Rioja include an increase in the planting of Graciano, which gives longevity and finesse to the finished wine, even if only added in small quantities, and a more pragmatic approach to the Garnacha. As high-profile bodegas from the North (Rioja Alta and Alavesa) use less Garnacha and more Tempranillo, at least one bodega in the South has produced a very pleasant, soft, early drinking (and modestly-priced) Rioja which is 100 per cent Garnacha and announces the fact on the label. This is exactly what Rioja needs: to fulfil the demand for cheaper wines with more Garnacha – and to say so – thus allowing the great wines to continue to improve by using more Tempranillo and Graciano.

The dull and wet summers of 1992 and 1993 which gave so much grief to northern Spain were, of course, welcomed with open water-butts in the South, and Montilla, to take just one example, registered 1993 as *Excelente* and one of its best years of the century. However, as from times of yore, the main business of

southern Spain is tasty, non-vintage everyday wines at very modest prices, and gentle but sustained growth is what has been achieved over the last couple of years.

So, to sum up, it finally seems to have clicked in the minds of Spain's best regions – and particularly Cava, Ribera del Duero and Rioja – that it really does pay to improve quality, and keep on improving it. This philosophy has been helped, of course, by the increasing quality of cheaper wines from areas of Spain which were formerly considered very ordinary. Work being done with the Airén and the Bobal in the Levant, the Parellada in Catalonia and the Viura in Navarra almost tempt me to say that there's no longer such a thing as an 'ordinary' grape, only 'ordinary' wine-making, but that is, perhaps, a little radical right at the moment.   **JOHN RADFORD**

CLASSIFICATIONS

Spain has the largest area under vine in the EU, but only 40 demarcated quality wine areas. The country is divided into 17 'Autonomías' and 50 provinces, as well as two offshore territories on the Moroccan coast. Some of these Autonomías consist of only one province (e.g. La Rioja, Navarra) and some consist of rather more – Castilla-Léon has nine provinces and Andalusia has eight. Fourteen of the Autonomías produce at least one quality wine, although some of the DO zones may overlap more than one province, or more than one Autonomía.

As with every country in the EU, Spain's wines divide into two grades: Table Wine (Vino de Mesa) and Quality Wine (Vino de Calidad Producido en Región Demarcada, or VCPRD). Each of these further subdivides as follows:

Table Wine

Vino de Mesa may not carry any kind of regional name, nor a vintage date, but may be blended from any region or regions of the bottler's choice. If the producer wants to put a vintage date on it – as with maverick winemakers such as the Marqués de Griñón in Toledo and the Yllera family in Rueda, then a legal nicety allows them to use a general regional name with no real meaning at all. In Griñón's case it's 'Vino de Mesa Toledo' (the name of a province); Yllera uses 'Vino de Mesa de Castilla-León (the name of the whole Autonomía).

Country Wines fall into two groups. Originally there were some 61 areas classified in various ways, but these have finally been organized into two groups of 28 (which leaves five unaccounted for).

The first 28 are fairly general large-area wines called **Vinos Comarcales** ('county' wines is the nearest equivalent in English). These have some local significance but no great pretension to quality. More important are the 28 **Vinos de la Tierra**: much smaller areas, more tightly controlled and, in many cases, with an ambition to go for DO status at some time in the future.

Quality Wine

Denominacion de Origen (DO) is roughly equivalent to the French AOC, except that it tends to be administered locally (rather in the manner of the Italian DOC) with a Consejo Regulador (Regulating Council) consisting of vineyard owners, winemakers, representatives from local and national government, oenologists and viticulturalists. Most decisions are made by the Consejo in the regions, and then subsequently sent for approval to INDO (the Instituto Nacional de Denominaciones de Origen) in Madrid.

Denominacion de Origen Calificada (DOC) is a new super-category (equivalent to the Italian DOCG) for wines which have a long tradition of high quality and are prepared to submit themselves to more rigorous quality scrutiny. There is considerable argument over what this scrutiny is, or should be, and there are a myriad theories about what Rioja ought to have done or could have done instead, but although the transition to DOC has attracted some criticism in and out of Spain, most bodegas are making a genuine effort to show that they're worthy of the new accolade. Sherry, Penedés and Ribera del Duero have been mooted as the next DOCs, but in best politician style, they're all hotly denying it. So it's probably true.

RED & ROSÉ WINES

Flying saucers have been spotted over many of Spain's best wine-producing areas, though made of stainless steel and with airtight 'manholes' top and bottom. These tanks are the very latest technology in red wine-making. The idea is that neither grape nor wines should be pumped, as this bruises and damages the end product. Nor is there any crushing. These *autoevacuaciones*, or self-emptying tanks, may look odd, but they're what it takes to combine the very best of old Spanish style with the pin-sharp accuracy of New-World wine-making.

GRAPES & FLAVOURS

BOBAL Good for deep-coloured, fruity red and stylish rosado wines in Utiel-Requena and Valencia. Reasonable acidity and relatively low alcohol keep the wines comparatively fresh and appetizing.

CARIÑENA A high-yielding grape (the Carignan of Southern France) producing dark and prodigiously tannic wine. It is believed to have originated in the region of the same name, south of Zaragoza, but plays only a small part in the DO wine which carries its name, and the region is now dominated by Garnacha and Bobal. Most Cariñena is grown in Catalonia, mostly as a beefy blender. It is also a minority grape in Rioja under the name Mazuelo. With its high tannin and acidity, and its aroma of ripe plums and cherries, it complements the Tempranillo so well – adding to its aging potential – that, each vintage, the Rioja bodegas fight over the little available.

GARNACHA This is Spain's – and the world's – most planted red grape variety. It grows everywhere, except Andalucía, and makes big, broad, alcoholic, sometimes peppery or spicy wines. The French, who know it as Grenache, moan about its lack of colour; but here in Spain, where burning heat and drought naturally restrict its yield, there's more dark skin in proportion to pale juice, and the wines turn out darker. They don't last well, but they can be delicious drunk young, whether as red, or fresh, spicy rosé. In Navarra the

presence of Garnacha is gradually giving way to Tempranillo and Cabernet. In the Rioja Baja, one or two bodegas are reacting to the increasing proportion of Tempranillo in the more expensive Rioja wines from the North, and producing a varietal Rioja Garnacha, which offers the triple benefits of early drinking, pleasant fruit and a modest price.

GRACIANO On the verge of extinction, Graciano has been rescued by the DOC upgrade in Rioja, where conscientious winemakers are seeking it out once again for the extra quality it gives to the wine.

MENCIA A grape native to Ribeiro and Bierzo. Believed to have a common ancestor with the Cabernet Franc, it is mainly used in light, fruity young wines, but older examples made in Bierzo before the DO was awarded indicate that it may have a future as a grape for oak aging.

MONASTRELL Spain's second most planted red variety, used to add body and guts to many Catalonian Tempranillo blends. Produces good crops of dark, tasty, alcoholic reds and rosés right down the eastern seaboard in Alicante, Jumilla, Almansa, Yecla and Valencia – usually dry and stolid but sometimes made sweet.

TEMPRANILLO The fine red grape of Rioja and Navarra crops up all over Spain even (for Vino de la Tierra) as far south as the province of Cádiz, but with a different name in almost every region (some may be a slightly different strain). It's Cencibel on the plains of La Mancha and Valdepeñas, Tinto Fino in Ribera del Duero; elsewhere it may be Tinto de Madrid, Tinto de Toro, Tinto del País ... It is being introduced into new areas (Cariñena, Somontano, the Rioja Baja...) and extended elsewhere. The wines have a spicy, herby, tobacco-like character, with plenty of sweet strawberry or sour cherry fruit, firm acidity and some tannin. Tempranillo makes vibrantly fruity wines for gulping down young, as well as more robust wines for longer aging – and its flavours mix brilliantly with oak. It's often blended, especially with Garnacha.

WINES & WINE REGIONS

ALICANTE, DO Heavy, rather earthy reds made in south-east Spain from the Monastrell grape which are mostly useful as blending wines.

ALMANSA, DO Falling between the high La Mancha plain and the near coastal plains of Alicante and Valencia, up-and-coming Almansa produces strong spicy reds from Monastrell and Garnacha, and even better reds from Tempranillo. The producer *Bodegas Piqueras* makes very good wines under the *Castillo de Almansa* and *Marius* labels.

AMPURDÁN-COSTA BRAVA, DO This part of Catalonia is a major supplier to the Costa Brava beaches. Seventy per cent is rosé, catering to the sun-freaks, but it also produces some so-called 'Vi Novell', supposedly modelled on the fresh, fruity style of Beaujolais Nouveau.

BIERZO, DO Emergent zone growing the possibly promising Mencía grape. Older wines are pre-DO blends, so the aging potential is pretty unknown.

BINISSALEM, DO Young and Crianza reds from Mallorca, made from the Manto Negro and Callet grapes; young *rosados*.

BULLAS, (DOp, 1982) Vino de la Tierra In the province of Murcia, great big heady Monastrell reds. DOp means provisonal DO (though the legal classification is still VdlT), but it's had the DOp since 1982 and not much has happened.

CALATAYUD, DO Mainly Garnacha reds, plus some Tempranillo, usually for drinking young. The area supplements neighbouring Cariñena and Campo de Borja, though it (generally) has slightly lower quality.

CAMPO DE BORJA, DO Situated in the heart of Aragón between Navarra and Cariñena. Hefty alcoholic reds made from Cariñena and Garnacha, now making way for lighter reds and very good rosés. *Bodegas Bordejé*, the *Borja* co-op and the *Santo Cristo* co-op look promising.

CARIÑENA, DO A lot of basic red from Cariñena, south-east of Rioja, finds its way as common *tinto* into Spain's bars, but the best co-ops (they make most of it) produce pleasant, full, soft reds. The main grape is the fat, jammy Garnacha, though a certain amount of Tempranillo firms up the better reds. Whites and rosés can be pleasant, but are mostly dull. The reds of the *Bodegas San Valero* co-operative are well made, sold here as *Don Mendo* and *Monte Ducay*.

CEBREROS, (DEp, 1986) Vino de la Tierra In Castilla-León, a source of good, honest local wines, mostly red and cheap. DEp means Provisional Denominación Específica. But it's still VdlT as far as the law's concerned.

> The price guides for this section begin on page 378.

CIGALES, DO Near Ribera del Duero, famed for rosados but with some serious reds as well, from Tempranillo/Garnacha mixes.

CONCA DE BARBERÁ, DO Catalonia's newest DO is in the highlands inland from Penedés, and has the potential for some excellent red wines. First seen in Britain is a Merlot from Concavins SA, which shows very well indeed what might be accomplished here. A group of plotters from Penedés (headed by Miguel Torres) are trying to annex this zone, though informed opinion suggests that their plans are doomed.

COSTERS DEL SEGRE, DO A virtual one-producer DO (Raïmat) in the Catalan province of Lérida. It's desert, but has been irrigated to grow cereals, fruit and vines, despite the fact that irrigation is officially banned both in Spain and the EC for DO wines and their like. But EC wine producers use two let-out clauses: if your vineyard is 'experimental', or if you can claim unusual local conditions, you can turn on the tap. *Raïmat Abadia*, based on Cabernet Sauvignon, Tempranillo and Garnacha and aged in oak, is normally good, as is *Raïmat Pinot Noir*. The *Raïmat Cabernet Sauvignon* is also very good – ripe but light, blackcurranty-oaky wine. The *Raïmat Tempranillo* isn't so very different. *Raïmat Merlot* is plummy and rich.

JUMILLA, DO Usually a palate-buster of a red from super-ripe Monastrell grapes grown in the dust bowls of Murcia. Much of it is sold in bulk for beefing up blends elsewhere. However, French investment is now creating a new fresh-flavoured red style. The *Condestable* brands, *Castillo de Jumilla* and *Con Sello*, are quite good and gentle as is the ripe, plummy *Taja* from French merchants Mahler-Besse. The *San Isidro* co-operative is the biggest in Spain.

LA MANCHA, DO Vast area south of Madrid. Only ten per cent red, most of which is pale semi-red plonk for the bars of Madrid. The reds *can* be enjoyable, yet so far only *Vinicola de Castilla, Cueva del Granero* and *Bodegas Rodriguez & Berger* are proving this with any regularity. *Arboles de Castillejo* from *Bodegas Torres Filoso* is a Tempranillo well worth a try. A huge government commission was established in 1993 to break the huge La Mancha DO into more manageable parts. It must report by the summer of 1996, at which time we may expect to see (probably) three new, smaller DO zones covering the plain.

MANCHUELA, (DOp 1982) Vino de la Tierra Mainly robust red wines made from the Bobal between Madrid and Valencia.

MENTRIDA, DO Strong, sturdy reds produced bang in the middle of Spain.

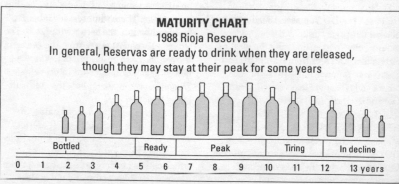

MATURITY CHART
1988 Rioja Reserva
In general, Reservas are ready to drink when they are released, though they may stay at their peak for some years

Bottled	Ready	Peak	Tiring	In decline

0   1   2   3   4   5   6   7   8   9   10   11   12   13 years

NAVARRA, DO This large region just north of Rioja grows the same grapes, but with more Garnacha. The officially-funded experimental winery here, EVENA, is one of the most impressive in Europe, and its influence is already showing, with Garnacha giving way to Tempranillo and Cabernet.

The best wine is the single estate *Magaña*, which has Cabernet and Merlot, not really DO-permitted varieties. Other potentially good names are *Chivite* and *Bodegas Principe de Viana,* which also uses the label *Agramont. Monte Ory* and *Bodegas Ochoa* are now much fresher. *Vinicola Navarra* makes old-fashioned, oaky reds – look for *Castillo de Tiebas* – and the modernized *Bodegas Irache* is producing both fruity and oak-aged styles.

PENEDÉS, DO Catalonia's leading wine region. The example set by Torres and other innovative winemakers is finally starting to filter down to the general run of bodegas, although there is still some way to go. And there are high spots. *Jean León's Cabernet Sauvignon* is one – a superbly weighty, impressively long-lasting red, though sadly lighter since 1980. *Torres* is another, from the rich, rather sweetly oaky basic reds, right up to the exciting Cabernet Sauvignon-based *Mas La Plana* and the 100% Pinot Noir *Mas Borras.* Other names to look out for are *Cavas Hill, Ferret i Mateu, Masia Bach, Mont Marçal, Vallformosa, René Barbier, Jaume Serra.*

PRIORATO, DO You need 13.5 degrees of alcohol here to get your DO. Cool, mountainous region, abutting the west of Tarragona. The reds from Garnacha and Cariñena are renowned – rich and full-bodied in style, and *Masia Barril, Scala Dei* and *de Muller* are worth trying.

RIBERA DEL DUERO, DO 'Ribera' means river bank, and this fine red wine region spreads out over the broad valley of the Duero (Portugal's Douro) and the smaller pine-clad valleys behind. The Tinto

---

RIOJA CLASSIFICATIONS

Rioja is divided into three geographical sub-regions: Rioja Alta, Rioja Alavesa and Rioja Baja: most wines will be a blend from all three. The wine's age, indicated on the label, falls into one of four categories.

Sin crianza Without aging, or with less than a year in wood; wine sold in its first or second year. (The words 'sin crianza' are not seen on the label.)

Crianza With a minimum of 12 months in wood and some months in bottle; cannot be sold before its third year. Whites will have had a minimum of six months in cask before bottling.

Reserva Selected wine from a good harvest with a minimum of 36 months' aging, in cask and bottle, of which 12 months minimum in cask. It cannot leave the bodega until the fifth year after the vintage. Whites have at least six months in cask, and 24 months' aging in total.

Gran Reserva Wine from an excellent vintage (supposedly) that will stand up to aging: 24 months minimum in cask and 36 months in bottle, or vice-versa. Cannot leave the bodega until the sixth year after the vintage. White wines have six months in cask and 48 months' aging in total.

Fino grape (alias Tempranillo) is by far the main one, sometimes mixed with Garnacha for drinking young, but used alone for the bigger reds. There's interest in Cabernet for blending into the better wines, too. The wines we see most of are from the *Bodegas Ribera-Duero* co-op at Peñafiel, where a new winemaker has meant improvements. The *joven* (young) reds show the soft fruit of the region.

Vega Sicilia is the famous name, an estate that has grown Cabernet, Merlot and Malbec to blend in with its Tinto Fino since early this century. These wines, which can be horribly expensive, taste like a mix of top Rioja and grand old-style

Piedmont, with great concentration. In fact the second wine, *Valbuena*, is often more enjoyable: rich, but with less wood aging – and less of an assault on the wallet. Two other bodegas offer lovely rich, oaked reds at rapidly rocketing prices – a disease that seems to be afflicting this DO. Look out for the unctuous, ripe, but over-oaky *Pesquera* from *Bodegas Alejandro Fernandez*, whose 1986 is the best recent year; for the delicious *Viña Pedrosa* from *Bodegas Perez Pascuas*; for *Bodegas Victor Balbas*; and for the *Ribera-Duero* co-op (the young reds, but not the more dubious Reservas). *Bodegas Monte-Vannos'* Reservas are also good.

RIOJA, DOC Classic reds that taste of oak and vanilla sweetness. Oak – and especially American oak, the type liked in Rioja – is full of vanilla, and wine leaches it out, taking up its buttery-vanilla-toffee aromas and flavours. The actual fruit in Rioja is usually rather light, sometimes peppery, with a strawberry jam sweetness.

Practically all the Rioja on sale here comes from firms who make or buy in wine from three distinct parts of the region and different grape varieties, blending and aging them to a 'house style'. Some use more of the more elegant Tempranillo, some more of the fatter, riper Garnacha, perhaps adding a little of the two minority grapes, Graciano and Mazuelo. The Rioja Alavesa region makes more delicate, scented wines; Rioja Alta is firmer, leaner, slower to show its character but slower to lose it too, and the lower, hotter Rioja Baja grows mostly Garnacha, which gets super-ripe and rather lumpish. There is now pressure from the authorities (as well as from the market) to use both new and old wood, both French and American, for aging, and to age for much shorter periods than in the past. The light has finally dawned on some bodegas that their wine actually ages very well in bottle. Best are *Bodegas Riojanas, Campo Viejo, El Coto, CVNE, Faustino, Lopez de Heredia, Marqués de Cáceres, Marqués de Murrieta, Martínez Bujanda,* *Montecillo, Muga, Olarra, La Rioja Alta Palacio, Campillo, Amerzola de la Mora,* and an improving *Marqués de Riscal*.

There is little credence given, as yet, to the 'estate' mentality, but it will come, as expectations rise and the over-achievers of the area determine to set an individual stamp on their wines. It's already worth trying to search out the wines from *Barón de Ley, Contino* and *Remélluri*.

SOMONTANO, DO The most exciting of Spain's newly demarcated regions in the cool foothills of the Pyrenees. A clutch of grape varieties make attractive, lightly scented reds, whites and rosés, and I've tasted some decent fizz. The *Cooperativa de Sobrarbe* under the *Camporocal* label is encouraging. *Covisa* have been doing well with both Spanish and foreign grapes.

TACORONTE-ACENTEJO, DO Spain's newest DO, on Tenerife. Mostly light reds, from the local Negramoll and Listán Negro.

TARRAGONA, DO The largest DO in Catalonia, to the south of Penedés. Originally known for high-strength dessert wines; now making undistinguished and unimpressive reds, whites and rosés.

TERRA ALTA, DO Hefty, frequently coarse red from west of Tarragona. Rather better at producing altar wine – *de Muller* is the world's biggest supplier.

TIERRA DE BARROS, (DOp 1979) Vino de la Tierra The great hope of Extremadura, one major bodega (Inviosa) has blazed a trail in export markets with its excellent Lar de Barros made from Cencibel and Cabernet Sauvignon. Other bodegas are following in the footsteps, and promotion to DO is a real prospect here.

TORO, DO This can make excellent, cheap, beefy, tannic but richly fruity reds from the Tinto de Toro – yet another alias for the Tempranillo. So far, the only really good wines come from *Bodegas Fariña*, whose *Gran Colegiata*, aged French-style in small oak barrels, is making waves here.

UTIEL-REQUENA, DO The reds, from the Bobal grape, are robust and rather hot and southern in style. The rosés *can* be better – delicate and fragrant.

VALDEORRAS, DO Galician region with young reds only, though good results are promised from the Mencía.

VALDEPEÑAS, DO Until recently the home of soft, unmemorable reds, this DO has improved When young the wines are often lightened with the white Airén grape. Crianza and others for aging in oak must, however, be made from 100% Cencibel (Tempranillo) and turn out deep and herby with good strawberry fruit – and excellent value at very low prices, even for Gran Reservas with a decade's aging. Look for the soft reds, aged in new oak, of *Señorio de los Llanos*, *Viña Albalí* from *Bodegas Felix Solis* and the young, fruity *Marqués de Gastañaga* and *Casa de la Viña*.

VALENCIA, DO Large quantities of reds, whites and rosés; fine for the beach. Some low-priced reds from *Schenk* and *Gandia Pla* can be good and the sweet Moscatels can be tasty and good value. *Castillo de Liria*, from *Gandia*, is an attractive red.

VINOS DE MADRID, DO Large area split into three parts around the capital: mainly young wines, plus some Crianza from Tempranillo and Garnacha.

YECLA, DO Sandwiched between Jumilla and Alicante, this dry region makes fairly full-bodied reds and more dubious whites. *La Purisima* co-op is the chief label we see.

WHITE WINES

The past year has seen a new interest in white wine from the North-West: from Galicia, from the northern Basque country, and from Penedés. Rueda lost the right to produce Cava on a technicality: the Catalans had insisted that only the traditional grapes plus Chardonnay could be used in Cava, and in Rueda they were using the Verdejo instead of the Viura (Macabeo). The Consejo Regulador in Rueda responded in 1993 by introducing a new wine to its canon: Rueda Espumoso. Made from at least 85 percent Verdejo, by the '*metodo tradicional*', with a minimum aging period of nine months it is, of course, Cava with a different grape.

GRAPES AND FLAVOURS

AIRÉN This plain and simple white grape hardly deserves its prominence, but it covers far, far more land than any other grape on earth. It holds sway over Spain's central plateau, where the summers are baking hot, irrigation is banned, and the vines are widely spaced to survive. As a result, the Airén must be a front-runner for another record: the *smallest* producer per hectare. Traditionally, these grapes have yielded tired, alcoholic, yellow plonk to service the bars of Madrid. But new, cool wine-making methods can transform it into some of the most refreshing basic white yet produced in Spain, with a delicious light apple, lemon and liquorice flavour.

ALBARIÑO The great white hope of the DO Rías Baixas, producing lovely, peachy, fresh and delicious wines with tremendous fruit and elegant acid balance. Some authorities believe that the grape is actually the Riesling of Germany taken to Galicia on the Camino de Santiago in the 17th century by German monks.

GARNACHA BLANCA A relation of the red Garnacha, and like the red, it makes wines high in alcohol, low in acidity and with a tendency to oxidize, so they are usually blended in with wines of higher acidity, like Viura. Good growers are grubbing it up, but its high yields keep it popular, especially in Navarra.

MALVASÍA This interesting, aromatic, flavourful grape tends, in Spain, to produce wines of low acidity that turn yellow and oxidize rapidly unless extreme care is taken. It is also low-yielding and prone to rot, so many growers in its traditional homelands of Rioja and Navarra have been ousting it in favour of the less interesting Viura. Only five per cent of Rioja is now planted with Malvasía, although there are hints of new interest from bodegas like *Marqués de Cáceres*. When well made, Malvasía wine is full-bodied, fairly strongly scented, spicy or musky, often with a hint of apricots, and sometimes slightly nutty. It blends well with Viura, which ups its acidity, but more and more wooded white Riojas are now based solely on Viura, which can't meld in oaky softness as successfully as Malvasía. Ten years ago, good white Rioja Reservas really *did* taste like white Burgundy – because of the high proportion of Malvasía in the blend. Still flying the flag for this style are the excellent *Marqués de Murrieta* and *CVNE*, with their *Monopole* and their Reserva.

MERSEGUERA Valencia's mainstay white grape, also grown in Alicante and Tarragona, produces light, delicately aromatic and characterful wines.

MOSCATEL The Muscat of Alexandria (Moscatel) is mostly grown in the south of Spain, where it overripens, shrivels and makes big, rich fortifieds. Valencia can make some extremely good, grapy, sweet white from it and *Torres* makes a good, off-dry, aromatic version mixed with Gewürztraminer in Penedés, as does *de Muller* in Tarragona.

PARELLADA Touted as the provider of all the perfume and finesse in Catalonia's whites and in Cava fizz, but Parellada doesn't honestly have a great deal to say for itself, except in the hands of the best producers. *Torres Viña Sol* is refreshing and lemony; other good examples include *Ferret i Mateu* and *Miret*.

VERDEJO This native of Rueda on the River Duero is one of Spain's more interesting white grapes. Nowadays it's used more for table wines than for Rueda's traditional fortifieds, and makes a soft, creamy and slightly nutty white, sometimes a touch honeyed, with good, green acidity and less alcohol than Viura. Not a world-beater, however.

VIURA The main white grape of Rioja, made nowadays apple-fresh and clean and, at best, rather neutral-flavoured; at worst it is sharp and grapefruity. It achieves similarly mixed results, under the name Macabeo, in Catalonia (where it also forms part of the Cava fizz blend). Made in this light, modern style, it's a wine for gulping down young, in its first year. But blended with Malvasía, topped up with a slug of acidity and left to age in oak barrels, the Viura can make some wonderful, rich, almost Burgundy-like white Riojas.

XAREL-LO One of the three main white grapes of Catalonia, heavier, more alcoholic and even less aromatic than the barely aromatic Parellada and Macabeo, with which it is generally blended. Some producers of Cava and still wines like to use it for extra body and alcohol, while others scorn it as coarse. It accounts for a third of all white plantings in Penedés. In Alella, it's called Pansá Blanca.

WINES & WINE REGIONS

ALELLA, DO Catalonian region gradually disappearing under the suburban sprawl, whose best wine is from the impressive firm of *Marqués de Alella*. The vines are found on granite slopes sheltered from the prevailing easterly wind. Its best-known wine is the off-dry, very fruity Marqués de Alella. Also look out for the light, pineapple-fresh *Chardonnay* and appley *Marqués de Alella Seco*, as well as the sparkling *Parxet*, which beats most of the famous Cavas hands down with its greengagey flavour.

BINISSALEM, DO Mallorca island DO making lightweight, beachfront whites, mainly from Moll, Xarel-lo and Parellada.

CAVA, DO The Spanish name for Champagne-method fizz. Around 95 per cent of it comes from Catalonia, and the authorities in Barcelona have been given the task of supervising the *Denominación de Origen* for the whole of Spain. Various other small vineyard enclaves have been granted the DO, odd patches of Rioja and Aragon for instance. When Cava was promoted to DO status, several regions lost the right to use the name, and their wines (some, admittedly excellent) must now be called *Metodo Tradicional*. However, the two biggest outsiders, *Bodegas Inviosa* in Almendralejo (Extremadura) and *Torre Oria* in Valencia have (supposedly temporary) permission to continue using the name, even though their grapes do not come from classified Cava vineyards. Their wines are good, and their financial and political clout is probably even better.

However, most Cava comes from the top right-hand corner of Spain, and it gets criticized in Britain for its earthy, old-fashioned style. There are those who criticize the grape varieties – Xarel-lo, Parellada and Macabeo – and a number of producers add Chardonnay to help the blend, but careful wine-making seems to be a bigger factor, as evidenced by the new generation of Cavas.

Some companies are starting to turn out fresher, less earthy Cavas by better wine-making and less excessive aging, and by including some Chardonnay; *Cavas Hill, Codorníu, Juve y Camps, Mont Marçal* and *Rovellats* look hopeful, though there's a distressing trend to raise prices with the use of Chardonnay. But most are stuck with their grape varieties, none of which will ever be renowned for its perfume or fruit. Most appetizing are *Cavas Hill Reserva Oro Brut Natur, Codorníu Première Cuvée Brut, Mont Marçal Cava Nature* (and *Chardonnay), Parxet, Raïmat, Segura Viudas* and *Rovellats, Freixenet* and its subsidiary company *Condé de Caralt*.

CHACOLÍ DE GUETARIA, DO Basque-country light, white seafood-type wine of mainly local interest (the local spelling is Getariako Txakolina), made from the (unpronounceable) Hondarribi Zuri grape.

COSTERS DEL SEGRE, DO Raïmat, virtually the only vineyard in the area, makes light, lemony, gently oaked *Raïmat Chardonnay*, as well as a good sparkler, *Raïmat Chardonnay Blanc de Blancs*.

LA MANCHA, DO Long dismissed as the most mediocre kind of base-wine producer, Spain's enormous central plateau – making 40 per cent of all Spain's wine – is now bringing in cool fermentation and is already drawing out unexpected fresh flavours – and still at a pretty rock-bottom price. The traditional wines were light yellow, thanks to creeping oxidation, but this has changed. Some we see here now are the new style, either bland, but fresh and fruity, or else quite surprisingly young and bright-eyed. But you have to catch them *very* young. In 1993 a new government commission was set up with a three-year brief to split La Mancha into (probably) three smaller DOs, each with its own Consejo Regulador, to speed up the quality process throughout the region. Best: *Casa la Teja, Castillo de Alhambra, Lazarillo, Señorio de Guadianeja, Viña Santa Elena, Yuntero, Zagarron.*

NAVARRA, DO Navarra's reputation for producing sub-Rioja was endorsed by its very ordinary, cool-fermented, neutral Viura wines which died quietly in the bottle on the shelf waiting for someone to buy them. However, young and fresh white Navarra is pleasant and slurpable, and serious work at EVENA and by certain bodegas is producing more exciting wines. New yeast strains, some maceration on the skins and a return to tradition is making its mark: look for *Agramont* from *Bodegas Principe de Viana*, which is fermented in new Alliers oak. This could be the future.

PENEDÉS, DO There was little to excite the export market in Penedés until quite recently. Indifferent winemaking for a voracious and undemanding market in Barcelona gave no incentive to experiment. Then along came Miguel Torres and Jean León who found that 'foreign' grapes could be made to produce excellent wines in the area. The next step was to apply the same exacting winemaking standards to the native varieties (of which there are 121) and this has been moderately successful in the hands of talented winemakers, like Torres, who extracts a lean, lemony, sharply refreshing flavour from his Parellada. Other good whites from local varieties come from *Cavas Hill, Ferret i Mateu* and *Mont Marçal*. *Torres* and *Masia Bach* have Riesling, Chenin, Chardonnay, Sauvignon and what have you; and *Jean León* makes a delicious oaky, pineappley Chardonnay.

RIAS BAIXAS, DO Three separate areas make up this DO on the Galician coast, north of Portugal. Val de Salnes, around Cambados makes whites from almost pure Albariño – fresh and fragrant when well made. *Martin Codax* is good. Further south, Condado de Tea and O Rosal make

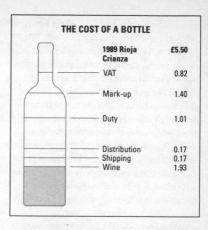

THE COST OF A BOTTLE

1989 Rioja Crianza	**£5.50**
VAT	0.82
Mark-up	1.40
Duty	1.01
Distribution	0.17
Shipping	0.17
Wine	1.93

Albariño-dominated wines, sometimes with a dash of Loureiro and Treixadura. As the wines become more fashionable in Spain, the prices are rising. *Bodegas Morgadio, Santiago Ruiz, Granja Fillaboa* and *Lagar de Cervera* are all good and worth a try.

RIBEIRO, DO Since this Galician area was granted DO status, a zone once known for flabby dry whites has been benefitting from investment. Fresh white wines made from Treixadura and Torrontes is a distinct improvement on the old regime, though as in nearby Rias Baixas, demand is causing prices to rise. A pleasant example at a reasonable price is *Casa Barco*, from *Bodega Alanis* (Thresher £3.49).

RIOJA, DOC The first DO to be upgraded to DOC, though the rules stay the same. Styles vary. White Rioja *can* be buttery and rich, slightly Burgundian in style. It used to be made from a blend of Viura and the richer, more interesting Malvasía, aged for several years in oak. Some were awful, tired and flat; some were wonderful. The style is now starting to make a comeback. *Marqués de Murrieta* still makes a very good example, and so, with rather less oak, does *CVNE* with its *Monopole* and *Reserva*, and *Bodegas Riojanas* with its *Monte Reál*. *Lopez de Heredia* makes an old-fashioned style, while *Navajas, Viña Soledad* from

Franco Españolas and *Siglo Gold* from *AGE* are all in the oak-aged mould. The best new-wave white Riojas are full of fresh, breath-catching raw fruit, with the acid attack of unsugared grapefruit.

RUEDA, DO This predominantly white wine region lies north-west of Madrid, by the river Duero. Rueda used to be famous, or notorious, for its heavy, oxidized, sherry-type wines made from the Palomino grape of Jerez – high on alcohol, low on fruit and freshness. But production of these *vinos generosos* is now really limited to a couple of bodegas, and the rest of the region has switched over to light table wines, picked early and fresh and fermented cool. They have a natural advantage in their local grape, the Verdejo, which makes soft, full, nutty wines, sometimes padded out with the dull Palomino, or sharpened up with the more acid Viura. Most are best young, but there are oaked versions, too. The most

interesting Ruedas are *Marqués de Griñon* and *Hermanos Lurton Sauvignon Blanc*, both made at *Bodegas Castilla La Vieja*. Others include *Marqués de Riscal*, who is also growing Sauvignon Blanc and re-discovering the use of Limousin oak, and *Alvarez y Diez*, which makes both old (*generoso*) and new, light wines. Rueda has also recently introduced a new *espumoso* to its range, made by the Cava method, from 85 percent Verdejo.

TACORONTE-ACENTEJO, DO Light wines from Spain's newest DO, on Tenerife. It produces a small but increasing supply of light young whites for the beach, made from Moscatel and Listán grapes.

VALDEORRAS, DO Galician region with undistinguished whites, fresh and fruity at their best, made from the Palomino and the Doña Blanca, but some useful work being down with the Godello promises well.

FORTIFIED WINES

Last year the tide seemed to have turned at last for sherry after a ten-year decline in exports. In Jerez there's a growing mood of optimism now that the blood-letting, closures, takeovers, redundancies and grubbing-up of vineyards are over. IDV has taken a minority stake in González-Byass, and Emilio Lustau (source of those superb *almacenista* sherries) has been sold to the quality-conscious Luís Caballero.

Over here, the uninteresting Croft Original still leads the field in sales, but at least some retailers are now stocking a few premium sherries (often in half-bottles) in addition to their normal ranges. All they have to do now is persuade people to trade up, though prices generally have risen anyway. High time too; though fine (dry, concentrated and complex) sherry is still ridiculously underpriced. A drive towards low prices, high volume and low quality was the cause of the decline, a decade and a half ago.

One consequence of higher prices for better sherry has meant that the other *vinos generosos of* Andalucia have been able to mop up the lower end of the market. Montilla and Condado Huelva have found themselves competing successfully with British 'sherry' (which will be called British Fortified Wine from January 1996), though whether they will ever be able to achieve much of an image by doing so is another matter. At least the cool, wet weather which has caused gloom in the North was good news in the deep South.

Málaga soldiers on. Perhaps a long-delayed comeback is just over the horizon – it's still, for me, one of the great pudding wines of the world. **JOHN RADFORD**

GRAPES & FLAVOURS

MOSCATEL Almost all Spanish Moscatel is the second-line Muscat of Alexandria rather than the top-quality Muscat à Petits Grains. Even so, it makes a lot of good wine – mostly rich and brown in Málaga, or fresh and grapy in Valencia. The Muscat de Chipiona from *Burdon* is wonderfully rich and peachy. Moscatel also sweetens cream sherries. One or two sherry bodegas are experimenting with a pure Moscatel fortified during fermentation (like port) and aged in oak. Early examples are encouraging, but it may not get the DO.

PALOMINO This is the dominant grape of the sherry region, making up all of the dry sherries, and an increasing proportion of the others. Although it produces great fortified wine it is not a great grape. It plays a minor role in Montilla-Moriles. As a table wine grape, it produces dull, fat stuff, but reacts brilliantly to the flor yeast which imparts to *fino* that characteristic bone-dry, stark-sour nose.

PEDRO XIMÉNEZ In decline in Jerez, where it used to be the chief component of sweet sherries. It is sometimes made into dessert wine, deeply coloured and thick. It constitutes 95 per cent of the nearby Montilla-Moriles vineyards, as well as providing richness in Málaga; otherwise used extensively for rather dull dry white wines in the south of the country.

WINES & WINE REGIONS

CONDADO DE HUELVA, DO Faces Jerez across the Guadalquivir river, with broadly similar climate and soils. Wines not unlike Montilla are made and mostly drunk locally, though some now reaches these shores. Tesco's *Tio Cani* is the sort of thing.

MÁLAGA, DO We don't see much Málaga here – in fact no-one sees much anywhere because Malaga's wine industry is beset by encroaching tourism. However, in the last century, Málaga was very popular and signs of revival have been noted. Málaga is usually full, brown and sweet in a raisiny, but not a gooey way and is slightly smoky too. There is some dry Málaga, but you'll have to take a long weekend on the Costa del Sol to see much. *Solera 1885* from *Scholtz Hermanos* is intense and raisiny while *Lagrima 10 Años* is sweet – and neither are expensive. *Bodega Lopez Hermanos is* also good.

MONTILLA-MORILES, DO Montilla wines are usually thought of as lower-priced – and lower-strength – sherry look-alikes but there is a great deal of fine wine made in Montilla-Moriles; the problem is getting any UK retailer to ship it. In general the dry wines, from Pedro Ximénez grapes, do not quite have the bite of really good sherry, but some of the mediums and sweets can outshine all but the best. In 1992 the Montilla exporters' association launched a campaign to the UK to try and interest people in their wine. If they have any sense, they'll go for the British Fortified Wine market with a vengeance.

SHERRY (JEREZ-XÉRÈS-SHERRY, DO) There are two basic sherry styles, *fino* and *oloroso*, each with sub-divisions. *Fino*, from Jerez or Puerto de Santa Maria, should be pale and dry, with an unnerving dry austerity. The tang comes from a layer of natural yeast, called flor, that forms on the surface of the wine in the barrels. The lightest, freshest wines are selected for *fino*, and they are less fortified than the heavier *oloroso* wines. *Fino* is usually drunk cool and fresh, often as an apéritif.

Manzanilla is a form of *fino* matured by the sea at Sanlúcar de Barrameda. It can be almost savoury-dry, and you might even imagine a whiff of sea salt – if you catch it young enough. Best: *Barbadillo, Caballero, Diez-Merito, Don Zoilo, Garvey, La Guita, Hidalgo, La Ina, Inocente, Lustau, La Riva, Sanchez Romate, Tio Pepe.* Good Puerto *fino* comes from *Burdon* and *Osborne*.

In Britain there can be a problem with freshness, as *fino* and *manzanilla* needs to be turned round within a year if it has 17 per cent alcohol, and six months if it has less. Own-brands tend to suffer most, but since 1992 producers must put a lot number on every bottle. Systems vary, but a common way is to print four figures to signify the year ('3' for 1993, '4' for 1994) and the day (001 for 1 January and 365 for 31 December), so 14 February 1994 would be expressed as 4045 or 0454) So one should be able to make a rough stab at the age of a bottle.

Real *amontillado* begins life as *fino*, aged in cask until the flor dies and the wine deepens and darkens to a tantalizing, nutty dryness. In the natural state, as drunk in Spain, it is *completely* dry, and a proper *amontillado* will usually say *seco* ('dry'), on the label. But we've adulterated the word in English to mean a bland, downmarket drink of no interest. But look out for *almacenista* sherries, unblended wine from small stockholders which can be wonderful.

Look out also for *Principe* and *Solear* (a *manzanilla pasada*) from *Barbadillo, La Goya Manzanilla Pasada* and *Amontillado Fino Zuleta* (*Delgado Zuleta*), *Amontillado del Duque* (*Gonzalez Byass*), *Hidalgo Manzanilla Pasada, Sandeman Bone Dry Old Amontillado, Valdespino's Amontillado Coliseo* and *Don Tomás.* (*Manzanilla pasada* is an old *manzanilla* beginning to take on *amontillado* characteristics.)

Real *olorosos*, made from richer, fatter wines without any flor, are deep and dark, packed with violent burnt flavours – and usually dry, though you may find *oloroso dulce* (sweet). In Britain most are sweetened with Pedro Ximénez or Moscatel. They usually come as 'Milk', 'Cream' or 'Brown'. Pale Creams are sweetened (inferior) *fino*, and are some of the dullest drinks around. For the real, dry thing, once again, look for *almacenista olorosos* from *Lustau.* There are a few good, concentrated sweetened *olorosos* around, like *Apostoles* and the fairly sweet *Matúsalem*,both from *Gonzalez Byass, Solera 1842 (Valdespino).* Dry: *Barbadillo, Don Zoilo, Sandeman, Valdespino Don Gonzalo, Williams & Humbert Dos Cortados.* Most are around a tenner, making these intense old wines one of today's great bargains.

WINERY PROFILES

ANTONIO BARBADILLO (Sanlúcar de Barrameda) ★★★★(★) Best *manzanilla* bodega. Principe is tangy, nutty, well-aged.

CAMPO VIEJO ★★★ Decent Riojas and soft, traditional Reservas.

VINICOLA DE CASTILLA (La Mancha) ★★★ Up-to-date producer turning out 14 million litres a year, including white and oaky red Señorio de Guadianeja. Soft red Castillo de Alhambra is good value.

CODORNÍU (Penedés) ★★★ Giant Cava company, owned by the Raventos family,

making some of the most likeably reliable fizzes. Good soft and honeyed Anna de Codorníu fizz, and a very good, creamy Chardonnay Cava.

CONTINO (SOCIEDAD VINICOLA LASERNA) (Rioja) ★★★★(★) Excellent, single-vineyard wine made from an estate half-owned by CVNE, half by private investors. Vines are predominantly Tempranillo, planted in one 45-hectare vineyard in prime Rioja Alta land. Big, plummy and spicily complex, Contino is made only as Reserva and Gran Reserva. If you see any '82, snap it up.

CVNE (Rioja) ★★★ Old-established, traditionally-inclined, but at the moment disturbingly unreliable bodega. Blanco Viura is one of the best modern white Riojas, and Monopole has nice oak. Try the Reserva white for a taste of good traditional Rioja.Best of the reds are the rare Imperial range (especially the '81).

DOMECQ (Jerez)★★★★(★)One of the oldest and most respected sherry houses, with top *fino* La Ina, Botaina *amontillado* and Rio Viejo *oloroso*. Also makes Rioja.

FAUSTINO MARTÍNEZ (Rioja) ★★★ A huge, family-owned bodega which makes good reds. Look out also for the new Campillo bodega.

FREIXENET (Penedés)★★High-tech Cava firm best known for Cordon Negro, but also making good value Carta Nevada, Vintage Brut Nature which includes some Chardonnay, and upmarket Brut Barroco.

GONZÁLEZ BYASS (Jerez)★★★★★Huge, family-owned company, producers of the best-selling *fino* Tio Pepe. GB also makes an impressive top range of wines, and a Rioja, Bodegas Beronia.

CAVAS HILL (Penedés) ★★(★) Table wines as well as fresh, clean Cava Reserva Oro Brut Natur. Look out for Blanc Cru and Oro Penedés Blanco Suave whites, and Rioja-style reds, Gran Civet and Gran Toc.

JEAN LEÓN (Penedés) ★★★★ Jean León makes some of Spain's most 'Californian' wines: super-oaky, pineapple-and-honey Chardonnay, and soft, blackcurranty Cabernet Sauvignon.

JULIAN CHIVITE (Navarra)★★★ One of the most export-minded and state-of-the-art bodegas in Navarra, making a clean white from Viura, attractive *rosado* from Garnacha, and a good Tempranillo-based red, all under the Gran Feudo label.

LOS LLANOS (Valdepeñas) ★★★ The brightest spot here: wonderfully soft, oaky reds. 1978 Gran Reserva is especially good.

LÓPEZ DE HEREDIA (Rioja) ★★★★ Rich, complex whites, Viña Tondonia and Viña Gravonia, and delicate, ethereal reds, Viña Cubillo and Viña Tondonia.

LUSTAU (Jerez) ★★★★ 'Reviving Traditional Sherry Values' with their wonderful range of *almacenista* wines.

MARQUÉS DE CÁCERES (Rioja) ★★★(★) Enrique Forner, who started this bodega in the mid-70s, trained in Bordeaux. Whites are cool-fermented and fresh, and reds have less wood aging than usual, but still keep an attractive style.

MARQUÉS DE GRIÑÓN (Toledo) ★★★★ Carlos Falco, the Marqués de Griñón, makes very good Cabernet in his irrigated, wire-trained vineyard, aided by advice from Professor Emile Peynaud from Bordeaux.

MARQUÉS DE MURRIETA (Rioja) ★★★★ A remarkable, ultra-traditional winery built into a hill outside Logroño. Red, rosés and whites are oak-aged far longer than in any other Rioja bodega; the Etiqueta Blanca wines, the youngest sold, spend at least two years in barrel, and are richly oaky, pungent and lemony. The red is soft and fruity-oaky, while the Reservas are deep and complex. The best wines of the very top years are sold as Castillo Ygay, and may sit in barrel for 40 years.

MARTÍNEZ BUJANDA (Rioja) ★★★ Wine is produced only from the family's own vineyards, and is very well made, from the super-fresh and lively Valdemar white to the strongly oaky Reserva and Gran Reserva Condé de Valdemar.

MONTECILLO (Rioja) ★★★(★) Since 1973, this has belonged to Osborne, the sherry company, who built a new winery to turn out an aromatic white Viña Cumbrero, a raspberry and oak red, Viña Cumbrero Crianza, and a Reserva, Viña Monty.

MUGA (Rioja) ★★★(★) This has a sternly traditional image. For reds, it does nothing but good, and the Crianza is fragrant and delicate, while the Prado Enea Reserva or Gran Reserva is more complex, but still subtle and elegant. It's not cheap, though.

VIÑA PESQUERA (Ribera del Duero) ★★★(★) Prices have shot up since American wine writer Robert Parker likened this to Château Pétrus. Made from Tinto Fino and Garnacha, it's good but not *that* good, oaky and aromatic, with rich savoury fruit.

PRINCIPE DE VIANA (Navarra)★★★(★) Innovative bodega which used to be a co-op, and became known as Bodegas Cenalsa. Agramont is its best-known UK brand, and look out for new Bodegas Guelbenzu, a Cabernet/Tempranillo estate in Cascante.

RAÏMAT (Costers del Segre) ★★★ The Raïmat Chardonnay Cava is honeyed, with grassy acidity. Abadía is an oak-enhanced blend of Cabernet, Tempranillo and Garnacha. Also Cabernet Sauvignon, Pinot Noir and Merlot.

LA GRANJA REMÉLLURI (Rioja) ★★★★(★) Single-estate wine; the Rodriguez family have completely rebuilt the winery, installing stainless steel fermentation tanks instead of the old wooden vats, and now make a fine, meaty Reserva, barrel-aged for two to three years.

LA RIOJA ALTA (Rioja) ★★★★
A traditional bodega, firm believer in long barrel-aging: over half the wines qualify as Reserva or Gran Reserva. Even the Viña Alberdi Crianza has a delightfully oaky flavour. They make two styles of Reserva, the elegant Viña Arana and the rich Viña Ardanza. In the best years, they make exceptional Gran Reservas.

RIOJANAS (Rioja) ★★★(★) One of the few still using the open *lagar* method of semi-carbonic maceration. Best reds are the Reservas: the light, elegant, plummy Viña Albina and the richer, more concentrated Monte Reál. White Monte Reál Crianza is soft and peachy, with just enough oak.

MIGUEL TORRES (Penedés) ★★★★ The best range of table wines in Spain. Viña Sol is a super-fresh modern white. Gran Viña Sol is half-and-half Parellada and Chardonnay, fresh and pineappley, enriched with hints of vanilla oak. Gran Viña Sol Green Label pairs Parellada with Sauvignon Blanc, like oakier Sancerre. The superstar white is Milmanda Chardonnay. Recent red additions are a Pinot Noir, Mas Borras, and a Merlot, Las Torres. Viña Esmeralda is Gewürztraminer and Muscat d'Alsace. Mas la Plana is Torres' top red, a Cabernet Sauvignon. Viña Magdala is equal parts of Pinot Noir and Tempranillo, Gran Sangredetoro is mainly Garnacha, and Coronas – a savoury Tempranillo – is the least exciting.

VALDESPINO (Jerez) ★★★★★ Another family-owned bodega making a range of top-class, dry sherries. Inocente is one of the last traditional *finos* at 17.5 degrees. Their Pedro Ximénez Solera Superior is one of the few examples of sherry's great sweetening wine bottled by itself. *Amontillados* and *olorosos* from here are about as good as you can get.

BODEGAS VEGA SICILIA (Ribera del Duero) ★★★★(★) Makers of Spain's most famous and expensive red wine. Vega Sicilia Unico, the top wine, is sometimes kept in barrel for as long as ten years. Younger wines, called Valbuena, offer a cheaper glimpse of Vega Sicilia's glories.

VICENTE GANDIA(Valencia) ★★(★) Perhaps this DO's most go-ahead producer. Fresh white Castillo de Liria and juicy red and rosado from Bobal.

PORTUGAL

Over a quarter of a million people in Portugal earn their living from viticulture, many of them small growers working to supply the enormous co-operatives. These people have been pushed and pulled in all directions over the eight years since Portugal joined the EU, and 1993–94 was no exception, with new regulations coinciding with a terrible harvest.

Ten years ago man, not nature, was being blamed for Portugal's tired, oxidized whites and tannic, astringent reds. The large co-ops smelled as bad as they looked – money was scarce and talent was missing. Then came 1986, and Portugal's accession to the EC. Huge amounts of EC money started flying around, and the wineries have, for the most part, made the most of it; all over the country stainless steel tanks have been shipped in, and new technology and vineyard renovation has become the order of the day. Oak, although still not widely used, is becoming accepted as a wine-making option, to the particular benefit of the reds.

While pursuing better wine-making, the Portuguese have kept in mind the value of their own grape varieties. These are turning out to be the country's greatest strength. Grapes such as Baga, Touriga Nacional, Maria Gomes and notably Periquita, are providing strikingly individual wines in a world all too full of Chardonnay and Cabernet Sauvignon. Nevertheless, in Britain we are still somewhat mystified by the top-quality styles; bowled over by upfront New World flavours, the enthusiast takes some getting used to the subtler, complex reds of Portugal, which often need several years' bottle-age to soften. Classy Portuguese reds won't really take off until the current generation grows out of knock 'em dead Aussie wines and searches for something a little more challenging.

Upgrading to the basement

Whether we understand them or not, we are beginning to drink a little more Portuguese wine – over the past 12 months the total British market share has increased from 1.8 to 2.3 per cent; and in the bargain basement Portugal suddenly seems unassailable. Wines priced around the £2 mark, such as Lezíria, Ramada and Planicie, took recession-hit Britain by storm last year. Sales of the Lezíria range, made at the huge Almeirim co-op in the Ribatejo region, have nearly reached the 300,000-case mark in Britain, and the Lezíria red, made predominantly from Periquita, is the best of the cheap and cheerfuls – fresh and very gluggable. It is clear that these wines are popular first and foremost because of their price, but the Portuguese, who are suffering a declining domestic market, are not complaining. Other co-ops busy upgrading their range include Redondo, Borba and Torres Vedras; at all three the enormous investments have been complemented by a better exchange of ideas among winemakers who have actually visited France, America and Australia to learn for themselves what the opposition is up to.

One step up the quality ladder, JP Vinhos is enjoying continued success with the Do Campo range, made by Australian Peter Bright in the Setúbal Peninsula, again using Portuguese varieties such as Fernão Pires, Rabo de Ovelha and Periquita. Bright, incidentally, has recently left JP Vinhos and has started his own operation making wine under the Bright Brothers label in the Ribatejo. The giant Esporão estate in Alentejo has had new life breathed into it by another Australian, David Baverstock, who is producing top quality in the medium-price bracket, and forward-thinking winemaker João Portugal Ramos is doing interesting things at Quinta de Pancas in Oeste. Sogrape, José Maria de Fonseca and Luis Pato continue to impress.

Portuguese classifications have always been baffling, but new regulations announced at the end of 1993 should make them a little easier to understand. Portugal now has a four-tier structure. DOC (Denominacão de Origem Controlada) replaced Região Demarcada as the top category from the 1990 vintage; the 13 DOCs are, in general, those considered historically important. Next is VQPRD, or Indicacão de Proveniencia Regulamentada (IPR), which roughly corresponds to the French VDQS bracket. This tier has been in increasing need of a shake-up. Some of the 31 areas are insignificant, others are due for rapid promotion to DOC, while the boundaries of some bisect important estates (José Maria de Fonseca, ludicrously, is one such divided property).

Further clarification has arrived in the shape of a new tier which falls just below IPR, and which should prove extremely important. Eight new Vinhos Regionais have been created, the equivalent of *vins de pays*. Wineries are allowed to put vintages and grape varieties on the labels; more importantly, consumers can start identifying wines in terms of large regions. The eight, from north to south, are Rios do Minho, Tras os Montes, Beiras, Estremadura, Ribatejo, Terras do Sado, Alentejo and Algarve. Some of these Vinhos Regionais, in particular Ribatejo and Alentejo, are playing an increasingly important role.

Rain of terror

With the human factor pulling its socks up, it seems sadly ironic that nature dealt such a cruel blow last vintage. The 1993 harvest was possibly the worst since 1956. The winter was dry, followed by abnormally heavy rains throughout April, May and June, and indeed throughout the harvest. Production in the northern and coastal regions was severely affected; in Vinho Verde, Douro and Bairrada the flowers frequently failed to set – and those berries that did form were attacked by rot. Across the country, production was down from the average of 8.5 million hectolitres to just 4.5 million – a 40 per cent decrease on 1992, which was itself a mean year. Ribatejo and Alentejo fared better by picking earlier or managing to avoid the most damaging rains. In the Douro it was the worst year for light wines since the demarcation came into effect in 1979. Stick to older vintages of Quinta de la Rosa, Quinta das Llamelas and Roederer-owned Duas Quintas to sample good Douro table wines.

Perhaps the poor vintage was no bad thing in the long term. Like a gangly child which has put on a spurt of growth, Portugal needs time to pause for rest and to consolidate its advances. Nineteen ninety-three will be a significant blip on the vintage charts, but excess stock will be reduced and prices stabilized as a result. What's more, the disastrous conditions have highlighted the wonders of new technology; for example, at Quinta dos Carvalhais, Sogrape's state-of-the-art winery in Dão, a rare optimistic note was hit following the harvest. The message was simple – we are on top of this. And after all, what's the point in buying new toys for your winery unless you get a chance to see what they can do when they have to?   SUSY ATKINS

WHITE WINES

Portugal is often thought of as being red wine territory. There used to be good reasons for this, unless you happened to enjoy flat, fruitless and probably oxidized dry whites. But it's amazing what a bit of cool fermentation and a dash of stainless steel can do for a wine – especially if it's made from some of the most unusual and promising grape varieties in Europe.

In the Vinho Verde region, Loureiro and Alvarinho make delicate, scented dry whites that are worlds away from the heavy-handed commercial blends, though 1993 was a wash-out. In the Douro the Viosinho and Gouveio grapes appear in Sogrape's peachy-smoky Reserva. Bairrada boasts the spicy Maria Gomes which crops up in the south as Fernão Pires. Sogrape, José Maria da Fonseca and JP Vinhos are the producers showing the most dexterity.

WINES & WINE REGIONS

ALENTEJO EU backing means that stainless steel and temperature control are now the norm, and it's going from strength to strength. The Roupeiro grape has been singled out as the best and *Esporão's* Aussie winemaker, David Baverstock, is making the most of its tropical, guava-like flavours. The *Redondo* co-op is also producing some good peachy whites.

BAIRRADA, DOC Some increasingly good dry whites from the Maria Gomes grape. *Sogrape*, maker of *Mateus Rosé*, has done the most to freshen up flavours. Try the crisp, floral *Quinta de Pedralvites*. Also very good: peachy *Sogrape Bairrada Reserva* and *Caves Aliança's* inexpensive dry white.

BUCELAS, DOC Popular in Wellington's day, this dry white was almost extinct, with *Caves Velhas* left as the sole producer. However, two new ones have appeared. Look out for *Quinta da Romeira* under the *Prova Regia* label.

DÃO, DOC White Dão was traditionally (and mostly still is) yellow, tired and heavy. But a few companies are now making a lighter, fresher, fruitier style, and now that the co-ops are losing the upper hand with production, others look set to follow suit. White *Grão Vasco*, now made in *Sogrape's*

shiny new winery at Quinta dos Carvalhais is a significant departure from tradition with its crisp lemon-zest appeal. Sadly, local regulations insist that the wine should be at least six months old before bottling, so it pays to catch the wine young. Look out for oak-aged Reservas in future.

DOURO, DOC Nearly all the best table wines are red, though the *Planalto* white from *Sogrape*, the Mateus-makers, is full and honeyed and good, as is its oaked *Douro Reserva*, and *Esteva* from *Ferreira* is clean and crisp. *Quinta do Valprado* Chardonnay, made by *Raposeira*, is big and honeyed.

RIBATEJO Until recently Portugal's second largest region concentrated on reds, but now the Almeirim co-op is turning out fresh, cheap whites under the *Lezíria* name, a good white for Safeway called *Falcoaria* and classier stuff under the *Quinta das Varandas* label. Australian Peter Bright is also making wine under his new Bright Brothers label at *Quinta da Granja*.

SETÚBAL PENINSULA The whole peninsula is now a Vinho Regional area, with the name of Terras do Sado. The best wines are produced on the limestone of the Arrábida hills where Peter Bright makes an oak-aged Chardonnay, *Cova da Ursa*.

The *João Pires* Muscat is also good. *José Maria da Fonseca* likes local grapes, though Chardonnay gives a lemony lift to the white *Pasmados*, and *Quinta da Camarate* boasts Riesling, Gewürztraminer and Muscat.

VINHO VERDE, DOC *Verde* here means green-youthful, un-aged, not the colour of a croquet lawn. Ideally, these wines are bone dry, positively tart, and brilliantly suited to heavy, oily Portuguese food. But we almost always get them slightly sweetened and softened, which is a pity, although it is in its peculiar way a classic wine style.

Most wines come from co-ops or are sold under brand names, but some larger private producers bottle their own. There is also some characterful single-quinta Vinho Verde. *Palacio da Brejoeira*, from the Alvarinho grape, is more alcoholic and full bodied, and expensive, for that matter, than the general run. Vinho Verde can be made from a variety of grapes, but there's often more Loureiro in the estate wines. Indeed, there's quite rightly a lot of interest in Loureiro, with its dry, apricotty, Muscaty aroma and taste. It is more attractive than the much-praised Alvarinho, and it gives the wines a much more tangy but fruity character. *Solar das Bouças* and *Quinta de Tamariz* are almost entirely Loureiro. *Quinta de Franqueira*, *Casa de Sezim* and *Terras de Corga* are also good. From the large firms *Gazela* is just off-dry and reliable. *Aveleda* also makes some good ones, including one made entirely from the Trajadura grape. Its best is called *Grinalda*, a perfumed blend of Loureiro and Trajadura grapes.

RED WINES

The rise and rise of Portugal's red table wines is revealing flavours that most of us never knew existed. If you want Cabernet or Merlot then Portugal is not the place to look, but if you want originality and adventure then just start at the Douro and work south. Portugal is blessed with a treasure trove of native grapes, but it's only with the advent of modern technology (heavily funded by the EU, and since that means you and me, we might as well enjoy the benefits) that they've been vinified in such a way as to keep their qualities right up to the glass. They used to be severely injured by the wine-making, and then aged until they were dead; no longer. The grapes, traditionally, used to be so mixed up in the vineyards that even their mothers couldn't identify them; they still are, but they are showing signs of getting sorted out. Grapes like Alfrocheiro, Aragonez, Baga, Castelão Frances and Touriga Nacional may not exactly roll off the tongue yet, but then neither did Cabernet Sauvignon until we all got to know it.

WINES & WINE REGIONS

ALENTEJO Unfettered by Portugal's legendary bureaucracy, the Alentejo comes on in leaps and bounds. With EU help the co-ops are showing more initiative here than anywhere else in the country. *Borba* led the way but *Redondo* is now living up to its name and producing some round, fruity reds. Roseworthy-trained David Baverstock deserves another mention, having left his job in the port trade to revitalise the vast *Esporão* estate at Reguengos de Monsaraz. The large *José Maria da Fonseca* company, a leading innovator, has invested a lot of time and energy in the region. Apart from *Fonseca*'s blends, and the *Tinto Velho* from the *JS Rosado Fernandes* estate, which Fonseca now owns, the best wines are from various co-ops. The reds from the *Redondo* co-op, with their big, brash grapy fruit show the potential waiting to be tapped. The upfront rich damson-and-raspberry fruit of the *Paço dos Infantes* from Almodovar shows the same marvellously untamed excitement. The *Borba* co-op, *Cartuxa, Esporão* and *Reguengos de Monsaraz* are producing reds with terrific fruit. Look also for *Quinta da Anfora*, which is a blend of reds from the region. The Rothschilds have bought a share of *Quinta do Carmo*, near Estremoz, and other foreign investors are looking.

ALGARVE The south coastal strip of the country, making undistinguished wines – mostly alcoholic reds. Once a *Região Demarcada*, it has now been split into four *Denominacãos de Origem Controlada*, Lagos, Portimão, Lagoa and Tavira. All deserve demotion from DOC status. Among producers, the *Lagoa* co-op is the best bet.

BAIRRADA, DOC In the flat land down towards the sea from the hilly Dão region, vineyards mingle with wheatfields, olive trees and meadows, and the wines frequently overshadow the more famous Dão reds. The wines are apt to be tannic, often the result of fermenting the wine with the grape stalks, but the Baga grape, the chief one in the blend, gives a sturdy, pepper, plum-and-blackcurrant fruit to the wine which can often survive the over-aging, and at ten years old, although the resiny bite and peppery edge are apparent, a delicious, dry fruit is more in command. The best Bairrada wines age remarkably well. Some growers, like *Luis Pato*, are experimenting with blending in a dollop of softening Cabernet Sauvignon.

Some Portuguese merchants will tell you that their own Garrafeira wines are based on Bairrada, though the label won't say so. That's probably true, because of the traditional Portuguese approach to high quality reds – buy where the grapes are best, blend and age at your company's cellars, and sell the 'brew' under your own name. Since 1979, however, the Bairrada region has been demarcated and bulk sales

have been banned, and the challenging, rather angular, black fruit flavours of the wines now sport a Bairrada label. *São João* produces wine of world class, though increasingly hard to find. *Aliança* and *Sogrape* (look for its *Nobilis*) are good. The best co-op is *Vilharino do Bairro*, and *Cantanhede* and *Mealhada* aren't bad. Encouragingly, single-estate wines are emerging, with *Luis Pato* the leader so far. He must be good because he's already had some of his wine turned down by the *Bairrada Região* as untypical because he'd used new oak instead of old.

COLARES, DOC Grown in the sand dunes on the coast near Lisbon from the doughty but scented Ramisco grape. Almost all the wine is vinified at the local Adega Regional, stalks and all, aged in concrete tanks for two to three years, then sold to merchants for further maturation and sale. The young wine has fabulous cherry perfume but is *numbingly* tannic. As it ages it gets an exciting rich pepper-and-bruised-plums flavour, but the 1974s are only just ready. The Adega no longer has a monopoly on Colares, but only *Carvalho, Ribeiro & Ferreira* shows interest in exploiting the new freedom, and it may be too late to save the region from extinction.

DÃO, DOC This upland eyrie, ringed by mountains, reached by steep, exotic, forest-choked river gorges, makes Portugal's most famous, if not always her most appetizing reds. They are reputed to become velvet-smooth with age. My experience is that they rarely achieve this and could do with less aging in wood and more in bottle. They are made from a mixture of six grapes, of which the Touriga Nacional is the best, and they develop a strong, dry, herby taste, almost with a pine resin bite.

The protectionist rules that allowed companies to buy only finished wine, not grapes, from growers, and that forbade firms from outside the region to set up wineries there, have been abolished and *Sogrape*, with its own winery in the region, is now making the most of it. Among the others, *Caves São João* deserves an honourable mention along with *Caves Aliança* and *José Maria da Fonseca* for its brand, *Terras Altas*. Other firms are persuading their co-op suppliers to leave the grape stalks out of the fermentation vats and make cleaner, more modern wines, but there's still a long way to go.

DOURO, DOC The Douro valley is famous for the production of port. But only a proportion of the crop – usually about 40 per cent – is made into port, the rest being sold as table wine. There is a glut of grapes for table wine at the moment and *Sogrape* (which owns *Ferreira*) is busy making the most of it. The other port companies are less keen to put their weight behind table wines, though behind the scenes one or two are trying them out based on Touriga Francesa, Touriga Nacional and Tinta Roriz; one producer is working with Cabernet Sauvignon. The flavour can be delicious – soft and glyceriny, with a rich raspberry-and-peach fruit, and a perfume somewhere between liquorice, smoky bacon and cigar tobacco. Look out for *Quinta da Cismeira, Quinta do Côtto, Quinta de la Rosa* from *Sogrape; Barca Velha, Reserva Especial* and *Esteva* from *Ferreira*.

OESTE Portugal's largest wine area, north of Lisbon (and largest wine area, full stop, in terms of volume) is dominated by huge co-ops, some of which are just beginning to do something about quality. *Arruda* makes strong, gutsy reds, *Alenquer* makes softer, glyceriny wine, while the *Óbidos* reds are drier, more acid, but good in a cedary way. *Torres Vedras'* reds are lighter than Arruda, with a climate more influenced by cool Atlantic air. Single-estate *Quinta de Abrigada* makes light, creamy whites and stylish damson and cherry reds, and *Quinta das Pancas* has some Chardonnay and some Cabernet. These two are the only private estates doing much so far, though *Paulo da Silva*'s *Beira Mar* and *Casal de Azenha* are both good Oeste blends. The region sub-divides into six IPR regions: Arruda, Alenquer, Óbidos, Torres Vedras, Alcobaça and Encostas d'Aire.

RIBATEJO Portugal's second largest region, in the flat lands alongside the Tagus, provides the base wine for some important brands and some of Portugal's

The price guides for this section begin on page 390.

best Garrafeira wines – in particular the *Romeira* of *Caves Velhas. Carvalho Ribeiro* and *Ferreira,* recently bought by Costa Pina, a subsidiary of Allied Lyons, also bottles some good Garrafeiras, and with multi-national backing its wines are likely to improve. The co-op at *Almeirim* markets good wine under its own name, including the price-busting *Lezíria,* and the *Torre Velha* brand isn't bad. The *Margaride* estate is the Ribatejo's leading estate. The wines are sold as *Dom Hermano, Margarides* and under the names of their properties, *Casal do Monteiro* and *Convento da Serra*. The wines are patchy, but can be very good. The region is being split up into six IPRs (*Indicação de Proveniencia Regulamentada*) the six being Almeirim, Cartaxo, Chamusca, Santarém, Tomar and Coruche.

SETÚBAL PENINSULA One of the most important wine regions in Portugal, and one with plenty of technical expertise at its disposal. *JP Vinhos* and *José Maria da Fonseca* are the leading lights, for reds and whites. Imports like Cabernet Sauvignon and Merlot are made as varietals and used in blends with local grapes like Periquita. The area around Setúbal is now a Vinho Regional called Terras do Sado.

VINHO VERDE, DOC Sixty per cent of all Vinho Verde produced is red, made from four different grapes, of which the Vinhão is best. The wine is wonderfully sharp, harsh even, is hardly ever seen outside the country and goes a treat with traditional Portuguese dishes like *bacalhau,* or salt cod. Adnams have the red from the *Ponte da Lima* co-op, for anybody feeling brave.

FORTIFIED WINES

Nineteen ninety-three was one of the poorest vintages on record in the Douro. Port shippers are already relating lurid tales of grape pickers slipping down the muddy terraces, and of wine samples so lacking in guts that they were almost transparent. At least they are being frank.

Those who picked at the end of September did well to do so, because it rained every single day from 2 to 17 October. Some medium-quality wines will have been made from the earlier pickings. At least we have the 1991s to coo over – the first generally declared port vintage since 1985, and one that seems likely to prove long-lived. At the time of writing, four houses have declared 1992s: Niepoort and Burmester, both of whom declared 1991s as well, and Fonseca and Taylor, who abstained over the 1991s (cynics please note that 1992 marks Taylor's tercentenary). The 1992s have marked fruit, lusher and fleshier than the 1991s. Sandeman has declared neither.

In Madeira last year legislation forced the eight exporters to use the words 'Rich', 'Medium Rich', 'Medium Dry' and 'Dry' on labels of those wines in which noble grapes form less than 85 per cent of the blend. The noble varieties are Sercial, Verdelho, Bual and Malmsey: the grapes which have given their names to the main styles of Madeira, but which have been widely supplanted in the wines (and in the vineyards) by the cheaper, lower-quality and all-purpose Tinta Negra Mole. The result is that a hotchpotch of poor and unknown vines are gradually being uprooted and replaced by the four noble varieties – which is good news – and the Tinta Negra Mole, which is slightly less good news. The popularity of Madeira has increased steadily over the past few years; sales in Britain were up three per cent last year. Most popular is the Malmsey style, and vintage Madeiras are enjoying a new vogue, albeit a small one.

GRAPES & FLAVOURS

Eighteen different grape varieties are used to make red and white ports, and of these the most important in terms of quality and flavour are the Roriz, Barroca, Touriga Francesa and Touriga Nacional among the reds, and the Malvasia Dorada and Malvasia Fina in the whites. The Moscatel is chiefly grown in Setúbal just south of Lisbon, where it makes a famous, but not particularly thrilling, sweet fortified wine.

WINES & WINE REGIONS

CARCAVELOS, RD Just when Carcavelos looked as if it was about to disappear for ever, along comes a new vineyard. *Quinta dos Pesos* is making a good, nutty, fortified rather like an aged Tawny port.

MADEIRA, RD Each Madeira style is supposedly based on one of four grapes, Malmsey (Malvasia), Bual, Verdelho and Sercial, though at the moment only the more expensive Madeiras really live up to their labels – the cheaper ones, up to 'five-years-old', are almost all made from the inferior Tinta Negra Mole. The EU is enforcing a rule that 85 per cent of a wine labelled with a grape variety should be made from it, so the cheaper Madeiras are likely to start calling themselves, more honestly, 'Pale Dry', 'Dark Rich', and so on.

The Malmsey grape makes the sweetest Madeira, reeking sometimes of Muscovado sugar, dark, rich and brown, but with a smoky bite and surprisingly high acidity that makes it positively refreshing after a long meal. The Bual grape is also rich and strong, less concentrated, sometimes with a faintly rubbery whiff and higher acidity. Verdelho makes pungent, smoky, medium-sweet wine with more obvious, gentle fruit, and the Sercial makes dramatic dry wine, savoury, spirity, tangy, with a steely, piercing acidity. To taste what Madeira is all about you need a ten-year-old, and, frankly, really good Madeira should be two or three times that age.

The move into Madeira by the Symington family (of port fame) should herald new investment – and better wines.

SETÚBAL, DOC Good, but always a little spirity and never quite as perfume-sweet as one would like, perhaps because they don't use the best Muscat. It comes in a six-year-old and a 25-year-old version, and the wines do gain in concentration with age – the 25-year-old does have a lot more character and less overbearing spiritiness – but the sweetness veers towards the cooked marmalade of southern French Muscats rather than the honeyed, raisined richness of the Australian versions. You can still occasionally find older wines like *José Maria da Fonseca*'s *1934,* or its intense, pre-phylloxera *Torna Viagem,* with a powerful treacle toffee character balanced by a sharp acidic tang.

PORT (DOURO, DOC) The simplest and cheapest port available in Britain is labelled simply 'Ruby' and 'Tawny'. Ruby is usually blended from the unexceptional grapes of unexceptional vineyards to create a tangy, tough, but warmingly sweet wine to knock back uncritically. It should have a spirity rasp along with the sweetness. Cheap Tawny at around the same price as Ruby is simply a mixture of light Ruby and White ports, and is almost never as good as the Ruby would have been, left to itself.

Calling these inferior concoctions 'Tawnies' is very misleading because there's a genuine 'Tawny', too. Proper Tawnies are kept in wooden barrels for at least five, but preferably ten or more years to let the colour leach out and a gentle fragrance and delicate flavour of nuts, brown sugar and raisins develop. Most of these more expensive Tawnies carry an age on the label, which must be a multiple of 10: 10, 20, 30 or even 40 years old, but the figure indicates a style rather than a true date: a 10-year-old Tawny might contain some 6-year-old and some 14-year-old wine. Lack of age on a Tawny label – however often it says 'Fine', 'Old', and so on – is a bad sign and usually implies a cheap Ruby-based blend, though there are some good brands like *Harvey's Director's Bin Very Superior Old Tawny* or *Delaforce's His Eminence's Choice*. Most Tawnies reach their peak at somewhere between 10 and 15 years, and few ports improve after 20 years in barrel, so don't pay inflated prices for 30- and 40-year-old wine. Try *Cockburn 10-year-old*, *Ferreira 10-* and *20-year-old*, *Fonseca 10-* and *20-year-old*, *Harvey's Director's Bin*, *Sainsbury's 10-year-old*. *Colheitas* – single-vintage Tawnies – are increasingly available, usually from Portuguese houses, and can be really delicious. *Calem* and *Niepoort* are good.

VINTAGE PORTS are the opposite of the Tawnies, since the object here is to make a big, concentrated rather than delicate mouthful. Vintage years are 'declared' by port shippers when the quality seems particularly good – usually about three times a decade. The wines are matured in wooden casks for two years or so, then bottled and left to age for a decade or two.

The final effect should have more weight and richness than a Tawny of similar age, since the maturation has taken place in the almost airless confines of the bottle, which ages the wines more slowly. There should also be a more exciting, complex tangle of flavours; blackcurrant, plums, minty liquorice, pepper and herbs, cough mixture and a lot more besides. Vintage port you get animated and opinionated about, while Tawny is more a wine for quiet reflection.

If you want a peek at what Vintage port can be like, buy Single-Quinta wine. Single Quintas (or farms) are usually from the best vineyards in the less brilliant years, but instead of being bottled and shipped after only two years or so, they are bottled after two years, stored for up to ten years, and shipped ready to drink. They are usually extremely good. Look for *Taylor's Quinta da Vargellas*, *Dow's Quinta do Bonfim*, *Warre's Quinta da Cavadinha*, *Fonseca's Quinta do Panascal* and *Quinta de la Rosa*.

Another good-value Vintage lookalike is Crusted port. This is a blend of wines from two or three vintages, shipped in cask and bottled slightly later than Vintage, at about three years old, so they retain the peppery attack of the top wines and also keep a good deal of the exotic perfumed sweetness of real 'Vintage'. They are called Crusted because of the sediment that forms after three or four years in bottle. More and more houses are producing Crusted ports, though the current collapse of the Vintage market means that both Crusted and Single Quinta look less good value when you can find the real thing for not much more.

Two other types of port like to think of themselves as vintage style. Vintage Character and Late Bottled Vintage are bottled four to six years after the harvest. Ideally, this extra time maturing in wood should bring about an effect similar to a dozen years of bottle-aging. Bottled at four years, and not too heavily filtered, it still can, but most VC and LB ports are too browbeaten into early decline and have as much personality as a pan of potatoes. The best, labelled with the year of bottling, are from *Fonseca, Niepoort, Smith-Woodhouse, Ramos-Pinto* and *Warre*. They are delicious, but can throw a sediment in the bottle, and may need decanting.

There are two styles of White port, dry and sweet. In general, the flavour is a bit thick and alcoholic, the sweet ones even tasting slightly of rough grape skins. But there are a few good dry ones, though I've never felt any great urge to drink them anywhere except in the blinding mid-summer heat of the Douro valley when they're refreshing with a few ice-cubes and a big splash of lemonade or tonic.

MATURITY CHART
Vintage Ports
1977 was always destined for the long term
1970 may now be enjoyed at its peak

1970

Bottled			Ready		Peak		Tiring	In decline
0	5	10	15	20	25	30	35 years	

1977

Bottled				Ready		Peak		Tiring	In decline
0	5	10	15	20	25	30	35	40 years	

1985 and 1991 are both good vintages to cellar,
but 1991 may mature relatively early

1985

Bottled			Ready		Peak		Tiring	In decline
0	5	10	15	20	25	30	35 years	

1991

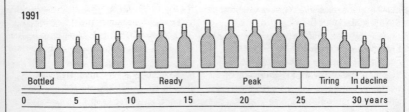

Bottled			Ready		Peak		Tiring	In decline
0	5	10	15	20	25	30 years		

PORT SHIPPER PROFILES

CÁLEM ★★★★ Important Portuguese shipper founded in the last century and still family owned. Cálem produce excellent 10, 20, 30 and 40-year old Tawnies, good Colheitas, and good Vintage port from the spectacular Quinta da Foz at Pinhão.

CHURCHILL GRAHAM ★★★(★) Established in 1981, the first independent port shipper to be founded in more than 50 years. John Graham is establishing a reputation for intense, concentrated wines which are made to last.

COCKBURN ★★★★ Shippers of the best-selling 'Fine Old Ruby' and 'Special Reserve'. At the forefront of research into viticulture in the Upper Douro. Recent Vintage ports have been stunning.

CROFT ★★(★) Quinta da Roeda near Pinhão forms the backbone of its Vintage wines, but many wines are over-delicate.

DELAFORCE ★★(★) The Tawny, His Eminence's Choice, is its best-known wine.

DOW ★★★★★ Quinta do Bomfim at Pinhão produces the backbone of Dow's firm-flavoured, long-living Vintage and has also been launched as a Single Quinta.

FERREIRA ★★★★ One of the best Portuguese-owned shippers, making elegant, early-maturing Vintages and two superb Tawnies; 10-year-old Quinta do Porto and 20-year-old Duque de Bragança. Bought by Sogrape in 1988.

FONSECA GUIMARAENS ★★★★★ Family-run shippers belonging to the Yeatman side of Taylor, Fladgate and Yeatman. Fonseca's wines are sweeter and less austere than Taylor's. The Vintage ports are often outstanding, and the quality of its commercial releases is reassuring.

GOULD CAMPBELL ★★★★ The name is used mainly for Vintage ports which tend to be ripe and mature relatively early.

GRAHAM ★★★★★ Usually rich and sweet. There is a Single Quinta, Quinta dos Malvedos, and fine Vintage styles.

NIEPOORT ★★★★★ Tiny firm run by a Dutch family with total commitment to quality. Aged Tawnies, traditional LBVs, Colheitas and long-lasting Vintage. It launched a new Single Quinta, Quinta do Passadouro, in 1994.

OFFLEY FORRESTER ★★★(★) Famous for 'Boa Vista' Vintage and LBV ports. Vintage is mostly based on its own Quinta da Boa Vista and can be insubstantial. Excellent Baron de Forrester Tawnies.

QUINTA DO NOVAL ★★★ Bought out last year by the French insurance group AXA. Noval's Nacional wines, made from ungrafted vines, are legendary and fetch a stratospheric price at auction. Other Noval wines don't attempt such heights, but are usually good, if light. Noval LB is widely sold, but isn't actually that special; the Tawnies and Colheitas are much better.

RAMOS-PINTO ★★★★ Delicious Tawnies from two quintas – Ervamoira and Bom Retiro. Elegant, nutty and delicate. Now owned by Louis Roederer of Champagne.

REAL VINICOLA ★★ Sells ports under seven different names including that of Royal Oporto. They can sometimes be good. Vintage is generally early maturing.

SANDEMAN ★★★ Currently being shaken up, and heading towards quality rather than quantity. It launched its first Single Quinta, Quinta do Vau, in 1993; and a new ruby port, Partners, in 1994.

SMITH WOODHOUSE ★★★★ Some delicious Vintage and LBVs. Concentrated Vintage wines which tend to mature early. Full-flavoured Crusted.

TAYLOR, FLADGATE AND YEATMAN ★★★★(★) Very high quality range, but some recent commercial releases have seen standards slip a bit, and their Vintage port

is no longer ahead of the field. Quinta de Vargellas is one of the best Single Quintas.

WARRE ★★★★★ The first port company in which the entrepreneurial Symington dynasty became involved. Warre produces serious wines: good LBVs and Vintage, fine 'Nimrod' Tawny. Quinta da Cavadinha has recently been launched as a Single Quinta.

PORT CLASSIFICATION

If you think that Burgundy and Bordeaux make a meal out of classifying their vineyards, just look at how rigidly port is controlled. Nothing is left to chance. The age of the vines is classified on a scale from 0 to 60 points. The level of upkeep of the vines is ruthlessly marked from –500 to +100 points. The objective is to score as many points as possible. The highest possible score would be +1680 points, while the bottom score possible would be a massively embarrassing –3430. The classification, based on points scored, is from A to F, and controls how many litres of juice per 1000 vines can be turned into port. The rest has to be made into table wine, which gives a smaller return.

The Vineyard Calculation

Productivity (Ranging from about 500 litres per 1000 vines to about 2000 litres; the lower the yield the higher the points scored.)
Worst: 0 points   Best: +80 points
Altitude (Ranging from a highest allowable altitude of 650 metres to a lowest of 150 metres.)
Worst: –900 points   Best: +150 points
Soil (Scored according to type. Schist scores best, granite worst.)
Worst: –350 points   Best: +100 points
Geographical position (Predetermined locations score different marks.)
Worst: –50 points   Best: +600 points
Upkeep of vineyard (Good housekeeping awards for various factors.)
Worst: –500 points   Best: +100 points
Variety and quality of grapes
Worst: –300 points   Best: +150 points
Gradient (From 1-in-6 to 1-in-30 – the steeper the better.)
Worst: –100 points   Best: +100 points
Shelter
Worst: 0   Best: +70 points

Age of vines (With 5-year-olds scoring 30; up to 25-year-olds scoring 60.)
Worst: 0   Best: +60 points
Distance root to root (The distance from the end of one vine's root to the start of the next root – too close is frowned upon.)
Worst: –50 points   Best: +50 points
Nature of land
Worst: –600 points   Best: +100 points
Aspect
Worst: –30 points   Best: +100 points

THE TOTAL

The experts then add up all these points and classify the vineyards according to score, allowing each group to make a certain number of litres of wine per 1000 vines, as follows:

A (1201 points or more)	600 litres
B (1001–1200 points)	600 litres
C (801–1000 points)	590 litres
D (601–800 points)	580 litres
E (401–600 points)	580 litres
F (400 points or less)	260 litres

PORT VINTAGES

Not every year produces a crop of fine enough quality for vintage-dated wine to be made, and a few houses may not make Vintage port even in a generally good year. It all depends on the quality the individual house has produced, although it is extremely rare for a house to declare two consecutive years. Announcing the intention to bottle Vintage port is known as 'declaring'. Five vintages were good enough in the 1980s, and 1991 was generally declared.

1992 Declared by four shippers: *Fonseca, Taylor, Niepoort* and *Burmester*. Rich, fruity wines, lusher and fleshier than the 1991s. Cynics note that 1992 was Taylor's tercentenary.

1991 Generally declared. A dry summer and an even drier economy mean that quantities will be small; the Vintage port market is in a poor state at the moment. *Dow*, for example, is declaring half the amount it declared in 1985.

1987 Four shippers, *Ferreira, Martinez, Niepoort* and *Offley*, chose to declare this small but good vintage. Coming so hard on the heels of the nearly universal 1985 declaration, most shippers opted instead for Single Quinta wines for medium term drinking.

1985 Declared by every important shipper. The quality is exceptionally good. The wines don't quite have the solidity of the 1983s but they make up for this with a juicy ripeness of fruit and unusually precocious signs of perfumes to come. Although *Taylor* isn't as outstanding as usual, several perennial under-achievers like *Croft* and *Offley* are very good, *Cockburn* is very attractive, and *Fonseca* is rich and lush. However, my favourites are *Graham, Warre, Dow, Gould Campbell* and *Churchill Graham*.

1983 Marvellous wine, strong and aggressive to taste at the moment, but with a deep, brooding sweetness which is all ripe, clean fruit. This won't be one of the most fragrant vintages, but it will be a sturdy classic in ten years' time. Prices have fallen, so buy now.

1982 Not as good as it was at first thought. It begins to look as though those shippers that declared 1982 in preference to 1983 made a mistake. *Croft* and *Delaforce* are already drying out, and most need to be drunk already.

1980 A good vintage, though excessively expensive when first offered. Although they were consequently unpopular, the wines are developing a delicious, drier than usual style. They should peak about 1995.

1977 Brilliant wine, now beginning to mature. The flavour is a marvellous mixture of great fruit sweetness and intense spice and herb fragrance.

1975 These in general don't have the stuffing that a true vintage style demands, but some have surprisingly gained weight and richness and are excellent for drinking now. *Noval, Taylor, Dow, Warre* and *Graham* need no apologies. Most of the others do.

1970 Lovely stuff, but, curiously, only cautiously praised. This is exceptional, balanced port, already good to drink, sweet and ripe with a fascinating citrus flash of freshness – and it'll last for ages. All the top houses are really special – led by *Fonseca, Taylor, Warre, Graham* and *Dow*, but lesser houses like *Calem* and *Santos Junior* are also excellent.

1966 They didn't rate this at first, but they do now. It's gained body and oomph and is now approaching its best. Doesn't *quite* have the super-ripe balance of the '70 or the startling, memorable character of the '63, but a very good year. *Fonseca* is the star at the moment.

1963 They call it the 'classic' year, and one can see why. It's big, deep, and spicy, with a remarkable concentration of flavours. One or two have lost a surprising amount of colour recently, but in the main it's so good that if you decide to see in the millennium with a bottle of *Fonseca, Taylor, Graham, Dow* or *Cockburn*... get my address from *Webster's*.

UNITED KINGDOM

Every year in early November I do the same thing. There I am, chatting to an English winemaker, and I ask how the harvest went. And every year I realise, a moment too late, that the vintage isn't over yet – it's too early. England is in the north of the wine world, and it harvests its grapes late. Last autumn saw the rain lashing down well before the grapes were picked.

After a record crop in 1992 of over 26,000 hectolitres, 1993 saw production slump by half. Some of Britain's growers didn't even bother to pick their miserable frost-bitten grapes while others soldiered on under sodden skies harvesting berries that one grower compared to mushy peas.

No wonder Commander Geoffrey Bond of the English Vineyards Association describes the situation as depressing. But the weather isn't the only thing to be depressed about. The record crop back in 1992 took Britain 1500 hectolitres above the 25,000 hectolitre threshold beyond which no EU country can plant more vines without a quality wine scheme along the lines of the French AC system. Brussels is determined to drain the European wine lake, and Britain, with just over 1000 hectares under vine, is to be treated exactly the same way as the Italians and Spanish who farm well over a million hectares of vineyards apiece.

All of which means, of course, more red tape. One grower grumbled bitterly that 'we now have 27 forms to complete and there are several thousand points of accuracy'. It's a common complaint, and one that could never have been foreseen by the late Major-General Sir Guy Salisbury-Jones who began the revival of English viticulture back in the 1950s when the European Union was no more than the fledgling Franco-German Coal and Steel community.

For sale: vineyard, one careful owner

There are other difficulties, too, currently facing the English wine industry. The recession has bitten hard and a number of committed growers, who in normal circumstances would have the wherewithal to see it through, have suffered terminal losses at Lloyds. Vineyards have been advertised in the glossy pages of *Country Life* and have changed hands at knock-down prices. Since 1 January 1993 the Single Market has also had an impact on English growers, many of whom earned an honest crust from farm gate sales. The irony of cars rushing through the Kent countryside laden with wine from the Calais *hypermarché* is not lost on Geoffrey Bond, who has been lobbying in tandem with the Wine and Spirit Association for a change in the British tax regime.

As if that were not discouraging enough, the EU has just unveiled its latest potentially catastrophic blow. In its continuing effort to limit production, Brussels has drawn up a scheme whereby minimum natural alcohol levels in northern Europe are to be increased from 5 to 7 per cent by volume for table wines and from 6 to 8 per cent for quality wine. On top of this, chaptalization (the addition of sugar during fermentation to increase alcoholic strength) is to be more tightly controlled with 1.5 and 2 per cent additional alcohol respectively set as the upper limit. Under the EU directive winemakers may only use rectified concentrated juice for chaptalization. You can see the logic of the restrictions.

Germany has been palming us off with thin, sugary Liebfraumilch for years. But England, with its small but courageous band of wine producers, believes it deserves to be treated differently. If the EU directive is adopted (and Geoffrey Bond fears the worst), in years like 1993 it would be almost impossible to make any wine at all.

After facing the capricious British weather for so long, you can be sure that England's growers and winemakers won't give up easily. The Denbies Estate in Dorking, Surrey, the country's largest vineyard, has recently staged a national advertising campaign with slogans like 'We left the French a frog in their throats' and 'We turned the Germans into sour krauts', all designed to make a Europhile wince. And although self-criticism is a tempting national trait (you won't find a Frenchman denigrating his native Bordeaux – unless, of course, he comes from Burgundy), quality is improving and prices have fallen. Economies of scale are developing: English Wine Growers Ltd is the country's first wine-making co-operative serving 20 small growers who would rather get their hands dirty in the vineyard than the winery.

At the other end of the spectrum eight of England's heavyweights, who are together responsible for 50 per cent of the nation's wine production, have joined together to form 'English Wine Producers', an association designed to give marketing clout to English wines at home and abroad. Supermarket buyers have been bullied into taking England seriously. Tesco, Sainsbury and Safeway have wines ranging from inexpensive medium-dry English blends to crisp, zesty single-estate wines for less than a fiver. For the full English experience, drink them in the rain.   RICHARD MAYSON

WHITE WINES

BACCHUS In Germany, this new crossing usually produces fat, blowsy, marmalade-Muscatty flavours. In England it is more likely to produce a sharp wine, with strong flavours of gooseberry, elderflower and orange rind. *Barkham, Partridge Vineyard, Three Choirs, Coddington and Shawsgate* are good; *Chiltern Valley's 1989 Noble Bacchus* showed that a warm summer can produce lusciously rich wines too.

FABER A crossing of Pinot Blanc and Müller-Thurgau, making fragrant wines with good acidity. One of the few varieties in which you can actually taste Riesling characteristics.

HUXELREBE A cross (of Gutedel, alias Chasselas, with Courtillier Musqué) that in Germany beetles to overripeness in no time at all. The wine there is usually rich, flat and grapy. In England it's generally the exact opposite, renowned for a grapefruit-pith taste and a greenish bite. For this reason it is often softened up by blending. *Headcorn's* version is almost as delicate as a German Mosel; *Lamberhurst* and *Biddenden* are fuller; *Staple St James* and *Pilton Manor* more grapefruity and smoky. *Nutbourne Manor's* is concentrated, *Astley* mixes it with Müller-Thurgau for Huxelvaner while *Three Choirs* late-picks it and tries to make a sweetie.

KERNER A bright, new German crossing of Riesling and Trollinger that has been producing good results. *Astley's* is light and *Oatley* mixes it successfully with Kernling for a gingery, apple-sweet wine in best Cox's Orange Pippin style.

MADELEINE ANGEVINE Basically this is a table grape, but it performs quite well in England, where its somewhat 'fruit-juicy' character is matched by good acidity, either in the green but refreshing, elderflower perfumed style of *Astley 1985* and '86, or the more honeyed but appley style of *Hooksway 1984*. *Sharpham* blends it with Huxelrebe and produces a flinty Loire lookalike.

MÜLLER-THURGAU This used to be the English workhorse. However, it has fallen from over one third of the acreage to 17.6 per cent. *Wootton, Bruisyard St Peter, Breaky Bottom, St Nicholas of Ash, Staple St James, Tenterden, St George's* are good. And it can make very attractive, slightly sweet wine (through the addition of *Süssreserve,* or unfermented grape juice, just before bottling), as at *Pulham* and *Rowney*.

ORTEGA German cross making fat, rich, grapy wine mostly in the Mosel, of all places, but better suited to England. *Hidden Spring* is concentrated, and *Biddenden*, in particular, makes a delicious, slightly sweet but tremendously fruity elderflower and apricot-tasting example. It is usually blended and rarely seen on its own.

REICHENSTEINER A real 'EU' grape, since it is a crossing of French Madeleine Angevine, German Müller-Thurgau and Italian Calabrese. Does this multi-coloured background make it an exciting, tempestuous grape? Sadly, it's rather more of a Brussels bureaucrat clone, taking up 12.7 per cent of the total acreage. It's usually pretty dull when dry, but made slightly sweet, it can develop a pleasant, smoky, quince-and-peaches taste which ages well. *Carr Taylor* and *Rock Lodge* use it for Champagne-method fizz, *Three Choirs '90 'New Release'* was 50/50

The price guides for this section begin on page 398.

Huxelrebe and Reichensteiner and *Nutbourne Manor*'s version is also good.

SCHEUREBE Silvaner crossed with Riesling, capable of producing good grapefruity, curranty wines in good years. *Thames Valley*'s late-harvest version is seductively good.

SCHÖNBURGER A *good,* pink grape. It makes a fat wine by English standards, with a pears-and-lychees flavour and good acidity. Dry versions like *Saxon Valley*'s need ripe fruit to balance the acidity, and it needs expert wine-making or it can end up tasting like bathroom detergent. The best are made by *Wootton, Carr Taylor, Coxley* and *Three Choirs*.

SEYVAL BLANC A French hybrid with 12.6 per cent of UK acreage, and falling slightly. *Breaky Bottom* is the most successful – dry and Sauvignon-like when young, honeyed like Burgundy after four to five years – but it is generally best blended with something more exotic like Schönburger or Huxelrebe, or made

sweetish. *Hambledon* blends it with Pinot Meunier and Chardonnay, *Three Choirs* with Reichensteiner and *Adgestone* with Reichensteiner and Müller, while *Tenterden* makes a very good oaked Reserve. *Thames Valley*, too, hits it with oak for its *Fumé; Hidden Spring* and *Headcorn* are also good.

OTHER WHITES Numerous other varieties are being tried. The most interesting are Gewürztraminer at *Barton Manor* on the Isle of Wight where it was planted in plastic tunnels in 1984, and Ehrenfelser, aged in a 4000-litre oak barrel, at *Penshurst; Wootton*'s Auxerrois is a pungent, salty-sappy wine, while *Tenterden* also achieves lean and nervy results with this variety. *Carr Taylor* has achieved good results with Pinot Blanc for its concentrated *Kemsley Dry*. There are also some efforts with Chardonnay, at, for example, the new, 250-acre *Denbies Estate* at Dorking in Surrey, England's biggest vineyard project yet. Chardonnay now has 26 hectares planted in England (Kerner has 25) and most of them are at *Denbies*.

RED & ROSÉ WINES

CABERNET SAUVIGNON *Beenleigh* in Devon has been growing this in plastic tunnels, along with Merlot, and the 1989 version is clean and fresh, if light.

PINOT NOIR There are now over 30 hectares and rising of the great Burgundy grape planted. So far, full reds have been difficult to achieve, but Kent has several patches making very good rosé – *Chiddingstone* blends it with Pinot Meunier to make a delicious wine redolent of eucalyptus; *Bodiam Castle* makes a tasty rosé blended with Blauburger, as well as a dry, honeyed Blanc de Pinot Noir white; *Biddenden* mixes it with Dornfelder and Gamay to produce a light, cherryish red; and *Tenterden*'s blend with Dunkelfelder

makes a gently honeyed, smoky, mango-flavoured pink. *Three Choirs* rosé from Pinot Noir has earthy raspberry-and-Morello-cherry fruit; *Conghurst* rosé is also good, with grapy, herbaceous flavours. Some estates, particularly *Denbies Estate*, have planted Pinot Noir for sparkling wine. *Denbies* also makes a nice light, scented rosé from it.

TRIOMPHE D'ALSACE There are only about 11 hectares planted to this hybrid, but the best examples have a fresh, raspberry-and-spice character like *Meon Valley*'s *Meonwara* or *Thames Valley*'s *Dry Red*. The trick, as with all reds in England, is to settle for a light, graceful wine and not to over-extract flavour.

EASTERN EUROPE

Eastern Europe, our great white hope for the future, is already looking a little disappointing. Not its fault, of course; perhaps ours, for expecting too much. Free market economics have not proved to be an instant panacea for nearly 50 years of Communism, and nationalism and pride mean that not all wineries are eager to be told what to do by Western winemakers. Yet from the Czech and Slovak Republics in the north and west to the CIS states of Moldova and Georgia in the east, the potential is still there.

Privatization continues apace, but most countries are hampered by lack of capital. Angela Muir, who has been barnstorming Eastern Europe on behalf of Kwik Save, reports that even Hungary (forward-thinking, but now with a newly-elected Communist government) is reluctant to give up control to outsiders. So for the moment Eastern Europe is a place for visitors; visitors like Muir herself and flying winemakers like Hugh Ryman and Kym Mylne who have cleaned up many an act in the vast state-owned wineries that still dominate production. The East is still a great source of value-for-money reds, but as commercial pressures strengthen, it will have to adopt a different approach if it is to reach the next rung on the quality ladder.   RICHARD MAYSON

HUNGARY

Hungary has been attracting attention in Britain, but its indigenous grape varieties are still a slightly unknown quantity, and it lacks the vast reserves of Cabernet and Merlot boasted by Bulgaria. The best vineyards are in the hills to the west around Lake Balaton. Look out for white wines from the Balatonboglar Winery. Tokaji is undergoing a long-awaited revivial with investment from Spain's Vega Sicilia, the Royal Tokaji Wine Company and Bordeaux interests.

BULGARIA

Among the old Soviet-dominated countries of Eastern Europe, Bulgaria was the first to take its wine industry seriously and begin exporting to the West. But since then things seem to have come to something of a standstill. There are plenty of good-value varietal reds from the Svishtov and Suhindol regions (Domaine Boyar is one of the most reliable exporters) but white wines from the coastal plains are much less interesting. A number of flying winemakers have arrived in Bulgaria to see what they can do but it will take more than an annual visit at the time of the harvest to improve handling. Many ripe, cleanly-made wines are marred by clumsy use of oak so, for the moment, go for the the brisk young Cabernets and Merlots.

ROMANIA

For decades Romania has been a *terra incognita* for most things, including wine. With its doors now flung wide open, it is clear that it has considerable potential. North and west of the Carpathians there are some good white wines from the Jidvei winery in the Tirnave region. Look out for a clean, grassy varietal Sauvignon under the Romanian Classic label. On the Danube plains to the south and east the vineyards of Dealul Mare are well stocked with Merlot, Cabernet and Pinot Noir. There are also some excellent indigenous varieties like the white Tamaoisa which produces luscious, botrytized wines at knock-down prices. There is also some fascinating botrytized Chardonnay. Wine-making in enormous state-owned wineries is still something of a lottery.

THE CZECH AND SLOVAK REPUBLICS

These two countries soak up most of the 1.3 milllion hectolitres of wine they produce, which leaves little for export. Two thirds of the former Czechoslovakia's vineyards are in Slovakia, but a severe spring frost there in 1993 did not help. Slovakia is gradually becoming more receptive to Western ideas, but unfortunately the vineyards of both republics are dominated by the uninspiring white Leanyka grape, a variety which is found with different names throughout Eastern Europe. There are workable quantities of Pinot Blanc and Pinot Gris and some Sauvignon, but they suffer from being vinified in state-owned wineries to the same formula.

CIS STATES

It is no wonder that Gorbachev was unpopular at home, since during his premiership he made his comrades uproot vineyard after vineyard. At around 18 million hectolitres, wine production in the former USSR is now about half what it was before he set to work. Vineyards are concentrated around the Black Sea in the states of Moldova and Georgia, both of which produce 6 to 7 million hectolitres apiece. Quality is patchy but Moldova produces some good old-fashioned beefy reds, and international whites with the help of Flying Winemakers.

SLOVENIA

Comment on most of the former Yugoslavia must, sadly, wait awhile, but Slovenia in the north is mercifully unaffected by the war. Since it gained its independence in 1991 it has looked mainly towards Italy and Austria for both inspiration and trade, and few wines of any quality (the better ones are usually made from Pinot Blanc and Pinot Gris) ever reach our shores. Prices are rarely competitive. That tired old stager Lutomer Laski Rizling is still among Britain's best-selling brands, although Slovenia can do much better than this.

EASTERN EUROPEAN CLASSIFICATIONS

BULGARIA In order of quality there are Country Wines (replacing the old Mehana, or bistro wines), Varietal Wines with Stated Geographic Origin (from 43 regions) and Controliran wines, from 27 zones. Special Reserves and Estate Selections are not official terms but indicate high quality.

HUNGARY 'Minosegi Bor' means 'Quality Wine', and is more or less equivalent to AC.

ROMANIA In order of quality there are VS (Vinul de Calitate Superioara, or Superior Quality);

VSO (Vinul de Calitate Superioara & Denumire de Origine, or Superior Quality with Appellation of Origin); VSOC (Vinul Superioara de Origine Controlata) which includes Spätlese, Auslese and TBA lookalike categories.

SLOVENIA All six Yugoslav republics shared a system. Premium (Kvalitetno) Wine is from a specific region. Select Wine (Cuveno or Vrhunsko Vino) can be from a single vineyard.

THE CZECH STATE, SLOVAKIA, CIS STATES No system of classifications.

For Further Information Contact:

**Laureate, 555 Stonefield Way, Ruislip, Middlesex, HA4 0HY,
United Kingdom. Telephone: 081 841 4134 Fax: 081 845 2072**

RED GRAPES & WINES

CABERNET SAUVIGNON Widely grown, and spans the quality scale. Bulgaria has the best; some oak-aged examples from Villanyi in Hungary, Kozhushny in Moldavia, and Dealul Mare and Murfatlar in Romania are rich, ripe and silky.

FRANKOVKA Native Czech grape yielding attractive grassy, peppery wines.

GAMZA Bulgarian grape, meaty, tarry, ripe wines. Often teamed with Merlot.

KADARKA Hungarian vine which yields spicy wine with good body and tannin.

KEKFRANKOS Thought to be the Gamay from Beaujolais. Also called Blaufrankisch.

MAVRUD Bulgarian; rich fruit, but can be rather tannic and unbalanced.

MELNIK Indigenous Bulgarian grape making concentrated, spicy reds.

MERLOT Widely grown. At its best it is young, brash, soft and blackcurranty. Bulgaria's Stambolovo and Sakar are good for older, oakier ripe Reserves. Romanian Merlots from Murfatlar and Dealul Mare can need about eight years to mellow.

PINOT NOIR Decidedly variable. There are occasional sightings of good examples from Moldova and Romania, but the bad far outnumber the good

ST LAURENT Soft, floral, damsony Austrian grape that can be delicious in Slovakia.

VRANAC Montenegran speciality, making robust reds.

WHITE GRAPES & WINES

ALIGOTÉ Light, dry wines in Romania, Bulgaria and Russia. Sometimes blended with Ugni Blanc.

CHARDONNAY Everywhere in all guises. Only Hungary seems to be getting the idea.

EZERJO Widely grown Hungarian; grassy, light wine, sometimes short on acidity.

FURMINT Hungarian; wines high in alcohol. Very susceptible to noble rot, and is the principal grape in Tokaji.

GEWÜRZTRAMINER Fair examples from Villanyi in Hungary, though balance is not always right.

IRSAY OLIVER Czech grape; gentle fruit and light spice; could use more acidity.

MUSCAT Usually the Ottonel variety, grown for medium-sweet and dessert wines.

PINOT BLANC Elegant from Nagyréde and Dunavár in Hungary; also some from the Czech State and Slovakia.

PINOT GRIS Full from Lake Balaton and Romania and smokier and rounder in the Czech Republic and Slovakia.

RIESLING Seldom exciting, but the Flying Winemakers in Hungary are beginning to get it right.

SAUVIGNON BLANC Best are from Slovenia and Gyöngyös in Hungary.

TRAMINER There's some attractive, zingy, aromatic Traminer from Moravenka in the Czech State and Slovenia.

WELSCHRIZLING (Same as Laski-, Olasz- and Riesling Italico.) Produces medium-dry, sometimes fruity, sometimes dirty wines, usually best avoided.

Introducing
The Bulgarian Vintners'

YOUNG WINES

Young fresh wines from Russe, Sliven, Haskovo and Svischtov.
Oak fermented reds and fragrant young whites from the new vintage.

The debut of *Debut*

UNITED STATES

Future wine historians (assuming that the neo-prohibitionists don't prevail and one can talk about wine in the future tense) may regard the 1990s as a turning point in the development of fine wines in the United States. There are so many changes and new directions that the mind boggles.

Perhaps one of the most important developments of the '90s is the realization that there is wine country beyond California. Wineries from Missouri and Ohio are taking gold medals at the San Francisco International Wine Expo and wine groupies from coast to coast are talking about that wonderful sparkling wine they had the other night from New Mexico. Judges at wine competitions across the country are discovering Colorado Chardonnay, Finger Lakes (New York) Riesling and Missouri Norton (an indigenous American grape).

Not that the Gallos and the Mondavis are going to be forced into early retirement, but if the United States is ever really to become a wine-drinking nation, it will be through this huge leap in quality of the smaller, regional producers.

There is also a sense of excitement among both winemakers and consumers about the success of wines based on grape varieties other than the Bordeaux and Burgundy standards. These are varieties that California winemaker Randall Grahm calls the meridional wines, which term Californians, with a fine disregard for geography, have extended to include northern Italy.

New releases are coming in every week of California Sangiovese, Syrah, Viognier, Nebbiolo, Marsanne, Grenache and any other variety that can claim some kinship with the southern sun, that beaker full of the warm south that Keats longed for. Even Robert Mondavi Winery, the Napa institution that some consider practically synonymous with California Cabernet, will have some small bottlings of what it calls alternative wines on the market before the end of the year.

There are also new plantings of the Spanish grape, Tempranillo, and California winemakers are charging around Spain and Portugal (which Grahm, the mad wizard of California wine-making, calls a 'museum of vines'), hunting for what might be the next trend.

Phylloxera's silver lining

Typically, Californians have also taken a multi-million-dollar disaster and turned it into a potential triumph. When the tiny root louse, *Phylloxera vastatrix*, began chomping its way through the vineyards of California a few years ago, there were grim predictions of the state's grape crop being wiped out. It wasn't the first time winegrowers in America and in Europe had had to deal with phylloxera. In the nineteenth century the disease almost completely destroyed the budding Californian industry and annihilated the vineyards of Europe. It was only the discovery that many native American grape rootstocks are tolerant of phylloxera that enabled the European vineyards to be replanted, since the traditional noble vines could everywhere be successfully grafted on to the resistant American rootstock.

However, a few years ago, a mutant strain of phylloxera realized that it could live quite happily on one of the most common of the rootstocks, and there were cries of doom and disaster.

Enter the silver lining. As the US economy improved in 1993, investment capital began flowing back into the wine industry and winegrowers on California's north coast began an aggressive replanting programme, including making great improvements in the vineyards above and beyond getting the rootstock right. One grower, Andy Beckstoffer, who farms over 2000 acres of premium wine grapes, has called the phylloxera outbreak 'the greatest opportunity we've ever had as grape growers. We are able to start from the ground up. It's an opportunity to do it right, to plant grape varieties where they should be growing.'

Two other highlights of the '90s should also be mentioned: one is the explosion of high-quality Champagne-method sparkling wines from California, with outstanding early releases from new producers like Jordan with its J sparkler, Domaine Carneros, Codorníu Napa and Gloria Ferrer as well as world class performances by Domaine Chandon, Mumm Napa, Scharffenberger and Schramsberg.

The other is the great potential for Pinot Noir in California from emerging areas like the Santa Maria Valley in Santa Barbara County and the 'Pinot Noir Belt' in cool northern Monterey County.

As for the 1993 vintage, no-one in California is issuing vintage-of-the-century claims. The Chardonnay is a bit of a let-down after the outstanding 1991 and 1992 vintages. The quality is average and, overall, a bit lightweight. However, in Washington, there has been a very enthusiastic response to the infant Chardonnays, Rieslings and Sauvignon Blancs, although there is still a question mark over the red wines of a very cool growing season and a heavy crop.

In Oregon, growers are very high on the Pinot Noir, which looks to be the best since the 1983 harvest, and when Oregon Pinot is good, it can be very, very good. In New York State, meanwhile, both red and white wines from Long Island are getting early rave reviews, with special praise for the Merlot. Riesling from New York's Finger Lakes region is also looking like a winner.   LARRY WALKER

RED GRAPES & FLAVOURS

BARBERA The Italian variety most grown in California. *Louis M Martini, Sebastiani* and *Bonny Doon* are good, as is *Monteviña* with an intense, blackberry-and-black-cherry wine; *Preston Vineyards* (Sonoma County) is also worth a try.

CABERNET SAUVIGNON Coming after a string of outstanding to good vintages in the 1980s, the '90s (with the possible exception of '93) are also looking very good in California. The 1985s are drinking well, but the '86s could do with a few more years in the cellar, although both have that wonderful upfront fruit quality that keeps

you reaching for another glass. The 1984s and 1987s are pure delight to drink now, with subtle flavours and soft centres, and shouldn't be kept much longer. Washington Cabernet takes on a much more intense fruit quality. For serious cellaring, good names are: *Beringer Reserve, Buena Vista, Burgess, Cain, Carmenet Reserve, Caymus Special Selection, Clos du Bois, Clos du Val, Conn Creek, Cuvaison, Diamond Creek, Dunn, Franciscan, Grgich Hills, Groth, Heitz Bella Oaks, William Hill, Inglenook Reserve Cask, Kenwood Artist Series, La Jota, Laurel Glen, Louis M Martini, Robert Mondavi Reserve* and *Opus One, Chateau*

Montelena, Newton, Raymond Reserve, Ridge Monte Bello, Sequoia Grove, Shafer Hillside Select, Spotteswoode, Stag's Leap Cask 23, Sterling Vineyards Diamond Mountain Ranch (California); *Ste Chapelle* (Idaho); *Fall Creek Vineyards, Llano Estacado, Messina Hof, Oberhellmann, Pheasant Ridge* (Texas); *Arbor Crest, Hogue Cellars, Chateau Ste Michelle, Staton Hills* (Washington). For a lighter Cabernet, the list is practically endless: *Beringer* (Napa Valley), *Caymus Liberty School, Chateau Souverain, Clos du Bois, Cosentino, Fetzer, Estancia, Foppiano, Kendall-Jackson, Wente* (California); *Columbia Crest* (Washington).

MERLOT In recent years Merlot has stepped out on its own. Once thought of here as mainly for blending with Cabernet Sauvignon, it has caught the fancy both of winemakers and the public. At its best, it shows lovely soft fruit with a perfumy, brambly edge that can be quite intriguing. Best are *Arrowood, Bellerose, Cuvaison, Duckhorn, Gundlach-Bundschu, Murphy-Goode, Newton, St Francis, Pine Ridge, Silverado, Sinskey, St Clement, Sterling, Vichon,* (California); *Bedell Cellars, Bridge-hampton, Peconic Bay* (New York); *Ch Ste Michelle, Columbia, Columbia Crest, Hogue Cellars, Leonetti, Paul Thomas* (Washington).

PETITE SIRAH Not the same as the great red Syrah grape of the Rhône or the Shiraz of Australia. It produces big, stark, dry, almost tarry wines – impressive, but usually lacking real style. *Ridge* is the exception, and in good years capable of making real Rhône Syrah blush. Also look for *Stag's Leap* and *Foppiano.*

PINOT NOIR It may be time to stop asking if California/Oregon can make great Pinot Noir, and start asking how many can be made. Oregon, after several bad years, seems to be getting back on track, while in California good to very good Pinot Noir is turning up all over the place: the Carneros region in Napa/Sonoma, the lower Russian

River Valley in Sonoma, north-eastern Monterey County and parts of Santa Barbara County. And there's Long Island, where an occasional flash of excellent Pinot can be seen. Try *Au Bon Climat, Acacia, Bonny Doon, Bouchaine, Byron, Calera, Carneros Creek, Chalone, Dehlinger, De Loach, Gary Farrel, Iron Horse, Lazy Creek, Mondavi, Saintsbury, Sinskey, Whitcraft, Wild Horse, Zaca Mesa* (California); *Bridge-hampton* (New York); *Adelsheim, Amity, Drouhin, Eyrie, Knudsen-Erath, Rex Hill, Scott Henry, Sokol-Blosser* (Oregon).

SYRAH/RHÔNE VARIETALS There has been an explosion of interest in the vines of the Rhône in California; they seem in many ways more suited to the climate than the Bordeaux or Burgundian grapes. Most eyes are on Syrah, but there is also Mourvèdre, Cinsaut, Grenache and Carignan, the last two of which used to be used in Central Valley jug wines. First results look good from *Bonny Doon, Duxoup, Kendall-Jackson, La Jota, McDowell Valley, Joseph Phelps Mistral* series, *Qupé, Santino* (California).

ZINFANDEL Its friends keep predicting a surge of interest in red Zinfandel because of the success of the light, sweet white or blush Zins, but so far it hasn't happened. Still, the wine can be good, either in the hearty, almost overpowering style or the lighter 'claret' style. Best of the big Zins are *Cline Cellars, Deer Park, Kendall-Jackson Ciapusci Vineyard, Preston Vineyards, La Jota, A Rafanelli, Ravenswood, Rosenblum, Shenandoah, Joseph Swan*. For a more elegant approach, try *Buehler, Buena Vista, Burgess, Clos du Val, Fetzer, Haywood, Kendall-Jackson Mariah Vineyard, Kenwood, Louis M Martini, Nalle, Quivira, Ridge*. Best for blush are *Amador Foothill, Beringer, Buehler, Ivan Tamas.*

The price guides for this section begin on page 400.

WHITE GRAPES & FLAVOURS

CHARDONNAY Winemakers are learning how to blend different areas for more balanced, rounded wines: offsetting the austerity of Napa Carneros, for example, with the tropical intensity of Sonoma County Russian River (*Louis M Martini*).

American Chardonnay will age, but look for the controlled, balanced fruit of *Acacia, Arrowood, Beringer, Buena Vista, Chalone, Chateau St Jean, Cuvaison, Dehlinger, Flora Springs, Franciscan, Kistler, Mondavi Reserve, Newton, Raymond Reserve, Simi* and *Sonoma-Cutrer* (California); *Bridgehampton* (NY); *Prince Michel* (Virginia). For more instant fun, try *Callaway, Clos du Bois, Estancia, Matanzas Creek, Kendall Jackson, Morgan, Mirassou, Phelps, Monterey, Parducci, Signorello, Wente Bros* (California); *Fall Creek* (Texas); *Chateau Ste Michelle, Columbia Crest, Hogue Cellars* (Washington).

GEWÜRZTRAMINER Looking up, but California still falls far short of Alsace. The problem is that the grape ripens too fast, too soon. A few people are beginning to get it right, making wines with that spiciness that keeps you reaching for another glass. Look for *Adler Fels* (sometimes), *Lazy Creek, Handley Cellars, Rutherford Hill, Obester* (California); *Llano Estacado* (Texas); *Columbia, Chateau Ste Michelle* (Washington).

RIESLING Like Gewürz, most Riesling in California has been planted in the wrong (warm) place. Riesling (in the US called Johannisberg or White) makes a dull wine then; it is the cooler areas of California, Oregon, New York and Washington that are beginning to show what it can do. Best are *Alexander Valley Vineyards, Konocti, Navarro* (California); *Lamoureux Landing, Wagner Vineyards* (NY); *Amity* (Oregon); *Chateau Morrisette, Prince Michel* (Virginia); *Hogue Cellars, Columbia Cellars, Chateau Ste Michelle, Kiona* (Washington).

SAUVIGNON BLANC/FUMÉ BLANC

Now being tamed; its tendency to extreme herbal/grassy tastes is now often moulded into complex spicy/appley fruit. If you are a fan of the big, grassy wines, those that smell like a field of new-mown hay, you'll like *Dry Creek Vineyards Reserve*, which carries that about as far as it can go. For more restraint look for *Ch St Jean, Ferrari-Carano, Hanna, Robert Mondavi, Murphy-Goode, Simi, Sterling, William Wheeler* (California); *Hargrave* (New York State); *Arbor Crest, Columbia* (Washington).

SÉMILLON Added to Sauvignon Blanc for complexity (*Clos du Val, Carmenet, Vichon*, California). For stand-alone Sémillon try *Alderbrook,R H Phillips, Ahlgren, Congress Springs* (California); *Chateau Ste Michelle* (Washington).

MATURITY CHART
1992 Carneros Chardonnay
The best Carneros Chardonnays have the elegance and balance to age well

Bottled	Ready	Peak	Tiring	In decline

| 0 | 1 | 2 | 3 | 4 | 5 | 6 | 7 | 8 | 9 | 10 years |

Wines of the Californias

T H E S T A T E O F T H E A R T

WINE REGIONS

CARNEROS (California) At the southern end of the Napa and Sonoma Valleys, snuggled against San Francisco Bay. Breezes from the Bay hold the temperature down and create an ideal climate for Pinot Noir and Chardonnay. Many of California's best Pinot Noirs come from here.

CENTRAL VALLEY (California) Once a vast inland sea, the Central Valley runs from the San Joaquin/Sacramento River Delta in the north to the unappealing flatlands of Bakersfield in the south, from the foothills of the Sierra range in the east to the coastal ranges in the west. It can be 110°F during the day, and hardly cooler at night. It's a brutal life, but with modern techniques there are some decent quaffs.

LAKE COUNTY (California) Grapes were grown in Lake County (north of Napa County and east of Mendocino County) in the last century; recently there has been a revival of interest with major plantings by *Louis M Martini, Konocti* and *Guenoc*. It's good Cabernet Sauvignon and Sauvignon Blanc territory, with warm days and cool nights, and a very long growing season.

LIVERMORE VALLEY (California) One of California's oldest vine-growing regions, this largely suburban valley has been enjoying a bit of a comeback. It was the first in California to put a varietal label on Sauvignon Blanc and the century-plus old *Wente Bros* winery in Livermore is increasingly good for that. The region is also proving good for Cabernet. Several small wineries have recently sprung up or been revived; early bottlings are promising.

MENDOCINO COUNTY (California) A rugged, coastal county with one major inland valley, and several cool east-west valleys running from the interior to the rocky coastline. This range of pocket climates makes it possible to grow a range of grapes, with Cabernet Sauvignon at its best in Round Valley in the interior but excellent Riesling, Gewürztraminer, Pinot Noir and Chardonnay doing well in the cool Anderson Valley, where Pacific fog and winds follow the Anderson River inland. This valley is also becoming a leading fizz district, with *Roederer US* making some outstanding bubbly and the tiny *Handley Cellars Brut* one of the best in California.

MISSOURI At the turn of the century this midwestern state was the third largest wine producer in the US. It's making a comeback, growing both standard vinifera grapes and a range of French hybrids like Vidal (which when handled right has the complexity of a Merlot) as well as native American grapes like Cynthiana/Norton. *Stone Hill Winery's* Norton red wine, made from a vineyard first planted in the mid nineteenth century, has been compared favourably to a Rhône wine. There are some very pleasing Rieslings made in the state (*Mount Pleasant Vineyard*) as well.

MONTEREY COUNTY (California) This came late to wine: only in the early '70s did pioneering plantings by *Mirassou* and *Wente Bros* begin to bear fruit. Early Cabernets had a distinct taste of green peppers and other less appealing vegetal smells. Now growers have found more suitable grapes, like Riesling, Chenin Blanc and Pinot Noir. Even Cabernet has made a comeback, on hillsides in the cool Carmel Valley.

NAPA COUNTY (California) There are several important sub-regions within Napa: Calistoga, Carneros, Chiles Valley, Howell Mountain, Mount Veeder, Oakville, Pope Valley, Rutherford, Spring Mountain and Stag's Leap. Some of these are formally designated viticultural regions. This is California's classic wine country. Napa's strong suit is red – Cabernet Sauvignon and Merlot – with Pinot Noir in Carneros.

NEW MEXICO Northern New Mexico grows mostly hybrid grape varieties but some interesting wines are coming from irrigated vineyards in the South. Good producers are *Anderson Valley*, especially for Chardonnay, and a fizz from *Devalmont Vineyards* under the Gruet label.

NEW YORK STATE The big news in New York continues to be Long Island, with outstanding Chardonnay and Pinot Noir. The Chardonnay is very different from those of California, with more austere flavours, a bit like ripe Chablis. There's also decent Chardonnay and outstanding Riesling from the Finger Lakes and the Hudson River Valley. The Lake Erie-Niagara region is lagging behind the other three, with more native grapes. Try the wines of *Bedell Cellars, Bridgehampton, Brotherhood, Hargrave, Lenz, Pindar* and *Wagner*.

OREGON Oregon has suffered from too much attention. Hyped by press notices of the 1983 vintage for Pinot Noir, perhaps too much was expected of Oregon, too soon. Now that the dust has settled a bit and Oregon winegrowers have begun to sort out the *terroir*, the early promise for Pinot Noir is showing signs of paying off. A new generation of winemakers, with the technical skills and cash capital that were sometimes lacking in the the Oregon pioneers, are showing what can be done on a consistent basis with Oregon Pinot Noir. Oregon's secondbest grape is Pinot Gris, which can often be charming. Riesling can also be quite good, although it is a little short on that floral intensity one expects in a great Riesling. For Pinot Gris, try *Adelsheim, Eyrie or Knudsen. Amity* and *Oak Knoll* have the best Riesling.

SAN LUIS OBISPO COUNTY (California) A Central Coast growing area with the best wines coming from cool regions in canyons opening in from the coast. There are sites here for Pinot Noir, Chardonnay and a few surprising old Zinfandel vineyards. Edna Valley is the chief sub-region with a deserved reputation for Chardonnay.

SANTA BARBARA COUNTY (California) This growing region just to the north of Los Angeles is divided into two major sub-regions, the Santa Maria and Santa Ynez valleys. Both are coastal valleys with openings to the Pacific which means that both day and night are fairly cool. There are some outstanding Pinot Noirs from both regions with some good Sauvignon Blanc and Merlot from the Santa Ynez Valley.

SANTA CRUZ MOUNTAINS (California) Just south of San Francisco, this has lured several people who believe it to be Pinot Noir heaven. Despite some occasional successes, the track record is spotty, but progress is being made. *Bonny Doon, David Bruce, Congress Springs* and *Santa Cruz Mountain Winery* have all made Pinot with various degrees of success. Surprisingly, for a cool climate region, some very good Cabernet has been made – notably from *Mount Eden* – but its Chardonnay is even better.

SIERRA FOOTHILLS (California) California's gold country was one of the busiest wine zones in the state in the last century but only a few Zinfandel vineyards survived Prohibition. These are the basis of the area's reputation today, plus good Sauvignon Blanc and Barbera. Sub-regions include Amador County, El Dorado County and Calaveras County. Best are *Amador Foothill Winery, Boeger Winery, Monteviña, Santino* and *Shenandoah Vineyards*.

SONOMA COUNTY (California) On the West Coast, people are beginning to realize that Sonoma's Chardonnay, long in the shade of Napa, need take a back seat to no-one. Sonoma Valley is the main sub-region, but there are many others, in particular Alexander Valley, Chalk Hill, Dry Creek,

Knight's Valley, and the Russian River Valley itself (including its sub-region Green Valley). In general, Cabernet and Chardonnay yield the best wines, usually a little fruitier and softer than in Napa.

TEXAS Texas wines continue to amaze. Major regions are the Austin Hills and the Staked Plains region of west Texas, centred around Lubbock. Cabernets from Texas have a drink-me-now rich fruitiness and the Chardonnays and Sauvignon Blancs are looking better every year. In short, it's goodbye Chateau Redneck. Best currently are *Fall Creek, Llano Estacado, Messina Hof, Oberhellmann* and *Pheasant Ridge*.

VIRGINIA Growing good wine grapes in Virginia's hot, humid climate is certainly a man-over-nature drama. Besides the heat and the humidity, there is also the occasional hurricane. Nevertheless, there are some good Rieslings and Chardonnays coming from the state. Top producers are *Chateau Morrisette, Ingleside Plantation* and *Prince Michel.*

WASHINGTON STATE There are those who believe that in the long run, the finest wines from North America may come from Washington State. There is an incredible intensity of fruit right across the board in all varietals that is simply astonishing. When the first serious wines started appearing only about 15 years ago, the best were Riesling and Chardonnay; but most recently, the Cabernets and Merlots can be outstanding, as can the Sauvignon Blanc and Sémillon, varieties which are taken very seriously in Washington. Good wineries include the following names: *Arbor Crest, Chateau Ste Michelle, Columbia Cellars, Columbia Crest, Hogue Cellars, Staton Hills.*

WINERY PROFILES

ACACIA ★★★(★) (Carneros/Napa) Acacia continues to produce attractive Pinot Noir and delightfully understated Chardonnay.

ADLER FELS ★★(★) (Sonoma) A quirky winery, taking chances that sometimes miss. Outstanding Gewürztraminer and an unusual Riesling sparkler that is a treat.

ARROWOOD ★★★★ (Sonoma) Cabernet is best at Richard Arrowood's winery.

AU BON CLIMAT ★★★★ (Santa Barbara) Fine Pinot Noir. The best is soft and approachable, with intense black cherry fruit. Chardonnay can also be impressive.

BEAULIEU VINEYARDS ★★★ (Napa) The top-of-the-line George de Latour Private Reserve Cabernet Sauvignon is still marvellous and capable of extended aging. The big surprise here is a lean, supple Carneros district Chardonnay.

There is also an inexpensive Beautour Cabernet, which is good value.

BERINGER ★★★★(★) (Napa) This always outstanding performer gets better and better. A fantastic 1986 Cabernet Reserve and 1988 Chardonnay Reserve, but also the low-priced, very drinkable Napa Ridge.

BETHEL HEIGHTS ★★★(★) (Oregon) Impressive, intense Pinot Noirs. The Reserves can be among Oregon's finest.

BONNY DOON ★★★★ (Santa Cruz) Randall Grahm makes some of the most delicious wines in California from his mountain-top winery a few miles from the Pacific. His work with Grenache (Cigare Volant) and Mourvèdre (Old Telegram) have opened new vistas for California winemakers. A new line of Italian-style wines under the Ca' Del Solo label is winning him more friends.

BRIDGEHAMPTON ★★★(★) (New York)
A first-class Chardonnay from Long Island vineyards as well as a fresh, light quaffable Pinot Noir and a fruity, forward Merlot.

BUENA VISTA ★★★(★) (Sonoma/Carneros)
Buena Vista has made a big comeback in recent years, with balanced, understated Merlot, Pinot Noir and Cabernet. A new line of Reserve wines adds intensity and depth. One of California's better Sauvignon Blancs is made from Lake County grapes.

CAKEBREAD CELLARS ★★★ (Napa)
Always sound, sometimes outstanding: one of the best Sauvignon Blancs.

CALERA ★★★★(★) (San Benito) Possibly the best Pinot Noir in California. Rich, intense wine. The Jensen Vineyard is the best. Also fine Viognier and Chardonnay.

CAYMUS ★★★★ (Napa) Benchmark California Cab which shows no sign of faltering. Also a good Zinfandel and good value wines under the Liberty School label.

CHALONE ★★★★(★) (Monterey) A reputation for individualistic Pinot Noir and big, buttery Chardonnay. Also some nice Pinot Blanc and Chenin Blanc.

DOMAINE CHANDON ★★★ (Napa) A producer of consistently good fizz, with the best being Chandon Reserve in magnum. Over-production in the mid-1980s may have hurt, but it seems back on track. Watch out for a new rosé sparkler.

CHATEAU POTELLE ★★★(★) (Napa) Run by two transplanted French wine buffs. Promising Sauvignon Blanc and Cabernet and an outstanding Zinfandel.

CHATEAU ST JEAN ★★★(★) (Sonoma) A Chardonnay specialist (look for Belle Terre and Robert Young vineyards), with interesting Gewürztraminer, Riesling, Sauvignon Blanc and Cabernet.

CHATEAU STE MICHELLE ★★★(★) (Washington) Consistently good to outstanding white and red with Cabernet Sauvignon and Merlot being the real strengths; a pretty good bubbly as well. Columbia Crest, which began as a good-value label, is now a stand-alone winery with terrific Cabernet Sauvignon.

CLOS DU BOIS ★★★(★) (Sonoma) Now owned by Hiram Walker-Allied Vintners, Clos du Bois makes consistently good Merlots, Chardonnays and claret-style Marlstone.

CLOS DU VAL ★★★(★) (Napa) Bordeaux-trained owner and winemaker Bernard Portet makes elegant, well-balanced reds, with an emphasis on austere fruit. Best wines from this underrated winery are Cabernet Sauvignon and Zinfandel.

COLUMBIA ★★★ (Washington) David Lake's pioneering winery, founded in 1962 by a group of university professors, makes a basketful of varietals including Sémillon, Gewürztraminer, Chardonnay and Riesling (especially Wyckoff vineyard); plus Syrah, soft, peppery Pinot Noir, seductive Merlot (Red Willow vineyard), and surprisingly ripe Cabernet Sauvignon (Otis vineyard).

CUVAISON ★★★ (Napa) Winemaker John Thacher turns out delicious but unpredictable Merlot, Pinot Noir and Cabernet, at best elegant and understated with unexpected layers of complexity.

DEHLINGER ★★★★ (Sonoma) Makes one of the best Pinots in North America from cool vineyards along the Russian River Valley County, just a few miles from the Pacific. Also good Cabernets including a good value Young Vine Cabernet.

DOMAINE MUMM ★★★★ (Napa) Winemaker Greg Fowler, who helped establish Schramsberg as the top gun in

American fizz, is now at Domaine Mumm and well on form. Early releases have been simply outstanding, especially the Brut and an impressive Blanc de Noirs.

DROUHIN ★★★★ (Oregon) With the 1991 Pinot Noir, this Oregon winery owned by the Burgundy wine firm, earned a fourth star, and has kept it with subsequent vintages. Only the winery's estate grapes are used. This is the Pinot Noir we have all been waiting for Oregon to make.

DRY CREEK VINEYARDS ★★★ (Sonoma) Big, herbal Fumé Blanc loaded with fruit. The reserve bottling ages nicely.

DUCKHORN ★★★ (Napa) Intensely flavoured, deep, rich Merlot and weighty Cabernet.

ELK COVE VINEYARDS ★★★(★) (Oregon) Perhaps the best Pinot Noir in Oregon, with the '90 Estate top of the list.

EYRIE ★★★ (Oregon) David Lett is Oregon's Pinot pioneer. He has spawned a whole industry, and his wines can still be some of the best: generally supple, light but flavoursome. Pinot Gris, though, forms the bulk of production.

FALL CREEK VINEYARDS ★★★ (Texas) These wines can hold their heads up anywhere: a delicious Proprietor's Red (Cabernet, Ruby Cabernet, Merlot and Carnelian), a charming Sémillon and a first-rate Cabernet Sauvignon.

FETZER ★★★(★) (Mendocino) Great value from this large Mendocino producer. Look for Cabernet from Lake County and several different Zinfandels (especially the Ricetti Vineyard). Sundial Chardonnay is tasty. A new line of wine made from organically-grown grapes is quite good.

FLORA SPRINGS ★★★(★) (Napa) Excellent Chardonnay and a fair blend of both Cabernets and Merlot called Trilogy. Soliloquy is a creamy, rich, floral white that belies its Sauvignon Blanc base.

FOPPIANO ★★★ (Sonoma) This historic family winery has been a bit up and down in recent years but a Reserve Zinfandel introduced in 1987 and a Reserve Petite Sirah are usually outstanding. A line of Cabernet Sauvignon under the Fox Mountain label is quite tasty with good aging potential. Riverside Farms is the downmarket value label.

FRANCISCAN ★★★★(★) (Napa) Winemaker Greg Upton with the support of co-owner Agustin Huneeus has taken this once down-at-heel property and brought it to the top. He does a terrific Chardonnay, Cuvée Sauvage, made using wild yeast, and his Cabernets are stunning. Estancia is a bargain second label.

HANDLEY CELLARS ★★★★ (Mendocino) Very good Chardonnay from family-owned vineyards in Sonoma's Dry Creek Valley and a terrific Brut sparkler that some say is one of the best in the West.

HEITZ ★★★ (Napa) The Martha's Vineyard Cabernet Sauvignon has a devoted following and fetches high prices, but it seems a bit of a dinosaur compared with the elegant, sleek Cabernets of today.

IRON HORSE ★★★★ (Sonoma) Terrific racy, incisive fizz, and now engaged in a joint venture with Laurent-Perrier of Champagne. Very good Pinot Noir and Chardonnay. Its second label, Tin Pony, is good value.

JORDAN ★★★★(★) (Sonoma) A rich, ripe Cabernet Sauvignon that ages well and a plausible 'wannabe Meursault' Chardonnay from this French lookalike winery in northern Sonoma. An outstanding sparkling wine called J was released in the spring of 1991.

KENDALL-JACKSON ★★★ (Lake) Owns what is probably the biggest Chardonnay vineyard in the world (1200 acres) in Santa Barbara. Smooth, rich, sometimes spicy Chardonnay is invariably seamless with a spoonful of sugar; Proprietor's Grand Reserve is intense and buttery. Juicy Sauvignon Blanc and rather dense Pinot Noir.

KENWOOD ★★★(★) (Sonoma) A consistent producer of well-above-average quality. The Jack London and Artist series Cabernets are outstanding, as is the Zinfandel and Sauvignon Blanc.

LAUREL GLEN ★★★★ (Sonoma) Winemaker Patrick Campbell makes only Cabernet Sauvignon at his Sonoma Mountain winery and it is very, very good Cabernet. With intense black cherry fruit, it's a treat for short-term drinking but there is every reason to believe it will age very well. He releases three wines, a regular bottling, 'Counterpoint', which is wine not quite good enough for the A-list cut and a wine called Terra Rosa which he blends from bulk wine purchases.

LOUIS MARTINI ★★★★ (Napa) A delightful range, from simple varietals to single vineyards. Sensationally drinkable Gamay Beaujolais; lively, fruity Barbera; very good Merlot; some glorious Cabernet Sauvignons (1985 Monte Rosso) that age well; excellent Petite Sirah; complex Pinot Noir and a rich, ripe Gewürz.

MAYACAMAS ★★★ (Napa) A reputation in the past for big, hard Cabernets that would take decades to come around. There are signs that the reputation is justified, but a lot of people are still waiting.

ROBERT MONDAVI ★★★★(★) (Napa) Mondavi's major strength is in reds: both the straight and Reserve Cabernets are among the best in the world, though Opus One reds seem to lack the Reserve's

intensity. Recent bottlings of Pinot Noir from Carneros are terrific.

NEWTON ★★★★ (Napa) Excellent, reasonably priced Chardonnay; cedary, cinnamon-spiced Cabernet and increasingly succulent Merlot.

PHEASANT RIDGE ★★(★) (Texas) Quite good Chardonnay and Sémillon; promising Cabernet Sauvignon in recent vintages.

PHELPS ★★★(★) (Napa) Best here is the Insignia Vineyard Cabernet Sauvignon but exciting things are happening with Rhône grapes, particularly Syrah, released under the Mistral label. Also a nice light touch with that most civilized of wines, Riesling.

RIDGE ★★★★(★) (Santa Clara) Benchmark Zinfandel. The Monte Bello Cabernets are also remarkable, with great balance and long-lasting, perfumed fruit. Petite Sirah from York Creek is brilliant, under-valued and under-appreciated.

ROEDERER ESTATE ★★★★ (Mendocino County) Located in the cool Anderson Valley, Roederer's first two releases of bubbly had wine lovers doing hand-springs. The style is unlike that of most California sparkling wine, austere with understated fruit. The brut and the rosé are terrific.

SAINTSBURY ★★★★ (Napa) A young Carneros winery with a growing reputation for Pinot Noir and Chardonnay. Garnet, from young Pinot Noir vines, is delicious.

SANFORD WINERY ★★★(★) (Santa Barbara) At its best, Sanford Pinot Noir can be a real treat, with spicy, lush, intense fruit. Good Sauvignon and Chardonnay.

SCHRAMSBERG ★★★★ (Napa) The best fizz in California can still come from here, but the challengers are rapidly gaining ground. The vintage sparklers age beautifully into lush, rich wines.

SHAFER ★★★★ (Napa) There's very good, very long-lived Cabernet Sauvignon and Merlot here, grown up on hillside vineyards.

SIMI ★★★(★) (Sonoma) Rich, sometimes voluptuous, always reliable Chardonnay. The concentrated Cabernet Sauvignons can be drunk young, but really need time. Reserves are excellent, as is Sauvignon Blanc.

SONOMA-CUTRER ★★★★ (Sonoma) Chardonnay from three different Russian River vineyards. The Les Pierres is a restrained classic made to age. Russian River Ranches is more forward and fruity while the Cutrer is rich, full and more in the California tradition.

STAG'S LEAP WINE CELLARS ★★★(★) (Napa) Look for fine, elegant Chardonnay with lean, appley fruit. The Cabernet Sauvignons with which this winery made

its reputation seemed to be missing a beat for a few years, but the straight 1987 bottling indicated a welcome turn for the better.

ROD STRONG VINEYARDS ★★★(★) (Sonoma) At this much underrated winery on the Russian River, Rod Strong makes some very fine Cabernet Sauvignon, Pinot Noir and Zinfandel from river-terrace vineyards.

TREFETHEN ★★(★) (Napa) Consistently good middle-of-the road Cabernet and Chardonnay. Best is a dry Riesling, one of the state's finest. Best value are the Eshcol reds and whites.

ZD WINES ★★★ (Napa) A source of Cabernet Sauvignon, Pinot Noir and Chardonnay, all of which have good intensity and depth. The Pinot Noir, especially, seems to get better with each vintage.

AUSTRALIA

It has been quite a year in Australia, but on the whole the wine industry has come out of it pretty well. Quite large parts of New South Wales were burnt to ashes, but with the exception of some vines in the Lower Hunter Valley the vineyards escaped unscathed. Then there were fears that the winemakers might be taxed to death by an increase in the domestic Wine Sales Tax, but that was all sorted out as well, in the end. But the biggest adventure of all is just beginning: Australia is developing its own *appellation* scheme.

British wine drinkers, who buy Australian wine by brand name anyway, might be tempted to say, 'So what?' But it is important, not least as a sign that Australian wine has finally grown up and left home. Part of the deal is that it will cease to call its sparkling wines Champagne, and its dry whites Chablis – and doing so always was the equivalent of taking your washing home to your mother.

It has all taken rather a long while to happen. Back in 1918 there was a call by W Percy Wilkinson, in a paper for the Royal Geographical Society of Australasia, for Australia to stop borrowing European wine names; but he suggested, as substitutes, Chabalia instead of Chablis, Portalia instead of port, Burgalia instead of Burgundy and Claralia instead of claret. Not surprisingly, the idea didn't catch on. It was not until 1988 that talks on the subject between Australia and the EC finally began, and Australia still wasn't all that keen.

Naming names

But exports proved the great spur. Australia wanted to export more and more wine, and it wanted to export it to the EC. The EC wanted Australia to play ball over nomenclature. The EC wasn't so bothered about exports to Australia (except for Champagne, which was very bothered indeed since it sells a lot there), but it was concerned about its exports to the US, and it suspected that on the subject of wine names the US and Australia were likely to make common cause.

So in the end there was flexibility on both sides. The EU will provide easier access for Australian wines (which even without it managed to increase their sales in Britain by 45.5 per cent last year) and it will allow the mention of up to five grape names on an Australian wine label (at the same time France is moving in the opposite direction, and removing varietal names from most AC wine labels). An Australian varietal wine need contain only 85 per cent of the grape named and Australian wines can name up to three regions on a label. EU wines can, needless to say, only name one.

But you'll be pleased to hear that the days of Australian Sancerre, St-Émilion and white Bordeaux are now over (no, I've never seen any either, but I've obviously been looking in the wrong places). Australian Malaga, Madeira, Hock and Chianti will also go by the end of 1997.

But what, I hear you ask, about Australian Chablis, port, sherry and Sauternes, all of which I and many others have seen on domestic labels? What indeed about Australian Champagne? Are the lawyers of (French) Champagne not the world's most hyperactive? Do they not turn snarling on the producers of expensive scent and of sparkling elderflower drink? Well, yes they do. But they will have to froth impotently at the mouth for a bit longer as far as Australia is concerned, because Australian Champagne (and port, Sauternes et al) will be perfectly legal for a while yet. In fact, for quite a while yet. In fact, until a date which has yet to be agreed.

It will be agreed, of course, because politicians have said so, and politicians are honourable men, are they not? Besides, if it shows no sign of happening the French will presumably go ape. And in the meantime attention will turn to the developing system of *appellations,* or Geographical Indications.

This, by any stretch of the imagination, is not an easy task. Once glance at the mistakes made in Europe shows how difficult it is to reconcile the need to make prestigious names exclusive and thus preserve their quality, with the desire of as many as possible of the local producers to share that prestige. There will be arguments over every single region, but Coonawarra will serve as an example.

Coonawarra has always claimed that it is special because of its *terra rossa* soil. The red soil in question extends in a narrow strip, surrounded by black and grey soil; and precisely where the line should be drawn depends, of course, on where your vineyards are. Australian wine companies are all buying vineyards like mad at the moment so as to be self-sufficient in grapes and thus immune to price changes: BRL-Hardy has bought 160 ha of Coonawarra; Katnook is busy planting bare Coonawarra land (over 300 ha by the end of 1996) and Penfolds already owns half of Coonawarra. The red soil extends over a very small area; Coonawarra (Greater Coonawarra, we should perhaps call it) already has much more than that planted with vines. Perhaps the *terra rossa* will prove to be not so important after all.   MARGARET RAND

WHITE GRAPES & FLAVOURS

CHARDONNAY The difficult feat is balancing the understandable desire of the winemakers to produce more sophisticated, subtle wines that need time in bottle to develop complexity, with the exuberant upfront ripe fruit and sweet oak style that is the British consumer's best friend. Winemakers and wine critics banging the lean and lissom cool climate drum should remember that Le Montrachet was never accused of subtlety while gaining its repuation as the world's greatest white wine, and they should also take note of how often it is warm climate Aussie Chardies that win the top medals at wine shows. Ripeness of fruit and oak spice are crucial to Aussie Chardie, so let's hope they don't throw the baby out with the billabong water. Best: *Petaluma* (Adelaide Hills); *Greenock Creek, Peter Lehmann* (Barossa); *Giaconda* (Beechworth); *Grosset* (Clare); *Katnook* (Coonawarra); *Hill Smith Estate, Mountadam, Seppelt Partalunga* (Eden Valley); *Bannockburn* (Geelong); *Frankland Estate, Howard Park, Plantagenet, Wignall's* (Great Southern); *Allanmere, Rosemount* (Hunter); *Tim Knappstein, Stafford Ridge* (Lenswood); *Wirra Wirra* (McLaren Vale); *Cape Mentelle, Cullen, Evans & Tate, Leeuwin Estate* (Margaret River); *Dromana Estate* (Mornington); *Eileen Hardy, Lindeman's* (Padthaway); *Piper's Brook* (Tasmania); *Coldstream Hills* (Yarra Valley); *Koonunga Hill* (various).

CHENIN BLANC This ripens to a much fuller, fruitier and blander style than its steelier Loire counterpart. *Moondah Brook* (Swan Valley) does a good example.

GEWÜRZTRAMINER GT should never be confused with Sydney's predilection for the oily, sweet and dim 'Traminer Riesling', often made of Muscat and Sémillon. Fine, faintly spicy cool-climate Gewürztraminers smelling of lychee-and-honeydew melon are made by *Brown Brothers, Delatite* and *Lilydale* (Victoria), and *Tim Knappstein* (Clare). *Orlando Wyndham's Flaxman's* (Eden Valley) is always good, as is *Tolley's* (Barossa).

MARSANNE In Central Victoria, both *Chateau Tahbilk* and *Mitchelton* have made big, broad, ripe Marsanne.

MUSCAT There are two types of Muscat in Oz: first, the bag-in-box *Fruity Gordo* or Muscat of Alexandria – fruity, sweetish, swigging wine, from a heavy-cropping lowish-quality grape grown in irrigated vineyards along the Murray River; second, Liqueur Muscat, made from the Brown Muscat, a strain of the top quality Muscat à Petits Grains, grown in Victoria. It is a sensation: dark, treacly even, with a perfume of strawberry and honeyed raisins. Best producers include *All Saints, Bailey's, Bullers, Campbells, Yalumba, Chambers, Morris* and *Stanton & Killeen*.

RIESLING This is Australia's most-planted premium white grape. It has long produced excellent flinty, lime-and-soft-lemon wines from the cooler regions like Clare and Eden Valleys, and now from Great Southern. The best of these wines will grow for 20 years in bottle without developing too much of the old kerosene aroma that many Australians learned to love. The hotter regions make full, off-dry wines akin to ripe, unwooded Sémillon. Some makers do fine botrytis-affected sweet Rieslings which are best had in bed, at either end of the day. Best: *Rockford* (Barossa); *Tim Adams, Jim Barry, Grosset, Tim Knappstein, Mitchell, Petaluma, Pike's* (Clare); *Heggie's, Hill Smith Estate, Lindeman's Leo Buring, Orlando St Helga, Seppelt Partalunga* (Eden Valley); *Frankland Estate, Howard Park* (Great Southern); *Henschke* (Lenswood or Eden Valley); *Piper's Brook* (Tasmania); *Delatite* (Victoria). Best botrytis-afffected wines: *Petaluma, Mt. Horrocks* and *St. Hubert's*.

SAUVIGNON BLANC There was an awful moment a year or so back when it seemed that Sauvignon would become as ubiquitous as Chardonnay. But it is fussier about where it lives. Picked early, in cool regions, it gives bright, zippy, gooseberry, grassy wines smelling of tomato leaves. Let it ripen more, or grow it somewhere hot, and the flavours will soar through delicately floral to jammy to overcooked to dead dull. Best: *Jim Barry, Pike's* (Clare); *Katnook* (Connawarra); *Hill Smith* (Eden Valley); *Bannockburn* (Geelong); *Frankland Estate, Wignall's* (Great Southern); *Stafford Ridge* (Lenswood); *Mount Hurtle, Wirra Wirra* (McLaren Vale); *Hardy's, Lindeman's* (Padthaway); *Bridgewater Mill* (various).

SÉMILLON Sémillon was among the first grapes grown in Australia, and it thrived in the Hunter Valley, where it was called Shepherd's Riesling for one century and Hunter Riesling for the next. In the Hunter it makes firm, almost watery young wines which grow into majestic butter-toast-and-marmalade beauties with ten or 20 years in bottle. It has also long been widespread in the Clare Valley. Clare Semi, as it is known to its friends, is fuller and more buttery in its youth. In Lenswood it has the force and body of Loire Sauvignon, and from Margaret River and Great Southern it is crisp and limy but buttery. It also makes fabulously rich, honeyed botrytized dessert wines, usually with some oak. In the Barossa they drink these at breakfast, with smoky bacon and eggs. Best: *Peter Lehmann, Rockford* (Barossa); *Grosset, Mitchell's, Mount Horrocks* (Clare); *Hill Smith Estate* (Eden Valley); *Brokenwood, Lindeman's, McWilliams, Petersen, Rothbury* (Hunter); *Knappstein* (Lenswood); *Evans & Tate, Moss Wood* (Margaret River); *Brown Bros* Best blends with Sauvignon: *St Hallett* (Barossa); *Brokenwood (Hunter); Cape Mentelle, Pierro* (Margaret River); *Wirra Wirra* (McLaren Vale). *Geoff Merrill* blends with Chardonnay. Best stickies: *Peter Lehmann, Tim Adams, de Bortoli.*

RED GRAPES & FLAVOURS

CABERNET SAUVIGNON This can be rich and chocolaty in the Barossa, austere and minty in Victoria's Pyrenees, full of moss, tobacco and cedar flavours in the Eden Valley, and dense, phenolic and black in the Hunter. Sometimes it can be all of these, sometimes it's nothing more than simple blackcurrant jelly. Makers give it their best, which often means too much wood. But when it's good, it's breathtaking. Best: *Greenock Creek, Peter Lehmann, Rockford, Seppelt's Dorrien* (Barossa); *Grosset, Tim Knappstein, Wendouree* (Clare); *Bowen Estate, Hollick Ravenswood, Katnook, Lindeman's Pyrus* and *St George, Leconfield, Orlando, Parker, Penley Estate, Petaluma, Wynns' Coonawarra* and *John Riddoch, Yalumba* (Coonawarra); *Heggie's, Henschke, Hill Smith Estate, Mountadam The Red, Seppelt's Partalunga* (Eden Valley); *Ch Tahbilk* (Goulbourn Valley); *Mt Langi-Ghiran* (Great Western); *Frankland Estate, Goundrey, Howard Park, Plantagenet* (Great Southern); *Brokenwood, Lake's Folly* (Hunter); *Ch Reynella, Shottesbrooke, Wirra Wirra* (McLaren Vale); *Cape Mentelle, Capel Vale, Devil's Lair, Leeuwin Estate, Moss Wood, Vasse Felix* (Margaret River); *Dromana Estate* (Mornington); *Taltarni* (Pyrenees); *Freycinet, Domaine A* (Tasmania); *Seppelt's Drumborg, Tisdall Mt Helen* (Victoria); *Coldstream Hills, Mount Mary, Seville Estate, St Hubert's, Yarra Yering* (Yarra); *Geoff Merrill, Penfold's* (various).

GRENACHE Forgotten for 20 years, while the young turks pursued Cabernet and Pinot, Grenache is back in the charts, with big, sweet, meaty, dense black wines of amazing fortitude and character. The best come from unirrigated, sunburnt bush vines, from the likes of *Rockford, Turkey Flat, Charles Melton* and *RBJ* (Barossa) and *d'Arenberg* (McLaren Vale). The Turkey Flat vines have been in constant production since 1847.

PINOT NOIR Because Australia for decades endured just the one clone of Pinot Noir – one that tasted like simple red berry jelly – all its Pinot tasted like simple red berry jelly. Now that a wider range of clones has been released from quarantine the story is changing rapidly. Best: *Ashton Hills, Hillstowe, Pibbin* (Adelaide Hills); *Giaconda* (Beechworth); *Mountadam* (Eden Valley); *Bannockburn* (Geelong); *Wignall's* (Great Southern); *Henschke, Tim Knappstein* (Lenswood); *Moss Wood* (Margaret River); *Freycinet, Spring Vale, Piper's Brook* (Tasmania); *Coldstream Hills, Mt Mary, St Hubert's, Tarrawarra, Yarra Yering* (Yarra).

SHIRAZ The most widely planted red vine in Oz, and the one which squeezes out the most distinctive flavours, in wines of the greatest opulence and longevity. Old gnarled Shiraz vines seem to slurp up sunlight, in return offering grapes with the dense, black iron intensity of Clare, the chocolate, earth and moss of the Barossa, the black pepper of the cooler bits of Victoria and WA, or the simple red berry sweetness of the over-irrigated, hot Murray Valley. Try: *Grant Burge Meshach, Greenock Creek, Peter Lehmann, Charles Melton, Rockford, St Hallett* (Barossa); *Jasper Hill, Passing Clouds* (Bendigo); *Cape Mentelle* (Cape Mentelle); *Tim Adams, Jim Barry, Mitchell, Wendouree* (Clare); *Bowen, Majella, Wynns, Zema* (Coonawarra); *Craneford, Henschke, David Wynn Patriarch* (Eden); *Bannockburn* (Geelong); *Ch Tahbilk* (Goulbourn); *Mt Langi-Ghiran* (Great Western); *Plantagenet* (Great Southern); *Brokenwood, Rothbury* (Hunter); *Craiglee* (Macedon); *Chapel Hill, Hardy* (McLaren Vale); *Dalwhinnie, Taltarni* (Pyrenees); *Bailey's* (Rutherglen); *Yarra Yering* (Yarra); *Hardy, Penfolds*.

The price guides for this section begin on page 407.

WINES & WINE REGIONS

The new Australian Geographical Indication system, at the time of writing being thrashed out in smoke-filled rooms all over the continent but not yet appearing on labels, has to encompass certain Australian peculiarities. The main one is the system of regional blending: that is, trucking grapes from several different regions, possibly in different states, for blending together. So the Australian system has more layers than most, starting with the most general designation, which is Produce of Australia. Anything sold solely under this *appellation* will not be able to have a grape variety or a vintage on its label.

The next most general is South-Eastern Australia, an appellation which already exists and is much seen; it covers, in fact, most of the wine producing areas of the country. Then there is the more specific State of Origin, and then zones. A zone is smaller than a state but larger than an individual region: Central South Australia incorporates both McClaren Vale and the Barossa, for example. Then come regions, like Barossa itself (not Barossa Valley, note: by dropping the Valley they can incorporate the Clare Valley with it). Finally there are sub-regions. In all there will be about 400 Geographical Indications.

ADELAIDE HILLS (South Australia) This includes numerous high country vineyards, like Ashton Hills and Lenswood, but only one major winery, *Petaluma*, since the whole region is an environmentally-fragile water catchment zone. And SA is the driest state in the driest continent.

BAROSSA VALLEY (South Australia) The heart of the wine industry, and a wonderful mix of huge wineries and small family vineyards planted originally by immigrants from Silesia. Most of Australia's wine passes through the Barossa, if only for bottling or aging. Big: *Penfold, Orlando-Wyndham.* Medium: *Peter Lehmann, Mildara-Blass.* Tiny: *Rockford, Greenock Creek, Charles Melton, Grant Burge.*

BENDIGO (Victoria) This 19th-century region, destroyed by phylloxera, has been replanted with excellent Cabernet, good Shiraz and some Pinot Noir. *Balgownie* is the leader, with *Chateau Le Amon, Craiglee, Harcourt Valley, Heathcote, Mount Ida, Passing Clouds* and *Yellowglen* important.

CANBERRA DISTRICT (ACT) In the Australian Capital Territory, with some modest wineries producing wines to match.

CENTRAL VICTORIA Goulburn Valley is the most important area, with *Chateau Tahbilk* producing big old-style Shiraz and Cabernet, and some interesting Marsanne. *Tisdall* makes superbly fruity Cabernet, Chardonnay and Sauvignon; *Mitchelton* is also good. *Delatite* makes delicate whites and intense reds in cool-climate conditions.

CLARE (South Australia) An upland complex of four valleys (Skillogallee, Clare, Watervale and Polish River), Clare is cool and dry and produces steely, limy Riesling (*Leo Buring, Tim Knappstein, Jim Barry, Pike's* and *Grossett*), soft, light Chardonnay (*Penfold*), rounded Sémillon (*Mitchell*) and long-living reds (*Wendouree, Knappstein, Skillogallee, Leasingham, Watervale*).

COONAWARRA (South Australia) A big, flat, wide-open landscape dotted with 300-year-old red gums with the famous cigar-shaped strip of *terra rossa* soil which is the heart of Coonawarra. This is Australia's most profitable red wine vineyard, and its incredibly expensive land is jam-packed with great names. In recent years, more white grapes have been planted, but these are best for sparkling wines. Coonawarra is best at Cabernet and unirrigated Shiraz.

Try: *Bowen, Brand's, Hardy/Reynella, Hollick, Lindeman's, Majella, Mildara, Orlando, Penfold, Penley, Petaluma, Rouge Homme, Rosemount, Wynns* and *Zema*.

EDEN VALLEY (South Australia) A network of upland valleys, home to some of Australia's oldest vineyards, like *Henschke's* 120-year-old Hill of Grace, and some of the newest and most high-tech (*Mountadam* and *Seppelt's Partalunga*). Most of the major Barossa companies take fruit from these rolling uplands. The *Yalumba* winery is here too, with its beautiful *Heggie's* and *Hill Smith Estate* vineyards.

GEELONG (Victoria) Best are intense Cabernets from vineyards like *Idyll* and *Bannockburn*, Pinot Noir from *Prince Albert* and *Bannockburn*, whites from *Idyll*.

GLENROWAN-MILAWA (Victoria) Famous for *Bailey's* torrid, palate-blasting reds from Cabernet and Shiraz and (more importantly) Liqueur Muscats. These are intensely sweet, the very essence of the overripe brown Muscat grape, full of an exotic tangle of orange and honey. *Brown Brothers* makes a wide range, but its best are from the Koombahla vineyard, and the high altitude Whitlands site.

GOULBOURN VALLEY (Victoria) One of Victoria's biggest premium regions, this houses *Mitchelton*, a medium-sized modern

winery, and *Tahbilk*, one of the nation's oldest, still making traditional intense reds and long-lived Marsanne. Tiny, highland, high-tech *Delatite* is nearby.

GRANITE BELT (Queensland) This sits on a 1000m-plateau: altitude and southern latitude allow grapes to be grown in a banana-and-mango belt. Most wines serve the captive local markets and some (*Ballandean, Koninos Wines, Rumbalara, Robinsons Family* and *Stone Ridge*) are good. *Ironbark Ridge* is one to watch.

GREAT SOUTHERN This huge, wild, breathtakingly remote region is host to just a handful of widely scattered vineyards, and even fewer wineries, but it is one of Australia's most promising. It has Rieslings as good as Clare and Eden Valley, and delightful limy Chardonnays. Its Shiraz is lithe and peppery, its Pinot lush and fleshy, and its Cabernet magnificent, full of cedar, spice, moss, fern and earth. Soon Cabernet from here will give those from Margaret River a very hard run for their money. The wineries are *Goundrey, Alkoomi, Plantagenet* and the new *Frankland Estate*. Also new is the stunning *Howard Park*, home of the *Madfish Bay* blends.

GREAT WESTERN (Victoria) Historic area best known as the source of base wine for *Seppelt's Great Western* fizz, but more exciting for its reds. Shiraz is superb, full of

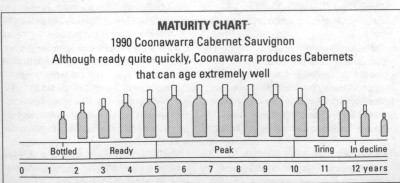

MATURITY CHART
1990 Coonawarra Cabernet Sauvignon
Although ready quite quickly, Coonawarra produces Cabernets that can age extremely well

Bottled	Ready		Peak		Tiring	In decline

| 0 | 1 | 2 | 3 | 4 | 5 | 6 | 7 | 8 | 9 | 10 | 11 | 12 years |

chocolate, coconut and cream as at *Cathcart Ridge*, or dry, liquoricy and with impressive pepper as at *Mount Langi-Ghiran*. *Best's*, *Montara* and *Seppelt* are other top names. There is also excellent Chardonnay from *Best's* and *Seppelt*, good Cabernet Sauvignon from *Mount Langi-Ghiran* and 'Vintage port' from *Montara*.

HUNTER VALLEY (New South Wales)
The Upper Hunter, home to *Arrowfield* and *Rosemount*, is hot and dry compared to the hot and wet sub-tropical Lower Hunter, with *Rothbury*, *Lindeman's*, *Brokenwood*, *Lake's Folly*, *McWilliam's*, *Petersen* and *Tyrrell*. It's not a good place to grow grapes (it produces only about five per cent of Australia's crop), but it's near Sydney, so the growers struggle on and forge some distinctive, long-lived Shiraz and Sémillon. Chardonnay also does reasonably well.

LOWER GREAT SOUTHERN (Western Australia) A vast, rambling area of great promise, especially round Mount Barker. *Alkoomi*, *Forest Hill*, *Goundrey*, *Howard Park* and *Plantagenet* are good. The whites are fragrant and appetizing, with zesty Riesling and Sauvignon, but the reds are best, with spicy, tobaccoey Cabernets.

MARGARET RIVER (Western Australia)
There have been masses of superb wines from here, like *Cape Mentelle*, *Cullens*, *Leeuwin Estate*, *Moss Wood*, *Sandalford*, *Redgate* and *Vasse Felix*. The best Cabernets have magnificent fruit with grassy acidity and are as good as top-line clarets. Pinot Noir sometimes does well. Chardonnay is often rich and barrel-fermented. Sémillon is frequently now made in an apple-fresh, but weighty style – though old-style ones age superbly. There is also some port-style wine and *Happ's* have planted Portuguese varieties which are looking interesting.

MCLAREN VALE (South Australia) This has recently forsaken thick, heavy reds for beautifully balanced reds and whites of positively cool-climate style. Great Cabernet, Shiraz and Chardonnay have already been produced, and much fine Sauvignon Blanc and Sémillon. Best: *Chapel Hill, Coriole, Richard Hamilton, Hardy's Chateau Reynella, Hillstowe, Hugo, Ingoldby, Geoff Merrill's Mount Hurtle, Norman's, Shottesbrooke, Wirra Wirra, Woodstock*.

MORNINGTON PENINSULA (Victoria)
One of the coolest Aussie wine zones, this is a weekend playground for the Melbourne rich. It has 80 vineyards and wineries, among the best of which are *Dromana, Stoniers Merricks* and *Moorooduc Estate*.

MUDGEE (New South Wales) Able to make good table wines owing to a late spring and cold nights. Though established on Shiraz (*Montrose* is outstanding) the best reds have been tarry, plummy Cabernets. But Chardonnay is even better, usually rich, soft and full of fruit-salad flavours. Best: *Montrose, Craigmoor, Huntington, Miramar*.

MURRUMBIDGEE IRRIGATION AREA/GRIFFITH (New South Wales)
The vast irrigated MIA provides 15 to 20 per cent of the total Australian crop. Most of it is bulk wine, but *McWilliams* makes some attractive wines, as does *de Bortoli*, including a Sauternes-style Sémillon.

PADTHAWAY (South Australia) High quality and increasingly important for whites, notably Chardonnay, Riesling and Sauvignon Blanc. Established in the 1960s when pressure on land in Coonawarra made wineries look elsewhere. Padthaway has some of the *terra rossa* soil which makes Coonawarra so special. Grapes are grown here for sparkling wine, and there is some excellent sweet Riesling. Best: *Hardy's, Lindemans, Seppelt*; major names like *Orlando* and *Penfolds* also use the grapes.

'PORT' Shiraz and other Rhône-type grapes are often used to make high-quality 'port'. Vintage is wonderful. One day they'll stop calling it port. Best: *Chateau Reynella, Lindeman's, Montara, Penfolds, Saltram, Seppelt, Stanton & Killeen, Yalumba.*

PYRENEES (Victoria) Very dry Shiraz and Cabernet reds, and mostly Sauvignon whites. Tops: *Dalwhinnie, Mount Avoca, Redbank, Taltarni, Warrenmang,* and for fizz, *Chateau Remy* and *Taltarni. Chateau Remy* also produces some very stylish Cabernet and Chardonnay.

RIVERLAND (South Australia) The grape basket of Australia – a vast irrigation project on the river Murray providing 38 per cent of the national crop. Dominated by the huge *Angoves* winery, and the even bigger *Berri-Renmano-Loxton* group (now part of BRL-Hardy), it makes enormous amounts of bag-in-box wines of consistently good quality. But it also yields fresh, fruity Rhine Riesling, Chardonnay, Sauvignon, Colombard, Chenin, Cabernet and Shiraz.

RUTHERGLEN (Victoria) The centre of the fortified tradition. The white table wines are generally dull, except for the reliably fine *St Leonards*. The reds are rich and robust. The fortifieds, either as *solera*-method 'sherries', as 'Vintage ports', or as intense, brown sugar-sweet Tokays, are all memorable. The true heights are achieved by Liqueur Muscats, unbearably rich but irresistible with it. Best: *Bullers, Campbells, Chambers, Morris, Stanton & Killeen.*

SPARKLING WINES Along with Pinot Noir, quality fizz is a Holy Grail here. In the lead are *Croser, Domaine Chandon* (called *Green Point* in the UK), *Yalumba D, Salinger* and *Jansz.* Cheaper: *Seaview, Angas Brut, Orlando Carrington.* Upmarket: *Seppelt's Blanc de Blancs* and *Pinot Noir / Chardonnay.* And try *Yalumba's Cabernet* and *Seppelt's Shiraz* (sparkling reds).

SWAN VALLEY (Western Australia) One of the hottest wine regions anywhere, this made its reputation on big, rich reds and whites, but even the famous *Houghton's Supreme* is now much lighter and fresher. Good names: *Bassendean, Evans and Tate, Houghton, Moondah Brook, Sandalford.*

TASMANIA Only tiny amounts, but there is some remarkable Chardonnay from *Pipers Brook* and *Tasmanian Wine Co,* and Cabernet from *Freycinet* and *Domaine A.* Pinot Noir can be terrific.

YARRA VALLEY (Victoria) This pretty valley could become Victoria's superstar. It is cold, and suits the Champagne grapes, Pinot and Chardonnay, plus Riesling and Gewürztraminer, and even Cabernet and Pinot for superb reds. The scale is quite small, the quality very high. Names to seek are: *Coldstream Hills, de Bortoli, Diamond Valley, Lillydale, Mount Mary, St Hubert's, Seville, Tarrawarra, Yarra Burn, Yarra Ridge, Yarra Yering* and *Yeringberg.*

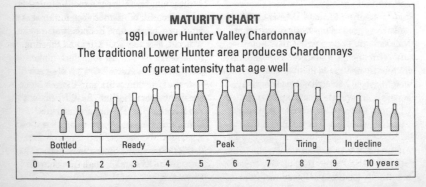

MATURITY CHART
1991 Lower Hunter Valley Chardonnay
The traditional Lower Hunter area produces Chardonnays
of great intensity that age well

Bottled	Ready	Peak	Tiring	In decline

0   1   2   3   4   5   6   7   8   9   10 years

WINERY PROFILES

TIM ADAMS ★★★★ (South Australia) Spectacular early results: spellbinding Sémillon and a dense, full-flavoured Shiraz. Tiny amounts but building a cult following.

BAILEY'S OF GLENROWAN ★★★★ (Victoria) Greatest of Australia's fortified winemakers, its 'Founder' Liqueur Muscat is an unbearably delicious concentration of sweet, dark flavours. Also reassuringly traditional Cabernet and Shiraz.

BANNOCKBURN ★★★★ (Victoria) Gary Farr, winemaker at Domaine Dujac in Burgundy, produces some of cool-climate Geelong's best wines: a rich Pinot Noir, full-bodied Chardonnay and Shiraz.

BAROSSA VALLEY ESTATES ★★(★) (South Australia) Berri-Renmano-Hardy-owned, this specializes in high-quality cheap wine.

JIM BARRY ★★★★ (South Australia) Clare Valley winery producing outstanding Chardonnay, Rhine Riesling, Sauvignon Blanc and a splendid Shiraz, The Armagh.

BASEDOW ★★★★ (South Australia) Old Barossa winery now surging ahead with big, oaky Chardonnay, fine Watervale Riesling, hearty, chocolaty Shiraz and Cabernet.

BERRI-RENMANO and HARDY★★★(★) (South Australia) This public company, which crushes 25 per cent of all Australian wine, is the result of last year's merger of Berri-Renmano and the family company of Hardy's. It's a powerful combination, with Berri's high standard, cheap own-labels and Hardy's impressive quality across the range from the Bird Series and Nottage Hill to Chateau Reynella and Eileen Hardy.

WOLF BLASS ★★★(★) (South Australia) Though now owned by Mildara, Wolf Blass still has a knack of producing what people like: wines of tremendous fruit and well-judged oak. Good Riesling, voluptuous Chardonnay and five styles of red which are, in rising price order, red, yellow, grey, brown and black label.

DE BORTOLI ★★★(★) (New South Wales) Shot to fame with an astonishing sweet 1982 botrytis Sémillon, and has since put together a string of well-priced basics. De Bortoli's new Yarra property makes some of the region's best Chardonnay, Cabernet and Shiraz.

BOWEN ESTATE ★★★★ (South Australia) The best value in Coonawarra: elegant Cabernet/Merlot and razor-fine Shiraz renowned for consistency and quality. Very good Riesling, Chardonnay.

BROKENWOOD ★★★★(★) (New South Wales) Small, high-class Hunter Valley winery noted for eclectic blends such as Hunter/Coonawarra Cabernet and latterly Hunter/McLaren Vale Sémillon/Sauvignon Blanc. Low-yielding Graveyard vineyard produces one of Australia's best Shiraz: concentrated, profound and long-living.

BROWN BROTHERS ★★★ (Victoria) Family firm, and a huge range of good wine. The best vineyards are the cool Koombahla and even cooler Whitlands; look for Muscat, Sémillon, Chardonnay, Koombahla Cabernet, Whitlands Gewürz and Riesling.

CAPE MENTELLE ★★★★(★) (Western Australia) Important Margaret River winery now part-owned by Veuve Clicquot with founder David Hohnen; also owns New Zealand's buzz winery Cloudy Bay. Excellent Cabernet and variations on the Sémillon/Sauvignon theme as well as Shiraz – and Zinfandel, of all things to find in Australia.

CHATEAU TAHBILK ★★★★ (Victoria) Historic Goulburn Valley winery with great traditional reds.

COLDSTREAM HILLS ★★★★ (Victoria) Aussie wine writer James Halliday opted for practising what he preached. World class Pinot Noir, exciting Chardonnay and Cabernet.

DELATITE ★★★★ (Victoria) 'A magic piece of dirt, it could grow anything' is how the owners describe the Delatite vineyard. The wines have an individuality of fruit plus superb wine-making which puts them in the top class. Dry Riesling is delicious, the sweet version superb, while Pinot Noir, Gewürz, Cabernet and Shiraz are brilliant.

DOMAINE CHANDON ★★★★ (South Australia) Moët & Chandon's Green Point Estate in the Yarra Valley released its second Champagne-method sparkler in the UK in 1993. Outstanding quality.

DROMANA ★★★(★) (Victoria) Excellent Chardonnay, promising Pinot Noir and Cabernet/Merlot in the Mornington Peninsula, as well as the good-value Schinus Molle label.

HENSCHKE ★★★★★ (South Australia) Old red vines, some of them 100 years old, that yield deep, dark, curranty wines of top class. Whites equally stunning – Riesling, Sémillon and Chardonnay.

HILL-SMITH/YALUMBA ★★★★ (South Australia) A large Barossa company producing good wines under the Yalumba and Hill Smith labels, and exceptional ones under the Signature, Heggie's and Pewsey Vale Vineyard labels, where dry and sweet Rieslings are some of the finest in Australia. Yalumba D is very good fizz.

HOLLICK ★★★ (South Australia) With vineyards on the best soils of Coonawarra, Ian Hollick and winemaker Pat Tocaciu

harvest some of the region's suavest reds; a soft and tobaccoey Cabernet/Merlot and an outstanding Cabernet *cuvée*, Ravenswood. They make fine Pinot and Chardonnay fizz and the district's most successful Riesling.

HOWARD PARK ★★★(★) (Western Australia) Expensive but superb, long-living wines. The Riesling is intense, perfumed and austere; the Cabernet deep and structured. Both need cellaring.

LAKE'S FOLLY ★★★★ (New South Wales) Tiny Hunter Valley winery making highly idiosyncratic Chardonnay and Cabernet, very exciting with age.

LEEUWIN ESTATE ★★★★ (Western Australia) Ultra-high profile, ultra-high prices for exciting Chardonnay and Pinot Noir, blackcurrant-and-leather Cabernet Sauvignon, good Riesling and Sauvignon.

LINDEMANS ★★★★ (Victoria) Remarkable firm, now part of Penfolds. Has land in the Hunter, Padthaway, Barossa and Coonawarra. Exceptionally good basic varietals, while Coonawarras, Padthaways and old-style Hunters are among Australia's finest. Coonawarra reds Limestone Ridge and St George are tip-top, as is the claret blend, Pyrus.

MCWILLIAMS ★★(★) (New South Wales) Old-fashioned giant now rapidly improving its quality. Though traditionally a Hunter company, much McWilliams wine now comes from Griffith in the MIA. Blends like the Hillside Colombard/Chardonnay show what can be done with fairly basic fruit.

CHARLES MELTON ★★★★ (South Australia) A 1000-case Barossa winery with Grenache-based Nine Popes and a Shiraz of exceptional concentration and character.

GEOFF MERRILL ★★★(★) (South Australia) Walrus-moustached, charismatic and irreverent Merrill combines an instinct for wine with marketing ability. He makes worthy Cabernet, full Chardonnay, crisp Sauvignon/Sémillon and thirst-quenching Grenache rosé at Mount Hurtle.

MILDARA BLASS★★(★) (South Australia) Based in the irrigated Murray River hinterland, but with large holdings in Coonawarra. Quality is erratic, though price is fair. It also owns Yellowglen and Balgownie in Victoria, Krondorf in SA and Morton Estate in New Zealand.

MITCHELTON ★★★(★) (Victoria) Wide range of styles in the Goulburn Valley, notably fine, full-flavoured Rieslings, good Chardonnay under the Preece label and the speciality of the house, Marsanne.

MOORILLA ESTATE ★★(★) (Tasmania) The first of the new-wave Tasmanian wineries, producing a polished range of crisp cool-climate wines. Pinot Noir is a speciality; aromatic Riesling, Chardonnay and Gewürztraminer are also good.

MOSS WOOD ★★★★ (Western Australia) Superbly original wines from one of Margaret River's best. Sémillon, with and without wood-aging, is some of the best in Australia. Pinot Noir is daring and delicious, Chardonnay less daring but just as delicious, Cabernet rich and structured.

MOUNTADAM ★★★★(★) (South Australia) David Wynn established this Adelaide Hills vineyard after selling Wynns in Coonawarra. His son Adam makes complex, Burgundian Chardonnay, substantial Pinot Noir, idiosyncratic Riesling, lean Cabernet.

MOUNT LANGI-GHIRAN ★★★★ (Victoria) Great Western winery making dry, intense Shiraz and long-lived Cabernet.

MOUNT MARY ★★★★ (Victoria) Finely structured Cabernet-based Bordeaux blend and a Pinot Noir improving with age. Tiny production, much sought-after.

ORLANDO ★★★ (South Australia) Barossa winery with fine quality at every level. Its boxed wine is outstanding, its RF Cabernet, Riesling and Chardonnay are usually the best in the price bracket, and St-Helga Riesling, St-Hilary Chardonnay and St-Hugo Cabernet are among the best.

PENFOLDS ★★★★★ (South Australia) The greatest red-winemakers in Australia, and now good in whites too. Its basics are clean and tasty, its varietals packed with flavour, and its special selection reds, culminating in the deservedly legendary Grange Hermitage, are superlative, hugely structured wines of world class. If you can't afford Grange, try Bin 28, Bin 128, Bin 389 or the new Bin 407 Cabernet Sauvignon.

PENLEY ESTATE ★★★★ (South Australia) Kym Tolley is a scion of the Penfolds and Tolley families, hence Penley. He planted his Coonawarra estate in 1988, but so far his award-winning Shiraz, Cabernet/ Shiraz and Chardonnay come from bought-in grapes.

PETALUMA ★★★★(★) (South Australia) The baby of Brian Croser is hitting its stride. Some of his Rieslings, sweet and dry, (Chardonnays, too) have been tip-top, and his Cabernet-based reds are now top quality. Also 'Croser' fizz.

PIPERS BROOK ★★★★ (Tasmania) Keenly-sought wines which combine classy design, clever marketing and skilful wine-making by Andrew Pirie. Steely aromatic Riesling, classically reserved Chardonnay, serious Pinot Noir and tasty, barrel-fermented Sauvignon Blanc are the best.

PLANTAGENET ★★★(★) (Western Australia) In an unglamorous apple-packing shed in chilly Mount Barker, John Wade and Tony Smith make a fine range. Noted for peppery Shiraz, melony/nutty Chardonnay, fine limy Riesling and elegant Cabernet Sauvignon.

ROCKFORD ★★★★(★) (South Australia)
The individuality of Rocky O'Callaghan's
wines, especially his Basket Press Shiraz,
has made him a Barossa cult.

ROSEMOUNT ★★★(★) (New South
Wales) The company which did more than
any to help Australia take the UK by storm
with Chardonnay, Fumé Blanc and
Cabernet. The last two are no longer so
good, though Chardonnay is on the way
back and the single vineyard Roxburgh and
Show Reserve Chardonnays are
impressive. Worldwide, the Chardonnays
have set new standards for affordable
quality. We are seeing surprising Pinot Noir
and excellent Sémillon and Shiraz.

ROTHBURY ★★★★ (New South Wales)
One of the leading Hunter companies
founded by the indomitable Len Evans. Its
wines went through a bad patch a few years
ago, but are now back on form with classic
flavours. The Chardonnay and Sémillon
are now some of the Hunter's best and
Pinot Noir and Shiraz increasingly good.

ST HALLETT ★★★★ (South Australia)
Big Bob McLean (a small winemaker in
only one sense), with Stuart Blackwell and
the Lindner family in the Barossa, makes
full, oaky Sémillon and Chardonnay and a
rich Shiraz, Old Block, from old vines.

ST HUBERTS ★★★★ (Victoria) Now
owned by Rothbury and back at the top.
Brilliant whites and reds; Chardonnay and
Cabernet Sauvignon are exceptional.

SEPPELT ★★★(★) (Victoria) Leading
makers of quality fizz from Champagne
grapes, peaking with Salinger. Also fruity,
easy-drinking styles. Now part of Penfolds.

SHAW & SMITH ★★★★ (South Australia)
Itinerant winemaker Martin Shaw and his
cousin, Michael Hill-Smith MW, make fine
Sauvignon Blanc and Chardonnay in the
Southern Vales. A duo to watch.

STONIERS MERRICKS ★★★ (Victoria)
Good Chardonnay and Cabernet from this
Mornington Peninsula winery.

TALTARNI ★★★ (Victoria) Remarkable
bone-dry, grassy-sharp Fumé Blanc; fine
Cabernet and Shiraz which soften (after
about a decade) into classy, if austere reds.
If it sounds rather French – well, the
winemaker grew up at Château Lafite.

TISDALL ★★★ (Victoria) Goulburn
winery making fresh, easy-to-drink reds
and whites and cool-climate, quality
classics from its Mount Helen grapes.

TYRRELL ★★★(★) (New South Wales)
Eccentrically brilliant Hunter winery which
sells 'port' and 'blackberry nip' to tourists
through the front door while making some
classic wines out the back. There has never
been a more exciting Aussie Chardonnay
than the Vat 47 of the early '80s, and for
years Tyrrell was the only maker of good
Pinot Noir. Vat 1 Sémillon is also excellent,
as is his 'plonk' – Long Flat Red and White.

VASSE FELIX ★★★★ (Western Australia)
One of the original Margaret River wineries.
Classic regional style of rich, leafy,
curranty Cabernet and spicy, fleshy Shiraz.

WIRRA WIRRA★★★★ (South Australia)
Fine, concentrated reds, whites and fizz;
exceptional Angelus Cabernet Sauvignon.

WYNNS ★★★★ (South Australia) Big,
oaky Chardonnay, refined Cabernet and
Shiraz from this Coonawarra company.
Top-line John Riddoch Cabernet is
expensive but worth every penny.

YARRA YERING ★★★★★ (Victoria)
Wonderful Yarra Valley winery, where
Bailey Carrodus labels his Cabernet-based
wine Dry Red No.1 and his Shiraz-based
wine Dry Red No.2: exceptional, powerful
and concentrated yet fragrant reds. Fine
Pinot Noir and Chardonnay as well.

NEW ZEALAND

After nearly a decade of spectacular growth New Zealand wine has finally reached a plateau, but not because nobody wants it. Instead the weather has imposed limits, simply by allowing only poor flowering in 1992 and 1993. As a result the harvest dropped from 14.3 tonnes per hectare in 1990 to 12.2 tonnes in 1991, 9.6 tonnes in 1992, and just 6.8 tonnes in 1993. The current year looks better: 12 tonnes is expected in 1994.

Not only has there not been much wine about, but it hasn't been that good either. Cool weather in 1992 and 1993, particularly in the South Island regions, has meant that Marlborough Sauvignon Blanc has been noticeably greener with less ripe fruit and more pronounced acidity. And in addition a strengthening New Zealand dollar has forced some winemakers to increase their prices in the face of exchange rate losses of nearly one-third in the space of a year.

Short supply, a drop in quality and increasing prices have not helped the image of New Zealand wines in Britain. Nevertheless (and surprisingly) demand for the leading wines has remained strong.

More and better

And British wine drinkers can expect their loyalty to be rewarded. There will be significant changes in both the quality and quantity of New Zealand wine in the years ahead – partly because the vineyard area will increase by one-third to over 8000 hectares when the vines planted in 1993 and 1994 begin to bear fruit. Producers will be able to reduce their dependence on contract grape growers – good for quality, since it gives them more control. In addition, phylloxera has forced an extensive replanting programme in most regions. Superior clones of classical European grape varieties are now replacing bulk vines such as the once-popular Müller-Thurgau; in fact Chardonnay has recently overtaken Müller-Thurgau as the country's most widely-planted variety. Vine maturity will provide another significant boost to quality in future: the 15-year optimum age at which vines produce both good, concentrated grapes and enough of them, has so far been achieved by only a tiny percentage of the nation's vines.

The number of New Zealand wine labels should also expand considerably over the next few years. There are already 150 wine producers, though British drinkers would be forgiven for not noticing this, since only three of them control 90 per cent of the country's production. Around 20 new producers apply for a licence to make wine each year. Most are very small lifestyle wineries but collectively they put a lot of pressure on a sluggish domestic market. Many will export a significant proportion of their output: they will have to, or drink it themselves.

Marlborough Sauvignon Blanc is still New Zealand's best known export wine style. Although it is popular with local wine drinkers there is growing interest in North Island Sauvignon Blanc which offers riper, more robust peach and nectarine flavours. The latter is more suited to oak maturation, too, and is a better bet for the cellar than the lighter, more piercing and aromatic South Island styles. The best North Island examples approach the oily richness of a good Pessac-Léognan from Bordeaux. **BOB CAMPBELL MW**

WHITE GRAPES & FLAVOURS

CHARDONNAY NZ grows wine in so many latitudes that styles range from the soft peaches-and-cream of Gisborne to the grapefruit of Hawkes Bay and the light, zesty wines of Marlborough. Auckland, Nelson, Wairarapa and Canterbury have less defined styles. Best: *Babich* (Irongate), *Cloudy Bay, Collards* (Marlborough, Hawkes Bay, Rothesay), *Cooks* (Hawkes Bay), *Corbans* (Marlborough), *Coopers Creek, Hunter's, Kumeu River, Matua Valley* (Judd Estate), *Morton Estate* (Blanc Label), *Nobilo* (Dixon, Marlborough), *de Redcliffe, Selaks, Te Mata, Vidal, Villa Maria.*

CHENIN BLANC Often overcropped but capable when grown on heavy clay soils of making impressive, full-bodied numbers like *Collards'*. On lighter soils it veers to delicacy and elegance – *Millton Vineyards'* organically grown one, for instance.

GEWÜRZTRAMINER Well suited to NZ's cool climate, Gisborne makes pungent, fleshy wines with strong lychees and apricot aromas. Fine, spicy and highly aromatic styles are produced in Central Otago, NZ's most southerly wine region, from *Rippon*. *Matawhero* put the variety on the map and makes fine examples. V*illa Maria* and *Robard & Butler* are good from Gisborne.

MÜLLER-THURGAU The mainstay of bag-in-the-box production. Good ones in bottle include a soft and fruity wine from *Nobilos,* and a more steely example from

Montana. Babich makes one of the best. Also good are *Collards* and *Matua Valley.*

RIESLING NZ Riesling (often called Rhine Riesling) used to be bland and sweetish. Now styles have polarized towards both dry and lusciously sweet wines, and quality has risen. The best dry Riesling is made by *Robard & Butler*, with *Giesen* and *Redwood Valley* also good. For off-dry wines try *Corbans Stonleigh, Montana, Coopers Creek, Millton* and *Babich*. The best sweet botrytis ones are made by *Villa Maria, Corbans, Coopers Creek* and *Palliser.*

SAUVIGNON BLANC Can be divided into the pungently aromatic and zesty South Island (mainly Marlborough) styles, and the fleshier, riper and softer wines of the North Island. Best of the South: *Hunter's, Wairau River, Jackson Estate, Neuford, Vavasour,* grassier *Montana Marlborough* and *Cloudy Bay (*which includes a dash of Sémillon). Best North Island: *Matua Valley, Vidal, Morton Estate, Palliser* and *Mills Reef.*

SÉMILLON NZ winemakers have until recently used a Swiss clone of Sémillon that seldom ripens well enough to lose its aggressively grassy flavours. It makes good blending wine but can overpower as a varietal. *Villa Maria* and *Collards* are the most successful. *Selaks'* Sauvignon Blanc/Sémillon is the best example of a Sémillon blend. New clones are now being planted. Watch this space.

RED GRAPES & FLAVOURS

CABERNET SAUVIGNON In the hotter North Island, Waiheke, Matakana, Hawkes Bay and Wairarapa can make good to great Cabernet in many years, but the cooler South Island is less consistent. Merlot is often added to soften the unripe fruit in cool years and to add complexity in good vintages. NZ's best Cabernet has

deliciously ripe berry flavours, often with a touch of mint. *Te Mata Coleraine* is the leader in stylishness, *Stoneyridge Larose* wins for concentration while *Vidals* and *Villa Maria Reserve* deserve an award for consistency. Other top wines include *Waimarama, Matua, Ararimu, Esk Valley, Heron's Flight, Te Motu* and *Delegats.*

MERLOT Mostly blended with Cabernet although there is an emerging band of top varietals including *Delegats'* (delicately plummy/peppery), *Corbans'* (rich and gamy) and the concentrated *Vidals*.

PINOT NOIR NZ might not keep many Burgundy producers awake at night but the best can hold their own in the New World. *Martinborough Vineyards* is closest to the Burgundy benchmark. *Ata Rangi*, also from the Wairarapa, makes more obviously New World Pinot Noir that relies on strong plum and cherry fruit. Others: *Waipara Springs, Rippon, Neudorf, Mark Rattray, Palliser* and *St Helena*.

WINES & WINE REGIONS

GISBORNE (North Island) They call this carafe country, because it yields the second highest grape tonnage after Marlborough. Above all it is home to Müller-Thurgau, which can yield 20 to 25 tons a hectare on the Poverty Bay alluvial flats. Matawhero is a high-quality sub-area, as are Tolaga and Tikitiki further north. Local growers and winemakers have dubbed their region the Chardonnay Capital of NZ to mark the high number of award-winning wines they have produced in recent years. Gisborne is also a spiritual home of Gewürztraminer with a consistent string of winners. Reds are less exciting although expanding vineyards of Pinot Noir are now being grown for good Champagne-method fizz.

HAWKE'S BAY (North Island) Potentially NZ's greatest wine region. Plenty of sun plus complex soil patterns help to give top Chardonnay, Cabernets Sauvignon and Franc and Merlot. It has been established for over 100 years and yet we are only now beginning to see what it can do. *Te Mata* is the region's leading resident winemaker with *Brookfields, Church Road, Esk Valley, Ngatarawa, Vidal* and *Waimarama* close behind. Top producers of Hawke's Bay wines outside the region include *Babich, Cooks, Matua Valley, Mills Reef, Morton Estate* and *Villa Maria*.

MARLBOROUGH (South Island) NZ's biggest region by far was established in '73 despite criticism that the vines would be killed by frost. In their haste many planted ungrafted vines, and now over half of the vineyards must be replanted. Sauvignon Blanc is the leader with Riesling and Chardonnay also doing well in the long, cool ripening conditions. Reds have fared less well although Pinot Noir is in great demand when it can be spared from the buoyant Champagne-method fizz industry. There's good botrytis wine here as well.

OTHER NORTH ISLAND Matakana, north of Auckland, has received overnight acclaim for its stylish reds. Waiheke, an island in Auckland harbour, has been hailed by some as NZ's top red region thanks to robust Bordeaux blends from *Stoneyridge, Te Motu* and *Goldwater*. *Kumeu River, Collards* and *Matua Valley* have shown that mainland Auckland can also produce the right stuff. Wairarapa is a small but significant region in the south of the North Island, and is home to *Martinborough Vineyards, Ata Rangi, Dry River* and *Palliser*, with Pinot Noir as the star.

OTHER SOUTH ISLAND Nelson has good performers in *Neudorf* and *Seifried*. Canterbury is dominated by the excellent *Giesen* and *St Helena* with *Waipara Springs* and the new *Mark Rattray Vineyards, Pegasus Bay* and *French Farm*. Central Otago is NZ's most southerly region; *Rippon, Gibbston* and *Chard Farm* are the leading producers.

The price guides for this section begin on page 416.

WINERY PROFILES

ATA RANGI ★★★★ Good Pinot Noir and an intense Cabernet/Merlot/Shiraz blend called Celebre.

BABICH ★★★(★) Fresh Fumé Vert (Chardonnay, Sémillon, Sauvignon Blanc), zesty Marlborough Savignon Blanc, elegant Irongate Chardonnay and Cabernet/Merlot.

CELLIER LE BRUN ★★★★(★)One of the three top fizz producers outside France.

CLOUDY BAY ★★★★★ Excellent, complex Sauvignon, fattened with a little Sémillon . Top Champagne-method fizz under the Pelorus brand. Chardonnay is also good.

COLLARDS ★★★★ A top Chardonnay maker. Buttery Chenin Blanc and luscious botrytized Riesling when the vintage allows.

CORBANS ★★★(★) Stoneleigh Sauvignon, Chardonnay and Riesling are reliable to very good. Cooks Winemakers Reserve Cabernet and Chardonnay are concentrated.

DELEGATS ★★★ A Marlborough range called Oyster Bay. Fine Chardonnay and Cabernet with a good botrytized Riesling.

GIESEN ★★★(★) Elegant dry and luscious sweet Riesling; big, buttery Chardonnay.

GROVE MILL ★★★(★) Weighty Riesling, rich Chardonnay. Top reds in good years.

HUNTER'S ★★★★(★) Top Sauvignon and elegant Chardonnay. Fizz with potential.

KUMEU RIVER ★★★★(★) Top Chardonnay – but not mainstream. Good North Island Sauvignon and Merlot/Cabernet.

MARTINBOROUGH VINEYARDS ★★★★ NZ's best-known Pinot Noir, big and complex Chardonnay, lovely Riesling.

MATUA VALLEY ★★★★ Top Ararimu Chardonnay and Cabernet. Luscious Sauvignon and Gewürztraminer.

MONTANA ★★★(★) Grassy Sauvignon. Top Champagne-method fizz (Deutz); good Chardonnay and botrytized Riesling. Church Road Chardonnay and Cabernet.

MORTON ESTATE ★★★★ Chardonnay, especially Black Label. Good Sauvignon and Gewürztraminer plus an impressive fizz. Reds good and improving rapidly.

NEUDORF ★★★★Remarkably Burgundian Chardonnay; good Sauvignon, Pinot Noir.

NGATARAWA ★★★ Good Chardonnay, Cabernet/Merlot and botrytized Riesling.

NOBILO ★★★(★) Good Dixon vineyard Chardonnay. Stylish Sauvignon. Popular White Cloud (Müller-Thurgau/Sauvignon).

PALLISER ★★★★ Good Sauvignon, Pinot Noir and concentrated Chardonnay.

C J PASK ★★★(★) Good reds and Chardonnay from excellent vineyard sites.

ST HELENA ★★★(★) Good Chardonnay, Pinot Gris and Pinot Blanc.

SELAKS ★★★★ Great Sauvignon and Sauvignon/Sémillon. Founder's Selection is the top label.

TE MATA ★★★★★ Coleraine and Awatea, are sought-after Cabernet/Merlot blends. Burgiundian-style Elston Chardonnay.

VAVASOUR ★★★★ Top Chardonnay and reds and very good Sauvignons.

VILLA MARIA ★★★★ Outstanding Vidal, Esk Valley and Villa Maria Reserve wines.

CHILE

The British wine drinker's love of Chile has been an on-off affair. Several years ago we were bewitched with our new discovery. True, only a handful of the wines reflected the perfect conditions they were said to enjoy, but we reckoned it would only take the Chileans a year or two to turn the rest around.

As is often the case with the most passionate of beginnings, disillusionment quickly set in. When the wines were good, they were very, very good, but many continued to be disappointingly patchy. In reality Chile is planted extensively with dull grapes such as Pais and Sauvignonasse, and many wineries are still lumbered with old beechwood barrels and poorly trained winemakers. The truth was that it would take something of a revolution to turn the quality around, and in the meantime there was always Australia... and so our affections moved on.

In the winery and the vineyard, Chile is still in the throes of that revolution. At the moment it is still a matter of picking and choosing carefully, but the country deserves more patience than we have previously accorded it.

The most exciting new region is the Casablanca Valley, some 80 kilometres north-west of Santiago, close by the cool Pacific Ocean. Casablanca was unheard-of five years ago when the winemaker at Concha y Toro began planting classic white varieties there. But word spread, and something like a gold rush started: latest figures show that over 1200 hectares have now been planted, while land prices have soared to US$10,000 per hectare. Although Casablanca vines are still youthful, wines produced from them reveal that the area is fulfilling its initial promise. The valley looks set to become Chile's foremost region for Chardonnay and Sauvignon Blanc, and even Gewürztraminer is doing well there.

Play it again, Ignacio

The chief architect of the region is Ignacio Recabarren, who is clearly emerging as the leading figure in Chilean wine-making. Mercurial and obsessive, Recabarren has coaxed more varietal character out of Chilean fruit over the past two or three years than anyone else had previously managed. Chile could do with more mavericks like Recabarren, who learnt much of his trade working vintages in California, Bordeaux and New Zealand (at Cloudy Bay). On the other hand wineries are increasingly coming under the influence of talented winemakers flying in from abroad. Famous names joining the throng are Hugh Ryman, now working at Montes, and Jacques Lurton, who has just begun to give a much-needed helping hand at San Pedro. Château Lafite-Rothschild (at Los Vascos), Franciscan Cellars of California, William Fèvre of Chablis and Bruno Prats of Château Cos d'Estournel are other major sources of finance and/or advice; while Miguel Torres' operation at Curico is blazing a trail. The results are, yet again, patchy, with Ryman's wines so far proving no better than those of Aurelio Montes, and Los Vascos heading down a strange path of French imitation, but it's worth keeping an eye on the progress these wineries make in the future.

Internally, Chile is making headway with the structure of its wine-making industry. The Wine Association, which represents 19 of the major wineries, has worked closely with the Chilean government to come up with tighter quality regulations, which, we are promised, will have come into effect by the time this book goes to press in 1994. At last we may be able to identify regional characteristics; changes mean that any wines carrying the name of one of the four recognized quality regions, Aconcagua, Maipo, Rapel or Curico, must contain at least 75 per cent fruit from that region. Further, a varietal wine must contain 85 per cent of the grape variety in any blend, and 'estate' wines must be 100 per cent estate produced and bottled. Chile would do well to soothe our suspicions by imposing these rules strictly– whether it does so or not remains to be seen. For the future, the Wine Association says it is eager to develop the *appellation* laws further to identify smaller sub-regions, such as Casablanca, currently part of the Aconcagua region.

All this helps matters – or will do when the new rules are finally imposed – but the Chileans still need to push for lower yields and better clones. When it comes to yields the pressure is on to keep prices down, but that doesn't mean we need a flood of hard-pressed or dilute wines – or that we will buy them whatever the price. Clones are a more complex problem – in order to plant better vines, and eliminate the use of dull domestic clones such as Sauvignonasse (still often passed off as Sauvignon Blanc), the Chilean government needs to relax its tight quarantine laws. This is a country terrified of phylloxera in the same way Britain fears rabies. Long may it remain free of the disease which is now decimating California, but may it also find ways of continuing to progress.   SUSY ATKINS

RED GRAPES & FLAVOURS

CABERNET SAUVIGNON This is the variety with which Chile arrived on our shelves some years ago. The best vines are those of the Maipo Valley. Chilean Cabernet at its best is marked by a remarkable depth of colour, intense, pure fruit character and a depth of flavour which is anything but jammy. Some lighter, juicy styles are now emerging. Venerable top-notch wines are to be had from: *Concho y Toro Don Melchor, Cousiño Macul (Antiguas Reservas), Errazuriz Don*

Maximimiano. Best of the new wineries: *Carmen, Cono Sur, Canepa*.

MERLOT On the up, with the best tasting of green peppers and crunchy black cherry fruit. Try *Errazuriz, Concha y Toro, Santa Carolina, Torréon de Paredes*.

PINOT NOIR Very little is produced; the best example available in Britain being *Undurraga*'s, the trail-blazing, aromatic *Cono Sur*.

WHITE GRAPES & FLAVOURS

CHARDONNAY Characteristically perfumed with ripe pineapple and greengage and a good dollop of sweet new oak, Chardonnay is now widely planted throughout the wine-growing regions – in particular in Curico, part of the Maule region. New trends have seen lighter, unoaked (or lightly oaked) Chardonnays with lime and lemon character emerging, particularly from the cool vineyards in the Casablanca Valley. Best: *Santa Rita,*

Carmen, Santa Carolina, especially its *Casablanca* label, *Vina Porta, Canepa* (under the brand names *Rowan Brook* and *Montenuevo*), *Concha y Toro*.

SAUVIGNON BLANC This is all too often a disappointment, lacking both freshness and the pungent varietal characterthat one looks for, which leads one to suspect that the inferior Sauvignonasse is still widely used. Widely planted, most particularly in the Curico region. Again, the cool Casablanca Valley is now producing better varietal character, with ripe gooseberry flavours and firm acidity. Winemaker Ignacio Recabarren makes by far the best examples from the *Santa Isabel* estate under his *Casablanca* label. Other good ones to look for include *Undurraga* and *Carmen*.

RIESLING Only minimal amounts of the great German grape are grown in Chile, and it's not being pursued with any great zeal. *Miguel Torres* makes a good Gewürztraminer/Riesling blend in Curico, however, *Santa Monica* makes a minerally varietal and *Santa Rita*'s example has good varietal character.

SÉMILLON This widely-planted grape is sold mostly on the domestic market or blended with Sauvignon Blanc and Chardonnay (for the simple reason that Sémillon grapes are a quarter of the price of Chardonnay). There are a couple of varietals available over here, though, from *Santa Monica* and *Canepa* (*Montenuevo* and *Peteroa* are the brand names to look for). Both wines display good peachy character and have some reasonable weight to them.

GEWÜRZTRAMINER Alsace's most famous grape is rare in Chile, but there is one deliciously soft and ripe example under the *Casablanca* label; *Torres* makes a blend with Riesling (see above).

WINE REGIONS

Grapes are grown in areas covering 12,000km of the length of Chile, but only a 600km strip in the centre of the country, the Central Valley, produces quality wine. Further north and south it is too hot or too cold, and fortified and table wines are produced. In the Central Valley the foothills of the Andes provide lots of promising microclimates, and the coolest of these (Casablanca is the latest star) are proving good for whites.

ACONCAGUA The furthest north of the quality regions, and the coolest, parts of it being close to the Pacific. Casablanca and Panquehue are its sub-regions.

Aconcagua is noted for its good white wines. Viticulture is concentrated in the valleys of rivers that start in the Andes and flow to the Pacific Ocean. *Errazuriz, Santa Carolina, Casablanca* and *Santa Emiliana* are all located here.

MAIPO, RAPEL AND MAULE In these regions grape growing is concentrated along the Central Valley, between the Andes to the east and the Coastal range to the west. Maipo is close to the sprawling city of Santiago and is famous for top-quality Cabernet Sauvignon production. However, the Upper Maipo Valley is being developed as a cooler sub-region which shows promise for whites. Of all the

regions Maipo produces the largest number of grapes for fine export wines. *Santa Rita, Undurraga, Cousiño Macul, Concha y Toro* are the names to look for.

Rapel, a little further south and warmer, also produces fine Cabernet. Rancagua is a sub-region that is increasingly recognized as a source of good reds. Rapel is home to *Los Vascos* and *Torréon de Parredes*.

Maule, following the map south, includes the Curico sub-region, proving good for Chardonnay, less good for Cabernet Sauvignon. *Montes, Torres* and *Santa Monica* wineries are all located here.

BIO-BIO lies south of Maule. It, too, is a recognized region, but little of its fruit is used for export wines. It is here that vast tracts of the Pais grape are grown to supply the domestic market.

WINERY PROFILES

CANEPA ★★★★ The company behind many of the best own-label Chilean wines on sale here, Canepa also produces the excellent Montenuevo and Rowan Brook. It is in the lead of the price/quality ratio change.

CONCHA Y TORO ★★★★ The largest Chilean wine exporter, with the emphasis on reds. Top of the range is Don Melchor Cabernet Sauvignon. Concha y Toro is based in Maipo and has a French winemaker, Gaetana Caron. Second label is Santa Emiliana (★★).

COUSIÑO MACUL ★★★★ Three generations of the Cousiño family work this nineteenth-century estate to produce reds, notably the single-vineyard Cabernet Antiguas Reservas.

ECHEVERRIA ★★★ Interesting, family-run boutique winery with Aurelio Montes acting as consultant. Easy-drinking Cabernet, crisp Sauvignon.

ERRAZURIZ ★★★(★) Family-run, with the help of Ignacio Recabarren as consultant winemaker. Owner Eduardo Chadwick would be wise to give him his head – at present the best are the Errazuriz reds, especially the Merlot and flagship Cabernet Don Maximiano. Second label Caliterra★★

LOS VASCOS ★★★ A 50 per cent buy-out by Lafite-Rothschild in 1988 has led, inevitably, to an Old-World style in the reds. Even the bottles look French – strange marketing indeed.

MONTES ★★★ Modern boutique winery with the influential Aurelio Montes as founding partner and winemaker. Part of the Discover Wine venture; Nogales is the sister label. The best is the Montes Alpha, made from Cabernet Sauvignon.

SAN PEDRO ★★(★) Large winery producing huge amounts for the domestic market and some inconsistent exports. New investment and the arrival of Jacques Lurton as winemaker should see a shake-up.

SANTA CAROLINA ★★★ With the help of Ignacio Recabarren and huge investment in a new winery, Santa Carolina pulled its socks up. Now Recabarren is moving on, and it remains to be seen whether quality will be maintained. The White Label wines are the best. Second label is Viña Casablanca (★★★★(★)), Recabarren's own project: a superb range from the Casablanca Valley.

SANTA MONICA ★★★(★) Small family-run winery with a good range of whites.

SANTA RITA ★★★ Large but unfocussed high-tech operation with excellent and erratic Cabernet Sauvignon (Medalla Real and Casa Real) and Chardonnay (Medalla Real). Sister label is Viña Carmen (★★★★).

TORRÉON DE PAREDES ★★★(★) Large winery based in Rapel. Good wines, particularly an award-winning Merlot.

TORRES ★★★ Miguel Torres makes a wide selection at his operation in Curico. Better than average whites include a good but lean oaked Chardonnay. He's also trying out grapes unusual to Chile.

UNDURRAGA ★★★ Beautiful nineteenth-century show-estate making wines from the Maipo Valley. Best are Merlot and Sauvignon Blanc.

VIÑA PORTA ★★★★ Excellent small winery making top-notch Chardonnay and Cabernet Sauvignon. In joint venture with California winery Clos Du Val, with new French winemaker Yves Pouzet at the helm.

SOUTH AFRICA

Everyday life in South Africa, even in the wine industry, is inseparable from politics. Although wine is currently experiencing a boom, in recent years it has been as hard hit by political turmoil as any other South African industry.

Nevertheless, South African white wines are looking better and better, with excellent value at the cheaper end, and some really top class Chardonnays emerging. The best South African sweet wines are also extremely good – being made from Riesling as well as Chenin Blanc – while those not quite in the top rank are, at the very least, good. Sauvignon Blanc is the other widely exported premium variety. Here the quality is more variable, from wishy-washy wines with little discernible flavour to grassy, concentrated ones from Constantia.

Sparkling wines are developing fast, too. From simple, fresh, clean fizz made from Chenin Blanc or other non-Champagne varieties, South African bubbly has progressed to sophisticated Chardonnay and Pinot blends with yeasty, lees-aged characters. The success rate so far is surprisingly good.

Pinotage: cook quickly

Red wines are more difficult to categorize. Cabernet Sauvignon has recently taken over from the undistinguished Cinsaut as most widely planted variety, with South Africa's own home-bred grape, Pinotage, in third place. Merlot, Shiraz and Pinot Noir plantations are small but growing. Traditionally, the Pinotage has been South Africa's multi-purpose grape, used to make everything from fizz and rosé to light reds and juicy, full-bodied ones. But it's these latter that it does best. Winemakers have now realized that the way to get rid of the undesirable acetone flavour that used to bedevil red Pinotage is to ferment it very hot for a short while to blow the acetoney character away, so Pinotage should become a much more exciting variety. Unfortunately, not everyone has caught on yet, so you still have to be very careful whose you buy.

With Cabernet Sauvignon, I believe South African winemakers have a fundamental problem. Almost all the serious wines taste austere when young, aging to cedary, tarry flavours after ten years or more. Never do you find the rich, ripe blackcurrant flavours of Cabernet from Bordeaux, Australia or even Italy. The problem lies in the vines, with only two clones of Cabernet available for planting, the old, tarry one, and a new, rather insubstantial, minty one. South Africa needs a greater range of Cabernet clones before its potential can be realized. Thank heavens, therefore, for Merlot, and its blends with Cabernet Sauvignon (and sometimes Cabernet Franc, Malbec, Petit Verdot and Shiraz). These represent the best route for Cape Cabernet at present.

South Africa also has a lot of work to do to convince us that the wines are worth the prices they ask for them. There's lots of good value, under-£3.50 white wine around, but there's an alarming gap from £3.50 to nearly £6 before real quality appears again. What we need is more good wines at £3.99 and £4.99. This would have been easy earlier this year, with the rand as weak as it has been. With the political situation after the election looking more stable, the rand may well strengthen, and the wines will become even more expensive. But then nobody would wish for the alternative. CHARLES METCALFE

WHITE GRAPES & FLAVOURS

CHARDONNAY Still the world's favourite grape, and certainly South Africa's. Here it runs the gamut from dilute and neutral to massively over-oaked, but along the way it makes most of the best dry whites, soft, ripe and buttery, with subtle oak flavours and firm acidity. Best: *Alphen, Avontuur Le Blush* (fermented in ex-Merlot barrels), *Backsberg, Graham Beck Lonehill, Bellingham Reserve, Blaauwklippen, Bouchard-Finlayson, Buitenverwachting, Danie De Wet Bateleur, Dieu Donne, Neil Ellis, Hamilton-Russell, Klein Constantia, Glen Carlou Reserve, Groot Constantia, De Leeuwen Jagt, Nederburg Auction, Simonsig, Stellenryck, Thelema, Vergelegen Les Enfants, Weltevrede, Zevenrivieren, Zevenwacht, Zonnebloem.*

CHENIN BLANC Known locally as Steen, Chenin Blanc is a South African speciality, and there's much more of it grown than anything else. It's used for every style of white from steely-dry to ultra-sweet, and is responsible for many of South Africa's best value, off-dry commercial whites. The best examples include: *Alphen Noble Late Harvest, Blaauwklippen Special Late Vintage, Fleur du Cap Noble Late Harvest, Nederburg Edelkeur.*

COLOMBARD Second only in quantity to Chenin Blanc in South Africa, Colombard makes crisp, commercial whites. A flowery freshness is about all they can ever aspire to.

MUSCAT Two types of the Muscat grape are grown in South Africa, Muscadel (a version of the high-quality Muscat-à-Petits Grains) and Muscat of Alexandria (known as Hanepoot). Muscadel can be red or white, and is always sweet. The best sweet Muscadels include: *KWV White Muscadel, Klein Constantia Vin de Constance, De Leeuwen Jagt Muscadel, Nederburg Eminence, Van Loveren Blanc de Noir, Van Loveren Red Muscadel, Vredendal Muscadel.*

RIESLING Riesling ripens every year here, but it keeps its acidity, and gives the best sweet Rieslings outside Germany. The dry and off-dry ones can be excellent, too. Best dry: *Buitenverwachting, Neetlingshof.* Best off-dry: *Klein Constantia, De Leeuwen Jagt, Liefland.* Best botrytized sweet Rieslings: *Danie De Wet Edeloes, KWV Noble Late Harvest, Nederburg Noble Late Harvest and Neetlingshof Noble Late Harvest.*

CLASSIFICATIONS AND WINE LAWS

Every bottle of wine sold in South Africa must bear the 'Wine of Origin' seal. This certifies, through vineyard inspection, cellar checking, analysis and an official tasting panel, the wine's area of origin, grape variety (or varieties) and vintage. Varietal wines must contain at least 75 per cent of the stated grape if sold on the domestic market, and 85 per cent if exported. Blends must state the grapes in descending order of proportion, and if any varieties are present under 20 per cent the percentage must be stated.

Chaptalization (addition of sugar to grape-must to increase the alcohol level) is not allowed, but acidification (addition of acidity) is.

To qualify as an 'estate', a producer must vinify his wines from grapes grown only on his property. Most then bottle and mature it on the estate, too, but this is not strictly essential.

'Methode Cap Classique' (MCC) is the new name for South African Champagne-method fizz. Best brands so far are *Graham Beck, Blaauwklippen Barouche, Boschendal, Charles de Fere Tradition, Pierre Jourdan, JC Le Roux Chardonnay* and *Pongracz.*

SAUVIGNON BLANC Constantia, Elgin and Durbanville are the only regions to get anywhere near the intense asparagus-and-gooseberry tastes of New Zealand examples. But South Africa has good Sauvignons in a softer, riper, more tropical fruit style, sometimes oaked, sometimes paired with Sémillon. Try *Bouchard-Finlayson, La Bri, Buitenverwachting, Neil Ellis Whitehall, Klein Constantia, KWV Cathedral Cellar, Mulderbosch, Swartland Co-operative, Thelema, Villiera, Zevenwacht Blanc Fume.*

RED GRAPES & FLAVOURS

CABERNET SAUVIGNON, CABERNET FRANC AND BORDEAUX BLENDS

There is now more Cabernet Sauvignon in South Africa than any other grape. If only there were better clones. Some clones have been cleaned of virus and so ripen earlier, but they still taste austere and tarry. Paarl and Stellenbosch are Cabernet's heartland, but stick to the blends with other Bordeaux grapes. Best Cabernets: *Avontuur Reserve, Bellingham, Blaauwklippen Reserve, Neil Ellis, Excelsior, Glen Carlou, Hartenberg, Liefland, Landskroon Cabernet Franc, Nederburg, Stellenryck, Swartland Co-operative, Thelema.* Blends: *Avontuur Baccarat, Buitenverwachting Grand Vin, Clos Malverne Auret, Fairview Charles Gerard Red Reserve, Glen Carlou Les Trois, Groot Constantia Gouverneur's Reserve, Klein Constantia Marlbrook, Lievland DVB, Nederburg Auction, Rustenberg Gold, Villiera Cru Monro, Zonnebloem Laureat.*

CINSAUT Recently overtaken by Cabernet as the most planted variety. Cinsaut's greatest claim to fame here is that, crossed with Pinot Noir, it produced the Pinotage. By itself it gives light, undistinguished red.

MERLOT Arrived in appreciable quantity only in 1985, but already making itself felt. By itself Merlot makes rich, ripe, easy reds – even better aged in new oak. Blended with Cabernet, it smooths over the austere edges to give most of the best reds. Good are *Avontuur Reserve, Bellingham, Bouchard-Finlayson, Boschendal, De Leuwen Jagt, Fairview Reserve, Glen Carlou, Meerlust, La Roche du Preez, Rusten-Vrede, Villiera, Zonnebloem.*

PINOTAGE This crossing of Pinot Noir with Cinsaut can be used to make either light and easy rosé or red, or reds that are a great deal more substantial. The best examples are dark and rich, with a unique damson and marshmallow perfume and flavour and are made to be drunk young. New barrel aging can help the best. Good examples: *Clos Malverne, Bellingham, Groot Constantia, Kanonkop, Nederburg, Simonsig.*

PINOT NOIR Most of South Africa's vineyards are too warm for great Pinot Noir. The cliff-top slopes above Hermanus are the furthest south and the coolest, and give Pinots of European elegance and subtlety. Why Walter Finlayson can do it at Glen Carlou on the (hotter) south-west outskirts of Paarl is a mystery. Maybe it's in the Finlayson genes, since he used to make it at Hamilton Russell in Hermanus, too. There are still not many successful Pinot Noirs in South Africa, but those that are good are very good: *Bouchard-Finlayson, Glen Carlou, Hamilton-Russell.*

SHIRAZ Shiraz used to be the grape South African winemakers forgot until they'd harvested their Cabernet. By that time it was often overripe and good only for port. Now a few are trying harder. As with Cabernet, growers are hampered by lack of really good clones, but Shiraz can make savoury, raspberry-fruited wines, perhaps lacking the fleshy sweetness of the best of the northern Rhône and Australia. Best: *Bertrams, Fairview, Groot Constantia, Hartenberg, La Motte, Lievland, Zonnebloem.*

WINES & WINE REGIONS

CONSTANTIA In Constantia, you have to wear a jersey if you get up early. Sea breezes and shade from the Constantiaberg give some of South Africa's most herbaceous Sauvignon Blancs (with a strong overtone of fig). It's hard to generalize with only three fully operational producers (*Buitenverwachting, Groot Constantia* and *Klein Constantia*), but the Chardonnays are very good, in a Burgundian style, and the Bordeaux blends rank among the best.

DURBANVILLE Cape Town is threatening the vineyards of Durbanville, just to the north-east of the city. A pity, since it's cool. Sauvignon Blanc is particularly good.

FRANSCHHOEK 'French Corner' was the valley where the Huguenots settled in the 17th century. It has the potential to make fine wines, but does not always do so. *La Bri* has good Sauvignon Blanc, *Boschendal* good Merlot and fizz, *Bellingham* several good wines (usually blends of Franschhoek and other regions' grapes), *Dieu Donné* good Chardonnay, *La Motte* good Shiraz, and *Clos Cabrière* a range of excellent fizz.

HERMANUS Or Walker Bay, Overberg, or whatever you like to call this region, is home to *Hamilton Russell* and *Bouchard-Finlayson*, two of South Africa's few good Pinot Noir producers. The cool, breezy slopes of the downlands above the seaside town of Hermanus are ideal for Chardonnay and Pinot Noir, in a more Burgundian style than elsewhere in the Cape.

OLIFANTS RIVER The Olifants River finishes its journey to the sea just west of Vredendal, with vineyards along its last 30 miles. Most are planted with white grapes, though styles vary from crisp Sauvignons and Chardonnays to unctuous sweeties made from various Muscats. Co-ops rule here, with the huge but good *Vredendal* co-op, plus *Lutzville, Klawer* and *Spruitdrift*.

There's also the co-op at *Citrusdal* and SA's highest winery, *Cederberg Cellars*.

PAARL Paarl Rock is the landmark here, and many of the best vineyards are on its lower slopes. The headquarters of the *KWV* is in the town of Paarl, as is the important *Nederburg*. There is also *Backsberg, Villiera, Glen Carlou, Fairview, De Leeuwen Jagt* and *Landskroon*, with good wines from almost every variety in the Cape. Villiera even has an extremely good Sauvignon, and Glen Carlou one of South Africa's best Pinot Noirs, despite the heat.

ROBERTSON Horse-breeding, brandy and stickies country. The valley, sheltered from the northern heat by the Langeberg and watered by the Breede River, is hot (35° to 40°C) in summer, but almost always cooled by a sea breeze in the afternoon. Chardonnay has been successfully pioneered by *Danie De Wet*. *Graham Beck* has a good Lone Hill Chardonnay as well as an excellent sparkler, and *Van Loveren* a reliable range of dry and sweet whites.

STELLENBOSCH The heart of the Cape wine industry. *Stellenbosch Farmers' Winery*, the *Bergkelder* and *Gilbeys* are all in or near the town. Both reds and whites are successful here, with the Devon Valley (*Clos Malverne* and *Bertrams*) very good for reds. Also try: *Avontuur, Blaauwklippen, Hartenberg, Kanonkop, Lievland, Meerlust, Mulderbosch, Neetlingshof, Neil Ellis, Rusten-Vrede, Simonsig, Thelema, Vriesenhof* and *Zevenwacht*.

SWARTLAND Called 'black land' because of the dark grey scrub that covers the hills, Swartland is hot and dry, with cereal crops outnumbering vineyards. Yields are very low, and Chenin Blanc, Sauvignon Blanc, Colombard and Pinotage do best. The *Swartland Co-operative* and *Allesverloren* estate are the region's best producers.

OTHER WINE REGIONS

ARGENTINA

Argentina is still the sort of place that makes people laugh when I mention it as a potential source of highly enjoyable wine – but it is, it is. Potential is, however, the operative word. Nature has done her bit with the right climate, if winemakers choose properly, but until very recently man was doing his best to mess it up by only making cheap and not very cheerful wines, in large quantities.

Slowly things are looking up, though. There are now some producers making good quality everyday wines that are temptingly cheap, and that can offer a change from the ubiquitous Chardonnay and Cabernet Sauvignon.

Some of these, if they are red, are made from Malbec, a grape grown in south-west France but not much regarded elsewhere. In Argentina the quality can vary somewhat but wines from *Trapiche* and *Norton* can be dark and exciting. The other French varieties are out in force as well, of course; *Flichman*, *Norton* and *Trapiche* Cabernets are worth a look, as are *Flichman*'s and *Norton*'s Syrah.

The indigenous white grape to look out for is Torrontes, an aromatic, lime-and-orange scented number especially good from *Michel Torino* or *Etchart* (who labels it *Cafayate*; try also the *Cafayate* Cabernet Sauvignon).

AUSTRIA

Austria has long been tired of people harking back to the scandal of 1985 – but the trouble is one has to start then, because it was the beginning of the Austrian renaissance, the transformation of a rather old-fashioned wine industry into something much better quality and much more interesting. We still don't see most of the good wines over here, but that's our loss, because the best are as good as you'll find anywhere. The cheap supermarket wines that we do see are not dissimilar to other cheap supermarket wines.

Austria's vineyards are all in the east of the country, and although the grapes are pretty similar to those of Germany and Alsace, not to mention much of central Europe (Riesling, Gewürztraminer, Welschriesling, Muskateller, Ruländer, Weissburgunder and some Chardonnay, plus the less usual Grüner Veltliner) the climate is warmer than most of Germany so the wines are fuller, and they're also made dry.

Pre-scandal it was sweet or sweetish wines that were popular in Austria, but this style was so tainted in the immediate aftermath that any grower with a survival instinct started fermenting out dry pronto. Even places with the rare ability to make botrytized wines every year without fail, like the Neusiedlersee Hügelland, have gained a reputation for well-structured, elegant dry wines. Nowadays, thankfully, sweet wines are more fashionable again, and rightly, because Austria is one of Europe's greatest sources of rich, balanced pudding wines.

The legacy of the scandal now takes the form of a new generation of growers determined to bottle their own wine, not send it to the merchants to deal with; and this new generation has bought enough stainless steel to keep an ailing steelworks in operation for years. It's all over the place, even in the tiniest family cellars that otherwise boast rows of ancient (but clean) wooden casks. Wine-making standards are high, even though some young growers seem to think that the place to go to learn about wine-making off-season is not Australia but, for some reason, South Africa.

Austria has four wine regions: Niederosterreich (or Lower Austria), Burgenland, Steiermark and Vienna itself, which boasts vineyards actually within the city boundaries. Lower Austria's finest area is the Wachau, a place of steep slopes and terraces overlooking the Danube, and of wines from the Grüner Veltliner and Rhine Riesling which can be as good as anything in Austria and, in the case of Riesling, as good as most of Germany too. These Rieslings are serious wines and deserve aging, but the Austrian fashion is for young wines and few of them make it past their second birthday.

Kamptau-Donauland, also in Lower Austria (the Austrians have an unfailing knack of giving their wine regions names that are completely unmemorable to anyone else) produces good Gruner Veltliner, and it is this grape that produces perhaps the most typical wine of Austria: light, dry and drunk within a year of the vintage at family-run inns known as Heurige.

It is the Burgenland, though, that is becoming established as Austria's top area. In the north there is a lake, the Neusiedlersee, which is broad and shallow and obligingly spreads humidity over a wide area to the east; it's almost impossible not to make botrytized dessert wines there. On the western bank there is botrytis in a fairly narrow strip along the lake shore but also plenty of dry whites too, and further south there are some decent reds. *Robert Wenzel*, *Georg Stiegelmar* and *Willi Opitz* are outstanding in Burgenland.

The driest of the dry come from Steiermark, or Styria. It's a beautiful, chilly, hilly area that borders Slovenia, and the fashion for dry wines that has gripped Austria for a decade has made Styria very trendy indeed. To an outside palate they can taste not merely dry but unripe, without enough body to balance the searing acidity. But the Austrians love them, and pay through the nose for them.

CANADA

Hybrid grapes, which are most easily able to withstand the climate, take up the bulk of Canada's vineyards. But there's a Vintners' Quality Alliance in Ontario, designed to improve quality. There have been dramatic improvements in white table wines and hopeful signs in some reds, and the sweet Ice Wines (the best are made from the hybrid Vidal grape) can be a delight.

CYPRUS

To describe many Cyprus wines as 'unexciting' is a compliment; all too often 'undrinkable' is the more appropriate term. There's Cyprus 'sherry' of course, but it's not much good (and not called 'sherry' for much longer, either). The table wines we see over here are frequently tired, flabby and oxidized. One reason is that the growers are paid according to the sugar levels in their grapes, which inevitably leads to too much sugar and not enough acidity; another reason is that the grapes take too long to get to the wineries, and start fermenting on the way.

Thankfully, a few bright spots are appearing in this otherwise depressing picture. The Xynisteri grape is one of them. When grown in the cooler, mountainous centre of the island it can produce fresh, lively whites – if it is handled properly. At present it accounts for some ten per cent of the vineyards, and is mostly not handled properly. *ETKO* makes a respectable version, called *Nefeli*, and *Keo* have a cool-fermented Xynisteri which is remarkably fragrant.

The other most widely planted native grape variety – in fact the most widely planted of all – is the black Mavro, which so far makes better raisins than it does wine. There is a debate going on as to whether Cyprus should move wholeheartedly towards French varieties like Cabernet Sauvignon and Chardonnay, and the government's research station at Limassol grows these and more. If the pioneering work on grapes and wine-making being done there were taken up by the big producers, then Cyprus would at last begin to fulfil its potential.

GREECE

Greece's wine-making history is rather more glorious than its present, and there are few companies making wines likely to appeal to international tastes. There is a whole raft of appellations, of which the Côtes de Meliton is the best all-round bet; Muscats are also generally sound, and sometimes excellent if from Samos.

Château Carras is a reasonable long shot at the classic Bordeaux blend, and is enthusiastically promoted and therefore quite expensive. *Tsantali* reds are also fairly reliable, and cheaper, and *Xinomavro Naoussis* is surprisingly good, with herby, slightly earthy fruit. *Gentilini* shows good international style, as does *Chateau Semili. Strofilia* Cabernet Sauvignons, both red and rosé, are very good.

For Retsina addicts (yes, they do exist), *Tsantali* and *Metaxa* have the authentic taste, and Sainsbury's own-label is good, with a little more resin.

INDIA

Money can buy you anything if you're a millionaire; even your very own Champagne lookalike. A perfectly good wine it is too, which is astonishing in a country that produces hardly any other wine. But when Bombay millionaire Sham Chougule decided he wanted to produce wine, he asked Piper Heidsieck to come and help; a state-of-the-art winery was built to process the grapes from high-altitude vineyards, and *Omar Khayyam* is the result. It's not cheap, though.

ISRAEL

If a whole country's wine industry specializes in making a particular sort of wine (kosher) for a captive worldwide audience (observant Jews) then two things are likely to happen. First, it will produce that wine to impeccable kosher standards; Jews the world over will be able to rely on the rabbinical signature on the label and will know that the wine has been produced in accordance with the strictest rules. Second, it will taste awful. That captive audience will be far more interested in the purity (in kosher terms) of the wine than in what it tastes like. Taste, traditionally, is a secondary consideration.

Then, the worldwide wine revolution being what it is, two more things will happen – and indeed have happened. First, California wine-making techniques will be brought in to make kosher wines that taste good enough to tempt non-Jews, too. And second, the biggest wine-making company in Israel (*Carmel*) will be forced to follow suit and invest US$8m in new equipment. The most attractive wines in Israel are however still made by the relative newcomer, the *Golan Heights* winery, whose *Yarden* wines are the best, followed by the *Golan* range. The Golan Heights winery has just invested $5m in new equipment, and although it has been mooted that the region, which is of great strategic importance, might one day be handed over as part of a peace agreement with Syria, negotiations are still far in the future.

LEBANON

Lebanese wine is, to all intents and purposes for us in Britain, *Château Musar*. There are other vineyards, to be sure, but it is *Musar* that is sought-after and admired; it is also Musar that puts the worries of most other winemakers firmly in the shade.

Frost and rot, the causes of most growers' sleepless nights, are not a problem for Serge Hochar of *Musar*. Civil war, on the other hand, is, and in 1984 he was not able to make a wine at all: the front line ran between the vineyards and the winery, and the grape-laden lorries were not able to cross it.

In other years the chances of a successful vintage have looked thin, yet the wine has been made. In 1989 the winery, the office and Hochar's apartment were all hit by shelling, yet the wine was good; in 1990 the grapes narrowly missed being caught by the blockade which began on 28 September. In 1991, by contrast, the winery was regarded locally as one of the safest places to be, and many of the villagers took shelter in the cellars.

The 1993 crop was healthy and was helped on by a hot spell just before the harvest, though the quantity is slightly down because of spring frost. The colour is rich and dark, says Serge Hochar, and the wines promise well.

Musar's style is, typically, big and powerful. For a time in the late sixties Hochar turned to making lighter wines more reminiscent of Médoc, but now the wines are huge again, and age superbly – Hochar in fact reckons they should be drunk at 15 years, and will be even better at 30. The trouble is, they're often so wonderful at seven, when they are released, that keeping them that long requires an awful lot of willpower.

LUXEMBOURG

Luxembourg's wines, from the banks of the Mosel, are of little other than local interest. They lack the body, the interest and the aging potential of the best of their neighbours further down the river in Germany, but are perfectly acceptable, with light, delicate fruit. Most are made from Müller–Thurgau, here called Rivaner, which accounts for half the area under vine. Other grapes grown are Elbling, Riesling, Auxerrois, Gewürztraminer and Pinot Gris, with the last two making some of the most interesting wines.

NORTH AFRICA

Forget all those jokes about Algerian Burgundy: the march of Islamic fundamentalism in North Africa means that the vineyard area is shrinking and output is falling. At this rate, any sort of Algerian wine could eventually be no more than a memory.

It wouldn't, it has to be said, be a particularly fond memory for most people. Algeria, Tunisia and Morocco did a great deal to beef up the weaker, weedier French wines in the years before such things became illegal, and independence from France in the fifties and sixties followed by the tightening up of EC rules in the seventies dealt all three countries a double blow.

The wines are still seen in Britain, however. Morocco makes some decent reds, like *Sidi Brahim*, made only from Cinsaut, and *Tarik*, a hot-climate blend of Cinsaut, Carignan and Grenache. Tunisia might have a name for its Muscats, if they were less generally oxidized, and Algeria, the biggest producer of the three in terms of quantity, can boast the Coteaux de Mascara, which makes heavy, rustic, rather coarse reds. All three countries have *appellation contrôlée* systems based on the French model. The term is *Appellation d'Origine Garantie* in Algeria and Morocco and *Appellation d'Origine Contrôlée* in Tunisia.

SWITZERLAND

Swiss wines may be labelled in French, German or Italian, but little is seen in Britain in any language. The most popular grape, the Chasselas, changes its name to Dorin in the Vaud, Perlan in Geneva and Neuchatel and Fendant in the Valais. Pinot Noir can be good, but like all Swiss wines (including some new releases of Chardonnay and, astonishingly, Syrah), it is light, clean, fruity and expensive.

TURKEY

Turkey's history of viticulture is rather more impressive than the wine itself. Although only three per cent of the total – huge – grape crop is made into wine, wine-making can be traced back some 4000 years – plenty of time in which to count the 1172 different grape varieties currently registered as being cultivated in the country.

It's hard positively to recommend Turkish wines or even any individual grape varieties, but *Buzbag* (red), *Villa Doluca* and *Doluca* (red and whites), *Hosbag* (red), *Villa Dona* (red and white) are brand names to consider.

ZIMBABWE

There is some wine made here, and some is even exported to Britain, under the name of *Marondera*. You could try it, just to prove to your friends that it exists.

PRICE GUIDES

Isuppose it could cross your mind that you don't need price guides – perish the thought, because if nobody wants a Price Guide I shall be back to doing pantomime at Northampton rep by next Christmas. But does that mean that you don't feel the need to know where to find the best price for a wine? That you don't want to find out what alternatives you can expect for the money you wish to spend? That you don't want to know if you're on to a super bargain? Surely not.

On expensive wines the price differences are often dramatic. On cheaper wines, the differences may be small but they're still worth knowing about. And our specially recommended wines may well be in limited distribution: it's of crucial importance to find out *where* the wines are stocked, as well as what the price differences are. By using these price guides judiciously, you should be able to drink *better* and more *cheaply* during the coming year.

● All prices are *per bottle inclusive of VAT*, unless otherwise stated. Remember that many merchants sell only by the case.

● Wines are listed in price bands and by vintage. Price bands run from the lowest to the highest. Vintages run from the most recent to the oldest. Within these categories the wines are listed in alphabetical order to help you find a particular wine more easily.

● Within the price bands, stockists are listed in brackets after each entry in ascending order of price. Occasionally, the same wine will fall into more than one price band, but before you get too agitated about variations in price, remember that wine warehouses, for example, often come out much cheaper because you have to buy by the case, they do not deliver, they do not have smart high street premises, and so on. Equally, there's no getting away from the fact that the price of a given wine sometimes varies wildly for no good reason.

● The claret prices are a special case. Specific prices are shown in ascending order by vintage. There *are* some dramatic price variations here – some are to do with keen pricing and the reverse; more often they will be because claret is now (for better or for worse) an investment medium and responsive to market pressures. A merchant buying wine *en primeur* in Bordeaux on Monday *afternoon* may pay 25 per cent more than the going rate that morning! Replacement stocks over the years will vary in cost and currency movements will also be a factor. So – for the sake of clarity – the prices we list were valid in the late spring/early summer of 1994.

● In the claret guide, all châteaux are listed alphabetically regardless of class. When a wine is quoted EC or IB, it means that the wine is offered on an *en primeur* basis (in Bordeaux or at the châteaux) or in bond (in the UK). All EC and IB prices are per dozen. The EC price simply includes the price of the wine in the bottle and excludes shipping, duties and taxes such as VAT. The EC price is usually payable when the wine is offered in the summer following the vintage.

The other costs (including VAT on both invoices) become payable when the wine is shipped. The *crus classés* and better *bourgeois* are shipped two years later, and the *petits châteaux* and the lesser *bourgeois* after a year. You should check the exact terms of sale with your merchant who will give you a projection of the final 'duty paid delivered' price at current rates of shipping, duty and VAT.

● Where merchants sell only by the case we have divided by 12 the VAT-inclusive price of a single case.

● When clubs (e.g. Les Amis du Vin) have both member and non-member prices we have used the *non-member* prices.

● Stars (★) denote wines that the editors consider particularly good value.

● To get the most out of the lists in the book, please remember that *Webster's* is a price GUIDE not a price LIST. An invaluable reference whenever you are ordering or buying wine, it is not meant to replace up-to-date merchants' lists. What it *does* do, however, is give you a unique opportunity to compare prices; to develop a sense of what you can reasonably expect to pay for any given wine; to spot a bargain; to work out exactly what you can afford – *and to find it*.

MERCHANT CODES

The following list of abbreviations enables you to identify the merchants from whose lists the wines in the price guides were selected. For more detailed information on each merchant, see the Merchant Directory on page 428.

AD	Adnams	CB	Corney & Barrow
AME	Amey's Wines	CHA	Châteaux Wines
AMI	Les Amis du Vin (also Cullen's)	CV	Celtic Vintner
ARM	John Armit Wines	DAV	Davisons
AS	Ashley Scott	DI	Direct Wine
ASD	ASDA	EL	Eldridge, Pope & Co
AUG	Augustus Barnett	EY	Philip Eyres
AUS	Australian Wine Centre	FA	Farr Vintners
AV	Averys	FIZ	Fine Wines of New Zealand
BAR	Barnes Wine Shop	GAL	Gallery Wines
BE	Bedford Fine Wines	GAU	Gauntleys of Nottingham
BEK	Berkmann Wine Cellars	GE	Gelston Castle Fine Wines
BER	Berry Bros & Rudd	GOE	Goedhuis & Co
BIB	Bibendum	GRE	Peter Green
BOD	Bordeaux Direct	HAL	Halves
BOR	Borg Castel	HA	John Harvey & Sons
BOT	Bottoms Up	HAC	Harcourt Fine Wine
BU	The Butlers Wine Cellar	HAH	Haynes Hanson & Clark
BUT	Bute Wines	HAW	Roger Harris Wines
BY	Anthony Byrne	HAY	Richard Harvey Wines
CAP	Cape Province Wines	HE	Douglas Henn-Macrae

HIC	Hicks & Don	SAI	Sainsbury
HIG	High Breck Vintners	SEC	Seckford Wines
HOG	J.E. Hogg	SO	Somerfield
KA	J.C. Karn & Son Ltd	SOM	Sommelier Wine Company
LAY	Lay & Wheeler	SUM	Summerlee Wines
LEA	Lea & Sandeman	TAN	Tanners
LO	London Wine	TES	Tesco
MAJ	Majestic Wine Warehouses	THR	Thresher
MAR	Marks & Spencer p.l.c.	TW	T. & W. Wines
MOR	Moreno Wines	UN	Unwins
MV	Morris & Verdin	VA	Valvona & Crolla
NA	The Nadder Wine Co Ltd	VIC	Victoria Wine
NI	James Nicholson	VIG	La Vigneronne
NO	The Nobody Inn	VIN	Vintage Wines
OD	Oddbins	WAI	Waitrose
PE	Thos. Peatling	WAT	Waterloo Wine Co
PEN	Penistone Court Wine Cellars	WCL	Winecellars
		WHI	Whitesides of Clitheroe
PIP	Christopher Piper Wines	WIC	Sunday Times Wine Club
PLA	Terry Platt	WIW	Wines of Westhorpe Ltd
RAE	Raeburn Fine Wines	WR	Wine Rack
RE	La Reserve España	WRI	Wright Wine Company
REI	Reid Wines	WS	Wine Society
RES	La Reserve	WW	Windrush Wines
ROB	Roberson	WY	Peter Wylie Fine Wines
SAF	Safeway	YAP	Yapp Brothers

RED BORDEAUX

d'Agassac *cru grand bourgeois exceptionnel Haut-Médoc*
1985 £8.45 (PE) £9.95 (GE)
1983 £11.69 (TW)
1982 £11.50 (GE) £11.85 (WHI)

Amiral-de-Beychevelle *St-Julien*
1988 £16.20 (WRI)

Andron-Blanquet *cru grand bourgeois exceptionnel St-Éstèphe*
1989 £10.90 (PIP)
1985 £10.70 (PIP)

l'Angélus *grand cru classé St-Émilion*
1990 £16.81 (BUT)
1989 £22.57 (BUT)
1985 £24.85 (PE)
1983 IB £130.00 (GOE)
1966 £28.20 (REI)

d'Angludet *cru bourgeois supérieur exceptionnel Margaux*
1992 £5.94 (HIC)
1992 EC £68.00 (SUM)
1991 £9.50 (BE)
1991 EC £77.00 (SUM)
1990 £11.99 (NI) £15.95 (VIG)
1990 EC £114.00 (SUM)
1989 £10.50 (AMI) £10.76 (BEK) £11.75 (CV) £11.75 (LAY) £12.95 (WS) £13.00 (HAY) £13.50 (PIP) £14.22 (TAN)
1989 magnum £26.00 (BE)
1988 £10.58 (GOE) £10.93 (EY) £11.75 (CV) £12.75 (BE) £12.95 (WS) £13.00 (HAY) £14.82 (TAN)
1987 £7.95 (PE) £9.70 (CV) £10.20 (BE)
1986 £14.30 (BE) £15.00 (BUT) £15.28 (CV)
1985 £14.30 (BE) £15.00 (GE)
1983 £17.95 (BAR)
1978 £14.60 (SOM) £17.63 (CV) £18.74 (BUT)

Anthonic *cru bourgeois supérieur Moulis*
1989 £10.68 (PEN)
1986 £11.03 (PLA)

Archambeau *Graves*
1990 £7.80 (WRI)

d'Arche *Graves*
1986 £9.00 (GOE)

d'Armailhac (was Mouton-Baronne-Philippe) *5ème cru classé Pauillac*
1990 £12.37 (BUT)
1989 £13.27 (BUT) £13.97 (NO) £13.99 (POR) £14.79 (PLA)
1988 £11.85 (GRE) £11.85 (SEC)
1986 £13.55 (PE) £15.24 (BUT)
1985 ★ £10.56 (PLA) £15.95 (RES) £16.00 (MV) £17.05 (ROB) £17.16 (TW)
1983 £14.95 (RES) £15.22 (PLA)
1982 £17.61 (PLA) £19.95 (RES)
1981 £17.50 (ROB)
1975 £14.39 (REI)
1962 £38.68 (FA)
1945 £160.00 (WY)
1941 £90.00 (WY)
1934 £70.00 (FA)
1929 £170.00 (WY)
1922 £130.00 (WY)

Arnauld *Haut-Médoc*
1987 £7.95 (GE)
1985 £8.95 (GE)
1982 £13.50 (PLA)

d'Arricaud *Graves*
1985 £6.99 (SEC)

l'Arrosée *grand cru classé St-Émilion*
1990 £20.00 (WS)
1989 £22.33 (GOE)
1988 £18.50 (GE)

Ausone *1er grand cru classé St-Émilion*
1990 £54.00 (AD) £59.97 (BUT)
1989 £61.51 (BUT)
1988 £60.99 (BUT)
1986 £47.14 (AV) £53.00 (AD)
1985 £49.93 (REI) £49.95 (AD) £57.00 (UN) £59.00 (ROB) £62.32 (BUT)
1983 £48.90 (UN) £52.88 (BEK) £55.00 (HAC)
1979 £70.00 (ROB)
1979 IB £495.00 (BIB)
1978 £62.50 (SOM)
1970 £88.13 (BIB)
1928 £275.00 (FA)

> *All châteaux are listed alphabetically regardless of class.*

Bahans-Haut-Brion *Graves*
1990 £12.95 (BU)
1989 £16.54 (BUT) £19.50 (WS)
1988 £14.95 (NI)
1986 £11.99 (NO)
1985 £23.51 (CB)

Batailley *5ème cru classé Pauillac*
1992 EC £70.00 (SUM)
1991 £11.95 (DI)
1991 EC £88.00 (SUM)
1990 £12.14 (HIG) £14.95 (DI)
1990 EC £114.00 (SUM)
1990 magnum £25.84 (HIG)
1989 £10.75 (BUT) £12.14 (HIG) £12.95 (SEC) £13.45 (BER) £14.75 (DI)
1989 magnum £25.45 (HIG)
1989 double magnum £62.64 (HIG)
1988 £9.75 (WS) £13.20 (BE)
1988 magnum £24.66 (HIG)
1988 double magnum £59.53 (HIG)
1986 £14.85 (DAV) £16.60 (DI)
1985 ★ £12.24 (GOE) £17.60 (BE) £18.95 (DI)
1983 £18.48 (BE)
1982 £24.95 (DI)
1982 IB £175.00 (BIB)
1975 £15.00 (WY) £18.00 (BU)
1974 £16.86 (BOR)
1970 £25.00 (WY) £25.07 (BUT) £27.50 (BU)
1966 £22.00 (WY) £30.00 (BU)
1961 £35.00 (BU) £59.00 (VIG)

Beau-Site *cru grand bourgeois exceptionnel St-Éstèphe*
1990 £8.42 (HIG) £10.30 (NI)
1989 £8.15 (BUT)
1988 £8.35 (WS)
1986 £8.95 (DAV)
1985 £12.10 (WRI)

Beaumont *cru grand bourgeois Haut-Médoc*
1991 £8.65 (HAC)
1990 £7.42 (GOE) £7.45 (SAI) £7.59 (WAT)
1989 £7.50 (WS) £7.91 (GOE) £7.95 (SEC) £7.99 (UN) £8.85 (GRE) £9.40 (WRI)
1988 £7.42 (GOE) £7.50 (HAY) £7.67 (LO) £7.99 (DAV) £8.26 (BE) £8.85 (GRE) £9.50 (WRI) £9.95 (RES)
1986 £9.95 (HAY) £10.99 (RE) £11.95 (WRI)

Beauséjour *1er grand cru classé St-Émilion*
1986 £10.85 (SEC)
1985 £11.95 (SEC) £19.34 (NO)

Belair *1er grand cru classé St-Émilion*
1989 £21.99 (BUT)
1988 £15.25 (LO)
1987 £13.33 (ARM) £19.95 (CB)
1986 £23.90 (CB)
1985 £20.95 (AD) £22.72 (BUT)
1983 £17.77 (NO)
1983 IB £160.00 (GOE)
1982 £18.95 (SOM) £20.04 (BUT)

Belgrave *5ème cru classé Haut-Médoc*
1989 £12.85 (NI) £13.95 (BAR)

Beychevelle *4ème cru classé St-Julien*
1990 IB £170.00 (FA)
1989 £20.56 (BUT) £26.61 (CB)
1988 ★ £14.75 (GRE) £17.15 (LO) £22.95 (DAV)
1986 £19.65 (PE) £22.50 (ROB) £22.50 (GAU)
1985 £18.27 (BY) £23.25 (GAL) £23.95 (AMI) £24.85 (PE) £27.75 (VIC)
1984 £19.50 (UN)
1983 £19.89 (WHI) £24.65 (AMI) £28.34 (AV)
1983 IB £150.00 (BIB)
1983 magnum IB £155.00 (GOE)
1982 £24.75 (VIC) £25.00 (WY) £25.91 (HIC) £26.45 (WHI) £28.45 (PE) £35.00 (RES) £35.25 (TW)
1982 IB £225.00 (BIB) £235.00 (GOE)
1981 £15.00 (WY) £18.50 (BU) £21.50 (GAL) £23.95 (BAR) £26.00 (ROB)
1981 IB £165.00 (WY)
1979 £27.50 (ROB)
1979 IB £165.00 (FA)
1978 £22.50 (BU) £25.00 (WY) £25.46 (FA) £35.00 (ROB)
1978 IB £245.00 (BIB)
1978 magnum £50.00 (WY)
1975 £38.25 (ROB)
1971 magnum £52.87 (REI)
1970 £49.95 (AD) £54.50 (ROB)
1970 IB £320.00 (FA)
1970 magnum £62.67 (FA)
1966 £40.00 (WY) £85.00 (ROB)
1966 IB £465.00 (WY)
1961 £80.00 (WY)
1959 £37.50 (BU) £100.00 (WY)

Blaignan *cru bourgeois Médoc*
1987 £7.95 (ROB)

le Bon-Pasteur *Pomerol*
1985 £22.05 (BUT)
1983 £19.50 (BE) £19.95 (RES)

Bourgneuf-Vayron *Pomerol*
1989 £14.10 (BUT)

Bouscaut *cru classé Pessac-Léognan*
1989 £11.99 (RAE)
1986 £9.95 (RAE)

Boyd-Cantenac *3ème cru classé Margaux*
1986 £14.40 (CV)
1982 £21.50 (ROB)
1982 IB £120.00 (BIB)
1970 £29.75 (HAC)
1967 £20.00 (VIG)

Branaire-Ducru *4ème cru classé St-Julien*
1989 £16.04 (BUT) £17.95 (GRE)
1989 IB £150.00 (FA)
1986 £18.90 (GAL)
1985 £17.52 (BUT) £18.50 (ROB) £19.95 (RES)
1983 £14.50 (AV) £15.95 (ROB) £16.96 (HOG) £17.84 (NI)
1982 £18.00 (WY)
1979 double magnum £88.13 (TW)
1978 £18.00 (WY) £21.40 (BEN)
1978 IB £150.00 (FA)
1975 £28.81 (AV)
1970 £22.00 (WY) £30.00 (RES)
1962 £29.50 (BU)
1961 £70.00 (GRE)

Brane-Cantenac *2ème cru classé Margaux*
1989 £16.58 (GOE) £17.99 (RAE)
1989 IB £175.00 (WY)
1988 £14.99 (RAE)
1985 £14.53 (BUT) £21.75 (VIC) £22.85 (WRI)
1982 £29.75 (GRE)
1982 IB £210.00 (BIB)
1979 £15.00 (WY) £15.67 (GOE)
1978 £16.50 (BU) £17.00 (WY) £17.62 (GOE)
1978 IB £265.00 (BIB)
1975 IB £195.00 (BIB)
1970 £23.00 (WY) £30.55 (TW)
1970 IB £240.00 (WY)
1966 £28.00 (WY) £40.00 (RES) £45.00 (VIG)
1961 £50.00 (WY)
1920 £130.00 (WY)

du Breuil *cru bourgeois supérieur Haut-Médoc*
1992 EC £49.50 (SUM)
1991 EC £58.00 (SUM)
1990 EC £68.00 (SUM)

Calon-Ségur *3ème cru classé St-Éstèphe*
1989 £14.60 (BE) £17.95 (ROB) £19.22 (AV) £24.50 (CB)
1988 £17.96 (BUT) £19.95 (BER) £19.95 (CB) £19.95 (NI)
1986 £20.50 (GAL)
1985 ★ £12.35 (BY) £17.94 (BUT) £18.50 (UN) £19.53 (AV) £23.95 (AMI) £25.00 (ROB)
1984 £15.00 (UN)
1983 £15.95 (ROB)
1982 £27.53 (NO)
1982 IB £225.00 (BIB)
1970 £29.00 (WY)
1966 £30.00 (WY)
1961 £53.00 (WY) £75.00 (ROB) £135.00 (RES)
1959 £99.00 (RES)
1945 £120.00 (WY)

de Camensac *5ème cru classé Haut-Médoc*
1990 £10.45 (WAT) £11.50 (SEC)
1988 ★ £9.67 (GOE)
1986 £11.60 (GAL)
1985 £13.35 (WRI) £14.95 (ROB)
1984 £9.50 (UN)
1983 £12.28 (PLA)
1975 £14.68 (PLA) £19.75 (ROB)
1970 £22.91 (REI) £29.50 (WRI)

Canon *1er grand cru classé St-Émilion*
1992 EC £62.00 (ARM)
1990 £9.58 (ARM) £21.68 (BUT)
1989 ★ £11.50 (SEC) £27.50 (AD) £29.85 (RAE) £30.00 (GOE) £30.63 (BUT) £30.69 (AV)
1988 £21.50 (HAY) £23.50 (RAE) £26.01 (BUT)
1987 £14.95 (RAE) £17.95 (SEC) £18.50 (RES)
1986 ★ £12.50 (ARM) £21.95 (RAE) £24.44 (BUT) £24.75 (CB)
1985 £28.00 (PIP) £28.49 (BUT) £35.00 (GAU)
1983 £29.09 (WHI)
1982 £45.88 (NO)
1979 £28.75 (ROB)
1959 £83.23 (FA)

Canon-la-Gaffelière *grand cru classé St-Émilion*
1989 £16.77 (BUT)
1986 £23.31 (BOR)
1961 £52.64 (TW)

Cantemerle 5ème cru classé Haut-Médoc
1989 £16.53 (BUT) £17.75 (LEA) £19.75 (ROB)
1988 £11.50 (SEC) £13.95 (ROB) £14.00 (GE)
1987 £8.99 (TES) £11.55 (PE)
1986 £15.65 (PE)
1985 £16.65 (PE) £18.95 (GRE) £19.50 (ROB)
1984 £14.80 (UN)
1983 £18.00 (HOG)
1982 £19.95 (AME) £20.52 (LO) £21.95 (BAR)
1982 IB £150.00 (BIB)
1981 £14.90 (HOG)
1979 £14.00 (WY)
1978 £15.00 (WY) £19.00 (HAC)
1978 IB £150.00 (WY)
1975 £19.73 (PLA) £27.50 (ROB)
1970 £21.54 (FA) £40.00 (ROB)
1966 £30.00 (WY) £41.89 (RE)

Cantenac-Brown 3ème cru classé
Margaux
1990 £13.41 (GOE)
1989 £16.50 (GOE)
1987 £12.57 (BY)
1983 £15.95 (ROB)
1982 £21.95 (ROB)
1970 £22.11 (BUT) £29.50 (ROB)

Carbonnieux cru classé Pessac-Léognan
1988 £10.33 (GOE)
1985 £14.85 (ROB)
1959 £60.00 (WY)
1957 £15.67 (FA)

de Cardaillan Graves
1985 £6.95 (DAV)

la Cardonne cru grand bourgeois Médoc
1991 £8.30 (HAC)
1989 £8.16 (HOG)
1987 £8.75 (ROB) £8.90 (PIP)

les Carmes-Haut-Brion Pessac-Léognan
1989 £15.95 (BUT)
1976 £13.22 (GOE)
1975 £17.62 (GOE)

Caronne-Ste-Gemme cru grand
bourgeois exceptionnel Haut-Médoc
1988 £7.75 (AMI) £8.22 (EL)
1986 £8.15 (WS) £8.46 (EL) £9.55 (NA) £9.69
   (AME) £10.58 (HA)
1985 £11.44 (BOR) £11.95 (BAR)
1983 £9.95 (BEN) £11.50 (BE)
1983 ½ bottle £5.95 (BU)
1982 £11.50 (GE)

**Carruades de Lafite (Moulin des
Carruades until 1987)** Pauillac
1990 £14.68 (HIG) £16.95 (DI)
1990 IB £125.00 (FA)
1989 £15.77 (BUT) £15.94 (LAY)
1989 IB £135.00 (FA)
1988 £17.90 (BUT) £17.99 (WR) £17.99 (BOT)
   £17.99 (THR) £19.80 (PIP) £21.24 (BY)
1986 £17.49 (BUT)
1985 £17.90 (BUT)
1984 £11.50 (ROB)
1981 £20.60 (WHI)
1980 £17.04 (TW)
1934 £140.00 (WY)

Castéra cru bourgeois Médoc
1985 £10.50 (GRE)

Certan-de-May Pomerol
1992 EC £190.00 (ARM)
1991 £16.00 (MV)
1990 IB £395.00 (FA)
1989 £37.53 (BUT) £37.78 (HAH)
1989 IB £250.00 (FA)
1988 £37.90 (GAU) £40.80 (BUT)
1987 £27.91 (CB)
1986 £42.95 (CB)
1986 IB £360.00 (GOE)
1985 £36.66 (GOE) £41.11 (BUT)
1985 IB £360.00 (FA) £360.00 (GOE)
1983 £33.25 (LAY)
1983 IB £240.00 (FA)

Certan-Giraud Pomerol
1989 £17.62 (BUT)
1985 £15.42 (ARM) £20.56 (REI)

Chasse-Spleen cru grand bourgeois
exceptionnel Moulis
1990 £14.95 (LAY)
1990 IB £160.00 (WY)
1989 £13.85 (NO) £14.52 (BUT) £14.65 (GRE)
   £16.31 (BY) £19.92 (BER)
1989 IB £155.00 (WY)
1988 £11.01 (NO) £11.95 (GRE) £14.74 (CHA)
   £16.86 (TAN)
1987 £11.46 (BY) £13.95 (ROB) £15.83 (TAN)
1986 £11.61 (BUT)
1986 magnum £24.25 (NO)
1985 £15.20 (BE) £19.75 (ROB)
1984 £10.95 (ROB) £16.50 (BY)
1983 £17.95 (BAR) £19.20 (AD) £19.42 (HA)
   £19.95 (RES)
1982 £16.80 (BUT) £18.90 (EY) £21.75 (PE)
1978 £27.95 (RES)

Chauvin *grand cru classé St-Émilion*
1990 £11.50 (GOE)
1989 £11.40 (HAM)
1988 £11.50 (RAE) £13.65 (WAT)
1986 £10.74 (BUT)
1982 £14.50 (BU)

Cheret-Pitres *Graves*
1990 £8.90 (CHA)
1989 £8.90 (CHA)

Cheval-Blanc *1er grand cru classé St-Émilion*
1992 EC £265.00 (ARM)
1989 £58.70 (BUT) £75.00 (ROB)
1989 IB £550.00 (FA)
1987 £28.95 (LO)
1986 £43.00 (AMI) £48.35 (CB)
1985 £44.06 (BEK) £47.50 (GOE) £50.00 (WY)
£55.06 (NO) £55.50 (PIP) £55.51 (BUT)
£55.70 (WHI) £64.99 (VIC) £65.00 (RES)
1985 IB £495.00 (BIB)
1984 £25.00 (WS) £38.00 (BER) £42.00 (UN)
1983 £49.90 (UN) £50.00 (WY) £55.00 (BER)
£65.85 (DAV) £75.00 (RES)
1983 IB £550.00 (FA)
1982 £82.59 (NO) £90.00 (BER) £115.00 (WY)
£140.00 (ROB)
1982 IB £1080.00 (FA) £1100.00 (BIB)
1981 £48.00 (BER) £51.08 (AV) £51.45 (NI)
£54.71 (VIN) £59.85 (DAV)
1979 £43.00 (WY) £50.00 (BE) £50.92 (FA)
£77.85 (DAV)
1978 £85.00 (ROB)
1975 £79.50 (DAV)
1975 IB £700.00 (FA)
1975 magnum £137.08 (FA)
1970 £78.00 (FA) £91.77 (NO) £125.00 (DAV)
£135.00 (ROB)
1970 IB £995.00 (BIB)
1970 magnum £160.00 (FA)
1966 IB £1100.00 (FA)
1959 £180.00 (WY)
1955 £210.00 (RES)
1953 £135.00 (WY)
1953 magnum £490.00 (WY)
1950 ½ bottle £30.00 (WY)
1949 £180.00 (WY) £367.19 (FA)
1949 ½ bottle £115.00 (WY)
1947 £185.00 (WY)
1947 IB £11,000.00 (FA)
1945 £375.00 (WY)
1943 £140.00 (WY)
1934 £150.00 (FA)
1929 magnum £1077.08 (FA)

Cissac *cru grand bourgeois exceptionnel Haut-Médoc*
1991 EC £74.50 (SUM)
1990 £9.68 (TAN) £9.95 (NI) £12.31 (AV)
1990 EC £84.00 (SUM) £86.35 (HAH)
1989 £8.95 (HAY) £11.55 (TAN) £11.83 (CB)
1988 £10.87 (EL) £11.30 (AV) £11.35 (WS)
£11.55 (TAN)
1987 £7.65 (PE) £9.75 (TAN) £9.95 (DI)
1986 £10.75 (BUT) £12.16 (HA) £13.35 (WRI)
1985 £9.95 (NI) £10.25 (PE) £11.53 (TAN)
£11.93 (EL) £11.99 (OD) £12.90 (WRI)
£12.95 (DI) £13.50 (RES)
1983 £12.34 (EL) £12.41 (HIC) £12.99 (HIG)
£13.20 (NI) £13.50 (DI) £16.50 (BE)
1982 £13.85 (SOM) £18.95 (BIB)
1981 £13.59 (NI) £15.50 (ROB)
1978 £16.61 (BUT)
1975 £15.86 (REI) £16.74 (EL)
1971 £12.75 (BU)
1970 £14.95 (BU) £20.25 (BUT) £21.56 (EL)
1969 £8.95 (BU)

Citran *cru grand bourgeois exceptionnel Haut-Médoc*
1988 £9.67 (BEK) £11.90 (PIP)
1987 £10.89 (SO)

Clarke *cru bourgeois Listrac*
1989 £10.79 (NI)
1988 £11.63 (PEN)
1985 £14.15 (PE)

Clerc-Milon *5ème cru classé Pauillac*
1989 £15.75 (BUT)
1987 £11.95 (RES) £13.33 (ARM)
1986 £18.04 (BUT)
1985 £15.95 (RES) £16.00 (GE) £17.57 (PLA)
£17.95 (LAY)
1983 £14.75 (ROB) £15.50 (WS)
1978 £26.35 (NA)
1970 £25.26 (REI)

Clinet *Pomerol*
1990 £33.00 (WY)
1990 IB £395.00 (WY)
1989 IB £780.00 (FA)
1982 £23.00 (WY)

> *Stars (★) indicate wines
> selected by the editors as
> particularly good value
> in their class.*

Clos Beauregard *Pomerol*
1982 £16.70 (BUT)

Clos des Jacobins *grand cru classé St-
Émilion*
1989 £19.56 (BUT)
1985 £17.95 (ROB) £20.75 (PE)

Clos du Marquis *St-Julien*
1990 £10.99 (OD) £11.15 (BUT)
   £11.17 (GOE)
1989 £12.95 (RAE)
1988 £10.99 (RAE) £11.79 (BUT) £14.69 (WR)
   £14.69 (BOT) £14.69 (THR) £17.60 (PIP)
1986 £12.42 (GOE) £21.25 (VIC)
1985 £11.89 (AV) £20.25 (VIC)
1984 £9.20 (VIC) £9.85 (ROB) £14.72 (BY)
1982 £22.80 (BEN)
1982 IB £160.00 (FA)

Clos Fourtet *1er grand cru classé St-
Émilion*
1989 £25.65 (BER)
1985 £20.48 (SUM) £22.50 (BER) £22.50 (PIP)
1982 £22.95 (RE)
1961 £60.00 (RES)
1949 £105.00 (WY)
1945 £130.00 (WY)

la Clotte *grand cru classé St-Émilion*
1989 £17.68 (CB) £20.62 (BUT)
1988 £12.63 (CB)
1986 £14.39 (CB)

Connétable Talbot *St-Julien*
1987 £10.99 (PE)
1985 £11.45 (PE)
1983 £11.55 (PE)

la Conseillante *Pomerol*
1990 IB £420.00 (FA)
1989 £42.44 (AV) £45.57 (BUT)
1988 £44.79 (AV)
1987 £20.95 (WHI)
1986 £31.48 (AV)
1985 £26.67 (GOE) £37.50 (AMI) £39.06 (PEN)
1985 IB £261.00 (GOE)
1984 £20.35 (AV)
1983 IB £195.00 (FA)
1982 IB £420.00 (FA) £450.00 (BIB)
1981 £35.00 (RES)
1981 IB £220.00 (FA)
1978 £22.90 (BUT)
1971 IB £290.00 (FA)
1970 £52.87 (REI)
1959 IB £1300.00 (FA)

Corbin *grand cru classé St-Émilion*
1989 £10.79 (BUT)
1985 £13.75 (ARM)

Cormeil-Figeac *grand cru St-Émilion*
1989 £8.65 (BUT) £9.99 (MAJ)

Cos d'Estournel *2ème cru classé St-
Éstèphe*
1991 IB £150.00 (GOE)
1990 £25.00 (WY) £25.46 (HIG) £28.58 (AV)
1990 IB £210.00 (FA) £260.00 (WY)
1990 magnum £54.83 (HIG)
1989 £21.95 (BE) £27.50 (BUT) £28.34 (AV)
   £32.00 (BER) £35.96 (CB)
1989 IB £220.00 (BIB) £260.00 (WY)
1988 £22.87 (BUT) £24.83 (GOE)
1987 £19.95 (RES)

1986 £22.15 (PE) £23.68 (BUT) £25.26 (TAN) £26.00 (BER) £31.90 (GAU)
1986 IB £260.00 (FA)
1985 £32.50 (AMI) £35.00 (WY)
1984 £13.75 (ROB) £18.20 (UN)
1983 £20.56 (GOE) £21.68 (BEK) £25.33 (HA) £26.00 (BER) £27.50 (AMI) £29.80 (PIP)
1982 £36.81 (NO) £48.47 (FA)
1982 IB £425.00 (GOE)
1982 double magnum £146.90 (NO)
1978 £27.50 (BU)
1975 £29.50 (BU)
1975 IB £220.00 (FA) £225.00 (BIB)
1970 £38.00 (WY) £39.17 (FA) £50.00 (OD) £50.04 (BUT) £50.85 (BEN) £65.00 (DI)
1966 £41.12 (FA)
1962 £58.00 (WY) £90.00 (RES)
1959 £115.00 (WY)
1955 £50.00 (VIG)

Cos Labory 5ème cru classé St-Éstèphe
1990 £15.94 (LAY)
1986 £9.65 (PE) £13.95 (ROB) £14.60 (PIP)
1985 £12.55 (PE) £16.06 (NO)
1985 magnum £33.60 (HAM)
1970 £19.50 (BE)

Coufran cru grand bourgeois Haut-Médoc
1990 £8.94 (BEK) £11.25 (GRE)

Couvent-des-Jacobins grand cru classé St-Émilion
1986 £13.65 (PE) £16.50 (PIP)

le Crock cru grand bourgeois exceptionnel St-Éstèphe
1990 £10.00 (GOE) £10.50 (GAU)
1989 £9.95 (RAE) £10.95 (BER)
1985 £9.45 (PE)

la Croix-de-Gay Pomerol
1990 £14.40 (BUT)
1989 £13.00 (BE) £15.52 (BUT)
1985 £15.95 (ROB)

la Croix-de-Pez St-Éstèphe
1989 £8.50 (BU)
1986 £10.76 (HA)

la Croix-du-Casse Pomerol
1989 £12.58 (BEK)

Croizet-Bages 5ème cru classé Pauillac
1970 £17.05 (BUT) £20.00 (BU)
1961 £75.00 (ROB)

Curé-Bon-la-Madeleine grand cru classé St-Émilion
1988 £10.75 (BU)

la Dame de Montrose St-Éstèphe
1990 £14.08 (GOE)
1989 £11.26 (BUT) £15.40 (PIP)
1985 £18.35 (BUT)

Dauzac 5ème cru classé Margaux
1988 £15.50 (WRI)

Desmirail 3ème cru classé Margaux
1989 £12.99 (RAE) £14.10 (HIG)
1988 £11.99 (RAE)
1981 £16.00 (WRI)

Deyrem-Valentin cru bourgeois Margaux
1989 £9.45 (HAM)
1988 £8.67 (EY)

Domaine de Chevalier cru classé Pessac-Léognan
1992 EC £123.00 (RAE)
1991 £16.99 (RAE)
1990 EC £185.00 (RAE)
1989 £27.75 (AD) £28.95 (RAE) £29.95 (BUT) £30.25 (GOE) £36.25 (CB)
1986 £23.63 (BUT)
1985 £23.31 (NO) £28.00 (BER) £33.25 (WHI)
1985 IB £185.00 (FA)
1984 £17.00 (WS) £18.95 (RAE)
1983 £20.56 (BEK) £21.60 (BE) £23.50 (CV) £24.00 (GE) £24.49 (REI) £27.50 (AD) £33.43 (CB)
1983 IB £175.00 (FA) £200.00 (GOE)
1982 £25.00 (WS) £27.53 (NO) £32.00 (BE) £38.90 (BUT) £39.95 (AD)
1982 IB £220.00 (FA) £227.00 (GOE)
1979 IB £195.00 (FA)
1978 £24.50 (HAC) £30.34 (BUT) £33.00 (WY)
1975 £25.21 (EY) £35.00 (RES)
1970 £45.00 (RES)
1970 IB £520.00 (FA)
1966 £50.00 (RES)

> *EC (ex-cellar) price per dozen, excl shipping, duty and VAT. IB (in bond) price per dozen, excl duty and VAT. All other prices, per bottle incl VAT.*

Domaine de l'Eglise *Pomerol*
1992 EC £81.00 (SUM)
1991 EC £106.00 (SUM)
1990 £13.70 (HIG) £16.50 (DI)
1990 EC £140.00 (SUM)
1989 £14.10 (HIG) £15.45 (BER) £16.71 (BUT)
  £16.95 (DI)
1988 £13.51 (HIG)
1986 £15.85 (DAV)
1985 £15.35 (WS)

Domaine la Grave *Graves*
1990 £5.67 (GOE) £6.25 (GE) £8.99 (HIG)
1989 £8.16 (GOE) £8.42 (HIG)
1986 £8.81 (TW)

la Dominique *grand cru classé St-Émilion*
1989 £17.77 (BUT) £19.22 (AV)
1986 £16.50 (BER) £17.95 (ROB)
1985 £14.95 (AMI) £17.42 (BUT)

Ducluzeau *cru bourgeois Listrac*
1988 £9.25 (AD) £9.58 (ARM)

Ducru-Beaucaillou *2ème cru classé St-Julien*
1990 £25.46 (HIG) £29.00 (AV)
1990 IB £195.00 (BIB) £235.00 (WY)
1990 magnum £54.83 (HIG)
1989 £23.45 (BE) £29.67 (BUT) £29.85 (RAE)
  £34.65 (BER) £39.42 (CB)
1989 IB £245.00 (BIB) £255.00 (WY)
1988 £21.50 (RAE) £23.50 (HAY) £24.13 (BUT)
  £26.44 (EL) £26.95 (LAY) £31.00 (BER)
1987 £19.95 (RES)
1986 £24.60 (BUT) £24.99 (PE) £29.00 (BER)
1986 IB £243.00 (BIB) £250.00 (GOE)
1985 £23.33 (GOE) £29.95 (BER) £29.99 (OD)
  £30.84 (BUT) £30.95 (PE) £31.50 (ROB)
1985 IB £225.00 (FA)
1984 £14.95 (SEC) £18.99 (PE) £19.60 (WS)
1983 £20.56 (BEK) £21.00 (SEC) £23.65 (PIP)
  £24.41 (BUT) £24.69 (VIC) £26.50 (RES)
  £26.50 (LAY) £27.10 (GAU) £27.95 (BAR)
  £29.09 (WHI) £29.20 (CB) £29.50 (BER)

1983 IB £210.00 (GOE)
1982 £46.25 (PE) £48.75 (GRE) £54.83 (NO)
  £54.95 (BEN)
1982 IB £395.00 (FA) £450.00 (GOE)
1982 double magnum £275.00 (WY)
1981 £28.95 (DAV) £29.67 (SUM) £39.95 (AMI)
1979 £29.95 (PE)
1979 magnum IB £190.00 (FA)
1978 £27.00 (BU) £36.05 (SUM) £38.95 (LAY)
1978 IB £300.00 (FA) £350.00 (BIB)
1976 £33.78 (TAN)
1975 £25.00 (WY) £27.00 (BU) £31.28 (AV)
  £40.00 (WS) £43.00 (DI) £45.00 (ROB)
  £45.00 (GRE)
1975 IB £245.00 (FA)
1975 jeroboam £350.00 (DI)
1970 £37.50 (BU) £56.80 (FA) £63.15 (BEN)
  £63.52 (TAN) £69.95 (AD) £75.00 (RES)
  £79.80 (NI)
1966 £53.85 (FA)
1961 £95.00 (BU) £105.75 (BIB) £195.00 (RES)
1961 IB £1450.00 (FA)
1943 £125.00 (ROB)
1924 £125.00 (WY)

Duhart-Milon-Rothschild *4ème cru classé Pauillac*
1990 £13.50 (BE) £14.95 (LAY)
1989 £15.50 (LAY) £17.12 (BUT) £20.30 (CB)
1987 £11.75 (ROB)
1986 £13.50 (SEC) £16.24 (BUT) £21.02 (PEN)
1985 £17.95 (ROB) £18.72 (PIP)
1983 £15.00 (GE)
1982 £19.50 (ROB)

Durfort-Vivens *2ème cru classé Margaux*
1985 £17.95 (ROB)
1978 £16.95 (RAE)

l'Église-Clinet *Pomerol*
1989 £22.60 (BUT)
1988 £19.00 (GE)

l'Enclos *Pomerol*
1990 £13.79 (WAT)
1989 £13.44 (BOR)
1988 £12.80 (GAL)
1986 £15.28 (CV) £15.75 (PIP)
1985 £17.75 (BUT)
1982 £20.31 (BUT)

l'Ermitage de Chasse-Spleen *Haut-Médoc*
1990 £11.40 (PIP)
1989 £7.70 (PEN)

l'Évangile *Pomerol*
1990 IB £420.00 (FA)
1987 £19.98 (CB)
1986 £30.00 (ROB)
1985 £40.84 (BUT)
1984 £20.03 (CB)
1983 IB £280.00 (FA)
1967 £35.00 (VIG)

Feytit-Clinet *Pomerol*
1990 £12.55 (TAN) £15.65 (AD)
1989 £17.80 (CB)
1987 £11.34 (EL)
1986 £14.20 (AD)
1985 £16.75 (AD)
1983 £16.00 (WS)
1959 £40.00 (ROB)

Les Fiefs-de-Lagrange *St-Julien*
1990 £11.17 (ARM)
1988 £10.69 (HOG) £11.00 (WS)
1985 £18.35 (BUT)

de Fieuzal *cru classé Pessac-Léognan*
1990 £14.16 (GOE)
1989 £16.68 (BUT) £16.71 (HAH) £18.96
  (BER)
1988 £12.99 (NI) £14.75 (BER)
1988 IB £120.00 (GOE)
1987 £9.15 (PE)
1986 £13.65 (PE) £16.70 (PIP)
1986 IB £120.00 (GOE)
1985 £14.15 (PE) £15.86 (TAN) £16.41 (BUT)
  £17.03 (REI) £17.95 (RES) £17.99 (NI)
  £18.10 (AD)
1983 £14.50 (WS) £15.95 (ROB) £16.10 (AD)
1982 £21.75 (PE)

Figeac *1er grand cru classé St-Émilion*
1990 IB £295.00 (BIB)
1989 £27.67 (BUT) £29.05 (AV)
1988 £24.08 (AV)
1987 £19.50 (RES)
1986 £27.56 (BUT) £27.70 (GAL)
1985 £28.93 (AV) £30.16 (BY) £30.29 (VIC)
  £30.50 (UN) £32.77 (BUT)
1985 IB £250.00 (BIB)
1984 £17.27 (AV)
1984 IB £155.00 (WY)
1983 £18.60 (GOE) £24.90 (UN) £32.00 (ROB)
  £35.00 (WS) £35.82 (HA) £37.69 (VIC)
1981 £35.00 (VIG) £36.71 (TW)
1976 £27.91 (FA)
1970 £56.80 (FA)
1959 £185.00 (RES)

la Fleur-Pétrus *Pomerol*
1992 IB £210.00 (CB)
1989 £41.65 (BUT)
1988 £28.08 (TAN) £32.98 (BUT)
1986 £39.50 (ROB) £41.19 (CB)
1985 £40.80 (BUT)
1970 £56.80 (FA)
1966 £65.00 (FA)
1947 £225.00 (ROB)

Fombrauge *grand cru St-Émilion*
1988 £8.24 (BOR) £10.65 (BER)
1986 £13.95 (BER)
1985 £13.23 (BUT)
1961 £55.00 (ROB)

Fonbadet *cru bourgeois supérieur*
Pauillac
1983 £12.50 (HOG)

Fonréaud *cru bourgeois Listrac*
1990 £8.19 (AV)
1989 £8.45 (NA)
1982 £11.95 (ROB)

Fonroque *grand cru classé St-Émilion*
1990 £12.00 (ARM)
1989 £14.58 (ARM) £15.80 (AV) £16.95 (CB)
1988 £12.20 (HA) £12.85 (CB)
1986 £12.50 (ARM) £13.92 (CB)
1983 £14.10 (CV)
1982 £17.21 (BUT)
1978 £10.87 (PLA)

les Forts-de-Latour *Pauillac*
1991 EC £120.00 (RAE)
1990 £17.92 (BUT) £22.95 (LAY)
1990 IB £190.00 (FA)
1986 £17.51 (HA)
1985 £27.10 (AD) £28.99 (TES) £29.95 (AMI)
1983 £19.65 (WHI) £23.50 (PEN)
1979 £21.10 (PIP)
1978 £28.35 (HA) £32.00 (AD) £36.25 (VIC)
1976 £22.50 (BU)
1975 £27.00 (HAM)
1975 IB £245.00 (FA)
1970 £45.23 (REI)
1967 £35.00 (VIG)

Fourcas-Dupré *cru grand bourgeois*
exceptionnel Listrac
1988 £10.86 (PIP) £11.70 (DI) £11.95 (BEN)
1986 £9.50 (GE)
1985 £10.40 (PIP)
1982 £17.50 (ROB)

Fourcas-Hosten *cru grand bourgeois exceptionnel Listrac*
1990 £8.75 (DI)
1989 £9.98 (BER)
1988 £9.00 (HIG)
1985 £11.95 (DI) £12.50 (ROB)
1983 £10.75 (BU)
1982 £18.85 (AV)
1949 £76.37 (REI)

Fourney *grand cru St-Émilion*
1988 £9.75 (NI)

Franc-Mayne *grand cru classé St-Émilion*
1987 £11.40 (BY)
1986 £10.26 (HOG)
1984 £9.13 (BY)
1983 £12.22 (BY)

de France *Pessac-Léognan*
1989 £7.99 (OD) £10.95 (LEA)

la Gaffelière *1er grand cru classé St-Émilion*
1975 £28.02 (REI)
1970 £30.00 (HOG)

la Garde *Pessac-Léognan*
1989 £8.03 (BEK)
1988 £7.95 (SEC)

le Gay *Pomerol*
1992 EC £105.00 (ARM)
1989 £23.45 (BUT)
1985 £18.00 (WY) £20.93 (BUT)
1983 £13.22 (GOE) £15.39 (BY)
1971 £44.00 (WY)
1970 £37.60 (TW)

Gazin *Pomerol*
1989 £19.36 (BUT) £20.98 (HAH) £25.91 (CB)
1988 £28.60 (CB)
1987 £13.48 (BY)
1983 £17.25 (AMI)
1981 magnum £37.50 (ROB)
1975 £16.16 (FA)
1955 £37.50 (BU)

> Stars (★) indicate wines
> selected by the editors as
> particularly good value
> in their class.

Giscours *3ème cru classé Margaux*
1989 £13.30 (BE) £17.95 (ROB)
1988 £17.13 (HIG)
1987 £14.95 (RES)
1986 £21.96 (PEN)
1985 magnum £41.50 (ROB)
1983 £21.10 (GAL)
1982 £22.20 (GAL)
1978 £40.00 (ROB)
1975 £25.21 (EY)
1975 IB £285.00 (GOE)
1973 £17.53 (BOR)
1970 £39.17 (GOE) £41.00 (WY)
£55.00 (ROB)
1970 magnum £68.00 (WY)
1966 £35.00 (WY)
1964 £49.95 (RES)
1961 £64.03 (REI) £65.00 (WY)
1959 £85.00 (WY)

du Glana *cru grand bourgeois exceptionnel St-Julien*
1988 £10.50 (BER)
1986 £12.25 (BER)
1975 £12.33 (PLA)

Gloria *cru bourgeois St-Julien*
1990 £11.99 (BUT) £12.96 (BEK)
£14.85 (CHA)
1989 £11.75 (BE) £14.38 (AV) £14.75 (PEN)
£16.78 (BER)
1988 £15.10 (BER) £17.18 (PIP)
1987 £12.95 (AMI)
1986 £11.55 (PE) £13.99 (MAJ)
£17.35 (NI)
1985 £20.00 (VIG)
1983 £17.20 (GAL)
£19.58 (BUT)
1982 £19.75 (BE) £25.13 (AV)
1970 £27.75 (ROB)

Grand-Corbin *grand cru classé St-Émilion*
1989 £11.66 (GOE)

Grand-Mayne *grand cru classé St-Émilion*
1990 £11.99 (OD)
1989 £12.50 (SEC) £12.69 (BUT)
1986 £13.82 (BEK)
1985 £13.95 (WS)

Grand-Pontet *grand cru classé St-Émilion*
1988 £10.67 (GOE)

Grand-Puy-Ducasse *5ème cru classé*
Pauillac
1990 £11.95 (SEC) £12.50 (DI)
1989 £11.50 (DI) £12.91 (GOE) £12.95 (GRE)
£14.39 (CB) £15.70 (WRI)
1988 £10.52 (PLA)
1985 £15.65 (PE) £16.75 (GRE) £17.50 (ROB)
1955 £37.50 (BU)
1948 £85.00 (WY)

Grand-Puy-Lacoste *5ème cru classé*
Pauillac
1990 £17.95 (LAY)
1989 £16.89 (BUT) £17.99 (RAE)
1988 £14.99 (RAE) £17.33 (GOE) £19.55 (DAV)
1987 £12.00 (WAI)
1986 £17.26 (BUT) £18.25 (LAY) £18.95 (AMI)
£19.25 (ROB)
1986 IB £140.00 (GOE)
1985 £19.41 (TAN) £20.95 (AD) £21.26 (BUT)
£22.75 (PE) £22.95 (AMI) £24.75 (WHI)
1984 £12.55 (PE) £17.00 (UN)
1983 £16.63 (REI) £21.00 (LO) £27.70 (BUT)
1982 £30.35 (WHI) £31.50 (LAY) £33.95 (AMI)
1981 £17.32 (BUT) £18.14 (HIC)
1978 £24.00 (GE) £24.95 (BAR) £25.95 (DI)
£26.97 (TAN) £29.00 (AD)
1975 £22.91 (PLA)
1975 IB £195.00 (BIB)
1970 £32.21 (TAN) £50.00 (RES)

la Grave-Trigant-de-Boisset *Pomerol*
1992 IB £145.00 (CB)
1989 £20.61 (CB) £22.72 (BUT)
1988 £15.35 (CB)
1986 £17.27 (CB)
1975 £23.50 (FA)

Graveyron *Graves*
1989 £5.92 (PEN)

Graviers d' Elliés *grand cru St-Émilion*
1983 £11.75 (ROB)

Gressier-Grand-Poujeaux *cru bourgeois*
supérieur Moulis
1988 £10.98 (NI)
1985 £10.25 (PE) £14.50 (ROB)
1981 £7.95 (GE)
1979 £12.15 (ROB)
1970 £24.27 (BUT)

Greysac *cru grand bourgeois Médoc*
1989 £6.08 (HOG) £6.95 (POR) £8.95 (ROB)
1987 £7.32 (BUT)
1985 £8.25 (PE)

Gros-Caillou *St-Éstèphe*
1989 £7.15 (BUT)

Gruaud-Larose *2ème cru classé St-Julien*
1989 £23.00 (WS) £24.08 (GOE) £26.23 (BUT)
1988 £22.39 (BUT) £23.05 (AV) £25.00 (PE)
1987 £12.49 (OD) £15.65 (PE)
1987 ½ bottle £5.85 (SEC)
1986 £17.50 (SEC) £20.00 (HAY) £23.40 (BEN)
£24.85 (PE) £25.50 (RES) £26.35 (WHI)
1986 IB £165.00 (FA)
1986 ½ bottle £14.95 (BEN)
1986 ½ bottle IB £165.00 (FA)
1985 £13.95 (DAV) £16.00 (WY) £18.99 (NI)
£20.12 (BUT) £22.05 (LO) £23.95 (AMI)
1985 IB £150.00 (FA)
1985 ½ bottle IB £155.00 (FA)
1985 double magnum IB £185.00 (FA)
1984 £14.65 (PE) £18.00 (UN)
1984 double magnum £85.00 (WY)
1983 £18.00 (WY) £18.50 (GE) £18.98 (HOG)
£19.50 (GRE) £20.95 (AME) £21.00 (LO)
£21.95 (BAR) £22.75 (PE) £22.80 (BEN)
£23.55 (HA) £23.55 (HA) £25.80 (PIP)
1983 IB £155.00 (FA) £160.00 (GOE)
1983 ½ bottle £8.00 (WY) £11.70 (BEN)
1983 ½ bottle IB £155.00 (FA)
1983 magnum £42.00 (LO) £45.60 (BEN)
1983 magnum IB £155.00 (FA)
1983 double magnum £75.00 (WY)
1983 double magnum IB £160.00 (FA)
1982 £27.85 (PE) £30.35 (GOE) £35.00 (WY)
£37.50 (ROB) £39.50 (LAY)
1982 IB £345.00 (BIB)
1981 £20.75 (PE) £23.00 (WS)
1979 £27.85 (PE)
1979 magnum £49.74 (PLA)
1978 £28.95 (PE) £31.50 (LAY) £34.50 (RES)
1978 jeroboam £135.00 (WY)
1976 £17.00 (WY) £27.03 (PEN)
1975 £25.26 (REI) £32.12 (NO)
1973 £13.59 (BOR)

1971 £26.43 (REI)
1970 £30.00 (BU) £31.33 (GOE) £44.95 (AMI)
1966 £40.00 (WY) £60.00 (ROB) £60.00 (WHI)
1966 magnum £100.00 (WY)
1962 IB £495.00 (FA)
1955 £90.00 (WY)
1953 IB £1350.00 (FA)
1947 ½ bottle £103.40 (TW)
1934 £110.00 (ROB)
1920 £155.00 (WY)
1920 magnum £390.00 (WY)
1916 £149.22 (TW)

Guillot *Pomerol*
1986 £14.95 (HIC)
1985 £12.50 (GE)
1983 £12.50 (GE)
1981 £11.00 (GE)

la Gurgue *cru bourgeois supérieur Margaux*
1989 £11.50 (ROB) £13.20 (BUT)
1988 £11.00 (GE)
1987 £9.11 (PLA)

Hanteillan *cru grand bourgeois Haut-Médoc*
1990 £8.50 (PIP)
1988 £8.50 (WS)
1987 £15.65 (PE)
1986 £9.99 (WHI)

Haut-Bages-Avérous *cru bourgeois Pauillac*
1989 £12.59 (BUT) £15.20 (BER)
1988 £12.36 (HA) £14.99 (BOT) £14.99 (WR) £14.99 (THR) £17.78 (BY)
1987 £13.85 (BY)
1984 £12.43 (BY)
1983 £13.50 (ROB)
1981 £15.46 (PEN)

Haut-Bages-Libéral *5ème cru classé Pauillac*
1990 £10.21 (BUT)
1989 £13.85 (GRE)
1988 £13.99 (TAN) £15.80 (GAL)
1987 £9.34 (PLA)
1986 £11.30 (BUT) £13.00 (GE)
1983 £15.84 (AV) £19.50 (WRI)
1979 £15.80 (PLA)

Haut-Bailly *cru classé Pessac-Léognan*
1989 £14.70 (NO) £18.94 (AV)
1988 £12.95 (RAE) £14.50 (HAY) £15.33 (GOE)

1986 £14.65 (PE)
1985 £18.98 (BUT)
1984 £15.31 (BY)
1982 £24.10 (AD) £26.50 (GRE)
1981 £15.00 (GE) £21.50 (ROB)

Haut-Batailley *5ème cru classé Pauillac*
1989 £14.00 (MV) £14.06 (BUT)
1989 IB £95.00 (WY)
1988 £13.83 (GOE)
1987 £15.50 (ROB)
1986 £11.95 (BUT) £13.50 (HOG)
1985 £11.75 (GOE) £13.59 (SEC) £14.24 (AV)
1984 £10.90 (UN)
1983 £15.60 (BE)
1983 magnum IB £145.00 (BIB)
1982 £19.09 (BIB) £21.25 (EY)
1979 magnum £26.00 (WY)
1978 £14.69 (FA)
1970 £28.00 (GE) £28.95 (ROB)

Haut-Brion *1er cru classé Pessac-Léognan*
1990 £45.12 (BUT) £47.99 (OD)
1990 IB £480.00 (FA) £495.00 (BIB)
1989 £65.10 (BUT) £88.27 (AV)
1989 IB £750.00 (FA)
1988 £47.29 (VIC)
1987 £29.99 (OD)
1986 £42.38 (BUT) £43.87 (CB) £45.00 (PE)
1985 £43.00 (SEC) £43.83 (BY) £49.50 (PIP) £51.86 (BUT) £53.60 (BE) £56.99 (OD) £58.30 (UN) £64.69 (VIC) £65.15 (PE)
1984 £29.99 (SEC) £38.50 (UN)
1983 £40.00 (HOG) £47.15 (PE) £49.00 (BER)
1982 £58.75 (REI) £60.00 (WY) £64.62 (FA) £66.08 (BUT) £69.99 (OD) £72.00 (BER) £75.00 (ROB) £91.69 (VIC) £99.88 (PEN)
1982 IB £650.00 (FA) £650.00 (BIB)
1981 £36.43 (BEK) £42.70 (PIP) £46.50 (BAR)
1981 IB £350.00 (FA)
1980 £25.75 (SEC)
1979 £75.00 (ROB)
1978 £50.86 (EY) £59.39 (BUT) £92.00 (ROB)
1978 IB £550.00 (FA) £585.00 (BIB)
1976 £47.98 (FA) £56.00 (BER)
1976 magnum £90.08 (FA)
1975 £60.00 (TAN)
1975 IB £540.00 (FA)
1972 £29.50 (BU)
1971 £58.00 (BER)
1971 IB £500.00 (FA)
1970 £49.00 (NI) £68.54 (FA) £75.00 (BU) £76.00 (WY) £110.00 (ROB)
1970 IB £680.00 (FA)
1970 double magnum £295.00 (WY)

1969 £35.63 (BUT)
1967 £59.00 (VIG)
1966 £83.00 (WY) £85.00 (BU) £89.85 (BUT)
1966 IB £950.00 (FA)
1964 £80.00 (GE) £120.00 (RES)
1964 IB £750.00 (FA)
1962 £120.00 (RES)
1961 £250.00 (FA)
1961 magnum £685.42 (FA)
1960 £59.00 (VIG)
1959 £150.00 (RES)
1955 £195.00 (BUT)
1949 £170.00 (WY) £244.79 (FA)
1949 magnum £485.00 (WY)
1948 £120.00 (WY)
1947 £140.00 (WY)
1947 IB £1850.00 (FA)
1937 £100.00 (FA)
1934 £130.00 (FA)
1929 £265.00 (WY) £470.00 (REI)
1928 £320.00 (WY) £395.00 (ROB)
1926 £310.00 (WY)
1924 £365.00 (WY)

Haut-Gardère *Pessac-Léognan*
1989 £8.07 (BUT)
1986 £5.95 (WAT)

Haut-Marbuzet *cru grand bourgeois exceptionnel St-Éstèphe*
1989 £15.95 (GRE) £16.95 (AME)
1989 IB £125.00 (BIB)
1988 £13.95 (WRI) £14.25 (SO) £15.95 (GRE)
1985 £13.71 (FA) £15.85 (WHI)

Haut-Pontet *grand cru St-Émilion*
1989 £12.83 (AV)

Haut-Sarpe *grand cru classé St-Émilion*
1985 £17.04 (CV)

Houissant *cru bourgeois supérieur St-Éstèphe*
1989 £7.95 (SEC)
1988 £7.05 (EL) £8.95 (AMI)
1986 £5.65 (PE)

d'Issan *3ème cru classé Margaux*
1991 £11.97 (CHA)
1990 £16.95 (DI)
1989 £18.34 (BER)
1988 £12.95 (RAE) £14.75 (GOE)
1986 £13.84 (BUT) £15.95 (AMI) £20.00 (VIG)
1985 £19.75 (BAR) £23.75 (ROB)
1982 £21.85 (NI)

Kirwan *3ème cru classé Margaux*
1992 £12.95 (WRI)
1990 £15.75 (DI) £15.75 (WRI)
1989 £12.95 (DI) £15.39 (WAT)
1988 £18.95 (WRI)
1983 £14.69 (PEN)
1982 £35.75 (WRI)

Labadie *cru bourgeois supérieur Médoc*
1990 £6.99 (SO)
1988 £7.80 (PIP)

Labégorce *cru bourgeois supérieur Margaux*
1989 £8.56 (BE)

Labégorce-Zédé *cru bourgeois supérieur Margaux*
1989 £11.50 (TAN) £13.08 (BUT)
1988 £9.99 (PE)
1987 £7.45 (PE)
1986 £10.75 (PE) £11.08 (BUT) £12.95 (DAV) £15.50 (ROB)
1983 £15.25 (EY)

Lacoste-Borie *Pauillac*
1990 £9.92 (AV)
1989 £9.83 (GOE)
1988 £8.25 (GOE) £10.58 (EL) £19.55 (DAV)
1986 £7.95 (PE) £9.50 (WS)

Lafite-Rothschild *1er cru classé Pauillac*
1990 £59.95 (LAY)
1989 £65.51 (PEN) £68.06 (AV)
1988 £52.62 (BUT) £59.29 (VIC)
1987 £34.99 (OD) £38.50 (ROB)
1986 £59.00 (MV) £60.15 (PE) £61.31 (BUT) £69.59 (VIC) £70.00 (ROB)
1986 IB £500.00 (FA)
1985 £45.63 (BY) £46.25 (GOE) £49.06 (BUT) £52.00 (WY) £52.88 (CV) £58.97 (VIN) £61.60 (UN) £69.15 (PE) £70.00 (AMI)
1985 IB £450.00 (FA) £495.00 (BIB)
1984 £34.00 (PE)
1983 £40.00 (WY) £49.00 (UN) £55.00 (BER)
1983 IB £420.00 (FA)
1982 £85.00 (WY) £95.42 (BUT) £110.00 (WS) £111.63 (EL) £115.00 (DI)
1982 IB £950.00 (FA) £950.00 (BIB)

All châteaux are listed alphabetically regardless of class.

1982 EC £880.00 (SOM)
1982 magnum IB £980.00 (FA) £1000 (WY)
1981 £58.49 (BY)
1981 IB £450.00 (FA)
1981 magnum £80.00 (WY)
1979 £77.85 (DAV)
1978 £57.50 (BU) £70.50 (FA)
1978 magnum IB £650.00 (FA)
1976 £83.23 (FA) £105.00 (ROB)
1975 £87.31 (BUT)
1971 £49.50 (BU)
1970 £75.00 (WY) £130.00 (ROB)
1970 IB £995.00 (BIB)
1970 magnum £275.00 (ROB)
1967 £35.74 (FA)
1966 £115.00 (WY) £139.18 (NO)
1964 £50.00 (WY)
1962 £124.00 (PE)
1961 £195.00 (FA) £275.00 (RES)
   £286.00 (OD) £399.00 (PE)
1961 ½ bottle £90.00 (WY)
1961 magnum £475.00 (FA)
1960 £30.00 (WY)
1959 £250.00 (FA)
1955 £120.00 (FA)
1953 £140.00 (WY) £250.00 (BIB)
1952 £70.00 (FA) £75.00 (WY)
1949 £155.00 (WY)
1948 ½ bottle £65.00 (WY)
1947 £140.00 (WY)
1947 ½ bottle £60.00 (WY)
1945 £570.00 (WY)
1943 £171.00 (WY)
1934 £200.00 (WY)
1931 £325.00 (WY)
1929 £270.00 (WY)
1928 £285.00 (WY) £342.71 (FA)
1923 £185.00 (WY)
1918 £220.00 (WY)
1914 £310.00 (WY)

Lafleur *Pomerol*
1992 EC £310.00 (ARM)
1989 £94.43 (BUT)
1989 IB £950.00 (FA)
1988 £70.49 (BUT)
1986 IB £735.00 (GOE)
1982 IB £1850.00 (FA)
1971 IB £1300.00 (FA)
1970 £55.00 (ROB)
1970 IB £1300.00 (FA)

Lafleur-Gazin *Pomerol*
1983 £18.61 (AV)
1982 £20.00 (WS)

Lafon-Rochet *4ème cru classé St-Éstèphe*
1990 £8.75 (LEA)
1989 £12.20 (GAL)
1986 £14.40 (GAL)
1985 £14.50 (GAL) £15.83 (ROB)
1982 £16.50 (HOG) £21.50 (WRI)
1981 £13.95 (RES)
1978 £15.95 (ROB)

Lagrange *Pomerol*
1989 £14.60 (BUT) £19.23 (AV)
1985 £14.95 (SEC) £16.21 (BUT)
1978 £16.00 (WY)

Lagrange *3ème cru classé St-Julien*
1989 £19.25 (BER)
1985 £22.00 (HA)
1983 £12.50 (SEC) £16.90 (HOG)
   £18.95 (ROB) £20.30 (GAL)
1982 £23.00 (ROB)
1979 £13.00 (WY)
1970 £32.00 (ROB)
1966 £41.12 (TW)
1962 £20.00 (WY)

la Lagune *3ème cru classé Haut-Médoc*
1990 £16.50 (DI)
1990 IB £175.00 (WY)
1989 £16.95 (NI) £17.95 (LAY) £18.75
   (ROB)
1989 IB £125.00 (FA) £150.00 (BIB)
1989 ½ bottle IB £130.00 (FA)
1988 £14.68 (HIG) £14.69 (CV) £15.05 (BEK)
1987 £12.48 (HOG) £13.00 (GAL) £15.50 (ROB)
1986 £13.66 (GOE) £14.15 (PE) £14.42 (BUT)
   £15.67 (HIG) £17.33 (HOG) £17.80 (GAL)
   £18.00 (HAY) £18.95 (BU) £19.28 (CHA)
1985 £18.75 (ROB) £19.42 (BUT) £19.50 (UN)
   £19.95 (AMI) £19.98 (EL) £22.56 (CHA)
1984 £16.10 (UN)
1983 £18.95 (DAV) £19.28 (BEK) £19.95 (LO)
   £22.50 (PIP)
1983 IB £135.00 (FA)
1983 magnum IB £155.00 (GOE)
1982 £27.00 (WY) £28.00 (BE) £33.96 (NO)
1982 IB £240.00 (GOE) £255.00 (BIB)
1981 £19.50 (HAC) £19.75 (BAR)
1979 £24.95 (BAR) £26.50 (GRE)
1979 magnum £52.00 (DI)
1978 £23.50 (DI) £24.75 (EY) £24.95 (BAR)
   £30.24 (BUT) £30.75 (ROB)
1975 £17.95 (BU) £19.79 (REI) £23.78 (BUT)
1975 ½ bottle £8.95 (BU)
1975 magnum £31.33 (FA)
1961 £79.50 (BEN)

Lalande d'Auvion *Médoc*
1989 £8.79 (CB)

Lalande-Borie *cru bourgeois supérieur St-Julien*
1990 £8.95 (LEA) £10.00 (GOE) £10.50 (MV)
1989 £11.66 (GOE)
1988 £10.20 (MV) £10.83 (GOE)
1986 £10.79 (BUT) £10.87 (CB) £13.00 (MV)
1983 £13.75 (WS)

de Lamarque *cru grand bourgeois Haut-Médoc*
1988 £10.95 (CB)
1986 £10.96 (CB)
1985 £11.62 (CB)
1975 £9.34 (PLA)

Lamothe-Bergeron *cru bourgeois Haut-Médoc*
1989 £9.25 (GRE)
1988 £9.35 (GRE) £9.83 (AV)

Lamothe-Cissac *Haut-Médoc*
1990 £6.99 (WW) £7.95 (DI)
1989 £7.65 (GAL) £8.35 (DI)

Lanessan *cru bourgeois supérieur Haut-Médoc*
1990 £10.49 (CHA) £10.95 (DI)
1989 £9.20 (MV) £9.44 (BUT)
1988 £11.95 (DI)
1986 £9.98 (BER) £11.50 (LO) £12.90 (DI)
1985 £12.83 (BEK) £15.52 (PIP) £16.99 (RE)
1983 £13.90 (DI)
1982 £18.95 (RES)
1979 £17.50 (ROB)

Langoa-Barton *3ème cru classé St-Julien*
1992 EC £88.00 (SUM)
1990 £13.67 (BUT) £16.94 (LAY) £16.97 (TAN)
1989 £11.75 (BE) £14.44 (SUM) £15.66 (GOE)
1989 IB £135.00 (BIB)
1988 £17.25 (LAY)
1987 £11.35 (TAN) £12.99 (TES) £13.75 (NI)
1986 £14.88 (BUT)
1985 £15.95 (SOM)
1983 £17.50 (BE)
1981 £20.25 (PE)
1976 £16.50 (BU)

Larcis-Ducasse *grand cru classé St-Émilion*
1990 £14.16 (BOR)
1985 £9.50 (GE)

Larmande *grand cru classé St-Émilion*
1989 £15.00 (MV) £15.60 (BUT) £16.44 (AV) £19.72 (BER)
1986 £12.42 (GOE) £14.95 (WS)
1985 £14.39 (BUT) £15.95 (WS)
1983 £20.00 (VIG)

Laroque *grand cru St-Émilion*
1989 £14.95 (VIG)

Larose-Trintaudon *cru grand bourgeois Haut-Médoc*
1989 £9.50 (DI)
1985 £10.53 (HA)

Laroze *grand cru classé St-Émilion*
1989 £12.49 (SAF)
1986 £12.50 (HIG)

Larrivet-Haut-Brion *Pessac-Léognan*
1989 £13.77 (BUT)
1985 £12.73 (BUT)

Lascombes *2ème cru classé Margaux*
1990 £12.00 (WAI) £13.50 (NI) £15.95 (ROB)
1989 £14.44 (SUM) £18.76 (VIN) £19.95 (ROB)
1988 £12.00 (WY) £13.99 (PE) £20.95 (ROB)
1986 £18.60 (NO) £22.95 (ROB)
1984 £13.95 (ROB)
1984 IB £106.00 (WY)
1983 £21.00 (RAE)
1982 £24.75 (GRE) £25.00 (WS)
1981 £21.35 (AMI) £24.05 (VIN)
1966 £32.00 (WY)
1961 £55.00 (WY)
1955 £55.00 (ROB)
1920 £80.00 (WY)

EC (ex-cellar) price per dozen, excl shipping, duty and VAT. IB (in bond) price per dozen, excl duty and VAT. All other prices, per bottle incl VAT.

Latour *1er cru classé Pauillac*
1992 £23.33 (HIC)
1992 EC £288.00 (RAE)
1991 £35.80 (RAE)
1990 IB £695.00 (BIB) £780.00 (FA)
1990 magnum £165.00 (VIG)
1989 £47.00 (PEN) £50.59 (BUT) £60.81 (CB)
  £65.00 (DI) £66.33 (TAN) £68.06 (AV)
1988 £39.50 (RAE) £41.70 (BY) £46.20 (NI)
  £48.81 (BUT) £49.64 (LAY)
1988 IB £410.00 (GOE)
1987 £26.85 (PE) £28.60 (RAE) £39.50 (ROB)
1987 IB £275.00 (WY)
1987 magnum £49.95 (SEC)
1986 £49.00 (MV) £52.00 (ROB) £60.15 (PE)
1986 IB £450.00 (BIB)
1985 £36.66 (GOE) £43.00 (WY) £56.67 (NO)
  £58.30 (UN) £59.00 (AMI) £60.00 (ROB)
1985 IB £365.00 (GOE)
1985 magnum £86.00 (WY)
1984 £33.50 (ROB) £40.50 (UN)
1983 £35.25 (FA) £36.23 (GOE) £43.00 (HOG)
  £50.94 (HA) £55.00 (BER) £55.00 (UN)
  £55.00 (ROB) £56.55 (PE) £56.75 (BEN)
1983 magnum £120.00 (ROB)
1982 £90.00 (WY) £95.00 (BU) £99.88 (PEN)

1982 IB £950.00 (FA)
1982 double magnum £550.00 (WY)
1981 £39.31 (BUT) £60.00 (ROB) £61.65 (PE)
  £61.75 (GRE)
1979 £59.95 (RES) £64.50 (GRE) £77.85 (DAV)
1979 IB £380.00 (FA) £420.00 (GOE)
  £450.00 (BIB)
1978 £88.00 (HOG) £90.00 (ROB)
1976 £90.00 (ROB)
1976 IB £400.00 (FA)
1976 double magnum £175.00 (WY)
1975 £70.00 (WY) £73.44 (FA) £79.85 (BUT)
  £130.00 (RES)
1975 IB £750.00 (BIB)
1975 magnum £152.75 (FA)
1971 £51.41 (GOE)
1970 £115.00 (WY) £120.00 (RES) £122.50
  (BUT) £123.96 (TW) £125.00 (AMI)
1970 magnum IB £1050 (BIB) £1350 (FA)

1969 £35.63 (BUT)
1967 £65.50 (RES)
1966 £32.00 (WY) £165.00 (ROB)
1966 IB £1500.00 (FA)
1962 £85.00 (BU) £122.40 (FA)
1961 £440.62 (GOE) £595.00 (ROB)
1961 IB £4750.00 (FA)
1959 £220.00 (FA)
1957 £45.00 (FA)
1956 £45.00 (FA)
1955 £120.00 (WY) £186.04 (FA) £230.00 (RES)
1955 IB £2750.00 (FA)
1954 £215.00 (WY)
1953 £490.00 (WY)
1952 £80.00 (WY)
1951 £151.00 (WY)
1949 £245.00 (WY) £330.00 (FA)
1948 £165.00 (WY)
1947 £140.00 (WY) £495.00 (ROB)
1945 £550.00 (WY) £550.00 (FA)
1943 £195.00 (WY)
1934 £210.00 (WY)
1918 £275.00 (WY)
1908 £275.00 (FA)

Latour-à-Pomerol *Pomerol*
1992 IB £184.00 (CB)
1989 £39.50 (CB)
1988 £17.14 (FA) £24.85 (CB) £28.72 (TAN)
1986 £26.56 (CB)
1982 £43.00 (WY)
1981 £25.00 (WY) £28.38 (BUT)
1975 £23.50 (FA)
1970 £55.00 (HAC)

Lavillotte *cru bourgeois Médoc*
1988 £8.95 (GE)
1986 £8.95 (GE)
1983 £9.95 (GE)
1981 £9.95 (GE)

Léoville-Barton *2ème cru classé St-Julien*
1992 EC £97.00 (SUM)
1990 £15.31 (SUM) £17.25 (SOM)
1990 EC £157.75 (HAH)
1989 £16.34 (SUM) £16.85 (AD) £17.00 (WS)
  £19.49 (LAY) £19.85 (TAN) £43.90 (NI)
1989 IB £150.00 (BIB)
1988 £14.25 (SUM) £14.28 (BY) £15.00 (GE)
  £17.99 (OD) £20.70 (AV)
1987 £13.30 (GAL) £13.33 (ARM)
1986 £14.90 (GAL) £16.05 (BUT) £16.50 (HAY)
  £16.95 (HOG) £17.95 (DAV) £18.95 (LAY)
1986 IB £165.00 (BIB)

1986 magnum £180.00 (WY)
1985 £15.85 (BY) £18.00 (WY) £19.00 (BE)
1985 IB £180.00 (WY)
1984 £11.35 (BE)
1984 IB £108.00 (WY)
1983 £17.50 (MV) £18.41 (LO) £18.60 (BEN)
£18.98 (NO) £19.90 (DI) £19.95 (LAY)
1983 IB £130.00 (FA)
1982 £27.95 (LAY) £31.55 (TAN) £32.00 (ROB)
1982 IB £240.00 (GOE)
1982 magnum IB £240.00 (GOE)
1981 £18.74 (PLA)
1979 magnum £30.00 (WY)
1978 £18.00 (BU) £28.95 (LAY) £32.00 (AD)
1975 £16.00 (WY) £27.95 (BEN)
1970 £30.00 (WY)
1970 magnum £65.00 (WY)
1970 magnum IB £360.00 (WY)
1966 £33.00 (WY) £47.00 (REI)
1961 £65.00 (WY) £95.00 (ROB) £112.50 (AD)
1960 £18.00 (BU) £19.58 (FA)
1955 £42.00 (WY)
1937 £85.00 (WY)

Léoville-Las-Cases 2ème cru classé St-Julien
1989 £34.22 (AV) £38.45 (BER)
1986 £27.41 (BUT) £30.95 (PE) £31.48 (AV)
1985 £25.43 (BY) £31.00 (BER) £31.64 (BUT)
£35.60 (VIC) £36.15 (PE) £37.99 (WHI)
1985 IB £253.00 (BIB)
1984 £16.59 (AV) £18.99 (PE) £19.60 (WS)
£22.00 (BER) £25.00 (UN)
1983 £18.60 (GOE) £23.96 (PIP) £26.26 (LAY)
£27.70 (GAL) £28.50 (CB) £29.09 (WHI)
£29.50 (AD) £34.00 (BER)
1983 ½ bottle £14.22 (HAL)
1982 £60.00 (PE) £69.50 (BEN)
1982 IB £600.00 (FA)
1982 ½ bottle IB £600.00 (FA)
1982 magnum IB £600.00 (FA)
1981 £29.63 (BY) £30.00 (ROB) £31.95 (AMI)
1981 IB £230.00 (GOE)
1978 £33.00 (WY) £45.00 (RES) £45.00 (ROB)
1978 IB £320.00 (FA)
1976 £30.50 (TAN)
1975 £28.00 (BU) £33.29 (FA) £33.49 (BEK)
£35.00 (WY) £39.96 (PIP) £47.50 (ROB)
1975 IB £330.00 (FA)
1971 £20.56 (BIB)
1970 £33.78 (GOE) £36.72 (FA) £41.12 (REI)
£43.28 (TAN) £50.00 (OD) £50.00 (WS)
£53.49 (AV) £65.00 (ROB) £66.70 (AD)
1970 IB £360.00 (FA)
1966 £79.29 (NI)

1964 £34.27 (FA)
1961 £100.00 (WY) £195.00 (RES)
1955 £105.00 (ROB)
1953 £159.00 (RES)

Léoville-Poyferré 2ème cru classé St-Julien
1992 EC £96.00 (RAE)
1990 £16.44 (BUT)
1990 EC £140.00 (RAE)
1989 £13.92 (GOE) £18.75 (ROB) £20.07 (HAH)
1988 £14.95 (RAE) £23.25 (RE)
1985 £15.37 (BY) £17.80 (UN) £34.25 (VIC)
1983 £15.67 (GOE) £17.00 (GE) £17.59 (BEK)
£21.22 (PIP) £21.50 (ROB) £25.85 (GRE)
1982 £21.54 (GOE) £25.95 (WS) £26.50 (TAN)
1981 £19.95 (GAL)
1978 £40.60 (VIC)
1970 £24.00 (WY)
1961 £65.00 (WY)
1959 £49.00 (GE) £98.00 (ROB)
1952 £49.00 (VIG)
1949 £85.00 (WY)

Lestage cru bourgeois supérieur Listrac
1990 £6.49 (WAT)
1959 £25.00 (BU)

Liversan cru grand bourgeois Haut-Médoc
1990 £11.89 (AV)
1989 £11.85 (NI) £12.28 (CB)
1988 £8.15 (PE) £9.44 (NI) £9.45 (BER)
1986 £11.69 (CB)

Livran cru bourgeois Médoc
1990 £5.95 (WAT) £6.10 (HOG) £6.30 (AS)

Loudenne cru grand bourgeois Médoc
1992 £3.52 (HIC)
1989 £8.15 (HOG)
1988 £7.43 (HOG)
1986 £6.82 (NO)

la Louvière Pessac-Léognan
1989 £12.08 (BUT) £13.12 (HAH)
1987 £10.11 (PLA)
1983 £12.48 (NI)
1979 £14.95 (AMI)

> Stars (★) indicate wines
> selected by the editors as
> particularly good value
> in their class.

Lynch-Bages *5ème cru classé Pauillac*
1990 £22.08 (GOE) £23.05 (AV) £25.00 (WY)
1990 IB £210.00 (FA)
1989 £24.58 (GOE) £26.29 (BUT) £31.15
  (BER) £33.04 (AV) £39.50 (ROB)
1989 IB £260.00 (FA)
1988 £18.99 (RAE) £20.00 (HAY) £32.20 (NI)
1987 £17.50 (GAL) £18.67 (BY)
1986 £19.99 (PE) £20.49 (BUT) £23.75 (DAV)
  £24.90 (GAU) £28.93 (AV)
1986 IB £245.00 (BIB)
1985 £18.86 (BY) £25.25 (VIC) £27.91 (GOE)
  £28.65 (BUT) £29.95 (AMI) £33.20 (PIP)
1985 IB £335.00 (BIB)
1984 £14.65 (PE) £15.70 (BY) £18.00 (UN)
1983 £21.21 (PEN) £24.40 (GAL) £27.61 (REI)
1982 £42.10 (FA) £45.00 (WY) £58.16 (TW)
1982 IB £385.00 (GOE)
1982 magnum IB £450.00 (FA)
1981 £28.00 (ROB) ·
1981 IB £225.00 (BIB)

1979 £18.00 (WY) £31.80 (PIP)
1978 £26.00 (WY)
1978 IB £250.00 (BIB) £300.00 (WY)
1978 magnum £50.00 (WY)
1976 £20.00 (WY) £22.52 (GOE)
1975 £23.00 (SOM) £28.95 (BEN) £45.00 (ROB)
1975 IB £250.00 (FA)
1970 £63.00 (WY) £69.52 (BUT) £70.50 (FA)
1966 £63.65 (FA)
1961 £95.00 (BU) £110.00 (WY) £175.00 (RES)
1945 £210.00 (WY)

Lynch-Moussas *5ème cru classé Pauillac*
1989 £10.95 (SEC) £10.99 (NI)
1980 £15.69 (BUT)
1978 £14.20 (GOE)

Magdelaine *1er grand cru classé St-Émilion*
1992 IB £176.40 (CB)
1988 £21.95 (TAN) £24.50 (BUT)
1987 £18.85 (CB)
1982 £48.00 (ROB)
1981 £20.47 (BUT) £24.00 (WY)
1975 £34.50 (BAR)

Malartic-Lagravière *cru classé Pessac-Léognan*
1985 £15.03 (BUT)
1973 £13.49 (BOR)
1971 £16.86 (BOR)

Malescot-St-Exupéry *3ème cru classé Margaux*
1990 £13.95 (VIG)
1989 £17.50 (DI)
1988 £11.95 (POR) £13.50 (DI) £14.50 (BU)
1986 £12.50 (HOG) £14.80 (WRI)
1985 £13.46 (HOG) £17.15 (TW) £17.60 (BE)
1983 £16.63 (HIC)
1982 £20.00 (BU)
1978 £15.84 (BOR)
1976 £17.75 (ROB)
1970 £29.96 (REI)

de Marbuzet *cru grand bourgeois exceptionnel St-Éstèphe*
1990 £9.70 (BUT) £9.91 (GOE)
1989 £12.41 (GOE)
1988 £10.66 (GOE)
1987 £7.00 (GOE)

Margaux *1er cru classé Margaux*
1991 £6.99 (MAR)
1989 £7.99 (SAF) £59.65 (AD)
1988 £46.99 (OD) £55.25 (VIC)
1986 £65.00 (DI) £69.50 (LAY) £75.00 (RES)
1986 IB £600.00 (FA)
1985 £37.50 (ROB) £50.00 (WY) £54.20 (UN)
  £54.50 (GRE) £58.75 (CV) £59.00 (AMI)
  £64.85 (VIC) £65.15 (PE)
1984 £38.50 (ROB) £40.50 (UN) £45.00 (BER)
1983 £48.00 (WY) £49.00 (UN) £56.51 (BUT)
  £59.00 (BER) £64.63 (EL) £69.10 (WHI)
  £70.00 (ROB) £73.25 (VIC)
1983 IB £550.00 (BIB)
1982 £90.00 (GAU) £110.12 (NO)
1982 IB £800.00 (FA) £895.00 (BIB)
1981 £43.34 (BUT) £48.00 (BE) £65.00 (ROB)
1977 £26.50 (BU)
1975 £49.50 (BU) £68.32 (BUT)
1970 £110.00 (ROB)
1970 IB £620.00 (FA) £625.00 (BIB)
1969 £30.00 (WY)
1966 £70.00 (WY) £140.00 (ROB)
1966 magnum IB £950.00 (FA)
1964 £60.71 (FA)
1962 £65.00 (BU) £70.50 (FA)
1961 £288.85 (FA)
1961 magnum £480.00 (FA)
1960 £35.00 (BU)

1955 magnum £240.00 (FA)
1953 magnum £660.00 (WY)
1950 magnum £293.75 (REI)
1949 £86.00 (WY)
1947 £120.00 (WY)
1945 £240.00 (WY) £480.00 (FA)
1945 magnum IB £6000.00 (FA)
1934 £175.00 (ROB)
1929 £295.00 (WY)
1926 £260.00 (WY)
1926 magnum £450.00 (FA)
1924 £180.00 (WY)
1918 £300.00 (WY)
1908 £430.00 (WY)

Marquis de Ségur *St-Éstèphe*
1985 £18.09 (BUT)

Marquis-de-Terme *4ème cru classé*
Margaux
1989 £13.00 (MV)
1988 £11.00 (MV) £12.99 (TES) £19.95 (VIG)
1985 £14.36 (BUT) £14.59 (SEC)
1983 £14.90 (HOG)
1982 £22.50 (RES)
1937 £55.00 (WY)

Martinet *grand cru St-Émilion*
1989 £8.75 (GE)
1988 £7.50 (GE)

Maucaillou *cru bourgeois Moulis '*
1990 £12.59 (NI)
1989 £11.95 (SAI) £12.95 (NI)
1988 £11.85 (NI)
1986 £12.95 (DAV)
1983 £10.50 (AMI)
1970 £19.50 (ROB)

Meyney *cru grand bourgeois exceptionnel*
St-Éstèphe
1989 £11.99 (UN)
1988 £9.99 (UN) £11.55 (PE)
1987 £7.95 (PE) £8.99 (SO) £11.50 (ROB)
1986 £11.65 (PE) £13.00 (HOG) £16.25 (GRE)
1985 £11.25 (PE) £13.15 (BUT) £15.00 (GOE)
    £16.25 (GRE) £16.70 (WRI) £17.50 (ROB)
    £17.95 (BEN)
1984 £8.95 (PE) £10.49 (UN)
1983 £14.50 (HOG) £14.65 (PE)
1982 £18.75 (WHI)
1981 £15.95 (RES)
1979 £13.50 (HOG)
1966 magnum £50.00 (WY)
1961 £48.47 (BIB)

Millet *Graves*
1988 £9.43 (HOG)

la Mission-Haut-Brion *cru classé Pessac-*
Léognan
1989 £57.44 (BUT)
1989 IB £550.00 (FA)
1989 magnum IB £560.00 (FA)
1986 £34.45 (AV) £35.22 (BUT) £39.99 (PE)
1985 £44.50 (AMI) £44.62 (BUT)
1984 £25.05 (AV) £35.00 (BER) £36.20 (UN)
1984 IB £165.00 (FA)
1983 £28.00 (WY) £34.00 (HOG) £35.50 (GRE)
    £36.80 (UN) £42.00 (BER)
1983 IB £285.00 (GOE)
1982 £60.00 (BER) £65.00 (WY) £70.00 (ROB)
1982 IB £595.00 (FA)
1981 £27.00 (WY) £37.50 (BER) £42.90 (PIP)
1981 magnum £52.00 (WY)
1981 magnum IB £295.00 (WY)
1980 £25.50 (ROB)
1979 £60.00 (RES)
1978 IB £750.00 (FA)
1976 £25.00 (WY)
1975 £225.00 (RES)
1970 £60.71 (GOE) £65.00 (BU)
1967 £25.00 (WY)
1966 £100.00 (WY) £122.40 (FA) £150.00 (RES)
1964 IB £950.00 (FA)
1962 £65.00 (BU)
1962 IB £780.00 (FA)
1955 £220.00 (FA)
1953 magnum IB £2750.00 (FA)
1950 £225.00 (RES)
1945 £400.00 (WY)
1945 magnum £800.00 (WY)
1945 magnum IB £5200.00 (FA)
1926 £300.00 (WY)
1920 £280.00 (WY)

les Moines *Médoc*
1989 £5.00 (HOG)
1988 £5.95 (RES)

Monbousquet *grand cru St-Émilion*
1959 £48.00 (ROB)
1955 £29.50 (BU)

Monbrison *cru bourgeois Margaux*
1990 £14.00 (GOE) £19.81 (BUT)
1989 £20.00 (VIG)
1985 £11.32 (BUT)

Monlot-Capet *St-Émilion*
1989 £9.95 (HAY)

Montalivet *Graves*
1989 £8.30 (PIP)
1988 £9.17 (ARM)
1986 £9.58 (ARM)

Montbrun *cru bourgeois Margaux*
1985 £9.99 (DAV)
1945 £40.00 (WY)

Montrose *2ème cru classé St-Éstèphe*
1990 imperial IB £450.00 (FA)
1989 £19.98 (PEN) £21.33 (BUT) £25.20 (CB)
   £27.00 (BER)
1988 £18.80 (EL)
1986 £16.99 (PE) £19.04 (PLA) £19.50 (BU)
1985 £16.58 (BY) £19.99 (MAJ) £24.75 (AMI)
   £24.85 (PE) £26.30 (WRI)
1984 £17.50 (UN)
1983 £23.69 (VIC)
1983 IB £130.00 (FA)
1982 £21.05 (BEK) £21.10 (GAL) £23.00 (WY)
   £23.88 (AV) £25.00 (BU) £26.90 (BE)
   £26.95 (GRE) £26.95 (AMI) £27.75 (WS)
   £29.60 (PIP) £31.50 (WRI)
1982 IB £220.00 (GOE) £235.00 (BIB)
   £240.00 (FA)
1981 £15.00 (WY) £23.20 (PIP)
1981 IB £155.00 (WY)
1980 £16.85 (BUT)
1978 £19.00 (WY) £23.64 (AV) £26.92 (TAN)
1975 £21.15 (EL) £27.95 (BEN) £35.00 (RES)
1970 £45.00 (WY) £56.66 (NO)
1966 £37.50 (BU) £40.00 (WY) £47.00 (PEN)
1966 ½ bottle £20.00 (WY)
1961 £65.00 (BU)
1928 £185.00 (WY)

Moulin-Haut-Villars *Fronsac*
1983 £7.08 (ARM)

Moulinet *Pomerol*
1976 £14.50 (BU)
1973 £18.68 (TW)

Mouton-Rothschild *1er cru classé*
   Pauillac
1991 IB £285.00 (BIB)
1990 £49.99 (OD) £53.85 (HIG)
1990 IB £495.00 (BIB)
1990 magnum £111.62 (HIG)
1989 £57.50 (BU) £60.01 (BUT)
1989 IB £595.00 (BIB)
1988 £45.00 (BU) £56.89 (NO) £69.00 (VIG)
1987 £45.00 (WY)
1986 £68.61 (BUT) £87.50 (VIC)

1986 IB £680.00 (GOE) £800.00 (FA)
1985 £48.75 (GOE) £55.00 (UN) £59.95 (AMI)
   £64.80 (VIC) £65.00 (ROB) £69.15 (PE)
1985 magnum IB £500.00 (FA)
1984 £31.00 (DI) £37.50 (ROB) £38.50 (UN)
   £39.00 (BER) £70.00 (WY)
1984 ½ bottle £29.08 (TW)
1983 £40.00 (WY) £45.00 (WAT) £45.00 (UN)
   £47.36 (PIP) £48.00 (WS) £48.47 (GOE)
   £55.26 (LO) £56.49 (VIC) £60.00 (ROB)
1983 IB £420.00 (FA)
1982 £117.50 (GOE) £119.30 (NO) £135.45
   (LAY) £155.00 (ROB)

1982 IB £1295.00 (FA)
1981 £46.25 (WHI) £59.85 (DAV) £61.65 (PE)
   £64.50 (GRE) £67.61 (VIN)
1981 IB £395.00 (FA) £595.00 (BIB)
1981 magnum £77.35 (FA)
1979 £65.80 (NI) £77.85 (DAV)
1978 £58.00 (WY) £58.26 (GOE) £71.50 (OD)
   £90.00 (ROB) £95.60 (DAV) £99.99 (VIC)
1978 IB £625.00 (BIB)
1978 magnum £120.00 (WY)
1978 magnum IB £580.00 (FA)
1978 double magnum £250.00 (WY)
1977 £29.50 (BU) £40.00 (WY)
1976 £68.00 (BER)
1975 £70.77 (BUT) £89.00 (GAU) £115.00 (ROB)
1975 IB £750.00 (BIB) £750.00 (FA)
1975 magnum £133.17 (FA) £155.63 (REI)
1974 £115.00 (WY)
1973 £75.00 (WY)
1973 double magnum £325.00 (WY)
1972 £57.00 (WY)
1971 £57.50 (BU) £60.00 (WY)
1970 £100.00 (WY) £105.64 (LAY) £107.71
   (FA) £127.00 (DAV) £145.00 (ROB)
1970 IB £1095.00 (BIB)
1970 ½ bottle £75.00 (VIG)
1968 £240.00 (WY)

1967 IB £480.00 (FA)
1966 IB £1600.00 (FA)
1966 magnum IB £1650.00 (FA)
1964 £110.00 (WY)
1964 magnum IB £950.00 (FA)
1963 £460.00 (WY)
1961 £400.00 (WY) £440.62 (FA)
1959 £300.00 (FA) £445.00 (ROB)
1955 £244.79 (FA)
1953 £420.00 (WY)
1952 £160.00 (FA) £190.00 (WY)
1950 £250.00 (FA)
1948 £640.00 (WY)
1947 £575.00 (WY)
1945 £1200.00 (FA)
1942 £335.00 (WY)
1937 £315.00 (WY)
1934 £245.00 (WY)
1928 £550.00 (WY)
1928 IB £6000.00 (FA)
1926 £750.00 (WY)
1921 £565.00 (WY)
1920 £380.00 (WY)
1909 £165.00 (WY)
1907 £390.00 (WY)

Nenin *Pomerol*
1990 £11.99 (OD) £12.95 (BU)
1990 IB £120.00 (WY)
1985 £15.70 (BE) £16.90 (UN)
1983 £12.50 (UN)
1982 £14.00 (WY)
1978 £18.00 (BU)
1970 £21.54 (FA) £35.00 (RES)
1966 £40.00 (RES)
1959 £85.00 (WY)
1949 £90.00 (WY)

Notton *Margaux*
1989 £8.09 (HOG) £8.75 (AMI) £9.75 (GRE)
1988 £9.37 (HOG) £10.03 (HA)

Les Ormes-de-Pez *cru grand bourgeois*
St-Éstèphe
1991 £9.99 (SAF)
1990 £11.54 (BUT) £14.26 (BY)
1989 £12.38 (BUT)
1988 £12.85 (BER)
1987 £14.07 (BY)
1986 £8.82 (SUM) £9.99 (PE) £11.00 (BUT)
   £18.39 (BY)
1985 £14.81 (BEK) £17.69 (PIP)
1983 £15.95 (BEN)
1982 £17.95 (BEN) £18.95 (RES)
1973 £9.75 (BU)

Palmer *3ème cru classé Margaux*
1992 EC £122.00 (SUM)
1991 £18.20 (BE)
1991 EC £184.00 (SUM)
1990 £24.00 (BE) £27.50 (NI) £29.94 (CV)
1990 IB £250.00 (BIB)
1990 EC £275.00 (SUM)
1989 £25.00 (BE) £28.21 (TAN) £28.86 (BUT)
   £29.99 (CV) £37.25 (NI) £38.00 (BER)
1989 IB £260.00 (FA)
1988 £26.50 (BE)
1988 IB £220.00 (GOE)
1987 £17.30 (BE) £17.63 (CV)
1986 £24.99 (PE) £25.00 (HAY) £26.95 (DI)
   £29.00 (BE) £29.38 (CV) £30.90 (BUT)
   £35.00 (BER) £39.75 (ROB)
1986 IB £240.00 (GOE) £275.00 (FA)
1985 £26.00 (WY) £27.84 (BUT) £27.91 (GOE)
   £29.20 (BE) £29.97 (CV) £30.95 (PE)
   £31.80 (BER) £32.50 (GAL) £32.70 (AMI)
   £41.25 (WHI) £41.50 (ROB)
1985 magnum £52.00 (WY)
1984 £15.21 (BOR) £19.50 (BER)
1983 £36.00 (BER) £39.00 (BE) £45.83 (CV)
1983 IB £395.00 (FA)
1982 £30.00 (BU) £33.00 (WY) £42.00 (BER)
   £43.50 (ROB) £49.85 (NI)
1982 IB £395.00 (BIB)
1981 £27.31 (BUT) £39.00 (ROB)
1978 £39.64 (LAY) £40.00 (WY) £45.00 (BU)
1978 IB £420.00 (FA)
1976 £45.00 (ROB)
1975 £35.00 (BU) £40.00 (WY) £43.08 (FA)
1975 IB £420.00 (FA)
1975 magnum £48.47 (BIB)
1970 £68.54 (GOE) £75.00 (WS) £75.00 (WY)
   £80.29 (FA) £105.00 (ROB)
1970 IB £800.00 (FA) £840.00 (WY)
1967 IB £275.00 (FA)
1966 £195.00 (ROB)
1966 IB £1300.00 (FA)
1964 IB £450.00 (FA)
1961 £210.00 (RES) £210.00 (WY) £334.87 (REI)
1960 £45.00 (VIG)
1959 £210.00 (ROB)
1950 IB £650.00 (FA)
1921 £150.00 (FA)

Pape-Clément *cru classé Pessac-Léognan*
1989 £21.15 (TAN)
1988 £19.87 (BUT) £22.00 (BER)
1985 £21.07 (BUT) £25.00 (BER)
1982 £20.75 (HAC)
1982 IB £175.00 (BIB)
1970 £22.00 (WY) £26.44 (FA) £30.39 (NI)

Patache d'Aux *cru grand bourgeois*
Médoc
1991 £6.49 (TES)
1989 £8.95 (GRE) £9.95 (ROB) £10.20 (PIP)
1985 £12.50 (ROB)
1982 £10.20 (BUT)

Pauillac de Château Latour *Pauillac*
1990 £12.22 (HA) £16.95 (BEN)

Pavie *1er grand cru classé St-Émilion*
1991 £18.99 (RAE)
1989 £19.75 (ROB) £21.58 (BUT) £22.47 (AV)
1989 IB £185.00 (BIB)
1987 £15.73 (PIP)
1986 IB £170.00 (GOE)
1985 £21.61 (BUT)
1983 £17.50 (HAC) £18.71 (BUT) £19.95 (RES)
   £23.50 (ROB)
1982 £31.25 (VIC) £32.40 (BE) £34.20 (PIP)
   £45.00 (ROB)
1982 IB £295.00 (BIB)
1975 £25.80 (BUT)
1970 £31.19 (BUT)
1924 £95.00 (ROB)

Pavie-Decesse *grand cru classé St-
Émilion*
1990 £13.25 (GOE)
1989 £13.49 (BUT)
1988 £12.75 (GE)
1985 £16.50 (PIP)

Pavillon-Rouge-du-Château Margaux
Margaux
1991 £11.99 (OD)
1990 £19.95 (DI)
1989 £22.99 (TES)
1987 £19.79 (PEN)
1986 £18.75 (DAV) £19.00 (WY) £26.50 (ROB)
1985 £19.27 (BUT)
1983 £26.10 (AD)

Pédesclaux *5ème cru classé Pauillac*
1986 £21.65 (BE)
1985 £19.95 (BUT)

Petit-Village *Pomerol*
1990 £24.08 (GOE) £25.08 (BUT)
1989 £28.08 (BUT) £29.92 (GOE)
1988 £23.22 (BUT)
1986 £20.66 (GOE) £22.90 (NI)
1986 IB £199.00 (GOE)
1985 £21.66 (GOE)
1985 IB £220.00 (GOE)

Pétrus *Pomerol*
1990 IB £2500.00 (FA)
1990 magnum IB £2600.00 (FA)
1989 £270.31 (CB)
1989 IB £2500.00 (FA) £2550.00 (BIB)
1988 £164.56 (CB)
1988 magnum IB £1350 (GOE) £1700 (FA)
1987 £176.25 (TW)
1986 magnum IB £1700.00 (FA)
1985 £258.15 (BUT) £260.00 (PE)
1985 IB £2400.00 (FA)
1983 £230.00 (PE)
1983 magnum £368.15 (REI)
1982 £344.55 (BUT) £399.00 (PE)
1982 IB £3900.00 (FA)
1982 magnum £750.00 (WY)

1982 magnum IB £4000.00 (FA)
1981 £206.00 (DAV)
1981 IB £1700.00 (FA)
1981 magnum IB £1700.00 (FA)
1980 £127.29 (FA)
1979 £181.13 (REI)
1978 IB £1900.00 (FA)
1975 IB £3300.00 (FA)
1975 magnum IB £3300.00 (FA)
1971 IB £3300.00 (FA)
1970 £155.00 (RES) £300.00 (BIB)
   £300.00 (WY)
1964 magnum £650.00 (FA) £750.00 (WY)
1961 £1450.00 (FA)
1959 £734.37 (FA)
1955 £4000.00 (FA)
1955 ½ bottle £270.25 (TW)
1953 £550.00 (FA)
1953 IB £9000.00 (FA)
1950 £650.00 (FA)
1949 £900.00 (FA)
1928 £1300.00 (FA)
1906 magnum £2400.00 (FA)

Peyrouquet *St-Émilion*
1989 £12.50 (GRE)

de Pez *cru bourgeois supérieur St-Éstèphe*
1988 £12.50 (WRI)
1986 £10.76 (HOG) £15.50 (WRI)
1985 £11.23 (NO)
1983 £17.56 (BUT)
1978 £15.18 (BIB) £22.95 (RES) £28.21 (BUT)
1971 £14.95 (BU)
1970 £25.00 (BU)

Phélan-Ségur *cru grand bourgeois exceptionnel St-Éstèphe*
1989 £12.20 (GAL) £16.95 (ROB)
1988 £11.49 (UN) £14.48 (BEK) £18.03 (PIP)
1982 £16.90 (HOG)
1981 £11.95 (PEN) £15.70 (WRI)
1980 £9.98 (PLA)
1979 £13.81 (PLA)
1959 £45.00 (ROB)

Pibran *cru bourgeois Pauillac*
1991 £9.49 (OD)
1990 £12.14 (BUT)
1989 £12.45 (BUT) £14.91 (GOE) £17.45 (CB)
1988 £10.91 (GOE) £12.00 (GE)
1987 £11.81 (BY)

Pichon-Longueville (called Pichon-Baron until 1988) *2ème cru classé Pauillac*
1990 £29.99 (CV)
1990 IB £260.00 (FA) £260.00 (BIB)
1989 £21.00 (GE) £27.08 (BUT) £31.50 (BER)
1989 IB £230.00 (BIB)
1988 £20.46 (BUT) £23.64 (AV)
1987 £21.25 (ROB)
1986 £20.00 (GE) £21.90 (GAU) £24.60 (ROB)
1985 £18.00 (BU) £21.30 (AMI)
1984 £16.61 (BOR)
1983 £32.50 (ROB)
1982 £16.50 (BU) £18.60 (GOE) £27.50 (HAM) £29.75 (GRE) £53.00 (WY)
1981 £20.75 (ROB)
1975 £44.00 (BE)
1970 £43.20 (RE) £69.30 (NI)
1966 £50.00 (RES)
1964 £22.50 (BU)
1961 £155.00 (RES)
1950 £25.00 (WY)
1949 £75.00 (WY)

Pichon-Longueville-Lalande (called Pichon-Lalande until 1993) *2ème cru classé Pauillac*
1992 IB £575.00 (GOE)
1990 £23.75 (SOM) £24.65 (LAY) £25.46 (HIG)
1990 IB £250.00 (BIB)
1990 magnum £54.83 (HIG)
1989 £25.00 (WY) £35.00 (BER) £37.74 (AV)
1988 £23.50 (HAY) £24.68 (CV) £39.50 (AV)
1987 £17.56 (BUT) £21.25 (ROB)
1986 £28.61 (BUT) £32.50 (ROB) £34.00 (VIC)
1986 IB £265.00 (GOE) £275.00 (BIB)
1985 £22.75 (PE) £26.00 (WY) £26.67 (GOE) £28.43 (HA) £30.00 (UN) £31.60 (AD) £31.95 (LAY) £32.50 (BER) £35.00 (RES)
1985 IB £235.00 (BIB) £240.00 (FA)
1984 £17.65 (PE) £18.60 (WS) £19.50 (RES)
1983 £22.50 (UN) £23.00 (WY) £25.10 (BEK) £27.50 (BU) £32.20 (PIP) £33.95 (WHI) £35.20 (VIC) £39.95 (RES)
1983 IB £250.00 (FA) £253.00 (BIB)
1983 magnum IB £300.00 (WY)
1982 £55.00 (WY) £56.25 (VIC) £70.00 (GAU)
1982 IB £485.00 (GOE) £575.00 (FA)
1981 £22.68 (BUT) £28.00 (WS) £29.00 (BE)
1979 £40.00 (WS)
1979 IB £270.00 (FA)
1978 £38.10 (EY) £41.79 (BUT) £45.00 (BU)
1978 IB £380.00 (FA) £385.00 (GOE)
1976 IB £255.00 (FA)
1975 £28.89 (BIB) £50.00 (WRI)
1970 £59.65 (LAY) £85.00 (ROB) £90.00 (RES)
1966 IB £600.00 (FA)
1964 £105.00 (ROB)
1964 IB £320.00 (FA)
1960 IB £300.00 (FA)
1959 IB £1100.00 (FA)
1958 IB £390.00 (FA)
1957 IB £300.00 (FA)
1956 IB £300.00 (FA)
1951 IB £500.00 (FA)
1950 £70.50 (FA)
1947 £110.00 (WY)
1942 IB £720.00 (FA)
1938 IB £750.00 (FA)

le Pin *Pomerol*
1990 £95.47 (BUT)
1989 £140.00 (WY)
1986 £103.39 (BUT)
1983 IB £1595.00 (BIB)
1982 IB £3500.00 (BIB)

Plagnac *cru bourgeois Médoc*
1989 £6.99 (UN)
1988 £7.05 (EL) £9.50 (BEN)
1987 £5.85 (PE) £7.99 (WHI)

Plince *Pomerol*
1985 £15.95 (ROB)

la Pointe *Pomerol*
1989 £11.20 (BE)
1986 £18.50 (BE)
1981 £18.21 (TW)
1980 £18.21 (TW)
1970 £17.14 (FA)
1945 £107.00 (WY)

Pontet-Canet *5ème cru classé Pauillac*
1989 £14.25 (BUT) £16.84 (HIG)
1989 magnum £34.85 (HIG)
1988 £15.66 (HIG)
1986 £12.95 (BER) £13.64 (HOG) £13.90
   (GAL)
1985 £15.33 (HOG) £19.50 (ROB)
1983 £15.00 (HOG) £19.25 (WRI)
1982 £14.00 (WS) £27.50 (ROB)
1953 £110.00 (WY)
1945 £73.00 (WY)

Potensac *cru grand bourgeois Médoc*
1990 £8.95 (LAY) £9.99 (CHA) £10.40 (AV)
1989 £8.12 (BUT) £8.25 (HAY) £9.95 (RAE)
   £11.75 (BU)
1988 £7.95 (HAY) £9.50 (RAE) £9.85 (SEC)
   £10.20 (LO) £12.95 (PIP)
1987 £8.99 (CHA)
1986 £8.65 (PE) £9.95 (SEC) £12.95 (DI)
   £16.95 (VIG)
1985 £5.79 (GOE) £9.95 (WS) £10.75 (SEC)
1983 £10.74 (CHA)
1982 £15.95 (BU) £20.75 (ROB)

Poujeaux *cru grand bourgeois
exceptionnel Moulis*
1989 £10.80 (TAN) £11.21 (BUT) £11.99 (NI)
   £12.33 (GOE)
1988 £8.60 (BEK) £10.50 (GOE) £11.51 (PIP)
   £15.50 (RES)
1986 £11.00 (HAY)
1983 £9.61 (BEK)
1982 £21.50 (ROB)
1982 IB £125.00 (GOE)

Prieur de Meyney *St-Estèphe*
1987 £8.45 (PE)

Prieuré-Lichine *4ème cru classé
Margaux*
1989 £16.14 (AV)
1988 £13.95 (ROB) £14.74 (CHA)
1986 £13.84 (BUT)
1985 £16.40 (GAL)
1982 £18.90 (GAL)
1975 £25.00 (ROB)

Ramage-la-Bâtisse *cru bourgeois Haut-
Médoc*
1989 £9.55 (BOT) £9.55 (WR) £9.55 (THR)
   £9.95 (AME) £9.95 (POR)
1988 £10.58 (CV)

Rausan-Ségla *2ème cru classé Margaux*
1990 £17.99 (OD) £26.17 (NO)
1989 £24.50 (WS)
1988 £30.43 (NO) £44.76 (BUT)
1986 £22.50 (RES) £22.98 (NO)
1985 £17.00 (GE) £32.50 (NO)
1983 £22.11 (AV)
1982 £16.50 (BU) £20.75 (ROB) £26.90 (GAL)
1976 £18.95 (ROB)
1959 £35.00 (BU)
1952 £49.00 (VIG)
1949 £85.00 (ROB)
1945 £110.00 (WY)

Rauzan-Gassies *2ème cru classé Margaux*
1988 £17.85 (DAV)
1985 £15.49 (SEC) £16.90 (GAL) £19.75 (ROB)
1983 £19.95 (ROB)
1978 £16.40 (BOR)
1970 £39.50 (ROB)
1961 £27.50 (BU) £69.00 (AMI)
1960 £18.00 (BU)
1945 £100.00 (WY)
1940 £70.00 (SEC)
1937 £95.00 (ROB)
1928 £95.00 (WY)

Réserve de la Comtesse *Pauillac*
1989 £11.64 (LAY) £16.00 (ARM)
1988 £10.98 (BUT) £12.46 (LAY) £13.99 (BOT)
   £13.99 (WR) £14.65 (BY)
1987 £16.33 (BY)
1986 £12.95 (LAY)
1984 £12.45 (VIC) £13.45 (BY) £13.85 (ROB)

Respide-Médeville *Graves*
1986 £11.70 (TW)

de Roquetaillade-la-Grange *Graves*
1990 £7.65 (LAY)
1988 £6.90 (BE)
1986 £6.99 (DAV) £7.94 (HOG) £8.23 (SUM)
   £8.50 (AMI)

Rouget *Pomerol*
1990 £14.29 (CB)
1985 £15.24 (BUT)
1981 £17.50 (ROB)
1961 £52.87 (REI)

St-Bonnet *cru bourgeois Médoc*
1990 £6.95 (NA)
1989 £7.74 (LAY)
1985 £8.43 (BUT)

St-Pierre *Lussac-St-Émilion*
1986 £12.14 (HOG)
1983 £19.05 (HOG)

St-Pierre *4ème cru classé St-Julien*
1989 £17.07 (BUT) £17.95 (ROB)
1987 £12.83 (BY)
1986 £15.01 (WAT)
1983 £18.00 (GAL)
1982 £22.80 (GAL) £27.80 (AD)
1979 £15.00 (GE)
1970 £36.50 (AD)
1961 £67.56 (REI)

de Sales *Pomerol*
1986 £12.95 (MAJ)
1985 £12.00 (WY)
1983 £16.03 (BEK) £16.60 (BUT) £17.30 (AV)
   £17.50 (PIP) £17.95 (ROB)
1975 £29.38 (TW)
1970 £30.00 (RES)

Sarget de Gruaud-Larose *St-Julien*
1989 £13.49 (POR)
1988 £12.95 (AME)
1987 £10.55 (PE)
1986 £11.99 (WHI) £15.65 (PE)
1985 £11.95 (LAY) £13.95 (DAV)
1984 £9.49 (POR) £11.55 (PE)
1983 £13.99 (PE)

Sénéjac *cru bourgeois supérieur Haut-Médoc*
1990 £8.10 (MV) £8.20 (SOM) £8.27 (TAN)
1989 £8.60 (BER) £8.75 (GE) £8.80 (MV)
1988 £9.75 (PIP) £9.75 (TAN)
1987 £7.93 (EL)
1986 £9.27 (PLA) £10.50 (MV)

la Serre *grand cru classé St-Émilion*
1989 £12.95 (RAE)
1986 £10.75 (PE)
1985 £12.65 (PE)
1978 £12.99 (SEC)

All châteaux are listed
alphabetically
regardless of class.

Siran *cru bourgeois supérieur Margaux*
1989 £12.33 (NI)
1988 £12.20 (NI) £16.95 (SOM)
1987 £9.40 (CV)
1986 £10.75 (PE) £19.15 (PIP)
1985 £18.95 (PIP)
1981 £19.32 (NI)
1964 IB £150.00 (FA)
1955 IB £300.00 (FA)
1952 IB £250.00 (FA)
1950 IB £250.00 (FA)
1947 IB £550.00 (FA)

Smith-Haut-Lafitte *cru classé Pessac-Léognan*
1989 £12.95 (SEC)
1987 £14.40 (RE)
1986 £17.50 (GRE)
1985 £14.44 (NO)
1983 £13.75 (GAL)

Sociando-Mallet *cru grand bourgeois Haut-Médoc*
1991 £10.99 (RAE)
1989 £12.95 (RAE) £14.58 (GOE) £14.70 (BUT)
   £16.00 (HAY)
1989 IB £135.00 (BIB)
1988 £11.83 (GOE) £13.50 (HAY)
1986 £14.50 (HAY)
1983 £12.24 (GOE)

Soutard *grand cru classé St-Émilion*
1985 £16.00 (GE) £17.85 (NO)
1983 £11.95 (SEC)
1981 £13.00 (GE)
1970 £15.50 (SEC)
1964 £28.00 (GE)

Taillefer *Pomerol*
1985 £15.80 (RE)

Talbot *4ème cru classé St-Julien*
1989 £17.68 (NO) £19.20 (BUT) £23.00 (BER)
1989 IB £130.00 (FA)
1989 ½ bottle £8.00 (WY)
1988 £13.99 (OD) £15.95 (ROB) £18.65 (PE)
1987 £13.75 (HAM) £14.70 (NI) £15.95 (ROB)
1986 £16.16 (PLA) £16.85 (DI) £18.62 (NO)
   £19.90 (BER) £20.60 (WHI) £22.75 (PE)
1986 IB £140.00 (GOE)
1985 £17.15 (BUT) £17.33 (PLA) £19.95 (LAY)
   £20.75 (PE) £20.75 (GRE) £21.50 (ROB)
   £22.50 (AMI) £22.70 (PIP)
1984 £12.55 (PE) £16.20 (UN)
1983 £18.49 (SEC) £19.99 (PE) £22.50 (ROB)

1983 magnum IB £140.00 (GOE)
1982 £21.50 (GAL) £24.85 (PE) £28.95 (LAY)
£30.00 (WY)
1982 IB £250.00 (BIB)
1981 £17.42 (BUT) £19.15 (PE) £23.75 (DAV)
£25.00 (ROB)
1979 £17.14 (GOE) £21.00 (LO) £29.50 (GAL)

1978 £20.00 (WY) £21.33 (BUT) £26.85 (PE)
£26.97 (TAN) £35.00 (ROB)
1978 IB £185.00 (BIB) £220.00 (WY)
1970 £25.00 (WY) £33.72 (BOR) £42.99 (RE)
£47.50 (RES)
1970 magnum £52.00 (WY)
1966 £29.37 (FA)
1966 double magnum £145.00 (WY)
1961 IB £595.00 (BIB)
1959 £90.00 (GAL) £95.00 (RES)
1949 £100.00 (WY)
1947 £140.00 (ROB)

Terre Rouge *Médoc*
1990 £6.70 (AD) £7.27 (AV)
1988 £7.16 (BUT) £7.33 (ARM)
1986 £8.17 (ARM)

Terrey-Gros-Caillou *cru bourgeois St-Julien*
1989 £10.16 (EY)
1988 £9.58 (GOE) £9.76 (BEK) £12.30 (PIP)
1982 £14.95 (NA)

du Tertre *5ème cru classé Margaux*
1989 £17.50 (BER)
1988 £16.95 (ROB)
1986 £15.80 (GAL)
1983 £15.95 (ROB) £16.39 (PLA)
1982 £24.75 (ROB)

Tertre-Daugay *grand cru classé St-Émilion*
1900 £125.00 (WY)

Tertre Rôteboeuf *St-Émilion*
1992 IB £199.00 (CB)
1991 £17.35 (CB)
1990 £22.08 (BUT) £23.09 (CB)
1986 £19.93 (BUT)

la Tour-Carnet *4ème cru classé Haut-Médoc*
1985 £12.95 (GRE)
1981 £10.65 (WAT)
1975 £17.95 (WRI)

la Tour-de-By *cru grand bourgeois Médoc*
1990 £7.25 (AMI) £8.87 (TAN) £9.40 (HIG)
£9.80 (HAM) £10.95 (GRE)
1989 £8.49 (UN) £8.99 (HIG)
1988 £7.49 (UN) £9.95 (PIP) £11.70 (BEN)
1987 £6.45 (PE) £7.35 (HAM)
1986 £7.95 (PE) £9.45 (WRI)

la Tour-de-Grenet *Lussac-St-Émilion*
1989 £7.45 (LAY)

la Tour-de-Mons *cru bourgeois supérieur Margaux*
1990 £8.95 (WS)
1982 £16.95 (BEN)

Tour-des-Combes *grand cru St-Émilion*
1990 £8.59 (WAT)
1988 £8.75 (AS)

Tour-du-Haut-Moulin *cru grand bourgeois Haut-Médoc*
1991 £9.25 (DI)
1990 £10.75 (DI)
1988 £9.08 (GOE) £10.95 (DI)
1986 £8.68 (BEK) £8.95 (GAL) £10.30 (PIP)
1985 £9.32 (BUT) £10.83 (GOE)

la Tour-du-Pin-Figeac *grand cru classé St-Émilion*
1986 £14.50 (BU) £15.50 (ROB)
1982 £14.69 (FA)
1959 £36.00 (ROB)

la Tour-Figeac *grand cru classé St-Émilion*
1990 £12.00 (BOR)
1985 £14.65 (PE) £14.70 (UN)

la Tour-Haut-Brion *cru classé Pessac-Léognan*
1989 £39.50 (LAY)
1985 £21.76 (AV) £30.00 (WS)

la Tour-St-Bonnet *cru bourgeois Médoc*
1990 £7.95 (POR) £8.19 (NA)
1989 £6.46 (EL) £6.54 (HOG) £7.25 (GRE)
£7.49 (UN) £7.63 (REI) £7.90 (BER)
1988 £7.75 (GRE) £7.95 (WRI) £9.95 (RES)
1986 £9.00 (BE)
1982 £11.00 (GE)

Les Tourelles de Pichon *Pauillac*
1990 £11.54 (BUT) £15.20 (HAH)
1989 £12.95 (RAE) £15.99 (BOT) £15.99 (WR)
£15.99 (THR)
1988 £11.08 (GOE) £20.16 (BY)
1987 £14.61 (BY)

Tronquoy-Lalande *cru grand bourgeois*
St-Éstèphe
1988 £9.40 (EL)

Troplong-Mondot *grand cru classé St-*
Émilion
1990 £15.01 (BUT)
1989 £15.16 (GOE) £15.45 (BUT)
1987 £11.00 (GE)
1986 £13.95 (DAV)
1982 £18.67 (AV)

Trotanoy *Pomerol*
1992 IB £240.00 (CB)
1990 IB £360.00 (FA)
1989 £47.47 (BUT)
1988 £36.24 (CB) £37.24 (BUT)
1986 £37.39 (CB) £38.43 (BUT)
1985 £55.58 (CB)
1984 £22.50 (BU)
1983 £32.95 (LAY) £37.63 (BUT)
1982 IB £850.00 (BIB)
1981 IB £320.00 (FA)
1980 £28.00 (WY)
1979 £31.33 (FA)
1979 IB £395.00 (BIB)
1978 £85.00 (ROB)
1976 £37.21 (FA)
1975 £78.33 (FA)
1970 IB £950.00 (FA)
1966 IB £900.00 (FA)
1957 £60.00 (ROB)
1955 £90.00 (ROB)

Trottevieille *1er grand cru classé St-*
Émilion
1992 EC £120.00 (SUM)
1991 EC £162.00 (SUM)
1990 £19.58 (HIG) £23.95 (DI)
1990 EC £215.00 (SUM)

1989 £19.40 (BUT) £19.58 (HIG) £21.00 (BER)
£24.90 (DI)
1988 £18.90 (BER)
1986 £19.00 (WS)
1983 £17.95 (DAV)
1947 £125.00 (ROB)

Verdignan *cru grand bourgeois Haut-*
Médoc
1985 £8.09 (BEK) £10.20 (PIP)
1976 £10.73 (BOR)

Vieux-Château-Certan *Pomerol*
1992 IB £90.00 (FA) £135.00 (BIB)
£135.00 (GOE)
1992 EC £150.00 (RAE)
1990 £26.33 (GOE) £29.95 (LAY)
£30.86 (BUT)
1990 EC £220.00 (RAE)
1989 £31.69 (BUT) £31.74 (TAN) £32.50 (RAE)
£35.00 (ROB) £36.44 (AV) £39.00 (BER)
1988 £27.78 (BUT) £28.50 (BER) £33.90 (GAU)
1988 IB £250.00 (GOE)
1988 magnum £50.00 (HAY)
1987 £16.65 (PE)
1986 £26.15 (PE) £27.85 (BUT) £28.33 (GOE)
£29.50 (BER) £35.00 (TAN)
1985 £20.00 (HAY) £32.00 (BER) £32.00 (PE)
£33.50 (PIP) £35.30 (UN)
1983 £30.00 (ROB)
1983 IB £250.00 (GOE) £275.00 (WY)
1978 magnum £50.00 (WY)
1976 £23.00 (WY)
1970 IB £360.00 (FA)

Vieux-Château-Landon *cru bourgeois*
Médoc
1990 £8.79 (CB)

Villegeorge *cru bourgeois supérieur*
exceptionnel Haut-Médoc
1986 £8.85 (HAM) £9.75 (RAE)

Villemaurine *grand cru classé St-Émilion*
1985 £13.36 (HA)

Villeneuve de Cantemerle *Haut-Médoc*
1989 £7.75 (WS)
1986 £8.99 (WHI) £10.75 (PE)

Vraye-Croix-de-Gay *Pomerol*
1989 £16.71 (BUT)
1985 £16.60 (EY)
1983 £14.95 (BU)
1982 £13.14 (BUT)

PETITS CHATEAUX

des Annereaux *Lalande-de-Pomerol*
1989 £8.50 (GRE) £9.25 (AME) £9.75 (BEN)
1988 £9.40 (CV) £10.50 (ROB)

de Barbe *Côtes de Bourg*
1990 £5.59 (DAV)
1988 £5.29 (EL)

Belair *1ères Côtes de Blaye*
1992 £4.75 (NA)

de Belcier *Côtes de Castillon*
1988 £6.25 (DAV) £7.49 (POR) £7.50 (AME)

Bertin *Montagne-St-Émilion*
1988 £6.72 (BUT)
1986 £6.33 (BUT)

Bonnet *Bordeaux Supérieur*
1992 £4.99 (EL) £6.29 (BOT) £6.29 (THR)
1991 £6.30 (NI)

Calon *Montagne-St-Émilion*
1955 £41.71 (TW)

Canon de Brem *Canon-Fronsac*
1992 EC £59.00 (ARM)
1990 £9.00 (MV) £9.00 (ARM) £10.95 (CB)
1989 £9.40 (MV) £10.67 (ARM) £11.50 (SEC)
1988 £8.50 (MV) £8.50 (ARM)
1986 £10.54 (CB)

Canteloup *1ères Côtes de Blaye*
1989 £7.67 (ARM)

la Claverie *Côtes de Francs*
1990 £8.40 (PIP)
1986 £6.57 (BEK)

Clos de l' Eglise *Lalande-de-Pomerol*
1985 £19.90 (BUT)

Clos des Templiers *Lalande-de-Pomerol*
1990 £8.40 (EL)

la Croix-des-Moines *Lalande-de-Pomerol*
1990 £10.99 (RAE)

de la Dauphine *Fronsac*
1990 £9.45 (CB)
1989 £7.70 (MV) £8.71 (BUT) £9.95 (CB)
1988 £8.95 (CB)

Durand-Laplagne *Puisseguin-St-Émilion*
1989 £6.65 (AD)

l'Escadre *1ères Côtes de Blaye*
1992 £2.20 (HIC)
1990 £5.95 (ROB)

le Gardera *1ères Côtes de Bordeaux*
1990 £6.95 (BEN)
1988 £5.95 (PE)
1987 £5.45 (PE)
1986 £5.65 (PE)

Grand-Mazerolles *1ères Côtes de Blaye*
1990 £5.34 (REI)
1985 £5.99 (PE)

Gros-Moulin *Côtes de Bourg*
1990 £4.54 (BEK)

Guionne *Côtes de Bourg*
1990 £4.86 (HOG) £5.67 (ARM)
1989 £5.42 (ARM)
1988 £4.85 (PE)
1986 £5.65 (PE)

Haut-Gillet *Montagne-St-Émilion*
1985 £6.17 (EL)

de Haut-Sociondo *1ères Côtes de Blaye*
1989 £4.95 (SUM)
1986 £5.99 (GRE)

du Juge *1ères Côtes de Bordeaux*
1991 £5.30 (GAL)
1990 £6.02 (AV)
1988 £4.92 (BY)

de Lussac *Lussac-St-Émilion*
1990 £7.50 (ARM)
1989 £6.67 (ARM)

du Lyonnat *Lussac-St-Émilion*
1989 £7.75 (AMI)
1988 £7.84 (BY) £7.87 (CV) £8.95 (ROB)

Macquin-St-Georges *St-Georges-St-Émilion*
1990 £6.50 (AD) £6.77 (TAN) £6.88 (HAH) £7.00 (AV) £7.50 (CB)
1989 £6.95 (CB)
1988 £6.25 (DAV) £6.92 (CB)

Mazeris *Canon-Fronsac*
1989 £11.50 (SEC) £11.57 (CB)
1988 £7.08 (ARM) £8.20 (MV) £9.51 (CB)
1987 £5.83 (ARM) £7.95 (GAL)
1986 £10.29 (CB) £11.67 (ARM)
1985 £10.00 (ARM) £14.95 (RE)

Méaume *Bordeaux Supérieur*
1990 £4.86 (HA) £4.99 (MAJ) £5.00 (BE)
£5.79 (NA) £5.99 (AME)

le Menaudat *1ères Côtes de Blaye*
1992 £5.56 (AV)

Mendoce *Côtes de Bourg*
1990 £5.49 (DAV)
1989 £5.49 (DAV)

des Moines *Lalande-de-Pomerol*
1988 £11.20 (AV)

Montaiguillon *Montagne-St-Émilion*
1989 £7.03 (BEK)

Pérenne *1ères Côtes de Blaye*
1991 £6.50 (PIP)
1990 £5.52 (BEK)

les Petits Arnauds *Côtes de Blaye*
1989 £5.07 (HOG) £5.89 (GRE)
1988 £5.99 (VIC)

Pitray *Bordeaux Supérieur Côtes de
Castillon*
1990 £6.75 (BU)
1990 IB £38.00 (BIB)
1989 £5.95 (WS) £6.69 (CB) £6.90 (PIP)
1988 £5.49 (PE) £5.95 (WS) £6.99 (SEC)

Plaisance *Montagne-St-Émilion*
1990 £4.45 (ASD)
1989 £5.95 (WS)

la Prade *Côtes de Francs*
1989 £8.29 (WW)

Puygueraud *Côtes de Francs*
1990 £7.18 (TAN)
1989 £7.69 (SEC) £8.21 (BUT)
1988 £9.25 (TAN)
1987 £8.16 (REI)
1985 £9.24 (BUT) £9.95 (VIG)

Richotey *Bordeaux*
1990 £5.77 (TAN) £6.20 (AD) £6.32 (CB)

la Rivière *Fronsac*
1991 £8.20 (BE)
1989 £9.10 (BE)
1988 £10.60 (BE)
1987 £8.99 (AME)
1986 £9.99 (PLA) £10.00 (BE) £10.50 (DI)
1983 £10.35 (BE) £10.56 (PLA)
1981 £13.81 (TW)
1979 £11.74 (PLA) £15.10 (TW)

Roquevieille *Côtes de Castillon*
1988 £5.58 (PEN)

Rouet *Fronsac*
1990 £5.95 (HAY)
1989 £6.50 (RAE) £7.83 (GOE)
1986 £6.45 (PE)
1985 £7.65 (PE)

Rousset *Côtes de Bourg*
1990 £5.20 (AD **1983** £8.99 (RE)

Segonzac *1ères Côtes de Blaye*
1992 £4.69 (DI)
1986 £6.75 (BÜ)

Siaurac *Lalande-de-Pomerol*
1989 £9.00 (ARM)

Sirius *Bordeaux*
1990 £5.95 (HAY)
1989 £5.99 (BOT) £5.99 (WR) £5.99 (THR)
£6.46 (HIC)
1988 £5.95 (GE)

de Sours *Bordeaux Supérieur*
1990 £5.75 (NI) £5.79 (MAJ) £6.80 (PLA)
£7.00 (CB) £7.50 (RES)
1989 £6.08 (GOE) £6.51 (BUT)

Tanesse *1ères Côtes de Bordeaux*
1985 £6.45 (PE)

Toumalin *Canon-Fronsac*
1988 £6.57 (EY) £6.95 (GE)
1986 £6.25 (GE)

Tour de l'Espérance *Bordeaux Supérieur*
1990 £4.62 (BY)
1989 £4.62 (BY)

Villars *Fronsac*
1989 £7.70 (MV) £9.95 (VIG)
1988 £7.49 (EY) £8.50 (MV) £9.95 (VIG)
1986 £8.30 (LAY) £8.95 (DAV)

WHITE BORDEAUX

DRY

Under £5.50

Non-vintage
Tertre de Launay (DAV)
1993
Bauduc (CV)
Bonnet (THR, WR, BOT)
Thieuley (SOM, MAJ, WS, AD)
1992
Bauduc (SUM)
Bauduc les Trois Hectares (CV)
Bonnet (NI, EL)
du Juge (GAL)
Fondarzac (ASD)
Moulin de Launay (EY, TAN, AD)
Thieuley (EY)

£5.50 to £6.99

1993
Thieuley (HIC, HAH)
1992
Bauduc les Trois Hectares (SUM)
Coucheroy (THR, WR, BOT)
de l'Étoile (AD, TAN)
Maitre d'Estournel (AD)
de Sours (MAJ, CB, PLA)
Thieuley (GOE, WCL)
1991
Coucheroy (NI)
de Sours (NI)
1990
Sirius (BE, THR, WR, BOT)
de Sours (SEC, BUT)
1989
Roquetaillade-la-Grange (BEK, BE)
1988
Cabannieux (WHI)
Sirius (GE)

£7.00 to £8.99

1993
Reynon Vieilles Vignes (WS)
1992
Cruzeau (EL)
la Grave (GE)
Reynon Vieilles Vignes (OD, WS)
1991
Doisy-Daëne Grand Vin Sec (OD)
la Grave (HAH)
1990
Cabannieux (ROB)

1989
Bauduc les Trois Hectares (PIP, NO)
Doisy-Daëne Grand Vin Sec (TAN)
Guiraud 'G' (BUT)

de Landiras (EY)
Roquetaillade-la-Grange (HIC)
1988
des Gravilles (RE)
1984
la Louvière (GE)
la Tour Martillac (RAE)

£9.00 to £11.99

1992
Rieussec 'R' (HAH)
1990
Couhins-Lurton (TAN)
la Louvière (BUT)
Montalivet (AD)
1989
Bouscaut (RAE)
la Grave (GOE)
la Louvière (NI)
Montalivet (TAN)
Rieussec 'R' (CB)
1985
Carbonnieux (REI)
Rieussec 'R' (BUT)

£12.00 to £14.99

1992
Carbonnieux (GE)
1990
Carbonnieux (GE)
Couhins-Lurton (REI, BIB)
la Louvière (OD)
1989
Bouscaut (BIB, BER)
Carbonnieux (GE, HAH)
Couhins-Lurton (AD)
la Louvière (BUT)
Smith-Haut-Lafitte (SEC)
la Tour Martillac (NI)

1988
la Grave (BUT)
1986
la Louvière (WS)
1985
Smith-Haut-Lafitte (BUT)
1981
Couhins-Lurton (RAE)

£15.00 to £19.99

1991
Pavillon Blanc du Château Margaux (ARM)
1990
Smith-Haut-Lafitte (OD)
la Tour Martillac (NI)
1989
Pavillon Blanc du Château Margaux
  (LAY, WY)
la Tour Martillac (GRE)
1988
Smith-Haut-Lafitte (NO)
la Tour Martillac (BUT)
1987
de Fieuzal (BER)
`L' de la Louvière (RAE, AD)
1982
Malartic-Lagravière (BUT)
1976
Roumieu (WY)

£20.00 to £29.99

1990
de Fieuzal (BUT, OD, AD)
Pavillon Blanc du Château Margaux (ARM)
1988
de Fieuzal (SEC, OD)
Pavillon Blanc du Château Margaux (WY)
1987
Haut-Brion Blanc (WY)
1985
'Y' d'Yquem (FA, REI)
1979
Laville-Haut-Brion (SEC)

£30.00 to £39.99

1992
Domaine de Chevalier (RAE)
1991
Domaine de Chevalier (RAE)
1990
Laville-Haut-Brion (OD)
1988
Haut-Brion Blanc (WY)
Laville-Haut-Brion (BUT)
'Y' d'Yquem (BUT, TW)

1985
Domaine de Chevalier (WS)
1983
Domaine de Chevalier (BER)
1982
Laville-Haut-Brion (ROB)

£40.00 to £49.99

1990
Haut-Brion Blanc (OD)
1989
Domaine de Chevalier (BUT)
1986
Domaine de Chevalier (BUT)
1983
Haut-Brion Blanc (WY)
1981
Haut-Brion Blanc (WY)
1978
'Y' d'Yquem (WY)
1967
Laville-Haut-Brion (WY)

£50.00 to £69.99

1983
Laville-Haut-Brion (BER)
1982
Domaine de Chevalier (TW)
1966
'Y' d'Yquem (VIG)
1964
'Y' d'Yquem (WY)
1949
Carbonnieux (WY)
1947
Olivier (WY)
1926
Pavillon Blanc du Château Margaux (WY)

£70.00 to £75.00

1989
Laville-Haut-Brion (BUT)
1967
Laville-Haut-Brion (VIG)

£90.00 to £99.99

1947
Laville-Haut-Brion (WY)

> *In each price band wines
> are listed in vintage order.
> Within each vintage they
> are listed in A–Z order.*

SWEET

Under £7.00

1990
Bastor-Lamontagne ½ bottle (WAI)
★ Clos St-Georges (SAI)
Marquis de Beausoleil St Croix du Mont (UN)
1989
de Berbec (OD, HIC)
Liot ½ bottle (HAL)
Terfort (VIG)
1988
Bastor-Lamontagne ½ bottle (BUT)
1986
Bastor-Lamontagne ½ bottle (EL)
1984
Coutet ½ bottle (NI)

£7.00 to £8.99

1992
Fayau (MV)
1990
Domaine de Noble (BIB)
du Juge (GAL)
Loupiac Gaudiet (HOG, HAH)
Rabaud-Promis ½ bottle (BIB)
Rayne-Vigneau ½ bottle (BUT)
des Tours (AD)
1989
Bastor-Lamontagne ½ bottle (SO)
Domaine de Noble (HIC)
Lousteau-Vieil (HAM)
1988
de Berbec (CV)
Coutet ½ bottle (WY)
Liot ½ bottle (HAL)
Rabaud-Promis ½ bottle (BUT, RAE)
1986
Coutet ½ bottle (BU, DI, LEA)
Rabaud-Promis ½ bottle (BUT)
1985
Coutet ½ bottle (DAV)
Filhot ½ bottle (DAV)

£9.00 to £11.99

1990
des Arroucats (CB)
Doisy-Dubroca ½ bottle (BAR)
Lamothe-Guignard (NI)
1989
Coutet ½ bottle (WY, SUM, BUT)
Liot (WS)
1988
Broustet (BUT)
Caillou (HAY)

la Chartreuse (HIC)
Guiteronde du Hayot (HOG)
les Justices ½ bottle (TW)
Liot (HAY, EL, GOE)
Lousteau-Vieil (PIP)
Rayne-Vigneau ½ bottle (WY)
St-Amand (PLA)
1987
St-Amand (PLA)
1986
Bastor-Lamontagne (NO, HOG, EL)
Filhot ½ bottle (HAL)
les Justices ½ bottle (TW)
Liot (EY)
de Malle (DAV)
Rieussec ½ bottle (GOE, BIB)
Romer du Hayot (HOG)
1984
★ Les Cyprès de Climens (VIC)
Rieussec ½ bottle (HAM)
1983
Filhot ½ bottle (DAV, WY)
Rayne-Vigneau ½ bottle (WY)
1979
Coutet ½ bottle (WY)
Doisy-Védrines (WY)
1978
Doisy-Daëne (WY)
1975
d'Arricaud (RAE)

£12.00 to £14.99

1990
Climens ½ bottle (BUT)
Doisy-Védrines (GOE)
Guiraud ½ bottle (BUT)
Liot (CB)
Rabaud-Promis (BIB)
Rayne-Vigneau (NI)
Rieussec ½ bottle (WY, OD)
1989
Bastor-Lamontagne (AME)
Lamothe-Guignard (GE, WS)
Rabaud-Promis ½ bottle (HAL, RAE)
Rieussec ½ bottle (OD, BUT, BUT)
Suduiraut ½ bottle (WY)
1988
d'Arche (GOE)
Climens ½ bottle (BAR)
Filhot (BIB, RAE)
Guiraud ½ bottle (BUT)
Lamothe-Guignard (LAY, GE, AD)
Rieussec (OD)
1987
Lafaurie-Peyraguey (PE)

1986
Climens ½ bottle (BUT)
St-Amand (GE)
1985
Coutet (DAV)
Filhot (DAV)
1984
Coutet (ROB)
Rieussec (DAV)
1983
de Malle (DAV)
Suduiraut ½ bottle (BIB)
1976
Filhot ½ bottle (WY)

£15.00 to £19.99

1990
Coutet (TAN)
Doisy-Daëne (BUT)
de Malle (BUT)
la Tour Blanche (NI)
1989
Broustet (BUT, LEA)
Coutet (BIB, HOG, PE, SUM)
Doisy-Daëne (GE, TAN, BER)
Filhot (BER)
Nairac (BE)
Romer du Hayot (AD)
Suduiraut (FA)
1988
Broustet (PIP)
Cantegril (AD)
la Chartreuse (TAN)
Climens (NI)
Coutet (HOG, PIP, BER)
Rabaud-Promis (RAE)
Rayne-Vigneau (EL)
Rieussec ½ bottle (WY, REI, NO)
1987
Rabaud-Promis (PE, AD)
1986
d'Arche (GE)
Coutet (DI, HOG)
les Justices (TW)
Lamothe-Guignard (EY)
Nairac (BUT)
Rabaud-Promis (BUT, WS)
Rayne-Vigneau (AD)
1985
Climens (BIB)
Lamothe-Guignard (LAY)
Suduiraut (AD)
1983
Climens ½ bottle (BU)
Coutet (GOE, BIB)

Filhot (DAV, WY, ROB)
Lamothe-Guignard (GE, BE)
Rabaud-Promis (HOG)
Rayne-Vigneau (HOG)
Rieussec ½ bottle (DAV)
Suduiraut (GOE)
la Tour Blanche (HOG)
1982
Rieussec (SEC, WAT)
la Tour Blanche (HOG)
1980
Lafaurie-Peyraguey (PLA)
1979
Rieussec (WY)
1978
Rayne-Vigneau (ROB)
1976
Coutet ½ bottle (WY)
1975
la Chartreuse (VIG)
1971
la Chartreuse (VIG)
Doisy-Védrines (WY)
1959
Climens (SEC)

£20.00 to £29.99

1990
Bastor-Lamontagne (BUT)
Climens (NI)
Filhot (NI)
Guiraud (BUT)
Rieussec (NI, LAY)
1989
Doisy-Védrines (ARM)
Guiraud (LEA)
Lafaurie-Peyraguey (BAR, BUT)
Rabaud-Promis (RAE, HAM)
Rayne-Vigneau (AD)
la Tour Blanche (BER)
1988
Doisy-Daëne (TAN)
Guiraud (BUT)
Lafaurie-Peyraguey (BUT)
de Malle (PIP, CV)
Suduiraut (BUT, HAY, BER)
la Tour Blanche (BUT, PIP)
1986
Climens (BUT)
Coutet (VIG, GRE, EY, ROB, AD)
Lafaurie-Peyraguey (BAR)
Rieussec (WY, BUT, NO, PIP, BU)
Sigalas-Rabaud (PIP)
1985
Guiraud (ROB)

Lafaurie-Peyraguey (PE)
Rieussec (DAV)
1983
Climens (WAT, WY, LEA, BIB, ARM)
Coutet (BE, LEA, DI, BEN, ROB, HA, TAN, AD)
Guiraud (BAR, LEA)
Lafaurie-Peyraguey (NO)
1981
de Malle (DI)
Rieussec (ROB)
1979
Rayne-Vigneau (DI)
1975
Coutet (REI)
Guiraud (PLA)
1971
Romer du Hayot (VIG)
1970
Filhot (BU)
Rayne-Vigneau (PLA)
1964
Guiraud (REI)

£30.00 to £39.99

1989
Climens (RAE, HAH, TAN)
Rieussec (TAN, RAE)
Sigalas-Rabaud (BER)
1988
Rieussec (BUT)
1984
d'Yquem ½ bottle (WY)
1983
de Fargues (FA)
Rieussec (BIB, WY, DAV, BUT, NI)
1982
Suduiraut (ROB)
1976
Rieussec (EY)
1975
Filhot (WY)
1969
Guiraud (VIG)

£40.00 to £59.99

1986
de Fargues (GOE)
1985
de Fargues (GOE, BUT)
1981
d'Yquem ½ bottle (UN)
1980
de Fargues (VIG)
1976
Climens (WY, NI)

1971
Rieussec (BIB)
1970
Rieussec (ROB)
Suduiraut (VIG)
1962
Sigalas-Rabaud (WY)
la Tour Blanche (ROB)
1961
Coutet (WY)
Doisy-Daëne (WY)
Guiraud (BIB)
1949
d'Arche (WY)

£60.00 to £89.99

1988
d'Yquem ½ bottle (WY, ARM)
1986
d'Yquem ½ bottle (BIB, WY)
1985
d'Yquem ½ bottle (TW)
1984
d'Yquem (WY, DI, BIB, OD)
1983
d'Yquem ½ bottle (BUT, WY)
1976
d'Yquem ½ bottle (WY)
1970
Gilette Crème de Tête (CB)
1961
Rieussec (WY)
1947
Rayne-Vigneau (WY)
1939
Rayne-Vigneau (WY)
1926
Lafaurie-Peyraguey (WY)
la Tour Blanche (WY)
1919
Sigalas-Rabaud (WY)

£90.00 to £119.99

1988
d'Yquem (FA, GOE, WY, CV)
1982
d'Yquem (WY)
1981
d'Yquem (UN, BU, WY)
1980
d'Yquem (WY)
1971
de Fargues (WY)
1966
Climens (BIB)

1955
Gilette Crème de Tête (TW)
1948
Coutet (WY)
Filhot (WY)
Rayne-Vigneau (WY)
1947
Coutet (WY)
Gilette (BEN)
1941
Rayne-Vigneau (WY)
1937
Coutet (WY)
Filhot (WY)
1935
la Tour Blanche (ROB)
1929
Filhot (WY)
1928
Climens (WY)
1923
Lafaurie-Peyraguey (ROB)
1921
Guiraud (WY)

£120.00 to £149.99

1988
Coutet (WY)
1987
d'Yquem (VIG)
1986
d'Yquem (BIB, WY, WS, BUT)
1985
d'Yquem (BUT, LAY, DI)
1983
d'Yquem (HA)
1943
Rieussec (WY)
1934
Filhot (WY)
1927
Climens (WY)
1924
Coutet (WY)
1923
la Tour Blanche (WY)

£150.00 to £199.99

1976
d'Yquem (WY)
1975
d'Yquem (BUT)
1969
d'Yquem (BUT)
1961

d'Yquem (BU)
1947
Rieussec (ROB)
1942
Climens (WY)
1924
Climens (WY)
1921
Filhot (WY)

£200.00 to £249.99

1971
d'Yquem (WY)
1949
Gilette Crème de Tête (TW)
1947
Climens (WY)
1934
Gilette Crème de Tête (TW)

£300.00 to £399.99

1967
d'Yquem (WY)
1962
d'Yquem (ROB)
1959
d'Yquem (NO)
1943
d'Yquem (WY)

£400.00 to £499.99

1955
d'Yquem (ROB)
1938
d'Yquem (WY)

Over £500.00

1953
d'Yquem (WY)
1944
d'Yquem (WY)
1919
d'Yquem (WY)
1918
d'Yquem (WY)

ROSÉ

Under £6.00

1993
de Sours Rosé (MAJ)
Thieuley Clairet (AD)
1992
de Sours Rosé (NI)
Thieuley Clairet (SOM)

BASIC BURGUNDY

RED

Under £5.00

1992
Bourgogne Rouge Cave de Buxy (WR, BOT, THR)
1991
Bourgogne Rouge Cave de Buxy (OD)
1988
Bourgogne Rouge Boisson-Vadot (BEK)

£5.00 to £6.99

1992
Bourgogne Coteaux de St-Bris, Brocard (AD)
1991
Bourgogne Rouge Faiveley (NO)
1990
Bourgogne Passe-Tout-Grains, Rion (MV)
Bourgogne Rouge Cave de Buxy (WAI)
Bourgogne Rouge Tasteviné, Bichot (DAV)
1988
Bourgogne Irancy, Bienvenu (HAM)
Bourgogne Rouge Tasteviné, Bichot (UN)
1986
Bourgogne Passe-Tout-Grains, Lejeune (RAE)
Bourgogne Passe-Tout-Grains, Vallet (BOR)

£7.00 to £7.99

1992
Bourgogne Rouge Jadot (WR, THR, BOT)
1991
Bourgogne Passe-Tout-Grains, Henri Jayer (SEC)
1990
Bourgogne Rouge Faiveley (DI)
Bourgogne Rouge Parent (CV)
1989
Bourgogne Rouge Jadot (VIC)
1988
Bourgogne Passe-Tout-Grains, Henri Jayer (RAE)

£8.00 to £11.00

1991
Bourgogne la Digoine Villaine (AD)
Bourgogne Rouge Coche-Dury (BEK)
Bourgogne Rouge Michel Lafarge (HAH)
1990
Bourgogne Rouge Georges Roumier (HAH)
Bourgogne Rouge Michel Lafarge (HAH, GOE)

WHITE

Under £6.00

1992
Bourgogne Aligoté Brocard (BEK)
Bourgogne Chardonnay A Bichot (UN)
1991
Bourgogne Aligoté Bichot (UN)
Bourgogne Chardonnay Sorin (HOG)
1990
Bourgogne Aligoté Brocard (WAI)

£6.00 to £7.99

Non-vintage
★ Crémant de Bourgogne Cave de Lugny (WAI, SO, MAR, OD)
1992
Bourgogne Aligoté de Bouzeron, Villaine (AD, TAN)
Bourgogne Aligoté Rion (MV)
Bourgogne Aligoté Rollin (BIB)
Bourgogne Blanc Latour (PEN)
Bourgogne Chardonnay Jadot (VIC)
1989
Bourgogne Aligoté de Bouzeron, Villaine (BUT)
1987
Bourgogne Aligoté Rollin (PE)

£8.00 to £9.99

1992
Bourgogne Chardonnay les Champs Perriers, Clerc (TAN)
1990
Crémant de Bourgogne Cave de Viré (CV)
1989
Bourgogne Blanc Brocard (WCL)
Bourgogne Blanc Leroy (BUT)
Bourgogne Blanc les Clous, Villaine (AD)
1988
Bourgogne Blanc Jobard (RAE)

£10.00 to £15.99

1992
Bourgogne Blanc Jobard (RAE)
1991
Bourgogne Blanc Jobard (MV)
1989
Bourgogne Blanc Domaine Leflaive (CB)
1986
Bourgogne Blanc Domaine Leflaive (BUT)

CÔTE D'OR

RED

Under £7.00

1992
Hautes-Côtes de Nuits, Caves des Hautes-
Côtes (TES)
1990
Hautes-Côtes de Beaune, Caves des
Hautes-Côtes (DI, WAI, TES)
Hautes-Côtes de Nuits, Caves des Hautes-
Côtes (OD)
Savigny-lès-Beaune Latour (WHI)
1988
Hautes-Côtes de Beaune, Caves des
Hautes-Côtes (OD)

£7.00 to £7.99

1991
Savigny-lès-Beaune Latour (PLA)
1990
Chorey-lès-Beaune Maillard (WAI)
1989
Santenay Latour (LO)

£8.00 to £8.99

1991
Côte de Beaune-Villages Drouhin (NI)
1990
Chassagne-Montrachet Latour (WY)
Hautes-Côtes de Nuits, Michel Gros (BY)
1989
Chassagne-Montrachet Latour (PLA)
★ Savigny-lès-Beaune Pavelot (GE)

£9.00 to £9.99

1991
Chassagne-Montrachet Henri Germain
(AD)
★ Gevrey-Chambertin Rossignol-Trapet (OD)
St-Aubin les Frionnes, Prudhon (TAN, HAY)
St-Aubin Sentier du Clou, Prudhon (BIB)
1990
Ladoix-Serrigny Drouhin (NI)
Meursault les Forges, Prieur-Brunet (EL)
Santenay la Maladière, Prieur (EL)
Savigny-lès-Beaune Faiveley (WAI)
1989
Fixin Gelin (PLA)
1988
Pernand-Vergelesses Rollin (RAE)
Santenay le Foulot, Domaine Prieur-
Brunet (EL)

£10.00 to £10.99

1991
Chorey-lès-Beaune Tollot-Beaut (AD, DI)
1990
Chorey-lès-Beaune les Beaumonts,
Machard de Gramont (WRI)
Chorey-lès-Beaune Tollot-Beaut (BEK)

Monthélie Garaudet (PIP)
St-Aubin les Argillières, Lamy-Pillot (ARM)
St-Aubin Sentier du Clou, Prudhon (NI)
1989
Aloxe-Corton les Chaillots, Latour (LO)
Monthélie Garaudet (WY)
St-Aubin les Frionnes, Prudhon (GOE)
1988
St-Romain Domaine Gras (ROB)
St-Romain Gras-Boisson (LEA)
Santenay Tasteviné, Bichot (UN)
Savigny-lès-Beaune Pavelot (DAV)
1987
Santenay Clos du Haut Village, Lequin-
Roussot (PLA)
Savigny-lès-Beaune les Lavières, Camus-
Bruchon (PE)

£11.00 to £11.99

1991
Gevrey-Chambertin Rodet (EL)
Marsannay Charlopin (HAH)
Savigny-lès-Beaune Pavelot (LAY)
1990
Marsannay Charlopin (WCL)
Santenay Drouhin (NI)
Santenay la Maladière, Girardin (BEK)
Savigny-lès-Beaune les Serpentières,
Drouhin (OD)
1989
Aloxe-Corton Latour (WY)
Auxey-Duresses Roulot (HAY)
Santenay Grand Clos Rousseau, Albert
Morey (BEK)
Savigny-lès-Beaune Pavelot (SAI)

1988
Monthélie Garaudet (WY)
Monthélie Monthélie-Douhairet (MV)
Morey-St-Denis Regis Bouvier (BEK)
St-Aubin les Frionnes, Prudhon (GOE)
Santenay Latour (PEN)
Savigny-lès-Beaune Bize (HAH)
1986
Chorey-lès-Beaune Tollot-Beaut (GRE)
1985
Hautes-Côtes de Nuits, Michel Gros
  (BUT, TW)
Santenay Latour (WHI)
1983
Beaune Clos des Fèves, Chanson (BUT)

£12.00 to £12.99

1992
Aloxe-Corton Rollin (RAE)
1991
Aloxe-Corton Drouhin (NI)
Gevrey-Chambertin Rossignol-Trapet (PIP)
Gevrey-Chambertin Trapet (BEK)
1990
Fixin Alain Guyard (NI)
Savigny-lès-Beaune Faiveley (DI)
Savigny-lès-Beaune Girard-Vollot (WCL)

1989
Beaune Vignes Franches, Latour (PLA)
Gevrey-Chambertin Trapet (BY)
1988
Beaune Vignes Franches, Mazilly (MV)
Chassagne-Montrachet Albert Morey (WY)
Gevrey-Chambertin Rodet (WHI)
Pernand-Vergelesses Île de Vergelesses,
  Chandon de Briailles (BEK)
Pommard les Cras, Belland (WAT)
Santenay Drouhin (ROB)
Savigny-lès-Beaune Latour (DAV)
1987
Vosne-Romanée les Violettes, Georges
  Clerget (BY)
1986
Meursault Clos de la Baronne, Manuel (CV)
Volnay Henri Boillot (ASD)
1983
Aloxe-Corton les Chaillots, Latour (WHI)
Gevrey-Chambertin Rodet (SAI)

£13.00 to £13.99

1991
Côte de Nuits-Villages Jayer-Gilles (AD)
1990
Aloxe-Corton Champy (HOG)
Beaune Clos du Roi, Chanson (POR)
Chambolle-Musigny Lignier (SOM)
Nuits-St-Georges Labouré-Roi (PIP)
1989
Beaune Vignes Franches, Latour (WY)
Nuits-St-Georges Rodet (PLA)
Savigny-lès-Beaune les Lavières, Chandon
  de Briailles (LEA)
1988
Beaune Grèves, Moillard (BE)
Beaune les Montrevenots, Jean-Marc
  Boillot (BEK)
Monthélie Parent (TAN)
Nuits-St-Georges Labouré-Roi (WY)
1987
Chassagne-Montrachet Champs-Gains,
  Jean Marc Morey (DAV)
Côte de Nuits-Villages Vallet (POR)
1986
Beaune Teurons, Jadot (GRE)
Latricières-Chambertin Trapet (BEK)
Vosne-Romanée Latour (WY)
1985
Chorey-lès-Beaune Tollot-Beaut (BUT)
Côte de Nuits-Villages Jayer-Gilles (PE)
1983
Beaune Blanches Fleurs, Tollot-Beaut (RAE)
Gevrey-Chambertin Chanson (BUT

£14.00 to £14.99

1991
Santenay Clos Tavannes, Domaine de la
Pousse d'Or (DI)
1990
Auxey-Duresses Roulot (ARM)
Beaune Bressandes, Henri Germain
(TAN, AD)
Monthélie Château de Monthélie,
Suremain (RAE)
Savigny-lès-Beaune les Lavières, Chandon
de Briailles (LEA)
Vosne-Romanée les Brulées, Henri
Jayer (EL)
1989
Aloxe-Corton Rollin (NI, RAE, BIB)
Beaune Clos des Ursules, Jadot (POR)
Gevrey-Chambertin Latour (LO)
Monthélie Château de Monthélie,
Suremain (RAE)
1988
Gevrey-Chambertin Trapet (BY)
1987
Beaune Clos du Roi, Tollot-Beaut (BEK)
Nuits-St-Georges Faiveley (GRE)
Nuits-St-Georges les Cailles, Michelot
(BEK)
Vosne-Romanée Engel (ROB)
1986
Nuits-St-Georges les Damodes,
Lescure (BE)
Nuits-St-Georges les Vaucrains,
Michelot (BEK)
Santenay Clos Tavannes, Domaine de
la Pousse d'Or (GOE)
1985
Pommard la Platière, Coche (RAE)
1983
Aloxe-Corton les Chaillots, Latour (WY)
Beaune Bressandes, Henri Germain (EY)
Chambolle-Musigny Georges Roumier
(RAE)
Meursault Clos de la Baronne, Manuel (CV)

£15.00 to £15.99

1992
Volnay Michel Lafarge (RAE)
1991
Volnay Frémiets, Marquis d'Angerville
(CB)
Vosne-Romanée Jean Gros (DI)
1990
Beaune Teurons, Rossignol-Trapet (BY)
Gevrey-Chambertin Latour (GAL)
Nuits-St-Georges Champy (HOG)

Santenay Clos Tavannes, Domaine de la
Pousse d'Or (DI)
Savigny-lès-Beaune les Lavières, Tollot-
Beaut (AD)
Vosne-Romanée Mongeard-Mugneret (GOE)
1989
Beaune Bressandes, Henri Germain (AD)
Côte de Nuits-Villages Jayer-Gilles (WS)
Gevrey-Chambertin Latour (PEN)
1988
Volnay 1er Cru, Michel Lafarge (BEK)
1987
Beaune Chouacheux, Machard de
Gramont (DAV)
Corton-Bressandes Tollot-Beaut (BEK)
Corton Tollot-Beaut (BEK)
Nuits-St-Georges Faiveley (DI)
Volnay Clos des Chênes, Michel Lafarge
(BEK)
1986
Beaune Grèves, Tollot-Beaut (HAY)
Chambolle-Musigny Faiveley (DI)
1985
Gevrey-Chambertin Leclerc (GOE)
1983
Aloxe-Corton Latour (PEN)

£16.00 to £16.99

1991
Gevrey-Chambertin Armand Rousseau (TAN)
Savigny-lès-Beaune les Vergelesses, Bize
(DI)
1990
Chassagne-Montrachet Champs-Gains,
Jean Marc Morey (PIP)
Gevrey-Chambertin Armand Rousseau (EL)
1989
Chambolle-Musigny Dujac (BUT)
Gevrey-Chambertin Rossignol-Trapet
(TW)
Morey-St-Denis Clos de la Bussière,
Georges Roumier (TAN)
Nuits-St-Georges les Hauts Pruliers,
Machard de Gramont (GAL)
Pommard les Épenots, Latour (PEN)
Savigny-lès-Beaune les Vergelesses,
Bize (DI)
Vosne-Romanée Engel (BEN)

*In each price band wines
are listed in vintage order.
Within each vintage they
are listed in A–Z order.*

1988
Beaune 1er Cru, Domaine du Château de
   Meursault (LO)
Beaune Clos des Ursules, Jadot (HA)
Beaune Épenottes, Parent (CV)
Chambolle-Musigny de Vogüé (WY)
Chambolle-Musigny Dujac (BUT)
Corton Latour (WY)
Nuits-St-Georges les Hauts Pruliers,
   Machard de Gramont (PLA)
1987
Gevrey-Chambertin Faiveley (DI)
Nuits-St-Georges Rion (MV)
Volnay Michel Lafarge (RAE)
1986
Clos de la Roche Dujac (BY)
Gevrey-Chambertin Vieille Vigne,
   Domaine des Varoilles (CHA)
Morey-St-Denis Olivier Leflaive (TW)
1983
Beaune Clos des Fèves, Chanson (RE)
Beaune Teurons, Domaines du Château de
   Beaune (PEN)
Corton Chanson (BUT)

£17.00 to £17.99

1990
Chambolle-Musigny Georges Roumier (EL)
Gevrey-Chambertin Rossignol-Trapet (HAH)
Nuits-St-Georges Robert Chevillon (GAU)
1989
Nuits-St-Georges Faiveley (GRE)
Pommard Clos Blanc, Machard de
   Gramont (AD)
Volnay Frémiets, Marquis d'Angerville (GE)
1988
Chambolle-Musigny Latour (PLA)
Corton-Grancey Latour (WY)
Savigny-lès-Beaune les Vergelesses,
   Bize (HAH)
Vosne-Romanée Engel (BEN)

£18.00 to £19.99

1991
Beaune Clos du Roi, Tollot-Beaut (DI)
Morey-St-Denis Dujac (DI)
Nuits-St-Georges Méo-Camuzet (GOE)
Pommard les Saussilles, Jean-Marc
   Boillot (GOE)
1990
Aloxe-Corton Drouhin (NI)
Aloxe-Corton Tollot-Beaut (LAY)
Chambolle-Musigny Lignier (VIG)
Gevrey-Chambertin Drouhin (NI)
Volnay Drouhin (NI)

1989
Aloxe-Corton Tollot-Beaut (AD)
Chambolle-Musigny de Vogüé (WY)
Gevrey-Chambertin Cazetiers, Armand
   Rousseau (AD)
Morey-St-Denis Dujac (AD)
Savigny-lès-Beaune la Dominode, Bruno
   Clair (BEN)
Volnay Michel Lafarge (WS)
1988
Chambolle-Musigny Dujac (BEN)
Gevrey-Chambertin Bachelet (GAU)
Nuits-St-Georges Faiveley (DI)
Pommard les Bertins, Lescure (PIP)
Volnay Champans, Gagnard-Delagrange (BY)
Volnay Michel Lafarge (RAE)
Vosne-Romanée Rion (MV)
1987
Beaune Teurons, Jacques Germain (WHI)
Gevrey-Chambertin Bachelet (ROB)
Morey-St-Denis Clos de la Bussière,
   Georges Roumier (ROB)
Morey-St-Denis Clos des Ormes,
   Lignier (BIB)
Pommard Lejeune (RAE)
Volnay les Caillerets, Domaine de la
   Pousse d'Or (ROB)
Volnay Santenots Matrot (CB)
Vosne-Romanée Rion (BEN)
1986
Corton Latour (VIC)
Latricières-Chambertin Trapet (BY)
Nuits-St-Georges Jadot (VIC)
Nuits-St-Georges les St-Georges,
   Faiveley (DI)
Pommard les Chaponniers, Parent (EY)
Savigny-lès-Beaune Marconnets, Bize (TW)
Volnay les Caillerets, Clos des 60 Ouvrées,
   Domaine de la Pousse d'Or (BY)
1985
Aloxe-Corton Voarick (BUT)
Volnay Santenots Rougeot (PE)
1982
Corton-Grancey Latour (SEC)
1979
Chambolle-Musigny Latour (PEN)
1978
Santenay Remoissenet (GRE)

> *Stars (★) indicate wines
> selected by the editors as
> particularly good value
> in their class.*

£20.00 to £22.49

1990
Chambolle-Musigny Dujac (BUT)
Gevrey-Chambertin Vieilles Vignes Alain
  Burguet (GAU)
Morey-St-Denis Dujac (TAN)
1989
Beaune Grèves, Moillard (WRI)
Échézeaux Mongeard-Mugneret (GOE)
Gevrey-Chambertin Vieilles Vignes Alain
  Burguet (GAU)
Nuits-St-Georges les Boudots, Méo-
  Camuzet (GOE)
Volnay Clos des Santenots, Prieur (BER)
Vosne-Romanée Jean Gros (BOT)
1988
Chambolle-Musigny Faiveley (GRE)
Corton Pougets, Jadot (HA)
Nuits-St-Georges Méo-Camuzet (RAE)
Volnay Santenots Lafon (MV)
Vosne-Romanée les Beaumonts, Domaine
  Rion (OD)
1987
Beaune 1er Cru, de Villamont (ROB)
Beaune Clos des Mouches, Drouhin (GRE)
Clos de Vougeot Noëllat (BEK)
Gevrey-Chambertin Lavaux-St-Jacques,
  Maume (PE)
1986
Volnay Caillerets Cuvée Carnot, Bouchard
  Père (VIC)
Volnay Clos des Ducs, Marquis
  d'Angerville (CB)
1985
Chambolle-Musigny la Combe d'Orvaux,
  Grivot (BUT)
Chambolle-Musigny Lignier (BUT)
Vosne-Romanée Jean Gros (BUT)
1983
Beaune Grèves, Tollot-Beaut (BUT)
Nuits-St-Georges Clos de Thorey,
  Moillard (PEN)

£22.50 to £24.99

1991
Latricières-Chambertin Trapet (OD)
Volnay les Caillerets, Clos des 60 Ouvrées,
  Domaine de la Pousse d'Or (DI)
1990
Nuits-St-Georges Clos de Forets St-
  Georges, Domaine de l'Arlot (OD)
Pommard les Épenots, Mme de Courcel
  (EL, WS)
Volnay les Caillerets, Marquis d'Angerville
  (EL)

1989
Morey-St-Denis Clos des Ormes,
  Faiveley (GRE)
Nuits-St-Georges Clos de Forets St-
  Georges, Domaine de l'Arlot (BY)
Nuits-St-Georges Clos de la Maréchale,
  Faiveley (BEN)
Volnay les Caillerets, Clos des 60 Ouvrées,
  Domaine de la Pousse d'Or (LAY)
1988
Latricières-Chambertin Trapet (BEK)
Mazis-Chambertin Armand Rousseau (TAN)
Nuits-St-Georges Clos de la Maréchale,
  Faiveley (DI)
Pommard Rugiens Domaine Courcel (EL)
Volnay Champans, Marquis d'Angerville
  (BEN)
Volnay Clos des Chênes, Michel Lafarge
  (PIP)
Volnay les Caillerets, Clos des 60 Ouvrées,
  Domaine de la Pousse d'Or (BY)
1987
Corton-Bressandes Tollot-Beaut (BY)
Nuits-St-Georges Richemone, Pernin-
  Rossin (RAE)
Vosne-Romanée les Chaumes, Rion (MV)
1986
Chambertin Trapet (BY)
Clos de la Roche Armand Rousseau (BUT)
Clos de Vougeot Grivot (WY)
Clos de Vougeot Méo-Camuzet (RAE)
Nuits-St-Georges Vignes Rondes, Rion (GRE)
Vosne-Romanée les Beaumonts, Domaine
  Rion (GAU)
1985
Vosne-Romanée Confuron-Cotetidot (ROB)
1983
Aloxe-Corton Tollot-Beaut (BUT)
Beaune Clos des Ursules, Jadot (BUT)
Latricières-Chambertin Trapet (BY)
Pommard les Argillières, Lejeune (BUT)

£25.00 to £27.49

1991
Chambertin Trapet (OD)
Volnay Clos de la Bousse d'Or, Domaine de
  la Pousse d'Or (DI)
1990
Beaune Clos des Mouches, Drouhin (NI)
Mazis-Chambertin Armand Rousseau (EL)
1989
Charmes-Chambertin Armand Rousseau
  (EL)
Clos de Vougeot Méo-Camuzet (GOE)
Clos de Vougeot Mongeard-Mugneret (GOE)

1988
Chambertin Trapet (BEK)
Charmes-Chambertin Armand Rousseau
(AD)
Clos de la Roche Armand Rousseau (EL)
1987
Corton Pougets, Jadot (VIC)
Gevrey-Chambertin Clos St-Jacques,
Armand Rousseau (BUT)
Gevrey-Chambertin Combottes, Dujac (BUT)
1986
Chambertin Clos-de-Bèze, Bruno Clair (WY)
Charmes-Chambertin Dujac (BY)
Clos St-Denis Dujac (BUT)
Latricières-Chambertin Ponsot (GOE)
Pommard Rugiens Domaine Courcel (EL)
Volnay Clos de la Bousse d'Or, Domaine de
la Pousse d'Or (GOE)

£27.50 to £29.99

1991
Corton-Bressandes Tollot-Beaut (DI)
Nuits-St-Georges les Boudots, Méo-
Camuzet (GOE)
Volnay Santenots Lafon (VIG)
1990
Charmes-Chambertin Armand Rousseau
(GOE)
Morey-St-Denis 1er Cru, Ponsot (ARM)
Nuits-St-Georges Clos de Forets St-
Georges, Domaine de l'Arlot (ARM)
Pommard Pezerolles Domaine de
Montille (HAH)
Volnay les Caillerets, Clos des 60 Ouvrées,
Domaine de la Pousse d'Or (DI)
Volnay Santenots Lafon (GOE)
Vosne-Romanée les Chaumes, Rion (GAU)
1989
Beaune Clos des Mouches, Drouhin (NO)
Chambolle-Musigny de Vogüé (BEN)
1988
Beaune Clos des Mouches, Drouhin (TW)
Beaune Cuvée Brunet Hospices de Beaune,
Patriarche (BER)
Chapelle-Chambertin Trapet (BEK)
Clos de Vougeot Noëllat (BEK)
Nuits-St-Georges Clos de Forets St-
Georges, Domaine de l'Arlot (BY)
Nuits-St-Georges Clos des Argillières,
Rion (GAU)
Nuits-St-Georges Vignes Rondes, Rion (GAU)
1987
Beaune Cuvée Maurice Drouhin, Hospices
de Beaune (BEN)
Charmes-Chambertin Dujac (BY, BUT)

1986
Chambertin Clos-de-Bèze, Faiveley (GRE)
Clos de la Roche Dujac (BUT)
Corton Maréchaudes, Chandon de Briailles
(TW)
Gevrey-Chambertin Clos St-Jacques,
Armand Rousseau (BUT)
Gevrey-Chambertin Combottes, Dujac (BY)
1985
Corton Bonneau du Martray (ROB)
Volnay les Caillerets, Domaine de la
Pousse d'Or (WS)
Volnay Santenots Lafon (BUT)

£30.00 to £34.99

1992
Échézeaux Henri Jayer (RAE)
1991
Bonnes-Mares Roumier (HAH)
Volnay Clos des Chênes, Michel Lafarge
(HAH)
1989
Bonnes-Mares de Vogüé (WY)
Bonnes-Mares Roumier (TAN)
Chambolle-Musigny les Amoureuses,
Roumier (TAN)
Charmes-Chambertin Dujac (BUT)
Corton Pougets, Jadot (WR, THR, BOT)
Volnay Clos de la Bousse d'Or, Domaine de
la Pousse d'Or (WR, BOT, THR)
1988
Clos de Vougeot Château de la Tour (EL)
Corton-Bressandes Tollot-Beaut (AD)
Gevrey-Chambertin Clos St-Jacques,
Armand Rousseau (BUT)
Gevrey-Chambertin Combottes, Dujac (BUT)
Latricières-Chambertin Trapet (BY)
Mazis-Chambertin Armand Rousseau
(GAU)
Nuits-St-Georges les Boudots, Méo-
Camuzet (GOE)
Ruchottes-Chambertin Armand Rousseau
(ROB)
1987
Charmes-Chambertin Bachelet (GAU)
Clos de la Roche Armand Rousseau (BUT)
Corton Clos des Cortons, Faiveley (GRE)
Échézeaux Domaine de la Romanée-Conti
(WY)
1986
Chambertin Armand Rousseau (WY)
Chambertin Ponsot (GOE)
Clos de la Roche Ponsot (MV)
Clos de Vougeot Méo-Camuzet (PE)
Clos St-Denis Dujac (BY)

1985
Charmes-Chambertin Armand Rousseau
(BUT)
Corton-Bressandes Michel Voarick (BUT)
Corton les Renardes, Michel Voarick (BUT)
Échézeaux Mongeard-Mugneret (BUT)
1983
Clos de Vougeot Moillard (PEN)
Échézeaux Domaine de la Romanée-Conti
(FA)

£35.00 to £39.99
1991
Bonnes-Mares Lignier (VIG)
Clos de Vougeot Méo-Camuzet (GOE)
1990
Clos de Vougeot Château de la Tour (EL)
Gevrey-Chambertin Clos St-Jacques,
Armand Rousseau (EL, GOE)
Grands-Échézeaux Mongeard-Mugneret
(GOE)
Mazis-Chambertin Faiveley (DI)
Nuits-St-Georges les St-Georges,
Faiveley (DI)
1989
Bonnes-Mares Dujac (BUT)
Chambolle-Musigny les Amoureuses, de
Vogüé (WY)
Clos de la Roche Armand Rousseau (BUT)
Clos de la Roche Dujac (BUT)
Clos de la Roche Vieilles Vignes,
Ponsot (GOE)
Clos St-Denis Dujac (BUT, TAN)
Latricières-Chambertin Ponsot (GOE)
1988
Charmes-Chambertin Dujac (BUT)
Clos de la Roche Armand Rousseau (BUT)
Clos St-Denis Dujac (BUT)
Corton Clos des Cortons, Faiveley (DI)
Échézeaux Faiveley (DI)
Musigny Prieur (EL)
1987
Bonnes-Mares Dujac (BUT)
Bonnes-Mares Roumier (BUT)
Clos de Vougeot Arnoux (WHI)
Échézeaux Jacqueline Jayer (BUT)

1986
Bonnes-Mares Roumier (BUT)
Clos de Vougeot Grivot (DAV)
1985
Clos de la Roche Armand Rousseau (BUT)
Corton Clos des Cortons, Faiveley (BIB)
Corton-Grancey Latour (WY)
Gevrey-Chambertin Clos St-Jacques,
Armand Rousseau (BUT)
Grands-Échézeaux Mongeard-Mugneret
(BIB)
Volnay Clos des Chênes, Michel
Lafarge (BUT)

£40.00 to £49.99
1990
Charmes-Chambertin Dujac (BUT)
Échézeaux Dujac (ARM)
Romanée-St-Vivant Domaine de la
Romanée-Conti (ARM)
1989
Clos de Vougeot Méo-Camuzet (BUT)
1988
Bonnes-Mares Dujac (BUT)
Bonnes-Mares Moillard (BER)
Chambertin Trapet (BY)
Chambertin Vieilles Vignes, Trapet (PIP)
Clos de la Roche Dujac (BUT)
Clos de la Roche Vieilles Vignes,
Ponsot (GOE)
Musigny Vieilles Vignes, de Vogüé (WY)
1985
Nuits-St-Georges Henri Jayer (BUT)

£50.00 to £59.99
1990
Bonnes-Mares Dujac (BUT)
Chambertin Clos-de-Bèze, Faiveley (DI)
Clos de la Roche Vieilles Vignes,
Ponsot (ARM)
Latricières-Chambertin Ponsot (GOE)
1989
Chambertin Armand Rousseau (BUT)
Grands-Échézeaux Domaine de la
Romanée-Conti (WY)
Musigny Vieilles Vignes, de Vogüé (WY)
Romanée-St-Vivant Domaine de la
Romanée-Conti (FA, WY)
1988
Chambertin Ponsot (GOE)
1987
Chambolle-Musigny les Amoureuses, de
Vogüé (TW)
Échézeaux Domaine de la Romanée-Conti
(BUT)

Grands-Échézeaux Domaine de la
    Romanée-Conti (WY)
1986
Grands-Échézeaux Domaine de la
    Romanée-Conti (WY)
Romanée-St-Vivant Domaine de la
    Romanée-Conti (WY)
1985
Chambertin Armand Rousseau (BUT)

£60.00 to £79.99

1991
Richebourg Domaine Gros (DI)
1990
Échézeaux Domaine de la Romanée-Conti
    (TAN, EL)
1989
Richebourg Domaine de la Romanée-Conti
    (FA)
Richebourg Domaine Gros (BY)
1988
Échézeaux Domaine de la Romanée-Conti
    (CB)
1987
Richebourg Domaine de la Romanée-Conti
    (WY)
Romanée-St-Vivant Domaine de la
    Romanée-Conti (BUT)
1986
Échézeaux Henri Jayer
    (BUT)
Richebourg Domaine de la Romanée-Conti
    (WY)
1985
Échézeaux Domaine de la Romanée-Conti
    (NO, BUT)
Musigny Vieilles Vignes, de Vogüé (PLA)
1983
Grands-Échézeaux Domaine de la
    Romanée-Conti (WY)

£80.00 to £99.00

1987
La Tâche Domaine de la Romanée-Conti
    (WY)
1985
Chambertin Ponsot (BIB)
Romanée-St-Vivant Domaine de la
    Romanée-Conti (WY)
Romanée-St-Vivant Cuvée Marey Monge,
    Domaine de la Romanée-Conti
    (BUT)
1983
Richebourg Domaine de la Romanée-Conti
    (WY)

£100.00 to £149.00

1989
La Tâche Domaine de la Romanée-Conti
    (WY)
1988
La Tâche Domaine de la Romanée-Conti
    (WY)
1985
Richebourg Domaine de la Romanée-Conti
    (BUT)
1985
La Tâche Domaine de la Romanée-Conti
    (TW)

£150.00 to £210.00

1988
Richebourg Domaine de la Romanée-Conti
    (NO)
1985
La Tâche Domaine de la Romanée-Conti
    (BUT)

£300.00 to £450.00

1989
Romanée-Conti Domaine de la Romanée-
    Conti (WY)
1987
Romanée-Conti Domaine de la Romanée-
    Conti (BUT)
1986
Romanée-Conti Domaine de la Romanée-
    Conti (BUT)

c. £551.00

1990
Romanée-Conti Domaine de la Romanée-
    Conti (EL)

c. £705.00

1988
Romanée-Conti Domaine de la Romanée-
    Conti (TW)

c. £1415.00

1990
Romanée-Conti Domaine de la Romanée-
    Conti (BUT)

WHITE

Under £10.00

1991
St-Aubin Prudhon (BIB)
1988
St-Romain Prieur-Brunet (EL)
1987
Santenay Blanc Lequin-Roussot (RAE)

£10.00 to £11.99

1992
Auxey-Duresses Diconne (BEK)
Auxey-Duresses Labouré-Roi (PIP)
Meursault Jean Germain (WS)
Meursault Michelot (OD)
Meursault Ropiteau (HOG)
Monthélie le Champ Fulliot, Garaudet
  (PIP)
St-Aubin la Chatenière, Roux Père
  et Fils (EL)
★ St-Aubin le Charmois, Olivier Leflaive
  (LAY)
1991
Pernand-Vergelesses, Olivier Leflaive (AD)
Pernand-Vergelesses Rollin (NI)
St-Romain Clos Sous le Château, Jean
  Germain (PLA)
1990
Pernand-Vergelesses Rollin (BIB)
1989
Pernand-Vergelesses Capron-Manieux (MV)
Pernand-Vergelesses, Olivier Leflaive (WS)
St-Aubin Prudhon (EY)
1988
Monthélie le Champ Fulliot, Garaudet (NO)
Pernand-Vergelesses Chanson (TAN)
Pernand-Vergelesses Laleure-Piot (GOE)

£12.00 to £13.99

1992
Puligny-Montrachet Labouré-Roi (EL)
1991
Meursault Bouchard Père (AME)
Meursault Latour (LO)
Meursault Michelot-Buisson (BEK)
1990
Meursault Latour (HOG, WHI)
1989
Chassagne-Montrachet Latour (HOG)
Puligny-Montrachet Latour (HOG)
1988
Pernand-Vergelesses Dubreuil-Fontaine
  (BY)
Pernand-Vergelesses Rollin (RAE)

1987
Meursault Clos des Meix-Chavaux, Jean
  Germain (GE)
Pernand-Vergelesses Vallet (BOR)
Puligny-Montrachet Grands Champs, Jean
  Germain (GE)
1986
Chassagne-Montrachet Latour (SEC)

£14.00 to £15.99

1992
Chassagne-Montrachet Drouhin (NI)
Meursault Jobard (LEA)
★ Puligny-Montrachet Carillon (OD)
Puligny-Montrachet Drouhin (NI)
1991
Meursault Clos des Meix-Chavaux, Jean
  Germain (HAH)
Meursault Drouhin (OD)
Meursault Genevrières, Latour (HOG)
Meursault Henri Germain (TAN)
Meursault Jobard (LEA)
Meursault Matrot (CB)
Puligny-Montrachet Latour (LO)
1990
Meursault-Blagny, Latour (FA)
Meursault l'Ormeau, Coche (BIB)
Puligny-Montrachet Latour (PEN)
1989
Meursault-Blagny, Latour (HOG)
Meursault Clos du Château, Château de
  Meursault (LO)
Meursault Genevrières, Latour (WY)
Meursault Latour (GAL, BEN)
Meursault Monatine, Rougeot (GOE, SEC)
1988
Puligny-Montrachet Carillon (ASD)
1987
Meursault les Luchets, Roulot (BUT)
Meursault l'Ormeau, Coche (RAE)
1985
Puligny-Montrachet Jean Germain (GE)

£16.00 to £17.99

1992
Chassagne-Montrachet Latour (WY)
1991
Chassagne-Montrachet les Caillerets,
  Jean-Marc Morey (EL)
Chassagne-Montrachet les Vergers,
  Colin (EL)
Puligny-Montrachet Carillon (LAY)
Puligny-Montrachet les Folatières,
  Latour (GAL)
Puligny-Montrachet Sauzet (BEK, EL)

1990
Bourgogne Chardonnay, Clos du Château
  de Meursault (VIN)
Meursault Charmes, Brunet (EL)
Meursault Henri de Villamont (ROB)
Puligny-Montrachet Grands Champs, Jean
  Germain (HAH)
St-Aubin Albert Morey (DAV)
1989
Chassagne-Montrachet Niellon (BUT)
1988
Chassagne-Montrachet Albert Morey (DAV)
Chassagne-Montrachet Drouhin (WY)
Meursault Clos du Cromin, Javillier (SUM)
Meursault Matrot (ARM)
1986
Meursault Charmes, Latour (SEC)
Puligny-Montrachet Carillon (GE)

£18.00 to £19.99

1991
Chassagne-Montrachet Sauzet (TAN)
1990
Meursault Genevrières, Latour (GAL)
Puligny-Montrachet Bouchard Père (AME)
Puligny-Montrachet Carillon (AD)
Puligny-Montrachet Olivier Leflaive (AMI)
Puligny-Montrachet Sauzet (PE)
1989
Chassagne-Montrachet Jadot (POR)
Chassagne-Montrachet les Vergers,
  Colin (EY)
Meursault les Vireuils, Roulot (HAY)
Puligny-Montrachet Grands Champs, Jean
  Germain (DAV)
1988
Chassagne-Montrachet les Vergers,
  Colin (GOE)
Chassagne-Montrachet Morgeot, Gagnard
  Delagrange (BY)
Meursault-Blagny, Latour (WY)
Meursault Michelot-Buisson (BY)
Puligny-Montrachet Clerc (BY)
Puligny-Montrachet Latour (PEN)
Puligny-Montrachet Olivier Leflaive (DI)
1987
Chassagne-Montrachet Domaine Leflaive
  (BEN)
Chassagne-Montrachet les Vergers,
  Colin (GOE)
Puligny-Montrachet Clerc (TW)
Puligny-Montrachet Domaine Leflaive (SEC)
1986
Meursault Jadot (VIC)
Meursault Poruzots, Germain (LEA)

£20.00 to £24.99

1992
Chassagne-Montrachet les Vergers,
  Colin (GOE)
Meursault Genevrières, Jobard (LEA)
Meursault Poruzots, Jobard (LEA)
1991
Meursault Genevrières, Jobard (LEA)
Meursault les Luchets, Roulot (ARM)
Meursault les Vireuils, Roulot (ARM)
Meursault Perrières, Domaine Leflaive (DI)
Meursault Poruzots, Jobard (LEA)
Puligny-Montrachet Clos de la Mouchère,
  Henri Boillot (DAV)
Puligny-Montrachet Domaine Leflaive (ARM)
1990
Chassagne-Montrachet la Boudriotte,
  Gagnard-Delagrange (HAH)
Chassagne-Montrachet les Embrazées,
  Albert Morey (EY)
Chassagne-Montrachet les Vergers,
  Colin (WS)
Meursault Genevrières, Jobard (LEA)
Meursault Jobard (MV, RAE)
Meursault Perrières, Prieur (VIG)
Puligny-Montrachet Clerc (VIN)
Puligny-Montrachet la Garenne, Thomas
  (WCL)
Puligny-Montrachet Domaine Leflaive
  (AD, GOE, CB, LAY)
Puligny-Montrachet les Folatières, Clerc (BY)
1989
Chassagne-Montrachet les Caillerets,
  Bachelet-Ramonet (BIB)
Chassagne-Montrachet Marquis de
  Laguiche (WY)
Corton-Charlemagne Olivier
  Leflaive (HAH)
Meursault-Blagny, Matrot (CB)
Meursault Clos de Mazeray, Prieur (WHI)
Meursault Jobard (RAE)
Meursault Santenots, Monthélie-
  Douhairet (BEN)
Puligny-Montrachet Carillon (ROB)
Puligny-Montrachet Domaine Leflaive
  (GOE)

Please remember that Webster's is a price GUIDE and not a price LIST. It is not meant to replace up-to-date merchant's lists.

1988

Chassagne-Montrachet la Romanée,
  Moillard (VIC)
Meursault-Blagny, Jadot (HA)
Meursault-Blagny, Matrot (ARM)
Meursault Genevrières, Jobard (RAE)
Meursault Henri Germain (AD)
Meursault Jobard (GAU)
Meursault Poruzots, Jobard (RAE)
Puligny-Montrachet Domaine Leflaive
  (GOE, TW, BIB)
Puligny-Montrachet les Chalumeaux,
  Matrot (ARM)
Puligny-Montrachet les Folatières,
  Drouhin (NO)

1987

Meursault Charmes, Matrot (ARM)
Puligny-Montrachet les Folatières,
  Clerc (PE)
Puligny-Montrachet les Perrières,
  Sauzet (PE)

1986

Chassagne-Montrachet les Vergers,
  Colin (GOE)
Meursault Genevrières, Latour (BUT)
Puligny-Montrachet Jadot (HA, VIC)
Puligny-Montrachet Labouré-Roi (CV)
Puligny-Montrachet Domaine Leflaive (BUT)
Puligny-Montrachet les Champs Gains,
  Clerc (PE)

£25.00 to £29.99

1992

Beaune Clos des Mouches, Drouhin (NI)
Corton-Charlemagne Olivier Leflaive (ARM)

1991

Corton-Charlemagne Latour (WY)
Puligny-Montrachet Clavoillon, Domaine
  Leflaive (ARM)
Puligny-Montrachet les Perrières, Sauzet
  (EL, TAN)

1990

Chassagne-Montrachet les Chaumes,
  Jean-Marc Morey (DAV)
Corton-Charlemagne Latour (FA, HOG)
Meursault Clos de la Barre, Lafon (GOE,
  GAU, VIG)
Meursault Poruzots, Jobard (MV, BIB)
Puligny-Montrachet Champ Canet, Sauzet
  (BEK)
Puligny-Montrachet Clavoillon, Domaine
  Leflaive (GOE, PE)
Puligny-Montrachet les Combettes, Prieur
  (WHI)
Puligny-Montrachet les Referts, Sauzet (BEK)

1989

Chassagne-Montrachet Jadot (THR, WR, BOT)
Corton-Charlemagne Bonneau du Martray
  (GOE)
Meursault Charmes, Domaine Leflaive (TW)
Puligny-Montrachet Champ Canet, Sauzet
  (WS)
Puligny-Montrachet Clos de la Garenne,
  Drouhin (WY)
Puligny-Montrachet Domaine Leflaive
  (ARM, BIB, DI, AD)
Puligny-Montrachet les Folatières,
  Drouhin (BEN)

1988

Chassagne-Montrachet les Chenevottes,
  Niellon (GAU)
Chassagne-Montrachet Marquis de
  Laguiche (WY)
Corton-Charlemagne Bonneau du Martray
  (GOE)
Puligny-Montrachet Champ Canet, Sauzet
  (ROB, GOE)
Puligny-Montrachet Clavoillon, Domaine
  Leflaive (GOE)
Puligny-Montrachet les Referts, Sauzet
  (GOE)

1987

Corton-Charlemagne Drouhin (ARM)
Corton-Charlemagne Olivier Leflaive (AMI)
Puligny-Montrachet les Pucelles, Domaine
  Leflaive (GOE)

1986

Meursault Genevrières, Jobard (BUT)
Meursault Poruzots, Jobard (BUT)
Puligny-Montrachet Clavoillon, Domaine
  Leflaive (PE)
Puligny-Montrachet les Folatières,
  Bouchard Père (PEN)

1985

Chassagne-Montrachet Morgeot, Henri
  Germain (AD)
Meursault Leroy (BEN)
Puligny-Montrachet Clerc (TW)

1983

Meursault Ampeau (CHA)
Puligny-Montrachet les Folatières,
  Latour (BUT)

£30.00 to £39.99

1992

Corton-Charlemagne Drouhin (NI)
Corton-Charlemagne Latour (WY)
Corton-Charlemagne Rollin (RAE)
Criots-Bâtard-Montrachet Olivier
  Leflaive (ARM)

1991
Bâtard-Montrachet Latour (WY)
Puligny-Montrachet les Combettes,
  Domaine Leflaive (ARM)
Puligny-Montrachet les Combettes, Sauzet
  (EL, TAN)
Puligny-Montrachet les Pucelles, Domaine
  Leflaive (ARM)
1990
Bâtard-Montrachet Latour (WY)
Beaune Clos des Mouches, Drouhin (BEN)
Corton-Charlemagne Drouhin (BEN)
Puligny-Montrachet les Pucelles, Domaine
  Leflaive (GOE, AD)
1989
Bâtard-Montrachet Albert Morey (BEK)
Bâtard-Montrachet Latour (WY)
Beaune Clos des Mouches, Drouhin (WY)
Corton-Charlemagne Olivier Leflaive (AD)
Corton-Charlemagne Rollin (BIB)
Meursault Clos de la Barre, Lafon (GOE)
Puligny-Montrachet Clavoillon, Domaine
  Leflaive (GOE, CB, BIB, ARM, AD, DI, PE)
Puligny-Montrachet les Combettes,
  Domaine Leflaive (ARM)
Puligny-Montrachet les Pucelles, Domaine
  Leflaive (EY)
1988
Corton-Charlemagne Drouhin (WY)
Corton-Charlemagne Latour (PLA, WY, EY,
  GAL)
Corton-Charlemagne Olivier Leflaive (GOE,
  AD, HAH)
Corton-Charlemagne Rollin (RAE)
Puligny-Montrachet Clavoillon, Domaine
  Leflaive (CB, BEN, ARM, PE)
Puligny-Montrachet les Combettes,
  Domaine Leflaive (GOE, ARM)
Puligny-Montrachet les Folatières,
  Latour (GOE)
Puligny-Montrachet les Pucelles, Clerc (TW)
Puligny-Montrachet les Pucelles, Domaine
  Leflaive (GOE, ARM)
1987
Bâtard-Montrachet Clerc (WY)
Bienvenues-Bâtard-Montrachet Bachelet
  (BIB)
Bienvenues-Bâtard-Montrachet, Domaine
  Leflaive (TAN)
Chassagne-Montrachet Marquis de
  Laguiche (TW)
Corton-Charlemagne Jadot (HA)
Corton-Charlemagne Rollin (RAE)
Puligny-Montrachet Clavoillon, Domaine
  Leflaive (ARM)

1986
Bâtard-Montrachet Albert Morey (EY)
Corton-Charlemagne Bonneau du Martray
  (GOE, GE, BUT)
Corton-Charlemagne Bouchard Père (PEN)
1985
Corton-Charlemagne Bonneau du Martray
  (BUT)
Puligny-Montrachet Clavoillon, Domaine
  Leflaive (HAY)
1983
Chassagne-Montrachet Marquis de
  Laguiche (WY)

£40.00 to £49.99

1992
Bâtard-Montrachet Olivier Leflaive (ARM)
1991
Bâtard-Montrachet, Domaine Leflaive (AD)
Bienvenues-Bâtard-Montrachet, Domaine
  Leflaive (ARM)
1990
Bienvenues-Bâtard-Montrachet, Domaine
  Leflaive (GOE)
Meursault Charmes, Lafon (GAU)
Meursault Perrières, Lafon (GAU)
Puligny-Montrachet les Combettes,
  Domaine Leflaive (ARM)
1989
Corton-Charlemagne Drouhin (WY)
Puligny-Montrachet les Pucelles, Domaine
  Leflaive (ARM, BIB, DI, BUT)
1988
Bâtard-Montrachet Gagnard-Delagrange
  (BY)
Beaune Clos des Mouches, Drouhin (TW)
Bienvenues-Bâtard-Montrachet Clerc
  (TW)
1987
Bâtard-Montrachet Olivier Leflaive (TW)
Chevalier-Montrachet Chartron (ROB)
Corton-Charlemagne Tollot-Beaut (ARM)
1986
Bâtard-Montrachet Latour (WY)
Chassagne-Montrachet Marquis de
  Laguiche (WY)
Corton-Charlemagne Latour (WHI, BIB)
1985
Bâtard-Montrachet Latour (WY)
Chassagne-Montrachet Marquis de
  Laguiche (WY)
Corton-Charlemagne Latour (VIC, WY, BUT)
1983
Puligny-Montrachet les Folatières,
  Drouhin (WY)

£50.00 to £69.99

1991
Chevalier-Montrachet, Domaine Leflaive
(ARM)
1990
Bâtard-Montrachet Olivier Leflaive (ARM)
Chevalier-Montrachet, Domaine Leflaive
(GOE, AD)
Chevalier-Montrachet les Desmoiselles,
Latour (WY)
1989
Bâtard-Montrachet, Domaine Leflaive (EY,
DI, GOE, BIB)
Bienvenues-Bâtard-Montrachet, Domaine
Leflaive (GOE)
Corton-Charlemagne Latour (AMI)
1988
Bâtard-Montrachet, Domaine Leflaive (EY)
Chevalier-Montrachet, Domaine Leflaive
(WY, HAY, GOE, ARM, REI, CB)
Chevalier-Montrachet les Desmoiselles,
Latour (WY)
Criots-Bâtard-Montrachet Blain-Gagnard
(BIB)
1986
Bâtard-Montrachet Olivier Leflaive (BEN)
Bienvenues-Bâtard-Montrachet, Domaine
Leflaive (BUT)
Chevalier-Montrachet Bouchard Père (PEN)
Criots-Bâtard-Montrachet Olivier
Leflaive (TW)
le Montrachet Thénard (BUT)
1985
Bienvenues-Bâtard-Montrachet
Remoissenet (WS)
Corton-Charlemagne Drouhin (WY)
1983
le Montrachet Château Herbeux (BUT)

£70.00 to £99.99

1991
le Montrachet Marquis de Laguiche (NI)
1990
le Montrachet Marquis de Laguiche (NI)
1989
Chevalier-Montrachet, Domaine Leflaive
(BIB, DI, GOE)
le Montrachet Latour (WY)
le Montrachet Thénard (WS)
1988
Bâtard-Montrachet Latour (VIN)
le Montrachet Latour (WY)
1986
Chevalier-Montrachet, Domaine
Leflaive (BUT)

le Montrachet Latour (BEN, BUT, WY)
le Montrachet Marquis de Laguiche
(WY)
1985
Bâtard-Montrachet, Domaine
Leflaive (BUT)
Chevalier-Montrachet les Desmoiselles,
Latour (TW)

le Montrachet Latour (BUT)
1983
le Montrachet Prieur (WY)
le Montrachet Thénard (WS)

£100.00 to £124.99

1989
le Montrachet Marquis de Laguiche (WY)
1988
le Montrachet Marquis de Laguiche (WY)
1987
le Montrachet Marquis de Laguiche (TW,
BUT)
1986
le Montrachet Marquis de Laguiche (BUT)
1985
le Montrachet Latour (WY)

£140.00 to £199.99

1984
le Montrachet Domaine de la Romanée-
Conti (WY)

£290.00 to £360.00

1990
le Montrachet Domaine de la Romanée-
Conti (EL)
1983
le Montrachet Domaine de la Romanée-
Conti (WY)

£400.00 to £499.99

1987
le Montrachet Domaine de la Romanée-
Conti (TW, BUT)
1986
le Montrachet Domaine de la Romanée-
Conti (BUT)

CÔTE CHALONNAISE

RED

Under £3.50

1990
Givry, Émile Voarick (WRI)

£6.50 to £8.99

1991
Rully Drouhin (OD)
1990
Mercurey Domaine du Meix-Foulot (CV)
Mercurey Latour (PEN)
1988
Givry Clos du Cellier aux Moines, Delorme
(WAT)
1987
Rully Clos de Bellecroix, Domaine de la
Folie (BUT)

£9.00 to £10.99

1991
Mercurey Domaine de la Croix, Jacquelet-
Faiveley (WRI)
Mercurey les Mauvarennes, Faiveley (BEN)
1990
Mercurey Domaine de la Croix, Jacquelet-
Faiveley (ARM)
Mercurey les Mauvarennes, Faiveley (DI)
Mercurey Maréchal (PIP)
1989
★ Mercurey Château de Chamirey (PLA, WHI)
1988
Mercurey Latour (PEN)
1987
Mercurey Sazenay, Suremain (GE)
1986
Mercurey Château de Chamirey (EL)
Mercurey les Veleys, de Launay (GE)
1983
Rully Domaine de l'Hermitage, Chanzy
(BUT)

£11.00 to £14.99

1991
Mercurey Clos du Roy, Faiveley (HAH)
1990
Mercurey Château de Chamirey (NO)
1988
Rully Clos de Bellecroix, Domaine de la
Folie (BUT)
1985
Mercurey Clos des Barraults, Juillot (BUT)

WHITE

Under £5.00

1991
Montagny 1er Cru les Coères, Bernard
Michel (ASD)

£6.00 to £6.99

1991
Montagny Château de Davenay, Picard (SAI)
Montagny Latour (HOG)

£7.00 to £7.99

1992
Montagny 1er Cru Alain Roy, Cave des
Vignerons de Mancey (BEK)

£8.00 to £8.99

1992
Montagny 1er Cru, Cave de Buxy (PIP, CV)
1990
Montagny 1er Cru Alain Roy, Cave des
Vignerons de Mancey (VIG)
Montagny Latour (WRI)
Rully la Chaume, Dury (HAM, SEC)
1989
Rully la Chaume, Dury (EY, HAY)

£9.00 to £10.99

1992
Montagny 1er Cru, Olivier Leflaive (CB)
1991
Mercurey Château de Chamirey, Rodet
(WHI, PLA)
Mercurey Émile Voarick (WRI)
Montagny 1er Cru, Olivier Leflaive (AD)
Montagny 1er Cru les Loges, Sarjeant
(DAV, TAN)
1989
Givry Ragot (ROB)
Montagny Château de Davenay, Moillard
(VIN)
1988
Rully Clos St-Jacques, Domaine de la Folie
(BUT)

£11.00 to £12.99

1991
Mercurey Clos Rochette, Faiveley (GRE)
Rully Grésigny, Cogny (AD)
1989
Mercurey Clos Rochette, Faiveley (DI)

MÂCONNAIS

RED

Under £5.00

1992
Mâcon Rouge Loron (UN, EL)

£5.00 to £5.49

1992
Mâcon-Supérieur Rouge, Cave de Buxy
(CV)

WHITE

Under £5.00

1993
Mâcon-Villages Cave Co-op. de Viré (SAF)
1992
Mâcon-Villages Rodet (MAR)
St-Véran Domaine St-Martin, Duboeuf
(BEK)
St-Véran Duboeuf (THR, BOT, WR)

£5.00 to £5.99

1993
Mâcon-Villages Duboeuf (NI)
1992
Mâcon-Lugny les Genièvres, Latour
(HOG)
Mâcon-Prissé Duboeuf (NI)
Mâcon-Villages Cave Co-op. de Viré (CV)
Mâcon-Villages Cave Co-op. Prissé (ARM)
Mâcon-Villages Loron (TAN)

£6.00 to £6.99

1993
St-Véran Château Fuissé, Vincent (AD)
St-Véran Domaine de la Batie, Duboeuf
(DAV)
1992
Mâcon Chardonnay Talmard (EY, AD, TAN)
Mâcon la Roche Vineuse, Merlin (BIB)
Mâcon-Lugny les Genièvres, Latour (LO,
PEN, GAL, BEN, PLA)
Mâcon-Prissé Cave Co-op. Prissé (HAH)
St-Véran Château Fuissé, Vincent (DI)
St-Véran Domaine de Vignemont (PEN)
1991
Pouilly-Loché Cave des Crus Blancs
(PLA)
St-Véran Latour (HOG)
1990
Mâcon-Lugny les Genièvres, Latour (WHI)

1989
Mâcon-Peronne Domaine de Mortier,
Josserand (SEC)
Mâcon-Viré Domaine des Chazelles (ASD)

£7.00 to £7.99

1993
Mâcon-Fuissé Thibert (LEA)
Pouilly-Fuissé Duboeuf (BEK)
1992
Mâcon Chardonnay Talmard (HAH)
Mâcon-Charnay Blanc Manciat-Poncet
(HAW)
Mâcon-Clessé Guillemot (HAH)
Mâcon-Lugny les Genièvres, Latour (TAN,
DAV, VIN)
Pouilly-Fuissé Dépagneux (WCL)
Pouilly-Loché Cave des Crus Blancs
(LEA)
St-Véran Domaine Deux Roches (HAH)
1991
Mâcon-Clessé Signoret (HAW)
Mâcon-Lugny les Genièvres,
Latour (HIG)
Mâcon-Viré Cuvée Spéciale, Bonhomme
(GE)
Pouilly-Loché Cave des Crus Blancs (HAW)
Pouilly-Vinzelles Mathias (PIP)
St-Véran Cave Co-op. Prissé (CV)
1990
Mâcon-Clessé Guillemot (TAN)
St-Véran Cave Co-op. Prissé (ARM)
1989
Mâcon la Roche-Vineuse, Lacharme (GAU)

£8.00 to £8.99

1993
St-Véran Domaine Deux Roches (BAR)
1992
Mâcon la Roche Vineuse, Merlin
(BEN, MV, WCL)
Pouilly-Fuissé Château Fuissé, Vincent
(DI)

Please remember that
Webster's *is a price
GUIDE and not a price
LIST. It is not meant to
replace up-to-date
merchant's lists.*

Pouilly-Fuissé Latour (HOG)
St-Véran Château Fuissé, Vincent
  (TAN, EL)
1991
St-Véran Château Fuissé, Vincent (WS)
1990
Mâcon-Lugny les Genièvres,
  Latour (WY)
Pouilly-Fuissé Loron (DI)
1989
Pouilly-Fuissé Domaine Béranger,
  Duboeuf (BEK)

£9.00 to £9.99

1992
Mâcon-Viré Goyard (RAE)
1991
Mâcon-Clessé Domaine de la Bon Gran,
  Thévenet (NO)
Mâcon Monbellet, Goyard (BIB)
1990
Mâcon-Viré Clos du Chapitre, Dépagneux
  (BEN)
1989
Mâcon Monbellet, Goyard (WS)
1986
St-Véran Latour (BUT)

£10.00 to £12.49

1992
Mâcon Monbellet, Goyard (WRI)
Pouilly-Fuissé Manciat-Poncet (HAW)
1991
Mâcon-Clessé Domaine de la Bon Gran,
  Thévenet (TAN)
Mâcon-Villages Domaine de la Bon Gran,
  Thévenet (AD)
Mâcon-Viré Goyard (EY)

£12.50 to £15.99

1992
Pouilly-Fuissé Château Fuissé, Vincent
  (TAN)
1991
Mâcon-Clessé Domaine de la Bon Gran,
  Thévenet (BEN, LEA)
1990
Mâcon-Clessé Thévenet (WW)
Pouilly-Fuissé Château Fuissé, Vincent
  (WS)
1988
Pouilly-Fuissé Château Fuissé, Vincent
  (VIG)
1986
Pouilly-Fuissé Domaine de l'Arillière (BUT)

£16.00 to £19.99

1992
Pouilly-Fuissé Château Fuissé Vieilles
  Vignes, Vincent (EL)
1990
Pouilly-Fuissé Château Fuissé, Vincent
  (AD)
1989
Pouilly-Fuissé Château Fuissé, Vincent
  (AD)
1988
Pouilly-Fuissé Château Fuissé, Vincent
  (RAE, TW)

1987
Pouilly-Fuissé Château Fuissé, Vincent
  (TW)
1986
Pouilly-Fuissé Corsin (BUT)

£20.00 to £29.99

1992
Pouilly-Fuissé Château Fuissé Vieilles
  Vignes, Vincent (DI)
1990
Pouilly-Fuissé Château Fuissé Vieilles
  Vignes, Vincent (AD)
1989
Pouilly-Fuissé Château Fuissé Vieilles
  Vignes, Vincent (EY)
1988
Pouilly-Fuissé Château Fuissé Vieilles
  Vignes, Sourice (NO)
Pouilly-Fuissé Château Fuissé Vieilles
  Vignes, Vincent (EY)
1986
Pouilly-Fuissé Château Fuissé Vieilles
  Vignes, Vincent (GOE, BUT)

*In each price band wines
are listed in vintage order.
Within each vintage they
are listed in A–Z order.*

CHABLIS

WHITE

Under £6.00

1992
★ Sauvignon de St-Bris, Defrance (EL)
1991
Sauvignon de St-Bris, Domaine des
   Remparts (HOG)
1989
Sauvignon de St-Bris, Sorin (WHI)

£6.00 to £6.99

1993
Chablis la Chablisienne (VIC)
1992
Chablis Bacheroy-Josselin (WAI)
Chablis Bonard (POR)
Chablis Bouchard Père (WAT)
Chablis Brocard (OD)
Chablis Domaine Ste-Anne, Louis Petit (BEK)
Chablis la Chablisienne (WAI, MAR)
Chablis Simonnet-Febvre (CHA)
Chardonnay Domaine des Remparts, Sorin
   (HIG)
Sauvignon de St-Bris, Domaine des
   Remparts (HIG)
1991
Chablis la Chablisienne (WAI)
1990
Chablis Domaine de Biéville, J Moreau (HOG)
Chablis Durup (EL)
Sauvignon de St-Bris, Defrance (VIG)

£7.00 to £7.99

1993
Chablis Domaine de Biéville, J Moreau
   (WHI)
Chablis Domaine du Valéry, Durup (TAN)
Chablis Vocoret (PLA)
1992
★ Chablis Bernard Defaix (SEC, HAM)
Chablis Château de Maligny, Durup (THR,
   BOT, WR)
Chablis Domaine des Manants, Brocard (AD)
Chablis Domaine Ste-Claire, Brocard (CV)
Chablis Droin (HAY)
Chablis Durup (HAH)
Chablis Gautheron (AME)
Chablis, J Moreau (DAV)
Chablis Laroche (PLA)
Chablis Louis Michel (NI)
Chablis Tremblay (PEN)

1991
Chablis Domaine Pico Race (GOE)
Chablis Grossot (LAY)
Chablis Latour (EY)
★ Chablis Légland (BIB)
Chablis Pautré (GAU)
Sauvignon de St-Bris, Renard (WRI)
1990
Chablis Château de Maligny, Durup (BY)
1988
Chablis la Chablisienne (GE)
1983
Chablis, J Moreau (HA)

£8.00 to £9.99

1992
Chablis 1er Cru, Laroche (PLA, DI)
Chablis Domaine de l'Églantière (PE)
Chablis Domaine Servin (WRI)
Chablis Drouhin (HIC, BEN)
Chablis Fourchaume, Domaine de Valéry
   (TAN)
Chablis Latour (PEN)
Chablis Montmains, Brocard (BEK, AD)
★ Chablis Vaillons, Laroche (PLA)
Chablis Vau Ligneau, Hamelin (BEK)
1991
Bourgogne Coteaux de St-Bris
   Chardonnay, Felix (ROB)
Chablis Château de Maligny, Durup (BY)
Chablis Domaine de l'Églantière (PE, POR)
Chablis Fûts de Chêne, Grossot (LAY)
Chablis Gautheron (UN)
Chablis Montmains, Domaine Pico Race
   (GOE)
Chablis Montmains, Louis Michel (NI)
Chablis Vaillons, Simonnet-Febvre (CHA)
1990
Chablis Fourchaume, Durup (EL)
Chablis Laroche (DI)
Chablis Montée de Tonnerre, Durup (EL)
Chablis Montmains, Louis Michel (OD)
Chablis Pautré (HIG)
Chablis Vaillons, J Moreau (HA)
Chablis Vaillons, Simonnet-Febvre (CHA)
Chablis Vocoret (BUT)
1989
★ Chablis Fourchaume, Domaine de
   Colombier, Mothe (ASD)
Chablis Latour (WY)
1987
Chablis Rémon (BOR)

£10.00 to £11.99

1992
Chablis 1er Cru, Pico Race (BAR)
Chablis Fourchaume, Laroche (PLA)
Chablis Montmains, Légland (BIB)
Chablis Vaudevey, Laroche (GRE)
1991
Chablis Côte de Léchet, Bernard Defaix (HAM)
Chablis la Forêt, Pinson (PIP)
Chablis Montée de Tonnerre, Domaine
　Servin (WRI)
Chablis Montée de Tonnerre, Louis Michel
　(OD)
Chablis Montmains, Brocard (EY)
1990
Chablis Daniel Defaix (VIG)
Chablis Fourchaume, Simonnet-Febvre (CHA)
Chablis la Forêt, Pinson (BIB)
Chablis Mont de Milieu, Pinson (BIB, PIP)
Chablis Montée de Tonnerre, Domaine de
　la Tour Vaubourg (GAL)
Chablis Montmains, Domaine de la Tour
　Vaubourg (GAL)
Chablis Vaudevey, Laroche (WHI)
1989
Chablis la Forêt, Vocoret (SEC)
Chablis Montmains, Brocard (CV)
Chablis Vaillons, Bernard Defaix (RAE)
Chablis Vaucoupin, J. Moreau (BER)
1988
Chablis Montmains, Louis Michel (GAU)
1986
Chablis Régnard (BUT)

£12.00 to £13.99

1992
Chablis 1er Cru, Drouhin (NI)
Chablis Fourchaume, Boudin (LEA)
Chablis Vaillons, Daniel Defaix (DAV)
1991
Chablis Fourchaume, Laroche (DI)
Chablis la Forêt, René Dauvissat (TAN)
Chablis Vaillons, Raveneau (HAH)
Chablis Vaillons, René Dauvissat (TAN)
1990
Chablis la Forêt, René Dauvissat (BUT)
Chablis Séchet, Louis Michel (BER)
Chablis Vaillons, Bernard Defaix (BER)
Chablis Vaudevey, Laroche (DI)
1989
Chablis Vaillons, Fèvre (BEN)
Chablis Vaudevey, Laroche (DI)
1986
Chablis Montée de Tonnerre, Louis Michel
　(BUT)

£14.00 to £16.99

1992
Chablis la Forêt, René Dauvissat (LEA)
Chablis Séchet, René Dauvissat (LEA)
1990
Chablis les Clos, Pinson (PIP)
1988
Chablis Côte de Léchet, Bernard Defaix
　(LAY, VIG, ROB)
Chablis les Clos, J Moreau (HOG)
Chablis les Lys, Daniel Defaix (TAN, VIG)
Chablis Vaillons, Daniel Defaix (VIG)
1987
Chablis Vaillons, Bernard Defaix (ROB)

£17.00 to £19.99

1991
Chablis Blanchots, Laroche (PLA)
Chablis Blanchots, Servin (DAV)
Chablis les Clos, Vocoret (VIN)
1990
Chablis les Clos, Droin (HAY)
Chablis les Clos, Pinson (BIB)
1989
Chablis Grenouilles, Louis Michel (GAU)
Chablis les Clos, Louis Michel (GAU)
Chablis Vaudésir, Gautherin (POR)
1988
Chablis Vaudésir, Louis Michel (GAU)
Chablis Vaudésir, Robin (BEK)
1987
Chablis les Clos, Pinson (WCL)

£20.00 to £24.99

1991
Chablis les Clos, René Dauvissat (LEA)
1990
Chablis Blanchots, Laroche (GRE)
Chablis Grenouilles, Droin (HAY)
1989
Chablis Bougerots, Laroche (NO)
1988
Chablis Blanchots, Laroche (DI)
1987
Chablis Blanchots, Laroche (WHI)
1986
Chablis Vaudésir, Fèvre (BUT)

£25.00 to £30.99

1992
Chablis les Clos, René Dauvissat (LEA)
1990
Chablis les Clos, Laroche (DI)
1989
Chablis les Clos, Pic (BER)

BEAUJOLAIS

RED

Under £4.50

1993
Beaujolais-Villages Cellier des Samsons
(WAI)
1992
Beaujolais-Villages Cellier des Samsons
(WAI)
1991
Beaujolais-Villages Domaine de la Ronze
(ASD)
Beaujolais-Villages Loron (UN)

£4.50 to £4.99

1993
Beaujolais-Villages Château de Néty (EL)
Beaujolais-Villages Château du Basty (OD)
Beaujolais-Villages Duboeuf (WR, THR, BOT)
1992
Beaujolais Loron (DI)
Beaujolais-Villages Cellier des Samsons
(BY)
Beaujolais-Villages Duboeuf (MAR, TES)
1991
Beaujolais-Villages Château du Bluizard
(TES)

£5.00 to £5.49

1993
Beaujolais Château de Tanay (HAW)
Beaujolais Château Gaillard, Sélection
Éventail (PLA)
Beaujolais Duboeuf (NI)
1992
Beaujolais-Villages Château Lacarelle
(POR)
1991
Beaujolais-Villages Château Lacarelle (WS)
Chénas Château de Chénas (WHI)
Juliénas Domaine des Mouilles, Duboeuf
(BEK)
Morgon Domaine des Montillets, Vermorel
Gaudet (AS)

£5.50 to £5.99

1993
Beaujolais Cave Beaujolais de St-Verand
(HAW)
Beaujolais-Villages Château des Vierres,
Duboeuf (DAV)

Beaujolais-Villages Château Lacarelle
(AME)
Beaujolais-Villages Rochette (HAY)
Brouilly Château de Nevers, Duboeuf (NI)
Fleurie Domaine des Quatre Vents,
Duboeuf (BEK)
Fleurie la Madone, Duboeuf (BEK)
Juliénas Pelletier (EL)
Morgon Domaine Jean Descombes,
Duboeuf (BEK)
Morgon le Clachet, Brun (EL)
1992
Beaujolais Lantignié, Domaine Joubert
(AD)
Beaujolais-Villages les Champs Bouthier,
Sapin (PEN)
Brouilly Large (CHA)
Chénas Domaine de la Combe Remont,
Duboeuf (LO)
Côte de Brouilly Joubert (TAN)
Juliénas Domaine Joubert (AD)
Juliénas Loron (UN)
1991
Beaujolais-Villages Château Lacarelle
(WCL)
Chénas Domaine de Chassignol,
Dépagneux (WS)
Juliénas les Envaux, Pelletier (CHA)
Morgon le Clachet, Brun (CHA)
Morgon Loron (UN)
1990
Morgon Jambon (ASD)

£6.00 to £6.49

1993
Brouilly Château de Nevers,
Duboeuf (DAV)
Brouilly Large (PLA)
Côte de Brouilly Domaine de Chavannes
(EL)
Morgon Domaine de Lathevalle,
Mommessin (AME)
Morgon Domaine Jean Descombes,
Duboeuf (THR, BOT, WR)
Morgon le Clachet, Brun (PLA)

---

*In each price band wines
are listed in vintage order.
Within each vintage they
are listed in A–Z order.*

1992

Beaujolais-Villages Cave des Producteurs
Juliénas (HAW)
Beaujolais-Villages Latour (AMI)
Brouilly Fessy (AMI)
Fleurie Château de Fleurie, Loron (TAN)
Juliénas Domaine de la Vieille Église,
Loron (DI)
Juliénas Domaine Joubert (TAN, EY)
Juliénas les Envaux, Pelletier (HIG)
Morgon Descombes, Duboeuf (LO)
Morgon le Clachet, Brun (HIG)

1991

Brouilly Château des Tours (WS)
Chénas Château de Chénas (HAW)
Juliénas Clos des Poulettes, Loron (GRE)
Juliénas Domaine du Grand Cuvage,
Duboeuf (DAV)
St-Amour Domaine du Paradis (BEK)

1988

Moulin-à-Vent Domaine des Héritiers
Tagent, Duboeuf (BEK)

£6.50 to £6.99

1993

Beaujolais Blaise Carron (HAW)
Beaujolais Garlon (HAW)
Brouilly Château des Tours (PIP)
Chiroubles Méziat (OD)
Fleurie Château de Fleurie, Loron (EL)
Fleurie Duboeuf (BOT, THR, WR, VIC)
Juliénas Pelletier (WRI)
Morgon Domaine Jean Descombes,
Duboeuf (NI)
Moulin-à-Vent le Vivier, Brugne (EL)

1992

Beaujolais-Villages Château du Grand
Vernay (HAW)
Brouilly Domaine de Saburin (PEN)
Brouilly Duboeuf (POR)
Brouilly Latour (HOG)
Chénas Domaine de Chassignol,
Dépagneux (BU)
Chénas Léspinasse (HAW)
Chiroubles Château de Raousset (BU, AME)
Chiroubles la Maison des Vignerons (AD)
Chiroubles Loron (TAN)
Fleurie Sélection Éventail, Domaine de
Montgénas (CHA)
Juliénas Domaine des Mouilles, Duboeuf
(BU)
Juliénas Léspinasse (HAW)
Morgon Fontcraine, Loron (GRE)
Moulin-à-Vent Brugne (CHA)
Regnié Noël (HAW)

1991

Chénas Domaine des Vieilles Caves,
Charvet (WS)
Chiroubles Château de Javernand,
Duboeuf (GRE)
Fleurie Château de Fleurie, Loron (EY)
Fleurie Verpoix (ASD)
Juliénas Domaine de la Vieille Église,
Loron (WRI)
Moulin-à-Vent Domaine de la Tour du
Bief, Duboeuf (BOT, WR, THR)
Moulin-à-Vent Loron (UN)

1990

Morgon Château Gaillard (RAE)
Morgon Côte de Py, Savoye (HIC)

1989

Côte de Brouilly Château Thivin (RAE)

£7.00 to £7.49

1993

Brouilly Château Thivin (AD)
Fleurie Sélection Éventail, Domaine de
Montgénas (PLA)
St-Amour les Bonnets, Bernard Patissier
(PLA)

1992

Chiroubles la Maison des Vignerons (HAW)
Fleurie Collin-Bourisset (BOR)
Fleurie Colonge (SOM, TAN)
Fleurie Domaine des Quatre Vents,
Duboeuf (LO)
Fleurie la Madone, Louis Tête (HOG)
Fleurie les Garans, Latour (HOG)
Moulin-à-Vent Domaine Charvet (TAN)
Moulin-à-Vent Domaine des Rosiers,
Duboeuf (LO)

1991

Chiroubles Château de Raousset (PIP)
Fleurie Cave Co-op. de Fleurie (CV)
Juliénas les Capitains, Louis Tête (HOG)
Morgon Aucoeur (HAW)
Moulin-à-Vent Domaine Lemonon, Loron
(WRI, DI)

1990

Brouilly Domaine de Saburin (WY)

1989

St-Amour Domaine du Paradis (BEK)

£7.50 to £7.99

1993

Beaujolais Cuvée Centenaire, Charmet
(HAW)
Brouilly Château des Tours (BEN, BIB)
Brouilly Michaud (MV)
Côte de Brouilly Château Thivin (DI)

Fleurie Château de Fleurie, Loron (GRE)
Fleurie Colonge (BIB)
Fleurie Domaine de la Presle, Mommessin
(AME)
Fleurie Domaine des Quatre Vents,
Duboeuf (NI, DAV)
Moulin-à-Vent le Vivier, Brugne (WRI)

1992
Brouilly Château des Tours (NO)
Brouilly Geoffray (HAW)
Côte de Brouilly Château Thivin (GRE,
HAW)
Fleurie Cave Co-op. de Fleurie (HAW)
Fleurie Château de Fleurie, Loron
(DI, WRI)
Fleurie Colonge (POR)
Fleurie Domaine de la Presle, Mommessin
(NA)
Juliénas Domaine de Berthets, Dépagneux
(ROB)
Juliénas les Capitains, Louis Tête (BAR)
Regnié Roux (HAW)
1991
Brouilly Jean Lathuilière (WCL)
Chiroubles Château de Raousset (NO)
Fleurie Cave Co-op. de Fleurie (HAW)
Fleurie la Madone, Duboeuf (GRE)
Juliénas Benon (HAW)
Moulin-à-Vent Domaine de la Tour du
Bief, Duboeuf (DAV, NI)
St-Amour Domaine des Billards,
Loron (GRE)
St-Amour Domaine des Pins, Echallier
(POR)
1990
Chénas Benon (HAW)
Côte de Brouilly Château du Grand
Vernay (HAW)
Morgon Bocuse (AMI)
Moulin-à-Vent Janin (HAY)
1989
Morgon Cave Bocabarteille,
Loron (WS)
St-Amour les Bonnets, Bernard
Patissier (PE)

£8.00 to £8.99

1992
Brouilly Château des Tours (ROB)
Brouilly Domaine de Saburin (WY)
Brouilly Jean Lathuilière (HAW)
Chiroubles Loron (ROB)
Fleurie Château de Fleurie,
Loron (AMI)
Fleurie les Garans, Latour (WY)
Fleurie Michel Chignard (MV)
Morgon Côte de Py, Savoye (VIG)
1991
Juliénas Condemine (HAW)
Moulin-à-Vent Janin (PIP)
1990
Fleurie les Garans, Latour (WY)
Juliénas Aujas (HAW)
Morgon Château Gaillard (BIB)

£9.00 to £11.49

1992
Fleurie Colonge (ROB)
1990
Moulin-à-Vent Château du Moulin-à-Vent
(HAW)
1985
Beaujolais-Villages Duboeuf (BUT)

WHITE

Under £6.00

1992
Beaujolais Blanc Duboeuf (BEK)
1991
Beaujolais Blanc Bully (TES)

£6.50 to £7.99

1993
Beaujolais Blanc Château des
Tours (PIP)
1991
Beaujolais Blanc Château des Tours (NO)
1990
Beaujolais Blanc Château des Tours (NO)

£8.50 to £8.99

1992
Beaujolais Blanc Charmet (HAW)

ROSÉ

Under £6.50

1992
Beaujolais Supérieur Rosé, Cave
Beaujolais du Bois d'Oingt (HAW)

CHAMPAGNE

SPARKLING WHITE

Under £10.00

Non-vintage
Bruno Paillard ½ bottle (HAL)
Moët & Chandon ½ bottle (PLA, TAN)
Veuve Clicquot ½ bottle (PLA)

£10.00 to £11.99

Non-vintage
Ayala (MAJ)
Bollinger ½ bottle (PLA, LEA)
★ Descombes (WR)
Duchâtel (UN)
Heidsieck Dry Monopole (LO, OD)
Moët & Chandon ½ bottle (WAT, POR, TES,
   WHI, OD, HAM)
★ de Telmont (MAJ)
Veuve Clicquot ½ bottle (LEA, ROB)

£12.00 to £13.99

Non-vintage
Alexandre Bonnet Prestige (HAY)
★ Beerens (BIB)
Blin (OD)
Bollinger ½ bottle (BEN, DI, BUT)
Canard-Duchêne (HOG, MAJ, LO)
★ Drappier Carte d'Or (WR, THR, BOT)
Ellner (DAV, LAY)
Jacquart Tradition (ASD)
Mercier (UN)
★ Pierre Vaudon 1er Cru (HAH)
★ Pol Roger (SOM)
Pol Roger White Foil (SOM)
★ Salon (EY)
Veuve Clicquot ½ bottle (BEN)

£14.00 to £15.99

Non-vintage
Canard-Duchêne (GRE, ROB)
Drappier Carte d'Or (BY)
George Goulet (VIG)
Georges Gardet (GOE)
★ Henriot Blanc de Blancs (BY)
★ Henriot Souverain (BY)
Joseph Perrier (HIC, PE)
Joseph Perrier Cuvée Royal (CV, ROB)
Lanson (PLA)
★ Laurent-Perrier (PLA)
Massé (BAR)
Mercier (ASD, POR, TES, WAI, SAF, DAV, WR,
   BOT, PE, VIC, THR, SUM, LAY, ROB, WHI)

Piper Heidsieck (SAF, NI, SO, TES, ASD, GRE)
Pommery (HAH, BIB)
★ 'R' de Ruinart (GOE, REI)
Salon (SOM)
Salon Blanc de Blancs (HAY)
The Society's Champagne (WS)
de Venoge (ROB)
de Venoge Cordon Bleu (GOE, EL)
1987
Heidsieck Dry Monopole (OD)
1986
Drappier Carte d'Or (BY)
★ Pol Roger (SOM)
1985
Duchâtel (UN)
de Telmont (MAJ)

£16.00 to £17.99

Non-vintage
Alfred Gratien (HAY)
Billecart-Salmon (AD, WW)
Canard-Duchêne (MV)
Charles Heidsieck (HOG)
Deutz (ARM, ROB)
George Goulet (PIP, BEN)
Heidsieck Dry Monopole (DI)
Henriot Blanc de Blancs (PEN, NO)
Jacquart Tradition (GAU)
Joseph Perrier (POR)
Joseph Perrier Cuvée Royal (HAM)
Lanson (HOG, WAI, ASD, UN, HA, POR, VIC, SO,
   BOT, WR, THR, TES, SAF, DAV)
Laurent-Perrier (BIB, UN, AMI, PE, LAY, MAJ,
   WR, THR, BOT, GOE, OD)
Moët & Chandon Brut Impérial (HOG, PLA,
   UN, POR)
Mumm Cordon Rouge (WR, THR, BOT, OD)
Perrier-Jouët (OD)
Pol Roger White Foil (BOR, PLA)
Pommery (HOG)
Thienot (AMI)
1986
Duval Leroy Fleur de Champagne (TAN)
Ellner (DAV)
1985
Bollinger ½ bottle (BAR)

£18.00 to £19.99

Non-vintage
Besserat de Bellefon Crémant (GRE)
Billecart-Salmon (BAR)
Bollinger (PLA, HOG, GOE, BU)

Bruno Paillard (BUT, ROB)
Bruno Paillard Blanc de Blancs (BEK)
Charles Heidsieck (TES, UN)
Joseph Perrier (TAN)
Lanson (WRI, PE, WHI, EL)
Laurent-Perrier (EL, VIC, PEN, CHA, MV, ROB,
   BAR, AD, WHI, ARM, CB)
Louis Roederer (PLA, HOG, GOE, NI, DAV, PE,
   GRE, TES, MAJ, OD)
Louis Roederer Rich (PLA, NI, MAJ)
Moët & Chandon Brut Impérial (EL, LAY,
   WRI, TAN, WAI, SAF, SAI, TES, ASD, DAV, VIC,
   WR, GRE, WHI, SUM, PE, WAT)
Mumm Cordon Rouge (VIC, UN)
Perrier-Jouët (WRI)
Pol Roger (REI, POR, ROB)

Pol Roger White Foil (GOE, HOG, GRE, PEN,
   OD, TES, WRI, UN, LEA)
Taittinger (BIB, HOG, LEA, POR, UN, TES)
Veuve Clicquot (HOG, PLA, GRE, HAY, WY, LO,
   LEA, WAI, BIB, UN, POR, DAV, MAJ, WHI, THR,
   BOT, TES, WR, OD)
1988
Perrier-Jouët (OD)
1986
Moët & Chandon (PLA)
Pol Roger Blanc de Chardonnay (SOM)
1985
★ Alfred Gratien (WS)
Canard-Duchêne (ROB)
Descombes (THR, WR, BOT)
Joseph Perrier (HIC)
Joseph Perrier Cuvée Royal (CV)
Piper Heidsieck (NI)
★ Salon Blanc de Blancs (AD)
de Venoge Blanc de Blancs (WHI)

£20.00 to £21.99

Non-vintage
Bollinger (GRE, PEN, TAN, CV, WCL, PIP, BE,
   POR, WRI, LEA, ASD, ARM, SUM, WHI, SAF,
   TES, MAJ, THR, OD, WR, BOT, DAV, PE, LAY)
Bruno Paillard Blanc de Blancs (GAU)
Louis Roederer (HAY, TAN, WR, BOT, THR,
   WRI, WCL, UN, BIB, LAY, WAI, WS, SUM, CV,
   AMI, WHI, LEA)

Moët & Chandon Brut Impérial (VIN)
Perrier-Jouët (PIP)
Pol Roger (WS, AMI)
Pol Roger White Foil (HAY, GE, TAN, BEN,
   HAM, HAH)
'R' de Ruinart (BEN)
Taittinger (ROB, LAY, WRI, ARM)
Veuve Clicquot (WCL, TAN, WRI, LAY, ROB)
Veuve Clicquot White Label Demi-Sec
   (WCL)
1988
Deutz (ARM)
1986
Lanson (PLA)
1985
Bruno Paillard (BEK)
Lanson (HOG)
Veuve Clicquot Gold Label (PLA)
1983
Bauget-Jouette (HIG)
Georges Gardet (GOE)

£22.00 to £23.99

Non-vintage
Bollinger (WAI, LO, AD, UN, WAT, CB, GAU,
   BEN, EL, BUT, DI, HAM, BAR, VIC, MV, HAH)
Gosset Brut Reserve (AMI)
Laurent-Perrier Ultra Brut (LEA)
Louis Roederer (HA, HAH, ARM, EL, AD, HIC,
   BEN, BAR, MV)
Louis Roederer Rich (PEN, BEN, ROB)
Perrier-Jouët Blason de France (NA)
Veuve Clicquot (MV, BEN, CB, ARM, VIC, HAH)
1988
Perrier-Jouët (PIP, AME)
Veuve Clicquot (GRE)
1986
Moët & Chandon (TAN, WAT, WHI, PE, TES,
   UN, WRI, OD, EL, VIC, DAV)
Pol Roger (PLA, HOG)
1985
Charles Heidsieck (PIP)
Dom Ruinart (GOE, PEN)
Joseph Perrier (HAM, SEC)
Lanson (HA, SO, THR, WR, BOT, WAI, VIC)
Laurent-Perrier (PLA, ARM, LEA, CHA)
Moët & Chandon (WY)
Thienot (AMI)
Veuve Clicquot (HOG)
1983
Lanson (WHI)
Moët & Chandon (BU)
Veuve Clicquot Gold Label (WY)
1982
Perrier-Jouët (PEN)

£24.00 to £25.99

Non-vintage
Bollinger (VIN)
Laurent-Perrier Ultra Brut (AD)
Louis Roederer (CB, GAU, VIN)
Mumm Crémant de Cramant Blanc de Blancs (ROB)
Veuve Clicquot (VIN)
1988
Laurent-Perrier (CB)
1986
Pol Roger (REI, GRE, PEN)
Veuve Clicquot (BIB)

1985
Bruno Paillard (YAP)
George Goulet (VIG, PIP)
George Goulet Crémant Blanc de Blancs (PIP)
Laurent-Perrier (AD, BAR)
Perrier-Jouët (AMI)
Taittinger (WAT)
Veuve Clicquot (LO, WCL, WRI, PE, CB, LEA, WR, UN, BOT, THR)
Veuve Clicquot Gold Label (LAY)
1983
George Goulet (VIG)
Lanson (PE)
Veuve Clicquot (WHI, WAT)
1982
Alfred Gratien Crémant (HAY)
1975
Veuve Clicquot (FA)
1966
Bollinger ½ bottle (BUT)

£26.00 to £27.99

Non-vintage
Perrier-Jouët Blason de France (PIP)
1986
Billecart-Salmon Cuvée N.F. Billecart (WW)
Louis Roederer (GOE)
Louis Roederer Blanc de Blancs (NI)
Pol Roger (TAN, LEA, BEN, HAM)
1985
Bollinger (HOG)

Louis Roederer (WCL)
Louis Roederer Blanc de Blancs (PLA)
Taittinger (ARM)
Veuve Clicquot (WS, HIC, ARM, EL, HAH)
Veuve Clicquot Gold Label (MV)
1982
Georges Gardet (HIC)
Veuve Clicquot Gold Label (GE)

£28.00 to £29.99

Non-vintage
Perrier-Jouët Blason de France (AMI)
1986
Billecart-Salmon (BAR)
Bollinger (GRE)
Louis Roederer (BIB)
Louis Roederer Blanc de Blancs (LAY)
1985
Bollinger (WCL, PIP, HIC, TAN, WRI, PE)
Louis Roederer (MV)
Veuve Clicquot Gold Label (PIP)
1983
Alfred Gratien (WS)
Bollinger (BU)
Louis Roederer (PEN)
1982
Pol Roger Blanc de Chardonnay (GRE)

£30.00 to £39.99

Non-vintage
Bollinger magnum (PLA)
Krug Grande Cuvée ½ bottle (LEA, BEN)
Lanson magnum (PLA, WRI)
Laurent-Perrier magnum (CHA)
Moët & Chandon magnum (TAN, TES, WAI, LAY, WRI, POR, WHI)
Perrier-Jouët magnum (ROB)
Pol Roger White Foil magnum (PEN)
Veuve Clicquot magnum (PLA)
1988
Perrier-Jouët Belle Époque (NA)
1986
Bollinger (DAV)
Louis Roederer (ARM, TAN, CB)
Louis Roederer Blanc de Blancs (BEN)
Pol Roger Blanc de Chardonnay (BEN, LEA)
1985
Billecart-Salmon Blanc de Blancs (WW)
Bollinger (MV, ARM, AD, HA, BE, BOT, WR, THR, EL, CB, BEN, TW, DI, BAR, WAT, VIC, HAH, VIN)
Bollinger Année Rare RD (BUT)
Dom Ruinart Blanc de Blancs (LEA)
Heidsieck Diamant Bleu (OD)
Pol Roger (VIN)

Pol Roger Blanc de Chardonnay (REI, PEN, WRI, AMI, VIN)
Pol Roger Cuvée Sir Winston Churchill (SOM)
Veuve Clicquot la Grande Dame (PLA)
1983
Dom Ruinart (MAJ)
Dom Ruinart Blanc de Blancs (BAR)
Louis Roederer (GAU)
Louis Roederer Blanc de Blancs (PEN)
1982
Bollinger RD (PLA)
Krug (ARM)
Pol Roger Blanc de Chardonnay (GE, ROB)
1981
Dom Ruinart Blanc de Blancs (VIC)
1979
Bruno Paillard (BUT)
1976
Bruno Paillard (BUT)
Laurent-Perrier Millésime Rare (CHA)

£40.00 to £49.99

Non-vintage
Bollinger magnum (LAY, TAN, AD, DI, BEN, LEA)
Pol Roger White Foil magnum (WRI, LEA, ROB, HAM)
Veuve Clicquot magnum (LEA)
1986
Perrier-Jouët Belle Époque (PIP)
1985
Dom Pérignon (PLA, HOG)
Dom Pérignon magnum (BU)
Lanson magnum (PLA)
Laurent-Perrier magnum (LEA)
Perrier-Jouët Belle Époque (WRI, OD, GRE, BE, WHI)
Pol Roger Cuvée Sir Winston Churchill (PLA, HOG, WRI)
Veuve Clicquot la Grande Dame (WY, GRE, GE, POR, LEA)
1983
Dom Ruinart Blanc de Blancs (PE)
1982
Bollinger RD (WCL, BIB, PIP, TAN, BEN, LEA, HAM, GAU, ROB)
Pol Roger Cuvée Sir Winston Churchill (GE)
Taittinger Comtes de Champagne Blanc de Blancs (DI, BUT)
1979
Bollinger Année Rare RD (BUT)
Bollinger RD (AD, DI)
1976
Bollinger Année Rare RD (BUT)

1975
Veuve Clicquot (VIG)
1971
Charles Heidsieck (BUT)
1966
Lanson (VIG)

£50.00 to £59.99

Non-vintage
Krug Grande Cuvée (AMI, VIC, REI, SEC, AD, EL, POR, WHI, LEA, BAR, WAT, LAY)
Laurent-Perrier Cuvée Grande Siècle (PEN, AD, CHA, CB, EL)
Pol Roger Cuvée Sir Winston Churchill (BEN)
1987
Louis Roederer Cristal (NO)
1986
Dom Pérignon (BIB)
Louis Roederer Cristal (GRE, BIB, PEN, ARM, CV, LAY, WRI, TAN)
Moët & Chandon magnum (UN)
Taittinger Comtes de Champagne Blanc de Blancs (WHI)
1985
Bollinger magnum (TAN)
Dom Pérignon (WY, HA, BY, ROB, PE, TAN, THR, WR, BOT, EL, WAT, OD, UN, WRI, DAV, CB, HAH, AMI)
Louis Roederer (WY)
Louis Roederer Cristal (PLA, NI, WCL, HAH, NO, BEN, OD, MAJ)
Perrier-Jouët Belle Époque (VIN)
Pol Roger Cuvée Sir Winston Churchill (TAN, ROB)
Taittinger Comtes de Champagne Blanc de Blancs (ROB)
Veuve Clicquot la Grande Dame (ROB)
1983
Dom Pérignon (WY, WHI)
Louis Roederer Cristal (NO)
Taittinger Comtes de Champagne Blanc de Blancs (LAY)
1982
Dom Pérignon (FA, TES)
George Goulet Cuvée de Centenaire (PIP)
Krug (GOE)
Louis Roederer Cristal (NO)
Pol Roger Cuvée Sir Winston Churchill (PEN)
1979
Bollinger RD (VIN)
1976
Taittinger Comtes de Champagne Blanc de Blancs (BUT)

£60.00 to £74.99

Non-vintage
Krug Grande Cuvée (PE, PEN, TAN, CB, BEN, BIB, HAH, ROB, VIN)
Louis Roederer Cristal (WS)
1986
Louis Roederer Cristal (AD, CB, LEA, ROB, LO)
1985
Bollinger magnum (LEA)
Dom Pérignon (VIC, VIN)
Louis Roederer Cristal (PE, EL, AMI, GAU)
1983
Dom Pérignon (SEC)
Louis Roederer Cristal (WY, VIN)
1982
Krug (AD, VIC, OD, TAN, BEN)
Salon (CB)
1979
Krug (GRE)
1978
Dom Pérignon (WY)
Louis Roederer Cristal (WY)
1976
Dom Pérignon (NO)
1975
Bollinger Année Rare RD (TAN, BUT)
1970
Bollinger magnum (BUT)

£75.00 to £99.99

Non-vintage
Bollinger jeroboam (LAY, TAN)
Pol Roger White Foil jeroboam (WRI)
Veuve Clicquot jeroboam (LEA)

1982
Bollinger Vieilles Vignes Françaises, Blanc de Noirs (GRE)
Krug (BIB, CB, DAV, HAH, ROB, TW, VIN)
Taittinger Collection Artist's Label (ROB)
1980
Dom Pérignon (SEC)
1979
Krug (NO)
1978
Dom Pérignon (BIB)

1975
Bollinger Année Rare RD (DI)
Krug (PEN)
1973
Bollinger Année Rare RD (AD)
1971
Dom Pérignon (WY)
1966
Dom Pérignon (WY)
Krug (BIB)
1947
Pommery (WY)

£100.00 to £125.00

Non-vintage
Lanson jeroboam (WRI)
Laurent-Perrier Cuvée Grande Siècle magnum (CHA)
Pol Roger White Foil jeroboam (LEA)
1986
Bollinger Vieilles Vignes Françaises, Blanc de Noirs (BEN)
1985
Dom Pérignon magnum (ROB)
1982
Pol Roger Cuvée Sir Winston Churchill magnum (REI)
1979
Pol Roger Cuvée Sir Winston Churchill magnum (VIN)
1964
Dom Pérignon (WY)
1959
Dom Pérignon (WY)
Krug (WY, FA)
1955
Dom Pérignon (WY)

£130.00 to £204.99

Non-vintage
Pol Roger White Foil methuselah (WRI, PEN)
1985
Bollinger jeroboam (LEA)
1982
Krug Clos du Mesnil Blanc de Blancs (ARM, BEN, ROB)
1980
Krug Clos du Mesnil Blanc de Blancs (GRE)
1975
Dom Pérignon magnum (WY)
1969
Dom Pérignon magnum (WY)
1955
Dom Pérignon (BIB)

c. £250.00

1961
Dom Pérignon magnum (WY)

£270.00 to £277.00

Non-vintage
Pol Roger White Foil salmanazar (PEN, WRI)

SPARKLING ROSÉ

Under £15.00

Non-vintage
Alexandre Bonnet Prestige (OD)
Bruno Paillard ½ bottle (HAL)
Mercier (VIC)

£15.00 to £19.99

Non-vintage
Ayala (AMI)
Bauget-Jouette (HIG)
★ Bricout (AME)
★ Bruno Paillard (BEK, YAP)
Canard-Duchêne (HOG, GRE, ROB)
Mercier (UN, ROB)
Piper Heidsieck (NI)
Pommery (BIB, ROB)
1986
Pol Roger (SOM)
1983
Jeanmaire (GOE)

£20.00 to £29.99

Non-vintage
Ayala (BEN)
Besserat de Bellefon Cuvée des Moines (GRE)
Billecart-Salmon (WW, BAR, OD)
Bricout (WCL)
Lanson (WHI, LAY, HA, VIC, PE, THR, BOT, WR, UN)
Laurent-Perrier (REI, PLA, BIB, LEA, POR, LO, AMI, GOE, LAY, CHA, UN, TAN, BOT, THR, OD, WR, MAJ, ARM, EL, WHI, ROB, GRE, CB, BAR, MV, WRI, PEN)
Louis Roederer (NI, BIB)
Pol Roger (PEN)
1986
Louis Roederer (LEA, AMI)
Moët & Chandon (GRE, UN)
Pol Roger (WRI)
1985
Bollinger (TAN)
Bruno Paillard (PIP)
George Goulet (PIP)

Moët & Chandon (WY, ROB)
Mumm Cordon Rosé (SEC)
Pol Roger (ROB)
1983
Veuve Clicquot (GRE)

£30.00 to £39.99

1986
Louis Roederer (BEN)
1985
Bollinger (BE, DI)
Veuve Clicquot (CB)
1983
Veuve Clicquot (ROB)

£40.00 to £49.99

Non-vintage
Laurent-Perrier magnum (CHA, LEA)
1986
Perrier-Jouët Belle Époque (NA)
1985
Perrier-Jouët Belle Époque (PIP, ROB)
1981
Dom Ruinart (GE, DI)

£55.00 to £79.99

Non-vintage
Krug (CB)
1979
Taittinger Comtes de Champagne (SEC)

c. £115.00

Non-vintage
Krug (WHI)

£140.00 to £160.00

1982
Dom Pérignon (BIB, LO, ROB)

STILL WHITE

Under £16.00

Non-vintage
Coteaux Champenois, Laurent-Perrier Blanc de Chardonnay (CHA)

STILL RED

Under £17.00

Non-vintage
Coteaux Champenois, Laurent-Perrier Pinot Franc, Cuvée de Pinot Noir (CHA)
1982
Coteaux Champenois, Bollinger Ay Rouge la Côte aux Enfants (GRE)

NORTHERN RHÔNE

RED

Under £6.00

1991
Crozes-Hermitage Cave de Vins Fins à
Tain-Hermitage (POR, AME)
1990
★Crozes-Hermitage Cave des Clairmonts (WAI)

£6.00 to £6.99

1991
Crozes-Hermitage Domaine des Entrefaux
(SUM, PIP)
1990
Crozes-Hermitage Cave des Clairmonts (MV)
Crozes-Hermitage Domaine des Entrefaux
(BY)
Crozes-Hermitage Jaboulet (OD)
1989
Crozes-Hermitage Delas (LO, CV)
1985
Crozes-Hermitage Domaine des Entrefaux
(BUT)

£7.00 to £8.99

1992
Crozes-Hermitage Graillot (BY, YAP, OD)
1991
Crozes-Hermitage Chapoutier (TAN)
Crozes-Hermitage Domaine des
Remizières, Desmeure (DAV)
Crozes-Hermitage les Meysonniers,
Chapoutier (DI)
St-Joseph Coursodon (THR, BOT, WR)
1990
Crozes-Hermitage Cave des Clairmonts,
Borja (HIC)
Crozes-Hermitage Domaine de Thalabert,
Jaboulet (HOG)
Crozes-Hermitage Domaine des
Remizières, Desmeure (RAE)
St-Joseph Cave Co-op. Agricole de St
Désirat-Champagne (YAP, WAI)
St-Joseph Delas (LO)
St-Joseph Deschants, Chapoutier (DI)
St-Joseph le Grand Pompée, Jaboulet
(HOG, OD)
1989
Crozes-Hermitage Domaine de Thalabert,
Jaboulet (WHI)
1988
St-Joseph Larmes du Père, Paret (ROB)

1985
Crozes-Hermitage les Meysonniers,
Chapoutier (BUT)
★ St-Joseph le Grand Pompée, Jaboulet
(HOG)

£9.00 to £10.99

1991
Cornas Coteau, Michel (BOT, THR)
Crozes-Hermitage Domaine de Thalabert,
Jaboulet (GRE, TAN)
Crozes-Hermitage Graillot (GAU)
Crozes-Hermitage les Meysonniers,
Chapoutier (PLA, GAU)
St-Joseph Grippat (YAP)
1990
Cornas Coteau, Michel (WR)
Cornas Jaboulet (HOG)
Crozes-Hermitage Domaine de Thalabert,
Jaboulet (OD, NI)
Crozes-Hermitage les Meysonniers,
Chapoutier (TAN)
St-Joseph le Grand Pompée, Jaboulet
(GRE, VIG)
1989
Cornas Michel (YAP)
St-Joseph Deschants, Chapoutier (GAU)
St-Joseph le Grand Pompée,
Jaboulet (PLA)
1988
Cornas Michel (YAP)
St-Joseph Gripa (GE)
1987
Cornas Jean Lionnet (GE)
Hermitage le Gréal, Sorrel (BIB)
St-Joseph Clos de l'Arbalestrier, Florentin
(RAE, BIB)
1986
Cornas Jaboulet (HOG, WS, GRE)
Cornas Michel (ROB)
1985
Crozes-Hermitage Domaine de Thalabert,
Jaboulet (BUT, HOG)
St-Joseph Deschants, Chapoutier (BUT)

£11.00 to £12.99

1992
Cornas Clape (YAP)
1991
Cornas Jaboulet (PLA)
St-Joseph Clos de l'Arbalestrier, Florentin
(GAU)

1990
Côte-Rôtie Seigneur de Maugiron, Delas (OD)
Crozes-Hermitage Domaine de Thalabert,
  Jaboulet (BUT, VIG)
1988
Cornas Noël Verset (GAU, RAE)
St-Joseph Clos de l'Arbalestrier, Florentin
  (AD)
1987
Cornas Noël Verset (WCL, RAE, HAY)
Hermitage la Chapelle, Jaboulet (EY)
Hermitage Marquise de la Tourette,
  Delas (PEN)
1986
Cornas Noël Verset (HAM)
Côte-Rôtie Barge (SEC)
Hermitage Domaine des Remizières (RAE)
Hermitage la Sizeranne, Chapoutier (EL)
1985
Cornas Jaboulet (HOG)
1984
Côte-Rôtie les Jumelles, Jaboulet (HA)
Hermitage Guigal (BU)
1983
Hermitage la Sizeranne, Chapoutier (BU)
1981
Hermitage Cuvée des Miaux, Ferraton (PIP)

£13.00 to £14.99
1992
Côte-Rôtie Champet (YAP)
1991
Cornas Clape (YAP, NI)
Côte-Rôtie Champet (YAP)
1990
Cornas Rochepertuis, Jean Lionnet (AD)
1989
Côte-Rôtie Burgaud (YAP)
1988
Cornas Clape (OD)
Côte-Rôtie Delas (WS)
1987
Côte-Rôtie Barge (GE)
Côte-Rôtie Burgaud (ROB)
Côte-Rôtie Guigal (BE)
Côte-Rôtie Jasmin (YAP)
1986
Cornas Jaboulet (VIC)
Côte-Rôtie Jasmin (FA)
Côte-Rôtie les Jumelles, Jaboulet (GRE)
1985
Cornas de Barjac (NO)
★ Côte-Rôtie Brune et Blonde, Guigal (FA)
Hermitage Domaine des Remizières (PE)
Hermitage Sorrel (BUT)

1984
Hermitage Chave (GOE)
Hermitage la Chapelle, Jaboulet (BUT, REI)
1983
Hermitage Domaine des Remizières (BUT)
Hermitage Jaboulet (WHI, HOG)

£15.00 to £16.99
1992
Cornas Clape (DI)
Côte-Rôtie Burgaud (YAP)
Côte-Rôtie Jasmin (YAP)
1991
Cornas Noël Verset (GAU)
Côte-Rôtie Burgaud (YAP)
Côte-Rôtie Jasmin (YAP)
Côte-Rôtie René Rostaing (AD, GAU)
1990
Cornas Clape (YAP)
Côte-Rôtie Champet (YAP)
Côte-Rôtie René Rostaing (BUT, HAH)
Hermitage la Sizeranne, Chapoutier (DI)
1989
Cornas de Barjac (LAY)
Côte-Rôtie Brune et Blonde, Guigal (BY, HAY)

Côte-Rôtie Champet (YAP)
Côte-Rôtie Jamet (GAU)
Côte-Rôtie Seigneur de Maugiron, Delas
  (PEN)
Hermitage Guigal (OD)
Hermitage la Sizeranne, Chapoutier (NO)
1988
Cornas de Barjac (NO)
Côte-Rôtie Barge (MV)
Côte-Rôtie Brune et Blonde, Vidal-Fleury
  (NO)
Côte-Rôtie les Jumelles, Jaboulet (HOG)
Hermitage la Sizeranne, Chapoutier (AD)
Hermitage le Gréal, Sorrel (GE)
Hermitage Sorrel (BY)
1987
Côte-Rôtie Côte Brune, Gentaz-Dervieux
  (EY)
1986
Côte-Rôtie Brune et Blonde, Guigal
  (GOE, NI)

Côte-Rôtie Guigal (GOE)
Côte-Rôtie Jamet (RE)
Côte-Rôtie les Jumelles, Jaboulet (HOG, PLA)
1985
Côte-Rôtie Chapoutier (BUT)
Côte-Rôtie les Jumelles, Jaboulet (RAE)
Hermitage Cuvée des Miaux, Ferraton
  (BUT)
1983
Côte-Rôtie Brune et Blonde, Guigal (FA)
Côte-Rôtie les Jumelles, Jaboulet (GAU)
Crozes-Hermitage Domaine de Thalabert,
  Jaboulet (BUT)
Hermitage la Chapelle, Jaboulet (WS)
1982
Hermitage Guigal (GOE)

£17.00 to £19.99
1992
Hermitage Grippat (YAP)
1991
Côte-Rôtie Jamet (BIB)
Côte-Rôtie la Viallere, Dervieux-Thaize
  (LAY)
Côte-Rôtie René Rostaing (BIB)
1990
Côte-Rôtie Chapoutier (DI)
Côte-Rôtie Gérin (THR, BOT, WR)
1989
Cornas les Ruchottes, Colombo (GAU)
Côte-Rôtie Chapoutier (DI)
Côte-Rôtie Delas (CV)
Côte-Rôtie Jasmin (YAP)
Hermitage la Sizeranne, Chapoutier
  (GAU, VIG)
1988
Cornas Clape (BUT, GAU)
Côte-Rôtie Brune et Blonde, Guigal (NI)
Côte-Rôtie Gentaz-Dervieux (WS)
Côte-Rôtie Guigal (WS)
Côte-Rôtie Jasmin (YAP)
Hermitage Chave (FA)
Hermitage Guigal (POR, AD)
Hermitage la Chapelle, Jaboulet (VIC)
1987
Hermitage Chave (GAU, WS)
1986
Cornas Clape (BUT)
Cornas Noël Verset (BUT)
Côte-Rôtie les Jumelles, Jaboulet (CB)
Hermitage Chave (WS)
Hermitage Guigal (BE)
Hermitage la Chapelle, Jaboulet
  (MV, WHI, HOG)
Hermitage la Sizeranne, Chapoutier (GRE)

1985
Hermitage Guigal (BY, PE, EY)
Hermitage la Chapelle, Jaboulet (FA, RAE)
Hermitage la Sizeranne, Chapoutier
  (BUT, DI)
1983
Côte-Rôtie Chapoutier (BUT)
1981
Côte-Rôtie Champet (YAP)
Hermitage Guigal (BUT)
1980
Côte-Rôtie les Jumelles, Jaboulet (WHI)

£20.00 to £24.99
1991
Côte-Rôtie Côte Brune, Gentaz-Dervieux
  (RAE)
Côte-Rôtie Gentaz-Dervieux (GAU)
Côte-Rôtie la Landonne, René Rostaing (BIB)
Hermitage Chave (YAP)
Hermitage la Chapelle, Jaboulet (GAU, TAN)
1990
Cornas les Ruchottes, Colombo (VIG)
Côte-Rôtie Côte Blonde, René Rostaing
  (BUT)
Côte-Rôtie Côte Brune, Gentaz-Dervieux
  (RAE)
Hermitage la Sizeranne, Chapoutier (MV)
1989
Côte-Rôtie Chapoutier (AD)
Hermitage la Chapelle, Jaboulet
  (HOG, GAU, VIG)
Hermitage la Sizeranne, Chapoutier (AD)
1988
Côte-Rôtie Burgaud (GAU)
Côte-Rôtie Chapoutier (GAU)
Côte-Rôtie Jamet (BUT)
Côte-Rôtie les Jumelles, Jaboulet (AD)
Hermitage Chave (YAP, GAU)
Hermitage la Chapelle, Jaboulet
  (GAU, HOG, HAH, VIG)
1986
Cornas Clape (AD)
Côte-Rôtie Côte Brune, Gentaz-Dervieux
  (BUT)
Côte-Rôtie Guigal (WS)
Hermitage Guigal (TW)
Hermitage la Chapelle, Jaboulet (AD)

> *In each price band wines
> are listed in vintage order.
> Within each vintage they
> are listed in A–Z order.*

1985
Cornas Clape (BUT)
Côte-Rôtie Brune et Blonde, Guigal (NI)
Côte-Rôtie les Jumelles, Jaboulet (BUT)
Hermitage la Chapelle, Jaboulet (HA, PIP, DI)
1983
Hermitage Guigal (TW)
1982
Hermitage Chave (BIB)
Hermitage la Chapelle, Jaboulet (NO)
1980
Hermitage la Chapelle, Jaboulet (ROB)

£25.00 to £29.99

1990
Côte-Rôtie la Landonne, René Rostaing (VIG)
Hermitage la Chapelle, Jaboulet (GAU, NI)
1989
Côte-Rôtie Côte Brune, Gentaz-Dervieux
  (FA)
Côte-Rôtie la Viallere, Dervieux-Thaize (VIG)
1986
Côte-Rôtie Jasmin (BEN, AD)
1985
Côte-Rôtie Burgaud (BUT)
1983
Côte-Rôtie Brune et Blonde, Guigal (BEN)

£30.00 to £39.99

1985
Hermitage Chave (BUT, AD)
1979
Hermitage la Chapelle, Jaboulet (GAU, PIP)
1971
Côte-Rôtie Champet (NO)

£40.00 to £60.00

1984
Côte-Rôtie la Landonne, Guigal (SEC)
Côte-Rôtie la Mouline Côte Blonde, Guigal
  (SEC, BUT)
1976
Hermitage la Chapelle, Jaboulet (HOG)
1971
Côte-Rôtie les Jumelles, Jaboulet (VIG)
1964
Cornas Jaboulet (WS)
1962
Côte-Rôtie les Jumelles, Jaboulet (REI)

£70.00 to £95.00

1987
Côte-Rôtie la Landonne, Guigal (GAU, VIG)
Côte-Rôtie la Mouline Côte Blonde,
  Guigal (GAU)

1986
Côte-Rôtie la Landonne, Guigal (GAU)
1982
Côte-Rôtie la Mouline Côte Blonde,
  Guigal (BUT)
1978
Hermitage Chave (NO)
Hermitage la Chapelle, Jaboulet
  (FA, BUT, REI)
1972
Hermitage la Chapelle, Jaboulet (BIB)

£110.00 to £150.00

1986
Côte-Rôtie la Mouline Côte Blonde,
  Guigal (TW, BUT)
1983
Côte-Rôtie la Mouline Côte Blonde,
  Guigal (GOE)
1955
Côte-Rôtie les Jumelles, Jaboulet (TW)

c. £188.00

1985
Côte-Rôtie la Mouline Côte Blonde,
  Guigal (BUT)

WHITE

Under £7.00

1992
Crozes-Hermitage Cave des Clairmonts (YAP)
Crozes-Hermitage Domaine des Entrefaux
  (BY, PIP)
1990
Crozes-Hermitage la Mule Blanche,
  Jaboulet (NI)
1989
Crozes-Hermitage la Mule Blanche,
  Jaboulet (HOG)

£7.00 to £8.99

1990
St-Joseph Courbis (BUT)
1988
Crozes-Hermitage Domaine des
  Remizières (RAE)
1987
★ Condrieu Vernay (SEC)

£9.00 to £11.99

1991
St-Joseph Clos de l'Arbalestrier,
  Florentin (GAU)
St-Joseph Grippat (YAP)

1988
Hermitage Chante-Alouette,
  Chapoutier (BER)
1986
St-Joseph Clos de l'Arbalestrier,
  Florentin (RAE)
1984
Hermitage Domaine des Remizières (PE)
St-Joseph Clos de l'Arbalestrier,
  Florentin (BUT)

£12.00 to £15.99

1992
Hermitage Chevalier de Stérimberg,
  Jaboulet (PLA)
Hermitage Grippat (YAP)
1990
Hermitage Chante-Alouette, Chapoutier
  (TAN)
Hermitage Chevalier de Stérimberg,
  Jaboulet (NI)
1989
Hermitage la Tourette Delas (PEN)
1988
Hermitage Guigal (BE)
Hermitage les Rocoules, Sorrel (BY)
1987
Hermitage Chevalier de Stérimberg,
  Jaboulet (WHI, VIG)
1986
Hermitage Chante-Alouette, Chapoutier (DI)
Hermitage Chevalier de Stérimberg,
  Jaboulet (GRE)
Hermitage Domaine des Remizières (PE,
  RAE)
Hermitage Guigal (BE)

£16.00 to £19.99

1992
Condrieu Coteaux de Chéry, Perret (AD, NI)
Condrieu Vernay (YAP)
1991
Condrieu Barge (MV)
Condrieu Château du Rozay Cuvée
  Ordinaire (YAP)
Condrieu Clos Chanson, Perret (ROB)
Condrieu Dumazet (BIB)
1990
Condrieu Delas (PEN)
Condrieu Guigal (MV)
Condrieu les Cepes du Nebadon, Paret (PE)
Hermitage les Rocoules, Sorrel (AD)
1989
Condrieu Barge (EY)
Condrieu Guigal (WAT)

1988
Hermitage Chave (YAP, WS, ROB)
Hermitage Chevalier de Stérimberg,
  Jaboulet (VIG, BEN)
1987
Condrieu Barge (BUT)
Hermitage Chave (GAU)
1986
Condrieu Barge (BUT)
1985
Hermitage Chante-Alouette, Chapoutier
  (BUT, AD)
Hermitage Chevalier de Stérimberg,
  Jaboulet (BEN)
Hermitage les Rocoules, Sorrel (BUT)

£20.00 to £24.99

1992
Condrieu Château du Rozay Cuvée
  Ordinaire (YAP)
Hermitage Chave (YAP)
1991
Condrieu Coteaux de Chéry, Perret (WW, NO)
Condrieu Pinchon (GAU)
Condrieu Vernay (YAP)
Hermitage Chante-Alouette, Chapoutier (GAU)
Hermitage Chave (YAP)
Hermitage les Rocoules, Sorrel (BIB)
1990
Hermitage Chante-Alouette, Chapoutier
  (GAU, VIG)
Hermitage Chave (YAP)
1989
Condrieu Dumazet (BEN)
Condrieu Guigal (EY)
Condrieu Vernay (EL)
1988
Condrieu Guigal (BUT)

£25.00 to £39.99

1991
Château Grillet (YAP)
Condrieu Coteau de Vernon, Vernay (YAP)
1990
Château Grillet (YAP)
1987
Condrieu Coteau de Vernon, Vernay (ROB)
1985
Condrieu Guigal (BUT)
Hermitage Chave (BUT)
1983
Château Grillet (NO)
Hermitage Chave (VIG)
1979
Hermitage Chante-Alouette, Chapoutier (VIG)

SOUTHERN RHÔNE

RED

Under £4.00

1992

Côtes du Rhône Domaine de la Renjardière (EL)

Côtes du Ventoux la Falaise (BU)

VdP des Coteaux de l'Ardèche Duboeuf (BEK)

1991

Côtes du Lubéron Cellier de Marrenon (GAL)

Côtes du Ventoux Pascal (LO)

1990

Côtes du Ventoux Jaboulet (HOG)

£4.00 to £4.99

1992

Côtes du Rhône Caves des Vignerons de Vacqueyras (TAN)

Côtes du Rhône Château St-Estève (SOM)

Côtes du Rhône Domaine St-Gayan (YAP)

★ Côtes du Rhône Parallèle 45, Jaboulet (HOG, OD)

Côtes du Ventoux Jaboulet (OD)

Côtes du Vivarais Domaine de Belvezet (TAN, AD)

Lirac Domaine les Garrigues (CHA)

1991

Côtes du Ventoux la Vieille Ferme (GRE, MV, ROB, LEA)

VdP des Coteaux de l'Ardèche Duboeuf (DAV)

1990

Coteaux du Tricastin Domaine de Grangeneuve (ASD)

Côtes du Lubéron Château Val Joanis (ASD)

Côtes du Rhône Château du Bois de la Garde, Mousset (ASD)

★ Côtes du Rhône Guigal (OD)

Côtes du Rhône Jaume (WS)

Côtes du Ventoux Jaboulet (NI)

Côtes du Ventoux la Vieille Ferme (SEC, AMI)

1989

Côtes du Lubéron Château Val Joanis (BE)

Stars (★) indicate wines
selected by the editors as
particularly good value
in their class.

£5.00 to £5.99

1992

Coteaux du Tricastin Domaine de Grangeneuve (YAP)

Côtes du Rhône Château du Grand Moulas (HAH, CV)

Côtes du Rhône-Villages Château du Grand Moulas (EY)

Côtes du Rhône-Villages Rasteau, Cave des Vignerons de Rasteau (GRE, CV)

1991

Côte du Rhône Laudun Rouge, Domaine Pélaquié (SUM)

Côtes du Rhône Guigal (HAY)

Côtes du Rhône Valréas, Bouchard (WS)

Côtes du Rhône-Villages Château du Grand Moulas (TAN)

Côtes du Rhône-Villages Sablet Château du Trignon (PLA)

1990

Coteaux du Tricastin Domaine de Vieux Micocoulier (WW)

Côtes du Lubéron Château Val Joanis (ROB)

Côtes du Rhône Château St-Estève (WS)

Côtes du Rhône Parallèle 45, Jaboulet (NI)

Côtes du Rhône Puyméras (YAP)

Côtes du Rhône-Villages Rasteau, Cave des Vignerons de Rasteau (POR)

Lirac les Queyrades, Mejan (AD)

Vacqueyras Caves Bessac (EL)

1989

Côtes du Rhône-Villages Sablet Château du Trignon (GAL)

Lirac les Queyrades, Mejan (TAN)

Lirac Sabon (WHI)

1988

Côtes du Rhône Cuvée Personnelle, Pascal (LO, YAP)

Côtes du Rhône Guigal (BE)

Côtes du Rhône Rascasses, Berard (WAT)

1987

Côtes du Rhône-Villages Château la Couranconne (BIB)

£6.00 to £6.99

1991

Côtes du Lubéron Château de Canorgue (YAP)

Côtes du Rhône Coudoulet de Beaucastel (OD)

Côtes du Rhône Guigal (MV)

Gigondas Domaine Raspail (HA)

1990

Côtes du Rhône Coudoulet de Beaucastel (SEC)

Côtes du Rhône Guigal (GOE, LAY, HIC, NI)

Côtes du Rhône-Villages Domaine Ste-Anne (LEA)

Côtes du Rhône-Villages Rasteau, Domaine la Soumade (PIP)

Lirac la Fermade, Domaine Maby (YAP)

Vacqueyras Jaboulet (HOG, EY)

Vacqueyras Pascal (DAV)

1989

Côtes du Rhône Château Redortier (PE)

Côtes du Rhône Guigal (ROB)

Vacqueyras Domaine la Garrigue (HIC)

Vacqueyras Domaine le Sang des Cailloux (PIP)

Vacqueyras Jaboulet (NI)

1988

Vacqueyras Cuvée Spéciale, Pascal (GAL)

Vacqueyras Pascal (YAP)

£7.00 to £7.99

1993

Châteauneuf-du-Pape Clos de l'Oratoire des Papes, Amouroux (DI)

1992

Côtes du Rhône-Villages Cuvée de l'Ecu, Château du Grand Moulas (AD)

1991

Châteauneuf-du-Pape Quiot (MAR, TES)

Côtes du Rhône Coudoulet de Beaucastel (GAU, ROB)

Lirac Domaine de Castel Oualou (GRE)

1990

Châteauneuf-du-Pape Delas (WAI)

Châteauneuf-du-Pape Domaine du Père Caboche (OD)

Gigondas Jaboulet (HOG)

Vacqueyras Domaine la Fourmone, Combe (TAN)

1989

Gigondas Domaine de Gour de Chaulé (HOG, EL)

Gigondas Jaboulet (HOG)

Vacqueyras Domaine de la Couroulu (HAM, POR)

1988

Gigondas Domaine du Cayron (BUT)

Gigondas Domaine du Grand Montmirail (YAP, GAL)

1986

Châteauneuf-du-Pape Quiot (SEC)

Gigondas Domaine du Grand Montmirail (DAV)

£8.00 to £8.99

1992

Gigondas Château du Trignon (PLA)

1991

Côtes du Rhône-Villages Cuvée St-Gervais, Domaine Ste-Anne (LEA)

1990

Châteauneuf-du-Pape Domaine de la Solitude (SO)

Côtes du Rhône Coudoulet de Beaucastel (GOE, BAR, BEN)

Gigondas Côtes de la Tour, Sarrazine (TAN)

Gigondas Guigal (MAJ)

1989

Châteauneuf-du-Pape Château des Fines Roches (ASD)

Châteauneuf-du-Pape Domaine Brunel (SAI)

Châteauneuf-du-Pape Domaine de Nalys (WW)

Gigondas Château du Trignon (GAL)

Gigondas Domaine du Cayron (BUT)

Gigondas Domaine St-Gayan, Roger Meffre (YAP, OD)

1988

Châteauneuf-du-Pape Château du Mont-Redon (SEC)

Châteauneuf-du-Pape Domaine du Père Caboche (YAP)

Vacqueyras Cuvée Spéciale, Pascal (VIN)

£9.00 to £9.99

1992

Châteauneuf-du-Pape Château de Beaucastel (GOE)

Châteauneuf-du-Pape Domaine Font de Michelle (WR, BOT, THR)

1991

Châteauneuf-du-Pape Château de Beaucastel (GOE)

Châteauneuf-du-Pape Domaine du Vieux Télégraphe (AD)

Châteauneuf-du-Pape Domaine la Roquette (BEK)

Châteauneuf-du-Pape Vieux Donjon (YAP)

1990

Châteauneuf-du-Pape Chante-Cigale (YAP, POR, CV)

Châteauneuf-du-Pape Delas (LO)

Châteauneuf-du-Pape Domaine de Montpertuis (EL)

Châteauneuf-du-Pape les Cailloux, Brunel (POR)

Châteauneuf-du-Pape les Cèdres, Jaboulet (HOG)

Gigondas Domaine du Cayron (AD)

Gigondas Domaine Raspail (LAY)

Gigondas Jaboulet (VIG)

1989

Châteauneuf-du-Pape Domaine du Père Caboche (YAP)

Châteauneuf-du-Pape Vieux Donjon (YAP)

1988

Châteauneuf-du-Pape Château des Fines Roches (BU)

Gigondas Domaine du Grand Montmirail (VIN)

Gigondas Domaine St-Gayan, Roger Meffre (YAP)

1987

Châteauneuf-du-Pape Clos des Papes, Avril (EY)

£10.00 to £11.99

1991

Châteauneuf-du-Pape Domaine du Vieux Télégraphe (LAY, HAH, DI)

1990

Châteauneuf-du-Pape Chante-Cigale (AME, BEN)

Châteauneuf-du-Pape Château de Beaucastel (LAY)

Châteauneuf-du-Pape Château du Mont-Redon (GAU)

Châteauneuf-du-Pape Château la Nerthe (OD)

Châteauneuf-du-Pape Domaine du Roquette (NO)

Châteauneuf-du-Pape Domaine du Vieux Télégraphe (HAH, TAN, AD)

Châteauneuf-du-Pape Domaine Font de Michelle (DAV, AME)

Châteauneuf-du-Pape Domaine Grand Veneur (VIG)

Châteauneuf-du-Pape la Bernardine, Chapoutier (DI, OD, FA, GRE)

Châteauneuf-du-Pape les Cèdres, Jaboulet (GRE, NI)

Châteauneuf-du-Pape Vieux Donjon (YAP)

Gigondas Domaine du Cayron (LAY)

1989

Châteauneuf-du-Pape Château de la Font du Loup (HOG)

Châteauneuf-du-Pape Domaine de Beaurenard (HA)

Châteauneuf-du-Pape Domaine du Vieux Télégraphe (TAN, SOM, POR)

Châteauneuf-du-Pape Domaine Grand Tinel (HAH)

Côtes du Rhône Château de Fonsalette (BUT)

Gigondas Domaine les Pallières (PIP)

Gigondas Guigal (NI)

1988

Châteauneuf-du-Pape Clos des Papes, Avril (HAY, BUT)

Châteauneuf-du-Pape Clos du Mont Olivet (WS)

Châteauneuf-du-Pape Vieux Donjon (YAP)

Côtes du Rhône Château de Fonsalette (HOG, BUT)

1986

Châteauneuf-du-Pape Domaine du Vieux Télégraphe (EY)

£12.00 to £14.99

1990

Châteauneuf-du-Pape Clos des Papes, Avril (GE, GAU, RAE)

Châteauneuf-du-Pape Clos du Mont Olivet (GAU)

1989

Châteauneuf-du-Pape Clos Pignan, Reynaud (BUT, VIG)

Châteauneuf-du-Pape Fleury (NA)

Châteauneuf-du-Pape Réserve, Sabon (BEN)

1988

Châteauneuf-du-Pape Château de Beaucastel (FA, GOE, NI)

Châteauneuf-du-Pape Clos Pignan, Reynaud (HOG, BUT)

Châteauneuf-du-Pape Domaine du Vieux Télégraphe (CV)

1987

Châteauneuf-du-Pape Château de Beaucastel (ROB)

1986

Châteauneuf-du-Pape Château de Beaucastel (FA)

Châteauneuf-du-Pape Clos des Papes, Avril (BUT)

Côtes du Rhône Château de Fonsalette (BUT)

1985

Châteauneuf-du-Pape Château de la Font
du Loup (HOG)

Châteauneuf-du-Pape Clos Pignan,
Reynaud (BUT)

Côtes du Rhône Château de Fonsalette (BUT)

£15.00 to £19.99

1990

Hermitage Bernard Faurie (HAH)

1989

Hermitage Bernard Faurie (PIP)

1986

Châteauneuf-du-Pape Château Rayas (HOG)

1985

Châteauneuf-du-Pape Château de
Beaucastel (ROB)

Châteauneuf-du-Pape Domaine de Mont-
Redon (GAU)

1981

Châteauneuf-du-Pape les Cèdres, Jaboulet
(WS)

£20.00 to £29.99

1988

Châteauneuf-du-Pape Château Rayas (BUT)

1985

Châteauneuf-du-Pape Château Rayas (BUT)

Châteauneuf-du-Pape Domaine du Vieux
Télégraphe (DI)

1983

Châteauneuf-du-Pape Château de
Beaucastel (BUT, ROB)

1978

Châteauneuf-du-Pape Clos du Mont Olivet
(LEA)

Châteauneuf-du-Pape les Cèdres, Jaboulet
(WS)

1976

Châteauneuf-du-Pape Domaine de la
Serrière (ROB)

£30.00 to £35.99

1992

Châteauneuf-du-Pape Château Rayas (DI)

1981

Châteauneuf-du-Pape Château de
Beaucastel (VIG)

> **Webster's** *is an annual
> publication. We welcome
> your suggestions for next
> year's edition.*

WHITE

Under £5.00

1992

Côtes du Lubéron la Vieille Ferme (MV,
GRE, ROB)

1991

VdP des Coteaux de l'Ardèche
Chardonnay, Latour (HOG)

1989

Côtes du Lubéron Château Val Joanis
(WHI)

£5.00 to £5.99

1993

★ Côtes du Rhône Domaine Pélaquié (BIB)

Côtes du Rhône Domaine St-Gayan (YAP)

1992

Côtes du Rhône Puyméras (YAP)

1991

Côte du Rhône Laudun Blanc, Domaine
Pélaquié (LAY)

Côtes du Rhône Guigal (NI)

1990

Lirac la Fermade, Domaine Maby (YAP)

1989

Côtes du Rhône Guigal (BE)

£6.00 to £9.99

1993

Châteauneuf-du-Pape Domaine de Mont-
Redon (WS)

1992

Côte du Rhône Laudun Blanc, Domaine
Pélaquié (SUM)

Côtes du Rhône Guigal (EY)

1988

Châteauneuf-du-Pape Domaine de Nalys
(BU)

1986

Châteauneuf-du-Pape les Cèdres,
Jaboulet (SEC)

£10.00 to £12.99

1992

Châteauneuf-du-Pape Domaine du Père
Caboche (YAP)

Châteauneuf-du-Pape Domaine du Vieux
Télégraphe (LAY)

1991

Châteauneuf-du-Pape Château de
Beaucastel (SEC)

1990

Châteauneuf-du-Pape Domaine de Nalys
(HOG, GRE)

£13.00 to £15.99

1992
Châteauneuf-du-Pape Domaine Font de Michelle (DAV, WR, BOT, THR)
Viognier Domaine Ste-Anne (LEA, TAN)
1991
Châteauneuf-du-Pape Domaine du Vieux Télégraphe (SOM)
1990
Châteauneuf-du-Pape Château de Beaucastel (GOE)
1988
Châteauneuf-du-Pape Domaine du Vieux Télégraphe (ROB)
1987
Châteauneuf-du-Pape Château de Beaucastel (BUT)
1986
Châteauneuf-du-Pape Château de Beaucastel (BUT)

£16.00 to £24.99

1992
Châteauneuf-du-Pape Domaine Grand Veneur (VIG)
1990
Châteauneuf-du-Pape Roussanne Vieilles Vignes, Château de Beaucastel (GOE, AD)
1989
Châteauneuf-du-Pape Château Rayas (BUT)
1988
Châteauneuf-du-Pape Roussanne Vieilles Vignes, Château de Beaucastel (NO)
1986
Châteauneuf-du-Pape Château Rayas (HOG)

£25.00 to £34.99

1991
Châteauneuf-du-Pape Roussanne Vieilles Vignes, Château de Beaucastel (VIG)
1988
Châteauneuf-du-Pape Château Rayas (BUT)

ROSÉ

Under £6.50

1992
Lirac Rosé la Fermade, Domaine Maby (YAP)
Tavel Château de Trinquevedel (EL)
1991
Côtes du Lubéron Château Val Joanis (ROB)
Tavel Château de Trinquevedel (HOG)

£6.50 to £7.99

1992
Tavel Domaine de la Genestière (PIP)
Tavel la Forcadière, Domaine Maby (YAP, PE)
1991
Tavel l'Espiègle, Jaboulet (HOG)

SPARKLING

Under £9.00

Non-vintage
Clairette de Die Brut Archard-Vincent (YAP)
Clairette de Die Tradition Demi-sec Archard-Vincent (YAP)

FORTIFIED

Under £7.00

1991
Muscat de Beaumes-de-Venise Domaine de Coyeux ½ bottle (BOT, WR, THR)
Muscat de Beaumes-de-Venise Jaboulet ½ bottle (OD)
1990
Muscat de Beaumes-de-Venise Domaine de Coyeux ½ bottle (AD)

£7.00 to £9.99

Non-vintage
Muscat de Beaumes-de-Venise Cave Co-op. de Beaumes-de-Venise (WHI, PLA)
Muscat de Beaumes-de-Venise Cuvée Pontificale, Pascal (DAV)
1992
Muscat de Beaumes-de-Venise Cave Co-op. de Beaumes-de-Venise (OD)
Muscat de Beaumes-de-Venise Domaine de Durban (YAP)
1991
Muscat de Beaumes-de-Venise Domaine de Coyeux (POR)

£10.00 to £12.99

Non-vintage
Muscat de Beaumes-de-Venise Perrin (PE, LEA)
1992
Muscat de Beaumes-de-Venise Domaine des Bernardins (PIP)
1990
Muscat de Beaumes-de-Venise Jaboulet (GRE)
1987
Muscat de Beaumes-de-Venise Domaine de Coyeux (RE)

LOIRE

DRY WHITE

Under £4.00

1993

Muscadet de Sèvre-et-Maine sur lie Carte d'Or, Sauvion (BEK)

Saumur Cave des Vignerons de Saumur (TES)

Sauvignon de Touraine Comte d'Ormont, Saget (MAJ)

★ Sauvignon du Haut Poitou, Cave Co-op. du Haut Poitou (WAI)

1992

Muscadet de Sèvre-et-Maine Château de la Dimerie (SAI)

★ Sauvignon de Touraine Confrérie d'Oisly et Thésée (OD)

1989

Saumur Blanc Château de Parnay Collé (WAT)

£4.00 to £4.99

1993

Chardonnay du Haut Poitou, Cave Co-op. du Haut Poitou (LO, DAV)

Muscadet de Sèvre-et-Maine Domaine des Hauts Pemions (CV)

Muscadet sur lie Chéreau, Domaine de la Mortaine (YAP)

Sauvignon du Haut Poitou, Cave Co-op. du Haut Poitou (SO, LO)

1992

★ Coteaux du Giennois Balland-Chapuis (OD)

Muscadet de Sèvre-et-Maine Fief de la Brie, Bonhomme (TAN)

Muscadet de Sèvre-et-Maine sur lie Château de la Ferronière (EL)

Muscadet sur lie Domaine des Pierres Noires (POR)

Saumur Cave des Vignerons de Saumur (AD)

Sauvignon de Touraine Comte d'Ormont, Saget (WHI)

Sauvignon de Touraine Domaine de la Garrelière (KA)

Sauvignon de Touraine Domaine Guy Mardon (VIC)

Sauvignon de Touraine Domaine Octavie, Barbeillon (KA)

1991

Muscadet de Sèvre-et-Maine sur lie Bossard (ASD)

1990

Sauvignon de Touraine Domaine de la Preslé (NI)

£5.00 to £5.99

1993

Muscadet de Sèvre-et-Maine sur lie Château de Cléray (PIP)

Muscadet de Sèvre-et-Maine sur lie Château de la Jannière (DAV)

Muscadet sur lie Château l'Oiselinière, Carré (WS)

★ Pouilly-Fumé les Loges, Saget (MAJ)

St-Pourçain Cuvée Printanière, Union des Vignerons (PIP)

Sauvignon de Touraine Confrérie d'Oisly et Thésée (HAH)

Sauvignon de Touraine Domaine de la Charmoise, Marionnet (BIB)

Sauvignon de Touraine Domaine de la Preslé (PIP)

1992

Muscadet de Sèvre-et-Maine sur lie Château de Chasseloir (AME)

Muscadet de Sèvre-et-Maine sur lie Clos des Bourguignons (HAH)

Muscadet de Sèvre-et-Maine sur lie Domaine de la Bretonnière (NI)

Muscadet de Sèvre-et-Maine sur lie Domaine des Dorices (GRE)

Muscadet de Sèvre-et-Maine sur lie Domaine des Hauts Pemions (EY)

Muscadet sur lie Château de la Galissonière (DI)

Pouilly-Fumé Saget (GRE)

Sancerre les Garennes, Brochard (WAT)

Vin de Thouarsais, Gigon (YAP)

1991

Menetou-Salon les Thureaux, Mellot (HOG)

Muscadet de Sèvre-et-Maine sur lie Château de Cléray (ROB)

Muscadet de Sèvre-et-Maine sur lie Thuaud (CHA)

1990
Anjou Blanc Sec Prestige, Tijou (HIG)
Menetou-Salon la Charnivolle, Fournier (BEK)
Muscadet de Sèvre-et-Maine sur lie Cuvée LM, Louis Métaireau (SOM)
Muscadet des Coteaux de la Loire Guindon (BIB)
Quincy Pierre Mardon (GE)
Saumur Blanc Domaine Langlois (DI)
Vouvray Château Moncontour (OD)
★ Vouvray Domaine de l'Épinay (ASD)

£6.00 to £6.99
1993
Pouilly-Fumé les Loges, Saget (GRE)
Quincy Jaumier (YAP)
Reuilly Beurdin (WCL)
Reuilly Robert & Gérard Cordier (YAP)
Touraine Azay-le-Rideau la Basse Chevrière (YAP)
Vouvray Jarry (YAP)
1992
Coteaux du Giennois Balland-Chapuis (SUM)
Menetou-Salon la Charnivolle, Fournier (PLA)
Menetou-Salon Pellé (SAI, THR, WR, OD, BOT)
Montlouis Domaine des Liards, Berger (YAP)
Muscadet de Sèvre-et-Maine sur lie Château de la Ragotière Black Label (VIN)
Muscadet de Sèvre-et-Maine sur lie Cuvée LM, Louis Métaireau (NI)
Muscadet de Sèvre-et-Maine sur lie Moulin de la Gravelle (GAL)
Pouilly-Fumé Bailly (WS)
Pouilly-Fumé Saget (MAR)
Quincy Pierre Mardon (AD)
Reuilly Beurdin (AD)
Sancerre Mellot (TES)
Sauvignon de Touraine Domaine des Corbillières (BUT)
Touraine Azay-le-Rideau Pavy (WS)
1991
Menetou-Salon Morogues, Pellé (WCL)
Muscadet de Sèvre-et-Maine sur lie Bossard (ROB)
1990
Vouvray Château Moncontour (NI)

£7.00 to £7.99
1993
Menetou-Salon Teiller (YAP)
Sancerre la Reine Blanche (WS)

1992
Menetou-Salon Domaine de Chatenoy (WRI, DI)
Menetou-Salon Morogues, Pellé (HIC, CV)
Menetou-Salon Pellé (GOE, EL, MV)
Menetou-Salon Roger (TAN)
Menetou-Salon Sauvignon, Rat (PE)
Muscadet de Sèvre-et-Maine sur lie Cuvée de Millénaire, Marquis de Goulaine (AV)
Muscadet sur lie Domaine de Chasseloir (GAL)
Pouilly-Fumé Domaine des Chailloux, Chatelain (BEK)
Pouilly-Fumé Domaine des Rabichattes (RAE)
Pouilly-Fumé les Loges, Saget (WHI)
Pouilly-Fumé Seguin Père et Fils (HAY)
Sancerre Clos de la Crêle, Lucien Thomas (EL)
Sancerre Domaine de la Garenne, Reverdy (HAY)
Sancerre Paul Prieur (HA)
Savennières Clos du Papillon, Baumard (GRE, NO, EL)
Savennières Domaine du Closel, Mme de Jessey (YAP)
Vouvray Clos du Bourg, Huet (WS, WAT)
Vouvray Clos Naudin, Foreau (DI)
1991
Menetou-Salon Pellé (GRE, HAH)
Pouilly-Fumé Domaine Coulbois (ASD)
Savennières Baumard (GRE, HOG)
Savennières Clos du Papillon, Baumard (HOG)
1990
Menetou-Salon les Thureaux, Mellot (GRE, AMI)
Pouilly-Fumé les Loges, Jean-Claude Guyot (YAP)
Sancerre Raimbault-Barrier (BU)
★ Savennières Clos du Papillon, Baumard (POR)
Savennières Domaine de la Bizolière (YAP)
Savennières Domaine du Closel, Mme de Jessey (WAT)
Vouvray Domaine Peu de la Moriette (PIP)

1989
Vouvray Château Moncontour (UN)
1988
Savennières Domaine du Closel, Mme de
  Jessey (WAT)
1986
Jasnières Caves aux Tuffières, Pinon (YAP)
1984
Vouvray Clos du Bourg, Huet (WAT, BIB)
Vouvray le Haut Lieu, Huet (RAE)
1980
Vouvray Clos Naudin, Foreau (AD)
1978
Vouvray Clos Naudin, Foreau (GE)

£8.00 to £9.99

1993
Pouilly-Fumé Seguin Père et Fils (BIB)
Sancerre André Dézat (TAN, POR)
Sancerre Chavignol, Delaporte (LEA)
Sancerre Clos des Roches, Vacheron (BEN)
Sancerre Domaine de Montigny,
  Natter (BIB)
Sancerre Domaine du Nozay, de Benoist (CB)
Sancerre Laporte (PIP)
Sancerre les Perriers, Vatan (YAP)
1992
Muscadet de Sèvre-et-Maine sur lie
  Château de la Ragotière Black Label (CV)
Pouilly-Fumé André Dezat (NI)
Pouilly-Fumé Château de Tracy (AD)
Pouilly-Fumé Château Fauray (BAR)
Pouilly-Fumé Domaine des Berthiers,
  Jean-Claude Dagueneau (SUM)
Pouilly-Fumé Domaine Thibault
  (TAN, POR, HIC)
Pouilly-Fumé Jean Pabiot (HAH, BAR)
Pouilly-Fumé la Loge aux Moines,
  Moreux (CB)
Pouilly-Fumé Seguin Père et Fils (RAE)
Sancerre Balland-Chapuis (PE, HIC)
Sancerre Clos du Roy, Millérioux (ARM, CB)
Sancerre Daulny (HAH)
Sancerre Domaine de Montigny, Natter
  (EY, WS, HAM)
Sancerre le Chêne Marchand, Roger (TAN)
Sancerre les Creux, Gitton (HIG)
Sancerre les Monts Damnés, Bourgeois (SOM)
Sancerre Roger (MV, BEN)
Sancerre Vacheron (AD, MAJ)
Savennières Château de Chamboureau,
  Soulez (YAP)
Savennières Château d'Epiré (YAP)
Savennières Clos du Papillon, Domaine du
  Closel (PIP)

1991
Pouilly-Fumé Seguin Père et Fils (ROB)
Sancerre Clos du Roy, Millérioux (HOG)
Sancerre Domaine de Montigny, Natter
  (LAY)
Savennières Clos de Coulaine (BIB)
1990
Menetou-Salon Montaloise (ROB)
Pouilly-Fumé les Loges, Saget (VIN, ROB)
Sancerre Comte Lafond, Château du Nozet
  (HOG)
Sancerre Laporte (DI)
Savennières Clos de Coulaine
  (HAM, RAE, BER)
Vouvray le Haut Lieu, Huet (HAM)
1989
Vouvray Brédif (KA)
Vouvray le Haut Lieu, Huet (RAE)
1988
Vouvray le Haut Lieu, Huet (WAT, GAU)
1987
Vouvray Clos du Bourg, Huet (NI)
1985
Vouvray Aigle Blanc, Poniatowski
  (GRE, ROB)
1983
Vouvray le Haut Lieu, Huet (AD, AV)
1976
Vouvray Château de Vaudenuits (UN)

£10.00 to £14.99

1992
Sancerre Cotat (VIG)
Sancerre les Romains, Gitton (HIG)
Savennières Clos du Papillon, Baumard
  (TAN)
1991
Pouilly-Fumé Château de Tracy (CB)
Pouilly-Fumé de Ladoucette, Château du
  Nozet (HOG, GRE, VIC, BER)
Pouilly-Fumé Didier Dageneau (TAN)
Pouilly-Fumé les Pechignolles (HIG)
Sancerre Clos des Roches, Vacheron (ROB)
Sancerre Comte Lafond, Château du
  Nozet (GRE)
1990
Pouilly-Fumé Cuvée Prestige, Châtelain
  (BEK)
Pouilly-Fumé de Ladoucette, Château du
  Nozet (WHI, ROB, AMI)
Savennières Clos du Papillon, Baumard
  (VIG)
Savennières Clos St-Yves (NO)
Savennières Roche-aux-Moines, Soulez
  (WS, YAP)

1988
Savennières Clos St-Yves (AV)

£15.00 to £19.99
1992
Savennières Coulée-de-Serrant, Nicolas
Joly (DI)
1991
Sancerre Chavignol la Grande Côte,
Cotat (GAU)
1990
Sancerre Chavignol la Grande Côte,
Cotat (AD)

£20.00 to £29.99
1990
Savennières Coulée-de-Serrant, Nicolas
Joly (YAP)
1989
Pouilly-Fumé Baron de L Château du
Nozet (BEN, WRI)
Pouilly-Fumé Silex, Didier Dagueneau
(BUT)
1988
Pouilly-Fumé Baron de L Château du
Nozet (ROB)
1971
Vouvray Clos du Bourg, Huet (RAE)
1969
Vouvray le Haut Lieu, Huet (GAU)

c. £50.00
1959
Vouvray Brédif (ROB)

SPARKLING

Under £7.00
Non-vintage
Saumur Brut Ackerman 1811 (DAV)
Saumur Brut Bouvet-Ladubay (HOG)
Saumur Rosé Ackerman 1811 (DAV)

£7.00 to £7.99
Non-vintage
Anjou Rosé Gratien & Meyer (HAY)
Crémant de Loire Brut Gratien & Meyer
(WS)
Crémant de Loire Château Langlois (HOG)
Diane de Poitiers Chardonnay du Haut
Poitou Brut (LO, AD)
Saumur Brut Ackerman 1811 (AME, BEN)
Saumur Brut Gratien & Meyer (HAY)
Vouvray Brut Jarry (YAP)
Vouvray Foreau (GE)

£8.00 to £10.99
Non-vintage
Crémant de Loire Château Langlois (BEN,
DI)
Montlouis Mousseux Brut Berger (YAP)
Montlouis Mousseux Demi-sec Berger (YAP)
Vouvray Brut Brédif (ROB)
Vouvray Méthode Champenoise, Huet
(RAE, EY)
1990
Saphir Bouvet-Ladubay (NI)

c. £12.00
1982
Vouvray Foreau (GAU)

SWEET WHITE

Under £7.00
1992
Coteaux d'Ancenis Malvoisie, Guindon (YAP)
1990
★ Vouvray Château de Vaudenuits (GRE)
1989
Coteaux du Layon Domaine des Saulaies
(BIB)
1988
Vouvray Brédif (GRE)
1982
Coteaux du Layon Beaulieu, Chéné (MV)

£7.00 to £8.99
1992
Coteaux du Layon Rablay Caves de la
Pierre Blanche (YAP)
1990
★ Coteaux du Layon Château de la
Roulerie (YAP)
1989
Coteaux du Layon Leblanc (RAE)
Vouvray Domaine Peu de la Moriette (TAN)
1987
Vouvray Château de Vaudenuits (RE)
1986
Coteaux du Layon Leblanc (RAE)
1985
★ Montlouis Moelleux Deletang (RAE)
★Vouvray Moelleux Bourillon Dorléans (MV)

> Stars (★) indicate wines
> selected by the editors as
> particularly good value
> in their class.

£9.00 to £12.99

1993
Vouvray Clos Naudin, Foreau (DI)
1992
Coteaux du Layon Clos de Ste-Catherine, Baumard (EL)
1990
Vouvray le Haut Lieu, Moelleux, Huet (HAM)
Vouvray Moelleux Jarry (YAP)
1989
Coteaux du Layon Clos de Ste-Catherine, Baumard (GRE, HOG)
Vouvray Aigle Blanc Réserve, Poniatowski (GRE)
1988
Coteaux du Layon Clos de Ste-Catherine, Baumard (HOG)
Quarts-de-Chaume Baumard (NO)
Vouvray Clos Baudoin, Poniatowski (GRE)

1986
Quarts-de-Chaume Baumard (HOG)
1985
Quarts-de-Chaume Château de l'Echarderie (NO)
Vouvray Clos du Bourg, Huet (WAT)
Vouvray Clos Naudin, Foreau (NO)
1983
Anjou Moulin Touchais (EL)
1982
Quarts-de-Chaume Baumard (HOG)
Vouvray Clos du Bourg, Huet (RAE)
1979
Quarts-de-Chaume Château de Bellerive (WAT)
1974
★ Quarts-de-Chaume Château de Bellerive (WAT)

£13.00 to £15.99

1989
Coteaux de l'Aubance Domaine de Bablut (AD)

Montlouis Moelleux Deletang (WS)
Quarts-de-Chaume Château de Bellerive (WS)
Vouvray Moelleux Bourillon Dorléans (MV)
1988
Quarts-de-Chaume Baumard (GRE, GAU)
Vouvray Clos du Bourg, Huet (AD)
1986
Quarts-de-Chaume Baumard (NO)
Vouvray Clos du Bourg, Huet (WS)
1985
Vouvray Clos Naudin, Foreau (HOG)
Vouvray le Haut Lieu, Moelleux, Huet (NO)
1981
Anjou Moulin Touchais (EL)
1979
Anjou Moulin Touchais (EL)
1971
Anjou Moulin Touchais (NO)

£16.00 to £19.99

1990
Bonnezeaux Château de Fesles (TAN)
Bonnezeaux la Chapelle, Château de Fesles (WS)
Quarts-de-Chaume Baumard (GRE, HOG, EL)
1989
Bonnezeaux Château de Fesles (NO)
Coteaux du Layon Clos de Ste-Catherine, Baumard (VIG)
Quarts-de-Chaume Baumard (HOG, GRE, NO)
Quarts-de-Chaume Château de l'Echarderie (YAP)
Vouvray Moelleux Bourillon Dorléans (VIG)
Vouvray Moelleux Huet (RAE)
1988
Bonnezeaux la Chapelle, Château de Fesles (MV)
Quarts-de-Chaume Château de Bellerive (NO)
1986
Vouvray Clos du Bourg, Huet (BIB)
1981
Anjou Moulin Touchais (ROB)
1979
Anjou Moulin Touchais (WRI)
1975
Anjou Moulin Touchais (EL)
1971
Coteaux du Layon Ravouin-Gesbron (AD)
1969
Anjou Moulin Touchais (NO)
1964
Vouvray Moelleux Bourillon Dorléans (MV)

£20.00 to £29.99

1990
Quarts-de-Chaume Château de Bellerive
(NO)
Vouvray Clos du Bourg, Huet (LAY, GAU)
Vouvray le Haut Lieu, Moelleux, Huet
(GAU)
1989
Bonnezeaux la Chapelle, Château de
Fesles (GAU)
Quarts-de-Chaume Baumard (GAU)
Vouvray Clos du Bourg, Huet (WS, LAY, AD)
Vouvray Clos Naudin, Foreau (HOG)
1967
Quarts-de-Chaume Baumard (NO)

£30.00 to £49.99

1990
Vouvray le Mont, Huet (GAU)
1989
Vouvray Cuvée Constance, Huet (BIB, BUT)
1970
Anjou Moulin Touchais (EL)
1969
Vouvray Clos du Bourg, Huet (AD)
1964
Bonnezeaux Château des Gauliers, Mme
Fourlinnie (YAP)
1959
Bonnezeaux Château des Gauliers, Mme
Fourlinnie (NO)
1953
Vouvray le Mont, Huet (WS)
1947
Anjou Moulin Touchais (NO)

£50.00 to £79.99

1959
Bonnezeaux Château des Gauliers, Mme
Fourlinnie (YAP)
Vouvray Clos du Bourg, Huet (NO, AD)
Vouvray Moelleux Bourillon Dorléans (MV)
1947
Bonnezeaux Château des Gauliers, Mme
Fourlinnie (NO)
1935
Bonnezeaux Château des Gauliers, Mme
Fourlinnie (YAP, NO)

---

*Webster's is an annual
publication. We welcome
your suggestions for next
year's edition.*

---

c. £90.00

1947
Vouvray Brédif (NO)

ROSÉ

Under £5.00

1993
Anjou Rosé Cellier de la Loire (NI)
1992
Coteaux d'Ancenis Gamay, Guindon (YAP)

£5.00 to £7.99

1992
Reuilly Pinot Noir, Beurdin (AD)
Touraine Azay-le-Rideau la Basse
Chevrière, Pavy (YAP)
Touraine Rosé Noble Jouée, Clos de la
Dorée (AD)
1990
Sancerre Rosé les Romains, Vacheron
(WHI)

£8.00 to £9.99

1993
Sancerre Rosé André Dezat (PIP)
Sancerre Rosé Delaporte (LEA)
Sancerre Rosé les Romains, Vacheron (BEN)
1991
Sancerre Rosé Cotat (AD)

c. £24.00

1961
Cabernet d'Anjou Domaine de Bablut
Demi-Sec (AD)

RED

Under £4.00

1993
Gamay du Haut Poitou Cave Co-op (WAI)
1992
Saumur-Champigny Caves des Vignerons
de Saumur (TES)
1991
Gamay du Haut Poitou Cave Co-op (LO)

£4.00 to £4.99

1993
Anjou Rouge Logis de la Giraudière,
Baumard (EL)
1992
St-Pourçain Union des Vignerons (YAP)
Saumur Cave des Vignerons de Saumur
(YAP)

1991
Gamay de Touraine Domaine de la
　Charmoise, Marionnet (RAE)
Saumur Cave des Vignerons de Saumur
　(AD)
1990
Anjou Rouge Logis de la Giraudière,
　Baumard (GRE)
1989
Bourgueil la Hurolaie Caslot-Galbrun (TES)

£5.00 to £6.99

1993
Chinon l'Arpenty Desbourdes (YAP)
Gamay de Touraine Domaine de la
　Charmoise, Marionnet (BIB)
1992
Anjou Rouge Logis de la Giraudière,
　Baumard (NO)
Chinon Château de Ligre (EL)
Coteaux d'Ancenis Gamay, Guindon (YAP)
Saumur Domaine du Langlois-Château (DI)
Vin de Thouarsais Gigon (YAP)
1991
Anjou Rouge Tijou (HIG)
1990
Bourgueil Clos de la Henry, Morin (AV)
Bourgueil Domaine des Ouches (WHI, HAM)
★ Bourgueil Vieilles Vignes, Lamé-Delille-
　Boucard (WAT)
St-Nicolas-de-Bourgueil Domaine du
　Fondis (TAN)
St-Nicolas-de-Bourgueil Mabileau (PLA)
★ St-Nicolas-de-Bourgueil Vieilles Vignes,
　Taluau (WAT)
1989
Bourgueil Caslot Jamet (WS)
Bourgueil Domaine des Raguenières (CV,
　WCL, HIG)
Saumur-Champigny Château de Parnay
　(WAT)
1986
Bourgueil Caslot Jamet (WS)

£7.00 to £8.99

1993
St-Nicolas-de-Bourgueil Clos de la Contrie,
　Ammeux (YAP)
1992
Menetou-Salon Domaine de Chateney,
　Clement (DI, VIG)
Menetou-Salon Rouge, Pellé (WCL)
1991
Chinon Domaine Dozon (PIP)
Sancerre Domaine du P'tit Roy (NI)

1990
Cabernet d'Anjou Clos de Coulaine (GAU,
　BIB, RAE)
Chinon Clos de l'Echo, Couly-Dutheil (WAT)
Menetou-Salon Rouge, Pellé (WS, WCL)
St-Nicolas-de-Bourgueil Taluau (WS)
Samur-Champigny Lavigne (TAN)
1989
Bourgueil Domaine du Grand Clos,
　Audebert (BER)
Bourgueil Vieilles Vignes, Lamé-Delille-
　Boucard (WAT)
Chinon Cuvée Prestige, Gouron (KA)
1988
Bourgeuil Cuvée Reserve, Druet (YAP)
Chinon Clos de l'Echo, Couly-Dutheil (WAT)
Chinon Olga Raffault (WS)
1987
Bourgueil Beauvais, Druet (BY)
1986
Chinon Clos de l'Echo, Couly-Dutheil (WAT)
1984
Bourgueil Grand Mont, Druet (BY)

£9.00 to £9.99

1993
Sancerre Delaporte (LEA)
1992
Sancerre André Dezat (PIP)
Saumur-Champigny Vieilles Vignes,
　Filliatreau (YAP)
1990
Bourgueil Domaine du Grand Clos,
　Audebert (LAY)
1989
Sancerre Domaine de Montigny,
　Natter (BIB)
1988
Bourgueil Grand Mont, Druet (MV)
Sancerre Clos du Roy, Millérioux (HOG)
1986
Bourgueil Grand Mont, Druet (BY)

£11.00 to £12.99

1992
Chinon Clos de la Dioterie, Joguet (AD)
1990
Bourgueil Beauvais, Druet (AD)
Bourgueil Grand Mont, Druet (YAP)
Sancerre Domaine de Montigny, Natter
　(LAY)

c. £15.50

1988
Bourgeuil Cuvée Vaumoreau, Druet (AD)

ALSACE

WHITE

Under £4.50

1993
★ Pinot Blanc Cave Co-op. Turckheim (WR, BOT, THR)
1992
★ Pinot Blanc Cave Co-op. Turckheim (OD, SO)
Sylvaner Dopff & Irion (EL)

£4.50 to £4.99

1993
Gewürztraminer Cave Co-op. Turckheim (BOT, WR, THR)
Pinot Blanc Tradition, Cave Co-op. Turckheim (CV, WCL, AME)
1992
Gewürztraminer Cave Co-op. Turckheim (SO)
Pinot Blanc Cave Co-op. Turckheim (LO, POR, NI)
Pinot Blanc Dopff & Irion (HOG, EL)
Pinot Blanc Ingersheim (DAV)
Pinot Blanc Kuehn (AS)
Pinot Blanc Seltz (WAT)
Pinot Blanc Tradition, Cave Co-op. Turckheim (GRE)
1989
Sylvaner Dopff & Irion (GRE)

£5.00 to £5.99

1993
Sylvaner Louis Gisselbrecht (PIP)
Tokay-Pinot Gris Tradition, Cave Co-op. Turckheim (AME)
1992
Gewürztraminer Dopff & Irion (HOG)
Gewürztraminer Seigneur d'Alsace, Dopff & Irion (EL)
Muscat Dopff & Irion (EL)
Muscat Réserve, Cave Co-op. Turckheim (OD)
Pinot Blanc Kuehn (NO)
Pinot Blanc Louis Gisselbrecht (PIP)
Pinot Blanc Muré (BEK, DI)
Pinot Blanc Producteurs de Beblenheim (HAH)
Riesling Cave Co-op. Turckheim (POR)
Riesling Réserve Cave Co-op. Turckheim (CV)
Riesling Seigneur d'Alsace, Dopff & Irion (EL)

Sylvaner Hugel (HOG)
Sylvaner Louis Gisselbrecht (WHI)
Tokay-Pinot Gris Cave Co-op. Turckheim (POR, LO, WCL, OD)
Tokay-Pinot Gris Dopff & Irion (EL)
1991
Muscat Muré (BEK)
Pinot Blanc Schlumberger (HOG)
Riesling Caves de Bennwihr (PE)
Sylvaner Schlumberger (PLA)
★ Sylvaner Vieilles Vignes, Ostertag (MV)
Tokay-Pinot Gris Dopff & Irion (HOG)
1990
Flambeau d'Alsace Hugel (DI)
Gewürztraminer Muré (BEK)
Pinot Blanc Hugel (HOG)
Sylvaner Hugel (DI)
Sylvaner Schleret (YAP)
1989
Riesling Dopff & Irion (GRE)
1988
Edelzwicker Rolly Gassmann (HAY, RAE, BIB)

£6.00 to £6.99

1992
Gewürztraminer Muré (DI)
★ Gewürztraminer Réserve Prestige, Cave Co-op. Turckheim (NI)
Gewürztraminer Schléret (YAP)
Muscat Louis Gisselbrecht (PIP)
Pinot Blanc Schleret (YAP)
Pinot Blanc Schlumberger (BEN)
Pinot Blanc Trimbach (BER)
Sylvaner Zind-Humbrecht (BY)
Tokay-Pinot Gris Louis Gisselbrecht (PIP)
1991
Pinot Blanc Rolly Gassmann (BIB)
Pinot Blanc Schlumberger (EY, HAH, PLA, NI, WRI)
Pinot Blanc Willy Gisselbrecht (BAR)
Riesling Louis Gisselbrecht (PE)
Riesling Rolly Gassmann (BIB)
Sylvaner Zind-Humbrecht (WR)

> *Please remember that* **Webster's** *is a price GUIDE and not a price LIST. It is not meant to replace up-to-date merchant's lists.*

1990
Gewürztraminer Caves de Bennwihr (PE)
Gewürztraminer Réserve, Cave Co-op.
  Turckheim (WCL)
Muscat Schleret (YAP)
Pinot Blanc Willy Gisselbrecht (ROB)
Riesling Louis Gisselbrecht (SOM, PIP)
Riesling Tradition, Kuentz-Bas (WS)
Sylvaner Vieilles Vignes, Ostertag (GAU)
1989
Riesling Blanck (AV)
Riesling des Princes Abbés, Schlumberger
  (HOG)
Riesling Schleret (YAP)
Sylvaner Faller (BUT)
1988
Pinot Blanc les Amours, Hugel (BUT)
Pinot Blanc Trimbach (BUT)
Riesling les Faitières (CHA)
1985
Sylvaner Hugel (TW)

£7.00 to £7.99

1993
Muscat Réserve, Trimbach (WS)
1992
Gewürztraminer Blanck (HAH)
Gewürztraminer Louis Gisselbrecht (PIP,
  HIC)
Gewürztraminer Sipp (PLA)
Muscat Blanck (AD)
Riesling Beyer (AME)
Riesling Sipp (PLA)
Sylvaner Vieilles Vignes, Ostertag (BAR)
Tokay-Pinot Gris Koehly (HAH)
Tokay-Pinot Gris Louis Gisselbrecht (WHI)
Tokay-Pinot Gris Sipp (PLA)
Tokay-Pinot Gris Wiederhirn (HIG)
1991
Gewürztraminer les Sorcières Dopff &
  Irion (HOG, EL)
Gewürztraminer Louis Gisselbrecht (ROB)
Gewürztraminer Sipp (WHI)
Muscat Wiederhirn (HIG)
Pinot Blanc Cattin (CB)
Riesling les Murailles, Dopff & Irion (EL)
Sylvaner Zind-Humbrecht (GAU)
Tokay-Pinot Gris les Maquisards, Dopff &
  Irion (HOG, EL)
1990
Muscat Zind-Humbrecht (BY)
Riesling Louis Gisselbrecht (TAN, HIC)
Riesling Réserve, Dopff & Irion (ROB)
Tokay-Pinot Gris Tradition, Kuentz-Bas
  (HOG)

1989
Gewürztraminer Tradition, Kuentz-Bas
  (BER)
Muscat les Amandiers, Dopff & Irion (HOG,
  GRE)
Muscat Schlumberger (NO)
Pinot Blanc Humbrecht (BUT)
Pinot Blanc Trimbach (BUT)
Riesling Hugel (HOG, WS)
Tokay-Pinot Gris les Maquisards, Dopff &
  Irion (GRE)
1988
Muscat Réserve, Heydt (CB)
Pinot Blanc Zind-Humbrecht (BUT)
Riesling Schoenenberg, René Schmidt
  (BER)
1985
Riesling les Murailles, Dopff & Irion (HOG)

£8.00 to £8.99

1992
Gewürztraminer Altenbourg, Blanck (AD)
Gewürztraminer Beyer (AME, NA)
★ Muscat Koehly (HAH)
1991
Gewürztraminer Rolly Gassmann (BIB)
Gewürztraminer Trimbach (HOG)
Gewürztraminer Willy Gisselbrecht (BAR)
Muscat Schlumberger (PLA)
Riesling Turckheim, Zind-Humbrecht (BY)
Tokay-Pinot Gris Schlumberger (EY, NI)
1990
Auxerrois Rolly Gassmann (BIB)
Gewürztraminer des Princes Abbés,
  Schlumberger (PLA, TAN, BEN)
Gewürztraminer Hugel (HOG, DAV)
Pinot Blanc Rolly Gassmann (TAN)
1989
Gewürztraminer Hugel (AD, DI)
Gewürztraminer Rolly Gassmann (HAY,
  HAM, RAE)
Muscat Réserve, Trimbach (GAU, ROB)
Riesling des Princes Abbés, Schlumberger
  (BEN)
Riesling Hugel (DI)

1988
Gewürztraminer Trimbach (BUT)
1985
Gewürztraminer Trimbach (BUT)

1984
Riesling Brand, Zind-Humbrecht (BY)

£9.00 to £10.49

1991
Muscat Clos St-Landelin, Muré (BEK)
Muscat Réserve, Trimbach (PLA)
Riesling Herrenweg, Zind-Humbrecht (BY)
Tokay-Pinot Gris Réserve, Trimbach (PLA)
Tokay-Pinot Gris Schleret (YAP)
Tokay-Pinot Gris Schlumberger (PLA, TAN,
  BEN, HIC)
1990
Gewürztraminer Tradition, Hugel (WS)
Muscat Réserve, Trimbach (BER)
Riesling Heimbourg Cave Co-op.
  Turckheim (WCL)
Riesling Schlossberg, Blanck (AD)
Riesling Turckheim, Zind-Humbrecht (WR)
1989
Gewürztraminer Herrenweg, Zind-
  Humbrecht (BUT)
Gewürztraminer Réserve, Trimbach (GAU)
Riesling Herrenweg, Zind-Humbrecht (BUT)
Riesling Réserve Particulière, Faller (BUT)
Riesling Rolly Gassmann (TAN)
Riesling Saering, Schlumberger (HOG)
Riesling Tradition, Hugel (AD)
Tokay-Pinot Gris Hatschbourg, Cattin (CB)
Tokay-Pinot Gris Tradition, Hugel (DI)
1988
Riesling Fronholz (SOM)
Riesling Réserve, Trimbach (TW)
Riesling Schoenenberg, Dopff au Moulin
  (HOG)
Riesling Tradition, Hugel (WS)
1986
Riesling Saering, Schlumberger (NI)
1985
Gewürztraminer Osterberg, Sipp (WHI)
Riesling Hugel (TW)

£10.50 to £12.99

1992
Gewürztraminer Fronholz Vendange
  Tardive, Ostertag (BAR)
Riesling Fronholz (BAR)
1991
Gewürztraminer Bollenberg, Cattin (CB)
Gewürztraminer Deiss (LEA, ROB)
Riesling Saering, Schlumberger (BEN)
Tokay-Pinot Gris Deiss (LEA)
Tokay-Pinot Gris Rolly Gassmann (TAN)
1990
Riesling Herrenweg, Zind-Humbrecht (WR)
Riesling Saering, Schlumberger (PLA, LAY,
  HIC)
1989
Gewürztraminer Hugel (PE)
Gewürztraminer Jubilee, Hugel (WS)
Gewürztraminer Réserve Particulière,
  Faller (BUT)
Riesling Kirchberg, Sipp (PLA)
Riesling Schlossberg, Domaine Weinbach
  (BUT)
Tokay-Pinot Gris Grand Cru Brand, Cave
  Co-op. Turckheim (POR)
1988
Gewürztraminer Goldert, Zind-Humbrecht
  (BY)
Gewürztraminer Jubilee, Hugel (HOG)
Gewürztraminer Réserve, Trimbach (BUT)
Riesling Brand, Zind-Humbrecht (BY)
1986
Gewürztraminer Seigneurs de
  Ribeaupierre, Trimbach (HOG)
Riesling Frédéric Emile, Trimbach (GRE)
Riesling Kitterlé, Schlumberger (HOG)
Riesling Tradition, Hugel (BEN)
1985
Gewürztraminer Clos Gaensbroennel, A.
  Willm (AMI)
Gewürztraminer Vendange Tardive, Sipp
  (BU)

£13.00 to £14.99

1992
Riesling Muenchberg, Ostertag (MV, WCL)
1989
Gewürztraminer Kessler, Schlumberger
  (PLA, BEN, NI)
Gewürztraminer Vendange Tardive, Cave
  Co-op. de Turckheim (POR)
Muscat Moench Reben, Rolly Gassmann
  (BIB, GAU)
Tokay-Pinot Gris Kitterlé, Schlumberger
  (AMI)

1988
Gewürztraminer Réserve Personnelle,
  Hugel (AV)
Riesling Frédéric Emile, Trimbach (HOG,
  GAU, WS, GRE)
Riesling Muenchberg, Ostertag (WCL)
Riesling Schoenenberg, Dopff au Moulin (VIG)
1986
Riesling Frédéric Emile, Trimbach (TW, BER)
1985
Gewürztraminer Altenbourg Vendange
  Tardive, Blanck (HAM)
1983
Gewürztraminer Réserve Personnelle,
  Hugel (BUT, DI, WRI)
Gewürztraminer Vendange Tardive,
  Sipp (BU)
Riesling Réserve Particulière, Faller (BUT)
Riesling Réserve Personnelle, Hugel
  (BUT, DI)
Riesling Trimbach (GAU)

£15.00 to £19.99

Non-vintage
Gewürztraminer Seigneurs de
  Ribeaupierre, Trimbach (GAU)
1991
Gewürztraminer Clos Windsbuhl, Zind-
  Humbrecht (GAU)
Gewürztraminer Herrenweg, Zind-
  Humbrecht (GAU)
Riesling Brand, Zind-Humbrecht (GAU)
1990
Muscat Goldert, Zind-Humbrecht (GAU)
Riesling Bergheim Burg Vendange
  Tardive, Deiss (LEA)
1989
Gewürztraminer Herrenweg Vendange
  Tardive, Zind-Humbrecht (BY)
Gewürztraminer Vendange Tardive,
  Sipp (PLA)
Gewürztraminer Vendange Tardive,
  Wiederhirn (HIG)
Riesling Altenberg de Bergheim, Koehly
  (BUT)
Riesling Frédéric Emile, Trimbach (GAU)

*Please remember that **Webster's** is a price GUIDE and not a price LIST. It is not meant to replace up-to-date merchant's lists.*

1986
Gewürztraminer Kitterlé, Schlumberger
  (GRE)
Riesling Kitterlé, Schlumberger (BEN)
1985
Gewürztraminer Kitterlé, Schlumberger
  (HOG)
Gewürztraminer Vendange Tardive,
  Wolfberger (SEC)
Riesling Frédéric Emile, Trimbach (TW)
Riesling Réserve Personnelle, Hugel
  (AV)
1983
Gewürztraminer Cuvée Christine,
  Schlumberger (REI)
Gewürztraminer Jubilee, Hugel (BEN)
Gewürztraminer Vendange Tardive,
  Wiederhirn (HIG)
Riesling Bergheim Burg Vendange
  Tardive, Deiss (REI)

£20.00 to £24.99

1989
Gewürztraminer Cuvée Exceptionelle,
  Schléret (YAP)
Gewürztraminer Kitterlé, Schlumberger (BEN)
Gewürztraminer Vendange Tardive,
  Zind-Humbrecht (ROB)
1985
Gewürztraminer Vendange Tardive,
  Hugel (DI)
1983
Gewürztraminer Vendange Tardive,
  Dopff & Irion (GRE)
Riesling Frédéric Emile, Trimbach (TW)
Riesling Vendange Tardive, Dopff & Irion
  (HOG, EL)
Tokay-Pinot Gris Vendange Tardive,
  Dopff & Irion (HOG, EL)

£25.00 to £29.99

1990
Gewürztraminer Herrenweg, Zind-
  Humbrecht (BY)
1989
Gewürztraminer Vendange Tardive,
  Hugel (WS)
1986
Gewürztraminer Cuvée Christine,
  Schlumberger (GRE, NI)
1985
Gewürztraminer Cuvée Anne Vendange
  Tardive, Rolly Gassmann (RAE)
Gewürztraminer Cuvée Christine,
  Schlumbergér (BU)

1983
Gewürztraminer Vendange Tardive,
Dopff & Irion (HOG, EL)
Gewürztraminer Vendange Tardive,
Hugel (HOG)

£30.00 to £39.99

1989
Gewürztraminer Cuvée Anne
Schlumberger (BU, GRE, GOE)
Gewürztraminer Cuvée Christine,
Schlumberger (BU)
1986
Gewürztraminer Cuvée Christine,
Schlumberger (TAN, VIG)
Gewürztraminer Hengst Vendange
Tardive, Zind-Humbrecht (BY)
Gewürztraminer Sélection de Grains
Nobles, Dopff & Irion (EL)
1985
Gewürztraminer Vendange Tardive,
Domaine Weinbach (BUT)
Gewürztraminer Vendange Tardive,
Hugel (TW)
1983
Gewürztraminer Sélection de Grains
Nobles, Dopff & Irion (HOG)
Gewürztraminer Vendange Tardive,
Hugel (BUT)
Gewürztraminer Vendange Tardive,
Trimbach (BUT)
Riesling Clos Ste-Hune, Trimbach (BUT)
Riesling Sélection de Grains Nobles, Dopff
& Irion (HOG, EL)
Riesling Vendange Tardive, Hugel (BEN)
Tokay-Pinot Gris Vendange Tardive,
Hugel (BEN)
1975
Riesling Frédéric Emile, Trimbach (VIG)

£40.00 to £49.99

1989
Gewürztraminer Cuvée Anne Vendange
Tardive, Rolly Gassmann (NO)
1983
Gewürztraminer Sélection de Grains
Nobles, Faller (BUT)
Riesling Frédéric Emile Vendange Tardive,
Trimbach (TW)
1976
Gewürztraminer Cuvée Christine,
Schlumberger (VIG)
Riesling Frédéric Emile Vendange Tardive,
Trimbach (VIG)
Riesling Vendange Tardive, Hugel (VIG, TW)

£50.00 to £59.99

1983
Gewürztraminer Sélection de Grains
Nobles, Heydt (CB)
Tokay-Pinot Gris Sélection de Grains
Nobles, Beyer (REI)
1976
Riesling Vendange Tardive Sélection de
Grains Nobles, Hugel (NO)
Tokay-Pinot Gris Vendange Tardive,
Hugel (TW)

c. £85.00

1976
Gewürztraminer Sélection de Grains
Nobles, Hugel (VIG)

c. £99.00

1989
Gewürztraminer Rangen Sélection de
Grains Nobles, Zind-Humbrecht (BY)

RED

Under £8.00

1992
Pinot Noir Louis Gisselbrecht (PIP)

£8.00 to £9.99

1992
Pinot Noir Beyer (NA)
1991
Pinot Noir Rolly Gassmann (BIB)
1990
Pinot Noir Hugel (WS, DI)
Pinot Noir l'Ancienne, Cave Co-op.
Turckheim (CV)
Pinot Noir Schleret (YAP)
1989
Pinot Noir Hugel (BUT)

£12.00 to £16.99

1990
Pinot Noir Herrenweg, Zind-Humbrecht (WR)
1985
Pinot Noir Réserve Personnelle, Hugel (TW)
Pinot Noir Réserve, Rolly Gassmann (BIB)

SPARKLING

Under £9.00

Non-vintage
Crémant d'Alsace Cuvée Julien, Dopff au
Moulin (HOG, LEA, GRE)
Crémant d'Alsace Dopff & Irion (EL)

LANGUEDOC/ROUSSILLON

RED

Under £3.00

Non-vintage
Coteaux du Languedoc Château
  Flaugergues (PE)
St-Chinian Rouanet (WAI)
VdP de l'Hérault, Domaine de St-Macaire
  (WAI)
1992
VdP de l'Aude Cabernet Sauvignon,
  Foncalieu (WAI)
★ VdP d'Oc Cépage Merlot, Domaine des
  Fontaines (WAI)
1991
★ VdP des Côtes Catalanes Château de
  Jau (OD)

£3.00 to £3.49

1993
VdP d'Oc Domaine Virginie sur lie (SOM)
1992
Costières de Nîmes Château de Nages (WAI)
VdP de la Cité de Carcassonne, Domaine
  Sautès le Bas (SAI)
VdP d'Oc Domaine Virginie sur lie (WAI)
1991
Côtes du Roussillon-Villages, Caramany (ASD)
Faugères l'Estagnon (WR, THR, BOT)
VdP de l'Hérault, Domaine de Chapître (MV)
1990
Corbières Château de Cabriac (ASD)

£3.50 to £3.99

Non-vintage
Fitou Mme Claude Parmentier (VIC)
1992
Corbières Château de Cabriac (DAV)
★ Coteaux du Languedoc Cépage Syrah,
  les Vignerons de la Carignano (OD)
★ Côtes de la Malepère Château de Festes
  (BEK)
★ VdP des Côtes de Thongue Cépage
  Syrah, la Condamine l'Évêque (WS)
1991
Corbières Château de Cabriac (EL)
Corbières Château de St-Jean (NA)
Côtes du Roussillon-Villages, Vignerons
  Catalans (GE)
Fitou Cave Pilote (EL)
Minervois Domaine de l'Abbaye de
  Tholomies (SAF)

Minervois Domaine de Ste-Eulalie (BOT,
  WR, THR)
VdP des Coteaux de Murviel, Domaine de
  Limbardie (DAV)
VdP du Gard Domaine Mas de Montel
  (BEK)
1990
Fitou Caves du Mont Tauch (HOG, MAR)
Minervois Domaine la Tour Boisée (WAT)
St-Chinian Domaine des Soulié (SAF)
1989
★ Minervois Château de Fabas (GE)

£4.00 to £4.99

1992
Côtes du Roussillon Château de Jau (OD)
Minervois Cuvée Émilie, Russol (BER)
VdP des Coteaux de Murviel, Domaine de
  Limbardie (SOM, MV, AD, TAN)
VdP des Côtes de Thongue Domaine Comte
  de Margon (AD)
1991
Corbières Château de Mandourelle (TAN)
Coteaux du Languedoc Domaine de
  l'Abbaye de Valmagne (EL)
★ Coteaux du Languedoc La Clape
  Château de Pech-Celeyran (TAN, AD)
Fitou Caves du Mont Tauch (GRE, NI)
Minervois Domaine de Ste-Eulalie (DAV, TAN)
St-Chinian Rouanet (HIG)
VdP des Côtes de Thongue Domaine Comte
  de Margon (ARM)
1990
★ Corbières, Château de Caraguilhes (SAF)
★ Coteaux du Languedoc La Clape
  Château de Pech-Celeyran (EY)
Coteaux du Languedoc Domaine de
  l'Abbaye de Valmagne (GRE)
Minervois Château de Gourgazaud (REI)
Minervois Château Villerambert, Julien
  (TAN)
VdP des Collines de la Moure, Domaine de
  l'Abbaye de Valmagne, Cuvée Cardinale
  (EL)
VdP des Côtes de Thongue, Clos Ferdinand
  (WCL)
1989
Corbières Chatellerie de Lastours (POR)
★ Coteaux du Languedoc La Clape
  Château de Pech-Celeyran (BER)
1988
Fitou Caves du Mont Tauch (AMI)

£5.00 to £6.99

1992
Costières de Nîmes Château de la Tuilerie (AV)
1991
★ VdP d'Oc La Cuvée Mythique, DuBernet/Vign. de Val d'Orbieu (NI)
★ VdP d'Oc Syrah, la Fadèze (LAY)
VdP du Mont Baudile, Domaine d'Aupilhac (AD)
1990
★ Collioure les Clos de Paulilles (OD)
★ Corbières Château de Lastours (WCL, BU)
Faugères Château de Grézan (POR)
Minervois Domaine de la Combe Blanche (CV, AME)
1989
Minervois Domaine de l'Abbaye de Tholomies (NI, BER)
1988
Minervois Château de Fabas (NO)
Minervois Domaine de la Combe Blanche (RE, WCL)

£7.00 to £9.99

1991
VdP de l'Hérault, Mas de Daumas Gassac (NI)

VdP des Coteaux de Murviel, Domaine de Limbardie (MV)
1990
Côtes du Roussillon Black Label, Domaine Sarda Malet (BIB)
★ Faugères Cuvée Spéciale, Gilbert Alquier (SUM)
VdP de l'Hérault, Mas de Daumas Gassac (POR, OD)
1989
Corbières Château de Lastours (ROB)
1987
Coteaux du Languedoc Prieuré de St-Jean de Bébian (VIG)

£10.00 to £14.99

1991
VdP de l'Hérault, Mas de Daumas Gassac (AD, BEN, ARM)

1990
VdP de l'Hérault, Mas de Daumas Gassac (BEN)
1989
VdP de l'Hérault, Mas de Daumas Gassac (HAM, GAU, VIG, WS)
1988
VdP de l'Hérault, Mas de Daumas Gassac (BUT, AMI, GAU, SEC)
1987
VdP de l'Hérault, Mas de Daumas Gassac (SEC, AMI)

c. £16.00

1984
VdP de l'Hérault, Mas de Daumas Gassac (ROB)

c. 25.00

1985
VdP de l'Hérault, Mas de Daumas Gassac (VIG)
1981
VdP de l'Hérault, Mas de Daumas Gassac (VIG)

c. £30.00

1982
VdP de l'Hérault, Mas de Daumas Gassac (VIG)

WHITE

Under £6.00

1993
★ VdP de l'Hérault Cépage Muscat Sec, du Bosc (WS)
1992
★ VdP d'Oc Cépage Chardonnay, Ryman (SAI)
★ VdP d'Oc Chardonnay, Fortant de France (WAI)
★ VdP d'Oc Chardonnay, Philippe de Baudin (also Chais Baumière) (SAI, WAI, CV)
1991
★ VdP d'Oc Chardonnay, Fortant de France (SAI)
1990
★ VdP d'Oc Cépage Chardonnay, Ryman (VIC)

£10.00 to £14.99

1992
VdP de l'Hérault, Mas de Daumas Gassac (SOM, NI)

1990
VdP de l'Hérault, Mas de Daumas Gassac
  (NO)
1987
VdP de l'Hérault, Mas de Daumas Gassac
  (NO)

£15.00 to £19.99

1993
VdP de l'Hérault, Mas de Daumas Gassac
  (BEN)
1992
VdP de l'Hérault, Mas de Daumas Gassac
  (NO, AD, BEN, ARM)
1991
VdP de l'Hérault, Mas de Daumas Gassac
  (HAM, GAU)
1989
VdP de l'Hérault, Mas de Daumas Gassac
  (BUT, AMI)

c. 22.00

1983
VdP de l'Hérault, Mas de Daumas Gassac
  (NO)

ROSÉ

Under £7.00

1992
Costières de Nîmes Château de la Tuilerie
  (AV)

£7.00 to £9.99

1991
VdP de l'Hérault, Mas de Daumas Gassac
  (BUT)
1987
VdP de l'Hérault, Mas de Daumas Gassac
  (BUT)

SPARKLING

Under £7.00

1991
Blanquette de Limoux Brut, Cave de
  Blanquette de Limoux (UN)
1988
Blanquette de Limoux Aimery, Cave de
  Blanquette de Limoux (HOG)

£8.00 to £8.99

1983
Blanquette de Limoux Sieur d'Arques
  (BER)

PROVENCE & CORSICA

RED

Under £4.00

Non-vintage
Coteaux d'Aix-en-Provence Château la Coste (WHI)
1993
VdP des Maures, Domaine d'Astros (BIB)
1992
VdP des Maures, Domaine d'Astros (SUM)

£4.00 to £6.99

Non-vintage
VdP des Sables du Golfe du Lion, Listel (PE)
1992
Coteaux d'Aix-en-Provence Château de Fonscolombe (PIP)

Coteaux d'Aix-en-Provence Château de la Gaude (YAP)
1991
Coteaux d'Aix-en-Provence Château de Fonscolombe (LAY)
Côtes de Provence les Maîtres Vignerons de St-Tropez (BEK)
1990
Coteaux d'Aix-en-Provence Domaine de la Vallonge (SOM)
1989
Côtes de Provence Domaine de Rimauresq (HOG)
1988
Bandol Mas de la Rouvière, Bunan (NI)
VdP des Sables du Golfe du Lion, Domaine du Bosquet (PEN)

£7.00 to £10.99

1991
Bandol Domaine Tempier (DI)
Côtes de Provence Domaine Richeaume (SAF)

1990
Bandol Mas de la Rouvière, Bunan (YAP)
Coteaux des Baux-en-Provence Mas de Gourgonnier (BEN)
1989
Bandol Château de la Rouvière, Bunan (YAP)
Bandol Cuvée Migoua (WS)
Bandol Domaine de Pibarnon (BEK, PIP)
Bandol Domaine Tempier (DI)
Coteaux d'Aix-en-Provence Domaine les Bastides Cuvée Speciale (WW)
1988
Bandol Cuvée Migoua (WS)
Bandol Mas de la Rouvière, Bunan (ROB)
Coteaux d'Aix-en-Provence Château Vignelaure (ROB)
1987
Bandol Château de la Rouvière, Bunan (NI)
1985
Bandol Château Vannières (NO)
Bandol Mas de la Rouvière, Bunan (NO)

£11.00 to £14.99

1992
Côtes de Provence Domaine de Trevallon (YAP)
1991
Côtes de Provence Domaine de Trevallon (YAP)
1990
Bandol Cuvée Migoua (GAU, WW)
Bandol Cuvée Tourtine (GAU, DI, WW)
Bandol Domaine Tempier (WW, DI)
Côtes de Provence Domaine de Trevallon (YAP)
1989
Bandol Cuvée Migoua (GAU)
Bandol Cuvée Tourtine (GAU)
Côtes de Provence Domaine de Trevallon (YAP)
Palette Château Simone (YAP, VIG)
1988
Palette Château Simone (VIG)

---

*Please remember that **Webster's** is a price GUIDE and not a price LIST. It is not meant to replace up-to-date merchant's lists.*

£15.00 to £19.99

1990
Coteaux d'Aix-en-Provence Domaine de Trévallon (VIG)
Côtes de Provence Domaine de Trevallon (GAU)
1988
Bellet Château de Crémat, Jean Bagnis (YAP)
1980
Palette Château Simone (VIG)
1979
Palette Château Simone (VIG)

WHITE

Under £7.00

Non-vintage
VdP des Sables du Golfe du Lion, Listel Blanc (PE)
1992
Côtes de Provence Mas de Cadenet (WW)
1991
Coteaux d'Aix-en-Provence Château de Fonscolombe (LAY)

£7.00 to £8.99

1992
Cassis Clos Ste-Magdeleine, Sack (YAP)
1991
Bandol Mas de la Rouvière, Bunan (YAP)

£13.00 to £14.99

1991
Palette Château Simone (YAP)
1989
Côtes de Provence Domaines Ott (PEN)
Palette Château Simone (VIG)

£15.00 to £16.99

1993
Bellet Château de Crémat, Jean Bagnis (YAP)
1990
Côtes de Provence Domaines Ott (ROB)
1989
Côtes de Provence Clos Mireille Blanc de Blancs, Domaines Ott (ROB)

ROSÉ

Under £7.00

Non-vintage
VdP des Sables du Golfe du Lion Gris de Gris, Domaine de Jarras (PE)

1991
Côtes de Provence Carte Noire, Vignerons de St-Tropez (WHI)

£7.00 to £9.99

1992
Bandol Mas de la Rouvière (YAP)
1991
Coteaux d'Aix-en-Provence les Baux Terres Blanches (VIG)

£12.00 to £14.99

1990
Palette Château Simone (VIG)
1989
Palette Château Simone (YAP)

VINS DOUX NATURELS

Under £9.00

1992
Muscat de Rivesaltes Domaine Cazes (WW)
1991
Muscat de Rivesaltes Château de Jau (GE)

£9.00 to £9.99

Non-vintage
Rasteau Domaine la Soumade (PIP)
1992
Muscat de Rivesaltes Domaine Cazes (BAR)
1991
Muscat de Rivesaltes Domaine Cazes (ROB)
1990
Muscat de Rivesaltes Domaine Cazes (ROB)
1989
Rasteau Domaine la Soumade (HAM)

£10.00 to £14.99

1992
Maury Mas Amiel (LEA)
1989
Muscat de Rivesaltes Domaine Cazes (VIG)
1978
Vieux Rivesaltes Domaine Cazes (ROB, VIG)

c. £23.00

1969
Maury Mas Amiel (VIG)

Webster's is an annual publication. We welcome your suggestions for next year's edition.

SOUTH-WEST FRANCE

RED

Under £3.50

1993
Côtes de Duras Seigneuret (WAI)
1992
★ Côtes de St-Mont, Producteurs Plaimont
  (SOM)
1991
Côtes de St-Mont, Les Hauts de Bergelle
  (SOM)
Côtes du Marmandais Château Marseau
  (WAI)
1990
Côtes du Marmandais Cave de Cocumont
  (SO)

£3.50 to £3.99

Non-vintage
VdP du Comté Tolosan, Domaine de
  Callary (PE)
1992
★ Côtes du Frontonnais Château Bellevue-
  la-Forêt (SAI)
1990
★ Côtes du Frontonnais Château Bellevue-
  la-Forêt (OD)
Madiran Domaine Laplace (MAJ)

£4.00 to £4.99

1992
Cahors Château de Gaudou (WCL)
Côtes de St-Mont, Les Hauts de Bergelle
  (TAN)
Gaillac Domaine de Labarthe (SOM)
1991
Côtes du Frontonnais Château Bellevue-
  la-Forêt (NI)
Tursan Domaine de Perchade-Pourruchot
  (WAT)
1990
★ Bergerac Château la Jaubertie (NI)
Buzet Tradition les Vignerons de Buzet (WW)
Cahors Château de Gaudou (SOM)
Côtes du Frontonnais Carte Blanche
  Château Montauriol (OD)
Côtes du Frontonnais Château Ferran
  (BEK, AME, WCL)
★ Gaillac Château Clement Termes (HOG)
1989
Cahors Château St-Didier-Parnac, Rigal
  (OD)

£5.00 to £5.99

1992
Marcillac Domaine du Cros, Teulier (AD)
1991
Madiran Domaine Damiens (BIB)
Pécharmant Château de Tiregand (SAI)
1990
Cahors Domaine de Paillas (BIB)
Cahors Domaine Pierre Sèche (BU)
1989
Bergerac Château le Barradis (WS)
Cahors Château de Haute-Serre (WS)
Cahors Domaine de la Pineraie (HOG)
Côtes du Frontonnais Château Ferran (ROB)
1988
Buzet Tradition les Vignerons de Buzet (PE)

£6.00 to £7.99

1992
Cahors Clos la Coutale (WW)
1990
Bergerac Domaine de la Raze (BOD)
Bergerac Reserve Château la Jaubertie (NO)
Cahors Château Lagrezette (BEK)
Côtes de Bergerac Château le Tour des
  Gendres (LEA)
1989
Côtes de St-Mont, Château de Sabazan (LAY)
1988
Cahors Château Cayrou d'Albas (WAT)
Cahors Clos de Gamot (WAT)
Madiran Cave de Crouseilles (SAI)

£8.00 to £11.99

1990
Madiran Château Montus (VIG)
1988
Cahors Château Lagrezette (ROB)
Madiran Château d'Aydie (PIP)
1985
Bergerac Reserve Château la Jaubertie (NO)

DRY WHITE

Under £3.00

1993
Côtes de Duras Croix du Beurrier (WAI)
VdP des Côtes de Gascogne Producteurs
  Plaimont (MAR)
1992
VdP des Côtes de Gascogne Producteurs
  Plaimont (SOM)

£3.00 to £3.49

1993
Bergerac Sauvignon Foncaussade (SAF)
★ VdP des Côtes de Gascogne Domaine
San de Guilhem (HOG)
VdP des Côtes de Gascogne Domaine de
Planterieu (WAI)
VdP des Côtes de Gascogne Domaine de
Tariquet (BOT, THR)
1992
Côtes de St-Mont, Les Hauts de Bergelle
(SOM)
VdP des Côtes de Gascogne Domaine de
Tariquet (WR)

£3.50 to £3.99

1993
Côtes de St-Mont, Producteurs Plaimont
(AD, TAN)
VdP des Côtes de Gascogne Domaine le
Puts (MAJ, CV)
1992
VdP des Côtes de Gascogne Domaine San
de Guilhem (MV)
VdP des Côtes de Gascogne Domaine de
Rieux (EY)
1991
VdP Charentais Cave St-André (ROB)
VdP des Côtes de Gascogne Domaine de
Rieux (PE)

£4.00 to £4.99

1993
Bergerac Sec Château de Tiregand (TAN)
1992
Pacherenc du Vic-Bilh Domaine du
Crampilh (WAT)

£5.00 to £5.99

1993
VdP des Côtes de Gascogne Domaine des
Cassagnoles (BOD, WIC)
1992
Bergerac Château Court-les-Mûts (BIB)
Bergerac Château la Jaubertie
(NI, HIG)
Bergerac Château le Fagé (BER)
Bergerac Domaine de Grandchamp (SAI)
Pacherenc du Vic-Bilh Domaine Damiens
(BIB, AD)
VdP des Côtes de Gascogne Domaine des
Cassagnoles (BEN)
1990
Bergerac Château la Jaubertie (NI)
Buzet Château Sauvagnères (PLA)

£6.00 to £6.99

1992
Bergerac Château la Jaubertie Cépage
Sauvignon (NI)
1991
Bergerac Château la Jaubertie (NO)
1989
★ Jurançon Sec Domaine Cauhapé (WAT)
Saussignac Château Court-les-Mûts (BIB)

£7.00 to £8.99

1992
Jurançon Sec Domaine Cauhapé (MV, AD,
WCL)

£10.00 to £11.99

1990
Jurançon Sec Domaine Cauhapé (VIG)

SWEET WHITE

Under £8.00

1990
Jurançon Moelleux Château Jolys (WHI)
Monbazillac Château Treuil-de-Nailhac
(WAT)
1989
Jurançon Clos Guirouilh (ROB)
Monbazillac Château Theulet (BAR)
1986
Jurançon Cru Lamouroux (HAY)

£8.00 to £8.99

1991
Monbazillac Château Theulet (ROB)
1986
Monbazillac Château Treuil-de-Nailhac
(WAT)

c. £16.00

1989
Jurançon Grains Nobles, Cave de Gan (REI)

c. £17.00

1990
Jurançon Moelleux Domaine Cauhapé (NO)

ROSÉ

Under £6.00

1993
★ Bergerac Château la Jaubertie (NI)
1992
Bergerac Château Court-les-Mûts (BIB)
Bergerac Château la Jaubertie (NI, VIC)

JURA & SAVOIE

JURA: RED

Under £4.50

Non-vintage
Bonchalaz Maire (ROB)

£6.00 to £7.50

1990
Côtes du Jura Pinot Noir/Trousseau,
  Boilley (WCL)
1988
Côtes du Jura Rouge Bourdy (AD)
1987
Côtes du Jura Rouge Bourdy (WS)

JURA: WHITE

Under £7.50

1990
Côtes du Jura Blanc Bourdy (WS)
1989
Côtes du Jura Cépage Savagnin, Boilley
  (PEN)

£8.50 to £9.99

1990
Chardonnay-Savagnin Château d'Arlay,
  Laguiche (SUM)
Côtes du Jura Cépage Savagnin, Boilley
  (WCL)
1989
Côtes du Jura Cépage Savagnin, Boilley (ROB)

£18.00 to £19.99

Non-vintage
Vin de Paille La Vignière, Maire 1/2 bottle
  (ROB, VIG)

£20.00 to £29.99

1986
Vin Jaune Château-Chalon, Bourdy (WS)
1985
Vin Jaune Château-Chalon, Bourdy (AD)
1983
Vin Jaune d'Arbois, Tissot (PLA)

> Stars (★) indicate wines
> selected by the editors as
> particularly good value
> in their class.

1982
Vin Jaune Côtes du Jura Château d'Arlay,
  Laguiche (REI)
1978
Vin Jaune Château-Chalon, Maire (ROB)

£30.00 to £35.00

1985
Vin Jaune Côtes du Jura Château d'Arlay,
  Laguiche (SUM)
1979
Vin Jaune Château-Chalon, Bourdy (WS)

c. £95.00

1934
Côtes du Jura Blanc Bourdy (WS)

JURA: ROSÉ

c. £4.50

Non-vintage
Vin Gris Cendré de Novembre Maire (HOG)

SAVOIE: RED

c. £5.50

1991
Mondeuse St-Jean de la Porte, J Perrier &
  Fils (AD)

SAVOIE: WHITE

Under £5.00

1992
Vin de Savoie Abymes (EL)

£5.00 to £6.49

1993
Apremont les Rocailles, Pierre Boniface (TAN)
1992
Seyssel Tacounière, Mollex (WS)
1991
Apremont les Rocailles, Pierre Boniface (PE)
1990
Apremont les Rocailles, Pierre Boniface (PE)

SAVOIE: SPARKLING

c. £6.50

Non-vintage
Seyssel Blanc de Blancs Mousseux
  Varichon & Clerc (EY)

GERMANY

Kab.	=	Kabinett
Spät.	=	Spätlese
Aus.	=	Auslese
BA	=	Beerenauslese
TBA	=	Trockenbeerenauslese

RHINE WHITE

Under £3.50

Non-vintage
Liebfraumilch Black Tower (SAF)
★ Rheingau Riesling, Schloss
  Reinhartshausen (SO)
1993
Niersteiner Gutes Domtal, Deinhard (HOG)
Niersteiner Gutes Domtal, Rudolf Müller
  (PEN)
1992
Rüdesheimer Rosengarten, Rudolf Müller
  (TAN)

£3.50 to £4.49

Non-vintage
Liebfraumilch Black Tower (SO, WHI)
Liebfraumilch Blue Nun (SO, UN, WHI)
Liebfraumilch Crown of Crowns (PE, WHI)
1993
Oppenheimer Krötenbrunnen, Rudolf
  Müller (CB)
1992
Bereich Johannisberg Riesling Kab., von
  Simmern (WHI)
Niersteiner Spiegelberg Riesling Kab.,
  Rudolf Müller (TAN)
1991
★ Kreuznacher Riesling Spät., Paul
  Anheuser (TES)
Liebfraumilch Blue Nun (WAI, DAV)
Niersteiner Gutes Domtal, Rudolf Müller
  (CB)
1990
Niersteiner Gutes Domtal, Rudolf Müller
  (HAH)

£4.50 to £5.49

1992
Wachenheimer Mandelgarten Müller-
  Thurgau Kab., Bürklin-Wolf (DI)
1989
★ Eltviller Sonnenberg Riesling Kab., von
  Simmern (WAT)

£5.50 to £6.49

1992
Mainzer Domherr Bacchus Kab., Guntrum
  (PIP)
Niederhauser Pfingstweide Riesling, Paul
  Anheuser (SUM)
Niersteiner Spiegelberg Kab., Guntrum
  (WRI, DAV)
1991
★ Binger Scharlachberg Riesling Kab.,
  Villa Sachsen (TES)
1990
Mainzer Domherr Bacchus Kab., Guntrum
  (WRI)
1989
★ Altenbamberger Rotenberg Riesling
  Kab., Staatliche Weinbaudomäne (EY)
Oppenheimer Schloss Müller-Thurgau
  Trocken, Guntrum (WRI)
★ Wachenheimer Rechbächel Riesling
  Kab., Bürklin-Wolf (ASD)
1988
★ Kiedricher Sandgrub Riesling Kab.,
  Schloss Groenesteyn (VIC)
Schloss Vollrads Blau-Gold, Matuschka-
  Greiffenclau (EL)

1986
Deidesheimer Herrgottsacker Riesling
  Kab., Deinhard (CV)
1985
★ Eltviller Sonnenberg Riesling Kab., von
  Simmern (RAE)
1983
★ Oestricher Doosberg Riesling Kab.,
  Schönborn (SO)

£6.50 to £7.49

1990
Johannisberger Erntebringer Riesling
  Kab., Balthasar Ress (SUM)
Niersteiner Oelberg Spät., Gessert (NI)

1989
★ Freinsheimer Goldberg Riesling Spät.,
Lingenfelder (OD)
Schloss Vollrads Grün-Gold, Matuschka-
Greiffenclau (EL)
1988
Geisenheimer Kläuserweg Riesling Spät.,
Ress (GE)
Kreuznacher Kahlenberg Riesling Spät.,
Paul Anheuser (CV)
1983
Oestricher Doosberg Riesling Kab.,
Schönborn (EL)

£7.50 to £8.49

1992
Forster Ungeheuer Riesling Kab.,
Bassermann-Jordan (GAU)
Rauenthaler Gehrn Riesling Kab.,
Staatsweingüter Eltville (HE)
1990
Kiedricher Sandgrub Riesling Kab.,
Schloss Groenesteyn (HOG)
Niederhauser Hermannsberg Riesling
Spät., Staatliche Weinbaudomäne (EY)
Oppenheimer Herrenberg Scheurebe Spät.,
Guntrum (WRI)
Schloss Böckelheimer Kupfergrube
Riesling Spät., Staatliche
Weinbaudomäne (EY)
Schloss Vollrads Blau-Silber, Matuschka-
Greiffenclau (HOG, EL)
1989
Forster Kirchenstück Riesling Kab.,
Bassermann-Jordan (BIB)
Niederhauser Hermannsberg Riesling
Spät., Staatliche Weinbaudomäne (EY)
Riesling Spät. Trocken, Lingenfelder (NI)
Schloss Böckelheimer Kupfergrube
Riesling Spät., Staatliche
Weinbaudomäne (EY)
1988
Forster Jesuitengarten Riesling Kab.,
Bassermann-Jordan (EY)
Forster Jesuitengarten Riesling Spät.,
Bassermann-Jordan (VIC)
Hochheimer Hölle Riesling Kab., Aschrott (AV)
Kreuznacher St-Martin Riesling Kab.,
Paul Anheuser (PE)
Niederhauser Hermannsberg Riesling
Spät., Staatliche Weinbaudomäne (EY)
Niersteiner Oelberg Riesling Kab., Heyl zu
Herrnsheim (HAC)
Niersteiner Pettenthal Riesling Spät.,
Balbach (VIC)

Wachenheimer Rechbächel Riesling Kab.,
Bürklin-Wolf (DI)
1987
Rüdesheimer Berg Roseneck Riesling Kab.,
Deinhard (PEN)
1986
Erbacher Marcobrunnen Riesling Kab.,
von Simmern (LAY)
Forster Jesuitengarten Riesling Kab.,
Bürklin-Wolf (GE)
Rauenthaler Baiken Riesling QbA Charta,
Verwaltung der Staatsweingüter Eltville
(HAC)
Ruppertsberger Gaisböhl Riesling Kab.,
Bürklin-Wolf (DI)
1985
Hochheimer Domdechaney Riesling Spät.,
Domdechaney Werner'sches (VIC)
Schloss Böckelheimer Kupfergrube
Riesling Spät., Staatliche
Weinbaudomäne (RAE)
1971
Grünstadter Höllenpfad Müller-Thurgau
Spät., Winzerkeller Leiningerland (HE)

£8.50 to £9.99

1993
Grosskarlbacher Burgweg Scheurebe Kab.,
Lingenfelder (HAC)
Rauenthaler Gehrn Riesling Spät.,
Staatsweingüter Eltville (HE)
Scheurebe Spät. Trocken, Lingenfelder
(AD)
Steinberger Riesling Kab.,
Staatsweingüter Eltville (HE)
1992
Traisener Rotenfels Riesling Spätlese,
Crusius (LAY)
1990
Kreuznacher Kahlenberg Riesling Spät.,
Paul Anheuser (ROB)
1989
Hochheimer Königin Victoria Berg
Riesling Kab., Deinhard (WHI)
Rauenthaler Baiken Riesling Spät.,
Staatsweingüter Eltville (HE)
Steinberger Riesling Kab.,
Staatsweingüter Eltville (HOG)

*Webster's is an annual
publication. We welcome
your suggestions for next
year's edition.*

1988
Deidesheimer Hohenmorgen Riesling
  Spät., Bassermann-Jordan (EY, RAE)
Forster Ungeheuer Riesling Spät.,
  Deinhard (PEN)
1983
Wachenheimer Gerümpel Riesling Spät.,
  Bürklin-Wolf (GRE)

1979
Grünstadter Höllenpfad Riesling Spät.,
  Winzerkeller Leiningerland (HE)

£10.00 to £11.99
1993
Rauenthaler Baiken Riesling Spät.,
  Staatsweingüter Eltville (HE)
1992
Freinsheimer Goldberg Riesling Spät.,
  Lingenfelder (HAC)
Riesling Spät. Trocken, Lingenfelder (AD)
Schloss Johannisberg Riesling Kab.,
  Metternich (BEN)
1990
Scheurebe Spät. Trocken, Lingenfelder
  (WCL)
1989
Freinsheimer Goldberg Riesling Spät.,
  Lingenfelder (WCL)
Rauenthaler Baiken Riesling Spät.,
  Staatsweingüter Eltville (WAT)
Schloss Böckelheimer Kupfergrube
  Riesling Spät., Staatliche
  Weinbaudomäne (HOG)
1988
Erbacher Marcobrunnen Riesling Spät.,
  Staatsweingüter Eltville (HE)
Forster Ungeheuer Riesling Spät.,
  Deinhard (BER)
Niersteiner Rehbach Riesling Spät., Heyl
  zu Herrnsheim (HAC)
1986
Niersteiner Oelberg Riesling Aus., Senfter
  (HOG)

1983
Rauenthaler Baiken Riesling Spät.,
  Staatsweingüter Eltville (HOG, GRE)
1979
Grünstadter Höllenpfad Scheurebe Aus.,
  Winzerkeller Leiningerland (HE)
1976
Grünstadter Höllenpfad Scheurebe Aus.,
  Winzerkeller Leiningerland (HE)

£12.00 to £14.99
1993
Erbacher Marcobrunnen Riesling Spät.,
  Staatsweingüter Eltville (HE)
1992
Schloss Böckelheimer Kupfergrube
  Riesling Spät., Staatliche
  Weinbaudomäne (BER)
1989
Niederhauser Hermannsberg Riesling
  Aus., Staatliche Weinbaudomäne (EY)
Schloss Böckelheimer Kupfergrube
  Riesling Aus., Staatsdomäne (EY)
1983
Wachenheimer Gerümpel Riesling Spät.,
  Bürklin-Wolf (WS)

£15.00 to £19.99
1985
Wachenheimer Rechbächel Riesling Aus.,
  Bürklin-Wolf (AD)
1979
Erbacher Marcobrunnen Riesling Spät.,
  Staatsweingüter Eltville (HAC)
1976
Schloss Böckelheimer Burgweg Riesling
  Aus., Pleitz (HE)

£20.00 to £29.99
1976
Niersteiner Kranzberg Riesling BA,
  Senfter (WRI)
Niersteiner Oelberg Riesling BA, Heyl zu
  Herrnsheim (HAC)
Oppenheimer Krötenbrunnen, Deinhard
  (PEN)

*Please remember that
Webster's is a price
GUIDE and not a price
LIST. It is not meant to
replace up-to-date
merchant's lists.*

c. £38.00

1985
Grosskarlbacher Burgweg Scheurebe TBA
½ Bottle, Lingenfelder (HAC)

RHINE RED

c. £12.00

1991
Spätburgunder QbA, Lingenfelder (HAC)
1990
Spätburgunder QbA, Lingenfelder (HAC)

MOSEL WHITE

Under £3.50

1992
Bereich Bernkastel Riesling, Schneider
(PLA, EL)
Piesporter Michelsberg Schneider (EL, PLA)
1991
Bereich Bernkastel Riesling, Schneider
(WHI)
Piesporter Michelsberg Schneider (WHI)

£3.50 to £3.99

1991
Piesporter Michelsberg Rudolf Müller (CB)
1990
Bereich Bernkastel, Rudolf Müller (PEN)
Wiltinger Scharzberg Riesling Kab.,
Zentralkellerei (TES)
1988
Deinhard Green Label (HOG)

£4.00 to £4.99

1991
Bereich Bernkastel, Rudolf Müller (CB)
Piesporter Michelsberg Rudolf Müller
(PEN)
1989
Deinhard Green Label (WHI)
Klüsserather St-Michael Riesling Spät.,
Rudolf Müller (BOR)
Ockfener Bockstein Riesling Spät., Rudolf
Müller (SAI)
1988
Deinhard Green Label (VIC)

£5.00 to £5.99

1992
Graacher Himmelreich Riesling Kab.,
Kesselstatt (ASD)
Trittenheimer Altärchen Riesling Kab.,
Weingut Hubertushof (HE)

1991
Trittenheimer Altärchen Riesling Kab.,
Weingut Hubertushof (HE)
1990
Deinhard Green Label (PEN)
Reiler Mullay Hofberg Riesling Kab.,
Rudolf Müller (TAN)
1988
★ Falkensteiner Hofberg Riesling Kab., F-
W-Gymnasium (VIC)
1986
★ Erdener Treppchen Riesling Spät.,
Monchhof (WAI)

£6.00 to £7.99

1993
Trittenheimer Apotheke Riesling Spät.,
Weingut Hubertushof (HE)
1992
Trittenheimer Apotheke Riesling Spät.,
Weingut Hubertushof (HE)
1991
Graacher Himmelreich Riesling Kab.,
F-W-Gymnasium (EL)
Scharzhofberger Riesling Kab., Kesselstatt
(EL)
Serriger Schloss Saarsteiner Riesling Kab.,
Schloss Saarstein (BIB)
Trittenheimer Apotheke Riesling Spät.,
Weingut Hubertushof (HE)
★ Wehlener Sonnenuhr Riesling Kab.,
Richter (SUM)
1990
Bernkasteler Lay Riesling Kab., Loosen (GE)
Graacher Himmelreich Riesling Spät.,
F-W-Gymnasium (EY)
★ Oberemmeler Hutte Riesling Spät., von
Hövel (EY)
Scharzhofberger Riesling Kab, Kesselstatt (BY)
Serriger Schloss Saarsteiner Riesling Kab.,
Schloss Saarstein (BAR)
Trittenheimer Apotheke Riesling Kab.,
Clusserath-Weiler (HOG)
1989
★ Brauneberger Juffer Riesling Kab.,
Kesselstatt (BY)
Scharzhofberger Riesling Spät.,
Kesselstatt (WAT)
Serriger Schloss Saarsteiner Riesling Kab.,
Schloss Saarstein (SUM)
★ Wehlener Sonnenuhr Riesling Kab.,
Loosen (EY)
1988
Serriger Antoniusberg Riesling Kab.,
Simon (WCL, ROB)

£8.00 to £9.99

1992
Wehlener Sonnenuhr Riesling Kab.,
  Richter (BER)
1990
Erdener Treppchen Riesling Kab., Loosen
  (EY)
Graacher Himmelreich Riesling Spät.,
  F-W-Gymnasium (TAN)
Scharzhofberger Riesling Spät.,
  Kesselstatt (NI)
Serriger Schloss Saarsteiner Riesling
  Spät., Schloss Saarstein (BAR)
★ Trittenheimer Apotheke Riesling Aus.,
  F-W-Gymnasium (EY)
Wehlener Sonnenuhr Riesling Kab.,
  Loosen (NO)
1989
Bernkasteler Lay Riesling Kab., Loosen
  (BER, ROB)
Eitelsbacher Marienholz Riesling Spät.,
  Bischöfliches Konvikt (PE)
Enkircher Steffenberg Riesling Spät.,
  Immich (GE)
Ockfener Bockstein Riesling Spät.,
  Staatlichen Weinbaudomänen (HOG)
Wehlener Sonnenuhr Riesling Kab., J.J.
  Prüm (NI)
1988
Bernkasteler Badstube Riesling Spät.,
  Heidemanns-Bergweiler (GRE)
Graacher Himmelreich Riesling Spät.,
  F-W-Gymnasium (ROB)
1985
Erdener Treppchen Riesling Kab., Dr
  Loosen (NO)
Scharzhofberger Riesling Spät., Hohe
  Domkirche (AD)
1983
Eitelsbacher Marienholz Riesling Spät.,
  Bischöfliches Konvikt (HOG)
Erdener Treppchen Riesling Spät., Dr
  Loosen (HAM)
Falkensteiner Hofberg Riesling Spät.,
  F-W-Gymnasium (GRE)

£10.00 to £11.99

1991
Maximin-Grünhäuser Abtsberg Riesling
  Kab., Schubert (LAY)
Wehlener Sonnenuhr Riesling Kab.,
  Deinhard (TAN)
1990
Bernkasteler Bratenhöfchen Riesling
  Spät., Lauerburg (BE)
Brauneberger Juffer Riesling Aus., Richter
  (SUM)
Erdener Treppchen Riesling Kab., Dr
  Loosen (NO)
Serriger Würzberg Riesling Spät., Simon
  (BE)
Wehlener Sonnenuhr Riesling Spät.,
  Deinhard (HOG)
1989
Maximin-Grünhäuser Abtsberg Riesling
  Kab., Schubert (WS)
Maximin-Grünhäuser Herrenberg Riesling
  Spät., Schubert (EY)
Scharzhofberger Riesling Spät., Hohe
  Domkirche (HOG)
1988
Graacher Himmelreich Riesling Aus.,
  F-W-Gymnasium (WHI)
Josephshofer Riesling Aus., Kesselstatt (NI)
Trittenheimer Apotheke Riesling Aus.,
  F-W-Gymnasium (VIC)
1986
Maximin-Grünhäuser Abtsberg Riesling
  Kab., Schubert (GRE)
1985
Erdener Treppchen Riesling Aus., Dr
  Loosen (NO)
1983
Bernkasteler Schlossberg Riesling Aus.,
  P.J. Hauth (HAC)
Dhroner Hofberger Riesling Aus.,
  Bischöfliches Priesterseminar (PE)
Erdener Treppchen Riesling Aus., Dr
  Loosen (NO)
Kaseler Nies'chen Riesling Aus.,
  Bischöfliches Priesterseminar (PE, GRE)

£12.00 to £14.99

1992
Maximin-Grünhäuser Abtsberg Riesling
  Spät., Schubert (WS)
Serriger Schloss Saarsteiner Riesling
  Spät., Schloss Saarstein (BIB)
1990
Maximin-Grünhäuser Herrenberg Riesling
  Spät., Schubert (EY)

Oberemmeler Hutte Riesling Aus., von
  Hövel (EY)
Wehlener Sonnenuhr Riesling Spät.,
  Deinhard (BEN)
1989
Maximin-Grünhäuser Herrenberg Riesling
  Kab., Schubert (GRE)
Wehlener Sonnenuhr Riesling Spät.,
  Prüm-Erben (DI)
1983
Bernkasteler Bratenhöfchen Riesling Aus.,
  Deinhard (PEN)
Dhroner Hofberger Riesling Aus.,
  Bischöfliches Priesterseminar
  (GRE)
Wehlener Sonnenuhr Riesling Aus.,
  F.W. Prüm (PE)

£15.00 to £19.99

1990
★ Graacher Himmelreich Riesling Spät.
  Eiswein, Bergweiler-Prüm (EY)
1989
Brauneberger Juffer Sonnenuhr Riesling
  Aus., Fritz Haag (VIG)
Wehlener Sonnenuhr Riesling Aus., S.A.
  Prüm-Erben (DI)
1988
Maximin-Grünhäuser Herrenberg Riesling
  Aus., Schubert (EY)
1983
Bernkasteler Bratenhöfchen Riesling Aus.,
  Deinhard (AD)
Bernkasteler Graben Riesling Spät.,
  Deinhard (AD)
Wehlener Abtei Eiswein, Schneider ½
  bottle (WHI)

£20.00 to £29.99

1989
Mulheimer Helenkloster Riesling Eiswein,
  Richter ½ bottle (SUM)
1987
Mulheimer Helenkloster Riesling Eiswein,
  Richter ½ bottle (SUM)
1985
Bernkasteler Doctor Riesling Spät.,
  Deinhard (PEN)

*Stars (★) indicate wines
selected by the editors as
particularly good value
in their class.*

£30.00 to £39.99

1990
Mulheimer Helenkloster Riesling Eiswein,
  Richter ½ bottle (BER, SUM)

£50.00 to £54.99

1983
Bernkasteler Graben Riesling Eiswein,
  Deinhard ½ bottle (AD)
1975
Bernkasteler Bratenhöfchen Riesling BA
  Eiswein, Deinhard (WRI)

c. £77.00

1976
Serriger Würzberg TBA, Simon (BOR)

c. £87.50

1983
Bernkasteler Graben Riesling Eiswein,
  Deinhard (TAN)

FRANKEN WHITE

£8.00 to £8.99

1988
Casteller Kirchberg Müller-Thurgau,
  Fürstlich Castell'sches Domänenamt
  (HAC, WCL)
Casteller Kirchberg Silvaner Trocken,
  Fürstlich Castell'sches Domänenamt
  (HAC)

BADEN WHITE

c. £7.00

1988
Rivaner, Karl Heinz Johner (HAC)

BADEN RED

c. £16.00

1987
Pinot Noir, Karl Heinz Johner (HAC)

GERMAN SPARKLING

Under £6.00

Non-vintage
Henkell Trocken (SAF)

£6.00 to £7.99

Non-vintage
★ Deinhard Lila Imperial Riesling (HOG)
Henkell Trocken (VIC, WHI, UN, WRI)

ITALY

NORTH-WEST RED

Under £4.00

1993
★ Spanna Travaglini (EL)
1988
★ Barbera d'Asti Viticoltori dell'Acquese (BUT)

£4.00 to £4.99

1992
Barbera d'Asti Viticoltori dell'Acquese (AD)
★ Dolcetto d'Acqui Viticoltori dell'Acquese (AD)

£5.00 to £5.99

1992
Barbera d'Alba Borgogno (DI)
1989
Inferno Nino Negri (HOG, GRE)
★ Sassella Nino Negri (HOG)
1988
Barolo Giacosa Fratelli (TES)
1983
Gattinara Berteletti (HOG)

£6.00 to £6.99

1992
Dolcetto d'Alba Ascheri (EL)
Dolcetto d'Alba Prunotto (EY)
1988
Barbera d'Asti Guasti Clemente (HOG)
★ Barolo Aliberti (BY)
Barolo Terre del Barolo (VIC)

£7.00 to £7.99

1992
Dolcetto d'Alba Prunotto (DI)
Dolcetto Sandrone (TAN)
1991
★ Nebbiolo d'Alba San Rocco, Mascarello (GRE, WCL)
1990
Ronco de Mompiano Pasolini (WCL)
1989
Barolo Ascheri (OD)
Barolo Fontanafredda (WHI, EY, THR, BOT, WR, DAV)
1987
Gattinara Travaglini (EL)
1985
Barbaresco Fontanafredda (PEN)

£8.00 to £9.99

1991
Barbera d'Alba Aldo Conterno (VA)
1990
Barbera d'Alba Conca Tre Pile, Aldo Conterno (POR, EY, SEC)
Barbera d'Alba Pio Cesare (DI)
Barolo Ascheri (AME, WCL)
Nebbiolo d'Alba San Rocco, Mascarello (ROB)
1989
Barbaresco Santo Stefano, Castello di Neive (VA)
Barolo Ascheri (GRE, HAM, VA)
Freisa delle Langhe Vajra (GRE, WCL)
1988
Barolo Pio Cesare (GRE)
Nebbiolo delle Langhe Vajra (WCL)
1987
Barolo Borgogno (DI)
Barolo Riserva Borgogno (ROB, PE)
Barolo Terre del Barolo (HAH)
1983
Barbaresco Gallina di Neive, Bruno Giacosa (RAE)

£10.00 to £12.49

1991
Barbera d'Alba Conca Tre Pile, Aldo Conterno (WCL, BEN)
1990
Vignaserra Voerzio (OD)
1989
Sfursat Nino Negri (GRE).
1988
Barolo Zonchera Ceretto (TAN)
1986
Barolo Marcenasco, Renato Ratti (PE)
1984
Barolo Zonchera Ceretto (NI)
1982
Barolo Riserva Fontanafredda (HOG)

£12.50 to £14.99

1990
Nebbiolo Il Favot, Aldo Conterno (POR)
1989
Barolo Prunotto (WS)
Barolo Zonchera Ceretto (DI, PIP)
1987
Barolo Bussia Soprana, Aldo Conterno (PIP)
Barolo Monprivato, Mascarello (DI, WCL)
Nebbiolo Il Favot, Aldo Conterno (WCL, PIP)

1986
Barolo Pio Cesare (DI)
Nebbiolo Il Favot, Aldo Conterno (WCL)
1983
Barolo Bruno Giacosa (RAE)
1982
Barbaresco Bruno Giacosa (HOG)
Barolo Riserva Fontanafredda (VIG)

£15.00 to £19.99

1991
Nebbiolo Il Favot, Aldo Conterno (WCL)
1990
Nebbiolo Il Favot, Aldo Conterno (SEC, NI)
1988
Barolo Monprivato, Mascarello (GE, REI,
    AME, LAY, WCL, POR, BEN)
Barolo Zonchera Ceretto (BER)
1987
Barbera d'Alba Vignarey, Gaja (TW)
Barolo Bussia Soprana, Aldo Conterno (WCL)
1986
Barolo Bussia Soprana, Aldo Conterno
    (TAN)
1985
Barbaresco Marcarini, Mascarello (WCL)
Barolo Bricco Rocche Brunate, Ceretto (NI)
1982
Barolo Lazzarito, Fontanafredda (GRE, VA)
1979
Barolo Montanello, Monchiero (WCL)
1978
Barolo Gattinera, Fontanafredda (HOG)

1967
Barolo Borgogno (WCL)
1964
Barolo Borgogno (WCL)

£20.00 to £29.99

1990
Barbera d'Alba Vignarey, Gaja (VA)
1989
Barolo Bussia, Prunotto (VIG)
Barolo Bussia Soprana, Aldo Conterno
    (GAU)

1988
Barolo Bussia Soprana, Aldo Conterno (NI)
Barolo Giacomo Conterno (VA)
Maurizio Zanella, Ca' del Bosco (VA)
1985
Darmagi Gaja (VA)
1984
Maurizio Zanella, Ca' del Bosco (VA)
1983
Maurizio Zanella, Ca' del Bosco (VA)
1982
Barolo Conca, Renato Ratti (AD)
1978
Barolo Borgogno (VA)
1974
Barbaresco Bricco Asili, Ceretto (WCL)
Barolo Montanello, Monchiero (WCL)
1971
Barolo Borgogno (VA)
Barolo Montanello, Monchiero (ROB, WCL)
Barolo Riserva Borgogno (GRE)
1970
Barolo Montanello, Monchiero (WCL)
1967
Barolo Ceretto (WCL)

£30.00 to £39.99

1986
Barbaresco Gaja (DI)
1984
Darmagi Gaja (VA)
1983
Darmagi Gaja (VA)
1970
Barbaresco Vigneto Montefico, Ceretto (WCL)
Barolo Ceretto (WCL)
Barolo Zonchetta, Ceretto (WCL)
1969
Barolo Mascarello (WCL)
Barolo Zonchetta, Ceretto (WCL)
1967
Barolo Mascarello (WCL)
1961
Barolo Borgogno (VA)

£40.00 to £59.99

1986
Barbaresco Sori San Lorenzo, Gaja (DI, TW)
1985
Barolo Conterno Riserva Speciale
    Monfortino (VA)
1982
Barbaresco Gaja (VA)
1968
Barolo Giacomo Conterno (WCL)

1964
Barolo Bussia, Prunotto (WCL)
1961
Barolo Pio Cesare (WCL)

£65.00 to £74.99
1989
Barbaresco Sorì Tildìn, Gaja (VA)
1986
Barbaresco Sori San Lorenzo, Gaja (NO)
1978
Barbaresco Gaja (TW)
1964
Barbaresco Gaja (WCL)

c. £150.00
1961
Barbaresco Gaja (VA)

NORTH-WEST WHITE

Under £6.00
1993
Chardonnay del Piemonte Viticoltori
dell'Acquese (WCL)
Moscato d'Asti Chiarlo (WAI)
1992
Moscato d'Asti Chiarlo (NI)

£6.00 to £7.99
1993
Favorita Deltetto (WCL)
1992
Favorita Deltetto (WCL)
1991
Gavi dei Gavi, la Scolca (DI)
1990
Gavi Fontanafredda (ROB)

£8.00 to £9.99
1993
Arneis del Piemonte San Michel, Deltetto
(WCL)
1992
Arneis del Piemonte Renesio, Damonte (AD)
Favorita Malvira (AD)
Moscato d'Asti la Spinetta-Rivetti (AD)

£10.00 to £19.99
1992
Arneis Blange Ceretto (VA)
Gavi dei Gavi, la Scolca (ROB)
1991
Arneis Blange Ceretto (ROB)
Chardonnay Rossj Bass, Gaja (VA)

£20.00 to £29.99
1989
Chardonnay Ca' del Bosco (ROB, WCL)
1988
Chardonnay Rossj Bass, Gaja (TW)

NORTH-WEST SPARKLING

Under £6.00
Non-vintage
Asti Spumante Baldovino (PLA)
Asti Spumante Martini (HOG, SAF, TES, POR)
Asti Spumante Sandro (WAT)
Gancia Spumante (VA)

£6.00 to £6.99
Non-vintage
Asti Spumante Martini (PLA, WAI, SO, BOT,
  WR, THR, WRI, UN, DAV, VIC, OD)
Gancia Pinot di Pinot (VA)

£7.00 to £7.99
Non-vintage
Asti Spumante Fontanafredda (VA)
Asti Spumante Martini (TAN, EL, VIN)

£10.00 to £14.99
1988
Mompiano Spumante Brut Pasolini (POR,
  WCL)

c. £25.00
Non-vintage
Franciacorta Brut, Ca' del Bosco (VA)

NORTH-EAST RED

Under £4.00
1992
Valpolicella Zonin (NA)
1991
Valpolicella Classico Negarine (SAI)

£4.00 to £4.99
1993
★ Bardolino Classico Ca' Bordenis (HOG)
Bardolino Portalupi (VA)
★ Valpolicella Classico Allegrini (WCL)

> *Stars (★) indicate wines
> selected by the editors as
> particularly good value
> in their class.*

1992

Bardolino Classico Superiore Masi (PIP)

★ Bardolino Classico Superiore Rizzardi (GRE)

★ Teroldego Rotaliano Gaierhof (WAI)

Valpolicella Classico Allegrini (POR)

Valpolicella Classico Superiore Masi (PIP)

Valpolicella Classico Superiore Rizzardi (GRE)

Valpolicella Classico Superiore Zenato (THR, WR, BOT)

1991

Bardolino Classico Superiore Masi (DI)

Bardolino Classico Superiore Rizzardi (HOG)

Valpolicella Classico Castello d'Illasi, Santi (HOG)

Valpolicella Classico Superiore Masi (DI)

Valpolicella Classico Superiore Rizzardi (HOG)

Valpolicella Classico Superiore Zenato (DAV)

1990

Valpolicella Classico Masi (OD)

Valpolicella Classico Superiore Villa Girardi (NI)

1989

Valpolicella Classico Superiore Masi (BY)

£5.00 to £5.99

1992

Bardolino Classico Ca' Bordenis (TAN)

Marzemino del Trentino Letrari (WS)

Molinara Quintarelli (BIB)

Valpolicella Classico Allegrini (GAL)

1991

Valpolicella Classico Castello d'Illasi, Santi (TAN)

1990

Maso Lodron Letrari (WS)

★ Valpolicella Classico Superiore Valverde, Tedeschi (AD)

Valpolicella Classico Tedeschi (LAY)

1989

★ Campo Fiorin Masi (OD)

1988

Valpolicella Classico Tedeschi (BEN)

£6.00 to £7.99

1992

★ Recioto della Valpolicella Classico Quintarelli (LEA)

1991

Bardolino Classico Superiore Rizzardi (ROB)

Teroldego Rotaliano Vigneto Pini, Zeni (DI)

1990

Cabernet Grave del Friuli, Collavini (VA)

Valpolicella Classico Palazzo della Torre, Allegrini (POR)

★ Valpolicella Classico Superiore La Grola, Allegrini (WS)

1989

Campo Fiorin Masi (PIP, VA)

Lagrein Dunkel Viticoltori Alto Adige (VA)

1988

Campo Fiorin Masi (NO, DI)

Castello Guerrieri (HOG)

Valpolicella Classico Superiore La Grola, Allegrini (POR)

1986

Valpolicella Classico Superiore La Grola, Allegrini (WAT)

£8.00 to £9.99

1991

Valpolicella Classico la Grola, Allegrini (WCL)

Valpolicella Classico Palazzo della Torre, Allegrini (WCL)

1990

★ Cabernet Sauvignon Puiatti (WCL)

Campo Fiorin Masi (LAY)

Palazzo della Torre, Allegrini (VA)

★ Pinot Nero Puiatti (WCL)

Valpolicella Classico la Grola, Allegrini (NO, VA)

Valpolicella Classico Superiore La Grola, Allegrini (BEN)

1989

Recioto Amarone Montresor (HOG)

Venegazzù della Casa Loredan-Gasparini (GRE, VA)

1988

Valpolicella Classico Palazzo della Torre, Allegrini (GAU, GAL)

1987

Valpolicella Classico Quintarelli (BIB)

Venegazzù della Casa Loredan-Gasparini (ROB)

1986

★ Recioto Amarone Zenato (VA)

1985

Recioto Amarone Negrar (EL)

£10.00 to £12.99

1990

Recioto Classico della Valpolicella Allegrini (WCL)

1988

Recioto Amarone Montresor (VA)

Recioto Amarone Tedeschi (DI, ROB)

Valpolicella Classico Superiore Quintarelli (AD)

1986
Recioto Amarone della Valpolicella
Allegrini (TAN, WS, AME, LEA)
1985
Recioto Amarone Bolla (VA)
Recioto Amarone Le Ragose (GRE)

£13.00 to £14.99
1986
Venegazzù della Casa Black Label,
Loredan-Gasparini (VA)
1978
Recioto Amarone Quintarelli (AS)

£15.00 to £19.99
1989
Recioto Amarone Masi (DI)
1988
Recioto Amarone Mezzanella, Masi (PIP)
Recioto Classico Capitel Monte Fontana,
Tedeschi (DI)
1986
La Poja, Allegrini (POR)
1985
Recioto Amarone Fieramonte, Allegrini
(WCL, VA)
Recioto Amarone Tedeschi (AD)

£30.00 to £34.99
1983
Recioto della Valpolicella Quintarelli
(WCL)
1979
Recioto della Valpolicella Classico
Quintarelli (AD)
Recioto della Valpolicella Riserva
Quintarelli (RAE)

NORTH-EAST WHITE

Under £4.00
1993
Lugana Santi (SAF)
Pinot Grigio Ca' Donini (VIC)
1992
Chardonnay Ca' Donini (ROB, WHI)
Soave Zonin (NA)
1990
Pinot Grigio Ca'vit (ROB)

£4.00 to £4.99
1993
Pinot Grigio Ca'vit (LO, TAN)
★ Soave Classico Superiore Masi (PIP)
Soave Classico Zenato (DAV)

1992
Lugana di San Benedetto, Zenato (SAI)
Pinot Grigio Ca' Donini (WHI, BAR)
Soave Classico Zenato (ASD, WAI)
1991
Soave Classico di Monteforte Santi (ROB)
Soave Classico Superiore Masi (DI)
1990
★ Pinot Grigio Tiefenbrunner (TES)

£5.00 to £5.99
1993
Lugana di San Benedetto, Zenato (DAV)
Soave Classico Tedeschi (LAY)
1992
Chardonnay Tiefenbrunner (AD)
Lugana Cà dei Frati (SOM)
Pinot Grigio Tiefenbrunner (WHI)
Soave Classico di Monteforte Santi (TAN)
★Soave Classico Monte Tenda, Tedeschi (AD)
Soave Classico Superiore Anselmi (GRE)
Soave Classico Tedeschi (BEN)
1991
Lugana Cà dei Frati (POR)
Soave Classico Pieropan (GRE)
Soave Classico Superiore Masi (REI)
Soave Classico Superiore Pieropan (POR)
1990
Chardonnay Tiefenbrunner (WHI)

£6.00 to £7.99
1993
Chardonnay EnoFriulia (WCL)
Chardonnay Lageder (NI)
Lugana Cà dei Frati, Dal Cero (WCL, BEN)
Pinot Grigio EnoFriulia (WCL)
Soave Classico Monte Carbonara, Tessari (AD)
Soave Classico Pieropan (WCL, BEN)
Soave Classico Superiore Anselmi (VA)
Soave Classico Superiore Pieropan (VA)
Tocai EnoFriulia (WCL)
1992
Chardonnay EnoFriulia (PIP)
Chardonnay Tiefenbrunner (TAN)
Gewürztraminer Tiefenbrunner (AD)
Lugana Cà dei Frati, Dal Cero (VA, LAY, TAN)
★ Pinot Grigio Collio, Puiatti (SOM)
Pinot Grigio Sortesele (BAR)
Soave Classico Col Baraca, Masi (PIP, VA)
Soave Classico Monte Carbonare, Di
Suavia (BIB)
Soave Classico Vigneto Calvarino,
Pieropan (EY, WCL, LAY)
Soave Classico Vigneto la Rocca, Pieropan
(AME)

1991
Pinot Grigio Lageder (BY, HIC)
Soave Classico Superiore Pieropan (SUM)
Soave Classico Vigneto la Rocca, Pieropan (WS)
1990
Chardonnay Vinattieri (BY)
Lugana Cà dei Frati, Dal Cero (GAL)
Soave Classico Superiore Pieropan (GAL)
Soave Classico Vigneto Calvarino, Pieropan (GAU)
1989
Lugana Cà dei Frati, Dal Cero (GAU)

£8.00 to £9.99

1993
Chardonnay Collio, Puiatti (WCL)
Pinot Bianco Collio, Puiatti (WCL)
Pinot Grigio Collio, Puiatti (WCL)
Sauvignon Collio, Puiatti (WCL)
1992
Chardonnay Collio, Puiatti (WCL)
Lugana Cà dei Frati (LEA)
Pinot Bianco Collio, Puiatti (LEA)
Pinot Bianco Jermann (NI)
Soave Classico Capitel Foscarino, Anselmi (VA)
1991
Soave Classico Vigneto la Rocca, Pieropan (AD, GRE, WCL, BEN)
1990
Soave Classico Vigneto la Rocca, Pieropan (GAU)
1989
Recioto di Soave Capitelli, Anselmi (OD)
1988
Recioto di Soave Capitelli, Anselmi (ROB)
Torcolato Vino Liquoroso Maculan (ROB)

£10.00 to £11.99

1992
Pinot Bianco Collio, Puiatti (BEN)
Pinot Bianco Jermann (VA)
Pinot Grigio Collio, Puiatti (BEN, NO)
Pinot Grigio Jermann (BAR)
1991
Pinot Grigio Collio, Puiatti (SEC)
Riesling Renano Collio, Puiatti (WCL)

> *In each price band wines*
> *are listed in vintage order.*
> *Within each vintage they*
> *are listed in A–Z order.*

1990
Pinot Bianco Collio, Puiatti (GAU)
Pinot Grigio Collio, Puiatti (GAU)
Ribolla Collio, Puiatti (WCL)
1989
Pinot Bianco Collio, Puiatti (WCL)

£12.00 to £14.99

1992
Pinot Grigio Collio, Felluga (VA)
1990
Chardonnay Jermann (REI)
Recioto di Soave le Colombare, Pieropan (WCL)

£15.00 to £24.99

1992
Vintage Tunina, Jermann (VA)
1988
Torcolato Vino Liquoroso Maculan (AD)
1987
Recioto di Soave Capitelli, Anselmi (BY)
1983
Vin de la Fabriseria Tedeschi (AD)

NORTH-EAST ROSÉ

c. £4.50

1993
Bardolino Chiaretto, Portalupi (VA)

NORTH-EAST SPARKLING

Under £8.00

Non-vintage
Alionza Frizzante di Castelfranco (BOD, WIC)
Prosecco di Conegliano Carpenè Malvolti (VA, LEA)

£14.00 to £17.49

Non-vintage
Berlucchi Brut (VA)
Ferrari Brut (VA)

CENTRAL RED

Under £4.50

1992
Chianti Rufina Tenuta di Remole, Frescobaldi (HOG)
★ Rosso Conero San Lorenzo, Umani Ronchi (NI)
Rosso Conero Umani Ronchi (WAI)

1991
★ Chianti Rufina Villa di Vetrice (GRE, AME, PIP, VA, WCL, WW)
★ Rosso Conero San Lorenzo, Umani Ronchi (VIC)
1990
★ Chianti Rufina Villa di Vetrice (SOM, ROB)
★ Parrina Rosso La Parrina (POR)

£4.50 to £4.99

1992
Chianti Classico Aziano, Ruffino (HOG)
Chianti Fattoria di Gracciano (BIB)
Chianti Rufina Riserva Tenuta di Remole, Frescobaldi (AMI)
Santa Cristina, Antinori (GRE, THR, VIC, WR, BOT)

1991
★ Chianti Classico Rocca delle Macie (MAJ, SAF, DAV)
Chianti Classico Ruffino (VA)
★ Chianti Rufina Riserva Villa di Vetrice (BAR)
Parrina Rosso La Parrina (AME, BAR, VA, WCL)
1990
Chianti Classico Rocca delle Macie (WAI)
Chianti Rufina Riserva Villa di Vetrice (THR, WR, BOT, AME)
Chianti Rufina Villa di Vetrice (HAH)
Parrina Rosso La Parrina (HAM, GAU)
1988
Chianti Rufina Riserva Villa di Vetrice (WCL)
Montefalco Rosso d'Arquata Adanti (OD)

£5.00 to £5.99

1992
★ Carmignano Barco Reale, Capezzana (WCL)
Chianti Classico Rocca delle Macie (NI)
Chianti Rufina Riserva Tenuta di Remole, Frescobaldi (VA)
Rosso di Montalcino Campo ai Sassi, Frescobaldi (AMI)
Santa Cristina, Antinori (LAY)

1991
Carmignano Barco Reale, Capezzana (SOM, ROB, AME)
Chianti Classico Castello Vicchiomaggio (LO)
Chianti Classico la Lellera, Matta (EL)
Chianti Classico Rocca delle Macie (VIG)
Chianti Classico San Felice (HOG)
Chianti Classico San Jacopo, Vicchiomaggio (PEN)
Chianti Classico Viticcio Landini (GAL)
Chianti Rufina Selvapiana (WCL)
Parrina Rosso La Parrina (LAY, BEN)
Rosso Conero San Lorenzo, Umani Ronchi (VA, GRE)
Rosso Conero San Lorenzo, Umani Ronchi (TAN)
Rosso di Montalcino Altesino (POR)
Rosso di Montalcino Campo ai Sassi, Frescobaldi (WAI)
1990
Chianti Classico Castello Vicchiomaggio (VIC)
Chianti Rufina Riserva Selvapiana (POR)
Chianti Rufina Selvapiana (THR, WR, BOT)
1989
Chianti Classico Felsina Berardenga (SOM)
Chianti Classico Villa Antinori (HOG)
Morellino di Scansano Poggio Valente (GAU)
Vino Nobile di Montepulciano Cerro (HOG)
1988
Chianti Rufina Riserva Villa di Vetrice (GAU)
Parrina Reserva, La Parrina (SOM)
Rosso Conero San Lorenzo, Umani Ronchi (BOT, WR, THR)

£6.00 to £6.99

1993
Carmignano Barco Reale, Capezzana (AD)
1992
Carmignano Barco Reale, Capezzana (DI)
Chianti Classico San Jacopo, Vicchiomaggio (DI)
Santa Cristina, Antinori (BUT)

1991
Chianti Classico Castello di Fonterutoli
(LEA)
Chianti Classico Castello di Volpaia (EY,
AD)
Chianti Classico Fontodi (WS)
Chianti Classico San Felice (GRE)
Chianti Rufina Selvapiana (DI, AD)
1990
Chianti Classico Rocca delle Macie (AV)
Chianti Classico Villa Banfi (PEN)
Chianti Classico Villa Cafaggio (GE)
Parrina Reserva, La Parrina (BAR)
Rubesco Torgiano Lungarotti (ROB)
1989
Chianti Classico Isole e Olena (WCL)
Chianti Classico Riserva Castello di
Nipozzano, Frescobaldi (HOG)
Chianti Classico Riserva Ducale, Ruffino
(HOG)
Chianti Classico Riserva Rocca delle Macie
(CV)
Chianti Classico Riserva Villa Antinori
(GRE, THR, BOT, WR, LAY, SAI, VA)
Chianti Classico Villa Antinori (MAJ)
Vino Nobile di Montepulciano Cerro (DI)
Vino Nobile di Montepulciano di Casale
(SAI)
1988
★ Carmignano Villa Capezzana (SOM)
Chianti Classico Riserva Rocca delle Macie
(WAI)
Chianti Classico Villa Antinori (DI)
Parrina Reserva, La Parrina (EY, OD)
1985
Chianti Rufina Riserva Villa di Vetrice
(AD, BY, WCL, GAU, GAL, BEN)
1980
Chianti Rufina Riserva Selvapiana (WCL)

£7.00 to £7.99
1992
★ Brusco dei Barbi Fattoria dei Barbi (BU)
Ornellaia Le Volte, Tenuta dell'Ornellaia
(AME)
Rosso di Montalcino Talenti (BIB)
1991
Chianti Classico Castello di Volpaia
(WCL)
Chianti Classico Felsina Berardenga (PIP,
AME, VA, WCL)
Chianti Classico Fontodi (BOT, WR)
Chianti Classico Isole e Olena (SOM)
Ornellaia Le Volte, Tenuta dell'Ornellaia
(POR, WCL)

1990
Carmignano Villa Capezzana (WS)
Chianti Classico Castello di Fonterutoli (WS)
Chianti Classico Castello di San Polo in
Rosso (AD)
Chianti Classico Felsina Berardenga (SEC)
Chianti Classico Isole e Olena (POR)
Chianti Classico Villa Cafaggio (WRI)
Chianti Rufina Selvapiana (BER)
Parrina Reserva, La Parrina (BEN)
Pomino Rosso Frescobaldi (VIC)
Rosso di Montalcino il Poggione (AD)
Vino Nobile di Montepulciano Riserva, Bigi
(GRE)
1989
Chianti Classico Isole e Olena (HAH)
Chianti Classico Riserva Antinori (LO)
Chianti Classico Riserva Villa Antinori
(BUT, LEA)
Chianti Classico Villa Antinori (TAN)
Chianti Rufina Castello di Nipozzano (VA)
Grifi Avignonesi (WAI)
Rubesco Torgiano Lungarotti (TAN)
Ser Gioveto, Rocca delle Macie (GRE, VA)
Vino Nobile di Montepulciano Bigi (VA)
Vino Nobile di Montepulciano Cerro (PE)
Vino Nobile di Montepulciano le Casalte (SOM)

1988
Chianti Classico Castello di Cacchiano
(GAU)
Chianti Classico Riserva Rocca delle Macie
(BAR, VIG)
Chianti Classico Riserva Villa Antinori
(NO)
Chianti Classico Villa Antinori (BUT)
Chianti Rufina Riserva Castello di
Nipozzano (ROB)
Chianti Rufina Riserva Selvapiana (WCL,
VA)
Parrina Reserva, La Parrina (GAU)
Rubesco Torgiano Lungarotti (HAH)
Vino Nobile di Montepulciano Riserva,
Cerro (AMI)

1987
Chianti Classico Castell'in Villa (CB)
Chianti Classico Felsina Berardenga (BOT, WR)
Chianti Rufina Riserva Castello di Nipozzano (WHI)
Morellino di Scansano Riserva, le Pupille (WS)
1986
Vino Nobile di Montepulciano Bigi (PEN)
1985
Chianti Classico Riserva Montagliari (WS)
Chianti Classico Riserva Villa Antinori (BUT)

£8.00 to £8.99

1992
Chianti Classico Isole e Olena (WCL, VA)
Chianti Classico Riserva Isole e Olena (LEA)
Ornellaia Le Volte, Tenuta dell'Ornellaia (VA)
1991
Chianti Classico Fontodi (WCL)

Chianti Classico Isole e Olena (WCL)
Ornellaia Le Volte, Tenuta dell'Ornellaia (PIP, BEN, LEA, REI)
Vino Nobile di Montepulciano le Casalte (WS)
1990
Carmignano Riserva, Villa Capezzana (BAR)
Chianti Classico Castello di Ama (WS)
Chianti Classico Isole e Olena (HAM)
Chianti Classico Pèppoli, Antinori (VA)
Chianti Rufina Riserva Selvapiana (WS)
Pomino Rosso Frescobaldi (AMI)
1989
Chianti Classico Isole e Olena (ROB)
Chianti Classico Pèppoli, Antinori (GRE)
Chianti Rufina Riserva Castello di Nipozzano (UN)
Vino Nobile di Montepulciano Baiocchi (WRI)
Vino Nobile di Montepulciano le Casalte (NO)

1988
Carmignano Villa Capezzana (AME, WCL)
Chianti Classico Isole e Olena (HIC)
Chianti Classico Riserva Castello di Volpaia (AD)
Chianti Classico Riserva di Fizzano, Rocca delle Macie (VA)
Chianti Classico Riserva Villa Banfi (PEN)
Ser Gioveto, Rocca delle Macie (NI)
Vino Nobile di Montepulciano Bigi (VIG)
1987
Chianti Classico Riserva di Fizzano, Rocca delle Macie (GRE, SO)
1986
Vino Nobile di Montepulciano Giovanni di Nicolo (NO)
1985
Carmignano Villa Capezzana (NO)

£9.00 to £9.99

1992
Chianti Classico Isole e Olena (BEN)
1990
Chianti Classico Isole e Olena (NI)
Chianti Classico Pèppoli, Antinori (WCL, LAY)
Chianti Classico Riserva Pèppoli, Antinori (TAN)
Vino Nobile di Montepulciano le Casalte (AD, AME, WCL, BEN)
1989
Chianti Classico Pèppoli, Antinori (WR, THR, BOT)
Chianti Classico Riserva Marchese Antinori (GRE)
Vino Nobile di Montepulciano Bindella (BIB)
Vino Nobile di Montepulciano le Casalte (TAN)
1988
Brunello di Montalcino Castelgiocondo (HOG)
Chianti Classico Castello di Cacchiano (BER)
Chianti Classico Riserva di Fizzano, Rocca delle Macie (VIG)
Chianti Classico Riserva Ducale, Ruffino (HOG)
1986
Chianti Classico Riserva Badia a Coltibuono (AME)
Chianti Classico Riserva Monsanto (RAE)
1985
Vino Nobile di Montepulciano Avignonesi (WAT)
1977
Chianti Rufina Riserva Villa di Vetrice (GAU)

£10.00 to £11.99

1990
Palazzo Altesi, Altesino (POR)
1989
Chianti Classico Castello di Volpaia (ROB)
1988
Brunello di Montalcino Castelgiocondo
(GRE, VA)
Carmignano Riserva, Villa Capezzana (WCL)
Chianti Classico Riserva Castello di
Volpaia (ROB)
Chianti Classico Riserva Fontodi (BEN)
Morellino di Scansano Riserva, le Pupille
(VA)
Vino Nobile di Montepulciano Trerose (DI)
1987
Chianti Classico Riserva Castello di
Cacchiano (WCL)
1986
Brunello di Montalcino Castelgiocondo (CV)
Chianti Classico Riserva Felsina
Berardenga (BER)
Chianti Classico Riserva Marchese
Antinori (DI)
Grifi Avignonesi (WAT)
Vino Nobile di Montepulciano Avignonesi
(WCL, VA)
1985
Ca' del Pazzo Caparzo (GRE)
Ghiaie della Furba, Capezzana (NO)
Tavernelle Villa Banfi (NO)

£12.00 to £14.99

1990
Cepparello, Isole e Olena (SOM)
Chianti Classico Riecine (WCL)
Palazzo Altesi, Altesino (DI)
Prunaio di Viticcio Landini (GAL)
1989
Brunello di Montalcino Argiano (WCL)
Cepparello, Isole e Olena (POR)
Tavernelle Villa Banfi (PEN)
1988
Brunello di Montalcino Altesino (POR, BY)
Brunello di Montalcino Argiano (WS, AME,
PIP, WCL)
Brunello di Montalcino Castelgiocondo (UN)
Brunello di Montalcino Fattoria dei Barbi
(GRE)
Brunello di Montalcino il Poggione (AD)
Brunello di Montalcino Talenti (BIB)
Brunello di Montalcino Val di Suga (DI)
Carmignano Riserva, Villa Capezzana (TAN)
Chianti Classico Riserva Vigneto Rancia,
Felsina Berardenga (WCL, BEN)

Coltassala Castello di Volpaia (AD)
Fontalloro, Felsina Berardenga (BY, WCL)
Grifi Avignonesi (REI)
Mormoreto Predicato di Biturica,
Frescobaldi (AMI)
Palazzo Altesi, Altesino (GAU)
I Sodi di San Niccolò, Castellare (AMI)
1987
Balifico Castello di Volpaia (AD)
Brunello di Montalcino Talenti (BIB)
1986
Cepparello, Isole e Olena (GAU)
Fontalloro, Felsina Berardenga (WCL)
Sangioveto Badia a Coltibuono (AD)
1985
Balifico Castello di Volpaia (BUT)
Bongoverno Farneta (NO)
Carmignano Riserva, Villa Capezzana (HAM)
La Corte, Castello di Querceto (RE)
Sangioveto Badia a Coltibuono (NO)
1983
Chianti Classico Riserva Rocca delle Macie
(BUT)
1981
Chianti Classico Riserva Monsanto (RAE)

£15.00 to £19.99

1991
Syrah Isole e Olena (WCL)
1990
Cabernet Sauvignon Isole e Olena (WCL)
Cepparello, Isole e Olena (WS, BAR, VA, WCL,
BEN)
Flaccianello della Pieve, Fontodi (BOT, WR,
BAR, WCL)
Quercia Grande, Capaccia (VA, OD)
Solatio Basilica Villa Cafaggio (GE)
Syrah Isole e Olena (WCL)
1989
Ornellaia Tenuta dell'Ornellaia (NO)
1988
Brunello di Montalcino Argiano (PE)
Brunello di Montalcino Poggio Antico (ROB)
Brunello di Montalcino Villa Banfi (PEN)
Ca' del Pazzo Caparzo (VA)
Cepparello, Isole e Olena (GAU, LEA, CB)
Chianti Classico Riecine (WCL)
Chianti Classico Riserva Riecine (WCL)
Chianti Rufina Montesodi, Frescobaldi (WCL)
Chianti Rufina Riserva Montesodi,
Frescobaldi (AMI)
I Sodi di San Niccolò, Castellare (DI, AD)
Solatio Basilica Villa Cafaggio (GE)
1987
Brunello di Montalcino Barbi (VIG)

1986
Coltassala Castello di Volpaia (VIG)
Fontalloro, Felsina Berardenga (BER)
Tignanello Antinori (GAU)
1985
Chianti Classico Castello Vicchiomaggio
(VIG)
Chianti Rufina Montesodi, Frescobaldi
(WHI, VA)
Tignanello Antinori (HOG)
1981
Tignanello Antinori (BUT)
1974
Chianti Classico Riserva Monsanto (RAE)

£20.00 to £24.99
1991
Ornellaia Tenuta dell'Ornellaia (WCL, DI,
BEN)
1990
Ornellaia Tenuta dell'Ornellaia (PIP, VA,
REI, POR, LEA)
Tignanello Antinori (LAY)
1989
Tignanello Antinori (WCL, VA, TAN, BER)
1988
Le Pergole Torte, Monte Vertine (VA)
Tignanello Antinori (THR, BOT, WR, HAH,
ROB, NO, BUT)
1987
Cabreo Predicato di Biturica Ruffino (VA)
Tignanello Antinori (DI)
1985
Brunello di Montalcino la Casa, Caparzo
(AMI)
Tignanello Antinori (BUT)
1982
Tignanello Antinori (BUT)

£25.00 to £34.99
1991
Sassicaia Incisa della Rocchetta (LAY)
1990
Grosso Senese, Il Palazzino (BU)
Ornellaia Tenuta dell'Ornellaia (BEN)
1989
Sassicaia Incisa della Rocchetta (VA, ROB)
1987
Sassicaia Incisa della Rocchetta (TAN, DI, BUT)
1986
Sassicaia Incisa della Rocchetta (GRE, GAU)
1985
Tignanello Antinori (NO)
1974
Rubesco Torgiano Lungarotti (RE)

£40.00 to £49.99
1990
Sassicaia Incisa della Rocchetta (REI, ROB,
VA, BEN, LEA, NO, BUT, CB)
1988
Sassicaia Incisa della Rocchetta (BUT)
Solaia Antinori (ROB, LAY)
1987
Solaia Antinori (DI)
1986
Solaia Antinori (WCL, CB)
1985
Sassicaia Incisa della Rocchetta (BUT)
Solaia Antinori (BUT)
1982
Sassicaia Incisa della Rocchetta (BUT)
1980
Sassicaia Incisa della Rocchetta (RE)
1977
Tignanello Antinori (RE)

£50.00 to £59.99
1982
Solaia Antinori (BUT)
1976
Sassicaia Incisa della Rocchetta (BUT)

c. £74.00
1977
Brunello di Montalcino Biondi-Santi (VA)

c. £106.00
1975
Brunello di Montalcino Biondi-Santi (VA)

CENTRAL WHITE

Under £4.00
1993
Orvieto Secco Conte Vaselli (TES)
1991
★ Frascati Superiore Colli di Catone (OD)

£4.00 to £4.49
1993
Orvieto Classico Amabile Bigi (VA)
Orvieto Secco Bigi (VA)
Verdicchio dei Castelli di Jesi Classico,
Umani Ronchi (VA)
1992
Frascati Superiore Gotto d'Oro (LO)
Frascati Superiore Monteporzio (HOG)
Galestro Antinori (HOG)
Orvieto Classico Abboccato Antinori (HOG)
Orvieto Classico Secco Antinori (HOG)

£4.50 to £4.99

1993
Frascati Superiore Gotto d'Oro (LAY)
Frascati Superiore Monteporzio (VA)
Galestro Antinori (BOT, THR, VA, WR)
★ Orvieto Classico Abboccato Antinori
(GRE)
Orvieto Classico Antinori (DAV)
Orvieto Classico Secco Antinori (GRE, WS,
WR, THR, BOT)
Verdicchio dei Castelli di Jesi, Brunori (BIB)
1992
Frascati Superiore Monteporzio (WAT)
Frascati Superiore Villa di Catone (WHI,
HAM)
Orvieto Classico Abboccato Antinori (ROB,
WR, BOT, THR)
Orvieto Secco Antinori (LO)
Vernaccia di San Gimignano San Quirico
(SAI)
1991
Orvieto Classico Amabile Bigi (WHI)
Orvieto Classico Secco Bigi (WHI)

£5.00 to £5.99

1993
Bianco Villa Antinori (LAY, THR, WR, BOT)
Frascati Superiore Colli di Catone (PIP)
Frascati Superiore Satinata, Colle di
Catone (AME)
Orvieto Classico Abboccato Antinori
(LAY)
Orvieto Classico Secco Antinori (LAY)
Orvieto Secco Antinori (PIP)
Verdicchio dei Castelli di Jesi Classico,
Casal di Serra (VA)
1992
Bianco Villa Antinori (TAN, LEA)
Frascati Superiore Satinata, Colle di
Catone (DI)
Orvieto Classico Abboccato Antinori (TAN)
Orvieto Classico Secco Antinori (TAN)
Orvieto Classico Vigneto Torricella, Bigi
(VA, OD)
Verdicchio dei Castelli di Jesi Classico,
Casal di Serra (EL, BAR, NI)
Vernaccia di San Gimignano Falchini (WRI,
RAE)

In each price band wines
are listed in vintage order.
Within each vintage they
are listed in A–Z order.

1991
Bianco Villa Antinori (DI)
Galestro Antinori (DI)
Orvieto Secco Antinori (DI)
1990
Vernaccia di San Gimignano San Quirico
(AMI)

£6.00 to £6.99

Non-vintage
★ Vin Santo Antinori (HOG, GRE)
1993
Frascati Superiore Satinata, Colle di
Catone (BEN)
Pomino Frescobaldi (VA)
Vernaccia di San Gimignano Teruzzi e
Puthod (WCL)
1992
Frascati Superiore Colli di Catone (NO)
Frascati Superiore Satinata, Colle di
Catone (EY, SEC, BY, WCL)
Orvieto Classico Vigneto Torricella, Bigi
(AD)
Pomino Frescobaldi (ROB)
Verdicchio dei Castelli di Jesi Classico,
Casal di Serra (VIC)
Verdicchio dei Castelli di Jesi Classico,
Fazi-Battaglia (TAN)
Vernaccia di San Gimignano Montenidoli
(BIB)
Vernaccia di San Gimignano Teruzzi e
Puthod (PIP, EY, HAM, BAR, HIC, ROB)
1991
Bianco Villa Antinori (HAH, BER)

£7.00 to £9.99

Non-vintage
Vin Santo Antinori (VA)
1993
Borro della Sala, Antinori (GRE)
Vernaccia di San Gimignano Teruzzi e
Puthod (BEN)
1992
Borro della Sala, Antinori (PIP)
Borro Lastricato Selvapiana (WCL)
Chardonnay Villa di Capezzana (WCL)
Pomino Frescobaldi (UN)
Vernaccia di San Gimignano Montenidoli
(AD)
1991
Borro della Sala, Antinori (WCL)
1990
Borro della Sala, Antinori (DI)
Orvieto Classico Terre Vineate, Il
Palazzone (WCL)

£10.00 to £12.49

1993
Vernaccia di San Gimignano Terre di Tufo,
Teruzzi e Puthod (WCL)
1992
Chardonnay I Sistri, Felsina Berardenga
(AME, WCL)
Chardonnay Isole e Olena (WCL)
1991
Chardonnay I Sistri, Felsina Berardenga
(HAM, LAY)
Vergena Sauvignon Blanc, Frescobaldi (AMI)
Vernaccia di San Gimignano Terre di Tufo,
Teruzzi e Puthod (SEC)
1990
Frascati Colle Gaio, Colli di Catone (WCL)
Frascati Superiore Colli di Catone (VA)
Pomino il Benefizio, Frescobaldi (AD, VA,
WCL, PIP)
1989
Pomino il Benefizio, Frescobaldi (AMI)
Vin Santo Antinori (GRE)

£12.50 to £14.99

1992
Chardonnay I Sistri, Felsina Berardenga
(BEN)
Vernaccia di San Gimignano Terre di Tufo,
Teruzzi e Puthod (BEN)
Vernaccia di San Gimignano Teruzzi e
Puthod (VA, LEA)
1991
Chardonnay I Sistri, Felsina Berardenga
(HIC)
1990
Chardonnay le Grance, Caparzo (AMI, LEA)
1989
Vin Santo Antinori (DI, LEA)
1987
Cabreo La Pietra Ruffino (HOG)
1986
Orvieto Classico Muffa Nobile, Barberani
(BU)
1979
Vin Santo Villa di Vetrice (WCL)

£15.00 to £19.99

1992
Cervaro della Sala, Antinori (LAY)
1991
Cervaro della Sala, Antinori (WCL)
1990
Cervaro della Sala, Antinori (VA)
1988
Vin Santo Selvapiana (LEA)

1987
Muffato della Sala, Antinori (RE)
1983
Orvieto Classico Pourriture Noble,
Decugnano dei Barbi (VIG)

CENTRAL ROSÉ

c. £7.00

1993
Carmignano Vinruspo Rosato, Capezzana
(WCL)

CENTRAL SPARKLING

Under £4.00

Non-vintage
Lambrusco Amabile Luigi Gavioli (HOG)
Lambrusco Bianco Ca' de Medici (WAI, WAT)
Lambrusco Ca' de Medici (WAI)
Lambrusco Grasparossa di Castelvetro (WAI)
Lambrusco San Prospero (GRE)

SOUTHERN RED

Under £4.00

1992
Montepulciano d'Abruzzo Umani Ronchi
(VIC)
1991
★ Cirò Classico Librandi (ASD)
★ Monica di Sardegna, C.S. di Dolianova
(WCL)
Montepulciano d'Abruzzo Bianchi (VA)
★ Settesoli Rosso (HOG)

£4.00 to £5.99

1992
Corvo Rosso Duca di Salaparuta (GRE)
Montepulciano d'Abruzzo Cornacchia (VA)
Montepulciano d'Abruzzo Umani Ronchi (NI)
1991
Corvo Rosso Duca di Salaparuta (HOG, TAN)
Montepulciano d'Abruzzo Illuminati (HOG)
Regaleali Rosso (GRE)
1990
Copertino Riserva, Cantina Copertina (DI,
VA, WCL)
Corvo Rosso Duca di Salaparuta (UN)
Regaleali Rosso (GE)
1989
Copertino Riserva, Cantina Copertino (BAR)
Salice Salentino Candido (OD, BAR, VA)
Salice Salentino Riserva Candido (PIP, AME,
WS, WCL, BEN)

1988
Salice Salentino Riserva Candido (POR, GE, SEC)
1987
Corvo Rosso Duca di Salaparuta (RE)

£6.00 to £8.99

1991
Corvo Rosso Duca di Salaparuta (DI)

Regaleali Rosso (PIP)
1990
Aglianico del Vulture, Fratelli d'Angelo
  (ROB, TAN)
Regaleali Rosso (TAN)
1989
Regaleali Rosso (DI, RE)

£10.00 to £14.99

1988
Regaleali Rosso del Conte (GE)
1977
Rosso Brindisi Patriglione, Taurino (WCL)

c. £20.00

1985
Montepulciano d'Abruzzo Valentini (WCL)

SOUTHERN WHITE

Under £4.00

1993
Settesoli Bianco (VA)
1992
Settesoli Bianco (HOG)
1991
Settesoli Bianco (ROB)

£4.00 to £5.99

1993
Corvo Bianco Duca di Salaparuta (VA)
Locorotondo (VA, WCL)
Regaleali Conte Tasca d'Almerita (VA)
Terre di Ginestra vdt (VA)

1992
Corvo Bianco Duca di Salaparuta (HOG, GRE)
Corvo Colomba Platino Bianco (HOG)
Regaleali Bianco (GRE)
Terre di Ginestra vdt (UN)
1991
Corvo Bianco Duca di Salaparuta (UN)
Pinot Bianco di Puglia, Vigna al Monte (AV)

£6.00 to £7.99

1992
Corvo Bianco Duca di Salaparuta (DI)
1991
Corvo Colomba Platino Bianco (DI)
Regaleali Bianco (DI, ROB)

£10.00 to £14.99

1991
Lacryma Christi del Vesuvio,
  Mastroberardino (DI)
1987
Trebbiano d'Abruzzo Valentini (WCL)

c. £18.00

1988
Corvo Bianco di Valguarnera Duca di
  Salaparuta (ROB)

SOUTHERN SPARKLING

c. £12.00

1992
Corvo Brut Cuve Close (VA)

SOUTHERN FORTIFIED

Under £8.50

Non-vintage
Josephine Dore de Bartoli (WCL, BEN)

£10.00 to £14.99

Non-vintage
Marsala Vigna la Miccia, de Bartoli (TAN, WCL)
Vecchio Samperi 10-year-old, de Bartoli
  (WCL, BEN)

£17.00 to £19.99

Non-vintage
Il Marsala 20-year-old de Bartoli (VA, WCL)
Vecchio Samperi 20-year-old, de Bartoli
  (VA, WCL)

c. £23.00

Non-vintage
Vecchio Samperi 30-year-old, de Bartoli (WCL)

SPAIN

RED

Under £3.50

Non-vintage
★ Vitorianas Don Darias, Vino de Mesa (TES, SAF)
★ Vitorianas Don Hugo, Alto Ebro, Vino de Mesa (WAI)
1990
Julián Chivite Gran Feudo, Navarra (HOG)
1987
★ Palacio de León, Vino de Mesa (VIC)

£3.50 to £3.99

1992
★ Felix Callejo Tinto F Callejo, Ribera del Duero (WAI)
1991
Fariña Colegiata, Toro (EL)
René Barbier, Penedés (PLA)
1990
El Coto, Rioja (DAV)
Fariña Colegiata, Toro (MAJ)
Torres Coronas, Penedés (HOG)
1989
Condé de Caralt, Penedés (MOR)
René Barbier, Penedés (CV)
★ Señorio de los Llanos Reserva, Valdepeñas (HOG, WS)
1988
Marqués de Murrieta Reserva, Rioja (WRI)
★ Señorio de los Llanos Reserva, Valdepeñas (NO)
★ Señorio de los Llanos, Valdepeñas (SOM)
1987
★ Señorio de los Llanos Reserva, Valdepeñas (TES)

£4.00 to £4.49

1992
Ochoa, Navarra (PLA)
1991
Ochoa, Navarra (EL)
Torres Sangredetoro, Penedés (TES, DI)
1990
Berberana Carta de Plata, Rioja (AME)
Marqués de Cáceres, Rioja (LO)
Torres Sangredetoro, Penedés (GRE)
1989
Fariña Colegiata, Toro (GAL)
Marqués de Cáceres, Rioja (HOG)
Torres Coronas, Penedés (TES)

1988
Julián Chivite Gran Feudo, Navarra (RE)
Julián Chivite Gran Fuedo Reserva, Navarra (HOG)
Señorio de los Llanos Reserva, Valdepeñas (GAL, ROB)
Señorio de Sarria, Navarra (GRE)

£4.50 to £4.99

1991
CVNE, Rioja (PLA)
Fariña Colegiata, Toro (DI)
1990
Berberana Carta de Oro, Rioja (NA)
CVNE, Rioja (CV, PEN, POR, WHI)
CVNE Viña Real, Rioja (CV)
El Coto Crianza, Rioja (ROB)
★ Fariña Gran Colegiata, Toro (OD)
1989
CVNE Viña Real, Rioja (MOR)
Marqués de Cáceres, Rioja (BE, CV, WHI, WS, GRE, DAV)
★ Raïmat Abadia, Costers del Segre (TES, VIC)

Siglo Saco, Rioja (GRE)
Torres Coronas, Penedés (EY, PEN, DI, CV, PE)
Torres Sangredetoro, Penedés (PEN)
1988
Campo Viejo Reserva, Rioja (VIC)
Campo Viejo, Rioja (WHI)
Señorio de los Llanos Reserva, Valdepeñas (LAY, BEN, RE)
Torres Gran Sangredetoro, Penedés (HOG)
1987
Campo Viejo Reserva, Rioja (THR, BOT, WR)
Condé de Caralt Reserva, Penedés (WCL)
Coto de Imaz Reserva, Rioja (DAV)
René Barbier Reserva, Penedés (PLA)
1986
Marius Tinto Reserva Piqueras, Almansa (HAM, LEA)

1985
Marius Tinto Reserva Piqueras, Almansa (RE)
1984
Señorio de los Llanos Gran Reserva, Valdepeñas (WS, MAJ)
Señorio de los Llanos Reserva, Valdepeñas (SOM)

£5.00 to £5.49

1990
★ Compania Vitivinicola Aragonesa Viñas del Vero Pinot Noir, Somontano (PLA)
CVNE, Rioja (BEK)
Marqués de Cáceres, Rioja (LAY)
★ Ochoa Tempranillo, Navarra (HOG)
Torres Coronas, Penedés (DAV, LAY)
1989
CVNE, Rioja (WAT)
★Fariña Gran Colegiata Reserva, Toro (TAN)
Fariña Gran Colegiata, Toro (EL)
Marqués de Cáceres, Rioja (EL, WCL, TAN, HAH, MOR)
Olarra Añares, Rioja (AS)
Raïmat Abadia, Costers del Segre (SAI)
Torres Coronas, Penedés (MOR)
Torres Gran Sangredetoro, Penedés (GRE, DI)
Torres Las Torres, Penedés (HOG)
1988
Cellers Scala Dei, Priorato (SOM)
CVNE Viña Real, Rioja (WHI)
1987
Berberana Reserva, Rioja (NA)
Condé de Caralt Reserva, Penedés (AME)
1986
Marius Tinto Reserva Piqueras, Almansa (TAN)
1984
Señorio de los Llanos Gran Reserva, Valdepeñas (PEN, BOR)
1980
Felix Solis Viña Albali Gran Reserva, Valdepeñas (SO)

£5.50 to £5.99

1991
Torres Las Torres, Penedés (DI)
1990
CVNE, Rioja (LAY, RE)
Felix Callejo Tinto F Callejo, Ribera del Duero (RES)
Ochoa Tempranillo, Navarra (PLA, CV, THR, WR, BOT, MOR)
Señorio de Sarria Cabernet Sauvignon, Navarra (GRE, GRE)

1989
Berberana Carta de Oro, Rioja (UN)
CVNE Viña Real, Rioja (ROB, RE, LEA, BIB)
Fariña Gran Colegiata, Toro (PE, AD, DI)
La Rioja Alta Viña Alberdi, Rioja (WAI)
Lan Crianza, Rioja (RE)
Ochoa Tempranillo, Navarra (MAJ)
Raïmat Abadia Reserva, Costers del Segre (HIC)
Raïmat Cabernet Sauvignon, Costers del Segre (WR, THR, BOT)
Torres Gran Sangredetoro, Penedés (LO, BOT, WR)
Torres Viña Magdala, Penedés (DI)
1988
Berberana Carta de Oro, Rioja (MOR)
Beronia, Rioja (PE)
Campo Viejo Reserva, Rioja (BEN)
Faustino V Reserva, Rioja (TES, GRE)
La Rioja Alta Viña Alberdi, Rioja (SOM)
Torres Gran Sangredetoro, Penedés (BE)
1987
La Rioja Alta Viña Alberdi, Rioja (POR)
Ochoa Cabernet Sauvignon, Navarra (HOG)
René Barbier Reserva, Penedés (ROB, RE)
★ Señorio de Nava Crianza, Ribera del Duero (SAF, ASD, FUL)
1986
Berberana Reserva, Rioja (MAJ)
Marqués de Cáceres Reserva, Rioja (LO)
1985
Beronia Reserva, Rioja (HOG)
Condé de Caralt Reserva, Penedés (WRI)
Ochoa Reserva, Navarra (HOG)
1984
René Barbier Reserva, Penedés (VIG)
Señorio de los Llanos Gran Reserva, Valdepeñas (PE, MOR, RE, BEN)

£6.00 to £6.49

1990
Ochoa Tempranillo, Navarra (EL, EY, AD, WCL, NO, REI)
1989
Compania Vitivinicola Aragonesa Viñas del Vero Pinot Noir, Somontano (SAF)
Ochoa Tempranillo, Navarra (WAT)
Torres Viña Magdala, Penedés (GRE, WHI)
1988
CVNE Viña Real, Rioja (VIG)
Faustino V Reserva, Rioja (WHI)
Marqués de Cáceres, Rioja (BER)
Marqués de Murrieta, Rioja (HOG)
Torres Gran Sangredetoro, Penedés (WRI, MOR)

1987
Berberana Reserva, Rioja (AME)
Señorio de Lazán Reserva Montesierra,
  Somontano (EL)
Señorio de Sarria Cabernet Sauvignon,
  Navarra (EL)
1986
Bodegas Riojanas Monte Real Reserva,
  Rioja (BY)
CVNE Reserva, Rioja (CV)
Marqués de Cáceres Reserva, Rioja (CV, HAH)

£6.50 to £6.99

1990
Compania Vitivinicola Aragonesa Viñas
  del Vero Pinot Noir, Somontano (BIB)
Ochoa Tempranillo, Navarra (TAN, RE, VIG)
1989
★ Felix Callejo Tinto F Callejo, Ribera del
  Duero (WS)
Raïmat Tempranillo, Costers del Segre (GRE)
Torres Las Torres, Penedés (ROB, PEN, MOR)
1988
Barón de Ley, Rioja (BOT)
Campo Viejo Gran Reserva, Rioja (OD)
La Rioja Alta Viña Alberdi, Rioja (DI, ROB)
La Rioja Alta Viña Ardanza Reserva, Rioja
  (NO)
Marqués de Riscal Reserva, Rioja (MOR, VIC)
Marqués de Riscal, Rioja (GRE)
Torres Gran Sangredetoro, Penedés (ROB)
Torres Mas Borras Pinot Noir, Penedés (GRE)
1987
Barón de Ley, Rioja (BOT, THR)
CVNE Reserva, Rioja (PLA)
CVNE Viña Real Reserva, Rioja (PIP)
Faustino V Reserva, Rioja (MOR)
Ochoa Cabernet Sauvignon, Navarra (CV)
Señorio de Sarria Cabernet Sauvignon,
  Navarra (WR)
1986
Barón de Ley, Rioja (WR)
Beronia Reserva, Rioja (OD)
CVNE Reserva, Rioja (PEN, WAT)
Torres Gran Sangredetoro, Penedés (GAU)
1985
Beronia Reserva, Rioja (RAE)
Campo Viejo Reserva, Rioja (RE)
Montecillo Gran Reserva, Rioja (OD)
Ochoa Reserva, Navarra (PLA, WAT, CV)
1983
Domecq Domain Reserva, Rioja (RE)
1982
Campo Viejo Gran Reserva, Rioja (VIC)
Ochoa Reserva, Navarra (PE)

£7.00 to £7.49

1989
Compania Vitivinicola Aragonesa Viñas
  del Vero Pinot Noir, Somontano (VIG)
1988
Marqués de Murrieta Reserva, Rioja (MAJ)
Marqués de Murrieta, Rioja (GRE)
Marqués de Riscal Reserva, Rioja (PEN)
Raïmat Merlot, Costers del Segre (GRE)
Torres Gran Coronas, Penedés (LO, BE)
1987
Bilbainas Viña Pomal Reserva, Rioja
  (SUM)
Marqués de Cáceres Reserva, Rioja (WHI)
Torres Gran Coronas, Penedés (PEN, EY)
1986
Fariña Gran Colegiata, Toro (VIG)
1985
CVNE Viña Real Reserva, Rioja (NO)
Ochoa Reserva, Navarra (BAR)
Raïmat Cabernet Sauvignon, Costers del
  Segre (GAU)
1984
Remelluri Reserva, Rioja (SOM)
1983
Olarra Cerro Anon Reserva, Rioja (RE)

£7.50 to £7.99

1989
Compania Vitivinicola Aragonesa Viñas
  del Vero Pinot Noir, Somontano (RE)
Raïmat Cabernet Sauvignon, Costers del
  Segre (GRE)
Raïmat Tempranillo, Costers del Segre
  (MOR)
1988
Contino Reserva, Rioja (PIP)
Faustino V Reserva, Rioja (RE)
Marqués de Riscal, Rioja (UN, PE)
Torres Gran Coronas Black Label (Mas La
  Plana), Penedés (SAI, DAV)
1987
Barón de Ley, Rioja (BAR)
CVNE Reserva, Rioja (LEA)
Ochoa Cabernet Sauvignon, Navarra (RE)
Torres Gran Coronas, Penedés (AMI, MOR)
1986
Barón de Ley, Rioja (RE)
CVNE Imperial Reserva, Rioja (PIP)
CVNE Reserva, Rioja (RE)
Marqués de Cáceres Reserva, Rioja (DI)
1985
Coto de Imaz Gran Reserva, Rioja (DAV)
CVNE Viña Real Reserva, Rioja (CV, WAT)
Ochoa Reserva, Navarra (RE, LEA)

1984
Bodegas Riojanas Monte Real Reserva,
  Rioja (MOR)
Contino Reserva, Rioja (CV)
Jean León Cabernet Sauvignon, Penedés (AMI)
Siglo Saco Gran Reserva, Rioja (GRE)
1982
Ochoa Reserva, Navarra (RE)
1981
Campo Viejo Gran Reserva, Rioja (SO)
Jean León Cabernet Sauvignon, Penedés (TAN)
1980
Campo Viejo Gran Reserva, Rioja (WHI)

£8.00 to £8.49

1989
Remelluri Reserva, Rioja (NO, WW)
Remelluri, Rioja (BIB)
1988
Marqués de Murrieta Reserva, Rioja (AD,
  WR, THR, BOT, AME)
Marqués de Murrieta, Rioja (WHI, WCL, BEN)
Muga Reserva, Rioja (EL)
Muga, Rioja (MOR)
Torres Gran Coronas, Penedés (HAH)
1987
CVNE Imperial Reserva, Rioja (CV)
Marqués de Murrieta Reserva, Rioja (WRI)
1986
Contino Reserva, Rioja (NO)
Faustino I Gran Reserva, Rioja (HOG)
La Rioja Alta Viña Arana, Rioja (HOG)
1985
CVNE Imperial Reserva, Rioja (POR)
CVNE Viña Real Gran Reserva, Rioja (PIP)
La Rioja Alta Viña Ardanza Reserva, Rioja
  (SOM)
1983
Berberana Gran Reserva, Rioja (AME)
1982
Marqués de Cáceres Gran Reserva, Rioja
  (CV, LO)
1981
CVNE Viña Real Reserva, Rioja (PLA)
Marqués de Cáceres Reserva, Rioja (PEN)

£8.50 to £8.99

1989
Remelluri, Rioja (TAN)
1988
Marqués de Murrieta Castillo Ygay Gran
  Reserva, Rioja (LAY)
Marqués de Murrieta Reserva, Rioja (MOR,
  PLA)
Marqués de Murrieta, Rioja (TAN, DAV)

1987
Contino Reserva, Rioja (CV)
Faustino I Gran Reserva, Rioja (GRE)
Marqués de Riscal Reserva, Rioja (RE)
Torres Viña Magdala, Penedés (RE)
1986
Contino Reserva, Rioja (PLA)
CVNE Imperial Gran Reserva, Rioja (MOR,
  PIP)
CVNE Imperial Reserva, Rioja (PLA, WS)
Faustino I Gran Reserva, Rioja (WHI)
La Rioja Alta Viña Arana, Rioja (WS)
La Rioja Alta Viña Ardanza Reserva, Rioja
  (HOG)
Marqués de Murrieta Reserva, Rioja (ROB)
1985
Contino Reserva, Rioja (PEN, CV)
CVNE Imperial Reserva, Rioja (WAT)
CVNE Viña Real Gran Reserva, Rioja (CV,
  PEN)
CVNE Viña Real Reserva, Rioja (RE)
Jean León Cabernet Sauvignon, Penedés (POR)
La Rioja Alta Viña Ardanza Reserva, Rioja
  (WS, POR)
Marqués de Cáceres Reserva, Rioja (RE)
Marqués de Murrieta Reserva, Rioja (RAE)
Mauro, Vino de Mesa (DAV)
Remelluri, Rioja (WS)
1984
Jean León Cabernet Sauvignon, Penedés (VIG)
1983
Berberana Gran Reserva, Rioja (DAV)
Lander Reserva, Rioja (RE)
1981
Contino Reserva, Rioja (CV)
CVNE Viña Real Reserva, Rioja (WS, CV)
Jean León Cabernet Sauvignon, Penedés
  (NO)
1980
Campo Viejo Gran Reserva, Rioja (MOR)
1978
Ochoa Reserva, Navarra (LEA)

£9.00 to £9.99

1991
Pesquera, Alejandro Fernandez, Ribera del
  Duero (OD)
1989
Marqués de Riscal Reserva, Rioja (BAR)
Pesquera, Alejandro Fernandez, Ribera del
  Duero (NI)
Remelluri Reserva, Rioja (MOR)
1988
Marqués de Murrieta Reserva, Rioja (NI,
  HAH)

1987
Contino Reserva, Rioja (EL, PLA, LAY)
CVNE Imperial Reserva, Rioja (AD, BAR)
Marqués de Griñon Cabernet Sauvignon,
  Rueda (GRE)
Priorato Extra, Masia Barril, Priorato (WCL)
Torres Gran Coronas, Penedés (RE)
1986
Contino Reserva, Rioja (WAT, VIC, WR, BOT,
  AD, MOR)
CVNE Imperial Reserva, Rioja (ROB, RE)
La Rioja Alta Viña Ardanza Reserva, Rioja
  (AD, AME, LAY)
Marqués de Griñon Cabernet Sauvignon,
  Rueda (NO)
Marqués de Murrieta Reserva, Rioja (PEN,
  RE)
Marqués de Murrieta, Rioja (AMI)
1985
CVNE Imperial Gran Reserva, Rioja (CV,
  PEN, POR, PIP)
CVNE Viña Real Gran Reserva, Rioja (GAL,
  PLA, ROB)
CVNE Viña Real Reserva, Rioja (BER)
La Rioja Alta Viña Ardanza Reserva, Rioja
  (GRE, SO, HAM, DI)
Marqués de Murrieta Reserva, Rioja (WRI)
Remelluri Reserva, Rioja (AD)
1984
Bodegas Riojanas Monte Real Reserva,
  Rioja (RE)
1983
Jean León Cabernet Sauvignon, Penedés
  (POR)
1982
CVNE Viña Real Gran Reserva, Rioja (CV)
CVNE Viña Real Reserva, Rioja (CV)
1981
Campo Viejo Gran Reserva, Rioja (RE)
CVNE Viña Real Gran Reserva, Rioja (CV)

£10.00 to £11.99

1990
Pesquera, Alejandro Fernandez, Ribera del
  Duero (ARM, TAN)
1988
Marqués de Griñon Cabernet Sauvignon,
  Rueda (WRI)
Pesquera, Alejandro Fernandez, Ribera del
  Duero (POR, AMI, PE)
Torres Mas Borras Pinot Noir, Penedés (DI,
  MOR, EY, PEN)
1987
Contino Reserva, Rioja (BIB, RE, LEA)
Faustino I Gran Reserva, Rioja (MOR)

1986
CVNE Imperial Gran Reserva, Rioja (TAN, BIB)
CVNE Imperial Reserva, Rioja (CB)
Faustino I Gran Reserva, Rioja (RE)
Marqués de Griñon Cabernet Sauvignon,
  Rueda (CB)
Marqués de Griñon Crianza, Rueda (MOR)
1985
Conde de la Salceda Gran Reserva, Rioja (TAN)
Contino Reserva, Rioja (BER, REI)
CVNE Imperial Gran Reserva, Rioja (REI,
  BIB, LEA, VIG)
CVNE Imperial Reserva, Rioja (GAL, BER)
CVNE Viña Real Gran Reserva, Rioja (RE,
  LEA, MOR, VIG)
Jean León Cabernet Sauvignon, Penedés (ROB)
La Rioja Alta Viña Arana Reserva, Rioja (RE)
La Rioja Alta Viña Ardanza Reserva, Rioja
  (MOR, BEN, RE, AMI)
Montecillo Gran Reserva, Rioja (RE, BAR)
Pesquera, Alejandro Fernandez, Ribera del
  Duero (NI)
1984
Marqués de Griñon Cabernet Sauvignon,
  Rueda (NO)
1982
Berberana Gran Reserva, Rioja (NA)
Contino Reserva, Rioja (CV)
CVNE Imperial Gran Reserva, Rioja (CV)
CVNE Imperial Reserva, Rioja (CV)
CVNE Viña Real Reserva, Rioja (GAL)
La Rioja Alta Viña Ardanza Reserva, Rioja
  (NO)
Marqués de Cáceres Gran Reserva, Rioja (DI)
Marqués de Cáceres Reserva, Rioja (MOR)
1981
CVNE Viña Real Reserva, Rioja (VIG)
1975
Bodegas Riojanas Monte Real Gran
  Reserva, Rioja (BY, MOR)
Bodegas Riojanas Viña Albina Gran
  Reserva, Rioja (MOR)
Marqués de Cáceres Gran Reserva, Rioja
  (CV)

£12.00 to £13.99

1990
Pesquera, Alejandro Fernandez, Ribera del
  Duero (ROB, HAM)
Pesquera Reserva, Alejandro Fernandez,
  Ribera del Duero (GRE)
1989
Pesquera Cosecha Especial, Alejandro
  Fernandez, Ribera del Duero (CB)
Remelluri, Rioja (RE)

1988
Pesquera Cosecha Especial, Alejandro
    Fernandez, Ribera del Duero (VIG)
Torres Mas Borras Pinot Noir, Penedés
    (GAU, RE)
1985
Julián Chivite Gran Fuedo Reserva,
    Navarra (MOR)
Marqués de Griñon Crianza, Rueda (RE)
Marqués de Murrieta Gran Reserva, Rioja
    (HAH)
Pesquera, Alejandro Fernandez, Ribera del
    Duero (BE)
1983
Marqués de Murrieta Gran Reserva, Rioja
    (HOG, MAJ)
Marqués de Murrieta, Rioja (GRE)
1982
Berberana Gran Reserva, Rioja (RE)
Conde de la Salceda Gran Reserva, Rioja
    (RE)
CVNE Imperial Gran Reserva, Rioja (LEA)
CVNE Imperial Reserva, Rioja (LEA)
CVNE Viña Real Gran Reserva, Rioja (VIG)
CVNE Viña Real Reserva, Rioja (VIG)
Jean León Cabernet Sauvignon, Penedés
    (PE)
La Rioja Alta Reserva 904 Gran Reserva,
    Rioja (SOM, HOG, POR)
1981
La Rioja Alta Reserva 904, Rioja (NO)
1980
Bilbainas Viña Pomal Gran Reserva, Rioja
    (SUM)
1979
Jean León Cabernet Sauvignon, Penedés
    (NO, POR)
1978
Bodegas Riojanas Viña Albina Gran
    Reserva, Rioja (RE)
1975
Berberana Gran Reserva, Rioja (BE)
1973
CVNE Viña Real Gran Reserva, Rioja (PLA,
    LEA)

£14.00 to £15.99
1988
Pesquera, Alejandro Fernandez, Ribera del
    Duero (RE)
Torres Gran Coronas Black Label (Mas La
    Plana), Penedés (VIG)
1987
Torres Gran Coronas Black Label (Mas La
    Plana), Penedés (HOG)

1983
La Rioja Alta Reserva 904 Gran Reserva,
    Rioja (WR, BOT, THR, LAY)
1982
CVNE Imperial Gran Reserva, Rioja (VIG)
CVNE Imperial Reserva, Rioja (VIG)
Jean León Cabernet Sauvignon, Penedés (POR)
La Rioja Alta Reserva 904 Gran Reserva,
    Rioja (BEN, PE)
1981
La Rioja Alta Reserva 904, Rioja (AMI)
1979
Jean León Cabernet Sauvignon, Penedés
    (REI, PEN, RE)
1978
Berberana Gran Reserva, Rioja (MOR)
Marqués de Murrieta Gran Reserva, Rioja
    (WCL)
1975
Berberana Gran Reserva, Rioja (RE)
Bodegas Riojanas Monte Real Gran
    Reserva, Rioja (RE)

£16.00 to £19.99
1988
Torres Gran Coronas Black Label (Mas La
    Plana), Penedés (CV)
1987
Torres Gran Coronas Black Label (Mas La
    Plana), Penedés (GRE, DI, NO, BU, EY)
Vega Sicilia 3rd year, Ribera del Duero (LAY)
1986
Vega Sicilia Valbuena 3rd year, Ribera del
    Duero (DI)
1985
Torres Gran Coronas Black Label (Mas La
    Plana), Penedés (GRE, NO, DI, PEN)
Vega Sicilia 3rd year, Ribera del Duero (NI)
Vega Sicilia Valbuena 3rd year, Ribera del
    Duero (PEN)
1984
Pesquera Reserva, Alejandro Fernandez,
    Ribera del Duero (VIG)
1983
Torres Gran Coronas Black Label (Mas La
    Plana), Penedés (NO, RAE, GRE, DI)
Vega Sicilia Valbuena 3rd year, Ribera del
    Duero (NO)
1982
Jean León Cabernet Sauvignon, Penedés (MOR)
La Rioja Alta Reserva 904 Gran Reserva,
    Rioja (RE, CB)
Marqués de Riscal Gran Reserva, Rioja (RE)
Torres Gran Coronas Black Label (Mas La
    Plana), Penedés (NO)

1978
Muga Prado Enea Reserva, Rioja (RE)
1975
Marqués de Murrieta Gran Reserva, Rioja
(MOR)

£20.00 to £29.99

1988
Vega Sicilia Valbuena 5th year, Ribera del
Duero (DI)
1985
Vega Sicilia Valbuena 5th year, Ribera del
Duero (DI)
1981
Torres Gran Coronas Black Label (Mas La
Plana), Penedés (NO)
1978
Marqués de Murrieta Gran Reserva, Rioja (CB)
Vega Sicilia Valbuena 5th year, Ribera del
Duero (NO)
1976
López de Heredia Viña Bosconia Gran
Reserva, Rioja (RE)
López de Heredia Viña Tondonia Gran
Reserva, Rioja (MOR, RE)
Torres Gran Coronas Black Label (Mas La
Plana), Penedés (NO)
1975
Marqués de Murrieta Gran Reserva, Rioja
(NO)
Torres Gran Coronas Black Label (Mas La
Plana), Penedés (NO)
1970
Bodegas Riojanas Monte Real Gran
Reserva, Rioja (GAU)
Marqués de Murrieta Gran Reserva, Rioja
(NO)
1942
Marqués de Murrieta Castillo Ygay Gran
Reserva, Rioja (BUT)

£30.00 to £49.99

1984
Vega Sicilia Valbuena 5th year, Ribera del
Duero (MOR, VIG)
1983
Torres Gran Coronas Black Label (Mas La
Plana), Penedés (VIG)
1982
Vega Sicilia Unico, Ribera del Duero (GRE)
1980
Vega Sicilia Unico, Ribera del Duero (PEN,
TAN)
1979
Vega Sicilia Unico, Ribera del Duero (DI)

1975
Marqués de Murrieta Castillo Ygay Gran
Reserva, Rioja (GRE)
Vega Sicilia Unico, Ribera del Duero (FA)
1973
La Rioja Alta Reserva 890 Gran Reserva,
Rioja (GAU)
1968
Marqués de Murrieta Castillo Ygay Gran
Reserva, Rioja (AMI, NO)
1964
Bodegas Riojanas Monte Real Gran
Reserva, Rioja (GAU)
Marqués de Murrieta Gran Reserva, Rioja
(MOR)

£50.00 to £64.99

1975
Vega Sicilia Unico, Ribera del Duero (DI,
GAU, MOR)
1968
Marqués de Murrieta Castillo Ygay Gran
Reserva, Rioja (AD, RE, ROB)
Vega Sicilia Unico, Ribera del Duero (FA)
1962
Vega Sicilia Unico, Ribera del Duero (DI, FA)
1950
Bodegas Riojanas Monte Real Gran
Reserva, Rioja (VIG)

£70.00 to £75.00

1968
Vega Sicilia Unico, Ribera del Duero (GAU,
ROB)
1962
Vega Sicilia Unico, Ribera del Duero (GAU)
1951
CVNE Viña Real Gran Reserva, Rioja (VIG)

£90.00 to £95.00

1972
Marqués de Murrieta Castillo Ygay Gran
Reserva, Rioja (AD)
1952
Marqués de Murrieta Castillo Ygay Gran
Reserva, Rioja (MOR, AMI)

WHITE

Under £3.50

Non-vintage
Castillo de Liria, Vicente Gandia, Valencia
(WAI, TAN)
Moscatel de Valencia Castillo de Liria,
Vicente Gandia, Valencia (WAI)

1992
Castillo de Liria, Vicente Gandia, Valencia (VIC)

£3.50 to £3.99
1993
El Coto, Rioja (DAV)
★ Hermanos Lurton Sauvignon Blanc, Rueda (SAI, VIC)
Marqués de Cáceres, Rioja (HOG)
1992
Barbadillo Castillo de San Diego, Vino de Mesa (HOG)
Hermanos Lurton Sauvignon Blanc, Rueda (VIC, WR, WR)
Marqués de Cáceres, Rioja (LO, CV)
Torres Viña Sol, Penedés (HOG, TES)
1991
Marqués de Cáceres, Rioja (WHI)

£4.00 to £4.99
Non-vintage
Los Llanos Armonioso, Valdepeñas (TAN, MOR)
1993
★ Alanis San Trocado, Ribeiro (PLA, OD)
★ Compania Vitivinicola Aragonesa Viñas del Vero Chardonnay, Somontano (PLA)
CVNE Viura, Rioja (PLA)
Marqués de Cáceres, Rioja (AD)
Olarra Seco, Rioja (PLA)
Torres Viña Sol, Penedés (DAV, LAY)
1992
CVNE, Rioja (BIB)
El Coto, Rioja (ROB, UN)
Marqués de Cáceres, Rioja (EY, GRE, EL, LAY, WCL, DI, NA, TAN)
Ochoa Seco, Navarra (RE)
Torres San Valentin, Penedés (DI)
Torres Viña Esmeralda, Penedés (HOG, GRE, LO, DI, EY)
Torres Viña Sol, Penedés (GRE, LO, WHI, BE, DI, WAT, PE, MOR, TAN)
1991
Cellers Scala Dei, Priorato (MOR)
Julián Chivite Gran Feudo Blanco, Navarra (RE)
Marqués de Cáceres, Rioja (HAH, AV)
Palacio de Bornos, Rueda (PE)
Torres San Valentin, Penedés (WHI)
1990
Barbadillo Castillo de San Diego, Vino de Mesa (PE, CV, WCL, TES)
CVNE Monopole, Rioja (PIP)

1989
Lan, Rioja (RE)
Marqués de Cáceres, Rioja (HOG, GRE)

£5.00 to £5.99
1993
Marqués de Alella, Alella (GRE)
Torres Gran Viña Sol, Penedés (LAY)
Torres Viña Esmeralda, Penedés (AME, CV)
1992
Marqués de Cáceres, Rioja (BER, RE, MOR, VIN)
Torres Gran Viña Sol, Penedés (LO, BE, CV, TAN)
Torres Viña Esmeralda, Penedés (NO, WR, BOT, THR, BE, WHI, DAV, WRI, PE, TAN, ROB, HAM)
1991
Alanis San Trocado, Ribeiro (SAF, ROB, RES)
★ Compania Vitivinicola Aragonesa Viñas del Vero Chardonnay, Somontano (SAF, ROB, RES, CB)
CVNE Monopole, Rioja (PLA)
CVNE, Rioja (RE)
Faustino V, Rioja (MOR)
Marqués de Alella, Alella (MOR)
Marqués de Riscal Superior, Rueda (MOR)
Torres Gran Viña Sol, Penedés (GRE, WHI, TES, DI, MOR, PE)
Torres Moscatel Malvasia de Oro, Penedés (NO)
Torres Viña Esmeralda, Penedés (MOR)
1990
CVNE Monopole, Rioja (CV, PE, WS)
Faustino V, Rioja (RE)
1989
CVNE Monopole, Rioja (PEN, PE, MOR, BEK)
1988
CVNE Monopole, Rioja (WAT)
CVNE Reserva, Rioja (CV)
1987
CVNE Reserva, Rioja (PIP)
1986
CVNE Reserva, Rioja (PEN)

£6.00 to £7.99
1992
Alanis San Trocado, Ribeiro (VIG)
Compania Vitivinicola Aragonesa Viñas del Vero Chardonnay, Somontano (VIG)
Muga, Rioja (EL, MOR)
Torres Fransola, Penedés (CV)
1991
Compania Vitivinicola Aragonesa Viñas del Vero Chardonnay, Somontano (RE)
Marqués de Alella, Alella (TAN)
Torres Fransola, Penedés (GRE, MOR, EY)

1990
CVNE Monopole, Rioja (LAY, TAN)
Marqués de Griñon, Rueda (MOR, WRI)
Raïmat Chardonnay, Costers del Segre (MOR)
Torres Fransola, Penedés (DI)
1989
CVNE Monopole, Rioja (RE, CB)
La Rioja Alta Viña Ardanza Reserva, Rioja
  (SAF)
Torres Milmanda Chardonnay, Penedés (DI)
1988
Bodegas Riojanas Monte Real, Rioja (RE)
La Rioja Alta Viña Ardanza Reserva, Rioja
  (ROB)
Marqués de Griñon, Rueda (RE)
Marqués de Murrieta Reserva, Rioja (WS)
Marqués de Murrieta, Rioja (HOG, GRE,
  BEN, WCL)
1987
CVNE Reserva, Rioja (MOR, RE)
Marqués de Murrieta Reserva, Rioja (MAJ,
  AD, WR, THR, BOT, AME, VIC)
Marqués de Murrieta, Rioja (DAV, MOR, WCL)
1986
Bodegas Riojanas Monte Real, Rioja (MOR)
Marqués de Murrieta Reserva, Rioja (WS)
Marqués de Murrieta, Rioja (WHI)
1985
CVNE, Rioja (WAT)

£8.00 to £10.99

1992
Lagar de Cervera Hermanos, Galicia (LAY,
  TAN)
1991
Lagar de Cervera Hermanos, Galicia (ROB)
1990
Castel de Fornos Vino Albarino, Bodegas
  Chavas, Rías Baixas (RE)
1989
Marqués de Murrieta Reserva, Rioja (PLA)
1988
Marqués de Murrieta, Rioja (TAN)
1987
CVNE Reserva, Rioja (VIG)
Marqués de Murrieta Reserva, Rioja (ROB,
  AMI)
1986
Marqués de Murrieta Reserva, Rioja (PEN)
Marqués de Murrieta, Rioja (NI)
1985
Marqués de Murrieta Reserva, Rioja (RAE,
  AV)
1984
Marqués de Murrieta, Rioja (TW)

£11.00 to £19.99

1991
Torres Milmanda Chardonnay, Penedés
  (NO)
1990
Torres Milmanda Chardonnay, Penedés
  (NO)
1989
Torres Milmanda Chardonnay, Penedés
  (GRE)
1988
Jean León Chardonnay, Penedés
  (REI)
Torres Milmanda Chardonnay, Penedés
  (NO)
1987
Jean León Chardonnay, Penedés (RE)
Torres Milmanda Chardonnay, Penedés
  (NO)
1986
Torres Milmanda Chardonnay, Penedés
  (NO)
1985
López de Heredia Tondonia Reserva, Rioja
  (MOR)
1984
Jean León Chardonnay, Penedés (MOR)
1983
Marqués de Murrieta Reserva, Rioja (NO)
1980
Marqués de Murrieta, Rioja (TW)
1976
Marqués de Murrieta Reserva, Rioja (BE)

£20.00 to £29.99

1990
Torres Milmanda Chardonnay, Penedés
  (PE)
1988
Torres Milmanda Chardonnay, Penedés
  (BE, REI, RE)
1976
López de Heredia Tondonia Gran Reserva,
  Rioja (RE)
1974
Bodegas Riojanas Monte Real, Rioja (VIG)
1970
Marqués de Murrieta Gran Reserva, Rioja
  (RE)
Marqués de Murrieta Ygay Gran Reserva,
  Rioja (NO, GRE, MOR)

c. £59.00

1948
Marqués de Murrieta, Rioja (VIG)

ROSÉ

Under £4.00
1992
Marqués de Cáceres Rosado, Rioja (LO, HOG)
1991
Marqués de Cáceres Rosado, Rioja (CV)

£4.00 to £4.99
1992
Marqués de Cáceres Rosado, Rioja (DI, NA)
Torres de Casta, Penedés (LO, BE, EY)
1991
Torres de Casta, Penedés (DI)

£5.00 to £5.99
1991
Faustino V Rosado, Rioja (MOR)
Marqués de Cáceres Rosado, Rioja (MOR)
Torres de Casta, Penedés (RE)
1990
Faustino V Rosado, Rioja (RE)
Marqués de Cáceres Rosado, Rioja (RE)
1985
Marqués de Murrieta Rosado, Rioja (NO)

c. £9.00
1987
Marqués de Murrieta Rosado, Rioja (MOR)

SPARKLING

Under £5.50
Non-vintage
Castellblanch Brut Zero, Cava (HOG)
Castellblanch Cristal Seco, Cava (WAI)
Jean Perico Brut, Cava (HOG)
Segura Viudas Brut, Cava (HOG)

£5.50 to £5.99
Non-vintage
Condé de Caralt Brut, Cava (CV, MOR)
Condé de Caralt Semi-seco, Cava (CV, MOR)
Freixenet Brut Rosé, Cava (PIP)
Freixenet Carta Nevada, Cava (PIP)
Freixenet Cordon Negro Brut, Cava (PEN, HOG)
Segura Viudas Brut, Cava (DI, OD)

> In each price band wines
> are listed in vintage order.
> Within each vintage they
> are listed in A–Z order.

£6.00 to £6.99
Non-vintage
Codorníu Brut Première Cuvée, Cava (VIC)
Condé de Caralt Blanc de Blancs, Cava (OD, MOR)
Freixenet Brut Rosé, Cava (CV, WHI, VIC)
Freixenet Carta Nevada, Cava (WHI, CV)
Freixenet Cordon Negro Brut, Cava (CV, POR, WAT, SAF, WHI, DAV, PE, LAY)
Marqués de Monistrol Brut, Cava (PE)
Marqués de Monistrol Rosé Brut, Cava (PE)
1990
Freixenet Cordon Negro Brut, Cava (PLA, EL)
1989
Freixenet Cordon Negro Brut, Cava (PIP, ROB)
1988
Castellblanch Brut Zero, Cava (MOR)
Freixenet Cordon Negro Brut, Cava (MOR, GAL)

£7.00 to £7.99
Non-vintage
Freixenet Carta Nevada, Cava (RE)
Freixenet Cordon Negro Brut, Cava (RE)
Raïmat Chardonnay Brut, Cava (VIC)
1990
Freixenet Cordon Negro Brut, Cava (TAN)
1988
Freixenet Brut Nature, Cava (MAJ, GAL)
Segura Viudas Brut, Cava (DI)

£8.00 to £10.99
1990
Codorníu Brut Première Cuvée, Cava (MOR)
1988
Codorníu Chardonnay Brut, Cava (MOR)
Condé de Caralt Brut, Cava (MOR)

OTHER FORTIFIED

Under £4.00
Non-vintage
Bodegas Alvear Medium Dry, Montilla (TAN)
Bodegas Alvear Pale Dry, Montilla (TAN)

c. £8.00
Non-vintage
Scholtz Solera 1885, Málaga (HOG)

£8.00 to £9.99
Non-vintage
Scholtz Lagrima 10 años, Málaga (GRE, TAN)
Scholtz Solera 1885, Málaga (GRE, PE, ROB)

SHERRY

DRY

Under £4.50

la Gitana Manzanilla, Hidalgo ½ bottle (HAL)

★ Valdespino Fino (WAT)

£4.50 to £4.99

Elegante, González Byass (HOG, WHI)

Fino Hidalgo (PLA, BIB)

Harvey's Luncheon Dry (HOG)

Lustau Fino (DI, MAJ)

★ Manzanilla de Sanlúcar, Barbadillo (AME, OD)

San Patricio Fino, Garvey (HOG)

Valdespino Fino (AS, LEA)

£5.00 to £6.99

Amontillado Napoleon, Hidalgo (AD, EY, NI, WS, WW)

Elegante, González Byass (TES, THR, BOT, WR, DAV, WAI, UN)

Fino de Balbaina, Barbadillo (HOG, PIP, AME, HIC, BAR)

Fino de Sanlúcar, Barbadillo (SUM, PIP, AME, HAY)

Fino Hidalgo (VIN, HAH, NI, LO)

la Gitana Manzanilla, Hidalgo (EL, HOG, OD, PLA, EY, WS, WAI, BIB, WW, HAH, LO, TW)

la Guita Manzanilla, Hidalgo (DI)

Harvey's Luncheon Dry (WHI, HA, BOT, WR, THR)

★ la Ina, Domecq (DAV, HOG, WHI, WRI, UN, WAT, HAH)

★ Inocente Fino, Valdespino (HOG, VIN, WS, WAT, WRI)

Lustau Dry Oloroso (DI)

Lustau Palo Cortado (AME)

Manzanilla de Sanlúcar, Barbadillo (SUM, PIP, PEN, GE, HAY, HIC, BAR, ROB, CB)

★ Manzanilla Pasada Solear, Barbadillo (SUM, HOG, WS, PIP)

Oloroso Especial, Hidalgo (EL)

Ostra Manzanilla (LAY)

San Patricio Fino, Garvey (PEN, ROB, HIG, WS, RE)

Tio Pepe, González Byass (HOG, WHI, WRI, OD)

Valdespino Fino (ROB)

£7.00 to £8.99

Amontillado Napoleon, Hidalgo (TW)

Don Zoilo Finest Fino (HOG)

Don Zoilo Pale Dry Manzanilla (HOG)

Fino Especial, Hidalgo (BIB, TAN, LAY)

Fino Quinta Osborne (RE)

la Guita Manzanilla, Hidalgo (HOG)

Harvey's Palo Cortado (HA)

la Ina, Domecq (EL, ROB)

Inocente Fino, Valdespino (WCL, AS, LEA, ROB, RE)

Jerez Cortado, Hidalgo (AD, TAN)

Manzanilla Pasada Almacenista, Lustau (DI)

Manzanilla Pasada de Sanlúcar, Hidalgo (TAN)

Manzanilla Pasada Solear, Barbadillo (AME, ROB, HIC)

Oloroso Dry, Hidalgo (AD, TAN)

Oloroso Especial, Hidalgo (LAY, WW)

Oloroso Seco Barbadillo (PIP)

★ Palo Cortado del Carrascal, Valdespino (WAT)

★ Palo Cortado, Valdespino (WCL, WS)

★ Tio Diego Amontillado, Valdespino (WAT, WS, WCL, LEA)

Tio Pepe, González Byass (TES, WR, BOT, THR, DAV, WAI, UN, ROB, EL, HAH)

Valdespino Manzanilla (RE)

£9.00 to £9.99

Don Zoilo Old Dry Oloroso (BAR)

Don Zoilo Pale Dry Manzanilla (BAR)

★ Don Zoilo Very Old Fino (AME, BAR)

★ Dos Cortados Old Dry Oloroso, Williams & Humbert (HOG)

Fino Especial, Hidalgo (TW)

la Guita Manzanilla, Hidalgo (RE)

Harvey's Palo Cortado (PLA)

la Ina, Domecq (HA)

Jerez Cortado, Hidalgo (WW, LAY, RE)

Lustau Dry Oloroso (RE)

Oloroso Especial, Hidalgo (TW)

Oloroso Seco Barbadillo (HOG)

Palo Cortado del Carrascal, Valdespino (ROB, LEA)

Tio Diego Amontillado, Valdespino (RE)

Tio Guillermo Amontillado, Garvey (RE)

£10.00 to £12.99

Don Zoilo Palo Cortado (HOG)

Lustau Palo Cortado (RE)

Manzanilla Pasada Almacenista, Lustau (PEN)

Manzanilla Pasada de Sanlúcar, Hidalgo (TW)

Palo Cortado, Don Beningo (HIC)

c. £15.50

Manzanilla de Sanlúcar Almacenista, Heredos de Arqueso (NO)

Oloroso de Jerez Almacenista, Guerrero (NO)

MEDIUM

Under £4.50

Amontillado Valdespino (WAT)

£4.50 to £4.99

Amontillado Lustau (DI, MAJ)

Amontillado Martial, Valdespino (HAH)

Amontillado Valdespino (AS, LEA, ROB)

Concha Amontillado, González Byass (HOG, WHI)

Harvey's Club Amontillado (HOG)

£5.00 to £6.99

Amontillado de Sanlúcar, Barbadillo (SUM, HIC, PIP, NO, HAY, BIB, SEC, BAR)

Amontillado Lustau (OD)

Caballero Amontillado, González Byass (TES)

Concha Amontillado, González Byass (WAI)

Dry Fly Amontillado, Findlater (WAI)

Dry Sack, Williams & Humbert (TES, HOG, WRI)

Harvey's Club Amontillado (WHI, TES, WR, BOT, THR, HA, WAI, WRI, ROB, DAV, HAH, OD)

Sandeman Amontillado (ROB)

Tanners Medium Sherry (TAN)

£7.00 to £10.99

Amontillado Almacenista, Lustau (DI)

Don Zoilo Amontillado (HOG, BEN)

Don Zoilo Finest Old Amontillado (ROB)

Harvey's Fine Old Amontillado (HA, PLA)

★ Oloroso de Jerez, Almacenista Viuda de Antonio Borrego (DI)

Palo Cortado, Barbadillo (SUM)

★ Principe Amontillado, Barbadillo (RE)

Solera 1842 Oloroso, Valdespino (LEA)

Viejo Oloroso, Valdespino (WS)

£11.00 to £12.99

Amontillado Almacenista, Lustau (PEN)

Oloroso Muy Viejo Almacenista, Lustau (PEN, ROB)

Palo Cortado, Barbadillo (PIP)

Sandeman Royal Corregidor Oloroso (HOG, LEA)

Sandeman Royal Esmeralda (HOG, LEA)

£15.00 to £19.99

Amontillado del Duque, González Byass (HOG, RAE, PE)

Apostoles Oloroso, González Byass (HOG, RAE, PE)

Coliseo Amontillado, Valdespino (HOG, WCL, LEA)

c. £21.50

Amontillado del Duque, González Byass (VIN)

Apostoles Oloroso, González Byass (VIN)

SWEET

Under £5.50

Bertola Cream (HOG)

Harvey's Bristol Cream (UN)

£5.50 to £6.99

Croft Original Pale Cream (WHI, HOG, WAI, TES, UN, ROB, DAV, OD, WRI, EL, VIN)

Harvey's Bristol Cream (WAI, HA, THR, BOT, WR, OD, TES, HOG, DAV, WHI, WRI, ROB)

Harvey's Bristol Milk (HA)

Harvey's Copper Beech (HA)

Sanlúcar Cream, Barbadillo (BAR, HIC)

£7.00 to £9.99

Don Zoilo Rich Old Cream (HOG)

Harvey's Bristol Cream (HAH, EL)

Lustau's Old East India (HOG, CV)

★ Pedro Ximenez, Barbadillo (PIP)

£17.00 to £19.99

Matusalem Oloroso, González Byass (HOG, RAE, OD, TES, WR, PE, THR, BOT, ROB)

£20.00 to £21.99

Matusalem Oloroso, González Byass (NO, VIN)

---

*Please remember that **Webster's** is a price GUIDE and not a price LIST. It is not meant to replace up-to-date merchant's lists.*

PORTUGAL

RED

Under £4.00

Non-vintage
Quinta de Cardiga Ribatejo (TES)
1991
Alentejo Borba Adega Co-operativa (UN)
1990
Dão Grão Vasco (DAV, PE)
Periquita J.M. da Fonseca (OD, TES, WAI)
1989
Bairrada Dom Ferraz (WAI)
Bairrada Reserva Caves Aliança (DI)
Dão Dom Ferraz (UN)
Dão Grão Vasco (GRE)
Periquita J.M. da Fonseca (MAJ)
1988
★ Bairrada Terra Franca (GRE)
1987
Bairrada Reserva Caves Aliança (MAJ)
Dão Reserva, Caves Aliança (DI)
1980
Garrafeira Caves Velhas (WCL)

£4.00 to £4.99

1992
★ Douro Quinta de la Rosa (PLA, GE, HAM, LEA, BEN)
★ Valle de Raposa (SAF)
1991
Bairrada Terra Franca (BEK)
★ Dão Duque de Viseu (BEK)
1990
Bairrada Reserva Caves Aliança (PEN)
Bairrada Terra Franca (SAI, BEK, SAF)
★ Dão Duque de Viseu (BEK, SAF)
Dão Reserva, Caves Aliança (PEN)
Dão Terras Altas J.M. da Fonseca (PIP)
Periquita J.M. da Fonseca (BOT, WR, AME, GRE, PE, TAN)
Tinto da Anfora João Pires (WAI, OD)
1989
Dão Reserva Dom Ferraz (WCL)
Dão Terras Altas J.M. da Fonseca (WHI, TAN)
Meia Pipa, João Pires (OD)
Periquita J.M. da Fonseca (WHI, POR)
1988
Pasmados J.M. da Fonseca (AME, GRE)
Periquita J.M. da Fonseca (ROB)
1987
Bairrada Terra Franca (ROB)

1986
Dão Terras Altas J.M. da Fonseca (GRE)
Tinto Velho Reguengos (TES)
1985
Dão Garrafeira Grão Vasco (GRE, PE)
Dão Porto dos Cavaleiros (WS)
Pasmados J.M. da Fonseca (POR)
1983
Bairrada Frei João (WRI)
Beira Mar Reserva, da Silva (WCL)
Dão Porto dos Cavaleiros (BU)

£5.00 to £5.99

1991
Douro Quinta de la Rosa (VIN)
1990
Quinta da Bacalhoa (SAI)
1989
Quinta da Camarate, J.M. da Fonseca (AME, AD)
Tinto da Anfora João Pires (MAJ, WCL)
1988
Quinta da Camarate, J.M. da Fonseca (PIP)
Tinto da Anfora João Pires (WRI)
1987
Bairrada Terra Franca (EY)
Dão Duque de Viseu (EY)
Quinta da Camarate, J.M. da Fonseca (POR, WHI, GRE, PE)
1986
Quinta da Camarate, J.M. da Fonseca (WCL)
1985
Bairrada Terra Franca (GRE)
Beira Mar Reserva, da Silva (AD)
1984
Garrafeira J.M. da Fonseca (TES)
Pasmados J.M. da Fonseca (WRI)
1982
Periquita Reserva J.M. da Fonseca (POR)
1980
Garrafeira da Silva (UN)

£6.00 to £7.49

1991
★Alentejo Vinha do Monte Sogrape (WS, SAF)
1990
Bairrada Luis Pato (BOT)
1989
Quinta da Camarate, J.M. da Fonseca (TAN)
Tinto da Anfora João Pires (WHI, WRI)
1986
Tinto Velho Reguengos (WRI, ROB)

1985
Bairrada Luis Pato (HAM)
1984
Garrafeira Particular Caves Aliança (DI)
1983
Beira Mar Reserva, da Silva (WS)
1982
Garrafeira J.M. da Fonseca (WHI, ROB)
1980
Quinta da Camarate Reserva, J.M. da
  Fonseca (WS)

£8.50 to £9.99
1988
Bairrada Luis Pato (BOT)
1984
★ Reserva Especial, Ferreira (OD)

£10.50 to £11.50
1990
Quinta do Côtto Grande Escolha,
  Champalimaud (AD)
1985
Quinta do Côtto Grande Escolha,
  Champalimaud (ROB, HAM)

c. £24.00
1985
Barca Velha, Ferreira (OD)

WHITE

Under £4.00
Non-vintage
Vinho Verde Aveleda (PEN, HOG)
Vinho Verde Casal Garcia (GRE)
Vinho Verde Casal Mendes Caves Aliança
  (DI)
★ Vinho Verde Chello Dry (SAI)
Vinho Verde Gazela (OD, GRE, DAV)
1992
Bairrada Caves Aliança (SO)
Dão Grão Vasco (OD, PE)
★ João Pires Branco (POR, SAI, TES, SAF,
  OD)
1991
Dão Terras Altas J.M. da Fonseca (MAJ)
1990
Bairrada Terra Franca (GRE)

£4.00 to £4.99
Non-vintage
Vinho Verde Aveleda (WHI)
Vinho Verde Casal Garcia (PE)
Vinho Verde Gazela (TAN, EL)

1993
★ Bairrada Quinta des Pedravites (OD)
Vinho Verde Aveleda (PIP)
1992
Dão Terras Altas J.M. da Fonseca (PIP)
Dry Palmela Moscato, João Pires (OD)
1991
Dão Dom Ferraz (WCL)
1989
João Pires Catarina (OD)
1985
Bairrada Terra Franca (BOR)

£5.00 to £5.99
1992
João Pires Branco (PIP)
1991
Bairrada Reserva Sogrape (SAF, GA)
João Pires Branco (WHI, GRE, AV, NO)
1990
Dão Grão Vasco (AV)
Planalto Reserva (GRE)

c. £7.00
1990
★ Cova da Ursa Chardonnay, J.P. Vinhos
  (TES, WR)
1989
João Pires Branco (VIN)

ROSÉ

Under £4.00
Non-vintage
Mateus Rosé (TES, VIC, SAI)

£4.00 to £4.99
Non-vintage
Mateus Rosé (WAI, SO, HOG, WHI, DAV)

£5.00 to £5.99
Non-vintage
Mateus Rosé (PE, UN, VIN)

FORTIFIED

Under £14.00
Non-vintage
Moscatel de Setúbal 20-year-old J.M. da
  Fonseca (NO)

c. £16.50
Non-vintage
Moscatel de Setúbal 20-year-old J.M. da
  Fonseca (TAN)

PORT

Under £6.50

Non-vintage
Cockburn's Fine Ruby (HOG, UN, WHI)
Cockburn's Fine Tawny (HOG)
Quinta do Noval Old Coronation Ruby (HOG)
Smith Woodhouse Fine Tawny (UN)
Smith Woodhouse Ruby (UN)
Warre's Ruby (WHI)
Warre's Tawny (WHI, VIC)

£6.50 to £6.99

Non-vintage
Cockburn's Fine Ruby (HA, THR, BOT, WR, VIC)
Cockburn's Fine Tawny (HA, UN)
Cockburn's Fine White (UN)
Dow's No. 1 White (HOG)
Graham Ruby (NI)
Quinta do Noval Late Bottled (HOG)
Sandeman Fine Old Ruby (WR, BOT, THR)
Sandeman Tawny (BOT, OD)
Warre's Warrior (WHI)
1984
Smith Woodhouse Late Bottled (UN)

£7.00 to £8.99

Non-vintage
Churchill Dry White (CV, LEA, WW)
★ Churchill's Finest Vintage Character (PIP, CV, GOE, LEA, WW)
Cockburn's Late Bottled (TES)
Cockburn's Special Reserve (UN, HOG, BOT, WR, WHI, THR, HA, WAI, VIC, OD)
Delaforce Special White Port (WR, BOT, THR)
Dow's Fine Ruby (ROB)
Dow's Fine Tawny (ROB)
Dow's No. 1 White (PEN)
Dow's Vintage Character (HOG)
Fonseca Bin 27 (HOG, BE, WCL, LO, WAI, WRI, HAM, ROB)
Quinta do Noval Late Bottled (WHI, GRE, WRI, TAN, UN)
Quinta do Noval Old Coronation Ruby (DAV)
Ramos-Pinto Ruby (BEN)
Ramos-Pinto Vintage Character (HAH)
Sandeman (OD)
Sandeman Fine Old White (EL)
Taylor Special Ruby (HAH)
Taylor Special Tawny (HAH, BEN)
Warre's Warrior (AME, TES, THR, WR, BOT, VIC, UN, DI)
1989
Martinez Crusted (ROB)

1988
Dow's Late Bottled (AME)
1987
Cockburn's Late Bottled (HOG)
Dow's Late Bottled (WAI, OD)
Ramos-Pinto Late Bottled (GRE)
1986
Cockburn's Late Bottled (HA, WHI, VIC)
Dow's Late Bottled (MAJ)
Graham Late Bottled (NI)
1985
Dow's Late Bottled (SUM)
1982
Warre's Quinta da Cavadinha ½ bottle (HAL)

£9.00 to £10.99

Non-vintage
Churchill (AV)
Churchill's Crusted Port (LEA)
Churchill's Finest Vintage Character (HAY, GAL, HIC, BAR)
Cockburn's Crusted (LEA)
Croft Late Bottled (BOT, WR, THR)
Delaforce His Eminence's Choice (HOG)
Dow's Crusted Port (PEN)
Dow's Vintage Character (PEN, WRI)
Gould Campbell (ROB)
★ Graham 10-year-old Tawny (NI)
Graham Late Bottled (TES, BOT, THR, WR)
Martinez Crusted (CV)
Quinta do Noval Late Bottled (ROB)
Sandeman Founder's Reserve (UN)
Taylor Chip Dry White Port (PLA, GRE, DAV, BEN)
Taylor Late Bottled (BOT, WR, THR)
1988
Dow's Crusted Port (AME)
★ Quinta de la Rosa (HAM)
Smith Woodhouse Crusted (WW)
1987
Churchill's Crusted Port (PLA)
Graham Late Bottled (GRE, WAT, TES, VIC, MAJ, TAN)
Smith Woodhouse Crusted (NO)
Taylor Late Bottled (WAI, VIC, UN)
1986
Taylor Late Bottled (ROB)
1985
Dow's Crusted Port (GRE)
Graham Late Bottled (HOG, REI)
★ Quinta do Noval (FA)
Taylor Late Bottled (HOG, ROB)

1983
★ Smith Woodhouse (PIP)
1982
Graham Late Bottled (BIB)
1980
Delaforce Quinta da Corte (OD)
Taylor ½ bottle (NO)

£11.00 to £12.99

Non-vintage
Cockburn's 10-year-old Tawny (HOG, HA)
Fonseca 10-year-old Tawny (HOG, PIP, WCL)
★ Quinta da Ervamoira 10-year-old Tawny
  (BEK, GRE, AME)
Tanners Crusted (TAN)
★ Taylor 10-year-old Tawny (EY, WHI, PLA)
Warre's 10-year-old Tawny (WHI)
Wellington Wood Port (BER)
1986
Churchill's Crusted Port (BUT)
Dow's Late Bottled (AV)
Martinez Crusted (AV)
1983
Dow (SEC)
Warre (GOE)

WARRE'S
1983
VINTAGE PORT
BOTTLED 1985
WARRE & C: L^o OPORTO
ESTABLISHED 1670
20% vol. PRODUCE OF PORTUGAL e 75 cl

1982
Churchill (NO)
Quinta da Eira Velha (ROB)
Quinta do Noval (POR, SEC)
Sandeman (LEA)
1981
Warre's Late Bottled (WHI, CV, PIP, WAI,
  PEN, WCL, DI)
1980
Royal Oporto (TES)
Sandeman (SEC)
1979
Warre's Late Bottled (NI, GOE)
1978
Royal Oporto (WAT)
1970
Martinez (BUT)

£13.00 to £14.99

Non-vintage
Dow's 10-year-old Tawny (ROB)
Quinta do Noval 10-year-old Tawny (UN, HAM)
Warre's Nimrod Old Tawny (WHI)
1987
Churchill's Quinta do Agua Alta (TAN)
1985
Delaforce (SEC)
Graham (FA)
Warre (SUM, BAR)
1983
Churchill's Quinta do Agua Alta (HAY)
Fonseca (SUM, WAT)
Royal Oporto (DI, WRI)
1982
Croft (GOE)
Royal Oporto (WAT)
Taylor Quinta de Vargellas (HOG, PLA, GRE)
Warre's Quinta da Cavadinha (WHI)
1981
Smith Woodhouse Late Bottled (ROB)
1980
Delaforce Quinta da Corte (POR)
Fonseca (BIB, WY)
Graham (BIB, SEC)
Warre (BIB)
1979
Graham Malvedos (NI)
Warre's Quinta da Cavadinha (GE)
1978
Fonseca Guimaraens (HOG)
1976
Graham Malvedos (NO)
1970
Croft Quinta da Roeda (GOE)

£15.00 to £16.99

Non-vintage
★ Cockburn's 20-year-old Tawny (HOG)
Dow's Vintage Character (BUT)
1991
Dow (HOG)
Graham (NI)
Smith Woodhouse (VIC)
1990
Graham Malvedos (LAY)
1985
Cockburn (BIB)
Dow (BIB)
Gould Campbell (DI)
Sandeman (BIB)
Taylor (GOE)
1984
Warre's Quinta da Cavadinha (AME)

1983
Cockburn (HOG)
Dow (LAY, HOG)
Graham (BIB)
Offley Boa Vista (BOT, WR, THR)
Smith Woodhouse (DI)
Taylor (HOG)
1982
Dow Quinta do Bomfim (AME)
Martinez (AD)
Sandeman (HOG)
Warre (NA)
1980
Dow (ROB)
Dow's Crusted Port (BUT)
Quarles Harris (HAH)
Taylor (WY, EL, HOG, POR)
1978
Croft Quinta da Roeda (CB)
Warre's Quinta da Cavadinha (CV, NO)
1975
Croft (BIB)
Graham (BIB, GOE)
Quinta do Noval (LEA)
1964
Fonseca (BUT)

£17.00 to £18.99

Non-vintage
Cockburn's Special Reserve (BUT)
Quinta da Bom Retiro 20-year-old Tawny
  (BEK, GRE)
1991
Quinta do Vesuvio (DI)
1985
Fonseca (BIB, HOG)
Offley Boa Vista (VIG)
Quinta do Noval (BUT)
1983
Gould Campbell (NO, PLA)
1982
Royal Oporto (UN)
1980
Gould Campbell (BER)
Warre (CV, ROB)
1979
Dow Quinta do Bomfim (ROB, REI)
Graham Malvedos (TAN, LAY, THR, WR, BOT)
1978
Quinta do Noval (PLA, PEN, EY, HAM, DAV)
Taylor Quinta de Vargellas (WRI, HAH, ROB,
  WR, BOT, THR, VIC, TAN)
1977
Gould Campbell (EL)
Smith Woodhouse (EL)

1976
Taylor Quinta de Vargellas (WR, BOT)
1975
Fonseca (WY, BUT)
Gould Campbell (BER)
Warre (BUT)
1970
Royal Oporto (BIB)
Smith Woodhouse (BIB)

£19.00 to £20.99

Non-vintage
Graham 20-year-old Tawny (NI)
Martinez 20-year-old Tawny (HIC)
Sandeman 20-year-old Tawny (WAI, LEA)
1985
Churchill (BUT)
Cockburn (PLA)
Taylor (BUT, HOG, SEC, NO)
1983
Cockburn (BUT)
1982
Quinta do Noval (VIC)
1980
Dow (DAV, BER)
Fonseca (ROB)
1978
Fonseca Guimaraens (VIG)
1977
Delaforce (OD)
Dow (SUM)
Warre (WY, BIB, BUT, GOE)
1975
Cockburn (BU, BER)
Delaforce (BER)
Dow (BUT)
Sandeman (BER)
Taylor (HAM)
1970
Cockburn (FA)
Croft (FA)
Sandeman (FA)
Warre (FA)

£21.00 to £22.99

Non-vintage
Fonseca 20-year-old (PLA, PIP)
Taylor 20-year-old Tawny (WHI)
1991
Cockburn (CB)
1985
Croft (VIG)
1983
Dow (DAV, GAU, NO)
Warre (UN, DAV, GAU, VIC)

1982
Churchill (ww)
Sandeman (TAN, UN)
1977
Croft (WAT)
Fonseca (BIB)
Gould Campbell (BER)
Quarles Harris (BUT, BER, AD)
1975
Croft (BER)
Fonseca (BER)
Quinta do Noval (VIC)
1970
Taylor ½ bottle (HAL)

£23.00 to £24.99

Non-vintage
Ferreira Duque de Braganca 20-year-old
    Tawny (WCL, NO)
1990
Quinta do Vesuvio (HAH)
1985
Cockburn (DAV)
Graham (DAV)
Warre (ROB, DAV)
1980
Taylor (BER)
Warre (VIC)
1977
Delaforce (WHI, POR)
Graham (FA, BIB)
Offley Boa Vista (VIC)
Smith Woodhouse (CV, ROB)
1975
Cockburn (ROB)
1970
Dow (FA)
Graham (BIB)
Quinta do Noval (BIB)
1966
Dow (FA)
Sandeman (FA)
1963
Offley Boa Vista (GOE)
1958
Quinta do Noval (FA)

> *Please remember that*
> ***Webster's*** *is a price*
> *GUIDE and not a price*
> *LIST. It is not meant to*
> *replace up-to-date*
> *merchant's lists.*

£25.00 to £29.99

Non-vintage
Quinta do Noval 20-year-old Tawny (HAM)
1977
Dow (DI, LAY, BUT)
Fonseca (HA, HOG)
Quarles Harris (VIG, DI)
Sandeman (BER)
Taylor (BIB)
1975
Croft (ROB)
Taylor (BER, DAV, ROB)
Warre (ROB)
1970
Cockburn (GAU)
Croft (BIB, WHI)
Delaforce (BER)
Rebello Valente (VIC)
Sandeman (BIB, BER)
Taylor (BIB, FA)
Warre (SEC, BIB, BUT)
1966
Croft (WY)
Gould Campbell (BER)
Offley Boa Vista (BER)
1960
Croft (FA)
Dow (WY)
Warre (FA)

£30.00 to £39.99

1977
Croft (BER, CB, DAV)
1967
Cockburn (VIG)
Quinta do Noval (VIG)
1966
Fonseca (BIB, WS, FA)
Graham (WS, DAV)
Rebello Valente (BUT)
Taylor (GOE, BUT, FA, BOR, WS, EY, DAV)
1963
Cockburn (TAN)
Croft (GOE, MV)
Dow (DI)
Martinez (WHI, EL)
Offley Boa Vista (SEC, DI)
Quinta do Noval (WY, FA, MV)
1960
Cockburn (BUT, DAV)
Graham (SUM)
Sandeman (BUT, ROB)
Taylor (WY, DAV, BUT)
1950
Cockburn (FA)

£40.00 to £49.99

1966
Quinta do Noval (CV)
Sandeman (ROB)
Warre's Warrior (DI)
1963
Sandeman (BIB)
Warre (BUT, BIB, WS, BAR, NI)
1960
Croft (ROB)
Warre (ROB)
1955
Cockburn (FA)
Croft (FA)
Martinez (POR)
Quinta do Noval (FA)
Sandeman (FA)

£50.00 to £74.99

Non-vintage
Taylor 40-year-old Tawny (GRE, PEN, UN, VIN)
1966
Fonseca (ROB)
Graham (ROB)
1963
Fonseca (FA, BIB, BUT)
Graham (WS, FA, DAV)
Taylor (FA, BIB, DAV, REI)
Warre's Warrior (DI)
1955
Gould Campbell (TW)
Taylor (BIB)
1952
Cálem (ROB)
1950
Croft (WY)
1944
Royal Oporto (TW)
1915
Gould Campbell (VIG)

£75.00 to £99.99

1963
Dow (ROB)
1955
Fonseca (VIG)
1947
Cockburn (WY)
1945
Ferreira (BIB)
1934
Sandeman (WY)
1920
Sandeman (FA)

£100.00 to £149.99

1948
Taylor (FA)
1947
Sandeman (WY)
1945
Quinta do Noval (BUT)
Rebello Valente (WY)
1935
Cockburn (WY)
1924
Dow (BEN)
1920
Dow (WY)
Warre (WY)
1908
Mackenzie (FA)

£150.00 to £199.99

1948
Graham (FA, BIB)
1945
Croft (WY)
1935
Taylor (FA)
1931
Warre (TW)
1927
Cockburn (WY)
Taylor (TW)
1924
Croft (WY)
1920
Taylor (WY)
1912
Cockburn (WY)
Croft (WY)

£220.00 to £250.00

1945
Taylor (WY)
1927
Fonseca (VIG)

c. £350.00

1945
Fonseca (ROB)

c. £470.00

1931
Quinta do Noval (TW)

c. £514.00

1963
Quinta do Noval Nacional (NO)

MADEIRA

Under £8.00

Non-vintage
Bual Henriques & Henriques (RE)
Bual Old Trinity House Rutherford &
 Miles (HAH)
Medium Dry Blandy (WAT)
Sercial Henriques & Henriques (RE)
Verdelho Henriques & Henriques (BU)

£8.00 to £9.99

Non-vintage
Bual Henriques & Henriques (BOR)
Bual Old Trinity House Rutherford &
 Miles (NA, BE)
Bual Reserve Rutherford & Miles (ROB)
Finest Old Malmsey Cossart Gordon (HAY)
Full Rich Blandy (HAH, NI, GRE, DAV, VIN)
Full Rich Good Company Cossart Gordon
 (CV, WCL, SEC)
Malmsey Henriques & Henriques (BOR)
Medium Dry Blandy (GRE, VIN)
Medium Rich Blandy (WAT, NI, TAN, THR,
 BOT, WR, VIN)
Medium Rich Cossart Gordon (PEN, WCL)
Rainwater Good Company Cossart Gordon
 (DI, SEC, AD)
Sercial Henriques & Henriques (PEN)
Sercial Old Custom House Rutherford &
 Miles (NA, AME, ROB)
Special Dry Blandy (NI, GRE, TAN, BOT, THR,
 WR, VIN)
Verdelho Henriques & Henriques (BOR, PEN)
Viva Dry Cossart Gordon (HAH, WCL, SEC)

£10.00 to £14.99

Non-vintage
10-year-old Bual Rutherford & Miles (NO)
10-year-old Malmsey Blandy (WAI, WAT, NI,
 NO, HOG)
10-year-old Malmsey Cossart Gordon (DI, GRE)
5-year-old Bual Cossart Gordon (SEC, DI,
 CV, GRE, HIC)
5-year-old Malmsey Cossart Gordon (DI,
 CV, GRE, AD)
5-year-old Sercial Cossart Gordon (DI, GRE)
Finest Old Bual Cossart Gordon (PIP)
Finest Old Malmsey Cossart Gordon (PIP)
Finest Old Sercial Cossart Gordon (PIP)
Full Rich Good Company Cossart Gordon (AV)
Rainwater Good Company Cossart Gordon
 (AV)
Viva Dry Cossart Gordon (AV)

£15.00 to £19.99

Non-vintage
10-year-old Malmsey Blandy (ROB, GRE)
10-year-old Malmsey Cossart Gordon (HIC, CV)
10-year-old Verdelho Cossart Gordon (HIC,
 CV)
Full Rich Good Company Cossart Gordon
 (RE)
Rainwater Cossart Gordon (RE)
Very Old Sercial Duo Centenary
 Celebration Cossart Gordon (HAH)

£20.00 to £49.99

Non-vintage
Malmsey Solera 1863 Leacock (NO)
1954
Bual Henriques & Henriques (LEA)
Malmsey Henriques & Henriques (LEA)
1950
Sercial Rutherford & Miles (GRE)
1934
Verdelho Henriques & Henriques (GRE, BU)

£50.00 to £64.99

1952
Rainwater Cossart Gordon (DI)
1950
Sercial Leacock (VIG)

£89.00 to £95.00

1934
Verdelho Henriques & Henriques (VIG)
1931
Medium Dry Blandy (VIG)
1920
Full Rich Good Company Cossart Gordon
 (DI)
1914
Medium Rich Cossart Gordon (DI)

£140.00 to £160.00

1930
Malmsey Quinta do Serrado (AD)
1927
Bual Quinta do Serrado (AD)

Stars (★) indicate wines
selected by the editors as
particularly good value
in their class.

UNITED KINGDOM

WHITE

Under £4.50

Non-vintage
Lamberhurst Sovereign (DAV)
1992
Denbies Surrey Gold (WAI)
1990
Three Choirs Seyval Blanc/Reichensteiner Dry (NO)

£4.50 to £4.99

Non-vintage
Denbies Surrey Gold (TES)
Lamberhurst Sovereign (DI)
1992
Denbies Surrey Gold (DAV)
Lamberhurst Priory Seyval Blanc (VIC)
1990
Chiddingstone Seyval/Kerner (DI)
Denbies Surrey Gold (VIC)
Three Choirs Medium Dry (NO)
1989
Pilton Manor Vintage Selection (HAC)
Wake Court (EL)

£5.00 to £5.99

1992
Three Choirs Müller-Thurgau/Reichensteiner (TAN)
1991
Astley Severn Vale (TAN)
Wootton Müller-Thurgau (WS)
1990
Biddenden Ortega (HAC)
Bruisyard St Peter Müller-Thurgau (BER)
★ Staple St-James Müller-Thurgau (HA)
Three Choirs Medium Dry (WS)
Wootton Schönburger (BER)
1989
Croffta (CV)
Heywood Madeleine Sylvaner (HAC)
Staple St-James Müller-Thurgau (BER)
Wraxall Müller-Thurgau/Seyval Blanc (AV)
1986
Penshurst Ehrenfelser (HAC)

£6.00 to £7.99

Non-vintage
English Vineyard (CB)
1991
Elmham Park Madeleine Angevine (HIC)

1990
Breaky Bottom Müller-Thurgau (HAC)
Breaky Bottom Seyval Blanc (WS, HAC)
Pulham Vineyards Magdalen Rivaner (TW)
Staple St-James Huxelrebe (HAC)
1989
Adgestone (BOR)
Chiddingstone Seyval/Kerner (BER)
Lamberhurst Schönburger (BER)
Pilton Manor Müller-Thurgau (AV)
Pilton Manor Seyval Blanc (HAC)
Staple St-James Huxelrebe (BER)
Wootton Schönburger (AV)
1988
Barkham Manor Medium Dry (CB)
Berwick Glebe (CB)
Pilton Manor Huxelrebe (HAC)

£8.00 to £9.99

1988
Lamberhurst Schönburger (PEN)
1987
Lamberhurst Schönburger (HAC)

RED

Under £6.00

1989
Biddenden Red (HAC)
1988
Westbury Light Red (HAC)
1986
Westbury Pinot Noir (HAC)

SPARKLING

Under £9.00

1989
Rock Lodge Impressario Brut (HAC)

c. £10.50

Non-vintage
Carr Taylor (HAC)

> *In each price band wines are listed in vintage order. Within each vintage they are listed in A–Z order.*

BULGARIA

RED

Under £2.50

Non-vintage
Russe Cabernet Sauvignon/Cinsaut (WIW)
★Suhindol Cabernet Sauvignon/Merlot (WIW)
Suhindol Merlot/Gamza (WIW)
1990
★ Suhindol Cabernet Sauvignon (WIW)

£2.50 to £2.99

Non-vintage
Bulgarian Cabernet Sauvignon/Merlot (DI,
　DAV, UN)
Bulgarian Merlot (PE)
Bulgarian Merlot/Gamza (WAI)
Pavlikeni Cabernet Sauvignon/Merlot (PE,
　GRE, VIC)
Petrich Cabernet Sauvignon/Melnik (MAJ)
1993
Bulgarian Cabernet Sauvignon (SAI)
1992
★ Assenovgrad Mavrud (SAF)
Suhindol Gamza (WIW)

1991
Bulgarian Merlot (GRE)
1990
★ Oriahovitza Cabernet Sauvignon
　Reserve (WIW)
Sakar Mountain Cabernet Sauvignon
　(WIW)
Suhindol Cabernet Sauvignon Reserve
　(WIW)
1989
Haskovo Merlot (ASD)
Suhindol Cabernet Sauvignon Reserve
　(WIW)
Svischtov Cabernet Sauvignon (ASD, MAR)
1988
★ ★ Assenovgrad Mavrud (WIW)
Bulgarian Cabernet Sauvignon (WAI)

£3.00 to £3.99

Non-vintage
Bulgarian Cabernet Sauvignon (PE)
Oriahovitza Cabernet Sauvignon Reserve
　(DI)
Russe Cabernet Sauvignon Reserve (VIC)
Svischtov Cabernet Sauvignon (LAY)
1988
Haskovo Merlot (TAN)
Plovdiv Cabernet Sauvignon (DAV)
Sakar Merlot (WIW)

WHITE

Under £3.00

Non-vintage
Burgas Muscat/Ugni Blanc (WIW)
Preslav Chardonnay (WIW)

1991
Khan Krum Chardonnay (WIW)
Preslav Chardonnay (OD)
1990
Khan Krum Chardonnay (WIW)

£3.00 to £3.99

Non-vintage
Khan Krum Chardonnay (DI)
1991
Novi Pazar Chardonnay (WIW)
1989
Khan Krum Chardonnay (PE, WHI)
1988
Khan Krum Chardonnay (WHI)

UNITED STATES

CALIFORNIA RED

Under £4.00

Non-vintage
E&J Gallo Cabernet Sauvignon (SAF)
E&J Gallo Dry Reserve (SAF, SO, VIC, PE)
Franzia Cabernet Sauvignon (VIC)

£4.00 to £4.99

1991
Fetzer Zinfandel (SAF)
Glen Ellen Cabernet Sauvignon (HOG, GRE)
1990
Fetzer Zinfandel (SOM, OD)
1988
Glen Ellen Cabernet Sauvignon (SO, WHI)
1987
E&J Gallo Zinfandel (UN)

£5.00 to £5.99

Non-vintage
Trefethen Eshcol Red (WHI)
1992
Quady Elysium Black Muscat ½ bottle (NA, UN)
Robert Mondavi Woodbridge Cabernet
    Sauvignon (THR, BOT, WR)
1991
Glen Ellen Cabernet Sauvignon (RE)
Robert Mondavi Woodbridge Cabernet
    Sauvignon (NI, WR, THR, BOT, WHI)
1990
Beaulieu Beautour Cabernet Sauvignon (SAI)
Franciscan Cabernet Sauvignon (OD)
Robert Mondavi Cabernet Sauvignon (HAH)
Robert Mondavi Woodbridge Cabernet
    Sauvignon (SEC)
Stratford Cabernet Sauvignon (MAJ)
1989
Beringer Zinfandel (BEK)
Fetzer Zinfandel (WHI)
Robert Mondavi Cabernet Sauvignon (VIC)
1988
Inglenook Cabernet Sauvignon (HOG)
Inglenook Petite Sirah (WRI)
Inglenook Zinfandel (VIC)

> *Stars (★) indicate wines
> selected by the editors as
> particularly good value
> in their class.*

£6.00 to £7.99

Non-vintage
Quady Elysium Black Muscat (NI)
Quady Elysium Black Muscat ½ bottle
    (SEC)
1992
★ Ca' del Solo Big House Red (SOM, MV, AD,
    TES, WCL)
Quady Elysium Black Muscat ½ bottle (NO,
    PEN)
1991
Cá del Solo Big House Red (POR)
Fetzer Zinfandel (DI)
Firestone Merlot (HOG, AMI)
Hawk Crest Cabernet Sauvignon (WW)
★ Saintsbury Garnet Pinot Noir (GE)
1990
Cá del Solo Big House Red (REI)
Firestone Cabernet Sauvignon (PIP)
Julius Wile Cabernet Sauvignon (PLA)
Quady Elysium Black Muscat ½ bottle (NO)
1989
Beringer Cabernet Sauvignon (PIP)
Beringer Zinfandel (PIP)
★ Carneros Creek Pinot Noir (WCL)
Firestone Cabernet Sauvignon (HOG, AMI)
Robert Mondavi Woodbridge Cabernet
    Sauvignon (BER)
1988
Pedroncelli Cabernet Sauvignon (LAY)
Sterling Cabernet Sauvignon (OD)
1987
Wente Bros Cabernet Sauvignon (PEN)

£8.00 to £9.99

1992
Carneros Creek Pinot Noir (ROB)
Quady Elysium Black Muscat ½ bottle
    (HAL)
Saintsbury Garnet Pinot Noir (BIB, HAH)
1991
★ Il Podere dell'Olivos Nebbiolo (MV)
Qupé Syrah Bien Nacido (SOM)
★ Ridge Paso Robles Zinfandel (AMI)
Robert Mondavi Pinot Noir (WAI)
1990
Clos du Bois Merlot (AMI)
Clos du Val Zinfandel (PE)
★ Jade Mountain La Provençale (POR)
Jade Mountain Mourvèdre (SOM)
Joseph Phelps Le Mistral (AMI)
Ridge Paso Robles Zinfandel (HOG, GE, BEN)

1989
Clos du Val Zinfandel (SOM, WAT)
Dry Creek Cabernet Sauvignon (GRE, CV)
Fetzer Barrel Select Cabernet Sauvignon (AMI)
Laurel Glen Cabernet Sauvignon (WW)

1988
Buena Vista Cabernet Sauvignon (WCL)
1987
Beringer Cabernet Sauvignon (SO)
Clos du Bois Cabernet Sauvignon (PE)
Dry Creek Cabernet Sauvignon (HOG)
Franciscan Cabernet Sauvignon (PEN)
Renaissance Cabernet Sauvignon (AD)
1985
Rutherford Hill Cabernet Sauvignon (HOG)

£10.00 to £11.99

1992
Il Podere dell'Olivos Nebbiolo (BEN)
Qupé Syrah Bien Nacido (BEN)
Saintsbury Pinot Noir (BIB)
1991
Au Bon Climat Pinot Noir (MV)
Newton Cabernet Sauvignon (NI)
Qupé Syrah Bien Nacido (PLA, BEN)
Ridge Geyserville Zinfandel (PIP)
Ridge Mataro (AMI)
Robert Mondavi Pinot Noir (GRE, TAN)
Saintsbury Pinot Noir (AD)
Sanford Pinot Noir (SOM, AMI, HOG)
Stag's Leap Cabernet Sauvignon (WW)
1990
Cá del Solo Barbera (WCL)
★ Calera Jensen Pinot Noir (PIP)
Fetzer Barrel Select Cabernet Sauvignon (DI)
Il Podere dell'Olivos Nebbiolo (WCL)
Jade Mountain La Provençale (BEN, WCL)
Jade Mountain Mourvèdre (MV, POR, WCL)
Laurel Glen Cabernet Sauvignon (DI)
Ojai Syrah (AD)
Robert Mondavi Pinot Noir (BEN)
Saintsbury Pinot Noir (WS, GE)
Shafer Merlot (AD)

1989
★ Bonny Doon Le Cigare Volant (RAE)
Fetzer Barrel Select Cabernet Sauvignon (LEA)
Newton Merlot (WCL)
Ridge Geyserville Zinfandel (ROB)
1988
Conn Creek Cabernet Sauvignon (NO)
Dry Creek Zinfandel (HAH)
Robert Mondavi Cabernet Sauvignon (GRE, PLA)
Shafer Cabernet Sauvignon (WS)
Simi Cabernet Sauvignon (CB, TAN, LAY)
1987
Clos du Val Pinot Noir (BEN)
Robert Mondavi Cabernet Sauvignon (ROB)
Rutherford Hill Merlot (AV)
1986
Newton Cabernet Sauvignon (AME)
Renaissance Cabernet Sauvignon (PEN)
Trefethen Cabernet Sauvignon (AMI)
1985
Newton Merlot (NO)
Rutherford Hill Cabernet Sauvignon (AV)
Rutherford Hill Merlot (WAT)
1984
Beaulieu Vineyard Pinot Noir (RE)
Ridge York Creek Cabernet Sauvignon (GAU)
Robert Mondavi Cabernet Sauvignon (HOG)
Robert Mondavi Oakville Cabernet Sauvignon (WHI)
Simi Cabernet Sauvignon (RE)

£12.00 to £14.99

1992
Qupé Syrah Bien Nacido (BER)
Saintsbury Pinot Noir (BEN)
1991
Au Bon Climat Pinot Noir (PLA, BEN, BAR)
Bonny Doon Le Cigare Volant (RAE)
Joseph Phelps Le Mistral (BEN)
Ojai Syrah (BEN)
Ridge Geyserville Zinfandel (GE, NO)
Saintsbury Pinot Noir (HAH, NI, DI)
Sanford Pinot Noir (NI, DI, WCL)
Stag's Leap Cabernet Sauvignon (DI)
1990
Au Bon Climat Pinot Noir (POR)
Bonny Doon Le Cigare Volant (MV, POR, RAE, PLA, BEN, VIG)
Newton Merlot (POR)
Qupé Syrah Bien Nacido (MV)
Saintsbury Pinot Noir (BER)
Sanford Pinot Noir (ROB)
Shafer Cabernet Sauvignon (BAR)

1989
Au Bon Climat Pinot Noir (ROB)
Carneros Creek Pinot Noir (BER)
Joseph Phelps Cabernet Sauvignon (AMI)
Qupé Syrah Bien Nacido (MV)
★ Robert Mondavi Cabernet Sauvignon
   Reserve (SEC)
Stag's Leap Cabernet Sauvignon (ROB)
1988
Clos du Val Cabernet Sauvignon (WS)
Cuvaison Cabernet Sauvignon (BY)
Sanford Pinot Noir (BEN)
Trefethen Cabernet Sauvignon (BER)
1987
Bonny Doon Le Cigare Volant (BUT)
1986
Carmenet Cabernet Sauvignon (ROB)
1984
Renaissance Cabernet Sauvignon (WHI)
1982
Simi Reserve Cabernet Sauvignon (CB)

£15.00 to £19.99

1991
Joseph Phelps Cabernet Sauvignon (LEA)
Lytton Springs Zinfandel (BER)
Newton Merlot (BEN)
Saintsbury Pinot Noir Reserve (GE, BIB)
1990
Joseph Phelps Syrah (BEN)
1989
Calera Jensen Pinot Noir (NO)
Cuvaison Cabernet Sauvignon (AMI)
Cuvaison Merlot (AMI)
Matanzas Creek Merlot (HAH)
1988
Au Bon Climat Pinot Noir (BUT)
Jordan Cabernet Sauvignon (LAY)
Qupé Syrah Bien Nacido (GAU)
Robert Mondavi Pinot Noir Reserve (WHI)
Stag's Leap Cabernet Sauvignon (BER)
1987
Sterling Cabernet Sauvignon Reserve (OD)
1986
Chalone Pinot Noir (AMI)
1984
Carmenet Cabernet Sauvignon (NO)
Mayacamas Cabernet Sauvignon (GAU)
1983
Freemark Abbey Cabernet Bosche (VIG)
1982
Acacia St Clair Pinot Noir (BUT)
Jekel Cabernet Sauvignon Private Reserve
   (BUT)
Mayacamas Cabernet Sauvignon (NO)

1980
Robert Mondavi Cabernet Sauvignon
   Reserve (WHI, GRE, VIG)
1976
Firestone Pinot Noir (BUT)

£20.00 to £29.99

1992
Saintsbury Pinot Noir Reserve (NI)
1989
Ridge Monte Bello Cabernet Sauvignon (AMI)
1988
Dominus Christian Moueix (MV)
Ridge Monte Bello Cabernet Sauvignon (AMI)
1987
Beringer Cabernet Sauvignon (ROB)
Dominus Christian Moueix (LAY, ARM)
1986
Dominus Christian Moueix (HAH, ARM)
1985
Heitz Bella Oaks Cabernet Sauvignon
   (BUT)
Robert Mondavi Cabernet Sauvignon
   Reserve (NO)
1983
Dominus Christian Moueix (ARM, BUT)
Robert Mondavi Cabernet Sauvignon
   Reserve (VIG)
1980
Ridge Monte Bello Cabernet Sauvignon
   (AMI)
Robert Mondavi Cabernet Sauvignon
   Reserve (NO, HOG)
1977
Robert Mondavi Cabernet Sauvignon
   Reserve (GAU)

£30.00 to £39.99

1990
E&J Gallo Cabernet Sauvignon (VIG)
1988
Dominus Christian Moueix (ARM)
Robert Mondavi Cabernet Sauvignon
   Reserve (BER)
1987
Mondavi/Rothschild Opus One (GRE, PE)
Robert Mondavi Cabernet Sauvignon
   Reserve (GAU)
1983
Mondavi/Rothschild Opus One (RAE)
1982
Heitz Martha's Vineyard Cabernet
   Sauvignon (NO, GRE)
1981
Mondavi/Rothschild Opus One (HOG)

1980
Ridge Monte Bello Cabernet Sauvignon
(BUT)
1978
Jekel Cabernet Sauvignon (BUT)
1975
Chalone Pinot Noir (BUT)
Robert Mondavi Cabernet Sauvignon (BUT)

£40.00 to £49.99
1990
Stag's Leap Cask 23 Cabernet Sauvignon
(WW)
1988
Mondavi/Rothschild Opus One (NO, TAN,
BEN, BUT)
1987
Mondavi/Rothschild Opus One (NO, PIP,
ROB, BUT, NI)
1986
Mondavi/Rothschild Opus One (NO, GRE, NI)
1985
Mondavi/Rothschild Opus One (NO, HAH, WHI)
1984
Heitz Martha's Vineyard Cabernet
Sauvignon (BUT)
Mondavi/Rothschild Opus One (NO)
1978
Ridge Monte Bello Cabernet Sauvignon (AD)

£50.00 to £59.99
1987
Mondavi/Rothschild Opus One (AMI)
1986
Mondavi/Rothschild Opus One (BUT)
1985
Mondavi/Rothschild Opus One (BUT)

£60.00 to £69.99
1985
Dominus Christian Moueix (BUT)
Heitz Martha's Vineyard Cabernet
Sauvignon (BUT)

CALIFORNIA WHITE

Under £4.00
Non-vintage
E&J Gallo Chenin Blanc (PE)
E&J Gallo French Colombard (SAF, SO, PE)
E&J Gallo Sauvignon Blanc (SAF, VIC, PE)
1991
E&J Gallo Chenin Blanc (DAV)
E&J Gallo French Colombard (DAV)
E&J Gallo Sauvignon Blanc (SAI)

£4.00 to £5.99
Non-vintage
Stratford Sauvignon Blanc (VIC)
Trefethen Eshcol (WHI)
1992
Dry Creek Chenin Blanc (GRE)
Glen Ellen Chardonnay (GRE)
Quady Essensia Orange Muscat ½ bottle
(NA)
Robert Mondavi Woodbridge Sauvignon
Blanc (NI, WHI)
Stratford Winery Chardonnay (WS)
1991
Firestone Riesling (AMI)
Glen Ellen Chardonnay (WHI)
Robert Mondavi Woodbridge Sauvignon
Blanc (EY, SEC)
1990
Beringer Fumé Blanc (BEK)
Clos du Val Chardonnay (WAT)
Julius Wile Chardonnay (PLA)
Robert Mondavi Sauvignon Blanc (HAH)
Sterling Chardonnay (OD)
Sterling Sauvignon Blanc (OD)
1989
Robert Mondavi Oakville Fumé Blanc (NI)
Stratford Winery Chardonnay (MAJ)
1988
Robert Mondavi Moscato d'Oro (WHI)

£6.00 to £7.99
Non-vintage
Quady Essensia Orange Muscat (NI)

Quady Essensia Orange Muscat ½ bottle
(HAM, SEC)
1992
Beringer Fumé Blanc (PIP)
★ Cá del Solo Malvasia Bianca (RAE, POR)
Dry Creek Chenin Blanc (ROB)
Firestone Chardonnay (SAI)
Hawk Crest Chardonnay (WW)

1991
Cá del Solo Malvasia Bianca (SOM)
Clos du Bois Sauvignon Blanc (GRE)
Clos du Val Chardonnay (LEA)
Dry Creek Fumé Blanc (CV)
★ Renaissance Riesling (AD)
Robert Mondavi Fumé Blanc (HOG, GRE)
Stag's Leap Sauvignon Blanc (WW)
1990
Dry Creek Chenin Blanc (ROB)
Dry Creek Fumé Blanc (GRE)
Firestone Chardonnay (HOG)
Preston Cuvée de Fumé (WS)
Quady Essensia Orange Muscat ½ bottle
  (NO, WHI, BEN)
Sanford Sauvignon Blanc (AMI)
Wente Bros Chardonnay (HOG)
1989
Clos du Bois Sauvignon Blanc (PE)
Dry Creek Chardonnay (HOG)
Dry Creek Fumé Blanc (HOG)
Quady Essensia Orange Muscat ½ bottle
  (ROB)
Wente Bros Chardonnay (SO, UN)
1988
★ Renaissance Riesling (PEN)

£8.00 to £9.99

1992
Il Podere dell'Olivos Arioso (MV)
Murphy Goode Fumé Blanc (AD)
Sanford Sauvignon Blanc (SOM)
1991
Beringer Chardonnay (BEK)
Cá del Solo Il Pescatore (MV)
Chateau St-Jean Fumé Blanc (PIP)
Clos du Bois Sauvignon Blanc (PE)
Dry Creek Chardonnay (EY)
Firestone Riesling (BER)
Il Podere dell'Olivos Arioso (WCL)
Murphy Goode Fumé Blanc (HAH)
Pedroncelli Chardonnay (LAY)
Saintsbury Chardonnay (GE)
Simi Sauvignon Blanc (CB, LAY)
1990
Buena Vista Chardonnay (WCL)
Dry Creek Fumé Blanc (DI)
Edna Valley Chardonnay (AMI, PIP, BEN)
Fetzer Barrel Select Chardonnay (AMI, DI)
Swanson Chardonnay (HOG)
1989
Clos du Bois Chardonnay (WHI)
Sanford Chardonnay (SOM)
Simi Sauvignon Blanc (TAN)
Swanson Chardonnay (AV)

1988
Edna Valley Chardonnay (HOG)
Grgich Hills Fumé Blanc (NO)
Newton Chardonnay (NO)
Renaissance Sauvignon Blanc (PEN)
Robert Mondavi Oakville Chardonnay (WHI)
Rutherford Hill Jaeger Chardonnay (AV)
Saintsbury Chardonnay (GE)
Sanford Sauvignon Blanc (HOG)
Swanson Chardonnay (PEN)
1987
Robert Mondavi Oakville Chardonnay (WHI)
Rutherford Hill Chardonnay (AV)
Shafer Chardonnay (WRI)
1986
Monticello Chardonnay (NO)
Saintsbury Chardonnay (AV)
1985
Renaissance Riesling Select Late Harvest
  ½ bottle (GAU)

£10.00 to £11.99

1992
Firestone Chardonnay (LEA)
Frog's Leap Chardonnay (MV)
Saintsbury Chardonnay (BIB)
1991
Grgich Hills Fumé Blanc (EL)
Newton Chardonnay (NO, POR, NI, GE)
Philip Togni Sauvignon Blanc (WW)
Robert Mondavi Chardonnay (PLA)
Stag's Leap Chardonnay (WW)
1990
Au Bon Climat Chardonnay (WCL)
Matanzas Creek Sauvignon Blanc (HAH)
Qupé Chardonnay (PLA, WCL, OD)
Simi Chardonnay (CB)
1989
Edna Valley Chardonnay (ROB, EY)
Robert Mondavi Chardonnay (TAN)
Simi Chardonnay (TAN)
1988
Sonoma-Cutrer Chardonnay (WRI)
1987
Robert Mondavi Fumé Blanc (VIG)
Sanford Chardonnay (HOG)
1979
Robert Mondavi Fumé Blanc (BUT)

> *In each price band wines
> are listed in vintage order.
> Within each vintage they
> are listed in A–Z order.*

£12.00 to £14.99

1992
Au Bon Climat Chardonnay (MV, PLA, BAR)
Shafer Chardonnay (BER)
1991
Au Bon Climat Chardonnay (POR)
Frog's Leap Chardonnay (BAR)
Sonoma-Cutrer Chardonnay (LEA)
1990
Au Bon Climat Chardonnay (ROB)
Cuvaison Chardonnay (AMI)
Edna Valley Chardonnay (WCL)
Jordan Chardonnay (LAY)
Qupé Chardonnay (MV)
Stag's Leap Chardonnay (ROB)
Torres Marimar Don Miguel Vineyard
    Chardonnay (NO)
1989
Acacia Chardonnay (AMI)
Iron Horse Chardonnay (NO)
★ Kistler Chardonnay Dutton Ranch (HAH)
Sanford Chardonnay (NI)
Stag's Leap Chardonnay (ROB)
Torres Marimar Don Miguel Vineyard
    Chardonnay (NO)
1988
Au Bon Climat Chardonnay (BUT)
Edna Valley Chardonnay (NO)
Robert Mondavi Oakville Reserve
    Chardonnay (WHI)
Simi Chardonnay (RE)
1987
Robert Mondavi Oakville Reserve
    Chardonnay (WHI)
1986
Robert Mondavi Chardonnay Reserve (GAU)
1983
Robert Mondavi Sauvignon Blanc Botrytis
    ½ bottle (HAL)

£15.00 to £19.99

1992
Bonny Doon Le Sophiste (MV, PLA)
Iron Horse Chardonnay (BER)
1991
Bonny Doon Le Sophiste (POR, AD)
Grgich Hills Chardonnay (EL)
Matanzas Creek Chardonnay (BAR)
Robert Mondavi Chardonnay Reserve (PLA)
Saintsbury Reserve Chardonnay (BIB)
1990
Kistler Chardonnay Dutton Ranch (NO)
Saintsbury Reserve Chardonnay (AD)
Sonoma-Cutrer les Pierres Chardonnay
    (HOG, PEN, AD)

1989
Chalone Chardonnay (AMI)
1988
Far Niente Chardonnay (NO)
Robert Mondavi Chardonnay Reserve (VIG)
Sonoma-Cutrer Chardonnay (ROB)
Sonoma-Cutrer les Pierres Chardonnay
    (SEC, ROB, AV)
1986
Alexander Valley Chardonnay (PEN)
1985
Joseph Phelps Johannisberg Riesling
    Selected Late Harvest ½ bottle (NO)
Mayacamas Chardonnay (NO)
Robert Mondavi Chardonnay Reserve (NO)
1984
Acacia Chardonnay (BUT)
1983
Joseph Phelps Johannisberg Riesling
    Selected Late Harvest ½ bottle (HAL)

£20.00 to £24.99

1992
Kistler Chardonnay Dutton Ranch (AD)
1989
Far Niente Chardonnay (AV)
1988
Simi Reserve Chardonnay (CB)

c. £35.00

1983
Robert Mondavi Sauvignon Blanc Botrytis
    (VIG)

CALIFORNIA ROSÉ

Under £4.00

Non-vintage
E&J Gallo White Grenache (SAF, VIC)

£4.00 to £4.99

Non-vintage
E&J Gallo White Zinfandel (PE)
1993
Robert Mondavi White Zinfandel (NI)
1992
E&J Gallo White Grenache (UN)

£5.00 to £5.99

1992
Robert Mondavi White Zinfandel (WHI)
1991
Robert Mondavi White Zinfandel (WHI)
1990
Robert Mondavi White Zinfandel (ROB)

CALIFORNIA SPARKLING

Under £9.00
Non-vintage
Cuvée Napa Brut Mumm (OD, POR)

£9.00 to £9.99
Non-vintage
Cuvée Napa Brut Mumm (ROB, SEC)

£15.00 to £19.99
1987
Schramsberg Blanc de Blancs (AD)
1986
Schramsberg Blanc de Blancs (ROB)
1984
Schramsberg Blanc de Noirs (AD)

c. £25.00
Non-vintage
Schramsberg J Schram (AMI)

OTHER USA RED

Under £7.00
Non-vintage
Cameron Pinot Noir (BIB)
1989
Columbia Pinot Noir (ASD)
1988
Covey Run Lemberger (HE)

£7.00 to £9.99
1987
Llano Estacado Cabernet Sauvignon (HE)
1986
Columbia Pinot Noir (PEN)
Elk Cove Estate Pinot Noir (HE)

£10.00 to £19.99
1991
Ponzi Pinot Noir (DI)
1990
Domaine Drouhin Pinot Noir (PLA)
Eyrie Vineyard Pinot Noir (WW, DI)
1989
Cameron Pinot Noir Reserve (BIB)
Domaine Drouhin Pinot Noir (HOG, LEA)
1988
Chateau Ste Michelle Cabernet Sauvignon
(WRI)

£20.00 to £24.99
1989
Domaine Drouhin Pinot Noir (VIG, WS, REI)

OTHER USA WHITE

Under £6.00
1993
Columbia Crest Sauvignon Blanc (SO)
1988
Fall Creek Emerald Riesling (HE)
1987
Covey Run Aligoté (HE)
1986
Texas Vineyards Johannisberg Riesling
(HE)

£6.00 to £7.99
1990
Hogue Cellars Fumé Blanc (ROB)
Salishan Chardonnay (WW)
Snoqualmie Semillon (ROB)
1989
Snoqualmie Semillon (WCL)
1988
Columbia Chardonnay (PEN)
Snoqualmie Muscat Canelli (WCL)

£8.00 to £9.99
1993
Adelsheim Pinot Gris (WW)
1992
Tyee Pinot Gris (WW)
1991
Ponzi Chardonnay (WW)
1990
Salishan Chardonnay (DI)
1988
Llano Estacado Chardonnay (HE)
1987
Elk Cove Estate Chardonnay Estate (HE)
1986
Salishan Chardonnay (WCL)

£11.00 to £15.99
1992
Adelsheim Chardonnay (WW)

1989
Cameron Chardonnay (BIB)
Eyrie Vineyard Chardonnay (ROB)

AUSTRALIA

RED

Under £4.00

1992
Berri Cabernet Sauvignon/Shiraz (WAI)
Orlando Jacob's Creek Red (HOG, GRE, WR, AUS, BOT, THR)
Tollana Cabernet Sauvignon/Shiraz (POR, THR, WR, BOT)
1991
Berri Cabernet Sauvignon/Shiraz (ASD)
Lindemans Shiraz Bin 50 (WAI)
Orlando Jacob's Creek Red (UN)
1990
Orlando Jacob's Creek Red (KA)

£4.00 to £4.99

1993
Rosemount Diamond Reserve Cabernet Sauvignon/Shiraz (NI)
1992
★ Baileys Bundarra Shiraz (OD)
Orlando Cabernet Sauvignon (DAV)
Penfolds Koonunga Hill Cabernet Sauvignon/Shiraz (SOM)
Penfolds Shiraz/Mataro Bin 2 (HOG, SOM, VIC, DAV)
Yalumba Oxford Landing Cabernet Sauvignon/Shiraz (NI)
1991
Lindemans Cabernet Sauvignon Bin 45 (POR, WHI)
Lindemans Shiraz Bin 50 (POR, WHI)
Orlando Cabernet Sauvignon (HOG, GRE)
Penfolds Koonunga Hill Cabernet Sauvignon/Shiraz (HOG, VIC)
Tyrrells Long Flat Red (PIP)
Wyndham's Shiraz Bin 555 (MAJ)
Yalumba Oxford Landing Cabernet Sauvignon/Shiraz (CV)
1990
Lindemans Cabernet Sauvignon Bin 45 (UN)
Lindemans Shiraz Bin 50 (UN)
Orlando Cabernet Sauvignon (SAI)
Orlando RF Cabernet Sauvignon (VIC, CV, AUS, SAF)
Yalumba Oxford Landing Cabernet Sauvignon/Shiraz (ASD)
1989
Penfolds Koonunga Hill Cabernet Sauvignon/Shiraz (AUS)
Rosemount Diamond Reserve Dry Red (CV)

£5.00 to £5.49

1992
David Wynn Cabernet Sauvignon (SOM)
Penfolds Koonunga Hill Cabernet Sauvignon/ Shiraz (THR, BOT, OD, SAF, TES, WR)
Rosemount Diamond Reserve Cabernet Sauvignon/Shiraz (LO)
Tyrrells Long Flat Red (TAN, AME)
1991
Brown Bros Shiraz (GRE)
Krondorf Shiraz/Cabernet Sauvignon (HOG)
Orlando RF Cabernet Sauvignon (LO, TAN)
Rosemount Diamond Reserve Dry Red (WHI)
Rouge Homme Shiraz/Cabernet Sauvignon (AME)
Wyndham's Cabernet Sauvignon Bin 444 (WHI)
1990
Basedows Shiraz (BIB)
Berri Cabernet Sauvignon (SO, UN)
David Wynn Pinot Noir (SOM)
Penfolds Kalimna Shiraz Bin 28 (HOG)
1989
Orlando Cabernet Sauvignon (KA)
Penfolds Kalimna Shiraz Bin 28 (AUS)
1988
Rouge Homme Shiraz/Cabernet Sauvignon (EY, GRE, HAM, WAT)

£5.50 to £5.99

1992
Basedows Cabernet Sauvignon (VIC)
Brown Bros Shiraz (NA)
Rosemount Cabernet Sauvignon (POR, GRE, WR, BOT, THR, NI, AME)
Rosemount Pinot Noir (POR, NI)
Rosemount Shiraz (POR, NI)
Rothbury Shiraz (AMI)
Wolf Blass Yellow Label Cabernet Sauvignon (HOG)
1991
Basedows Shiraz (VIC)
McWilliams Hanwood Cabernet Sauvignon (RE)
Mildara Cabernet Sauvignon/Merlot (PEN)
Penfolds Kalimna Shiraz Bin 28 (PIP)
Rothbury Shiraz (SOM)
Tyrrells Pinot Noir (SAF)
1990
Chateau Reynella Cabernet Sauvignon (CV)
★ Penfolds Coonawarra Shiraz Bin 128 (SOM, HOG)

Penfolds Koonunga Hill Cabernet
 Sauvignon/Shiraz (UN)
Rosemount Cabernet Sauvignon (VIC)
Rosemount Pinot Noir (GRE)
Yalumba Oxford Landing Cabernet
 Sauvignon/Shiraz (ROB)
1989
Baileys Bundarra Shiraz (NO)
Taltarni Shiraz (WHI, SOM)
1988
Brown Bros Cabernet Sauvignon (DI)
Brown Bros Shiraz (DI)
Brown Bros Shiraz/Cabernet Sauvignon (DI)
★Coldstream Hills Cabernet Sauvignon (CV)
Rosemount Cabernet Sauvignon (CHA)
Rosemount Pinot Noir (CHA)
Rosemount Shiraz (CHA)
Rothbury Shiraz/Cabernet Sauvignon (SEC)
1984
Idyll Cabernet Sauvignon/Shiraz (HOG)

£6.00 to £6.49

1993
David Wynn Cabernet Sauvignon (WCL)
David Wynn Pinot Noir (WCL)
1992
Best's Victoria Shiraz (BOR)
David Wynn Cabernet Sauvignon (HIC, AD)
Wynns Shiraz (WCL)
1991
Brown Bros Cabernet Sauvignon (PIP, POR)
Brown Bros Shiraz/Cabernet Sauvignon (WHI)
Penfolds Coonawarra Shiraz Bin 128 (WR,
 BOT, THR)
Peter Lehmann Cabernet Sauvignon (WAI)
Rosemount Cabernet Sauvignon (WHI)
Rosemount Hunter Valley Shiraz (WHI)
Wolf Blass Yellow Label Cabernet
 Sauvignon (POR)
Wyndham's Pinot Noir Bin 333 (WHI)
1990
Brown Bros Shiraz/Cabernet Sauvignon (WHI)
Chateau Tahbilk Shiraz (WS)
Penfolds Coonawarra Shiraz Bin 128 (TES)
Rosemount Hunter Valley Shiraz (WHI)
Wolf Blass Cabernet Sauvignon (WHI)
1989
Brown Bros Cabernet Sauvignon (WHI)
1986
Taltarni Merlot (WHI)

£6.50 to £6.99

1992
Mitchell Peppertree Shiraz (TAN, EY)
Rothbury Shiraz (WCL)

1991
Jamiesons Run Coonawarra Red (BE)
Knappstein Cabernet Sauvignon/Merlot (AMI)
★ Mount Langi Ghiran Shiraz (SOM)
Taltarni Merlot (POR)
Taltarni Shiraz (POR)
1990
Baileys Bundarra Shiraz (WRI)
Brown Bros Cabernet Sauvignon (PE, AD,
 PEN, AUS)
Brown Bros Shiraz (SEC)
Coriole Sangiovese (WS)
David Wynn Pinot Noir (DI)
De Bortoli Cabernet Sauvignon (OD)
Knappstein Cabernet Sauvignon (OD)
Penfolds Cabernet/Shiraz Bin 389 (HOG)
Penfolds Coonawarra Shiraz Bin 128 (WHI)
1989
Basedows Cabernet Sauvignon (BIB)
Chateau Reynella Cabernet Sauvignon (SO)
Chateau Tahbilk Cabernet Sauvignon (GRE)
Lindemans Cabernet Sauvignon Bin 45
 (BUT)
★Orlando St Hugo Cabernet Sauvignon (HOG)
Taltarni Shiraz (AUS)
Wolf Blass Yellow Label Cabernet
 Sauvignon (BY, SAF)
1988
Brown Bros Shiraz (AUS)
Lindemans Shiraz Bin 50 (BUT)
Rosemount Hunter Valley Shiraz (BUT)
1987
Lindemans Shiraz Bin 50 (BUT)

£7.00 to £7.49

Non-vintage
Penfolds Cabernet/Shiraz Bin 389 (SO)
1992
Jim Barry Cabernet Sauvignon (TAN)
1991
Coriole Shiraz (TAN)
Jamiesons Run Coonawarra Red (DAV)
Penfolds Coonawarra Shiraz Bin 128 (WCL)
Wolf Blass Yellow Label Cabernet
 Sauvignon (NO)
1990
Jamiesons Run Coonawarra Red (PEN)
Mount Langi Ghiran Shiraz (POR)
Taltarni Shiraz (PLA)
1989
Taltarni Cabernet Sauvignon (SAF)
1988
Campbells Shiraz (NO)
Coriole Cabernet Sauvignon (WS)
Rouge Homme Cabernet Sauvignon (HAY)

£7.50 to £7.99

1993
Coldstream Hills Pinot Noir (BEK)
1992
★ Charles Melton Nine Popes (SOM)
1991
Cape Mentelle Shiraz (POR)
Charles Melton Shiraz (POR, WCL)
Mount Langi Ghiran Shiraz (PIP, AME, GRE, WCL)
Penfolds Cabernet/Shiraz Bin 389 (OD)
Tasmanian Wine Company Pinot Noir (SOM, POR)
Tim Adams Shiraz (AUS)
Wyndham's Shiraz Bin 555 (RE)
1990
Charles Melton Shiraz (SOM)
Coldstream Hills Cabernet Sauvignon (BEK)
Rosemount Show Reserve Cabernet Sauvignon (TES, GRE)
Tasmanian Wine Company Pinot Noir (LEA)
1989
Penfolds Cabernet/Shiraz Bin 389 (AUS, POR)
Penfolds Coonawarra Cabernet (POR)
Rouge Homme Cabernet Sauvignon (AME, LEA, DI)

1987
Geoff Merrill Cabernet Sauvignon (WRI)
Penfolds Cabernet/Shiraz Bin 389 (DAV)
Taltarni Cabernet Sauvignon (PLA)
1986
Rouge Homme Cabernet Sauvignon (SEC)
Seppelt Cabernet Sauvignon Black Label (GAU)
Taltarni Cabernet Sauvignon (AME)
Taltarni Merlot (PLA)
Wynns Coonawarra Cabernet Sauvignon (HA)

£8.00 to £8.49

1992
★ St Halletts Old Block Shiraz (AUS)
1991
Coldstream Hills Pinot Noir (CV)
Penley Estate Coonawarra Cabernet Sauvignon/Shiraz (AUS)

1990
Cape Mentelle Zinfandel (POR)
Tyrrells Vat 9 Winemakers Selection Shiraz (HOG)
1989
Bannockburn Pinot Noir (AMI)
Cape Mentelle Shiraz (CV)
1988
Brown Bros Koombahla Cabernet Sauvignon (WRI, AUS)
Capel Vale Cabernet Sauvignon (AME)
1987
Knappstein Cabernet Sauvignon (GAU)
Orlando St Hugo Cabernet Sauvignon (CV)
Rosemount Show Reserve Cabernet Sauvignon (CHA)
1986
Penfolds Cabernet/Shiraz Bin 389 (AV)
Rosemount Show Reserve Cabernet Sauvignon (BUT)
1980
Wynns Coonawarra Cabernet Sauvignon (VIC)

£8.50 to £8.99

1992
Charles Melton Nine Popes (WCL)
Coldstream Hills Pinot Noir (PIP)
1991
Cape Mentelle Shiraz (PLA, AD)
Charles Melton Nine Popes (REI)
St Halletts Old Block Shiraz (LAY)
Tasmanian Wine Company Pinot Noir (PLA)
1990
Katnook Cabernet Sauvignon (BIB)
Mitchell Peppertree Shiraz (NO)
St Halletts Old Block Shiraz (REI, NO)
Tasmanian Wine Company Pinot Noir (SEC)
1989
Jamiesons Run Coonawarra Red (NO)
Plantagenet Shiraz (KA)
1988
Basedows Cabernet Sauvignon (TAN)
Jamiesons Run Coonawarra Red (NO)
Penfolds St-Henri Shiraz/Cabernet (SOM)
Plantagenet Shiraz (KA)
Wolf Blass President's Selection Cabernet Sauvignon (HOG)
1984
Redgate Cabernet Sauvignon (RAE)

£9.00 to £9.99

1991
Cape Mentelle Cabernet Sauvignon (NI)
Charles Melton Shiraz (GAU)
Mount Edelstone Shiraz (WS)

1990
Cape Mentelle Cabernet Sauvignon (GRE)
Eileen Hardy Shiraz (SAF, OD)
Lindemans Hunter Valley Shiraz (OD)
Lindemans Limestone Ridge Shiraz/
  Cabernet Sauvignon (POR, BOT, THR, WR)
★ Lindemans Pyrus (POR, SAI, OD)
Lindemans St George Cabernet Sauvignon
  (BOT, THR, WR)
Mount Edelstone Shiraz (AUS)
★ Mountadam Pinot Noir (SOM)
Petaluma Coonawarra Cabernet
  Sauvignon (OD)
★ Rockford Basket Press Shiraz (WCL, AUS)
Tim Adams Shiraz (TAN)
1989
Lindemans St George Cabernet Sauvignon
  (POR, OD)
★ Rockford Basket Press Shiraz (GAU, POR)
Vasse Felix Cabernet Sauvignon (AMI, MAJ)
Wolf Blass President's Selection Cabernet
  Sauvignon (GRE)
1988
Cape Mentelle Shiraz (BUT)
Cyril Henschke Cabernet Sauvignon (LAY)
Lindemans Limestone Ridge
  Shiraz/Cabernet Sauvignon (UN, AUS)
★ Lindemans Pyrus (AUS)
Lindemans St George Cabernet Sauvignon
  (AUS)
Orlando St Hugo Cabernet Sauvignon
  (BAR, UN)
Petaluma Coonawarra Cabernet
  Sauvignon (AMI, WR, BOT, THR)
1987
Moss Wood Cabernet Sauvignon (NO)
1980
Idyll Cabernet Sauvignon/Shiraz (HOG)

£10.00 to £10.99

1992
Coldstream Hills Pinot Noir (ARM)
1991
Hollick Coonawarra Cabernet
  Sauvignon/Merlot (BER)
Lake's Folly Cabernet Sauvignon (LAY)
Moss Wood Cabernet Sauvignon (GAL)
Penley Estate Coonawarra Cabernet
  Sauvignon (AUS)
1990
Cape Mentelle Cabernet Sauvignon (PLA,
  TAN, KA)
Charles Melton Shiraz (NO)
Rockford Basket Press Shiraz (WS, BEN,
  VIG, ROB)

1988
Eileen Hardy Shiraz (NO)
Moss Wood Cabernet Sauvignon (RAE)
1987
Cape Mentelle Cabernet Sauvignon (RAE)
Petaluma Cabernet Sauvignon/Merlot (NO)
1986
Cape Mentelle Cabernet Sauvignon (WCL, RAE)
Rouge Homme Cabernet Sauvignon (ROB)
Wynns Cabernet Sauvignon (TAN)
1985
De Bortoli Shiraz (NO)

£11.00 to £11.99

1992
Mountadam Pinot Noir (HIC, BOT, WR)
1991
Pipers Brook Pinot Noir (HOG)
1990
Bannockburn Pinot Noir (BEN)
Moss Wood Pinot Noir (GAL)
Mountadam Pinot Noir (NO)
Tarrawarra Pinot Noir (NO)
1989
Cape Mentelle Cabernet Sauvignon (BEN)
Penley Estate Coonawarra Cabernet
  Sauvignon/Shiraz (NO)
1988
Cape Mentelle Cabernet Sauvignon (RE, BUT)
Mountadam Pinot Noir (AME)
Penfolds Magill Estate Shiraz (HOG, SOM)
Petaluma Cabernet Sauvignon/Merlot (ROB)
1987
Lake's Folly Cabernet Sauvignon (AUS)
1985
Lindemans Pyrus (AV)
1984
Katnook Cabernet Sauvignon (NO)
1980
Brown Bros Family Reserve Cabernet
  Sauvignon (PIP)

£12.00 to £13.99

1991
Mountadam Pinot Noir (NO)
1990
Lindemans Pyrus (BER)
Penfolds Cabernet Sauvignon Bin 707
  (HOG, SOM)
Penfolds Magill Estate Shiraz (BOT, THR,
  WR)
Penley Estate Coonawarra Cabernet
  Sauvignon (LAY)
Petaluma Cabernet Sauvignon/Merlot (BEN)
Pipers Brook Pinot Noir (PEN, BEN)

1989
Penfolds Magill Estate Shiraz (POR, PIP)
Vasse Felix Cabernet Sauvignon (GRE)
Yarra Yering Dry Red No.2 (Shiraz) (ROB)
1988
Cyril Henschke Cabernet Sauvignon (WCL)
Dalwhinnie Cabernet Sauvignon (NO)
Vasse Felix Cabernet Sauvignon (LEA)
Yarra Yering Dry Red No.1 (Cabernet) (WCL)
1987
Cape Mentelle Cabernet Sauvignon (RE)
Moss Wood Cabernet Sauvignon (RE)
Tyrrells Pinot Noir (AV)
1986
Geoff Merrill Cabernet Sauvignon (WAT)
Penfolds Magill Estate Shiraz (AD)
Rosemount Kirri Billi Cabernet Sauvignon (BUT)
Rosemount Kirri Billi Merlot (BUT)
1985
Petaluma Cabernet Sauvignon/Merlot (NO)
1981
Chateau Tahbilk Cabernet Sauvignon (NO)

£14.00 to £15.99
1990
Mountadam Cabernet Sauvignon (NO)
Penfolds Cabernet Sauvignon Bin 707 (BY, PIP, POR, NO, OD, WR, TES, BOT, THR)
Yarra Yering Dry Red No.1 (Cabernet) (SOM, POR)
Yarra Yering Dry Red No.2 (Shiraz) (SOM, POR)
1989
Penfolds Cabernet Sauvignon Bin 707 (WR, THR, BOT, UN)
1988
Dromana Estate Cabernet/Merlot (BUT)
1986
Wolf Blass Black Label Cabernet Sauvignon (OD, POR)
1985
Lindemans Limestone Ridge Shiraz/Cabernet Sauvignon (NO, RAE)
Wolf Blass Black Label Cabernet Sauvignon (NO)

£16.00 to £19.99
1991
Yarra Yering Dry Red No.1 (Cabernet) (BEN)
Yarra Yering Dry Red No.2 (Shiraz) (BEN)
1990
Hollick Ravenswood Cabernet Sauvignon (TW)
1989
Yarra Yering Dry Red No.1 (Cabernet) (ROB, VIG)

1986
Penfolds Cabernet Sauvignon Bin 707 (NO)
1982
Vasse Felix Cabernet Sauvignon (VIG)

£20.00 to £29.99
1991
Jim Barry The Armagh Shiraz (TAN)
1990
Yarra Yering Pinot Noir (BEN)
1989
Yarra Yering Pinot Noir (NO)
1987
Penfolds Grange (SOM, BY)
1981
Penfolds Grange (HA)

£30.00 to £39.99
1988
Penfolds Grange (HOG, NO, POR, AD, WCL, WAT, BEN)
1985
Penfolds Grange (BER, NO)
1983
Penfolds Grange (BER, NO)
1982
Penfolds Grange (NO)
1978
Penfolds Grange (BUT)

WHITE

Under £4.00
1993
Nottage Hill Chardonnay (WAI)
Orlando Jacob's Creek Semillon/Chardonnay (HOG, LO, UN)
Penfolds Semillon/Chardonnay Bin 21 (POR)
1992
★ Hill-Smith Old Triangle Riesling (ASD)
Nottage Hill Chardonnay (ASD)
Orlando Jacob's Creek Semillon/Chardonnay (TES)
1991
Orlando Jacob's Creek Semillon/Chardonnay (AUS)

£4.00 to £4.49
1994
Orlando Jacob's Creek Semillon/Chardonnay (DAV)
1993
Hardy Bird Series Chardonnay (NO)
Nottage Hill Chardonnay (CV)

£4.50 to £4.99

1993
Basedows Semillon (VIC)
★ Brown Bros Dry Muscat (PIP)
Lindemans Chardonnay Bin 65 (POR, SOM,
    SAI, OD, BOT, MAR, THR, SAF, WR)
★ Mitchelton Un-oaked Marsanne (OD)
Orlando RF Chardonnay (DAV)
Penfolds Koonunga Hill
    Semillon/Chardonnay (OD, WAI, DAV)
Penfolds Semillon/Chardonnay Bin 21
    (BOT, THR, WR)
Pewsey Vale Riesling (TES)
Seaview Chardonnay (POR)
Tyrrells Long Flat White (PIP)
Yalumba Oxford Landing Chardonnay
    Yalumba Oxford Landing Chardonnay
    (HOG, NI)
1992
Brown Bros Dry Muscat (HOG)
Hardy Bird Series
    Gewurztraminer/Riesling (CV)
Hill-Smith Chardonnay (MAJ)
Lindemans Chardonnay Bin 65 (NO, UN)
Mitchelton Un-oaked Marsanne (ASD)
Orlando RF Chardonnay (HOG)
Penfolds Semillon/Chardonnay Bin 21
    (HOG, TES)
1991
Lindemans Sauvignon Blanc Bin 95 (WHI)
Orlando RF Chardonnay (SAF, AUS)
Yalumba Oxford Landing Chardonnay (ASD)
1990
Orlando RF Chardonnay (CV)
Tyrrells Long Flat White (AUS)
1989
Brown Bros Dry Muscat (DI)

£5.00 to £5.49

1993
Nottage Hill Chardonnay (WAT)
Wynns Chardonnay (SOM)

1992
Hardy Collection Chardonnay (SAI)
Penfolds South Australia Chardonnay (WHI)
Rothbury Chardonnay (HOG)
Wyndham's Chardonnay Bin 222 (MAJ)

1991
Basedows Semillon (BIB)
Houghton Gold Reserve Chardonnay (HOG)
Leasingham Chardonnay (MAJ)
Wyndham's Chardonnay Bin 222 (WHI)
1990
Rosemount Diamond Reserve
    Semillon/Sauvignon Blanc (WHI)
1986
★ Petersons Semillon (BEK)

£5.50 to £5.99

1993
Allandale Sutherland Chardonnay (AUS)
Basedows Chardonnay (VIC)
Rosemount Chardonnay (OD, LO, POR, DAV,
    NI, BOT, THR, WR)
Rosemount Fumé Blanc (LO, GRE, NI)
Rosemount Hunter Valley Chardonnay (AME)
Rothbury Brokenback Chardonnay (SOM)
Rothbury Chardonnay (DAV)
1992
Chateau Reynella Chardonnay (CV)
Len Evans Chardonnay (MAR)
Mitchelton Wood-Matured Marsanne (WAI)
Penfolds South Australia Chardonnay (WR,
    THR, BOT)
Rosemount Chardonnay (TES)
Tyrrells Old Winery Chardonnay (SAI)
Wyndham Estate Oak-Aged Chardonnay (MAJ)
Yalumba Oxford Landing Chardonnay (EY)
1991
Brown Bros Dry Muscat (EY, ROB)
Penfolds South Australia Chardonnay (MAJ)
Rosemount Chardonnay (VIC)
Rothbury Chardonnay (EY, AMI)
1990
Brown Bros Sauvignon Blanc (DI)
Leasingham Semillon (NO)
Rosemount Fumé Blanc (WHI)
1989
Brown Bros Sauvignon Blanc (WHI)
Brown Bros Semillon (DI)
Rosemount Fumé Blanc (CHA)
Rosemount Wood-Matured Semillon (WCL)
1987
Brown Bros Semillon (WHI)

£6.00 to £6.49

1993
Brown Bros Sauvignon Blanc (PIP)
David Wynn Chardonnay (WCL, AD)
David Wynn Riesling (WCL)
De Bortoli Chardonnay (WIC)
Wolf Blass Chardonnay (POR, GRE, WHI)

1992
Brown Bros Finest Reserve Victorian
    Muscat (TAN)
David Wynn Chardonnay (HIC)
Wolf Blass Chardonnay (WHI)
Wyndham's Chardonnay Bin 222 (TAN)
1991
Chateau Tahbilk Marsanne (PLA)
Mitchelton Wood-Matured Marsanne (SAI)
Rosemount Fumé Blanc (WHI)
Wyndham Estate Oak-Aged Chardonnay (WHI)
1990
Chateau Tahbilk Marsanne (NO)
Penfolds South Australia Chardonnay (HOG)

£6.50 to £6.99

1993
Jamiesons Run Chardonnay (BE)
Peter Lehmann Semillon (BER)
Pewsey Vale Riesling (ROB, WCL, BEN)
Rothbury Chardonnay (BEN, WCL)
Shaw & Smith Sauvignon Blanc (SOM)
Shaw & Smith Un-oaked Chardonnay (SOM)
1992
Basedows Chardonnay (BIB)
Best's Chardonnay (BOR)
Brown Bros Dry Muscat (BER)
David Wynn Riesling (DI)
De Bortoli Chardonnay (OD)
Jamiesons Run Chardonnay (SO)
Orlando St Hilary Chardonnay (HOG)
Shaw & Smith Sauvignon Blanc (POR)
Tyrrells Old Winery Chardonnay (AV)
1991
Brown Bros Semillon (PIP)
Penfolds South Australia Chardonnay
    (SOM, OD)
Wirra Wirra Sauvignon Blanc (AUS)
Wolf Blass Chardonnay (VIC)
1990
Bridgewater Mill Chardonnay (AMI)
Brown Bros Semillon (PE)
Hardy Collection Chardonnay (WAT)
Lindemans Chardonnay Bin 65 (BUT)
Mitchelton Wood-Matured Marsanne (WRI)
Rosemount Chardonnay (BUT)
Wolf Blass Chardonnay (AUS)
1989
Rosemount Chardonnay (BUT)
1988
Rouge Homme Chardonnay (HAY)
1987
Brown Bros Semillon (AUS)
1986
Hill-Smith Semillon (GE)

£7.00 to £7.49

1993
Cape Mentelle Semillon/Sauvignon Blanc (AD)
Lindemans Chardonnay Bin 65 (RE)
1992
Rosemount Show Reserve Chardonnay (WAI)
Wynns Chardonnay (POR)
1991
Jamiesons Run Chardonnay (NO)
Wirra Wirra Chardonnay (AUS)
1990
Cape Mentelle Semillon/Sauvignon Blanc (NO)
Knappstein Chardonnay (OD)

£7.50 to £7.99

1993
Cape Mentelle Semillon/Sauvignon Blanc
    (PLA, NI, DAV)
Shaw & Smith Sauvignon Blanc (WCL, AME,
    BEN, AD, ROB, BAR)
Shaw & Smith Un-oaked Chardonnay
    (WCL, NI)
Wirra Wirra Chardonnay (OD)
1992
Coldstream Hills Chardonnay (BEK)
Henschke Semillon (LAY)
Lindemans Padthaway Chardonnay (WR,
    BOT, THR)
Mildara Chardonnay (TAN)
Penfolds Padthaway Chardonnay (POR)
Rosemount Show Reserve Chardonnay (LO,
    SAI, POR, GRE, OD, WR, THR, BOT)
1991
Brown Bros Chardonnay (PE)
Knappstein Chardonnay (AMI)
Lindemans Padthaway Chardonnay (TES)
Rosemount Show Reserve Chardonnay (SAF)
Shaw & Smith Chardonnay (SOM)
Shaw & Smith Sauvignon Blanc (NO)
Simon Whitlam Chardonnay (WAI)
1990
Henschke Semillon (NO, AUS)
Wynns Chardonnay (THR, WR)
1989
Cape Mentelle Semillon/Sauvignon Blanc (CV)
Rothbury Reserve Chardonnay (AMI)
1988
Mitchelton Chardonnay (NO)
Rockford Semillon (AUS)
Rouge Homme Chardonnay (DI)
1987
McWilliams Mount Pleasant Elizabeth
    Semillon (RE)
Penfolds South Australia Chardonnay (WAT)
Rouge Homme Chardonnay (SEC)

£8.00 to £8.99

1993
Rosemount Show Reserve Chardonnay (NI)
1992
Cape Mentelle Chardonnay (NI)
Cape Mentelle Semillon/Sauvignon Blanc (EY)
Capel Vale Chardonnay (BAR)
Moss Wood Semillon (RAE, SEC)
Moss Wood Wooded Semillon (NO, RAE)
1991
Cape Mentelle Chardonnay (GRE)
Cape Mentelle Semillon/Sauvignon Blanc
  (WCL)
Coldstream Hills Chardonnay (CV)
Henschke Semillon (WCL)
Katnook Chardonnay (BIB)
Krondorf Chardonnay (VIC)
Moss Wood Semillon (ROB)
Petaluma Rhine Riesling (NO, AUS)
Tim Adams Semillon (BAR)
1990
Mitchelton Reserve Marsanne (NO)
Penfolds Padthaway Chardonnay (NO)
Plantagenet Chardonnay (WCL)
Rockford Semillon (WCL)
1989
Rosemount Show Reserve Chardonnay (CHA)
1986
Rosemount Show Reserve Semillon (BUT)

£9.00 to £9.99

1993
Petaluma Rhine Riesling (BEN)
1992
Cullens Chardonnay (NO, OD)
Petaluma Chardonnay (OD)
1991
Moss Wood Wooded Semillon (DAV)
Mountadam Chardonnay (WR, BOT)
Shaw & Smith Chardonnay (WCL, BEN, SEC,
  BAR, AUS)
1990
Krondorf Chardonnay (NO)
Petaluma Chardonnay (AMI)
Schinus Molle Chardonnay (NO)
Shaw & Smith Chardonnay (NO)
Tyrrells Vat 1 Semillon (AV)
1989
Cape Mentelle Chardonnay (NO, RAE)
Schinus Molle Sauvignon (BUT)
Simon Whitlam Chardonnay (GAU)

£10.00 to £12.99

1992
Moss Wood Wooded Semillon (VIG)

1991
Lakes Folly Chardonnay (LAY)
Petaluma Chardonnay (NO, ROB, WCL, NI, GOE)
Pipers Brook Chardonnay (GRE, PLA, WW)
Tyrrells Vat 47 Chardonnay (AV)
1990
Cape Mentelle Chardonnay (ROB, BUT)
Dromana Estate Chardonnay (BER)
Moss Wood Wooded Semillon (VIG)
Mountadam Chardonnay (WCL, HIC)
Pipers Brook Chardonnay (SOM, PEN, ROB, AUS)
1989
Moss Wood Semillon (RE)
Mountadam Chardonnay (GAU)
Petaluma Chardonnay (AUS)
Pikes Polish Hill River Sauvignon Blanc (BUT)
1988
Petaluma Chardonnay (NO)
Pokolbin Chardonnay (WRI)
1987
Lindemans Padthaway Chardonnay (BUT)

£13.00 to £15.99

1991
Rosemount Roxburgh Chardonnay (WHI)
1989
Rosemount Roxburgh Chardonnay (POR)
Yeringburg Marsanne (VIG)
1988
Rosemount Roxburgh Chardonnay (GRE,
  CHA, SAF)
1987
Rosemount Giants Creek Chardonnay (BUT)
1986
Rosemount Whites Creek Semillon (BUT)

£16.00 to £18.99

1991
Rosemount Roxburgh Chardonnay (BOT,
  THR, AME)
1990
Rosemount Roxburgh Chardonnay (NI)
Yalumba Chardonnay (NO)
1989
Yarra Yering Chardonnay (NO)
1987
Yarra Yering Chardonnay (BEN)

SPARKLING

Under £5.50

Non-vintage
Angas Brut (SOM, AUS)
Angas Brut Rosé (AUS)
Seaview (LO, AUS)

£5.50 to £5.99

Non-vintage
Angas Brut (NI, BAR, THR, OD, BOT, SAI, MAJ, WR)
Angas Brut Rosé (CV, NI, WAI, BAR, THR, OD, BOT, MAJ, WR, TES)
Taltarni Brut Taché (SOM)

£6.00 to £7.99

Non-vintage
Taltarni Brut (AD, PLA, WHI, HOG, AUS)
Taltarni Brut Taché (POR, WHI, HOG, AUS, AME)
Yalumba D (NI)
1989
★ Yellowglen Brut (PEN)

£8.00 to £9.99

1991
Croser (OD)
★Green Point Brut Domaine Chandon (CV, EY)
1990
Croser (SOM)
Green Point Brut Domaine Chandon (TES)
Seppelt Salinger Brut (SAI)
Seppelt Sparkling Shiraz (OD, TES)
Yalumba D (OD)
1989
★Green Point Brut Domaine Chandon (HOG)
1987
Seppelt Sparkling Shiraz (POR, NO, ROB)

£10.00 to £13.99

Non-vintage
Schinus Molle Chardonnay/Pinot Noir (BUT)
Seppelt Salinger Brut (DI)
Yalumba D (AUS)
1990
Green Point Brut Domaine Chandon (WHI)
Seppelt Salinger Brut (OD, TES, THR, BOT, AME, BEN)
1988
Croser (ROB)
Seppelt Salinger Brut (POR, SEC, DI)
1987
Yalumba D (AD)

SWEET & FORTIFIED

Under £5.00

1994
Brown Bros Orange Muscat & Flora ½ bottle (NA)
1993
Brown Bros Muscat Late Picked (HOG)
Brown Bros Orange Muscat & Flora ½ bottle (AD, GRE, PIP, POR, WR, PE, BOT, THR)

1992
Brown Bros Orange Muscat & Flora ½ bottle (BY, UN, PE)
1991
Brown Bros Orange Muscat & Flora ½ bottle (DI)

£5.00 to £5.99

1992
Brown Bros Muscat Late Picked (GRE, TES, WRI, PE, MAJ)
Brown Bros Noble Late Harvest Riesling ½ bottle (WAT, WHI)
Brown Bros Orange Muscat & Flora (ROB)
1991
Brown Bros Orange Muscat & Flora (AUS)
1990
Brown Bros Muscat Late Picked (DI, BY)
1989
Brown Bros Muscat Late Picked (SEC)
1988
Brown Bros Orange Muscat & Flora ½ bottle (SEC, PEN)
1982
Brown Bros Noble Late Harvest Riesling (MAJ)
Brown Bros Noble Late Harvest Riesling ½ bottle (GRE, BY, PIP)

£6.00 to £7.49

Non-vintage
Yalumba Museum Release Rutherglen Muscat (AUS)

£8.00 to £9.99

Non-vintage
Baileys Founder Liqueur Muscat (AME)
Baileys Liqueur Muscat (BAR)
Chambers Special Liqueur Muscat (NO)
Morris Liqueur Muscat (CV, GRE, KA, NO, WCL, BAR)
Stanton & Killeen Liqueur Muscat (AUS)

£10.00 to £12.99

Non-vintage
All Saints Rutherglen Liqueur Muscat (GAU)
Baileys Founder Liqueur Tokay (AUS, NO)
Brown Bros Liqueur Muscat (PIP)
Campbells Rutherglen Liqueur Muscat (NO, ROB, AUS)
Chambers Rosewood Liqueur Muscat (AD, RAE, SEC, GAU, TAN)

c.£17.00

Non-vintage
Bleasedale 16-year-old Verdello (BAR)

NEW ZEALAND

RED

Under £5.50

1992
Cooks Cabernet Sauvignon (WHI)
Montana Marlborough Cabernet
   Sauvignon (BOT, THR, WR, GRE)
1991
Cooks Cabernet Sauvignon (GRE, TES, WHI)
Montana Marlborough Cabernet
   Sauvignon (VIC, TES, KA, WAT)
1990
Cooks Cabernet Sauvignon (KA, DAV, VIC)

£5.50 to £6.99

1992
★ C J Pask Roy's Hill Red (TAN, LAY)
1991
Cooks Hawke's Bay Cabernet Sauvignon (AS)
Stoneleigh Marlborough Cabernet
   Sauvignon (WHI)
1990
Babich Henderson Valley Pinot Noir (HOG)
Nobilo Pinotage (GRE)
Redwood Valley Estate Cabernet
   Sauvignon (HOG)
Stoneleigh Marlborough Cabernet
   Sauvignon (TES, KA, WHI)
Villa Maria Cabernet Sauvignon (VIC)
1987
Nobilo Pinotage (WHI, AV, WRI)

£7.00 to £8.99

1992
Hunter's Pinot Noir (PIP)
Matua Valley Cabernet Sauvignon (BOT,
   THR, WR)
1991
Hunter's Pinot Noir (POR)
Ngatarawa Cabernet/Merlot (ROB)
Te Mata Coleraine Cabernet
   Sauvignon/Merlot (NA)
1989
Matua Valley Cabernet Sauvignon (NI)
1988
St-Nesbit Cabernet Sauvignon/Cabernet
   Franc/Merlot (FIZ)

£9.00 to £10.99

1992
Hunter's Pinot Noir (DI, ROB)
★Martinborough Pinot Noir(SOM,LAY,AME,OD)

1991
C J Pask Cabernet Sauvignon (EY, TAN, HAH)
Cloudy Bay Cabernet Sauvignon/Merlot
   (NO, WCL, BUT)
Delegat's Cabernet Sauvignon (BEN)
Palliser Estate Pinot Noir (CV, WR, BOT, OD,
   THR)
1990
Cloudy Bay Cabernet Sauvignon/Merlot (AD)
Hunter's Pinot Noir (KA)
1989
Cloudy Bay Cabernet Sauvignon/Merlot (NI)
Matua Valley Cabernet Sauvignon (KA)
1988
Cloudy Bay Cabernet Sauvignon/Merlot (CV)
1987
St-Nesbit Cabernet Sauvignon/Cabernet
   Franc/Merlot (WAT)
1985
Ngatarawa Cabernet/Merlot (NO)
1984
Nobilo Concept One (AV)

£11.00 to £14.99

1991
Palliser Estate Martinborough Vineyard
   Pinot Noir (SEC, WCL)
1990
Cloudy Bay Cabernet Sauvignon/Merlot(BUT)
Kumeu River Merlot/Cabernet Sauvignon(BEN)
1988
Martinborough Pinot Noir (BUT, GAU)
Te Mata Coleraine Cabernet
   Sauvignon/Merlot (NO)
1987
Te Mata Coleraine Cabernet Sauvignon(AME)

£15.00 to £18.99

1993
Stonyridge Larose Cabernet (FIZ)
1991
Stonyridge Larose Cabernet (AD)
1988
Stonyridge Larose Cabernet (NO)

WHITE

Under £4.00

1993
Nobilo White Cloud (SAI, GRE)
1992
Nobilo White Cloud (VIC)

1991
Cooks Chenin Blanc (WHI)
1989
Cooks Riesling/Chenin Blanc (KA)

£4.00 to £4.99

1994
Montana Marlborough Chardonnay (DAV)
Montana Marlborough Sauvignon Blanc(DAV)
1993
★ Delegat's Sauvignon Blanc (HOG)
Montana Marlborough Chardonnay (THR,
  WR, OD, GRE, BOT)
Montana Marlborough Sauvignon Blanc(HOG,
  SAI, SAF, BOT, ROB, OD, TES, GRE, THR, WR)
Nobilo Sauvignon Blanc (TES)
1992
Cooks Hawke's Bay Chardonnay (DAV, WAI)
Cooks Sauvignon Blanc (GRE, LO)
Montana Marlborough Chardonnay (HOG,
  ASD, ROB, WHI, VIC, SAF, KA, TES)
Montana Marlborough Sauvignon Blanc
  (SO, WHI, VIC, KA, ASD)
Nobilo Marlborough Sauvignon Blanc(GE, GRE)
Nobilo White Cloud (DAV, AV)
1991
Cooks Hawke's Bay Chardonnay (KA)
Cooks Sauvignon Blanc (KA)
Cooks Semillon (WHI)
Matua Valley Late Harvest Muscat ½
  bottle (NI)
Montana Marlborough Chardonnay (WHI)
Montana Marlborough Sauvignon Blanc(WHI)
1990
Cooks Chenin Blanc (KA)
Cooks Semillon (KA)
★ Matua Valley Late Harvest
  Gewürztraminer ½ bottle (LEA)

£5.00 to £5.99

1993
Aotea Sauvignon Blanc (SUM, ROB, FIZ, MV)
Babich Hawke's Bay Sauvignon Blanc (HOG)
Collards Chenin Blanc (BIB)
Coopers Creek Marlborough Sauvignon
  Blanc (NA)
Hawke's Bay Chardonnay (EL)
Matua Valley Brownlie Sauvignon (NI)
Montana Marlborough Chardonnay (PIP)
Montana Marlborough Sauvignon Blanc(EL)
Selaks Sauvignon Blanc (SOM)
Stoneleigh Marlborough Sauvignon Blanc
  (GRE, THR, WR, BOT)
Vidal Sauvignon Blanc (VIC)
Villa Maria Sauvignon Blanc (WAI)

1500
Aotea Sauvignon Blanc (KA)
Delegat's Chardonnay (HOG)
Matua Valley Chardonnay (NI)
Montana Marlborough Sauvignon Blanc
  (SEC, WAT, UN)
Morton Estate Sauvignon Blanc (BEK)
1991
Babich Gisborne Semillon/Chardonnay(PEN)
C J Pask Roy's Hill White (TAN)
Mills Reef Sauvignon Blanc (HOG)
Nobilo Gewürztraminer (WHI)
1990
Delegat's Sauvignon Blanc (CV)

£6.00 to £6.99

1993
Cloudy Bay Sauvignon Blanc (HAH)
Collards Marlborough Sauvignon Blanc(BIB)
Collards Rothesay Sauvignon Blanc (BIB)
Morton Estate Sauvignon Blanc (PIP)
Redwood Valley Sauvignon Blanc (HOG)
Wairau River Sauvignon Blanc (SOM)
1992
Babich Gisborne Semillon/Chardonnay(WRI)
Babich Hawke's Bay Chardonnay (HOG)
Coopers Creek Chardonnay (NA)
Matua Valley Sauvignon Blanc (PLA)
Millton Gisborne Chardonnay (SAF)
Nobilo Gisborne Chardonnay (AV)
Redwood Valley Late Harvest Rhine
  Riesling ½ bottle (FIZ)
Stoneleigh Chardonnay (GRE, TES)
Vidal Sauvignon Blanc (HOG, KA)
1991
Collards Rothesay Chardonnay (BIB)
Morton Estate Chardonnay (BEK)
Redwood Valley Late Harvest Rhine
  Riesling ½ bottle (WAT, ROB, LEA)
Stoneleigh Chardonnay (KA, WHI)
1990
Redwood Valley Late Harvest Rhine
  Riesling ½ bottle (KA, RE)
Selaks Sauvignon Blanc (PE)
1989
Delegat's Chardonnay (CV)
1988
Stoneleigh Marlborough Sauvignon Blanc(SO)

Stars (★) indicate wines
selected by the editors as
particularly good value
in their class.

£7.00 to £7.99

1993
Dashwood Sauvignon Blanc (OD)
Jackson Estate Marlborough Chardonnay (WW)
Jackson Estate Marlborough Sauvignon
  Blanc (GRE, WAI, CV, PLA, PIP, WHI, DAV,
  WW, WRI, WR, BOT, THR, TES)
Te Mata Castle Hill Sauvignon Blanc (WS, AME)
1992
Jackson Estate Marlborough Chardonnay
  (TAN, CV, WAI)
Morton Estate Chardonnay (PIP)
Selaks Kumeu Estate Sauvignon Blanc (AD)
Wairau River Sauvignon Blanc (SEC, WR)
1991
Dashwood Sauvignon Blanc (NO)
Esk Valley Sauvignon Blanc (KA)
Hunter's Gewürztraminer (HOG)
Mills Reef Chardonnay (HOG)
Morton Estate Chardonnay Reserve (BEK)
Nobilo Sauvignon Blanc (PEN)
1990
Ngatarawa Chardonnay (HOG)
Nobilo Gisborne Chardonnay (HAM)

£8.00 to £8.99

1993
Cloudy Bay Sauvignon Blanc (WAT)
Hunter's Sauvignon Blanc (HOG, GRE, POR,
  CV, LO, PIP)
Vavasour Oak-Aged Reserve Sauvignon
  Blanc (BOT, THR)
1992
Cloudy Bay Sauvignon Blanc (KA)
Dashwood Chardonnay (HAH)
Jackson Estate Marlborough Sauvignon
  Blanc (NO)
Kumeu River Sauvignon Blanc (FA)
Martinborough Vineyards Chardonnay (WCL)
Ngatarawa Sauvignon Blanc (LEA)
Palliser Estate Sauvignon Blanc (BUT)
Redwood Valley Chardonnay (HOG, FIZ)
Selaks Chardonnay (PE)
Te Mata Castle Hill Sauvignon Blanc (WRI)
Vavasour Oak-Aged Reserve Sauvignon
  Blanc (OD, WR)
Wairau River Chardonnay (SOM)
1991
Palliser Estate Martinborough Vineyard
  Sauvignon Blanc (BUT)
Redwood Valley Sauvignon Blanc (WAT)
Rongopai Te Kauwhata Chardonnay (PIP)
1990
Nobilo Dixon Chardonnay (AV)
Selaks Founders Reserve Chardonnay (SOM)

£9.00 to £10.99

1993
Elston Chardonnay (NA)
Palliser Estate Martinborough Vineyard
  Sauvignon Blanc (BUT)
1992
Cloudy Bay Chardonnay (NI, CV, GOE, WCL)
Hunter's Chardonnay (POR, PIP, BEN)
Hunter's Sauvignon Blanc (GAU, KA, NO)
Hunter's Wood-Aged Sauvignon Blanc
  (TAN, BEN, DI)
Palliser Estate Chardonnay (HAH)
1991
Babich Irongate Chardonnay (HOG, TAN)
Cloudy Bay Chardonnay (NO)
Hunter's Sauvignon Blanc (DI)
Kumeu River Chardonnay (NO, FA)
Martinborough Vineyards Chardonnay (LAY)
Mills Reef Chardonnay (FIZ)
Ngatarawa Chardonnay (LEA)
1989
Babich Irongate Chardonnay (PEN)
Giesen Chardonnay (KA)

£11.00 to £12.99

1992
Te Mata Elston Chardonnay (BOT, AME, WR)
1990
Palliser Estate Chardonnay (BUT)
Te Mata Elston Chardonnay (NO)
1989
Vidal Reserve Chardonnay (FIZ)
Villa Maria Reserve Chardonnay (HA)
1988
Martinborough Vineyards Chardonnay
  (GAU, BUT)

£13.00 to £15.99

1992
Elston Chardonnay (BEN)
Kumeu River Chardonnay (BEN)
1990
Kumeu River Chardonnay (UN)

SPARKLING

Under £7.00

Non-vintage
Lindauer Brut (WHI, SAI, TES, THR, BOT, WR, POR)

£7.00 to £9.99

Non-vintage
★ Daniel Le Brun Brut (NO)
Deutz Marlborough Cuvee (HOG, ROB, TES,
  OD, THR, BOT, WR)

CHILE

RED

Under £4.00

1992
Caliterra Cabernet Sauvignon (AME)
Concha y Toro Cabernet Sauvignon/Merlot (NI)
Concha y Toro Merlot (WAI)
1991
Caliterra Cabernet Sauvignon (SAI, DAV)
Concha y Toro Cabernet Sauvignon (WAI, NI)
Concha y Toro Cabernet Sauvignon/Merlot (HIC)
Concha y Toro Merlot (NI)
Santa Rita 120 Cabernet Sauvignon (OD)
Undurraga Cabernet Sauvignon (GRE)
1990
Caliterra Cabernet Sauvignon (ASD)
★ Villa Montes Cabernet Sauvignon (SAF)

£4.00 to £4.49

1991
Caliterra Cabernet Sauvignon (CV, OD)
Concha y Toro Cabernet Sauvignon/Merlot (EY)
Torres Cabernet Sauvignon (HOG)
Undurraga Cabernet Sauvignon (GE)
Villa Montes Cabernet Sauvignon (PLA)
1990
Caliterra Cabernet Sauvignon (WAT)
Concha y Toro Cabernet Sauvignon (GRE)
Santa Helena Siglo d'Oro Cabernet Sauvignon (HOG)
Santa Rita 120 Cabernet Sauvignon (BIB)
1989
Santa Rita 120 Cabernet Sauvignon (WHI)
1988
Santa Rita 120 Cabernet Sauvignon (WHI)
1987
Concha y Toro Cabernet Sauvignon (VIC)

£4.50 to £4.99

1992
Errázuriz Panquehue Cabernet Sauvignon (OD)
Los Vascos Cabernet Sauvignon (GRE)
1991
Concha y Toro Merlot (UN)
Los Vascos Cabernet Sauvignon (HOG)
San Pedro Merlot (ROB)
Torres Curico Cabernet Sauvignon (AME)
Undurraga Cabernet Sauvignon (WRI, LEA)

1990
Concha y Toro Cabernet Sauvignon (EY, HAM)
Errázuriz Panquehue Cabernet Sauvignon (GRE, VIC)
Santa Rita Cabernet Sauvignon Reserva (TES)
Torres Cabernet Sauvignon (GRE, PE)
Torres Santa Digna Cabernet Sauvignon (DI)
Undurraga Cabernet Sauvignon (AV, UN, BEN)
Undurraga Pinot Noir (GRE, TES)
Villa Montes Cabernet Sauvignon (GRE)
1989
Cousiño Macul Don Luis Red (NI)
Undurraga Cabernet Sauvignon (SUM)
Undurraga Cabernet Sauvignon Reserve Selection (GRE)
Viña Carmen Cabernet Sauvignon (WAI)
1988
Santa Rita 120 Cabernet Sauvignon (DI)
Viña Linderos Cabernet Sauvignon (NO)

£5.00 to £5.99

1992
Los Vascos Cabernet Sauvignon (PLA, LAY, BEN)
1991
Canepa Estate Oak-Aged Cabernet Sauvignon (WIC)
Concha y Toro Merlot (TAN)
Los Vascos Cabernet Sauvignon (HIC, LEA)
1990
Concha y Toro Cabernet Sauvignon (TAN)
Concha y Toro Casillero del Diablo (GRE)
Concha y Toro Merlot (OD)
Los Vascos Cabernet Sauvignon (WHI)
Santa Rita Cabernet Sauvignon Reserva (BIB)
Undurraga Pinot Noir (AV, WRI)
Villa Montes Cabernet Sauvignon (BER)
1989
Castillo de Molina Cabernet Sauvignon (ROB)
Montes Cabernet Sauvignon (TAN, WRI)
Santa Rita Cabernet Sauvignon Reserva (AD, LAY)
1988
Cousiño Macul Antiguas Reservas Cabernet Sauvignon (GRE)
Montes Cabernet Sauvignon (GRE)
Santa Rita Cabernet Sauvignon Reserva (DI)
Undurraga Cabernet Sauvignon Reserve Selection (EY, PEN, AV, BEN, LEA)

£6.00 to £6.99

1990
Cousiño Macul Antiguas Reservas
    Cabernet Sauvignon (AD)
Los Vascos Cabernet Sauvignon (ARM)
Santa Rita Cabernet Sauvignon Medalla
    Real (BIB)
1989
Cousiño Macul Antiguas Reservas
    Cabernet Sauvignon (TAN, NI, MOR)
Cousiño Macul Cabernet Sauvignon (HAM)
Santa Helena Seleccion del Directorio
    Cabernet Sauvignon (WRI)
Santa Rita Cabernet Sauvignon Medalla
    Real (SAF)
1988
Cousiño Macul Antiguas Reservas
    Cabernet Sauvignon (EY)
Cousiño Macul Cabernet Sauvignon (SOM,
    HIC)
Marqués de Casa Concha Cabernet
    Sauvignon (GRE)
Santa Rita Cabernet Sauvignon Medalla
    Real (DI)
Santa Rita Cabernet Sauvignon Reserva
    (ROB)

£7.00 to £8.99

1990
★ Montes Alpha Cabernet Sauvignon (DAV)
1989
Concha y Toro Cabernet Sauvignon (EY)
Marqués de Casa Concha Cabernet
    Sauvignon (TAN)
★ Montes Alpha Cabernet Sauvignon (AD,
    PLA, WRI, LAY)
1988
★ Montes Alpha Cabernet Sauvignon (OD,
    TES, VIC)
1987
Concha y Toro Cabernet Sauvignon (NO)

WHITE

Under £4.00

1994
★ Villa Montes Sauvignon Blanc (TES)
1993
Caliterra Chardonnay (DAV, AME)
Caliterra Sauvignon Blanc (GRE, AME, DAV)
Concha y Toro Sauvignon Blanc/Semillon (NI)
Undurraga Sauvignon Blanc (PEN, GRE)
1992
Caliterra Chardonnay (ASD)
Caliterra Sauvignon Blanc (OD)

£4.00 to £4.99

1993
Caliterra Sauvignon Blanc (CV)
Concha y Toro Chardonnay (NI, GRE)
Errázuriz Panquehue Chardonnay (OD)
Montes Chardonnay (TES)
Santa Rita 120 Sauvignon Blanc (BIB)
Torres Sauvignon Blanc (HOG, AME, TAN)
Undurraga Sauvignon Blanc (HIC, WRI, BEN)
Villa Montes Sauvignon Blanc (VIC, PLA)
1992
Caliterra Chardonnay (CV, OD)
Caliterra Sauvignon Blanc (WAT)
Concha y Toro Chardonnay (UN)
Cousiño Macul Chardonnay (GRE)
Santa Rita 120 Sauvignon Blanc (DI)
Undurraga Chardonnay (GRE)
Undurraga Sauvignon Blanc (EY, SUM, AV, UN)
Villa Montes Sauvignon Blanc (GRE)
1991
Errázuriz Panquehue Chardonnay (GRE, VIC)
Torres Santa Digna Sauvignon Blanc (DI)
1990
Caliterra Chardonnay (WAT)
Torres Bellaterra Sauvignon Blanc (DI)

£5.00 to £5.99

1993
Montes Chardonnay (WRI)
Undurraga Chardonnay (WRI, BEN)
Villa Montes Chardonnay (PLA)
1992
Concha y Toro Sauvignon Blanc/Semillon
    (TAN)
Montes Chardonnay (ROB)
Santa Rita Sauvignon Blanc Reserva (BIB)
Undurraga Chardonnay (EY, AV)
1991
Concha y Toro Chardonnay (OD)
1990
Cousiño Macul Chardonnay (NI)

£6.00 to £6.99

1993
Santa Rita Chardonnay Medalla Real (BIB)
1992
Santa Rita Chardonnay Medalla Real (ROB)
1991
Marqués de Casa Concha Chardonnay (GRE)
Santa Rita Chardonnay Medalla Real (DI)

c. £8.50

1991
William Fèvre Chardonnay, Santa Rosa
    del Pera (HIC)

SOUTH AFRICA

RED

Under £4.00

1992
Pinotage Culemborg Paarl (WAI)
1991
KWV Cabernet Sauvignon (DAV)
1990
KWV Cabernet Sauvignon (HOG, WR, UN,
THR, BOT)
KWV Pinotage (DAV, THR, UN, WR, BOT)
KWV Roodeberg (WAI, BOT, DAV, WR, CAP, THR)
KWV Shiraz (HOG)
1989
KWV Pinotage (HOG, DI)
KWV Roodeberg (UN, DI, VIC)
KWV Shiraz (UN)
1988
KWV Cabernet Sauvignon (DI)
KWV Roodeberg (HOG, GRE)

£4.00 to £4.99

1992
Drostdy Hof Rouge Select (TAN)
1991
Backsberg Cabernet Sauvignon (WAI, CAP)
★ Backsberg Pinotage (HOG, CAP)
Fairview Pinotage (CAP)
1990
Backsberg Cabernet Sauvignon (HOG)
Backsberg Pinotage (CAP)
Nederburg Pinotage (LO)
1989
Diemersdal (CAP)
Fairview Pinotage (WRI)
KWV Cabernet Sauvignon (EY, GRE, KA)
Nederburg Baronne (CAP)
Nederburg Edelrood (CAP, HOG)
Nederburg Paarl Cabernet Sauvignon
(HOG, CV, LO)
Nederburg Pinotage (WRI)
1988
Nederburg Paarl Cabernet Sauvignon
(POR, KA)
Nederburg Pinotage (HOG, CAP)
1987
Nederburg Pinotage (KA)

£5.00 to £5.99

1991
Backsberg Klein Babylonstoren (CAP)
Rustenberg Dry Red (CAP, TAN)

1990
Delheim Pinotage (SEC)
Groot Constantia Pinotage (CAP)
Nederburg Paarl Cabernet Sauvignon (TAN)
Rustenberg Dry Red (AV, HAM)
Zonnebloem Pinotage (CAP)
Zonnebloem Shiraz (CAP)
1989
Backsberg Pinotage (AD)
Groot Constantia Shiraz (CAP)
Zonnebloem Cabernet Sauvignon (CAP)
Zonnebloem Shiraz (CAP, GRE)
1988
Diemersdal (KA)
Klein Constantia Shiraz (HOG)
KWV Laborie (DAV)
KWV Shiraz (AV)
Zonnebloem Cabernet Sauvignon (CAP, BU, GRE)
Zonnebloem Pinotage (CAP)
1987
Klein Constantia Shiraz (GRE, AV)

£6.00 to £7.99

1992
★ Hamilton Russell Pinot Noir (PIP)
Kanonkop Pinotage (TES)
1991
★ Hamilton Russell Pinot Noir (HOG, WHI,
EY, LAY, AV, GAU, TAN)
Kanonkop Pinotage (CAP)
1990
Allesverloren Tinta Barocca (CAP)
Backsberg Klein Babylonstoren (KA)
Groot Constantia Cabernet Sauvignon
(CAP, DAV)
★Hamilton Russell Pinot Noir (GRE, WHI, HAM)
Kanonkop Pinotage (EY, HAM)
Klein Constantia Cabernet Sauvignon
(HOG, CAP)
Zandvliet Shiraz (CAP)
1989
★Hamilton Russell Pinot Noir (WAT, GAU, ROB)
Rustenberg Cabernet Sauvignon (GRE)
1988
Allesverloren Tinta Barocca (DI, CAP)
Backsberg Cabernet Sauvignon (BUT)
Fleur du Cap Roodebloem (CAP)
Groot Constantia Cabernet Sauvignon (KA)
Groot Constantia Heerenrood (CAP)
Meerendal Pinotage (DI)
Meerlust Rubicon (HOG)
Rustenberg Cabernet Sauvignon (HOG, AV, CAP)

1987
Klein Constantia Cabernet Sauvignon
  (HOG, EY, AV, AD, TAN)
1986
Uitkyk Carlonet (HOG)
Zandvliet Shiraz (DI)

£8.00 to £9.99

1990
Neil Ellis Cabernet Sauvignon (AD)
Stellenryk Cabernet Sauvignon (CAP)
1989
Rustenberg Gold (GRE, AV)
1987
Stellenrych Collection Cabernet (WRI)
1986
Blaauwklippen Cabernet Sauvignon (BUT)
Meerlust Cabernet Sauvignon (HOG)
1982
Backsberg Cabernet Sauvignon (PEN)
1980
Zonnebloem Shiraz (CAP)

£10.00 to £12.99

1987
Backsberg Klein Babylonstoren (BU)
Meerlust Cabernet Sauvignon (WRI)

1986
Meerlust Rubicon (WRI)
Warwick Farm Cabernet Sauvignon
  (VIG)
1985
Overgaauw Tria Corda (VIG)
1984
Meerlust Cabernet Sauvignon (DI)

c. £18.00

1974
Zonnebloem Pinotage (GAU)

WHITE

Under £4.00

1993
KWV Chenin Blanc (MAR, HOG, WAI, WR,
  THR, DAV, BOT, VIC)
KWV Sauvignon Blanc (MAR, HOG, WAI, DAV,
  VIC, WR, THR, BOT)
1992
KWV Chenin Blanc (GRE, CAP, UN)
KWV Sauvignon Blanc (CAP, UN)
1991
KWV Chenin Blanc (DI)
KWV Riesling (UN, GRE)

1990
KWV Chenin Blanc (CAP)
KWV Riesling (DI)

£4.00 to £5.99
1993
Backsberg Sauvignon Blanc (HOG, CAP)
Klein Constantia Sauvignon Blanc (GRE, HOG, EY)
1992
Backsberg Chardonnay (HOG, WAI)
Backsberg Sauvignon Blanc (CAP, WRI)
KWV Laborie (CAP)
Nederburg Stein (CAP)
Rustenberg Chardonnay (HOG)
de Wetshof Rhine Riesling (CAP)
1991
Klein Constantia Sauvignon Blanc (CV, CAP)
KWV Steen (PEN)
Nederburg Stein (HOG, LO)
Rustenberg Chardonnay (AV)
1990
Klein Constantia Chardonnay (HOG)
Koopmanskloof Blanc de Marbonne (CAP)
1989
Backsberg Sauvignon Blanc (BUT)
KWV Cape Foret (PEN)
Zonnenbloem Gewürztraminer (CAP)
1986
KWV Steen Special Late Harvest (PEN)

£6.00 to £7.99
1993
Hamilton Russell Chardonnay (GRE, EY)
1992
Hamilton·Russell Chardonnay (HOG, TAN, GAU, DI, LEA)
le Bonheur Sauvignon Blanc (CAP)
Neil Ellis Sauvignon Blanc (LEA)
l'Ormarins Sauvignon Blanc (WRI)
Uitkyk Carlsheim (CAP)
1991
Backsberg Chardonnay (WRI)
Hamilton Russell Chardonnay (WAT, ROB, AV)
Klein Constantia Chardonnay (EY, CAP)
Neil Ellis Sauvignon Blanc (ROB)
1989
Hamilton Russell Chardonnay (HAM)
l'Ormarins Sauvignon Blanc (DI, VIN)

£8.00 to £9.99
1992
de Wetshof Chardonnay (CAP)
1990
Nederburg Edelkeur ½ bottle (BU)

1988
Klein Constantia Vin de Constance ½ litre (HOG, GRE)
de Wetshof Chardonnay (DI)

ROSÉ
Under £5.00
1993
Nederburg Rosé (CAP)
1992
KWV Cabernet Sauvignon Blanc de Noir (WHI)
Nederburg Cabernet Sauvignon Blanc de Noir (CAP)

SPARKLING
Under £5.50
Non-vintage
Nederburg Premiere Cuvée Brut (HOG)

£5.50 to £6.99
Non-vintage
KWV Mousseux Blanc Cuvée Brut (CAP)
Laborie Blanc de Noir (CAP)
Nederburg Sparkling Première Cuvée Brut (KA)

c. £10.00
Non-vintage
JC Le Roux Sauvignon Blanc (CAP)

FORTIFIED
Under £4.50
Non-vintage
Mymering Pale Extra Dry (HOG)
Renasans Dry Amontillado (HOG)

£4.50 to £4.99
Non-vintage
Cavendish Fine Old Ruby (HOG)
Mymering Pale Extra Dry (CAP, DI)
Onzerust Medium (CAP, DI)
Renasans Pale Dry (CAP, DI)

£5.00 to £6.99
1979
Cavendish Vintage (CAP)
1963
Cavendish Vintage (HOG, CAP)

c. £9.00
1966
Cavendish Vintage (CAP)

OTHER WINE REGIONS

ARGENTINA

Under £5.50

1990
Trapiche Cabernet Sauvignon Reserve
(PLA)

c. £7.00

1983
Cavas de Weinert Cabernet Sauvignon
(BUT)

£8.50 to £10.00

1985
Cavas de Weinert Cabernet Sauvignon (CV,
LEA, ARM)
Mendoza Cabernet Sauvignon (NO)

AUSTRIA

Under £4.00

1990
Grüner Veltliner Lenz Moser Selection (WAI)

£4.00 to £5.50

1990
Grüner Veltliner Lenz Moser Selection
(PEN, ROB)
Pinot Blanc Lenz Moser Selection (PEN)

CANADA

Under £5.50

1992
Inniskillin Maréchal Foch Red (GRE)

£6.00 to £6.99

1992
Inniskillin Chardonnay (GRE)
1988
Inniskillin Maréchal Foch Red (AV)
Inniskillin Riesling (ROB)

£7.00 to £7.99

1989
Inniskillin Chardonnay (AV)
1988
Inniskillin Chardonnay (DI)

c. £10.00

1987
Inniskillin Pinot Noir Reserve (AV)

CYPRUS TABLE WINES

Under £4.00

Non-vintage
Aphrodite Keo White (TES, WHI)
Othello Keo Red (WHI)
St-Panteleimon Keo White (WHI)

£4.00 to £4.99

Non-vintage
Aphrodite Keo White (UN, DI)
Othello Keo Red (UN, DI)
St-Panteleimon Keo White (UN, DI)
Thisbe Keo White (WHI)

GREECE RED

Under £4.00

Non-vintage
Mavrodaphne Patras, Kourtaki (WAI)
1991
★ Nemea, Boutari (OD)

£4.00 to £5.99

Non-vintage
Demestica Achaia Clauss (DI)
Mavrodaphne Patras, Botrys
(NO, TAN)
Mavrodaphne Patras, Kourtaki (RE)
1988
Nemea, Kouros (UN)

£6.00 to £6.99

1990
Château Carras (DI)
1987
Château Carras (NO, DI)
★ Château Carras Côtes de Meliton
(CV, WS, TAN)

£7.00 to £7.99

1990
Château Carras (NO)
1981
Château Carras (NO)

---

*In each price band wines
are listed in vintage order.
Within each vintage they
are listed in A–Z order.*

GREECE WHITE

Under £3.00

Non-vintage
Retsina Kourtaki (WAI)

£3.00 to £4.49

Non-vintage
Demestica Achaia Clauss (DI)
Retsina Kourtaki (OD, VIC)
Retsina Metaxas (DAV, AD, PE)
Retsina Tsantali (TAN)
1991
Patras, Kouros (WAI)

HUNGARY WHITE

Under £3.50

1993
Gyöngyös Estate Chardonnay (SO)
Gyöngyös Estate Sauvignon Blanc (SO, SAF)

£3.50 to £3.99

1993
Gyöngyös Estate Chardonnay (PLA)
Gyöngyös Estate Sauvignon Blanc (PLA)
1988
Tokay Szamorodni Dry ½ litre (WIW)
Tokay Szamorodni Sweet ½ litre (WIW)
1986
Tokay Szamorodni Dry ½ litre (WIW)

£5.00 to £7.99

Non-vintage
Tokay Aszú 3 Putts ½ litre (DI, PE)
Tokay Aszú 4 Putts ½ litre (DI)
1988
Tokay Szamorodni Dry ½ litre (AD)
Tokay Szamorodni Sweet ½ litre (UN)
1986
Tokay Aszú 3 Putts ½ litre (WIW, BU)
Tokay Szamorodni Dry ½ litre (BU)
Tokay Szamorodni Sweet ½ litre (BU)
1983
Tokay Aszú 3 Putts ½ litre (VIG)
Tokay Aszú 5 Putts ½ litre (POR)
Tokay Szamorodni Dry ½ litre (ROB)
1982
Tokay Aszú 5 Putts ½ litre (OD)
1981
Tokay Aszú 3 Putts ½ litre (AD)

£8.00 to £13.99

Non-vintage
Tokay Aszú 5 Putts ½ litre (DI, LAY)

1988
Tokay Aszú 3 Putts ½ litre (GRE)
Tokay Aszú 5 Putts ½ litre (PLA)
1983
Tokay Aszú 4 Putts ½ litre (VIG)
Tokay Aszú 5 Putts ½ litre (AD, UN, VIG)
1981
Tokay Aszú 5 Putts ½ litre (GRE, TAN, ROB)

£30.00 to £65.00

1963
Tokay Aszú Muskotalyos ½ litre (AD)
1957
Tokay Aszú 3 Putts ½ litre (BU)
Tokay Aszú 6 Putts ½ litre (AD)
Tokay Aszú Essencia ½ litre (GRE)
1956
Tokay Aszú 4 Putts ½ litre (AD)
Tokay Aszú 5 Putts ½ litre (AD)

HUNGARY RED

Under £3.00

Non-vintage
Hungarian Cabernet Sauvignon (WHI)
1992
Villany Cabernet Sauvignon (ASD, SAF)

£3.00 to £4.99

Non-vintage
Eger Bull's Blood (SO, PE)
1983
Hungarian Merlot (WIW)

c. £6.00

1991
Palkonya Cabernet Sauvignon (BOD)

ISRAEL

Under £5.00

Non-vintage
Carmel Cabernet Sauvignon (SAF)
Palwin No. 10 (SAF)
1992
Carmel Petite Sirah Shomron Israel (MAR)

£5.00 to £6.99

Non-vintage
Palwin No. 4 (SAF, RE)
1993
Yarden Cabernet Sauvignon White
  Harvest (WRI)
1992
Golan Mount Hermon Dry White (WRI)

£7.00 to £8.99

1991
Yarden Chardonnay (WRI)
1990
Gamla Galilee Cabernet Sauvignon
  (WRI)
1987
Gamla Galilee Cabernet Sauvignon (ROB)

LEBANON RED

Under £7.50

1987
Château Musar (GRE)
1986
Château Musar (GRE, POR)
1985
Château Musar (SO)

£7.50 to £7.99

1987
Château Musar (GE, CHA, CV, PEN, POR, PLA,
  LO, MAJ, AMI)
1986
Château Musar (GAU, CHA, WHI, NI, DI)
1985
Château Musar (GRE)

£8.00 to £9.99

1988
Château Musar (LAY, BEN)
1987
Château Musar (TAN, AD, WRI, BAR, ROB,
  BUT, NA, AV)
1986
Château Musar (BAR, ROB, BUT, UN,
  BEN)
1985
Château Musar (CHA, DI, WRI, ROB,
  BUT)
1983
Château Musar (WHI, CHA,
  DI)
1982
Château Musar (POR, CV, WHI)

£10.00 to £11.99

1982
Château Musar (WRI, ROB,
  BEN)
1981
Château Musar (GE, POR, CHA, ROB,
  AMI)
1980
Château Musar (POR, GRE, CHA)

£12.00 to £18.99

1979
Château Musar (CHA, VIG)
1978
Château Musar (CHA, GRE, NI, AMI)

£20.00 to £29.99

1977
Château Musar (CHA, AMI)
1975
Château Musar (GAU, POR, CHA, WRI, AMI)

c. £36.00

1970
Château Musar (GAU)

c. £52.00

1972
Château Musar (CHA)

LEBANON WHITE

Under £6.50

1992
Château Musar Blanc (GRE)
1989
Château Musar Blanc (GRE)

£6.50 to £7.49

1991
Château Musar Blanc (GE, WRI)
1990
Château Musar Blanc (AD)
1989
Château Musar Blanc (WRI)

c. £8.50

1989
Château Musar Blanc (VIG)

LUXEMBOURG

c. £7.00

Non-vintage
Cuvée de l'Ecusson Brut (EL)

MEXICO

Under £5.00

1991
★ L A Cetto Petit Sirah (PLA, CV)
1988
★ L A Cetto Cabernet Sauvignon (CV)
1987
L A Cetto Cabernet Sauvignon (PLA)

MOLDOVA

Under £5.00

1987
★ Negru de Purkar (NO)

£5.00 to £7.99

1988
Negru de Purkar (VIG)
1987
Directors' Reserve Cuvée Kamrat,
   Kozhushny Winery (NO, AD, VIG)
1986
Negru de Purkar (NO, BU)
1984
Kodru, Krikova Winery (BU)

£8.50 to £10.99

1979
Negru de Purkar (AD, VIG)
1978
Negru de Purkar (POR, BAR)
1975
Negru de Purkar (POR, BU)

ROMANIA

Under £3.50

Non-vintage
Pinot Noir Dealul Mare (PE)
1992
Romanian Sauvignon Blanc (GRE)
1988
Classic Pinot Noir (GRE)

£3.50 to £4.49

1988
Romanian Pinot Noir (BU)
1986
Romanian Cabernet Sauvignon
   (BU)
★ Tamaioasa (GRE)
1984
Romanian Cabernet Sauvignon
   (BU)

c. £8.00

1960
★ Tamaioasa (BU)

SLOVENIA WHITE

Under £3.50

Non-vintage
Lutomer Laski Rizling (ASD, UN)

MERCHANT DIRECTORY

Abbreviations used in the Merchant Directory are as follows. **Credit cards** Access (AC), American Express (AE), Diners Club (DC), Switch (S), Visa/ Barclaycard (V). The following services are available where indicated: **C** cellarage, **EP** *en primeur* offers, **G** glass hire/loan, **M** mail order, **T** tastings and talks.

ADNAMS (AD)

(Head office & mail order) The Crown, High St, Southwold, Suffolk IP18 6DP, (0502) 724222, fax (0502) 724805;
The Cellar & Kitchen Store (Southwold collection), Victoria St, Southwold, Suffolk IP18 6JW;
The Wine Shop, South Green, Southwold, Suffolk IP18 6EW;
The Grapevine, 109 Unthank Rd, Norwich NR2 2PE, (0603) 613998
Hours Mail order: Mon–Fri 9–5, Sat 9–12.
Cellar & Kitchen Store: Mon–Sat 10–6.30.
The Wine Shop: Mon–Sat 10–7.15.
The Grapevine: Mon–Sat 9–9.
Credit cards AC S V.
Discounts £3 per case if collected (off mail order price).
Delivery £5 1 case, free 2 or more cases mainland UK.
Minimum order 1 mixed case.
C EP G M T
There's hardly an interesting wine that Adnams doesn't have. Pretty well every region is represented, too, including China, should you want to risk it. Brilliant on Australia, New Zealand, California, Germany, Italy, Bordeaux, Burgundy, Rhône, Alsace, Loire, French country – well, everything really. Excellent spirits, too, plus olive oils, vinegars (including the fabulous Valdespino sherry vinegar), ties and tasting blazers. All this, plus Adnams-owned The Crown, The Swan and The Cricketers, makes Southwold worth a detour.

AMEY'S WINES (AME)

83 Melford Road, Sudbury, Suffolk CO10 6JT, (0787) 377144
Hours Tue–Sat 10–7.
Credit cards AC V.
Discounts 5% off purchases of 12 or more bottles.
Delivery Free within 20 miles of Sudbury, min order £50
G
A varied and well-thought-out list; what is it about East Anglia that seems to attract so many good merchants? Strengths here are Australia, plus the south of France and middle-range Italy; fizz is good too, as is sherry.

LES AMIS DU VIN (AMI)

The Winery, 4 Clifton Rd, London W9 1SS, 071-286 6475;
Mail order: 430 High Road, London NW10 2HA, 081-451 0469 (24 hour)
Hours Clifton Rd: Mon–Fri 10.30–8.00, Sat 10–6.30.
Credit cards AC AE DC S V.
Discounts 5% unsplit cases for non-members, 10% for members (5% per bottle).
Delivery Free 3 or more cases, otherwise £3.95 London, £5.50 nationally. **C EP G M T**

The codes given in brackets on these pages beside the merchants' names are those by which the merchants are listed in the price guides (pages 262-427). They are also listed on page 263.

*Long on French wine, especially
Champagne, Bordeaux, Rhône and
Languedoc-Roussillon, though the
New World and Italy are strong as
well, and there's a good selection of
half bottles. Classic names feature in
the list: Guigal, Château de
Beaucastel, Opus One; and wines from
the south of France often have equally
immaculate pedigrees – good names
like Château de Fabas and Roger
Vergé's Côtes de Provence. There's not
much excitement under £5, though.*

JOHN ARMIT WINES (ARM)

5 Royalty Studios, 105 Lancaster
Road, London W11 1QF, 071–727
6846, fax 071–727 7133
Hours Mon–Fri 9–6.
Credit cards AC V.
Delivery Free 3 or more cases.
Minimum order 1 unmixed case.
C EP M T

*Getting a list out of this merchant was
like getting blood out of a stone, but
perhaps you may have better luck.
John Armit has positioned himself
firmly at the top of the market, without
outstanding selections from classic
regions and an interesting sprinkling
from elsewhere. But polish up your
gold card: 'inexpensive' here means up
to £10 a bottle, or £120 a case.*

ASDA (ASD)

(Head office) Asda House, Southbank,
Great Wilson Street, Leeds LS11 5AD,
(0532) 435435, fax (0532) 418666
Hours Mon–Fri 9–8, Sat 8.30–8, open
most bank hols, selected stores open
Sunday.
Credit cards AC S V. **T G**
*A smaller selection than some
supermarkets but unexpectedly good,
with a well-chosen and often
unconventional fine wine section.*

ASHLEY SCOTT (AS)

PO Box 28, The Highway, Hawarden, Deeside, Clwyd CH5 3RY, (0244) 520655
Hours 24-hr answerphone.
Discounts 5% unmixed case.
Delivery Free in north Wales, Cheshire, Merseyside.
Minimum order 1 mixed case. **G M T**
There's a small, pretty standard range here and nothing really catches the imagination. This is a club, not a shop, with a 24-hour answering machine.

AUSTRALIAN WINE CENTRE (AUS)

Down Under, South Australia House, 50 Strand, London WC2N 5LW, 071-925 0751, fax 071-839 9021
Hours Mon–Fri 10–7, Sat 10–4.
Credit cards AC AE V.
Discounts 5% 1 case cash, collected.
Delivery Free anywhere in UK for orders over £75, otherwise £6.50. **G M T**
A list written by and for enthusiasts. You'll see some of these wines (though by no means all) elsewhere, and not all the top names are here, but any Aussie wine fan could have a very good time here. In January 1995 they'll be moving premises, but at the time of writing they didn't know where.

AVERYS (AV)

7 Park St, Bristol BS1 5NG, (0272) 214141, fax (0272) 221729
Hours Mon–Sat 9–7.
Credit cards AC S V.
Discounts By negotiation.
Delivery Free 1 or more cases or within 5 mile radius of central Bristol, otherwise £5.50 per consignment.
C EP G M T
Long-established, and with a strong mail order side. Averys was a New World pioneer, but the Old World is strong, too. Good house Champagne.

BARNES WINE SHOP (BAR)

51 High St, Barnes, London SW13 9LN, 081-878 8643
Hours Mon–Sat 9.30–8.30, Sun 12–2.
Credit cards AC S V.
Discounts 5% mixed case, larger discounts negotiable.
Delivery Free in London.
Minimum order 1 mixed case or magnum (for delivery).
C EP G M T
A well-chosen, high-quality range from pretty well everywhere, with no reliance on famous names for the sake of it. Prices are pretty good.

BEDFORD FINE WINES (BE)

Faulkner's Farm, The Marsh, Carlton, Bedford MK43 7JU, (0234) 721153, fax (0234) 721145
Hours Office hours or by arrangement.
Discounts On preferred wines.
Delivery Free in Bedford, Luton and St Albans areas, £80 minimum order.
Minimum order 1 mixed case.
EP G M T
Claret (back to 1970) is the biggest single section here; other regions are less well represented, though French country wines look interesting. Some good Germans, too. The New World doesn't seem to be exactly a passion, with just two from New Zealand and three each from Australia and South Africa.

BENNETTS (BEN)

High Street, Chipping Campden, Glos GL55 6AG, (0386) 840392
Hours Mon–Fri 9–1, 2–5.30, Sat 9–5.30.
Credit cards AC V
Discounts On collected orders only.
Delivery Free 2 cases or more in England and Wales.
Minimum order 1 case.

This list has just about everything you could want, providing you want something French, Italian or to a lesser extent Australian. Other sources – Spain, Portugal – are good, but you wouldn't go out of your way. California is interesting, though, with names like Ridge, Calera, Bonny Doon and Qupe.

BERKMANN WINE CELLARS (BEK)

12 Brewery Rd, London N7 9NH, 071-609 4711
Hours Mon–Fri 9–5.30, (Sat 10–2 for occasional tasting). Closed bank holiday weekends.
Credit cards AC V.
Discounts £1 per case collected.
Delivery £3 less than 3 cases or £200 in value (excl vat) for all areas within M25, or £6 for Home Counties.
Minimum order 1 mixed case.
C EP G M T
Berkmann is the wholesale side, Le Nez Rouge the retail side. It's a very strong list that looks mostly towards France: excellent in most areas, and Burgundy lovers will think they've gone to heaven. It has recently expanded its New World section, with Beringer from California and Santa Monica from Chile, and with all the pride of a new parent it seems keen to emphasise these and play down its traditional strengths. Can't think why – its New World list is fine, but its French stuff is terrific.

BERRY BROS & RUDD (BER)

3 St James's St, London SW1A 1EG, 071-396 9600, fax 071-396 9611;
The Wine Shop, Hamilton Close, Houndmills, Basingstoke, Hants RG21 2YB, (0256) 23566, fax (0256) 479558
Hours St James's St: Mon–Fri 9.30–5. The Wine Shop: Mon–Fri 9–5, Sat 9–1.
Credit cards AC DC S V.
Discounts 3–7.5% according to quantity.
Delivery Free 1 case or more.
C EP G M T
There's a historically correct 250-year-old shop in St James's, a rather less romantic address in Basingstoke and now a decidedly commercial duty free branch at Heathrow's Terminal 3. You can order in advance, and collect before take-off. The list is excellent; claret prices are average, but other regions can look a bit extravagant.

BIBENDUM (BIB)

113 Regents Park Rd, London NW1 8UR, 071-722 5577
Hours Mon–Thur 10–6.30, Fri 10–8, Sat 9.30–6.30.
Credit cards AC AE V.
Delivery Free London, northern England, otherwise £6.97 up to 5 cases.
Minimum order 1 mixed case.
C EP G M T

A top class list, and a merchant that inspires confidence. There's more everyday stuff at around a fiver or less than there used to be, but the glories of the list are the fine wines. There's the best of California, Australia, France, Italy and Spain, and quite a lot of new stuff this year, too.

BORDEAUX DIRECT (BOD)

(Head office & mail order) New Aquitaine House, Paddock Rd, Reading, Berks RG4 0JY, (0734) 481718, fax (0734) 461493
Hours Mon–Fri 10.30–7 (Thur until 8), Sat 9–6; 24-hr answerphone. Mail order: Mon–Fri 9–7, Sat & Sun 10–4.
Credit cards AC AE DC S V.
Discounts Special offers.
Delivery Free for orders over £50.
G EP M T
The original 'direct from the vineyard' company. Mostly mail order, but there are five shops in the Thames Valley. Bordeaux Direct offers a particularly good range of French country wines, also well-priced drinking from Chile, Eastern Europe and Spain, from a rapidly-changing list. Sister company to the Sunday Times Wine Club.

BORG CASTEL (BOR)

Samlesbury Mill, Goosefoot Lane, Samlesbury Bottoms, Preston, Lancs PR5 0RN, phone & fax (025 485) 2128
Hours Mon–Fri 10–5, Thu 7–9.30pm, first Sun of month 12–4.
Discounts 6 or more cases.
Delivery Free 1 case or more within 30 mile radius.
C G M T
On this fairly-priced list most is from France and Germany. A good range from the Rhône and the Loire, and Alsace is represented by the reliable co-op at Turckheim.

BOTTOMS UP (BOT)

(Head office) Sefton House, 42 Church Rd, Welwyn Garden City, Herts AL8 6PJ, (0707) 328244, fax (0707) 371398
Hours Mon–Sat 9–10 (some 10.30), Sun 12–3, 7–10.
Credit cards AC AE S V.
Discounts 10% mixed cases wine, 17.5% mixed cases Champagne.
Delivery Free locally (all shops).**G T**
The largest shops of the Thresher chain.

BUTE WINES (BUT)

Mount Stuart, Rothesay, Isle of Bute PA20 9LR (0700) 502730, fax (0700) 505313.
2 Cottesmore Gardens, London W8 5PR, 071-937 1629.
Delivery (per case) £8.50 for 1, £10.50 for 2, £12.50 for 3, £13.50 for 4, free 5 or more.
Minimum order 1 case. **EP M T**

No shop at either address, but stock is held on Bute, and in London, Glasgow and Corsham. Much emphasis on classic names. Half a dozen top Alsace producers are here in depth, and a few famous names from Italy. There's also a decent sprinkling of New World, while Bordeaux and Burgundy are strongest of all.

BUTLERS WINE CELLAR (BU)

247 Queens Park Rd, Brighton BN2 2XJ, (0273) 698724, fax (0273) 622761
Hours Tue–Wed 10–6, Thu–Fri 10–7, Sat 9–7
Credit cards AC S V.
Delivery Free locally 1 case or more, free mainland England and Wales, some parts of Scotland 3 or more cases; otherwise (per bottle) £4.50 for 1, £5.50 for 2–3, £6.50 for 4–6, £7.50 for 7–12, £8.50 for 13–24, £10 for 25–35, 36 or more free.
G M T
Bin-ends are the mainstay of this shop – and what bin ends. Geoffrey and Henry Butler make a speciality of anniversary years – but not all are terrifically expensive. There's a rapid turnover, and a new list comes out every six weeks. They also have the sort of wine that's for drinking, not just giving – with a quirky, always good, and often excellent range of wines from just about everywhere. Plenty are priced at under a tenner.

ANTHONY BYRNE (BY)

88 High St, Ramsey, Huntingdon, Cambs PE17 1BS, (0487) 814555, fax (0487) 814962
Hours Mon–Sat 9–5.30.
Credit cards AC V.
Discounts 5% mixed case, 10% unsplit case.
Delivery £6 less than 5 cases, free 5 or more cases. **C M T**

A list packed with well-selected wines from Burgundy, Alsace, the Loire, the south of France, Italy, Australia, New Zealand... Pudding wines are a passion, and this is one of the few places to sell the extraordinary Château Gilette from Sauternes. There's also some sweet Pacherenc from Gascony – go on, surprise your friends.

CAPE PROVINCE WINES (CAP)

1 The Broadway, Kingston Rd, Staines, Middx TW18 1AT, (0784) 451860/455244, fax (0784) 469267
Hours Mon–Sat 9–9, Sun 12–1.
Credit cards AC S V.
Delivery £6 locally and London, UK mainland varies with quantity.
Minimum order 6 bottles.
M T
South African wines, as you might guess, are the be all and end all of this list, so it should be coming into its own now. There are Nederburg auction wines and rare vintages as well as plenty of others.

CELTIC VINTNER (CV)

73 Derwen Fawr Road, Sketty, Swansea SA2 8DR, (0792) 206661, fax (0792) 296671
Hours Mon–Fri 9–6, other times by arrangement.
Discounts Negotiable.
Delivery Free South Wales, elsewhere at cost.
Minimum order 1 mixed case.
C EP G T
An informative and stimulating list. Balance is the key; with Spain, for instance, you don't just get Torres (which would be no hardship), you get CVNE and Réné Barbier as well. Burgundy looks interesting, and there are quite a few half bottles for the abstemious (or possibly the greedy who want to try everything).

CHÂTEAUX WINES (CHA)

11 Church St, Bishop's Lydeard,
Taunton, Somerset TA4 3AT, phone &
fax (0454) 613959
Hours Mon–Fri 9–5.30, Sat 9–12.30.
Credit cards AC S V.
Discounts Negotiable.
Delivery Free UK mainland 1 case or
more.
Minimum order 1 case (usually
mixed).
C EP M T
*A short list of decent producers without
much variety, but there are oddities
like red and white Coteaux
Champenois from Laurent Perrier.
Laurent Perrier Champagne also
comes in big sizes, up to the 16-bottle
balthazar. Châteaux Wines have no
shop; everything is mail order.*

CORNEY & BARROW (CB)

12 Helmet Row, London EC1V 3QJ,
071-251 4051;
194 Kensington Park Rd, London
W11, 071-221 5122;
31 Rutland Sq, Edinburgh EH1 2BW,
031-228 2233;
Belvoir House, High St, Newmarket
CB8 8OH, (0638) 662068;
Corney & Barrow (Scotland) with
Whighams of Ayr, 8 Academy Street,
Ayr KA7 1HT, (0292) 267000
Hours Mon–Fri 9–5.30; 24-hr
answerphone.
Credit cards AC V.
Delivery Free London 2 or more
cases, elsewhere free 3 or more cases.
C EP G M T
*Sole UK importer of Château Pétrus
and the Domaine de la Romanée
Conti, which gives you some clue to the
rest of the list. All the Moueix wines are
here, plus a range of petits châteaux.
There's also a glittering cast of
Burgundy producers. Australia is
represented by Penfolds Grange and
Parker Estate, Italy by the super-
Tuscan Sassicaia. At the quirkier end
there are a couple of Canadians, and
Israelis from Baron Wine Cellars. C&B
say they are not pricy. Well, wine like
Pétrus doesn't come cheap, and if you
have to ask the price you can't afford it.
Don't expect bargains.*

DAVISONS (DAV)

(Head ofice) 7 Aberdeen Road,
Croydon, Surrey CR0 1EQ, 081-681
3222, fax 081-760 0390;
76 shops around the south-east.
Hours Mon–Sat 10–2, 5–10.
Credit cards AC S V.
Discounts 8.5% mixed case.
Delivery Free locally.
EP G T
*Strong on claret, petits châteaux,
Burgundy and vintage ports bought en
primeur. The strengths have always
been in the classic areas, but these are
now joined by wines from Australia,
Chile, Spain and Portugal. Often very
good prices.*

DIRECT WINE (DI)

5–7 Corporation Square, Belfast,
Northern Ireland BT1 3AJ, (0232)
243906, fax (0232) 240202
Hours Mon–Fri 9.30–6 (Thu till 8),
Sat 9.30–5.
Credit cards AC V.
Discounts 5% 6 unmixed bottles, 5%
1 mixed case, 7.5% 1 unmixed case.
Delivery Free in Northern Ireland 2
or more cases.
C EP M T
*This list specializes in Europe, with a
nice balance of good everyday wines
and some seriously fine ones from
Bordeaux, Burgundy, the Rhône and
Alsace. Good Germans and Italians
can be found here, too. From Spain
there's good value, tasty Toro, up to the
rather pricier Vega Sicilia.*

ELDRIDGE, POPE (EL)

(Head office) Weymouth Ave, Dorchester, Dorset DT1 1QT, (0305) 251251
Mail order: (0800) 378757.
Hours Mon–Sat 9–5.30.
Credit cards AC V.
Discounts On application.
Delivery £5 less than 2 cases, free 4 or more cases or £120 in value.
C G M T
Oodles of mouth-watering wines from the classic to the rare, from Bordeaux to Mexico. How can one resist wines like The Chairman's Exuberantly Fruitful New World Sauvignon? There are four J.B. Reynier Wine Libraries which turn into wine bars at midday – you buy your wine (often in half bottles) at retail prices in one part of the shop and take it in to lunch with you, and you have the whole list to choose from.

PHILIP EYRES (EY)

The Cellars, Coleshill, Amersham, Bucks HP7 0LW, (0494) 433823, fax (0494) 431349
Hours Usually Mon–Fri 8–10, Sat variable; answerphone out of hours.
Credit cards AC V.
Delivery Free within south Bucks, Windsor & Ascot, Berkhamsted, Bicester, Highgate & Hampstead areas, £6.50 central London 1 case, free 2 or more; otherwise £10 UK mainland 1 case, £6.50 2–3 or free 4 or more. Delivery on special offers charged separately.
Minimum order 1 case.
EP
There's a new and bigger list this year, owing to an association with Oxfordshire merchant S H Jones. Strengths are Europe, particularly Germany, with some really superb producers.

FARR VINTNERS (FA)

19 Sussex St, London SW1V 4RR, 071-828 1960, fax 071-828 3500
Hours Mon–Fri 10–6.
Credit cards AC V.
Discounts Orders over £2000.
Delivery £8.50 London; (per case) £3.50 Home Counties, minimum £10.50; £3.75 rest of England and Wales, minimum £11.25; £5.60 Scotland, minimum £16.80 or give 48 hours notice of collection.
Minimum order £250 plus vat.
Farr Vintners are fine wine brokers, but hold a great deal of stock as well, even though they have no shop. This is not the place to come for a bottle of Aussie Chardonnay for supper. It is, however, the place for a splendid selection of serious wines at competitive prices. All the first growths and their equivalents are here, plus top Burgundies, Rhônes, ports and a few from elsewhere. Also large sizes, for when you want an imperial of Lafite '59 (a snip at £3000).

FINE WINES OF NEW ZEALAND (FIZ)

PO Box 476, London NW5 2NZ, 071-482 0093, fax 071-267 8400
Hours Mon–Sat 9–5.
Credit cards AC V.
Discounts 2 or more cases.
Delivery £9 mixed case except for special offers.
Minimum order 1 mixed case.
M T
Small, quality-minded mail order outfit that pioneered many successful names here. Look for Redwood Valley, Vidal, Matua Valley, Ngatarawa, Ata Rangi, Aotea, Stonyridge... one could go on. Lovely pudding wines in half bottles, and the irresistably-named Chanel Chardonnay from Mission, for the designer freak with everything.

GALLERY WINES (GAL)

Gomshall Cellars, The Gallery, Gomshall, Surrey GU5 9LB, (0483) 203795, fax (0483) 203282
Hours Mon–Sat 10–6, (Fri till 8).
Credit cards AC S V.
Discounts 10% per case.
Delivery Free 2 or more cases within 25 miles Gomshall, otherwise £6 per consignment.
Minimum order 1 bottle. **C G M T**
Last year this appeared in Webster's as Lorne House Vintners, but ownership, premises and name have changed since. The fine wine list is the most interesting part, with mid-priced Spanish wines and good-value Moldovan Cabernet as well as fine claret.

GAUNTLEYS (GAU)

4 High St, Exchange Arcade, Nottingham NG1 2ET, (0602) 417973, fax (0602) 509519
Hours Mon–Sat 9–5.30.
Credit cards AC S V.
Delivery Free within Nottingham area, otherwise £6.50 per case + vat.
Minimum order 1 case.
C EP (not Bordeaux) **G M T**
A class list of all the wines you'd most like to have: excellent French, Italian, Spanish, Australian (including four liqueur Muscats), New Zealand, South African, port and sherry.

GELSTON CASTLE (GE)

Castle Douglas, Scotland DG7 1QE, (0556) 503012, fax (0556) 504183
Hours Mon–Fri 9–6.
Delivery Free within 25 miles of Castle Douglas 1 case or more, £7 rest of mainland UK; free for orders over £150.
Minimum order None, but mixed cases carry a surcharge of £4 per case.
C EP G M T

A traditional, knowledgeable list from which it would be all too tempting to spend a great deal of money. Lots of brilliant German wines, everyday and fine clarets, plus Rhônes and Burgundies. There's more from Italy and the New World this year, and a small but varied list of half bottles.

GOEDHUIS & CO (GOE)

6 Rudolf Place, Miles Street, London SW8 1RP, 071–793 7900, fax 071–793 7170
Hours Mon–Fri 9–6.30.
Credit Cards AC V.
Delivery Free 3 or more cases in London, 5 or more cases UK mainland.
Minimum order 1 case.
C EP G M T

A to-the-point, no-nonsense list of fine Bordeaux and Burgundy, plus a few Rhônes, ports, well chosen Champagne and the odd wine from elsewhere. There is also an interesting-looking Bottle Bank scheme for building up a cellar and spreading the cost over a year: there are nine cellar plans to choose from, starting from under £35 a month and rising to over £130.

PETER GREEN (GRE)

37A-B Warrender Park Rd, Edinburgh EH9 1HJ, 031-229 5925
Hours Mon–Fri 9.30–6.30, Sat 9.30–7.
Discounts 5% most unsplit cases.
Delivery Free in Edinburgh, elsewhere £6 1 case, £4 each additional case.
G M T
If you're planning a visit here, go early in the day, because you'll need plenty of time for browsing. Everything looks terrific: Italy, Spain, France, Germany, New World and, yes, appropriately for Scotland, malt whiskies, too...

HALVES (HAL)

(Mail order) Wood Yard, off Corve St, Ludlow, Shropshire SY8 2PX, (0584) 877866, fax (0584) 877677;
(Shop) The Wine Treasury, 899-901 Fulham Road, London SW6 5HU, 071-371 7131, fax 071-371 7772
Hours Mail order: Mon–Fri 9–6, Sat 9–12;
Shop: Mon–Sat 11–9
Credit cards AC AE S V.
Discounts £2.40 per case for delivery of 2 or more cases to a single address; 5% on all unmixed cases.
Delivery Free to mainland UK, £5 per case for off-shore islands, Northern Ireland and Eire.
Minimum order 1 mixed case of 24 half bottles. **C EP G M T**
There's a retail shop this year, which is good news, and as it's shared with Halves's partner it has full bottles as well. There's a stunning range of about 300 wines in half bottles – things like Condrieu, Alain Graillot's Crozes-Hermitage and Calera Jensen Pinot Noir as well as clarets and Champagne.

HAMPDEN WINE CO (HAM)

8 Upper High Street, Thame, Oxon OX9 3ER, (0844) 213251, fax (0844) 261100
Hours Mon–Wed, Sat 9.30–5, Thu–Fri 9.30–5.30.
Credit Cards AC AE S V.
Discounts 5% off all mixed cases.
Delivery First order £4 per case nationwide, £2 per case subsequently; orders over £150 free.
G M T
Not an enormously long list, but a very well-chosen one that manages to take in most countries of the world. Loire wines in particular look good, as does Portugal, and there are some excellent Burgundy growers.

HARCOURT FINE WINE (HAC)

3 Harcourt St, London W1H1DS, 071-7237202, fax 071-723 8085, answerphone 071-724 5009
Hours Mon–Fri 9.30–6, Sat 11–4.30.
Credit cards AC AE DC V.
Discounts 5% mixed case, additional for larger quantities.
Delivery Free in London 3 or more cases.
G M T
Once known as the English Wine Shop and still stockists of wines from over 45 English vineyards. There is a selection of French and German wine, too, and French brandy from vintages in the last century.

ROGER HARRIS (HAW)

Loke Farm, Weston Longville, Norfolk NR9 5LG, (0603) 880171/2, fax (0603) 880291
Hours Mon–Fri 9–5.
Credit cards AC AE DC V.
Discounts (per case) £2 for 2, £2.50 for 3, £3 for 5, £4 for 10.
Delivery Free UK mainland.
Minimum order 1 mixed case.
M T
What the Sunday colour supplements would call 'the Specialists' Specialist' – Beaujolais utterly dominates the list and the working life of Roger Harris. Only Champagne, some Mâconnais and a little Coteaux du Lyonnais get a look-in besides. A high-quality specialist list.

JOHN HARVEY (HA)

12 Denmark St, Bristol BS1 5DQ, (0272) 275010, fax (0272) 275001
Hours Mon–Fri 9.30–6, Sat 9.30–1.
Credit cards AC AE DC S V.
Delivery Free 4 cases or more UK mainland, no mixed cases.
C EP G T

Sherry (Harvey's), port (Cockburn's), and claret are the strengths of this traditional list. There are regular en primeur offers for claret and Burgundy, as well as wines from other parts of the world (often rather serious ones like Penfolds Grange from Australia) to vary the classic British sideboard tray.

RICHARD HARVEY (HAY)

Bucknowle House, Bucknowle, Wareham, Dorset BH20 5PQ, (0929) 480352, fax (0929) 481275
Hours By arrangement.
Discounts 5% 6 or more cases.
Delivery Free within 30 miles 3 or more cases.
Minimum order 1 case.
C EP G M T
It's an appointment-only set-up, but worth it for the wine – every producer listed is good quality. The sherries are Barbadillo, the port Churchill Graham, the Chilean wine Montes. An associated company opened in Cherbourg last year at La Maison du Vin, 71 avenue Caruot, Cherbourg 50100 (tel: 010 33 33 43 39 79; fax: 010 33 33 43 22 69). Much of the Richard Harvey list is available at duty-free prices there. Order through the British office and collect the wines in France, and so beat the chancellor without destroying the British wine trade.

HAYNES HANSON & CLARK (HAH)

Sheep St, Stow-on-the-Wold, Gloucs GL54 1AA, (0451) 870808;
36 Kensington Church Street, London W8 4BX, 071-937 4650 & 071-937 9732, fax 071-371 5887
Hours Sheep St: Mon–Sat 9–6. Kensington: Mon–Sat 9.30–7.
Credit cards AC S V.
Discounts 10% unsplit case.
Delivery Free central London, Gloucs, elsewhere 5 or more cases.
Minimum order Warehouse only 1 case.
EP G M T
An extremely knowledgeable, helpful merchant famous for its Burgundies but with excellent Bordeaux as well. Also go there for Loire, Rhône, delicious house Champagne, a good range of New World and reliable, honest advice.

DOUGLAS HENN-MACRAE (HE)

81 Mackenders Lane, Eccles, Aylesford, Kent ME20 7JA, (0622) 710952, fax (0622) 791203
Hours Mail order & phone enquiries only, Mon–Sat to 10pm.
Credit cards AC S V.
Delivery Free UK mainland 10 cases, otherwise £8 plus vat per order.
Minimum order 1 case.
M T

All the companies listed in the Merchant Directory have wines featured in the Price Guides (pages 262-427).
*Abbreviations used in the Directory are as follows: **Credit Cards** Access (AC), American Express (AE), Diners Club (DC), Switch (S), Visa/Barclaycard (V).*
*The following services are available where indicated: **C** cellarage, **EP** en primeur offers, **G** glass hire/loan, **M** mail order, **T** tastings and talks.*

With lots of new stuff on offer, this list looks less wierd than it used to, and more full of wines you'd actually want to buy. Württemberg is still here, but joined by good Mosels, Rheingaus and Pfalzes – though in case anyone thinks Henn-Macrae has thrown in the towel and gone commercial, he's offering things like Pinot Noir Auslese and Müller-Thurgau Spätlese 1971 (which he says is wonderful). Excellent Oregon, Washington State and Texas, too.

HICKS & DON (HIC)

(Head office) Blandford St Mary, Dorset DT11 9LS, (0258) 456040, fax (0258) 450147;
Park House, Elmham, Dereham, Norfolk NR20 5JY, (0362) 668571/2, fax (0362) 668573;
The Old Bakehouse, Alfred St, Westbury, Wiltshire BA13 3DY, (0373) 864723, fax (0373) 858250
Hours Mon–Fri 9–5.
Credit cards AC S V.
Discounts Negotiable.
Delivery 1–2 cases £3 per case, 3 or more cases free UK mainland.
Minimum order 1 mixed case.
C EP G M T
Strong on opening offers of claret, Burgundy, cru Beaujolais, port and the Rhône. Sherries are as strong as ever – all are from that excellent Sanlúcar house, Barbadillo. It's a well-chosen list, and prices are often good. They also have their own English wine, Elmham Park, and they have William Fèvre's Chardonnay from his Chilean venture.

HIGH BRECK VINTNERS (HIG)

Bentworth House, Bentworth, Nr Alton, Hants GU34 5RB, (0420) 562218, fax (0420) 563827
Hours Mon–Fri 9.30–5.30, other times by arrangement.

Credit cards AC V.
Delivery (south-east) £6 for 1 case, £4 for 2, 3 or more free; (rest of England) £9 for 1, £6 for 2, £4 for 3, 4 or more free.
Minimum order 1 mixed case.
EP G M T
A largely French selection of small growers, just one or two per region, and often exclusive to High Breck. There's André Sorin from Sauvignon de St Bris, Gitton from the Loire (single vineyard Sancerres and his Côtes de Gien) and various clarets. Italy is mostly Antinori, Spain is Berberana and there's not much from the New World, but if you're feeling peckish you could snack on smoked sea trout or air dried Cumbria ham.

J.E. HOGG (HOG)

61 Cumberland St, Edinburgh EH3 6RA, 031-556 4025
Hours Mon–Tue, Thu–Fri 9–1, 2.30–6; Wed, Sat 9–1.
Credit cards S
Delivery Free 12 or more bottles within Edinburgh. **G T**
There's a reliance on well-known names here, but since they're reliable, top names that's no misfortune. Burgundy is from the likes of Bouchard Pere, Moreau, Louis Latour, Champy; Alsace is Hugel, Schlumberger, Dopff et Irion, Trimbach and so on. Germany is distinctly interesting, Spain and Portugal have a token presence and there are goodies from New Zealand.

J.C. KARN & SON (KA)

7 Lansdown Place, Cheltenham, Glos GL50 2HU, (0242) 513265
Hours Mon–Fri 9.30–6, Sat 9.30–1.30.
Credit cards AC V.
Discounts 5% mixed case (cash).
Delivery Free in Glos.
G M T

There's no wine list here; instead J C Karn relies on a turnover of small parcels 'acquired in legitimate fashion' apparently, in case one had any doubts on the matter.

LAY & WHEELER (LAY)

(Head office & shop) 6 Culver St West, Colchester, Essex CO1 1JA, (0206) 764446, fax (0206) 560002
Wine Market, Gosbeck's Road, Shrub End, Colchester, Essex CO2 9JT, (0206) 764446
Hours Culver St: Mon–Sat 8.30–5.30. Wine Market: Mon–Sat 8–8.
Credit cards AC S V.
Discounts 5% 10 or more mixed cases.
Delivery Free locally 1 case, elsewhere 2 or more cases. **C EP G M T**
An informative, well-produced list with lots of information about growers and vintages.New this year are 'drink until' dates as well as 'drink from'. The selection is outstanding. There are the best growers of Burgundy (names like Carillon and Jacqueline Jayer) and in fact just about everywhere.

LEA & SANDEMAN (LEA)

301 Fulham Road, London SW10 9QH, 071–376 4767, fax 071–351 0275; 211 Kensington Church Street, London W8 7LX, 071–221 1982, fax 071–221 1985
Hours Mon–Fri 9–8.30, Sat 10–8.30.
Credit Cards AC AE S V.
Discounts On selected cases.
Delivery Free to UK mainland south of Perth on orders over £150.
Minimum order None. **G M T**

The codes given in brackets on these pages beside the merchants' names are those by which the merchants are listed in the price guides (pages 262-427). They are also listed on page 263.

The sort of local wine merchant everybody should have, with a terrific selection of really well-chosen wines. The emphasis is on the middle to top of the market, and among other goodies there are the wonderful sherries of Valdespino.

LONDON WINE (LO)

Chelsea Wharf, 15 Lots Rd, London SW10 0QF, 071-351 6856; freefone orderline (0800) 581266
Hours Mon–Fri 9–9, Sat 10–7, Sun 12–3.
Credit cards AC AE DC S V.
Discounts 5% per case.
Delivery Free in central London; quotes available for nationwide delivery.
EP G M T
A sound commercial list with plenty of variety. Prices are competitive.

MAJESTIC (MAJ)

(Head office) Odhams Trading Estate, St Albans Road, Watford, Herts WD2 5RE, (0923) 816999, fax (0923) 819105; 18 London branches plus Acocks Green, Amersham, Birmingham, Bletchley, Bristol, Bushey, Cambridge, Chichester, Croydon, Gloucester, Guildford, Ipswich, Maidenhead, Newbury, Northampton, Norwich, Oxford, Poole, Reading, St Albans, Salisbury, Stockport, Sunningdale, Swindon, Taunton
Hours Mon–Sat 10–8, Sun 10–6.
Credit cards AC AE DC S V.
Delivery Free locally.
Minimum order 1 mixed case.
EP G M T
Good Champage selection– their house fizz, De Telmont, is particularly good value. Keen prices generally, and it's good to see a greater number of distinctly good wines again. The Loire looks interesting, as does the Rhône and Germany.

Oddbins

During the '80's Oddbins created a rare phenomenon — the consumer-friendly wine merchant. It's difficult to feel over-awed by Oddbins staff or an Oddbins shop, and you can't help but notice that, when other high street chains smarten up, they usually start by trying to adopt the mix of laid-back expertise and breezy street-cred that we call Oddbins-isation.

Oz Clarke, The Daily Telegraph

MARKS & SPENCER (MAR)

(Head office) Michael House, Baker Street, London W1A 1DN, 071-935 4422; 280 licensed stores all over the country
Hours Variable.
Discounts 12 bottles for the price of 11.
M
The list has expanded but overall it's still relatively unexciting, covering a fairly narrow range of commercial flavours. It's sound, though, and the Chablis is very good.

MORENO WINES (MOR)

11 Marylands Rd, London W9 2DU, 071-286 0678, fax 071-286 0513; 2 Norfolk Place, London W2 1QN, 071-706 3055
Hours Marylands Rd: Mon–Sat 10–9, Sun 12–3.
Norfolk Place: Mon–Fri 10–8, Sat 10–8.
Credit cards AC S V.
Discounts 5% mixed case.
Delivery Free locally, elsewhere 5 or more cases.
G M T
Moreno has one of the broadest ranges of Spanish wines in the country. There's Toro, Rueda, Somontano, Valencia and others, treats such as Vega Sicilia, Bodegas Riojanas and CVNE; Albariño for when you're feeling rich, plus sherry and brandy.

MORRIS & VERDIN (MV)

28 Churton St, London SW1V 2LP, 071-630 8888
Hours Mon–Fri 8–6. Closed bank hols.
Discounts 5 or more cases.
Delivery Free central London, elsewhere 5 or more cases.
Minimum order 1 mixed case.
C EP G M T
Excellent, really imaginative list, majoring on Burgundy: names like Rion, Bachelet, Ponsot. Also Ostertag from Alsace, Au Bon Climat, Ca' del Solo, Qupé and Bonny Doon from California, some Aussies and NZs and lots of French country wines. There's a great emphasis on quality at all levels here.

THE NADDER WINE CO (NA)

Hussars House, 2 Netherhampton Road, Harnham, Salisbury, Wiltshire SP2 8HE, (0722) 325418; fax (0722) 421617
Hours Mon–Fri 9–7, Sat 10–3.
Credit cards AC S V.
Discounts 5% on orders over £100 (2.5% credit cards), 7.5% over £500 (5% credit cards).
Delivery Free within 50 miles of central London & Salisbury for orders of £50 or over; free UK mainland min 10 cases; otherwise at cost.
Minimum order 1 case.
G M T
There's quite a lot of scope here if you want mid-level clarets. Burgundy is almost entirely from Bouchard Aîné, Alsace is Leon Beyer and Spain is Berberana and Marqués de Cáceres. There's not a huge variety from anywhere, and not a great range of producers, but plenty of good drinking even if the list overall doesn't make the heart sing.

All the companies listed in the Merchant Directory have wines featured in the Price Guides (pages 262-427).
*Abbreviations used in the Directory are as follows: **Credit Cards** Access (AC), American Express (AE), Diners Club (DC), Switch (S), Visa/Barclaycard (V).*
*The following services are available where indicated: **C** cellarage, **EP** en primeur offers, **G** glass hire/loan, **M** mail order, **T** tastings and talks.*

JAMES NICHOLSON (NI)

27A Killyeagh St, Crossgar, Co. Down,
Northern Ireland BT30 9DG, (0396)
830091, fax (0396) 830028
Hours Mon–Sat 10–7.
Credit cards AC DC V.
Discounts 5–10% mixed case.
Delivery Free Northern Ireland;
otherwise £5 per case or £3 per case
3 cases or more.
Minimum order 1 mixed case.
C E P G M T

*A pretty comprehensive list of lots of
all the best names. Rhônes are very
good (white Coudoulet de Beaucastel
and other good whites, plus Guigal,
Jaboulet and Colombo), as are Italians,
Californians (Carneros Creek, Ridge,
Sanford, Newton, Saintsbury) and
Bordeaux (good middle range names).
There's also Drouhin's Oregon Pinot
Noir. There are lots of good producers
from Germany.*

THE NOBODY INN (NO)

Doddiscombsleigh, Nr. Exeter, Devon
EX6 7PS, (0647) 52394, fax (0647)
52978
Hours Mon–Sat 12–2 & 6–11, Sun
12–2 & 7–10.30; or by appointment
Credit Cards AC AE S V.
Discounts 5% per case
Delivery 1 case £7.98, 2 cases £4.69
each, 3 cases £3.40 each, 4–9 cases
£2.20 each, 10–16 cases £1.89 each,
17–40 cases £1.60 each; thereafter 90p.
G M T

*It seems rather unfair that some people
should have the pleasure of living in
Devon and be able to shop and eat at
the Nobody Inn as well, but I suppose
that's life. There's a passion for sweet
wines here, including what must be the
national collection of sweet Loires.
Everything else is good too, with
terrific New World wines.*

ODDBINS (OD)

(Head office) 31–33 Weir Road, London
SW19 8UG, 081-944 4400; 186 shops.
Hours Mon–Sat 9–9, Sun (not
Scotland) 12–2, 7–9. Closed Christmas.
Credit cards AC AE S V.
Discounts 5% split case wine; 7 bottles
Champagne and sparkling wine for
the price of 6 (if £5.99 or above).
Delivery Available locally most shops.
Free with 'reasonable' order. **EP G T**

By subscribing to Oddbins' magazine, The Catalyst, you can get reductions on selected wines as well as things like vintage reports and general winey news and gossip. The fine wine shops have spread to London's Notting Hill Gate and to Edinburgh. Oddbins probably still has the best range of the high street chains.

THOS. PEATLING (PE)

(Head office) Westgate House, Bury St Edmunds, Suffolk IP33 1QS, (0284) 755948, fax (0284) 705795.
Hours Variable.
Credit cards AC AE S V.
Discounts 5% mixed case.
Delivery Free in East Anglia, elsewhere free for delivery of 2 or more cases.
C EP G M T
Strong Peatling points have always been clarets, but the New World wines are getting better all the time. The clarets include umpteen famous names plus some good bourgeois growths and second wines. Of other French wines Burgundies look rather good, including Bernard Defaix's Chablis, and Rhônes look interesting. There's some Apremont from Savoie, too, for anyone nostalgic for their skiing holiday. New World treats include Mountadam from Australia and Mondavi's Cabernet Reserve.

PENISTONE COURT WINE CELLARS (PEN)

The Railway Station, Penistone, South Yorkshire S30 6HG, (0226) 766037, fax (0226) 767310
Hours Mon–Fri 9–6, Sat 10–3.
Delivery Free locally, rest of UK mainland charged at cost 1 case or more.
G M
Burgundies are mostly Louis Latour, Rhônes are Delas and Beaujolais is Paul Sapin. Austria however looks more inspired and there are some good names in Spain. There are the excellent California wines of Renaissance in Yuba County, which are not easy to find, and plenty of good Champagne from lots of top producers..

CHRISTOPHER PIPER (PIP)

1 Silver St, Ottery St Mary, Devon EX11 1DB, (0404) 814139, fax (0404) 812100
Hours Mon–Sat 9–6.
Credit cards AC S V.
Discounts 5% mixed case, 10% 3 or more cases.
Delivery Free in south-west England for 4 or more cases, elsewhere free for 6 or more cases.
Minimum order 1 mixed case.
C EP G M T

Particularly strong in crus bourgeois *and* petits châteaux *clarets, with very good – though not necessarily the most famous – classed growths. White Bordeaux is good, particularly Sauternes. A lot of leg-work has gone into the Burgundy list recently, and there are some superb growers here. The Loire and the Rhône are good, as is Italy, and sherry is from Barbadillo. A good, well-thought-out list with plenty of depth.*

TERRY PLATT (PLA)

Ferndale Road, Llandudno Junction, Gwynedd LL31 9NT, (0492) 592971, fax (0492) 592196
Hours Mon–Fri 8.30–5.30
Credit cards AC S V.
Delivery Free locally, or in mainland UK with minimum order of 3 cases.
Minimum order 1 mixed case.
G M T
There are a couple of Welsh wines on this list, plus Bouzy Rouge, Mexican, Argentinian and Canadian (though no Canadian Icewine). More conventionally, there are good ranges from the Loire, Spain and California, with lots of unfamiliar growers to try.

PORTLAND WINE COMPANY (POR)

16 North Parade, off Norris Road, Sale, Cheshire M33 3JS, 061–962 8752, fax 061–905 1291;
152a Ashley Road, Hale WA15 9SA, 061–928 0357;
82 Chester Road, Macclesfield SK11 8DL, (0625) 616147
Hours Mon–Sat 10–10, Sun 12–3, 7–9.30
Credit cards AC S V.
Discounts 10% off 12 mixed cases, 5% off 6 mixed cases.
Delivery Free locally.
Minimum order None.
G M T

Italy is a star here, as is Australia; The Rhône and the Loire are both quite short but good, and Burgundy is interesting. There are some nice Spanish wines.

RAEBURN FINE WINES (RAE)

23 Comely Bank Rd, Edinburgh EH4 1DS, phone & fax 031-332 5166
Hours Mon–Sat 9–6.
Credit cards AC S V.
Discounts 5% unsplit case, 2.5% mixed case.
Delivery Price negotiable, all areas covered.
C EP G M T
The Scots have always liked their claret, and this is one of the places they come to buy it. Most of this first-class list is French – Burgundies are from the likes of Michel Lafarge, Méo-Camuzet and Jean-Marc Boillot, there are top Rhônes and Alsace, and goodies from south-west France like Alquier's Faugères. Look out too for Quintarelli's Recioto di Valpolicella and excellent Californians.

REID WINES (1992) LTD (REI)

The Mill, Marsh Lane, Hallatrow, Nr Bristol BS18 5EB, (0761) 452645, fax (0761) 453642
Hours Mon–Fri 9–5.30.
Delivery Free within 25 miles of Hallatrow (Bristol), and in central London.
C G M T
There's claret back to 1929 here, and Sauternes back to 1893, and the list is larded with comments (as in 'These halves of Rieussec '87 are pretty naff', or 'The prize for the most cynically made wine in this list goes to this over-oaked, over-priced and absurdly labelled white wine'). But then they can afford to be honest: it's an outstanding list.

LA RESERVA ESPAÑA (RE)

Unit 6, Spring Grove Mills,
Manchester Road, Linthwaite,
Huddersfield, HD7 5QG, (0484)
846732
Hours Mon–Sat 9.30–5.30
Credit cards AC AE V
Discounts10% off 1 mixed case.
Delivery Free six cases or more.
Minimum order 1 mixed case.
G M T
*Spain is the major attraction here,
with Rioja, Ribera del Duero and Jerez
heading the list. There are smaller
selections from less Spanish regions.
The rest of the world is there as well,
and there is some good stuff,
particularly from Italy.*

LA RESERVE (RES)

56 Walton St, London SW3 1RB, 071-
589 2020, fax 071-581 0250
Hours Mon-Fri 9.30-9, Sat 9.30-7
Credit Cards AC AE S V
Discounts 5% per case except accounts
Delivery Free 1 case or more Central
London & orders over £200 UK
mainland. Otherwise £7.50. **C EP G T**
*As well as a separate old and rare list
there's an excellent selection of
Burgundies, Rhônes, Italians and
names like Kistler and Calera from
California.*

ROBERSON (ROB)

348 Kensington High St, London W14
8NS, 071-371 2121, fax 071-371 4010
Hours Mon–Sat 10–8, Sun 12–3.
Credit cards AC AE S V.
Delivery Free locally 1 case or more.
G M T
*There's a terrific, if expensive, selection
here –claret back to 1924, and depth
and breadth in most other areas, too.
Europe is stronger than the New
World but the latter is well-chosen.*

SAFEWAY (SAF)

(Head office) 6 Millington Road,
Hayes, Middlesex UB3 4AY, 081-848
8744
Hours Mon–Sat 8–8 (Fri till 9), Sun
10–4 (selected stores).
Credit cards AC S V.
G
*A list that is strong in English,
Eastern European, Australian, South
African and French country wines and
a bit patchy elsewhere. You need a
huge branch to see much of a range,
though.*

SAINSBURY (SAI)

(Head office) Stamford House,
Stamford St, London SE1 9LL, 071-
921 6000
Hours Variable, many open late.
Credit cards AC S V.
T
*The country's largest wine retailer.
There's a sound list enlivened by a
vintage selection of fine wines
available from 290 main stores with
the widest selection of 400 wines
available in 60 branches and 10
Savacentres.*

SECKFORD WINES (SEC)

2 Betts Ave, Martlesham Heath,
Ipswich, Suffolk IP5 7RH, (0473)
626681, fax (0473) 626004
Hours Tue–Sat 10–6
Credit cards AC S V.
Delivery Free locally.
Minimum order 1 mixed case
G M T
*A well-balanced, well-chosen list from
which one could happily stock quite a
large cellar. Most things look
interesting, but particularly those from
the Rhône, the red Burgundies and
French country wines. Italy's worth
investigating, too.*

SOMERFIELD/GATEWAY (SO)

(Head office) Somerfield House, Hawkfield Business Park, Whitchurch Lane, Bristol BS14 0TJ, (0272) 359359
Hours Mon–Sat 9–8, variable late opening Friday all stores.
Credit cards AC S V. **T**
All the Gateway stores are going to change their name to Somerfield. 675 stores throughout the UK in all, about 40 of which have the full list. A further 80 have the full list excluding the finer Wine Rack range. Quality is patchy, but there are some good clarets and southern French.

SOMMELIER WINE CO (SOM)

23 St George's Esplanade, St Peter Port, Guernsey, Channel Islands, (0481) 721677, fax (0481) 716818
Hours Tue–Thu 10–5.30, Fri 10–6, Sat 9–5.30; answerphone out of hours.
Credit cards AC S V (Grapevine only).
Discounts 5% 12 or more bottles.
Delivery Free 1 unmixed case.
G M (locally) **T**
Excellent and still improving. France, Italy, Australia and just about everywhere are terrific (not much fortified, though). Look for Californian Rhône Rangers and rarities like Pieropan's Passito della Rocca.

SUMMERLEE WINES (SUM)

64 High St, Earls Barton, Northants NN6 0JG, phone & fax (0604) 810488; (Office) Freddy Price, 48 Castlebar Rd, London W5 2DD, 081-997 7889, fax 081-991 5178
Hours Mon–Fri 9–2; answerphone out of hours.
Delivery Free England & Wales 5 or more cases, or Northants, Oxford, Cambridge & London 2 or more cases; otherwise £6.50 per consignment 1–4 cases. **C EP G M**

A fairly short, knowledgeable list of excellent clarets and Germans, plus good sherry, port, Faugères and vin jaune. Freddy Price takes the trouble to seek out wines, and it shows.

SUNDAY TIMES WINE CLUB (WIC)

New Aquitaine House, Paddock Road, Reading, Berks RG4 0JY, (0734) 481713, fax (0734) 461953
Hours Mail order, 24-hr answerphone.
Credit cards AC AE DC S V.
Discounts On special offers.
Delivery Free for orders over £50.
EP M T
Associate company is Bordeaux Direct. Membership fee is £10 per annum. The club also runs tours and tastings and an annual festival in London. The Club does monthly promitions to its members featuring around 150 wines each, and about a quarter of that list changes every month.

T. & W. WINES (TW)

51 King St, Thetford, Norfolk IP24
2AU, (0842) 765646
Hours Mon–Fri 9.30–5.30, Sat
9.30–1.00.
Credit cards AC AE DC V.
Delivery Free UK mainland 2 or
more cases.
C EP G M
*An extraordinary selection of fine, old
and rare wines – Burgundies (which
are a speciality) dating back to 1949,
clarets back to 1916 and half bottles of
all sorts back to 1944. Terrific Rhônes,
Australians, Californians, Tokaji and
most other things as well, including
lots of anniversary years.*

TANNERS (TAN)

26 Wyle Cop, Shrewsbury, Shropshire
SY1 1XD, (0743) 232400;
4 St Peter's Square, Hereford HR1
2PJ (0432) 272044;
36 High Street, Bridgnorth WC16
4DB, (0746) 763148;
The Old Brewery, Brook St, Welshpool
SY21 7LF, (0938) 552542;
36 Mytton Oak Rd, Copthorne,
Shrewsbury (0743) 366387
Hours Mon–Sat 9–6.
Credit cards AC S V.
Discounts 5% 1 mixed case wine
(cash & collection), 5% 5 or more cases
assorted bottles of wine, 7.5% 10 cases
(mail order).
Delivery Free local delivery 1 mixed
case or more or nationally for orders
over £75, otherwise £6 per order.
C EP G M T
*Wide-ranging and adventurously
chosen list – good on classic areas like
Burgundy and claret, but also the New
World. Terrific things from everywhere, in fact. The German selection
has names like von Simmern and Bischöfliches Priesterseminar as well as
the increasingly ubiquitous Dr Loosen.*

TESCO (TES)

(Head office) Delamare Road,
Cheshunt, Herts EN8 9SL, (0992)
632222, fax (0992) 630794; 406
licensed branches
Hours Variable (open Sunday).
Credit cards AC S V.
*Wide range, and no longer regarded as
runner-up to Sainsbury's in quality
terms. Lots of New World wines and
good on Italy, Germany and French
vins de pays too.*

THRESHER (THR)

(Head office) Sefton House, 42 Church
Street, Welwyn Garden City, Herts
AL8 6PJ, (0707) 328244, fax (0707)
371398
Hours Mon–Sat 9–10 (some 10.30),
Sun (not Scotland) 12–3, 7–10.
Credit cards AC S V.
Discounts Available on quantity.
Delivery Free local, selected branches.
G T
*Excellent Champagne list and good
French wines generally; Australia and
New Zealand are also varied, with
producers like Mountadam, Petaluma,
Martinborough Vineyards and
Palliser Estate.*

UNWINS (UN)

(Head office) Birchwood House,
Victoria Road, Dartford, Kent DA1
5AJ, (0322) 272711/7; 300 specialist
off-licences throughout the south-east
of England
Hours Variable, usually Mon–Sat
10–10, Sun 12–3, 7–10.
Credit cards AC AE DC S V.
Discounts 10% mixed case.
G M T
*Thorough though not always
adventurous list that covers just about
everywhere. Quality is rather uneven,
so choose carefully.*

VALVONA & CROLLA (VA)

19 Elm Row, Edinburgh EH7 4AA,
031-556 6066
Hours Mon–Wed 8.30–6, Thu-Fri
8.30–7.30, Sat 8.30–6. Closed 1–6 Jan.
Credit cards AC AE S V.
Discounts 5% mixed case.
Delivery Free locally for orders over
£25. Mail order £7.45 per case, £3.35
4 cases or more, free 8 or more. **G M T**
*Italophiles should instantly move to
Edinburgh. V&C have wines from all
over Italy, from the cheap to the
serious, plus Champagne, port and
over 4500 food lines and 40 olive oils.*

VICTORIA WINE (VIC)

(Head office) Brook House, Chertsey
Road, Woking, Surrey GU21 5BE,
(0483) 715066; over 1530 branches
throughout Great Britain (including
Augustus Barnett and Haddows)
Hours Variable, usually Mon–Sat 9–6
(high street), 10–10 (local shops), Sun
12–3, 7–10.
Credit cards AC AE S V.
Discounts 5% mixed case, 7 bottles
for the price of 6 on most Champagnes.
G T
*Over 500 wines are available, though
many need to be ordered in advance
through the list, which is much better
than the shelves in most branches.*

LA VIGNERONNE (VIG)

105 Old Brompton Rd, London SW7
3LE, 071-589 6113
Hours Mon–Fri 10–9, Sat 10–7.
Credit cards AC AE DC S V.
Discounts 5% mixed case (collected).
Delivery Free locally, £10 mainland
England & Wales for orders under
£100, £5 for £100–£200, free over £200;
mainland Scotland £16 for under £150,
£8 for £150–£300, free over £300.
C EP G M T

*Fascinating and very personal list,
strong on classic and southern French
– also the place for exceptional Loire
and Alsace, Canadian Icewine, top
Californians and Aussies. Not cheap.
There's also a monthly fine and rare
wines list, which is not just Bordeaux
and Burgundy but also old Loires,
Vega Sicilia and old solera Priorato.*

VINTAGE WINES (VIN)

116/118 Derby Rd, Nottingham NG1
5FB, (0602) 476565/419614
Hours Mon–Fri 9–5.15, Sat 9–1.
Credit cards AC V.
Discounts 10% mixed case.
Delivery Free within 60 miles. **G M T**
*Useful merchant with traditional taste
who takes particular care with his
house wines.*

WAITROSE (WAI)

(Head office) Doncastle Rd, Southern
Industrial Area, Bracknell, Berks
RG12 4YA (0344) 424680; 108 licensed
shops.
Hours Mon–Tue 9–6, Wed 9–8, Thu
8.30–8, Fri 8.30–9, Sat 8.30–6.
Discounts 5% for any whole case of
wine. **G**
*Waitrose is less devoted to own-label
wines than some supermarkets and in
most areas of its wide-ranging list is
remarkably adventurous. Bordeaux
and Burgundy, both red and white,
are particularly strong – look here for
good-value pudding wines. The New
World is also good, as is fizz.*

WATERLOO WINE CO (WAT)

6 Vine Yard, Borough, London SE1
1QL, 071-403 7967, fax 071-357 6976
Hours Mon–Fri 10–6.30, Sat 10–5
Credit cards AC S V.
Delivery Free 5 cases or more.
G T

There's a passion for the Loire here but there are goodies from other places besides: Penfolds Grange from Australia, well-chosen Germans, Hamilton Russell from South Africa and something called Diocletian Prosek from Yugoslavia. It's dessert wine, apparently.

WHITESIDES OF CLITHEROE (WHI)

Shawbridge St, Clitheroe, Lancs BB7 1NA, (0200) 22281, fax (0200) 27129
Hours Mon–Sat 9–5.30.
Credit cards AC V.
Discounts Dependent on amount, 5% unmixed case.
G M T
Good Loires and a sound though not necessarily imaginative selection from elsewhere, though Bordeaux is good. Don't let the look of the list put you off.

WINDRUSH WINES (WW)

The Ox House, Market Square, Northleach, Cheltenham, Glos GL54 3EG, (0451) 860680, fax (0451) 861166;
3 Market Place, Cirencester, Glos GL7 2PE, (0285) 650466;
25 High Street, Hungerford, Berks RG11 0NF, (0488) 686850
Hours Northleach: Mon–Fri 9–6.
Cirencester: Mon–Sat 9–5.30.
Hungerford: Mon–Sat 10–8.
Credit cards AC S V.
Discounts In bond and ex-cellar terms available.
Delivery Free locally, elsewhere £6 for up to 2 cases, free for 3.
Minimum order 1 bottle.
C EP G M T
Specialists in fine single-estate wines. While the emphasis lies on France, they also have a reputation for the best wines from California and the Pacific North-West. Look out for delicious Billecart Salmon Champagne and The Eyrie Vineyard from Oregon.

WINE RACK (WR)

(Head office) Sefton House, 42 Church Street, Welwyn Garden City, Herts AL8 6PJ, (0707) 328244, fax (0707) 371398
Hours Mon–Sat 9–10 (some 10.30), Sun 12–3, 7–10.
Credit cards AC AE S V.
Discounts 5% mixed cases wine, 12.5% mixed cases Champagne.
Delivery Free locally, all shops.
G T
Part of Threshers; but smarter and with a wider, generally more upmarket range. Eighty stores across the country.

WINE SOCIETY (WS)

(Head office) Gunnels Wood Rd, Stevenage, Herts SG1 2BG, (0438) 741177, fax (0438) 741392;
Showroom: (0438) 741566
Hours Mon–Fri 9–5; showroom Mon–Fri 9–6, Sat 9–1.
Credit cards AC V.
Discounts (per case) £1 for 5–9, £2 for 10 or more, £3 for collection.
Delivery Free 1 case or more UK mainland and Northern Ireland. Collection facility at Hesdin, France at French rates of duty & vat.
C EP G M T
You have to be a member to buy wines from this non-profit-making co-operative, but lifetime membership is very reasonable at £20. They offer an outstanding range. France is the backbone, but there are also masses of good and adventurous wines from California, Germany, Italy, Spain and Portugal, plus goodies like sun-dried tomatoes and olive oil. In spite of its rather safe image, this is one of the country's more enterprising wine merchants. Quoted prices include delivery, which makes them rather good value.

WINECELLARS (WCL)

153–155 Wandsworth High St,
London SW18 4JB, 081-871 3979
Hours Mon–Fri 11.30–8.30, Sat
10–8.30.
Credit cards AC S V.
Discounts 10% mixed case.
Delivery Free within M25 boundary,
or 2 cases UK mainland.
Minimum order 1 mixed case.
C G M T
*One of the most exciting ranges of wine
in London, and Britain's leading Italian
specialist. Each year the list gets
bigger and better and includes books,
coffee, even pasta flour and wonderful
olive oil. But it's not all Italian:
Australia is strong, as are – well, most
places, really. The California selection
is well-chosen and out of the ordinary.
Regular tastings are held, including
many non-Italian subjects.*

WINES OF WESTHORPE (WIW)

Marchington, Staffs ST14 8NX, (0283)
820285, fax (0283) 820631
Hours Mon–Fri and most weekends
9–6.30.
Credit cards AC S V.
Discounts (per case) £2.60 for 5–10,
£3.20 for 11–20.
Delivery Free UK mainland 2 or
more cases.
Minimum order 1 mixed case.
M T
*Eastern European specialists: a good
range of Bulgarian wines plus
Hungarians and a few Chileans. The
Australian section, from Tatachilla
Hill and d'Arenberg, has expanded.
There's a sweet red sparkling wine
from Hungary, too. But the Bulgarian
wines are still the main point of it all,
and have the royal warrant of King
Simeon II, exiled king of the
Bulgarians. Bet their rivals are really
jealous.*

WRIGHT WINE CO (WRI)

The Old Smithy, Raikes Rd, Skipton,
N. Yorks BD23 1NP, (0756) 700886
Hours Mon–Sat 9–6.
Discounts Wholesale price unsplit
case, 5% mixed case.
Delivery Free within 30 miles. **G**
*There are some pretty unusual wines
here, tucked into a list that is anyway
good. Sparkling red Burgundy? Pinot
Beurot from the Hautes Côtes de
Nuits? This is the place. There are also
more conventional treats from
Burgundy and Alsace in particular,
and lots of half-bottles.*

PETER WYLIE FINE WINES (WY)

Plymtree Manor, Plymtree,
Cullompton, Devon EX15 2LE,
(0884) 277555, fax (0884) 277557
Hours Mon–Fri 9–6.
Discounts Unsplit cases.
Delivery Free London 3 or more
cases, UK mainland 1 case £10,
2 cases £6.50 per case, 3 or more cases
£4 per case. **C M**
*Claret (back to 1890) and Sauternes
are the specialities, followed by
Burgundy, Champagne and port.
Madeira features too. There are plenty
of older vintages for the buff to wallow
in, since mature wines are a speciality.*

YAPP BROTHERS (YAP)

The Old Brewery, Mere, Wilts BA12
6DY, (0747) 860423, fax (0747) 860929
Hours Mon–Fri 9–5, Sat 9–1.
Credit cards AC V.
Discounts 6 or more cases.
Delivery £3 for under 2 cases.
C EP G M T
*Rhône and Loire specialist of 25 years
standing. Splendid wines: in the
Rhône, particularly, it has few rivals.
The south of France and Champagne
are excellent as well.*

REGIONAL DIRECTORY

LONDON

Les Amis du Vin	AMI
John Armit	ARM
Australian Wine Centre	AUS
Barnes Wine Shop	BAR
Berkmann Wine Cellars	BEK
Berry Bros & Rudd	BER
Bibendum	BIB
Bottoms Up	BOT
Bute Wines	BUT
Corney & Barrow	CB
Davisons	DAV
Farr Vintners	FA
Fine Wines of New Zealand	FIZ
Goedhuis & Co	GOE
Harcourt Fine Wines	HAC
Haynes Hanson & Clark	HAH
Lea & Sandeman	LEA
London Wine	LO
Moreno Wines	MOR
Morris & Verdin	MV
La Reserve	RES
Roberson	ROB
Summerlee Wines	SUM
Unwins	UN
La Vigneronne	VIG
Waterloo Wine Co	WAT
Winecellars	WCL

SOUTH-EAST AND HOME COUNTIES

Bedford Fine Wines	BE
Berry Bros & Rudd	BER
Bordeaux Direct	BOD
Bottoms Up	BOT
Butlers Wine Cellar	BU
Cape Province Wines	CAP
Philip Eyres	EY
Gallery Wines	GAL
Douglas Henn-Macrae	HE
High Breck Vintners	HIG
Unwins	UN

The Sunday Times Wine Club	WIC
Wine Society	WS

WEST AND SOUTH-WEST

Averys	AV
Bottoms Up	BOT
Châteaux Wines	CHA
Eldridge, Pope & Co	EL
John Harvey & Sons	HA
Haynes Hanson & Clark	HAH
Richard Harvey Wines	HAY
Hicks & Don	HIC
J.C. Karn	KA
Nadder Wine	NA
The Nobody Inn	NO
Christopher Piper	PIP
Reid Wines	REI
Windrush Wines	WW
Peter Wylie	WYL
Yapp Brothers	YAP

EAST ANGLIA

Adnams	AD
Amey's Wines	AME
Anthony Byrne	BY
Corney & Barrow	CB
Roger Harris Wines	HAW
Hicks & Don	HIC
Lay & Wheeler	LAY
Thos. Peatling	PE
Seckford Wines	SEC
T. & W. Wines	TW

MIDLANDS

Gauntleys	GAU
Halves	HAL
Summerlee Wines	SUM
Tanners	TAN
Vintage Wines	VIN
Wines of Westhorpe	WIW

NORTH

Borg Castel	BOR
Penistone Court Fine Wines	PEN
La Reserva España	RE
Whitesides of Clitheroe	WHI
Wright Wine Company	WRI

WALES

Ashley Scott	AS
Celtic Vintner	CV
Terry Platt	PLA

SCOTLAND

Bute Wines	BUT
Corney & Barrow	CB
Gelston Castle	GE
Peter Green	GRE
J.E. Hogg	HOG
Raeburn Fine Wines	RAE
Valvona & Crolla	VA

CHANNEL ISLANDS

Sommelier Wines	SOM

NORTHERN IRELAND

Direct Wine	DI
James Nicholson	NI

COUNTRYWIDE

ASDA	ASD
Augustus Barnett	AUG
Majestic	MAJ
Marks & Spencer	MAR
Oddbins	OD
Safeway	SAF
Sainsbury	SAI
Somerfield	SO
Tesco	TES
Thresher	THR
Victoria Wine	VIC
Waitrose	WAI
Wine Rack	WR

Oz Clarke's Wine Guide is an annual publication: we welcome any suggestions you may have for the 1996 edition. Send them to Webster's, Axe and Bottle Court, 70 Newcomen Street, London SE1 1YT.

INDEX

ACKNOWLEDGEMENTS

Our thanks go to Wink Lorch for the Cost of a Bottle and the Maturity Charts, to Philip White for his work on Australia, to all those who sent us their wine lists, and everyone who kindly supplied wines for our tasting.

NOTES